# RULERS AND VICTIMS

# RULERS AND VICTIMS

## THE RUSSIANS IN THE SOVIET UNION

### GEOFFREY HOSKING

THE BELKNAP PRESS OF
HARVARD UNIVERSITY PRESS
Cambridge, Massachusetts
London, England
2006

Library of Congress Cataloging-in-Publication Data

Hosking, Geoffrey A.
Rulers and victims : the Russians in the Soviet Union / Geoffrey Hosking.
p. cm.
Includes bibliographical references and index.
ISBN 0-674-02178-9 (alk. paper)
1. National characteristics, Russian.   2. Russians—Ethnic identity.
3. Nationalism—Russia (Federation).   4. Soviet Union—History.
5. Soviet Union—Ethnic relations.
I. Title: Russians in the Soviet Union.   II. Title.
DK510.34.H67 2006
305.800946—dc22      2005057215

# CONTENTS

# PREFACE

One dramatic image has remained in most people's minds from the final days of the Soviet Union: Boris Yeltsin standing on top of one of the tanks sent by the Soviet "Emergency Committee" in August 1991 to storm the White House, the Russian parliament building. As see in television footage aired around the world, Yeltsin condemned the coup as an attempt to "remove from power the legally elected authorities of the Russian Republic." He called on "the citizens of Russia to give a fitting rebuff to the putschists" and on all officials to "unswervingly adhere to the constitutional laws and decrees of the President of Russia." His defiant and courageous stand inspired Russians to come by the thousands to camp around the White House and defend it from possible assault. The junta decided not to open fire on them and the coup collapsed.

The final and decisive conflict, then, was not between Communism and anti-Communism, as the whole history of the USSR might have led one to expect, but rather between Russia and the Soviet Union. How could that be? How could it confront itself? That is the question which underlies this book.

My attempt to answer it, though, dates from long before 1991. One evening in 1969, as I was about to travel on the overnight train from Moscow to Leningrad, a friend gave me a book to read that she warmly recommended. At first I was not impressed: it was a novel by the Vologda writer Vasilii Belov, of whom I had never heard, and the title—*Privychnoe delo,* or "Business as Usual"—was not especially promising. But once I started reading, I found the text so gripping that I did not get much sleep that night. It concerned a collective farm somewhere in the Russian north, and the travails of a farmer devoted to his wife, his children, and the land, but so alienated by the local bureaucrats and their procedures that he decides to break with the village and seek a new life in the town.

What the book revealed to me was that there was a way of being Russian that was un-Soviet. Like most people, I had gotten used to thinking of the Soviet Union as essentially Russian. Russian was its main language, spoken with native fluency even by the non-Russians I met as a graduate student. Russian writers dominated all the bookshops. Russia's history—including that of the tsars—permeated the university curriculum, even if to my eyes the "era of feudalism" and the "era of capitalism" seemed incongruous labels to fix on the country's past.

On the other hand I knew from my undergraduate studies at Cambridge that there was another Russia, one not acknowledged in Moscow. Some of its sons and daughters, long cut off from their homeland yet still devoted to it, had been among our teachers. I had enjoyed Boris Pasternak's novel *Doctor Zhivago,* which was a best seller in the West but was not to be seen in any Soviet bookshop. I had read Anna Akhmatova's poem cycle *Requiem* and poetry by Osip Mandelstam, none of which was to be found even in the otherwise comprehensive catalogues of Moscow's Lenin Library. So I knew that there was a suppressed Russia whose culture was found only in emigration. Moreover, in the Soviet Union itself I had seen the Orthodox Church, bearer of the Russian national faith, conducting its services discreetly and unannounced, attended mainly by old women and inquisitive foreigners like myself.

Belov, however, was something new to me: the novel revealed a non-Soviet Russian culture that emanated, not from the church or from sophisticated non-Marxist intellectuals, but from ordinary Russian people, from the peasants whose voices had so long been silent, or at least unheard. One of my abiding early impressions of Soviet life had been the condition of the Russian villages—mostly seen from trains and buses. The muddy cart tracks that passed for roads and the ramshackle wooden huts with corrugated iron roofs did not correspond with my image of a superpower's agricultural economy. Could this be the same country that had launched Sputnik and that bristled with nuclear weapons and intercontinental ballistic missiles?

Reading Belov opened my eyes to the reasons for the apparent incongruity. Later I got to know other "village prose" writers, a unique generation of village lads who had undergone the demanding training of the Gorkii Literary Institute and had emerged able to do what no one else could: chronicle the transformation of the village that had taken place before their eyes. Though censorship inhibited them from complete frankness, I learned from them what no historian could then recount, how the collectivization of agriculture had disrupted the moral traditions of the village and demoralized its population. It turned out that in the ostensibly modernizing Soviet Union many people hankered after a form of social solidarity that was now lost.[1]

Since that time the fate of the Russians in the Soviet Union has haunted me. Most non-Russians regarded them as the ruling nation; most Russians, for their part, consciously or not, looked on the Soviet Union as their country. Yet in many ways, as I could see, Russians had suffered from the depredations of the Soviet decades as much as, if not more than, other peoples. In the late 1980s, some Russians even began to declare that they had been the victims of the Soviet Union, betrayed by the non-Russians they had striven to help. What was the truth?

Writing about the Russians in the Soviet Union is tricky. As I hope this book makes clear, Russian identity is diffuse and has a number of aspects that do not harmonize easily: ethnic, imperial, civic, and cultural. Until 1932 Russian identity was not acknowledged in any official document, and only non-Russians were represented in the People's Commissariat of Nationalities. Even after that date, when it was officially recorded as "entry no 5" in the internal passport that every adult had to carry, most Russians still attributed no great importance to their ethnic identity: in their eyes it still had fluid boundaries and merged readily with that of other peoples, especially the Ukrainians, Belorussians, Jews, and the non-Russian peoples of the Soviet Russian Republic, like the Chuvashi and the Mari. Many of the experiences of Russians described in this book were shared by non-Russians, for example in the Stalinist terror, in the collectivization of agriculture, or in the Second World War. That does not disqualify them as part of the Russian life story, but it is the Russians' experience of Soviet existence that I have tried to capture. In the field of culture, I have treated literature much more than the other arts, partly because it is what I know best, and partly because it has been the art form in which Russians have felt their national identity is most fully expressed.

My subject matter is, then, somewhat blurred in outline. Its importance, however, is incontestable. At a time when the fate of post-Soviet

Russia is still in many ways open and undecided, it is imperative to try and understand what the Soviet Union meant to Russians, what effect it had on their national identity, and how it shaped the formation of the Russian Federation after 1991.

This book is in some ways a sequel to my earlier work *Russia: People and Empire, 1552–1917,* published in 1997. Yet the subject matter is very different: to begin with, the new state was not even called after Russia anymore. As a result, I have structured this book differently, giving much more weight to Russians' personal experiences and to the informal features of Russian life.

I want to thank warmly my colleagues Pete Duncan, Stephen Lovell, Robert Service, and my daughter Katya, who have read all or part of an earlier draft and offered helpful and insightful comments that have improved the text considerably. I am grateful to the British Library and the library of the School of Slavonic and East European Studies, University College London; the archive of the Davis Russian Research Center, Harvard University; The State Archive of the Russian Federation (GARF); The Russian Center for the Preservation and Study of Documents of Contemporary History (RTsKhIDNI); and The Russian State Archive of the National Economy (RGANI). I owe a special thanks to the reading room attendants at the Archive of the Library of Russians Abroad *(Biblioteka-fond Russkogo Zarubezhia),* who actually served me glasses of tea while I pored over their documents; their collection, despite its title, contains a large number of personal papers deposited in response to an appeal by Aleksandr Solzhenitsyn for materials reflecting the lives of ordinary people in the Soviet Union.

Sonia Bogatyreva lent me the Belov novel that launched my search for Russia in the Soviet Union. Liudmila Chernichenko offered constant support and invaluable assistance with archives. My wife, Anne, and my daughters, Katya and Janet, comforted and sustained me through the seemingly endless process of research and writing. I also owe much to Kathleen McDermott and Christine Thorsteinsson of Harvard University Press, who saw the book through the publication process with tact and understanding.

I am greatly indebted to the Leverhulme Foundation, whose award of a Personal Research Chair made the research and writing of this book possible.

I am grateful for permission to use material from two of my previously published articles: "The Second World War and Russian National Consciousness," *Past and Present*, no. 175 (May 2002), 162–187; and "Forms of Social Solidarity in Russia and the Soviet Union," in Ivana Marková, ed., *Trust and Democratic Transition in Post-Communist Europe* (Oxford University Press for the British Academy, 2004), 47–62.

# INTRODUCTION

In 1993, during the first parliamentary elections to take place in the post-Soviet Russian Federation, the politician who seemed to capture most succinctly and forcefully Russians' mood—and the incongruity of their recent history—was the leader of the Liberal Democratic Party, Vladimir Zhirinovskii:

> For most of the twentieth century, our nation has been in transit. We travelled in carts, rattling over country roads and potholes. We smashed the Germans and sent men into space, but in the process destroyed families and lost our sense of history. . . . We mutilated our country. We turned it into a backward place, compelling the Russian nation, which at one time had occupied the vanguard, to retreat. We drove the population underground by economic, legal and psychological pressure. And today we're being told we cannot manage without the help of foreigners.[1]

Whatever one may think of Zhirinovskii as a politician, there is little doubt that—as his electoral success witnessed—he was articulating the mixture of resentment, bewilderment, and humiliation that many Russians felt. They could not understand why, given their nation's great and generally recognized achievements, Russia was impoverished and degraded by the final decade of the twentieth century. They had been the foremost people of a great state, allegedly leading humanity to a wonderful future, and now suddenly they were the victims of the collapse of that state, apparently backward and poverty-stricken, dependent on the handouts of other nations.

There is indeed something paradoxical and as yet poorly understood about the Russians' fate in the Soviet Union. By now we have histories of all the major nationalities of the Soviet Union, and a good many of the minor ones too—but not, so far, of the Russians. They were the "unmarked" Soviet people, the zero option of the USSR. Most Russians accepted this situation and identified themselves unthinkingly with the Soviet Union. They would sometimes refer to non-Slavs as *natsmeny*— "national people." Rather like the American term "ethnic," it implied that Russians themselves had no ethnic identity. A similar message was implicit in a ditty about the first cosmonaut that was popular in the 1960s:

> Kak khorosho, chto Iu. Gagarin,
> Ne tungus i ne tatarin,
> On ne khokhol i ne uzbek,
> A nash sovetskii chelovek.

> What a good thing that Iu. Gagarin
> Is not a Tungus or a Tatar,
> Not a Ukrainian and not an Uzbek,
> But one of us, a Soviet man.[2]

Most non-Russians and nearly all foreigners also assumed the Soviet Union was Russia. The non-Russians in the USSR generally regarded the Russians as their masters. Some accepted the fact, others resented it, but few questioned whether it was really the case. Russians, for their part, could never understand this viewpoint. They felt they had rescued all the Soviet (and European) nations from Nazi rule, and then assisted them at considerable cost in rebuilding their economies and constructing socialism. They were helpful comrades, not occupiers, still less tyrants. Why were they now treated with resentment and disdain?

Not everyone shared the consensus view, however, and some people even felt that the USSR was in a sense counterposed to Russia. Irina Kantor, a Jew who was an Orthodox believer, recalled as a child asking her father to show her Russia. He took her across to a map on the wall and pointed to the Soviet Union. She replied, "That's not Russia! Show me

Russia!" Then he pointed to the boundaries of the Russian Federation, the RSFSR. "I thought for a moment. If one removed the incomprehensible word 'Federation,' then that should be Russia all right. . . . But no, that was not Russia. Where was it? I stared at the map long and hard, but in vain." Her Russia was not a state nor a bounded territory on the map but a state of mind, an ideal for which she longed, though as a Jew she did not understand why.[3]

As a preface to her first published book of poems, Irina Ratushinskaia wrote an essay, "My Homeland," which reflects an uncertainty about her national identity similar to Kantor's. In her passport her nationality was listed as "Russian." But she had been brought up in Odessa, in the Ukrainian Soviet Republic, and had never set eyes on geographical Russia until she was an adult. Perhaps then she was Ukrainian? But she spoke and wrote in Russian, and in her home town virtually no one used Ukrainian. Perhaps she should accept what she was told at school, that her homeland was the Soviet Union. But she did not feel that she could identify equally with the wild mountains of the Caucasus, the mild Baltic coast, the frigid Siberian taiga, and the arid steppes of Kazakhstan. Nor did she feel much attachment to the Soviet culture propagated in the classroom. She came to the conclusion that her real homeland was Russian literature, not the one taught at school, but the one she discovered quite suddenly at the age of twenty-four: the unpublished poets Mandelstam, Tsvetaeva, and Pasternak. Or alternatively her homeland was God, Whom, she explains, "I did not seek. God found me Himself, helped me to survive and rescued my soul."[4] This identification with a language, a culture, or a religion rather than with a territory, a state, or a country is common, especially among Russian intellectuals.

We should pause, though, before assuming that such feelings of uncertainty and ambivalence about one's national identity are peculiar to Russia. They are commoner than one might think, especially among major ethnic groups that identify themselves with an overarching state. Such dominant ethnicities assume both power over and responsibility for smaller ethnic groups, and so they tend to take nationality for granted and to merge their identity with some larger ideal.[5] Most large European nations have gone through at least one period in their history when they assumed that their religion, their civilization, their political system, or their way of life was especially beneficial, and that it ought to be spread to the whole of humanity. The sixteenth-century Spaniards, having just expelled the Muslims from the Iberian peninsula, tried to take their mode of Catholicism to much of Europe (provoking revolution in the Netherlands) and across the ocean to South America. The French forcefully transported their ideal of the civic nation across most of Europe in the first decade of the nineteenth century. The Germans attempted something similar for ethnic nationhood and Kultur in the first half of the twentieth. As for Britain/England, for most of the eighteenth and nineteenth centuries its leaders and many of its ordinary people took for granted that their country had a duty to disseminate Protestant Christianity, free trade, and parliamentary government throughout the world. Today, the United States is the world's leading missionary nation, assuming both the right and the duty to spread its culture and its style of market economy—the "Washington consensus"—to the whole planet.[6] Thus Russians' twentieth-century belief that they had an analogous right and duty to spread socialism throughout the world is not at all unusual: it is part of the norm for large nations.

Anthony Smith, perhaps currently the foremost theorist of ethnic identity, sees the idea of sacred mission as a normal constituent of nationalism. He argues that "nationalism . . . draws much of its passion, conviction and intensity from the belief in a national mission and destiny; and this belief in turn owes much to a powerful religious myth of ethnic election." This belief has its origin in the idea of a "chosen people . . . a particular people as a vessel chosen by a deity for a special religious task or mission in the world's moral economy. By performing that mission, the elect will be set apart and sanctified, and their redemption, and that of the world, will be assured."[7]

Among the characteristics of such missionary nationalism, Smith highlights the following:

1. a belief in the moral superiority of the missionary community, conditional upon fulfilling the covenant and carrying out the mission;
2. confidence in the "radical reversal" of the community's "hitherto lowly or marginal status in the world" through fulfillment of its mission;
3. reinforcement of the strict boundary "against outsiders who . . . have no part in the sacred mission and its duties. . . . Election myths may also be used against insiders who reject the mission";
4. mobilization of the people as a whole, not just the elites. "Everyone

must be drawn into the communal task, so that the energies of the whole people can be engaged; and this in turn requires a high degree of popular participation in the special destiny of the people."[8]

All four characteristics apply to the Soviet Union. The Soviet leaders and many Soviet citizens believed in the superiority of their community and were confident that they were fulfilling their "covenant" with history by raising up the humble and oppressed (both themselves and other victims of global imperialism). They took pride in elevating Russians, hitherto one of the most backward of European peoples, to a global position of economic and scientific leadership. Their ideology, and their practice in such fields as education and propaganda, laid great stress on the mobilization of whole peoples, not just elites. The most doubtful category is the third: for part of its history the Soviet Union eagerly accepted outsiders as citizens. From the mid-1930s, however, the Soviet authorities erected and maintained very strict border controls; for fear of admitting spies and other enemies, they discriminated against Jews and deported entire ethnic groups (Chechens and Crimean Tatars, among others) whom they suspected of being internal enemies.

It might be argued, though, that the Soviet Union was not the Russian nation, and that full-blooded Russian nationalism was never the policy of the Soviet state; indeed, at times, as we shall see, the state actively disadvantaged Russians.

This, too, is less unusual than it might appear. A common characteristic of all forms of national messianism, historically speaking, is that on the face of it they were not very national, or at least that they subordinated nationhood to the supranational ideal: Catholicism in the case of the Spaniards, liberty, equality, and fraternity in the case of the French, Protestantism and free trade in the case of the British. In his recent study of English national identity, Krishan Kumar takes up Smith's category of "missionary nationalism." He describes it as "a nationalism that finds its principle not so much in equating state and nation as in extending the supposed benefits of a particular nation's rule and civilization to other people." In Kumar's conception, "the key feature of imperial or missionary nationalism is the attachment of a dominant or core ethnic group to a state entity that conceives itself as dedicated to some large cause or purpose, religious, cultural or political." In such cases, "nationalism and cosmopolitanism were not opposed but complementary." In practice, Kumar

uses the terms "imperial" and "missionary" nationalism almost inter-
changeably. "Empires," he states, "though in principle opposed to claims
of nationality, may be carriers of a certain kind of national identity which
gives to the dominant groups a special sense of themselves and their
destiny."[9] These formulations certainly apply to Russians in the Soviet
Union. They help to explain why many Russians deny that the category
of nationhood applies to them at all, and assert that the Soviet Union was
not an empire.

The wider mission may well entail a degree of self-abnegation. As
Smith observes, "In the great polyethnic empires we frequently encounter
conflicts between the universal pretensions of faith and empire [on the
one hand, and on the other] the heritage and interests of its culturally
dominant population."[10] As we shall see, those conflicts were acute in the
case of Soviet Russians, and sometimes left them feeling humiliated and
cheated even within the Soviet Union, let alone after it collapsed.

The term "missionary nationalism" used by Smith and Kumar assists us
in looking for a way to describe adequately the apparent contradictions of
Russian national consciousness. It helps to explain why Russians on the
whole do not regard their identity as being circumscribed by physical
boundaries, why they associate it with an "idea," and why they tend to reject the notion that it is adequately embodied in any particular territory
or state formation, seeing it instead as a spiritual or cultural entity.

In this sense the Russian situation is like that of dominant ethnies in
general. Until recently social scientists did not usually use the terms "ethnos" or "ethnie" for the English in the United Kingdom, the French in
France, or the Jews in Israel. "Ethnicity" was confined to minorities, who
had no state or only a subordinate one, and whose "ethnic" characteristics
therefore stood out by contrast to the dominant "political" ethos of the
ruling people. Recently, however, as decolonization and democratization
have swept across the world, and as European states have fragmented with
the end of the Cold War, peoples who took their state-bearing status and
their cultural dominance for granted have had for the first time to justify
or defend their situation, and in the process to rediscover their own hitherto unchallenged and therefore sometimes half-forgotten ethnic traditions.[11]

The failure to recognize ethnicity in a dominant group has been especially acute in the case of Russia. In most Western languages there is only
one word for "Russian," but the Russians themselves have two: *russkii,*

which refers to the people, the language, the culture, and the ethnos; and *rossiiskii*, which refers to the state, the empire, and the multinational territory. The difference is as important as that between "English" and "British," or—in some ways an even closer parallel—between "Turkish" and "Ottoman." If we neglect to draw these distinctions, we make elementary mistakes in writing about these peoples.

A corollary of this indiscriminate approach to Russia is that Westerners often write as if Russians, unlike other peoples, were not entitled to their own national consciousness, because by definition it is bound to be overbearing and chauvinistic. Now, admittedly, Russian national consciousness does tend to take on imperial or supraethnic forms: that is one of the main themes of the book that follows. But historically such an attitude has been associated with many other peoples as well; in any case, it hardly becomes an English or American scholar to chide the Russians for it. We should not automatically denigrate Russian national feeling as pernicious.

This book has been written in the overlap between two distinguished interpreters of Russian national identity, both of whom have deeply influenced my thinking, though they appear to hold almost diametrically opposed views: the émigré philosopher Nikolai Berdiaev and the Soviet dissident and novelist Aleksandr Solzhenitsyn.

In a celebrated study of the "Russian idea," Berdiaev asserted that, apart from the Jews, the Russians were the most messianic of peoples, and that Communism was merely the latest manifestation of this mentality. The Russian Empire, he argued, was sustained by the myth of the "Third Rome," the idea that Moscow was the successor of Rome and Byzantium as the bearer of the universal Christian idea: "Russia was the only Orthodox empire *(tsarstvo)*, and in that sense an ecumenical empire, like the first and second Romes."[12] The Soviet Union, in a paradoxical continuation of this tradition, was the Third International: "The messianic idea of Marxism, preaching the mission of the proletariat, combined with and became identical with the Russian messianic idea. In the Russian Communist revolution what became dominant was not the empirical proletariat but the idea, the myth of the proletariat. . . . Leninism-Stalinism is not classical Marxism. Russian Communism is a distorted variant of the Russian messianic idea. It proclaims light from the East to illuminate the bourgeois darkness of the West."[13]

Scholars have been divided in their approach to Berdiaev. Many see him as a source of snappy and serviceable quotes to highlight aspects of Russian thought or behavior. Few, however, have taken his equation of Third Rome and Third International wholly seriously. I believe his insight is very valuable, especially his contention that messianic consciousness generates an "imperialist temptation," so that a doctrine which starts out as universal becomes associated with a particular state, a particular form of rule, a particular national culture, and thus loses its universality.[14] I do not, though, accept his assertion that messianism is peculiar to the Russians; on the contrary, as I have argued, most large European nations have gone through at least one messianic period. In this respect Russia is a typical European nation. What distinguishes Russia is not its messianic mission as such, but rather the complex and contested nature of that sense of mission, and the attitude to it of both the state and the people.

Solzhenitsyn appears to say the opposite from Berdiaev, that the Soviet messianic ideology was not intrinsic but alien to Russian culture, that it came from outside, from the West, and undermined Russia's identity. Actually, both are right. There are two forms of Russian messianism, Christian and socialist, and the attitude of the ordinary people to both has been at times enthusiastic, at times restrained and suspicious. Solzhenitsyn's great insight was that in Russia people and empire were distinct, that the Russian people were separable from the Soviet Union and that their interests were not best served by spreading socialism throughout the world. He believed that Russians had been burdened with a universal ideology that was impeding their development as a nation. Thus far I agree. But I do not accept that Marxism was alien to Russia. It coalesced with Russian traditions of collectivism, and it retained specifically Russian messianic features that it shed in most of Europe. In any case, the split between people and empire in Russia had taken place before 1917; it was widened, but not created, by Marxist ideology.[15]

Russians' identity, as often happens, was formed in reaction to an "Other," in this case Western Europe, whose great power interactions from the late seventeenth century formed the context in which Russia developed. Unlike other world civilizations reacting against the West, however, Russia had no long-established religious or civilizational tradition as a distinct foundation on which to construct and validate its resistance, no equivalent of Islam, Confucianism, or the variety of Indian traditions that we normally call "Hinduism."[16] Its national creed, Orthodox Christianity, was one variant of the dominant Western religion. It had to borrow many of its foundation concepts from the West, though these were then reinterpreted and reconfigured through the practices of both the Russian state and the Russian people.

As part of its self-demarcation against the West, Russia actually generated two messianic ideas, one associated with Orthodoxy, the other with socialism. The two proved incompatible, indeed bitterly opposed to each other. Furthermore, each of them overlapped only partially with the community spirit of the Russian people. In the twentieth century the conflict between these three powerful forces burst into the open and reached its climax. That is why Russia's twentieth-century history has been so turbulent.

# 1

# MARXISM AND THE CRISIS
# OF RUSSIAN MESSIANISM

How did the idea take root that the Russians were a "chosen people" with a universal mission?

The concept of Moscow as the Third Rome, with a special mission to bring true Christianity to the whole of humanity, was born in the sixteenth century, after the fall of Byzantium. Although it sounds like an imperial project, the idea actually took shape in the church. In fact it was never really adopted by Muscovite tsars or by later Russian emperors, who feared that it would accord too much political influence to clergymen. They increasingly saw Russia as a European great power and a north Eurasian empire, not as a theocratic state.

The myth was, however, embodied in daily readings from the pulpit of Russian churches, and it seems to have resonated with ordinary people. It was cherished especially among the Old Believers. But it was widespread too, among peasants, merchants, clergymen of the official church, and even at times statesmen. The latent sentiment persisted that Russia was in some way a holy empire, chosen by God for a great mission.[1]

The subordination of the church to the state was deepened during the eighteenth and nineteenth centuries. Peter the Great abolished the patriarchate, symbol of the church's independent standing, and instead brought the church under the Holy Synod, which was in effect a department of state often headed by a layman. He and his successors also expropriated the church lands, the source of its self-sufficient wealth. They wanted the church to concentrate on the secular functions of providing education and tending to social welfare. In effect they carried out an abortive Protestant revolution within the church, but without the essential Protestant conditions of a literate, Bible-reading population and parish autonomy. The Bible was not even available in modern Russian (only in archaic Church Slavonic) until the 1870s. Adrian Hastings has emphasized the influence of Bible translation in generating a national language and in strengthening national identity among Christian peoples. In Russia it played such a role in the middle ages, but a declining one by the eighteenth and nineteenth centuries, since the scriptures were not available in the vernacular.[2] In this way modernization and the imperatives of empire actually delayed and obstructed the formation of Russian national consciousness.

## Popular Traditions of Social Solidarity

It is one thing to talk about state and church, quite another to consider the life of local communities far from the centers of power. Right up to the late nineteenth century Russia was overwhelmingly a country of small towns and villages, scattered over a huge territory, many of them at the margins of viable agriculture. For that reason the members of Russian communities were highly interdependent. From an early stage they had to generate collective arrangements that would provide for mutual support and help in their isolated and vulnerable situation. They developed a system known as *krugovaia poruka*—literally "circular surety," but perhaps best translated as "joint responsibility." All members of the community had to accept shared liability for settling conflicts, preventing crime, apprehending criminals, and maintaining common facilities.

Analogous systems can be found in the villages and small towns of most of medieval Europe— for example in England as tithings or frankpledge, and in France as the basis of the monarchy's tax-collecting system.[3] Most, however, were displaced or absorbed in the sixteenth to eighteenth centuries as monarchies became more powerful.[4] In Russia the opposite happened: with the coming of absolute monarchy "joint responsibility" was actually strengthened. The state took over *krugovaia poruka* as an administrative device, which helped it to restrain crime, collect taxes, and raise recruits for the army. If one household failed to pay its dues, the others had to make up the shortfall; if one recruit absconded or was found to be unsuitable for military service, then the community had to provide another in his place. This system greatly simplified the job of tax-collectors and recruiting sergeants.[5] It also made social life in both towns and villages more secure and predictable, since it meant that no individual or household faced misfortune on its own: the rest of the community was usually there as back-up. Everyone was a member of an interdependent collective bound by personal ties to someone in authority.

To achieve the level of consensus required to make such a system work, the community needed an open and accessible decision-making process. This was the function of the *selskii* or *posadskii skhod,* the village or town assembly, which normally consisted of all heads of households. It elected from among its own members a *starosta* (elder), who presided over its meetings, saw that decisions were implemented, and represented the community in dealings with the outside world and the authorities. Decisions in the assembly were taken by consensus, not by voting. Mutual agreement was important because decisions were supposed to reflect the crucial concept of *pravda:* this meant "truth," but also everything that was morally right, just, fair, and in accordance with God's law. Small-scale criminal charges and civil disputes within the community were settled by a court of older and respected villagers or townsfolk, the "best people," as written documents call them, chaired by the elder. Its findings also reflected *pravda,* though interpreted in such a way as to cause minimum damage to the economic life of the community as a whole.[6]

Both as social custom and administrative device, *krugovaia poruka* had profound implications for the Russians' view of life, especially for their attitude to law, property, and authority. For Russians law reflected consensus and *pravda,* and rights belonged to households and communities rather than to individuals. The tsar as an authority figure was also supposed to guarantee *pravda:* as the saying went, "God is found not in strength, but in *pravda.*" Ordinary people recognized, though, that his servitors were fallible and sinful, and they regarded them with reserve: "God is in his heaven, and the tsar is far away."[7]

*Krugovaia poruka* especially affected the life of the village. Peasants regarded the land as God's. It was given to human beings to use for their subsistence but did not belong to anyone in particular. It was a resource available to all who worked on it, along with their dependants, according to need. In keeping with that concept, many village communities periodically redistributed land among households to reflect changing family size and needs. Larger families would receive more land but would have to pay correspondingly higher taxes; smaller ones would lose land but also pay lower taxes. The key was to ensure that each household had enough to feed itself and discharge its obligations. The economic ideal was sufficiency. Both the indigent and the wealthy were regarded with distrust: the indigent because they were suspected of sloth and were a burden on the rest of the community, the wealthy because they were suspected of underhand practices that contravened *pravda* and might be a threat to their colleagues. As a popular saying had it, "Wealth is a sin before God; poverty is a sin before one's fellow villagers."[8]

Even after the money economy became generally accepted, in the second half of the nineteenth century, and peasants became accustomed to buying and selling land, they continued to assume, incongruously, that a basic minimum would always be available to them, should they need it, especially in emergencies like war, revolution, or famine.[9]

Because villagers were so interdependent, it was generally accepted that households should help each other out in difficulties, whether caused by shortage of food, sickness, theft, fire, or other contingency. Bread would be put aside for a starving family, herbs would be provided for the sick, neighbors would rally round and help with the harvest. There was no direct, equivalent exchange of services, but a general expectation that help given now would entitle one to receive help, of any kind needed, in the future. This mutual aid, known as *pomochi,* was not altruism but shared self-interest born of the fact that any household's misfortunes could affect the whole community.[10] Interdependence had its dark sides, too: villagers kept a close watch on one another's lives and constantly exchanged information. Gossip, often malicious, sustained the fabric of rural life, since heavy drinking, stealing, or marital discord could wreck the economic life of a household and therefore weaken the whole community. In this way communities of joint responsibility policed their own members.

*Krugovaia poruka* profoundly affected the outlook of Russians in all spheres of life. It was egalitarian and democratic, in that all households made their contribution to decision-making, yet also hierarchical and authoritarian, in that they were represented by their older, male members. Women and younger men were disadvantaged, and their interests were frequently poorly defended.[11] Joint responsibility generated community spirit and ensured that everyone could survive, yet it also squeezed out the gifted, deviant, or eccentric and generated its own internal splits and conflicts. It created dense networks of mutual obligations that were comforting yet required constant vigilance. In emergencies and difficulties—and there were to be plenty of those in the twentieth century—Russians tended to reproduce communities of joint responsibility adapted to the context in which they found themselves. Workers, for example, would enroll in an *artel*, a kind of labor cooperative, to live and work together and sign contracts with employers jointly. In the absence of effective institutions and laws, such communal associations were badly needed.

## Ukraine and Belorussia

Another aspect of ethnic Russia mattered greatly to the rulers. During the seventeenth and eighteenth centuries the Russian state absorbed a large number of East Slav communities—Ukrainians and Belorussians—who for centuries had lived under Polish or Lithuanian rule. Some of them were Orthodox, but many belonged to the Uniate (Greek Catholic) or even Roman Catholic faith. Their spoken dialects were related to the speech of Russian peasants, though with some alien vocabulary and syntax. Their culture was also similar, though they were far less likely than their Russian counterparts to practice mutual redistribution of land: individual plots would survive in the same family for generations, which meant that Ukrainian and Belorussian peasant households tended to feel a more intense attachment to a particular smallholding than did the Russians.[12]

The status of the Ukrainians and Belorussians was crucial to both the tsarist and later the Soviet state. They were numerous: at 22.4 million in 1897 the Ukrainians were "the largest non-dominant ethnic group in Europe," while the Belorussians added another 5.9 million people.[13] If both could be counted as Russians, then Russians constituted a considerable majority of the population in the state called after them, and offered a sound basis for the building of a Russian nation-state. If, however, they were acknowledged to be separate peoples, then Russians were in a minority in tsarist Russia and barely in a majority in the early Soviet Union. This was a serious matter, since, as Alexei Miller has pointed out, the Russian-Ukrainian encounter was "not the interaction of two shaped nations, but a rivalry between different projects of nation-building."[14] Moreover, behind the calculations of all Russian rulers hovered the threat of Poland, whose culture remained resilient, even when there was no independent Polish state. Russian rulers never altogether lost the fear that Poles were on the alert to claim Ukrainians and Belorussians for an alternative national project.

For that reason the tsarist regime abolished distinct Ukrainian institutions and referred to the geographical area as "Little Russia." It did its best to prevent the emergence of a printed Ukrainian literary culture. In 1863 an imperial decree prohibited the publication of books in Ukrainian, with the gloss that "there never has been a distinct Little Russian language, and there never will be one. The dialect which the common people use is Russian contaminated by Polish influence." P. A. Valuev, the minister responsible for the decree, advised the tsar that "permitting the creation of a special literature for the common people in the Ukrainian dialect would signify collaborating in the alienation of Ukraine from the rest of Russia."[15] A similar veto was laid on Belorussian, for the same reasons.[16]

At the beginning of the twentieth century the prospects for the formation of a distinct Ukrainian or Belorussian nation did not appear bright. The great majority of Ukrainians were illiterate peasants, while the Ukrainian nobles had more or less completely assimilated to the Russian imperial culture. In the larger towns of Little Russia few elites were Ukrainian: they were mostly Russian, Polish, German, even Greek or Armenian, while the urban masses were often Jewish. The clergy owed their loyalty to a Russian church that had no separate Ukrainian jurisdiction.

All the same, in the small towns and villages, and at the lower end of the professions, especially in the zemstvos (local government assemblies), there were a fair number of educated professional people, lawyers, doctors, feldshers (auxiliary medics), schoolteachers, and civil servants, who regarded themselves as Ukrainian; many of them were the sons and daughters of peasants or clergymen. Their focus on the local economy, health, and education gave a social welfare coloring to Ukrainian nationalism at this stage. In 1905–1907, when censorship relaxed, they launched Ukrainian-language newspapers and journals, founded scholarly societies, agricultural cooperatives, and political parties, and even for a time gained representation in the State Duma. At this time Ukrainian national sentiment focused on a number of themes: on the sixteenth-to-eighteenth century Dnieper Cossack institutions, with their own democratic self-government; on Ukrainian literature, especially the figure of Taras Shevchenko, the serf-poet who became a kind of Ukrainian Robert Burns; on the right to use Ukrainian in public life; and on the need for radical land reform so that Ukrainian peasants could make a good living from their holdings.[17]

The period 1914–1921 transformed the Ukrainian situation. The First World War sharpened perception of ethnic distinctions throughout Europe, not least in Russia, where, for example, the empress's German origin—scarcely noticed before the war—made her an object of suspicion. Little Russia was close to the front line throughout, and many Ukrainians became refugees; the aid organizations which offered help were mostly ethnically marked, that is, they emphasized attachment to the regional culture and language.[18] In the army, too, officers and men became more conscious of their ethnic origins, even while remaining on the whole steadfastly loyal to the tsar. Large numbers of junior officers were promoted, and the Little Russians among them came from precisely the social strata where Ukrainian feeling was strongest.[19]

As a result of these developments, after the fall of the tsar there was a sudden proliferation of Ukrainian associations of various kinds, which took most contemporaries by surprise. At the head was the Ukrainian Rada, the national equivalent of the All-Russian Congress of Soviets. When an All-Ukrainian Rada convened in Kiev in April 1917 it had delegates from zemstvos, army units, cultural-educational societies, professional associations, and peasant cooperatives. In May the Rada demanded home rule for Ukraine, separate representation in peace negotiations, and the formation of separate Ukrainian army units. A Ukrainian Military Congress met and set about creating a national army. After the fall of the Provisional Government in November, the Rada in its Third Universal (a term denoting a Cossack decree) proclaimed the independence of the Ukrainian People's Republic. This was real nation-building, however sudden and unexpected.[20]

The edifice could not be completed, though, because of the civil war. The first independent regime lasted only three months before it was overthrown by Russian-backed Reds, and soon afterward the whole country was occupied by the Germans. Over the next three years at least eight different kinds of regime ruled temporarily over substantial regions of Ukraine, but none was able to consolidate itself or even claim the adherence of most of the population. As Geoff Eley has commented, the "fragmentation of the polity and civil society" was "akin to the warlordism that dominated provincial China in the 1920s and 1930s."[21] The greatest weakness of Ukrainian nationalists was that they did not have the full backing of Ukrainian peasants, most of whom wanted land reform more than anything else and were prepared to accept land from whichever rulers offered it. In any case, the new Ukraine was torn between the great power ambitions of Germany, Soviet Russia, and Poland, as well as between its own irreconcilable political factions.[22]

All the same the memory of an independent state, however fragmented and embattled, thereafter remained a powerful factor in the Ukrainian self-image, especially since its memory was spectrally revived in 1922 in the shape of the Ukrainian Soviet Socialist Republic—not an independent state and not all of Ukraine, but still a real institution and a haunting reminder of what might be achieved. No longer could anyone simply take it for granted that Ukrainians would peacefully acquiesce in domination by Russians, of whichever political hue.

For Belorussians the situation was less clear. In 1897 a mere 2 percent of them lived in towns of more than 2,000 inhabitants, and among them there were almost no professional people; the urban population was mostly Jewish, Polish (in the west), and Russian (in the east). Ninety percent of Belorussians were engaged in agriculture, and modern Belorussian was largely a peasant dialect. In the second half of the nineteenth century Catholic intellectuals of peasant origin began to use it as a literary language, and this development, as we have seen, worried tsarist officials enough to ban Belorussian along with Ukrainian. It was revived after the 1905 revolution in the weekly journal *Naša Niva* (Our Cornfield, 1906–1915), whose content focused on the hard life of the peasants: this was what Belorussian intellectuals saw as their ethnic identity.[23]

In the turmoil of revolution and civil war, Belorussians attempted to establish a separate republic, at one stage in tandem with the Lithuanians, but there was no history of continuous independence, however embattled, between 1917 and 1921, as there was in Ukraine. In 1919, however, the Bolsheviks in Moscow sanctioned the creation of a Belorussian Soviet Republic, with its capital in Minsk, to parallel the one they were trying to establish in Ukraine. The idea seems to have been to create "buffer republics" between Soviet Russia and its neighbors to the west, a move that was also in line with Lenin's policy of setting up counterweights to "Great Russian chauvinism." Whatever the motive, the plan was opposed by some local Bolsheviks, who objected that Belorussia was not a nation and that there was no point in artificially engendering local nationalism.[24]

## Socialist Messianism

During the nineteenth century writers and thinkers revived the latent Russian messianic tradition and reformulated it in contemporary terms, as an assertion of Russia's special mission, distinct from that of the West. The Slavophiles maintained that Russians alone had withstood a damaging tide of individualism, atheism, and rationalism that had swept through Western Europe and was weakening the moral fiber of its peoples. Russians had retained a primeval sense of community, which the Slavophile theologian and historian Aleksei Khomiakov defined as *sobornost*, and with it a simple but deep Christian faith. According to the Slavophiles these characteristics equipped Russia potentially to heal the spiritual sickness of the West. They disapproved of the tsarist state, which they felt had absorbed much of the spiritual malady of the West, and they believed that Russia would have to be purified before it could shoulder such a mission. In the long run, however, they were confident that, cleansed of its impurities, Russia would be able to restore true Christianity to the more advanced and sophisticated but corrupted West.[25]

The Slavophiles attributed particular importance to the survival of the village commune. As we have seen, the Russian state had preserved the commune, with its *krugovaia poruka,* as a convenient device for the administration of the common people. Konstantin Aksakov, however, took a much more idealistic view: he called the commune "a moral choir . . . a union of the people, who have renounced their egoism, their individuality, and who express their common accord; this is an act of love and a noble Christian deed."[26] For the Slavophiles *sobornost* became the foundation ideology which gave Russia its distinctive faith and strength.

Shorn of its link with Orthodoxy, this outlook could easily be transmuted into a form of socialism. Between the 1860s and the 1890s, a whole pleiad of thinkers staked out a new concept of socialism, which took Marxism as its point of departure but rejected the idea that the revolution could only be led by the proletariat of the leading industrialist nations. On the contrary, they asserted, the peasants of Russia had distinct advantages: they still had their own primitive institutions, in which fundamental principles of socialism, like democratic self-government and property-sharing, were taken for granted. They had the potential to convert this rudimentary, unwitting socialism into modern, conscious socialism and avoid the evils of capitalism altogether. On the basis of a contemptuous reference by Lenin, these thinkers have gone down to posterity as "Populists" *(narodniki).* They differed from one another on whether the transition from primitive to modern socialism would come about through violent popular revolution (Mikhail Bakunin), through peaceful propaganda by educated and "conscious" people (Petr Lavrov), or with the help of a small elite that would seize power on behalf of the people (Petr Tkachev). But they all agreed that the peasant commune and its working-class equivalent, the artel, would form the basic building block of the new society.[27]

Most populists were atheists, but some explicitly professed Christianity of an nonecclesiastical kind. Andrei Zheliabov, organizer of the assassination of Alexander II in 1881, stated at his trial: "I deny Orthodoxy, although I affirm the essence of the teachings of Jesus Christ . . . All true Christians must fight for the truth, for the rights of the humiliated and the weak, and, if necessary, even suffer for them. This is my faith."[28]

It might be thought that Marxism, as a doctrine that, unlike Populism, was proletarian and internationalist, would repudiate any form of messianism associated with peasants or with a special Russian mission. Marx himself, however, was not always dogmatic about the course revolution might take. In 1881 he wrote to the Populist Vera Zasulich about the peasant commune: "special research has convinced me that this community is the mainspring of Russia's social regeneration."[29] He and Engels were in any case not immune from nationalism: they had a tendency to favor the larger European nations, and especially the Germans, as "progressive," while they considered "reactionary" and even "counter-revolutionary" the attempt of smaller ethnic groups to assert their national status in 1848–1849.[30] The notion of particular nations as bearers of social progress was not, then, wholly alien to the Marxist tradition.

Marxism was, moreover, partly Jewish in origin. Indeed, its founder was Jewish, and it proved especially appealing to Jews in Russia. They participated in the Russian revolutionary movement in strikingly large numbers from the 1870s onward. Most Jewish revolutionaries had reacted strongly in their adolescent years against the apparent rigidity and provincialism of their ethnic and religious heritage. Deprived of their family background and hating the autocracy, they found a spiritual home among the Russian socialists, who accepted them without prejudice and enabled them to participate in a struggle for an international brotherhood freed of all ethnic and racial stigmas. They entered this new and congenial environment while retaining certain core elements of their Jewish identity, notably the hope of bringing salvation to humanity. Lev Kogan-Bernshtein, before he was executed for his part in the Irkutsk rising of 1888, stated in his final speech: "By working all my life in the Russian revolutionary party, I worked for the destitute Jewish masses fully convinced that their fate is closely connected with the fate of all peoples living on the territory of Russia, and that the liberation of the Jewish people from political oppression can be realised only with the liberation of all Russia."[31]

At any rate, Jewish Marxists played a major role in promoting international revolution in Russia. It was the Jew Aleksandr Parvus-Helfand who first mooted the idea that the Russian proletariat might prove to be in the vanguard of European social revolution. Trotskii followed him, prophesying in June 1905 that the Russian working class would be "the initiator of the liquidation of world capitalism." The Russian bourgeoisie, he asserted, was so weak that the proletariat would have to take over the task of carrying out even the bourgeois revolution, which it would accomplish with the help of the peasants, who would be mounting their own revolution against feudalism. Thereafter, though, the Russian workers would lose the support of all peasants but the poorest, and, to take the revolution further, to the socialist stage, they would need support from abroad. They would get it from the proletariat of the more advanced European countries, who, inspired by the Russians' example, would by then have seized power in their own countries. Together with their Russian brethren they would declare a "republican United States of Europe," which in its turn would be the foundation for the "United States of the World."[32]

This intoxicating scenario of Russia as the flashpoint for world revolution inspired Lenin and helped his ideas to crystallize at a crucial stage. It inspired his vision of a Russian revolution of the proletariat and poor peasants sparking off a world revolution against imperialism. Here was the kernel of the Soviet Union's universal mission.

## Russian Popular Religion

The relationship of the ordinary Russian people to both forms of messianism, Orthodox and socialist, is hard to gauge. Students and young radicals, inspired by Lavrov, went out to the villages in the 1870s, both to learn from the peasants' primordial wisdom and to preach to them about how they could create true socialism in their villages. They got a mixed reception: many peasants welcomed their help, especially in the areas of medicine and education, and they were readily persuaded that the present landowning arrangements were inequitable. But they were prepared to accept a redistribution of land only if it was bestowed by the tsar, that is, in a moral and political framework that was already familiar to them. Socialist ideas seemed outlandish to them, or at least acceptable only if reframed in the language of the New Testament.[33]

Russian peasants were Orthodox believers and they attended Orthodox church services; indeed, if asked which nation they belonged to, most would probably have answered *pravoslavnyi*—Orthodox. All the same, their attitudes and practices were only loosely contained within the confines of the state church, a situation that worried the clergy. Some peasants were attracted to doctrines that prophesied the achievement of a truly Christian life on earth, to be achieved in the land of the "white waters" or in the sunken city of Kitezh. Some of these visions seemed to derive distantly from the ideal of the Third Rome. The Believers in Christ (*Khristovovery*), whose existence is first attested in the early eighteenth century, held that Christ was occasionally reincarnated in members of their own community who led an exemplary life. They would gather in their own congregations, in a private home or sometimes out of doors, wearing white garments. Divine worship would begin with their own "Christ" reading from the scriptures. On special occasions they would conclude the service with a *radenie*, a frenzied dance during which they would prophesy in tongues, like Muslim Dervishes or American Shakers. The Castrates (*skoptsy*), first attested in the late eighteenth century, tried to attain spiritual purity by more drastic means, mutilating themselves in order to achieve freedom from earthly and fleshly desires.[34]

Besides, many peasants remained Old Believers. By the early twentieth century, two hundred and fifty years or so after the schism that gave birth to their movement, the Old Belief claimed perhaps as many as one-sixth of all Orthodox believers.[35] It was influential even among those peasants who did not acknowledge membership in an Old Believer community. Frederick Conybeare, an American anthropologist who investigated popular religion in the 1910s, concluded that the strength of the Old Belief "lies less in its overt adepts than in the masses who mutely sympathize with it. . . . In many regions, among the *petit peuple* we meet with the singular opinion that official orthodoxy is only good for the lukewarm, that it is a worldly religion through which it is barely possible to attain salvation, and that the true and holy religion is that of the Old Believers."[36]

Russian socialists of the mid-nineteenth century hoped they might be able to forge some kind of link with the Old Believers—who, like them, were alienated from the official state and church. They soon found, however, that there was no basis for an alliance, so remote from socialism was the Old Believers' outlook. V. I. Kelsiev, a young socialist who visited their communities in the 1860s to inquire into their convictions, reported that not only they but the people as a whole "continue to believe today that Moscow is the Third Rome and that there will be no fourth. So Russia is the new Israel, a chosen people, a prophetic land, in which shall be fulfilled all the prophecies of the Old and New Testaments, and in which even the Antichrist will appear, as Christ appeared in the previous Holy Land. The representative of Orthodoxy, the Russian tsar, is the most legitimate emperor on earth, for he occupies the throne of Constantine."[37] These expectations might be messianic, but they were a long way from nineteenth-century socialism, of whatever variety.

Unlike the Old Believers, most peasants remained loyal to the official church, but their relationship with it was tense and, by the early twentieth century, evolving quite rapidly as peasants were becoming better educated and gaining experience of both urban and military life. Their religious culture was more homely and pragmatic than that of the sectarians. It combined narratives and symbols derived from Orthodoxy with rituals that celebrated local holy sites, marked the passage of the seasons and the agricultural cycle, and bestowed a deeper meaning on the events of family life.[38] Peasants were building new churches and chapels to house their own "wonder-working" icons, to commemorate a particular event, or to mark a holy place. They were organizing local festivals to supplement the country-wide ones in order to celebrate deliverance from an epidemic or a fire, or to mark the day of a saint they particularly cherished. As in Western countries, women were taking a greater part in religious life, generating narratives derived from their own spiritual experience and evoking the Virgin Mary—or, as Russians nearly always call her, the Mother of God—as guide, protector, and intercessor for women, the poor, and the weak. These demotic initiatives were regarded with misgivings by many clergymen, especially the bishops, who had come up through monasteries and had little experience of parish life. In generating their own versions of the Christian narrative, peasants became more insistent on the right to run their own parish affairs, a stance that was warmly welcomed by some clergymen but was regarded with distaste and suspicion by others.[39]

Overall, then, we may say that peasants' perceptions of religion were changing fast before 1917, as they became more literate and their links with urban culture became closer. Many of them were moving away from the official church, but that did not necessarily mean they were ready to embrace the socialism of intellectuals. They were partly engaged with both kinds of messianism, Orthodox and socialist, but not fully with either.

## The Orthodox Church

In most societies one of the principal mediators of national memory is the national church. For Russians this was especially true, for the Orthodox Church was a cardinal feature of their national identity. Their faith was, in their own eyes, what distinguished them from Germans, Poles, Jews, and Turks.

As we have seen, however, in the early twentieth century the Orthodox Church was under pressure both from rival faiths and from its own parishioners. Within the church, too, few clergymen, whether from the white (parish) or the black (monastic) clergy, were content with their situation. In answer to a questionnaire circulated by the Holy Synod in 1905, nearly all the bishops expressed dissatisfaction and recommended reform. They felt that the church did not have sufficient independence from the state, that it was poverty-stricken and unable to operate properly under what some called a "Protestant Caesaropapist" regime.[40]

Nearly everyone agreed, then, that reform was essential. But the clergy was split on what kind of reform was needed. There were two main approaches. One, which we may call that of the "episcopal conservatives," called for renewal of the church from above: they recommended the restoration of the patriarchate as the symbolic head of the church, and of the *pomestnyi sobor* (local council) as its sovereign assembly. Supporters of this viewpoint believed the bishops should play the leading role in the *sobor*. The other approach focused on the parish: it maintained that the white (parish) clergy and parish councils should be given more power to take their own decisions, appoint their own priests, and manage their own finances. The proponents of this line may be called "parish liberals" or "congregationalists," as they believed that revival would come from below. They mostly wanted the church to lift the ban on white clergymen becoming bishops, so that parish concerns would be better reflected at the higher levels of the church. Some of them also wanted to conduct parts of the liturgy in modern Russian (rather than Church Slavonic), to make them easier for ordinary people to understand.[41]

The division between these two reformist camps was sharp, and feelings between them sometimes bitter. They reflected indirectly the division in Russian society between the elites and the ordinary people. "Parish liberals" tended to sympathize with the peasants and workers of their parishes, and some of them inclined toward socialism, which they regarded as the contemporary embodiment of Christianity. Father Gapon, the organizer of the January 1905 St. Petersburg workers' demonstration, was one of them. In 1905 a group of thirty-two St. Petersburg clergymen published a petition calling for reform on "congregational" lines, and joined with a group of lay Christian socialists to form a Union for Church Regeneration with a wider social reform agenda.[42]

In 1905–1906 the church set about reforming itself, and the opposing camps had the opportunity to debate these issues at length in a so-called pre-conciliar consultative commission. The commission was intended to prepare the way for a full-scale *pomestnyi sobor,* whose convening would itself mark the first step to overhauling the church's structure. At a late stage, however, the tsar countermanded his order for the meeting of the *sobor.* All the reform plans fell by the wayside, but their supporters nonetheless continued to believe passionately in them.[43]

In the eyes of many believers the church, for all its defects, remained the bearer of the national messianic idea. At the celebration of the festival of the Kazan icon of the Mother of God in 1907, Archpriest Ioann Vostorgov declared that "Divine Providence, calling us Russian Slavs . . . into the bosom of the Church of Christ, in the very geographic placement of our country on the border between Europe and Asia, East and West, laid upon us a great mission: to carry the treasure of Christ and the true faith we have received to remote eastern and northern Europe, and further into Asia, to struggle with the darkness of paganism . . . to enlighten the wild tribes of aliens [*inorodtsy*] and to have them join in the Kingdom of God and in the life of enlightened humanity."[44]

## Dostoevskii and Russian Messianism

One figure stood at the crossroads of both Christian and socialist forms of messianism: the novelist Fedor Dostoevskii. His view of European civilization was similar to that of the Slavophiles: it was rationalist, individualist, mercenary, and atheist. He came to believe that Russia could provide healing for the West's spiritual ailments "in the form of God's *pravda,* in the form of the Truth of Christ which will surely some day be realized on earth and which is preserved in its entirety in Orthodoxy."[45]

In his regular newspaper column, "Diary of a Writer," Dostoevskii offered what may be called the classic definition of messianic nationalism: "Every great people believes—and must believe if it wishes to be alive for long—that the salvation of the world is to be found in it and in it alone, that it lives in order to stand at the head of the peoples, attach them all to itself in unity, and lead them in a harmonious choir to the ultimate goal, predestined for them all."[46]

With the Serbian rebellion of 1876–1877 against Ottoman rule, Dostoevskii hoped that the opportunity had come to turn his vision into reality. He attacked the government's failure to take the side of the insurgents against their oppressors. Russia's mission, he urged, was to act as the leader of the Slav peoples, to conquer Constantinople, and to inaugurate a reign of "eternal peace" in the Slav spirit: "Our war . . . is the first step to the attainment of that eternal peace in which we are fortunate enough to believe, and to the achievement of a *genuinely* caring prosperity for humanity."[47]

The intensity of Dostoevskii's convictions led him to conceive an abiding hatred of the rival messianic people, the Jews. He was not the first Russian to feel this way, but his anti-Semitism was unusually vehement. In his *Diary of a Writer* he stigmatized the Jews as marked by "materialism, a blind, carnivorous hunger for *individual* material security, a thirst for personal accumulation of money by any means."[48] He misquoted the Old Testament to imply that they were aiming at the physical conquest of the world and the enslavement of other peoples.[49] The Dostoevskian temptation has remained latent within Russian nationalism. Whenever the Russian universalist messianic dream falters, some Russians are always tempted to blame the Jews.

Dostoevskii came closer than any other Russian thinker to combining the two forms of messianism, the Christian and the socialist, to reconciling empire and people in one syncretic vision. He believed that the empire had a special mission thanks to its size and might, and that the people had too thanks to their humility, their readiness to accept suffering, and their tolerance of other cultures and faiths. In his vision, empire and people together could save Europe, restore true Christianity, and defeat socialism at its own game.

Dostoevskii's reconciliation of apparent incompatibles, his breathtakingly ambitious vision of Russia's future as the harbinger of universal humanity, have made him an eternally attractive thinker for Russians. No one has so well articulated for them what they felt their national identity ought to be. In an indirect sense, this vision was the unacknowledged foundation for the messianic premise of the Soviet state. It is no accident that from the 1960s onward Dostoevskii became the favorite author of many Russian intellectuals.

## The Desacralization of the Monarchy

What defeated Orthodox messianism and gave the socialist version its chance was the fall of the Romanov dynasty. Up to the early twentieth century the linchpin of the Russian political system had been the tsar. The original concept of authority that sustained him was Byzantine: the monarch was God's anointed and was considered sufficiently holy to have priestly powers. But he was not held to be an actual God, and therefore he had a partner, the church. It was the function of the church to remind the monarch of God's law in any given circumstance; it was the function of the monarch to exercise physical authority and to protect church and people. This was the *symphony*, the enmeshing of two distinct but mutually reinforcing forms of authority.

From the eighteenth century, however, the emperor (as the tsar now significantly retitled himself) claimed absolute authority, including in areas that had previously belonged to the church. He no longer acknowledged the church as forming a restraint on his power. Symbolically, this assertion of absolute power was accomplished when Peter the Great abolished the patriarchate in 1700 and in effect became head of the church himself. At the festive entry into St. Petersburg following his victory over the Swedes at Poltava in 1709, Peter was greeted with words formerly reserved for the patriarch: "Blessed be He who cometh in the name of the Lord!"[50]

The great majority of Russian people, however, including the clergy, continued to regard the emperor as a Byzantine *vasileus,* a figure of great power, but still answerable to God's law. There was thus a latent contradiction in the image of the tsar (as he was still usually known) held by the people and church on the one hand and by the bureaucracy and educated strata on the other. This contradiction was not fatal as long as the tsar could project himself as a powerful military leader, holding his own among the European powers, extending and defending his huge realm. He was able to accomplish that for the eighteenth and the first half of the nineteenth century. But then came defeat in the Crimean War in 1856: the first sign that his authoritative aura was beginning to fade. The disjuncture between the holy God-fearing Byzantine monarch and the amoral but all-powerful emperor began to become obvious and troubling. Significantly, this was the moment when the radical political opposition turned against the monarchy on principle and the first attempts were made to assassinate the tsar.[51]

In the early twentieth century the discrepancy between the two images of the tsar became much more serious, and ultimately fatal. Until then most workers and peasants—whatever they might think of bureaucrats, police, and landowners—had remained faithful to the image of their ruler as a holy figure abiding by God's law. As discontent among workers mounted, the first attempt to organize them for political action was made by a priest, Father Gapon of St. Petersburg. Gapon believed that if the tsar were alerted to the deprivation and oppression in which workers lived, he would come to their defense and issue decrees limiting the capitalists' exploitation of them. His movement was a kind of revivalist crusade. When the workers demonstrated in the capital city in January 1905, they carried not only a petition calling for more legal rights but also icons and portraits of the tsar. However, they were not received in audience by the tsar, as they had hoped. Instead, nervous soldiers opened fire on them, and a massacre resulted in which some two hundred workers were killed. This was even more of a disaster than it appeared at first sight, for it destroyed the hope of a revived urban Orthodoxy in partnership with a renewed and popular monarchy. Moreover, with the easing of censorship, the newspapers began to carry reports of the massacre that spread throughout the empire, including the villages, and provoked widespread unrest.[52] A sacral link between monarch and people had been severed. When tested, the monarch had behaved, not like the *vasileus* who observed God's law, but like a tyrant who did not.

This was the decisive moment when most politically active workers turned away from Christianity to one or another form of socialism. One scholar who has studied the writings of workers in the post-1905 period notes that they remained religious, but in an eclectic spirit, using themes derived from Christianity, but in a metaphorical or symbolic manner, and combining them with motifs from other religions and from revolutionary

socialism: "They typically viewed human existence . . . as a mythic journey through suffering toward deliverance from affliction, evil, even death.
Images of martyrdom, crucifixion, transfiguration and resurrection remained part of their creative vocabulary, as did narrative attention to suffering, evil and salvation." A poet of the Petrograd Proletkult (a worker's
cultural organization of 1917) wrote: "As God we proclaim Man, as the
Mother of God—the Machine, and as Jesus the Messiah—the Conscious
Socialist Hero."[53]

In February 1917 the monarchy was not merely overthrown; it was discredited and shorn of its sacred aura. This was quite unlike the situation
in France after the 1789 revolution, when many people were prepared to
fight for the monarchy, which as a result was actually restored in 1815. In
Russia a vacuum remained where the tsar had been. In the civil war none
of the White leaders, whatever their private views, called for the restoration of the monarchy because they knew that to do so would be to jeopardize public support for their cause. It is difficult to exaggerate the disori-
entation this absence generated. The source of power, hierarchy, law and
order, tradition, and stability had been eliminated. The social memory
not only of Russians but of most non-Russians too had been loosed from
its moorings. Everyone had to operate in a political, legal, and moral
framework no longer guaranteed by the state.

## Russian Socialism and Revolution

The vacuum was filled by Russian messianic socialism. Why, among the
European nations, was it Russia that generated a specifically socialist form
of messianism? Here the long survival of *krugovaia poruka* was decisive.
Russians were accustomed to a modest standard of living, and they were
accustomed to helping each other out in difficulties. They had never fully
accepted private property, individualism, and legalism. Egalitarianism,
joint responsibility, and mutual aid were ideals and habitual practices that
came naturally to most of them. The revolutionary movement of peasants
and workers in 1905–1907 and in 1917 was impelled partly by material
self-interest, but also by their own vision of *pravda*, that is, equality, justice, and self-rule. When in 1905 the tsar invited village assemblies to
put forward their own proposals for reform, the most popular demand
was for private ownership of land to be abolished, and for all land to be
transferred to those who worked it. As the resolution of an assembly in

Volokolamsk district, Moscow province, put it, "Land should be used only by those who cultivate it, in their families or in mutual associations, but without hiring labor, and in such quantity as they are able to cultivate."[54]

Urban workers had a more developed view than peasants of civil rights and democratic processes, but they too supported the peasant demand for the land, and supplemented it with their own demand for electing workers to factory supervisory committees. In the autumn of 1905 they improvised for themselves the urban equivalent of the village assembly, the soviet of workers' deputies. Soviets were elected by the employees of all the major industrial enterprises of any given city; they would assemble in a large building—or sometimes even on a river bank. Not only deputies but also their constituents could attend and speak, and deputies could be recalled at any time by their electors and replaced.[55] This was the closest thing to direct democracy that could be devised in the urban environment.

These were the features of Russian society which the Populists had always emphasized, and their view was cogent, given the nature of Russia's economy and its relationship to society and government. Capitalism and its related social institutions were less developed in Russia than in any other part of Europe save the Balkans. One indication of this mindset can be seen in the official and public reaction to the food-supply crisis during the First World War. Whereas the other combatant states used the commercial market to ensure that cities and armies were fed, both the Russian government and the voluntary associations sought grain through non-profit cooperative organizations that kept prices low. One result was that grain deliveries declined seriously by early 1917, precipitating the crisis that brought down the tsarist regime.[56]

When the tsar was overthrown in February 1917 and succeeded by the Provisional Government, strange transformations took place among Russia's political parties. The Kadets, who had long stood for liberal democracy and self-rule for the nationalities, now clung to the forms of an authoritarian empire and insisted on continuing the war; in the Provisional Government they refused to grant Ukraine autonomy and delayed the convening of a Constituent Assembly, because they feared undermining the Russian state. Even more surprisingly, the Mensheviks (Marxist socialists) and the Socialist Revolutionaries (Populist socialists) did the same—though the process caused a fatal split in the latter party.[57] Whatever political party found itself responsible for the fate of Russia was in thrall to the inherited form of the Russian state and was loath to tamper with it for fear of triggering a total breakdown of law and order. In 1917 only the Bolsheviks did not feel the same responsibility for Russia, and so they were free to launch their own slogans calling for an end to the war, for peasants to seize the land, for soldiers to take control of the army, and for nationalities to determine their own future, even though they knew these aims entailed the destruction of the state. Once they were themselves in power, though, the Bolsheviks also became subject to the same imperial imperatives, as we shall see.

In October 1917 the final collapse of government, army, police, and judiciary gave the peasants the opportunity to put their vision of land, law, and local government into practice. The new Bolshevik government explicitly gave them their head: borrowing the very words of a peasant congress of June 1917, it abolished private landownership and transferred all rural land to village and volost land committees for redistribution among peasant households. This decree at last satisfied the peasants' centuries-old longing to own all the land and run village affairs themselves. Sometimes peacefully, sometimes by violence, the village assemblies took over the land and the manor houses, dividing them up among themselves according to criteria worked out separately in each village.[58] Meanwhile in the cities, workers voted deputies to factory committees that undertook the supervision of industrial enterprises and usually ended up by expropriating the owners; and they elected delegates to city soviets whose armed detachments carried out the seizure of power. That is why the post-revolutionary government was called the "worker-peasant authority" *(rabochekrestianskaia vlast)* and the state was referred to as Soviet Russia, later the Soviet Union. Actual power, though, passed into the hands of the Bolsheviks, mainly because they were the only political party which was prepared at that juncture to sacrifice the existing Russian state to popular aspirations.[59]

The process of revolution demonstrated the degree of embitterment and alienation that existed between the people and the privileged, educated classes of old Russia. Whatever the niceties of Marxist class analysis, the term *burzhui* was applied indiscriminately to old-regime landowners, merchants, priests, lawyers, professors, and army officers—anyone who looked well-dressed or well-fed. As Orlando Figes has remarked, *burzhui* denoted "not so much a class as a set of popular scapegoats, or internal enemies, who could be redefined almost at will to account for the break-down of the market, the hardships of the war and the general inequalities of society." "We should exterminate all the *burzhui*," declared one factory worker in January 1918, "so that the honest Russian people will be able to live more easily." Trotskii recommended they be rounded up and made to shovel snow from the streets or clean out barrack-room latrines. Under the slogan "Loot the looters!" (*grab nagrablennoe!*) workers, peasants, and soldiers took over factories, marched on manor houses, and requisitioned bourgeois apartments with the explicit approval of the new regime. "I've spent all my life in the stables," a former servant declared at a political rally, "while they live in their beautiful flats and lie on soft couches playing with their poodles. No more of that, I say! It's my turn to play with poo-dles now; and as for them, it's their turn to go and work in the stables."[60]

Peasants also interpreted the land redistribution as a blow against the privileged. When the future writer Konstantin Paustovskii visited his aunt's estate in the Polese district of Belorussia, the driver of his horse and cart asked him when the "general permit" would "come through . . . for us peasants to take the land and be masters and to stick all the big and little masters in the backside with our pitchforks and send them all to the devil's mother?"[61] Actually, peasants did sometimes admit the former landowner to their community and award him a fair peasant-size plot of land, provided he turned himself into a peasant by cultivating it himself without hired labor. By contrast, landowners who resisted expropriation of their estate might be murdered along with their families, or at best driven to the nearest railway station and dumped there with a warning never to return. In Usman district of Tambov province, for example, Prince Boris Viazemskii was seized in his manor house by a crowd of peas-ants and subjected to a kangaroo court which initially resolved he should be sent to the front, "so that he can learn to fight as the peasants have done." But from the public bench at the court there were shouts of "Let's kill the Prince, we're sick of him!"; and before he got as far as the railway station, a drunken mob fell upon him and murdered him.[62]

Whatever happened to the landowners, peasants would then set about looting the manor house—usually starting with the wine cellars, con-fiscating tools and utensils that might be useful, and then smashing pic-tures, furniture, books, musical instruments, and anything else that re-called a more cultured way of life than they led themselves. Finally they would burn down the manor to ensure that the *barin*'s departure was final.

In September and October 1917 alone, one-fifth of the manors in Penza province were destroyed.[63] This was an orgiastic clearout of the cultivated, Europeanized milieu which had made peasants feel both alienated and exploited.

The October revolution was, then, both a conspiratorial seizure of power conducted by Lenin and the Bolsheviks and also a mass movement inspired by the egalitarian self-governing practices of peasants and workers—joined now by soldiers. The two aspects of the revolution intersected and overlapped. The socialist outlook did have quite a lot in common with the aspirations of workers and peasants: they shared, for example, the view of profit as immoral and of property as illegitimate except where it was justified by manual labor. But the people's outlook actually stemmed mainly from Christianity and from customary peasant practices rather than from any kind of theoretical socialism, even though by now quite a few workers and peasants had learned to frame their aims in socialist language.

By the same token, the underlying worldview of Marxist intellectuals was at a considerable remove from that of the ordinary Russian people. One can appreciate the difference if one considers the outlook of the young Ukrainian Jewish Communist Lev Kopelev in the early 1920s:

> World revolution was absolutely essential, so that justice should at last triumph, so that prisoners should be freed from bourgeois jails, so that the hungry should be fed in India and China, so that lands taken from the Germans and the Danzig "corridor" should be restored and our Bessarabia taken away from Romania . . . So that afterward there should be no more frontiers at all, no capitalists or fascists anywhere. So that Moscow, Kharkov, and Kiev should be as large and well-equipped as Berlin, Hamburg, or New York. So that we should have skyscrapers and streets full of cars and bicycles, so that all workers and peasants should go around in good-quality clothes, with hats and watches . . . And so that there should be airplanes and airships everywhere.[64]

There was a small area of overlap between this outlook and that of the Russian peasant, but its whole mental context, with its orientation to the modern, urban, international world, was completely different.

Both sides—peasants and socialist intellectuals—were determined to get their way, and ultimately they were bound to clash. When that happened, in the late 1920s and early 1930s, their conflict destroyed the traditional Russian way of life, but also transformed Marxism beyond recognition.[65]

Shortly after the revolution, all the same, the two forms of messianism were unexpectedly combined in one single poem by Aleksandr Blok. Called *The Twelve*—indicating a detachment of Red Guard soldiers, but also suggesting the apostles—it ends with the figure of Jesus Christ leading the soldiers through the streets of Petrograd:

> Thus they advance with state-bearing step,
> Behind them a hungry cur,
> Whilst at their head with blood-red flag,
> Invisible in the snowstorm,
> Impervious to the bullets,
> At a gentle pace above the blizzard,
> In the pearly scattering of snow,
> With a wreath of white roses,
> Before them all walks Jesus Christ.[66]

This ending surprised Blok himself. In a letter answering criticism of it, he replied: "I don't like the end of *The Twelve* either. . . . When I'd finished, I was surprised myself. Why Christ? Could it really be Christ? But the more I looked, the more clearly I saw Christ. And that's when I made a note of it for myself: unfortunately *Christ*. Christ and no one else." In his creative imagination, Blok was drawing on both the Bible—especially the Book of Revelation—and the recent culture of his own country. In so doing, he was coming up with dualistic apocalyptic imagery that well reflected the dual and contradictory nature of the Russian revolution.[67]

Among the Bolshevik leaders themselves, Anatolii Lunacharskii was the most effusive in his celebration of a specifically *Russian* revolution. He contrasted Russia with the United States, where mechanization enabled people to live a more leisured life, but where human beings had been taken over by machines and by the petty selfishness of capitalism. Russian workers, by contrast, he claimed, might appear backward and clumsy, but they had already shown that they could humanize industrial labor: "Our 'New America' will aim to use the labor of machines to make human life elegant and enjoyable."[68] Conceding that American workers were more efficient and pragmatic than their Russian counterparts, he nevertheless concluded, looking at the October revolution, that "the Russian working class was able, bleeding and offering enormous sacrifices, to rise from the depths of autocracy and barbarism to the position of avant-garde of humanity."[69] The theme of "America minus capitalism plus a humane culture" was to remain a dominant motif in the Soviet self-image.

## The Whites

One might have expected the White armies, or at any rate their leaders during the civil war of 1917–1921, to have acted as bearers of the Russian national idea against international socialism. That turned out not to be the case, for a number of reasons.

The main problem was the heritage of the empire. Russia was not a nation but an empire, and its identity was firmly linked to the person of the tsar. As we have seen, however, both the person and the myth of the tsar had been thoroughly discredited by 1917.

What, then, were the Whites fighting for? Senior White officers had received their training in the old Imperial Army, in a milieu that deliberately eschewed politics as something illegitimate. They were therefore both ignorant and contemptuous of it. Their propaganda was vague, confusing, and to many people threatening. They readily confused liberalism, socialism, and non-Russian nationalism as part of a single conspiracy, probably master-minded by the Jews, to destroy Russia.[70] The only formula on which they could all agree was "Russia, one and indivisible." But that simplified slogan suggested different things to different people: there was no agreed formulation of what "Russia" meant. Some, especially in the early stages of the civil war, were fighting for the prematurely dissolved Constituent Assembly as the only body that could claim to have been legitimately elected by the Russian people. But for most Whites the assembly was itself far too left-wing in its composition to be acceptable as a political icon.

Paradoxically, then, the Reds were fighting for (relatively) established institutions, the soviets, which at least in some sense represented the aspirations of the great mass of Russians. By contrast the Whites, the ostensible conservatives, created raw, unstable institutions and were proposing a vague and quixotic ideal with little popular support. Most peasants, workers, and soldiers feared that the Whites would deprive the peasants of their recently won land and self-government, bring back the capitalists, and let foreigners rule Russia. In another paradox, by seeking support from Russia's former World War I allies, the Whites, for all their devotion to "Russia," actually appeared unpatriotic, while the Reds, who had no foreign allies, could warn that imperialists were trying to crush the young Russian socialist state. Incongruously, the Reds were thus able, when it suited them, to pose as the party of patriotism.

Russian messianism came, then, in two configurations, Orthodox and socialist, both of which partially intersected with the outlook of the people, but neither of which fully met their needs. The revolution meant the apparent victory of the socialist variety. The Soviet Union then became the forum for a double struggle: between Communism and Orthodoxy, and between Communism and the Russian people. The first ended in initial victory but ultimate defeat for the Communists; the second was inconclusive, but each side was profoundly changed by the other.

# 2

# THE EFFECTS OF REVOLUTION
# AND CIVIL WAR

## Communists in Power

Among the great empires that fell after the First World War, the Russian and Ottoman were in some ways remarkably alike. They both straddled the borders of Christianity and Islam, both had a multiethnic ruling class, both professed a potentially universal religious faith, and both had a majority peasant population that bore the main burdens of empire. After 1922, however, their fates were completely different. The heartland of the Ottoman Empire became a Turkish nation-state, and with the abolition of the Caliphate it abandoned its sponsorship of a universal religion. The Russians, on the contrary, restored their empire almost completely; they abandoned one universal religion but took up another that was even more ambitious in its earthly claims.

The victorious Bolsheviks combined the multiethnic outlook of the imperial state with the messianism of the former Russian religious and political opposition. This was the first time, at least since the seventeenth century, that the Russian state had been messianic in its official outlook. In its new character as the Soviet Union, it was the bearer of the one true faith, Marxist socialism, which it aimed to carry to the entire world under the slogan "Workers of the world, unite!" That they had to achieve their task in the crucible of civil war only confirmed the Bolshevik leaders in their conviction that the transformation of society was both necessary and possible. No sooner had they seized power than they began implementing that transformation in the name of the people.

In appearance, then, this was a truly popular government, devoted to giving the people what they wanted. Yet it did so by destroying civil society and intermediate institutions, so that nothing remained between the regime and the people. For that reason extreme democratism was accompanied by extreme authoritarianism. Alongside the new people's courts the government set up an Extraordinary Commission for Struggle with Counter-Revolution and Sabotage—the Cheka, as it is commonly known—in essence the new regime's secret police, answerable to no popularly elected institution. To run all branches of the economy, a Supreme Council of the National Economy (Vesenkha) was created, which absorbed the new factory workers' committees and took charge of all commercial operations. Peasants now had their own land, but the grain grown on it was soon subject to compulsory requisition. In the armed forces, the soldiers' committees were absorbed into the regime's new "political departments" under "political commissars"; officers from the old army returned to take command and restored full military discipline, including the death penalty. The imperatives of the new-style universal empire took precedence over the creation from below of a national community.

Lenin saw no contradiction between democracy and dictatorship. The term "dictatorship of the proletariat" comfortably embraced both, and they were amalgamated in his thinking by the absolute desirability and popularity of the aims the Bolsheviks were pursuing. He believed that it would be sufficient to transfer the commanding heights of the capitalist economy to workers and peasants for exploitation to end and for the fruits of production to be available to the great majority of the people—provided they acted efficiently and ruthlessly.[1] "Comrade workers," he exhorted on November 5, 1917,

remember that *you yourselves* are administering the state. Nobody is going to help you if you do not yourselves unite and take over *all* affairs of state. Rally round your soviets: make them strong. . . . Institute strict revolutionary order, suppress without mercy the anarchic excesses of drunken hooligans, counter-revolutionary cadets, Kornilovites, etc. Institute rigorous supervision over production and accounting over products. Arrest and deliver to the tribunal of the revolutionary people anyone who dares to raise his hand against the people's cause.[2]

These were the tones of the millennial revolutionary, confident that, after a final decisive trial of strength, deliverance and the reign of peace and plenty were at hand.

The first draft program of the Communist Party envisaged a similar combination of spontaneous self-organization from below with ruthless dictatorship from above to eliminate the privileged social classes and establish complete social equality along with full communal self-government. It foresaw the end of the individual domestic economy, to be replaced by "joint catering for large groups of families." It recommended replacing the labor market with "universal compulsory labor service," and trade with "planned, organized distribution," which would eventually make money unnecessary, though in the meantime all banks would be controlled by the state.[3] In his book *The ABC of Communism,* written to put the party's program in plain words for the masses, Nikolai Bukharin explained that there would no longer be commodities but only products, and they would be "neither bought nor sold; they will simply be stored in communal warehouses, and subsequently be delivered to those who need them. In such conditions money will no longer be required."[4] In appearance the egalitarian principles of the Russian village commune were now to be applied universally by the state. But at the level of a whole country this could be accomplished only by a centralized, highly authoritarian, and well-informed government—one, moreover, working on principles that had only limited points of contact with the popular worldview and peasant custom. The domestic, social, and economic institutions of Russia were to be uprooted and replaced by a paternalist police state.

To ensure that this method of rule not be confused with parliamentary democracy, the new regime in January 1918 closed down the institutional child of the February revolution, the Constituent Assembly, which had been newly elected on the most generous franchise Russia had seen up to that time. The Bolsheviks received a respectable number of votes, but the largest single party in the Assembly was the Socialist Revolutionaries, the party of peasant self-government. Lenin claimed that the Assembly represented only "bourgeois democracy" and must yield to "democratic institutions of a higher order," the soviets. This was the first sign that the two revolutions of 1917 were set to clash with each other.

The early utopian Communist declarations also asserted categorically that the advance toward socialism meant the end of the nation and the nation-state:

National enmity and ill-feeling are among the means by which the
proletariat is stupefied and by which its class consciousness is
dulled. . . . The worker who, under capitalism, proclaims himself
a patriot, is selling for a copper or two his real fatherland, which
is socialism; and thereby he becomes one of the oppressors of the
backward and weak nations. . . . No matter what tongue the workers
of other lands may speak, the essential feature of their condition
lies in this, that they are all exploited by capital, that they are all
comrades, that they all suffer alike from poverty, oppression and injustice.[5]

Only the international proletariat could create a truly humane world:
"The proletariat today is the true savior of mankind from the horrors
of capitalism, from the barbarities of exploitation, from colonial policy,
incessant wars, famine, a lapse into savagery and brutalization, from all
the abominations that are entailed by financial capital and imperialism.
Herein lies the splendid historical significance of the proletariat."[6]

The ultimate vision was intoxicating: a superior human species, capable
of assimilating and surpassing the greatest cultural and scientific achievements of the past. Trotskii evoked his dream at the end of his book *Literature and Revolution:*

Man will make it his purpose to master his own feelings, to raise his
instincts to the heights of consciousness, to make them transparent,
to extend the wires of his will into hidden recesses, and thereby to
raise himself to a new plane, to create a higher social-biological type
or, if you please, a superman. . . . Man will become immeasurably
stronger, wiser, and subtler; his body will become more harmonized,
his movements more rhythmic, his voice more musical. The forms of
life will become dynamically dramatic. The average human type will
rise to the heights of an Aristotle, a Goethe, or a Marx. And above
this ridge new peaks will rise.[7]

To begin the work of creating an international proletarian state, in
1919 Soviet Russia founded the Communist International, or Comintern. From the outset the Comintern drew a clear distinction between the
old socialism of Western Europe, which merely strove to improve workers'
conditions within existing bourgeois societies, and the new revolution-

ary socialism, which aimed to transform the world. The Comintern denounced "reformist" and "opportunist" socialist leaders who had let their parties become "subsidiary organs of the bourgeois state," and it called for the overthrow of fraudulent parliamentary regimes in favor of "a new and higher workers' democracy." In 1920 it placed twenty-one conditions before European socialist parties who wished to join it, among which were issuing propaganda laying bare the bogus nature of existing democracies and preparing for an armed seizure of power.[8] In most countries only a small minority of socialists were prepared to satisfy these conditions and to join Communist parties, that is, parties affiliated with the Comintern. Their small number underlined the contrast between the messianic universalist socialism of Soviet Russia and the pragmatic, parliamentary, nation-bound socialism prevalent in most of Europe.

## Civil War and Chaos

In messianic thinking, deliverance is preceded by the apocalypse. The events of 1917–1921 bore out this expectation. As the historian Lynne Viola has commented, "Three of the four horsemen of the apocalypse—war, famine and disease—stalked the Russian land in an all too literal orgy of death and destruction."[9] Social capital and national memory were destroyed on an unprecedented scale. The development of civilized society was halted and reversed. The monarchy was abolished and discredited, the Orthodox Church disestablished, weakened, and divided. For a messianic political party, such devastation was not a disaster but an opportunity. Bolsheviks had always accepted that they could not create a new society without a destructive upheaval. But for most of the Russian people this transformation entailed a drastic decomposition of their society, a descent into a formlessness and chaos that were to leave their mark on them for decades—in a sense throughout the Soviet period.

Whereas international war tends to unite a society, civil war fragments it brutally. In Russia in 1917–1921 centralized power disintegrated, for all the Bolsheviks' authoritarianism. The empire dissolved into separate regions and discrete ethnic territories, sometimes even just individual villages, left to fend for themselves in a world where neighbors were at best untrustworthy, at worst intent on pillage and murder. Economic life lost its variety and its multiple interconnections and became crude and poverty-stricken; money, the bearer of community trust par excellence, lost most of its value and its power to inspire confidence. Ordinary services and facilities, which people had come to take for granted, simply collapsed. In the cities the end of the German war entailed the abrupt cessation of military manufacture and precipitated the unraveling of the industrial economy, soon followed by that of the auxiliary economic branches which had serviced and supplied it. Hundreds of thousands of workers were laid off and left without alternative sources of income. Over the next couple of years rail and water transport deteriorated drastically, and supplies of food and fuel became more and more haphazard. In January 1920 the anarchist Emma Goldman returned to St. Petersburg, whose "gaiety . . . vivacity and brilliancy" had impressed her in her youth. The city she found not only had a new name, Petrograd, but also looked quite different, and it appalled her: "It was almost in ruins, as if a hurricane had swept over it. The houses looked like broken old tombs upon neglected and forgotten cemeteries. The streets were dirty and deserted; all life had gone from them. . . . The people walked about like living corpses. . . . Emaciated, frost-bitten men, women and children were being whipped by the common lash, the search for a piece of bread or a stick of wood."[10]

Heating and lighting were reduced to a minimum, so that by 1921 an observer in Kharkov reported that people were "living four, five, six, even seven to a room without lights, without running water and without adequate fuel."[11] Much of Russia lies well north of Kharkov, and what the deprivation meant in the dark, cold winters at those latitudes can scarcely be imagined. When they could, people warmed themselves at improvised stoves known ironically as *burzhuiki* (implying a comfortable bourgeois hostess), which they fed with rubbish, worn-out clothes, books, and paper as fuel. Medical services and public hygiene virtually ceased, so that malnourished, exhausted, and stressed townsfolk were left to face disease unaided. Epidemics of typhus and cholera swept in destructive waves through the cities. Many people left, especially those in the more northern cities, which were remote from the grain-growing regions and hence most acutely threatened by hunger and disease. At times their precipitate exodus overwhelmed the already overstretched transport services: one train left Petrograd so crowded that it overbalanced while crossing a bridge, toppled over, and plunged into the River Neva with the loss of hundreds of lives.[12] Petrograd's population fell from 2.5 million in 1917 to 700,000 in 1920.

Apart from disease, people daily faced unfamiliar and pressing hazards, notably hunger and physical attack. They became fearful and suspicious; in order to survive they often had to react by emergency action or improvised and violent self-defense. A volatile temperament, swift reflexes, and readiness to fight at a moment's notice became positive attributes. In September 1918 the writer Mikhail Prishvin noted in his diary: "I can feel even the best and cleverest people, scholars included, beginning to behave as if there were a mad dog in the courtyard outside."[13] People were prepared to take greater risks than before, to act in a less rational, more impulsive manner, simply because situations were unfamiliar and perplexing, and because completely safe courses of action did not exist. Naturally, courtesy faded too, and coarse, aggressive behavior became the norm. People thought in cruder ways. When reverses happened, they did not seek a sophisticated explanation, but took the one which lay closest to hand and which their political superiors usually encouraged: namely, that misfortunes were caused by "enemies" who should be resisted at all costs and if possible destroyed, while good fortune was due to "comrades" who should be supported wholeheartedly. Such interpretations performed the vital function of inspiring hope, for they suggested that a favorable outcome could be reached by an uncomplicated line of conduct. They shaped the Russian mentality for much of the twentieth century.

The brutalization and impoverishment of everyday life were extremely distressing for members of the upper classes, who had been brought up to expect high standards of courtesy, forbearance, and tolerance from fellow human beings. Many of the elites concluded that normal life had become impossible and emigrated. Most ordinary people, however, were unable to do so, or chose to stay behind in the country they loved or had become accustomed to. Their lot was hard. In January 1919 the historian Iurii Gote walked all the way across Moscow to buy thirty eggs and three pounds of rice: "The journey around Moscow during business hours in the morning . . . produced a frightening impression on me—it is likely that the invasion of Genghis Khan affected the towns subjected to him in approximately the same way: all the windows have been boarded, everything has been killed, everything has stopped."[14]

The artefacts and practices of bourgeois life were losing their value and meaning. University meetings were chaired by party activists, people whose faces "exuded lack of culture." Parlor curtains were taken down to exchange for potato flour; when Gote was interrogated by the Cheka in an expropriated house, it was "in the old bedroom . . . with Corinthian columns and a marvellous mirror." Gote's own apartment was requisitioned by the local authorities, and an alien family was moved into his dining room, so that, he recalls, "I retained the impression that someone was going to the toilet all day behind me." Princess Sofia Volkonskaia suffered the same fate:

> A notice came from the "house committee" telling us to be ready to receive two new lodgers in our flat. We were, it appeared, occupying more space than was allotted to us according to Soviet law. Recriminations were of no avail. The couple thus forced on us—a young man and his wife—seemed quite nice, but . . . they were Communists. . . . Nothing could be more disagreeable than this living in close contact (having to cook our dinners on the same stove, to use the same bathroom devoid of hot water, etc.), with people who considered themselves a priori and in principle as our foes. Nothing could be more irritating than the feeling of being, even at home, under the constant eye of the enemy. "Take care," "Shut the door," "Do not talk so loud; the Communists may hear you." Pin-pricks? Yes, of course. But in that nightmare life of ours every pin-prick took on the dimensions of a serious wound.[15]

People became exiles in their own homes. Gote, at least, decided he could stand it no longer and moved into his workroom in the Rumiantsev Museum. A stable, calculable life had been transformed into a jumble of unforeseeable events: "I had thought that we would move from our apartment on Bolshoi Znamenskii only into the other world, but that shows what human expectations are worth; the Bolsheviks came and wrecked them all." So devastating was this bonfire of all cultural and social capital that Gote, a professional historian and an Orthodox believer, confessed one day to his diary that "there is neither religious nor historical feeling in me; the one and the other have been destroyed in me by what is going on."[16]

Gote, though thoroughly shaken up, managed somehow to survive in the new life of unpredictability and privation. Not so Igor Nilaev, an engineer in Petrograd who saw his factory closed down, his bank account sequestered, and rooms in his apartment handed over to worker families. Everything that had rendered his life meaningful had vanished, and he wandered around the one room left to him, muttering, "Whatever has happened to us?" Eventually he was taken to a psychiatric hospital, where he died.[17]

For peasants and workers the changes did not perhaps demand as radical a transformation of cultural attitudes as they did for the bourgeois and professional strata, but they did engender behavioral patterns that were archaic and simplified. They too divided the world into "right" and "wrong," "white" and "black." At the big Motovilikha armaments works outside Perm in December 1918 the workers proclaimed to the world: "Our revolutionary conscience and duty command us to take revenge on all persecutors of the Russian and International revolution, whether they are conscious persecutors—the bourgeoisie and capitalists—or unconscious ones—ignorant workers and peasants."[18] Their rhetoric is noteworthy for the assumption that whole classes of people were enemies, whether or not they intended to be. Civil war combined with ideology to impose a crude simplification of the categories by which everyone understood social life and politics.

The new regime abolished private trade in agriculture as part of its program of leaping straight to a socialist society. Soon, though, it had to recognize that without such trade there would be mass starvation. The paradoxical result was that almost everyone became a trader in a small way, either as seller or as buyer, often as both. But the "trade" that resulted was quite different from the orderly market of pre-1917 times. It was the most primitive form of commerce, barter, in which elaborate and fast-changing calibrations of comparative value become everyone's preoccupation and a perpetual subject of conversation. Bourgeois townsfolk who had little to offer, and whose most precious heirlooms had been abruptly devalued, were reduced to desperate expedients. Baroness Meyendorff sold a diamond brooch in order to buy a sack of flour, while Princess Golitsyna hawked home-made pies and the wife of General Brusilov boxes of matches.[19] Emma Goldman witnessed the ultimate degradation, city girls "selling themselves for a pound of bread, a piece of soap or chocolate. The soldiers were the only ones who could afford to buy them because of their extra rations."[20]

Workers were in a relatively favorable position, as long as their factories remained open: to obtain wares with which to trade, they would pilfer equipment or products from the workplace. Alternatively, to forestall such theft, employers would pay them, not in worthless currency, but in goods they could exchange on the market. Some of them would set up rudimentary workshops where they could hastily fashion or repair vitally needed objects: boots, overcoats, stoves, ovens, and so on. In special demand were axes, ploughshares, primus stoves, pen-knives, and cigarette lighters: townsfolk carrying such items would flood outward, cluttering up all available trains, especially those going south-eastward toward the main arable regions. Peasants with sackfuls of produce would take the reverse route and set up their stalls in the cities, where they could command a good price or exchange rate. The authorities could do little to control these "bagmen"—and anyway, to do so would mean condemning the entire urban population to starvation.[21]

That towns survived at all testifies to Russians' remarkable capacity to improvise viable ways of living in extreme adversity. They were able to revive rudimentary technologies and to restore more archaic forms of human association, even though the adaptation was neither easy nor congenial. The means they deployed to do so marked their social institutions for decades to come.[22]

Daily life was scarcely less harsh in the small towns and villages, whether under Red or White rule. In April 1919 Ataman Dutov of the Orenburg Cossack Army wrote from Troitsk, in the Urals, to his commander-in-chief, Admiral Kolchak:

> In the front-line zone and especially in the regions liberated from the Bolsheviks, local government does not exist. Local taxes do not get paid, and the officials have dispersed. Almost all hospitals in the villages are closed, since there are no medicines, the staff are not paid, and there are no resources to keep hospitals going. The schools are not working: there are no teachers, since they haven't been paid for half a year or more. . . . There is no agricultural production, the roads and bridges are unrepaired, everything is falling apart. In the villages there is no calico, no sugar, no paraffin. People drink herbs and samogon [home-brewed vodka], and they light tapers to see by.[23]

By that time a similar picture could have been painted for much of small-town and rural Russia.

It is true that the villages were in some ways better off than the towns: at least it was possible to grow food there. Besides, long-established *kustarnyi* (cottage industry) skills, though superseded by modern industry, had not been lost altogether, so that the basic amenities of life—clothes, furniture, and implements—could still be improvised locally, using axes and chisels instead of lathes and circular saws. On the other hand, the village was remote and undefended; in the absence of a firm central government it was vulnerable to any armed men who might turn up. For example, on the night of November 2–3, 1918, the settlement of Kishki in Ufa guberniia was alarmed by the appearance of a detachment of sixty horsemen of unknown status. They demanded thirty puds (nearly 500 kilos) of oats, three cartloads of hay, and a slaughtered ram. They took vodka from an old man, beating him up when he resisted. Finally they called for "wenches" *(devki)*. The leader of the band exclaimed, "If I die, so be it, but I'm going to have a good time first!" *(Umru tak umru, no poguliaiu.)*[24] That kind of attitude was common: life seemed short and cheap, and all moral restraints had been withdrawn.

Besides, the greatest attraction of the village—that it produced food—inevitably drew it into the circle of violence. Both Whites and Reds treated peasant households as passive sources of food supplies for the army and the cities. The authorities' pillaging of the village is reflected in a peasant woman's letter of August 1920 from Cherdyn district to her son: "They're taking butter away by force, we've given them four pounds, and now they want to take the cow. They're confiscating grain two sheaves out of three, and potatoes two buckets for them, one for us, and turnips the same. They took all our butter, didn't leave us any, and said if we didn't have any butter we should borrow some and give it to them. They told me to go and get some, or I would be arrested. Fedia, it's all just like last year, and I don't know who to complain to."[25] No one cared whether the peasants themselves had enough to live on and to guarantee the next season's sowing, even though the simplest reasoning would have suggested that they were the source of next year's food too. People's calculations had become so primitive and short-sighted that such considerations were now off the radar.

Some villages declared themselves "independent republics" and set about defending their "sovereign territory," with "Green" militias; one in Orel guberniia actually surrounded itself with barbed wire and trenches.[26] In Tambov guberniia in 1920, local authorities succeeded one another with bewildering rapidity, as the following story illustrates: "On September 25 there was always a fair in Okri, the next village. That day, reckoning that all policemen would be there keeping order, an armed detachment suddenly appeared out of the forest in our village. They quickly carried all the tables and cupboards out of the Volrevkom [district revolutionary committee premises] and set the building alight. Then the horsemen began to prance around the main square, shooting in the air to intimidate us. . . . The villagers made themselves scarce. No one came out to greet their new rulers. And the rulers, having circled the square a few times, galloped off into the forest." Two days later the Reds returned, took two village lads, made them dig their own graves, and then shot them. "Now we no longer knew whom to acknowledge and whom to obey. Each morning we would come out of our huts, look around, and ask one another in whispers, 'Who's in charge today, the Greens or the Reds?'"[27]

Even when governments established themselves, things were not necessarily better. Each successive regime viewed its predecessor as wholly "black" and would arrest all its employees and supporters on the strength of no more than a single denunciation. Under the Reds mere social origin might suffice to be imprisoned or even executed. In a further escalation of lexical malignity, the language of prophylactic hygiene was deployed to designate whole social classes. In December 1917 Lenin called for a "war to the death against the rich, the idlers, and the parasites" in order to "cleanse the Russian land of all vermin, of fleas—the crooks, of bed-bugs—the rich—and so on. In one place they will put in prison a dozen rich men . . . in another they will be put to cleaning latrines. In a third they will be given yellow tickets [the mark of the prostitute] after a term in prison, so that while they are harmful everyone can keep an eye on them. In a fourth one out of every ten idlers will be shot."[28]

In September 1918 in Kungur, Perm guberniia, the Cheka shot sixteen people simply because they had once been tsarist policemen, members of the Kadet Party or of the Union of Russian People—and two nuns were included for good measure. In Perm itself forty-two hostages were shot on September 15, and thirty-seven more at the start of October. The atmosphere was such that "if one heard next door a thud, scuffles, or a despairing cry, one froze and stared into the darkness, waiting in terror for a knock on one's own door."[29] This kind of casual and unreflecting violence, directed against whole categories of people, continued throughout the civil war and left its mark long afterward. It inculcated the habit of assuming that all problems could be solved by labeling entire collectives as enemies and annihilating them.

## Demographic Effects

World war, revolution, and civil war had a devastating effect on Russia's demographic health, and therefore on the family. Millions of young men were killed between 1914 and 1921. Although no one could foresee it at the time, the outbreak of the First World War plunged Russia's peoples into a period of turbulence exceeding anything they or their ancestors had experienced in their earlier history. The First World War was merely the initial stage. During the course of the war, 17.6 million men passed through the barracks, trenches, naval bases, and hospitals of the armed services. Of those, 11.4 million (60.6 percent) never returned, that is to say, they died or were lost without a trace. This percentage of losses is higher than for the German and Austro-Hungarian armed services, both of which suffered heavily in the course of a war in which they were defeated. The losses were particularly heavy among the officers and men of the standing army of 1914, in other words, among the bearers of the old imperial service ethos. Civilian casualties of the war are impossible to assess accurately, but deaths were probably in the range of 2 to 3.5 million.[30]

Between 1918 and 1922 the catastrophic population decline continued, as a result of fighting in the civil war, Red and White terror, epidemics, people fleeing their homes (including some 2 million who left the country altogether and went into emigration), the collapse of economic life, the requisition of food supplies, and the devastation of cities. Finally a drought in the main arable regions in 1920 drastically reduced harvest yields in 1921 and 1922. Famine resulted in the middle and lower Volga basin, as well as in parts of the Urals, Kazakhstan, and western Siberia. It has been estimated that the population of the area covered by the new Soviet republics in 1922 had declined by 11 to 15 million since autumn 1917. If one also takes into account the lost births compared with pre-1914 projections, then the total demographic loss must have been in the order of 20 million.[31]

The losses were especially heavy in the cities and non–black earth regions of the Russian republic; they were less so in Ukraine and the black-earth regions, while the population rose slightly in the Urals and lower Volga, and considerably in Siberia and Kazakhstan—areas to which refugees were fleeing. Russians had suffered huge losses, yet paradoxically they had became a majority within their own state territory for the first time in at least 200 years.[32]

The deaths, as we have seen, eliminated young men disproportionately. Their wives, mothers, and daughters were left alone, many of them without male support, to run smallholdings, allotments, and workshops. Since gender roles in villages and small towns were traditionally very sharply delineated, men often belittled the economic efforts of women taking over these roles. On the other hand, partly because of the shortage of able-bodied men and partly because of the social programs of the new regime, women gained a real influence in the village assemblies, from which previous custom had debarred them. They became shakers and movers in rural and small-town life to an unprecedented degree.

Whenever marriage could be sustained right through all the emergencies, it was immensely valuable as a pooling of economic and emotional resources, and people, especially women, clung to it. They regarded Bolshevik attempts to undermine the family and the church, which offered sacral backing for the family, with extreme misgivings. Inevitably, though, many nuclear families came to grief, either because one spouse died, or because the vicissitudes of war and revolution drove the partners apart. In those circumstances, there was a reversion toward an older pattern of kinship, with extended families grouping together for mutual support. This development was short-lived and was reversed by the mid-1920s, but it showed that Russian family arrangements could, if necessary, be quite flexible.[33]

## Destruction of Memory

An indispensable component of any community's identity and solidarity is memory. Although memory is an individual attribute, it is stocked with material much of which is shared with other members of the community, especially those in one's immediate social milieu. It offers the daily grid against which all experiences and impressions are checked and validated. Overlapping and shared memories enable people to communicate readily with others of similar background. Memory "reduces the complexity and restricts the uncertainty of our social environment," enabling people to trust one another without elaborate and irksome precautions.[34]

Memory is not necessarily shared by the nation as a whole. It is determined partly by one's home town or village, region, social class, religion, or ethnic affiliation. Prerevolutionary Russia had an especially fragmented and contested cultural memory; there was no ideal image of the country shared by all social classes and all nationalities. The most widely accepted elements of a common culture were the tsar and the Orthodox Church. By 1917, however, the monarchy had not only fallen but had also become largely discredited, while the church was about to face a devastating assault.

Perhaps the most powerful mediator of memory is the family. From the outset the Communists set out to undermine it, both in order to weaken the sense of property and to free women to play a more active role in society. Under their legislation, church marriages lost their civil significance, and any stable cohabitation, registered or not, was considered a family. The distinction between legitimate and illegitimate children was abolished, so that the few remaining inheritance rights could be claimed by any offspring. Abortion was available on demand, and divorce could be obtained simply by informing the other partner. Probably this legislation did less than revolution and war to undermine families, but it exacerbated the instability of domestic life in the 1920s and thereby further weakened the culture-preserving role of the family.

Abstract ideas, such as religion or nationhood, can become part of the cultural memory, but they need to be symbolized in specific images or practices and related to particular times and places. The content of memory, whether actualized in images, stories, songs, dances, shrines, ceremonials, or customs, bestows a certain emotional coloring and symbolic content to a community's sense of itself. The past is not simply reproduced; it also reconstitutes itself selectively in each succeeding generation, a process that entails forgetting as well as remembering—especially those past happenings that no longer speak to the needs of the contemporary community.[35] As a leading theorist of cultural memory has commented, "Only a *significant* past is remembered; only a *remembered* past becomes significant."[36]

What is remembered is determined partly (though certainly not wholly) by the authoritative discourses passed down from above, by the rulers. The Communists actually intended to destroy social memory in order to have, as it were, vacant cultural building sites on which to erect their own temples. As Barbara Misztal has commented, they "dismantled the traditional value-generating institutions, disintegrated families and undermined many previous values, such as responsibility, freedom and autonomy."[37] Russians' cultural memory, already divided and vulnerable, was drastically further degraded. Society became a shapeless structure: the social "rule book" consisted of more or less blank pages on which new ideals, norms, and practices could be inscribed at will. The Bolsheviks assumed this task with enthusiasm, self-confidence, and a considerable theoretical baggage, assembled in the underground and refashioned during the civil war. The question was how far they could succeed in "fixing" the new reality on the various strata of the population. Older people found the unfamiliar context difficult to adjust to; many younger people, by contrast, whatever their social origin, attempted to align themselves with it in order to secure a place where they could find a fulfilling role as individuals.

For the time being, though, in the absence of an agreed cultural memory or a reliable communications system, information and a sense of community were mediated by other means, primarily rumor and gossip. Rumors offer a substitute both for reliable information and for a stable community. As a cultural historian has commented, "Rumours are interpretations; in situations of great uncertainty, they seem to offer coherence."[38] They even create an artificial togetherness when individuals are terrified of being isolated and overwhelmed: "In a rumour one is not alone; that is its ambivalent promise. It is always connected with the fears, hopes and expectations of people. . . . Whoever hears a rumour and passes it on joins the linear sequence of 'people' who constitute the 'they,' the agents of collective speech." Gossip then processes rumor and gives it a context; it is the mechanism by which a society maintains its norms, or tries to restore them if they have been undermined.[39]

The natural milieu for rumor is wartime, when fear and distortion of information are at their height. A civil war, being especially disruptive of inherited norms and regular communications, makes rumor and gossip even more imperative than a national war. Soldiers exchange their own narratives in rest areas, field kitchens, and hospitals just behind the lines; these are then embroidered, magnified, commented on, and conveyed in letters to the rear, where they undergo the same processes yet again.[40] In the words of James Scott, "Life-threatening events such as wars, epidemic, famine and riot [all present in Russia then] are among the most fertile social sites for the generation of rumors. Before the development of modern news media and wherever, today, the media are disbelieved, rumor might be virtually the only source of news about the extra-local world."[41] These wartime conditions became more or less permanent features of life in the Soviet Union, and they created a continuing tendency to exaggeration, distortion, and sometimes outright fantasy masquerading as information. As the poet Anna Akhmatova observed tartly a decade and a half later, "We live in the pre-Gutenberg era."[42]

## Militarization of Life

Strange though it may sound, the best way for young men to cope with life's chronic instability was to enroll in the Red Army. It was by no means a haven of security, of course, but at least in its ranks one had a weapon to defend oneself with, and a better chance of being regularly fed. By 1920 the Red Army was no less than five million strong. In its early stages, though, it had proved difficult to muster. The Bolsheviks had begun by trying to extend the recruitment practices of the Red Guards, that is, to create a volunteer citizen militia, but few men came forward, and they had to replace the projected volunteer force with a conscript army. Conscripting did not prove easy either: in its early days the Red Army was plagued by desertions caused by war-weariness and by enlisted men's understandable worries about their families. By 1919, though, the Soviet authorities had devised a means of easing such concerns and accomplishing mobilization successfully: they offered new recruits tangible benefits. In a world that had become desperately insecure they guaranteed weapons, military training, a regular food supply, and rudimentary social security for their families in the form of the *paek*, or basic rations, as well as access for their children to education and a first claim on any spare land, for example, that confiscated from deserters. This was the best arrangement available at the time: the Red Army man fought for the state, and in return the state eased his material worries and took over some of his family obligations. In a way this was a kind of social contract, and it played a large part in constituting the new Soviet political community.[43]

As a result of this arrangement, a very high proportion of the young men who survived the civil war had been militarized at a decisive stage in their lives—in fact we may say that they experienced modernization as militarization. The Red Army had widened their horizons, taught many of them to read, and given them an insight into forms of social and political organization and a familiarity with modern technology. It had also cut them off from their childhood backgrounds, so that not infrequently soldiers were prepared to suppress peasant risings even in their own home provinces. Their training and wartime experience left a permanent mark on their concept of the political community. Whether they were initially recruited in the First World War or the civil war their commanders aimed in training to eradicate peacetime "weaknesses," to subordinate them to strict discipline and inure them to controlled violence, to encourage the comradely bonding of small fighting units, and to foster physical fitness and masculine qualities like courage, strength, stamina, and dexterity. In the Red Army, or in the preliminary training corps, Vsevobuch, they also received political education aimed at inspiring them with the image of their political community as the "toilers," regardless of ethnic origin.

Their "enemies" were the "former" social classes—merchants, landowners, priests, "kulaks" [wealthy peasants], and so on—and also the foreign imperialists, the "interventionists" who had invaded their country. For decades thereafter, these master images, positive and negative, dominated the imaginations of most young Soviet men.[44]

Some of these men, thus formed by wartime experience, moved on to become influential political figures in the succeeding years; indeed, former Red Army soldiers formed the backbone of the party and the soviets for a decade or two thereafter—the "cadres," as they were symptomatically called. Their outlook did much to shape the public rhetoric and the authoritative mentalities of Soviet society. They simply assumed that military organization and discipline were the natural way to deal with social problems. The language and outlook of military campaigns dominated their discourse: every social and economic program became a "front" to be taken by "assault," while those who did not pull their weight were "deserters" or even "enemies," against whom a life-or-death "struggle" was natural and legitimate. One killed because otherwise one would be killed.[45]

This militarization of socialism helps to explain why, despite the ostensible Bolshevik promotion of female equality, women soon sank into a kind of second-class citizenship. This was not just inherited prejudice: the dominant ethos of the militant, muscular, energetic proletarian was decidedly masculine. Bolsheviks came to mistrust women as confined by tradition, the body, and *byt* (everyday routine), everything that was to be overcome in the creation of socialism.[46]

The solidarity of military campaigns also colored the personnel patterns of the new regime. The comrades with whom one had shared broth around a bivouac fire became the closest associates in civilian life. When one of them was appointed to a people's commissariat or regional party secretaryship, he would invite his buddies of yesteryear to join his staff, as the people he knew best and trusted.[47] Their shared memories, both embellished and disinfected, became the sacred texts of the new regime, and were imbibed by the young and ambitious of the succeeding generation. Veterans' networks became the working model of party-state administration. There were no veterans' associations as such, but Sheila Fitzpatrick has aptly suggested that "the Bolshevik Party itself took the place and performed the functions of a veterans' organization."[48] This was the origin of the nomenklatura system of public appointments which soon created a new and unusually rigid ruling class.

There was no straightforward ethnic content to this image of the political community: that is why I do not call it a "nation," and the Soviet authorities did not either.[49] Certain national stereotypes did hover in the background, though. The great majority of Red Army soldiers were Russian, as the army drew most of its manpower from Russian villages and the big Russian industrial cities. There were many Ukrainians and Belorussians too, though of course some Ukrainians fought against the Reds for the independence of Ukraine. The Red Army was also a partial reincarnation of the old Imperial Army: many imperial officers served in it, and they welcomed the opportunity to recreate a properly disciplined Russian army, which in their opinion the Provisional Government had fatally undermined. The territory the Red Army was fighting to reclaim was, with a few modifications, the former Russian Empire, so that old-fashioned Russian patriotism was an acceptable motive for service within it. This was especially true from the spring of 1920, when the newly independent Poles, centuries-old rivals for dominance in the western regions, invaded Soviet territory. General Brusilov, who had hitherto stayed aloof from the civil war, issued an appeal in *Pravda*, urging his fellow imperial officers to drop their grudges against the Bolsheviks, to "forget egoistic feelings of class struggle" and join the Red Army: "It is now your duty to defend our beloved Russia with all your strength, and to give your lives to save her from irretrievable subjugation"; otherwise "our descendants . . . will say we have forgotten our own Russian people and destroyed Mother Russia."[50]

Non-Russians were drafted into the Red Army too, and many of them served with conviction to defend their homeland against the openly Russifying Whites. They did not join separate ethnic units, however. At least initially they were assigned to all-Soviet units in which they served together with people of other nationalities, with Russian as the language of command. Only in peacetime after the civil war did the 12th Party Congress of 1923 try to draw on specific ethnic loyalties by creating ethnic units, with a native language of command.[51]

The structure of the new society was in large part determined by practices which had evolved as a result of war. From 1914 onward the state—whether in its incarnation as tsarist regime, Provisional Government, White military rule, or Soviet republic—had systematically collected far more detailed information about its subjects than ever before. To determine liability for military or civilian service, eligibility for rations or other aid, to spot potential spies or internal opposition, everyone had to be identified and classified. These practices were common to all governments fighting the First World War. They used this information to learn about the moods and intentions of different categories of the population, and wherever possible to affect those moods. One might see this as a manifestation of the general tendency during the war to shift from a territorial concept of rule to a managerial one, to forms of government seeking "to manage populations, not just to rule territories."[52]

During the civil war in Russia it became extremely difficult for any regime to accomplish such information work systematically. All the same, by 1919 the Soviet authorities had some ten thousand officials opening and analyzing citizens' mail and compiling "summaries on the population's mood."[53] They extended this effort when peace returned, and they used the results to determine the status of their citizens. The positive, didactic aspect of their intelligence work was especially prominent, starting with regular "political enlightenment" sessions in the Red Army. Such instruction was necessary partly because the regime's aim was to transform society, and partly because society had in any case lost its bearings and its memory.[54] The result was the erection of what one scholar has called "the propaganda state," whose output replaced social memory and blocked the articulation of alternative viewpoints. In a real sense it supplanted civil society and the public realm, so that "the Soviet people ultimately came not so much to believe the Bolsheviks' world view as to take it for granted."[55] Statements about society, whether true or untrue, were henceforth active forces shaping everyone's activity and view of themselves.

These instruments of social policy were then taken up and used by the new supreme authority, the Communist Party, which was not a political party in the traditional sense, but, in the words of one historian, "a messianic order, burdened with the task of purifying society in the name of the future community." The party deployed administrative classification as a tool of social engineering. As civil war ended and society settled down, the shape of the new social hierarchy became determined by differential access to various levels and types of education. Prospective students would fill out special questionnaires designed to elicit vital information such as social origin, party affiliation, work experience, and role during the civil war. Special commissions would then examine the questionnaires in order to assign priorities. They would look for inconsistencies and question applicants on them. Preference would be given to party and Komsomol (Communist Youth) members, to workers and their children, to poor peasants and their offspring, and to active participants on the Red side of the civil war. From time to time purge commissions would re-examine a student's credentials along with progress in his or her studies, and might decide on expulsion. The "correct" composition of one's biography and avoidance thereafter of "incorrect" behavior became key skills.[56]

This social framework encouraged a habit of denunciations. As the director of the Leningrad Institute of Communications Engineers said, "Everybody was asked to forward written denunciations of those who they believed had no place in the workers' faculty. Interrogation took place in group meetings where denunciations were read aloud and cross-examinations took place. . . . Denunciations were seen neither as ignoble betrayals of colleagues nor as personal affairs but as the duty of every conscientious citizen."[57] Here the needs of the new order coincided with habits left over from "joint responsibility." Politics no longer concerned the conflict of ideas or the clash of articulated social, ethnic, or economic interests; rather it was about advancement or nonadvancement in the environment of monopoly patronage and in the context of a socialist messianic worldview.

## Popular Rejection of Communism

By 1920 the popular rebellion that had brought the Communists to power had more than run its course. Peasants, workers, and soldiers had achieved their dream of acquiring the land and productive resources, of governing their own lives—but had then seen their dream snatched away again by the new rulers. The contrast was so marked that some confused activists, recalling the short-lived liberties of 1917, actually coined the slogan "Long live the Bolsheviks! Death to the Communists!"—evidently not having registered that the party had changed its name.[58] There was good reason for their confusion. The grain they produced had been taken away by their former benefactors at gunpoint, their horses had been requisitioned and their sons conscripted for the Red Army, while their communal assemblies had become village soviets presided over by Communists. In the factories "workers' control" no longer meant anything: they had either been closed down or turned into fortresses of "commissarocracy," disciplined assembly lines of military production. In the army soldiers' assemblies had been brusquely abolished and replaced by "political departments" headed by political commissars with revolvers at their hips. "All power to the soviets," the slogan for which the masses had fought, had become a distant memory.

Peasants reacted by obstructing grain collections. If requisition squads arrived, they would turn them away or even murder them. Gradually peasants began using the weapons they had acquired during the years of fighting: they would form "green" bands in the forests and marshes, from where they would venture out to attack grain stores or Soviet offices. Whole regions of the middle and lower Volga, the Urals, and Siberia slipped out of Communist control. In Tambov, perhaps the worst-affected province, peasants demanded the restoration of the Constituent Assembly, the restoration of civil liberties and genuine soviet elections, an end to grain requisitioning, and a return to free trade.[59]

In late winter 1920–1921 the unrest spread to the towns. The immediate reason was a cut in the bread ration, but the striking workers of Petrograd and Moscow soon issued a set of demands remarkably similar to those of the peasants. If Communists tried to attend strike meetings, they would be expelled as traitors to the socialist cause. In February 1921 a socialist but anti-Communist Assembly of Plenipotentiaries launched a general strike in Petrograd, proclaiming: "We, the representatives of factories and socialist parties in Petrograd, despite much that we disagree on, have united on the basis of the following goals: overthrow of the Bolshevik dictatorship, free elections to the soviets, freedom of speech, press and assembly for all, and the release of political prisoners."[60]

The strikers' demands were taken up by the sailors of the Baltic Fleet in their garrison at Kronstadt, the island naval base just outside Petrograd. At a public meeting one sailor reported visiting his family's farm and finding that the cow had just been requisitioned: "When I and my brother return home from serving the Soviet Republic people will sneer at our wrecked farm and say 'What did you serve for? What has the Soviet Republic given you?'"[61] The sailors issued their own manifesto, repeating the workers' demands and adding their own for the abolition of political departments in the army and navy.[62] From the Communists' point of view this was a shattering blow. The Baltic sailors had been pioneers of soviet democracy, prominent among the stormtroopers of the October revolution, so their rejection of the Communist leaders now marked the desertion of the "truest of the true." Besides, the heavy artillery of their battleships was capable of causing destruction in Russia's largest industrial city.

What the peasants, workers, and sailors were demanding was a return to the original ideal for which they had fought in 1917, and which they had then called "soviet power": ownership of the land, the right to trade, to govern themselves, and freely to elect their own representatives to higher political authorities. Communist leadership had been rejected by its own grass roots, had lost the popular support on which it had depended. Lenin was right to call this crisis the most critical the regime had yet faced, "undoubtedly more dangerous than Denikin, Iudenich, and Kolchak combined."[63] He used the regime's new special security troops to crush the Kronstadt rebellion, but he also, for the first time, compromised with his enemies, by restoring certain elements of private enterprise and free trade in what became known as the New Economic Policy. He combined concessions, however, with an actual tightening of the political regime: non-Communist parties were finally banned, and even factions within the Communist Party were declared illegitimate. Thus the two revolutions of 1917 finally parted company, and the Communists prepared to continue their drive to save the world by means of naked coercion.

## The Orthodox Church

The ideas of the ecclesiastical reformers, frustrated in 1905, resurfaced in 1917 with all the bitterness of long delay. The end of the Romanov dynasty decapitated the church and so made reform at last unavoidable. The long-awaited local council (pomestnyi sobor), the first for more than two hundred years, convened in Moscow in August. It soon became apparent that the episcopal party had the upper hand over the parish-based reformers. The sessions were held in an increasingly tense political situation, with news coming in of the Bolsheviks' seizure of power in Petrograd. Within earshot of the cannons booming around the Kremlin in November, the delegates voted to restore the patriarchate and the pomestnyi sobor as the church's governing bodies. By a strange coincidence, then, Russia's two forms of messianism both reached their flowering at exactly the same time. The man the council elected as patriarch (the final stage was decided by lot) was Tikhon, who a few months earlier had become the first popularly elected Metropolitan of Moscow. He was a conciliatory figure, one who supported the parish liberals as well the episcopal conservatives, and he had much experience of leading the church in a hostile environment, having earlier served in Alaska, Poland, and Lithuania. He had, however, no sympathy whatsoever for socialism.[64]

The Communists, as the rival messianic movement, had no intention of allowing the church to rebuild its popular support. The government closed down the *sobor* and then broke the church's link with the state in a drastic manner quite unlike that recommended by either set of ecclesiastical reformers. A decree of January 1918 deprived the church of its status as a legal person, which meant that henceforth it could not own property and its central organization lost all administrative powers. These handicaps meant that parishes were thrown on to their own devices and resources. Ironically, they had gained their independence, as reformers had long aspired, but as legally helpless, isolated, and under-resourced bodies, pale shadows of what the "parish liberals" had envisaged.

Even worse followed. During the civil war many churches were simply closed or destroyed, while their parish priests were arrested or killed as members of a hostile social class. Anything like a full congregational life became extremely difficult to conduct. Patriarch Tikhon reacted by anathematizing "the confessed and secret enemies of Christ" who sow "anger, hatred and destructive accusations instead of brotherly love." He called on believers to defend the church against attack and expressed confidence that "the enemies of the Church of Christ will be shamed and scattered by the force of the cross of Christ."[65] He did not, however, specifically name the Soviet regime or call for armed resistance to it. Clergy who had escaped abroad were less cautious. They convened their own *sobor,* at Karlovci, in Yugoslavia, which called for the overthrow of the atheist Communist regime and the restoration of the monarchy. They thereby gave the Bolsheviks a good pretext for regarding the church inside Russia as "counter-revolutionary."

After the civil war, the Bolsheviks held back from a frontal assault on the church, fearing that it was likely to prove counterproductive in the face of the strongly held beliefs of most peasants and a good many workers. The famine of 1921–1922 in the Volga basin did, however, give them the opportunity to proceed in a more subtle manner, by splitting the church from within. The regime demanded that the church surrender its numerous valuables, chalices, plates, vestments, and the like, held in churches up and down the country, to raise funds for the famine relief effort. In reply Tikhon took the line that the church was prepared to sacrifice valuable objects for the cause of famine relief, but not those consecrated for liturgical use; and he insisted that parish councils should decide for themselves how their funds should be used.[66] Many reformers within the church denounced this attitude as narrow-minded and unworthy of an organization professing Christian ideals. A group of Petrograd clergy recommended a complete surrender of valuables to the government under the supervision of parish representatives.[67]

Even the "renovationists," those clergy who wished to cooperate with the regime, were themselves divided about what they wished to achieve and what kind of church they envisaged for Soviet Russia. Some of them took a broadly traditional view that the church should do its best to work with the government, as it had under the tsars, while introducing reforms to bring it more into line with modern society and closer to socialist ideals. The leader of this tendency was Bishop Antonin Granovskii, a one-time oriental scholar who joined the priesthood relatively late in life.

Some renovationists, however, actually wanted to reshape the church as an active advocate of socialism and a positive ally of the Communist regime. Aleksandr Vvedenskii, the most prominent among them, came from an intelligentsia family and trained at the St. Petersburg Spiritual Academy only after completing a degree in philology. He was ordained in 1914, having resolved to devote his life to renewing the apostolic mission of the priesthood by bringing about the reconciliation of science and faith and by preaching "the Gospel in atheist language." He was a flamboyant figure who believed that priests needed to attract congregations by enacting divine service as a dramatic spectacle. In his first service in 1914 he recited the Cherubim's Prayer (normally not heard by the congregation) as if it were a declamatory verse by a currently fashionable decadent poet; eventually the presiding bishop stepped in and asked him to desist.[68]

The clergy, then, was internally split in facing the regime's pressure. As for the great majority of believers, they resisted change of any kind. Because the society around them was undergoing such upheavals, they wished to preserve the church as a rock of stability and a custodian of fixed cultural memory. When activists of the GPU (as the Cheka was now called) turned up at churches to confiscate sacred vessels, they were often met by large crowds of parishioners determined to obstruct them. In one case, in Shuia, an industrial town not far from Moscow, a mêlée resulted in which four or five people were killed, including a Red Army soldier. Lenin regarded this clash as an ideal pretext to mount an assault on the church, with the famine as political cover. He wrote to the Politburo recommending that "the greater the number of representatives of the reactionary clergy and reactionary bourgeoisie we manage to shoot on this basis, the better. It is precisely now that we should deliver a lesson to [believers] so that they dare not even think about resistance for several decades."[69] His comrades nevertheless decided that a proper trial should be held, but the result was what Lenin wanted: five of the Shuia resisters were shot; even more seriously, so too was Metropolitan Veniamin of Petrograd for resisting confiscation of valuables in Petrograd parish churches. Tikhon was confined to house arrest and a court case was prepared to charge him with counter-revolutionary activity.

During the next few months the renovationists acted fast to profit by the sidelining of Tikhon. With the authorities' support, they set up a new Supreme Church Administration and issued an appeal (whose wording was approved by the Politburo) calling on all clergy to join them. They were awarded a cathedral in Petrograd for Bishop Antonin. Initially the renovationists were able to attract a good many parishes, mostly on the initiative of priests who either accepted their aims or sought the regime's favor. Some priests who resisted transfer to the renovationists were arrested. The plight of Tikhon's supporters at this time is illustrated by the situation that awaited a new bishop, Valerian, when he arrived to take over in Smolensk: "In our cathedral, as in other Tikhonite churches, there were no episcopal vestments, nor the sacred vessels needed for a bishop's ordination." The renovationists in the Trinity Monastery had some of these objects, though and the congregation managed to borrow them from well-disposed monks there. Such had been the turnover of clerical personnel, however, that there was no deacon available who knew how to conduct the service of greeting and solemnly installing a new bishop. So the service was improvised, but it was attended by a large and appreciative congregation.[70]

The reaction of most congregations to the renovationists was at best skeptical. In many parishes there was mass resistance to them from the outset. People suspected that changing the words of services would deprive them of their sacred character. The reform that aroused the greatest opposition was the introduction of the new calendar. It entailed the omission of thirteen days, and ordinary believers objected that they would have to slight certain saints by skipping their festivals. Parish priests warned that persisting with the reformed calendar would drive a good many parishioners into the arms of the Old Believers.[71]

The main reason for resistance to reform, however, was the well-founded impression that the renovationists were operating in league with the secret police. The spectacle of clergymen who resisted the reformers being arrested, tried, and sometimes shot naturally created the worst possible impression. In Moscow, the GPU reported, believers thought the reformers were working with the Communists to destroy the church in order to help the Jews. In Lipetsk believers refused to enter renovationist churches "for fear of receiving the mark of the Anti-Christ." In Leningrad oblast "members of the parish council in the village of Begunitsa vigorously agitated against the renovationist movement, saying 'Renovationist priests are commissars in cassocks. They support Soviet power because it pays them. They betray the people. They don't believe in God; they burn icons and rob churches. God has sent Soviet power to punish us for our sins. If people will pray as they did in the past, then the Lord God will deliver us from all this evil.'"[72]

The reformers, then, had minimal support within congregations. Worse still, they were split among themselves, along the old fault line between congregational and episcopal reformers. This rift reached a dramatic climax at a church service in September 1922, when Bishop Antonin suddenly turned away as Father Vladimir Krasnitskii approached him for a blessing, exclaiming for all to hear: "Christ is not among us!"[73]

The regime did not wish the renovationists to achieve their aims, either. What Communists wanted was not a new church of sincere believers who combined Christianity with socialism; rather they wanted to weaken and eventually destroy the existing church. Even Lunacharskii, a former "God-builder" and of all leading Bolsheviks the most inclined to a neoreligious worldview, wrote to Lenin in April 1921 remarking that the church was falling apart and that "we must help this process but by no means allow the church to regenerate and take some renewed form. . . . The party's stake is in communism and not in religion."[74] He recommended that the party avoid all contact with the church and leave it to the Cheka to handle priests and believers. Renovationists, however sympathetic to socialism, were to be kept at arm's length, since the best way to destroy the church was by splitting it from within. That was the purpose the renovationists fulfilled, especially in their early years; once they had performed that task, the regime no longer had any use for them.

Once the church was split, Tikhon no longer represented such a threat, and the authorities decided in June 1923 to free him and to allow him to operate under sufferance. As the price for his release he was required to issue a statement renouncing his implacable hostility to the regime. He asked believers to join with him in "praying for help to the Workers' and Peasants' Government in its labors for the good of the whole people," and not to undertake "antigovernment activity" or to hope for the return of the monarchy. He condemned the "harmful counter-revolutionary activity" of the Karlovci émigré church and finally broke all ties with them. Because of the church's fraught situation, he had secretly appointed three deputies who could replace him in an emergency. When he died in April 1925, however, the authorities would not permit a proper *pomestnyi sobor* to be held, and so there was no fully legitimate successor to him. All his three designated deputies were arrested, but one of them had further appointed Sergii, Metropolitan of Moscow, as his deputy beforehand.

On this basis Sergii took over as acting patriarch, and in 1927 he made a declaration of loyalty that satisfied the regime, although some of its wording was ambiguous. On the one hand, he said: "We wish to be Orthodox believers, and at the same time to claim the Soviet Union as our civil motherland, whose joys and successes are our joys and successes, and whose misfortunes are our misfortunes." Here Sergii was specifically pledging loyalty not to the regime but rather to the "motherland." However, the name of that motherland now contained a political term, "Soviet," rather than an ethnic or geographical one, "Russia." In any case, in another place Sergii added: "We need to show not only in words but also in deeds that . . . the most loyal adherents of Orthodoxy can be true citizens of the Soviet Union, loyal to the Soviet authorities *(sovetskoi vlasti)*." He also instructed clergy to pray for the regime.[75]

On the grounds that he had sworn allegiance to an atheist regime, a substantial number of Orthodox believers refused thereafter to acknowledge Sergii's authority. They accused him of declining to pray for bishops who had been deposed and arrested, of setting up an uncanonical temporary Holy Synod (supreme church administration) with the support of the GPU, and of using it to transfer bishops from one diocese to another. Metropolitan Iosif, whom he had dismissed from the Leningrad diocese, refused to lay down his charge, even though he was confined to a monastery in Rostov, and wrote to his followers: "The church's authority is in a state of slavery." When a delegation of Iosif's supporters came to Sergii, urging that the Soviet regime should not be obeyed because it was the creation of the Anti-Christ, Sergii replied that the rule of the Anti-Christ was prophesied to last for three years, whereas Soviet power had already lasted for ten: "Yes, we are persecuted, and we are retreating! But in return we have preserved the unity of the church." This, of course, was not true: in Leningrad, sixty-one out of one hundred parishes declared for Iosif.[76]

Sergii made his compromise in order to ensure that the church, however besieged, would survive as an organization. He believed that "if an individual part of the church body falls into schism, that will be less destructive for the Russian Orthodox Church than its wholesale fragmentation as a result of its illegal situation in the Soviet state."[77] He hoped that the church would preserve its moral and liturgical autonomy and be able to continue its customary wide range of social and educational activities. The regime soon disillusioned him. A law on "religious associations" of April 1929 forbade all ecclesiastical activities other than divine service. There were to be no religious processions, Sunday schools, prayer meetings, Bible study groups, no hospitals, almshouses, or old people's homes. Clergymen were forbidden to officiate outside their registered parish, so there could be no missionary activity. The church was to be allowed no central organization, and even parishes were not recognized as juridical persons—which meant, for example, that they could not so much as conclude a contract with a builder for repair work to their church building. Contradictorily, parishes were nevertheless treated like enterprises in the private economy, which paid very high taxes. To make it more difficult for ordinary people to attend church, the working week was calibrated in *dekady*, ten days, which meant that only one week in seven would one's day off fall on a Sunday.[78]

The long-term result of the failed reformist challenge was fateful for the church. Most Orthodox believers have to the present day retained the impression that serious reform or modernization inside the church is synonymous "with 'renovationism,' that is, with schism, treachery, and betrayal."[79] The church was robbed of its middle ground. As parishes were closed down and whole cities left with minimal religious provision or none at all, most people retreated into religious inactivity, though they might retain some kind of deistic belief: the unpublished 1937 census actually found that 57 percent of the population was still prepared to admit to belief in God, despite the dangers of making such a declaration.[80] The minority who remained staunch practicing believers retreated into a highly conservative and literalist version of their faith, impervious to all innovations. Since they were not allowed to do more than conduct weekly divine service, that become the entire public content of religion, unconnected with social, charitable, or educational activity. Nor was the church able to absorb young people, in the newly literate generations coming out of schools all over the Soviet Union. Congregations consisted increasingly of the old and uneducated. The link between the church and normal social activity had been completely broken, and thereby a cardinal element of Russian national consciousness fatally weakened.

## Creating a New Memory

From the outset the Bolsheviks were conscious of the importance not only of destroying tradition but also of creating their own social memory and fixing it by means of symbolic representations and celebrations that would appeal to ordinary people, such as public holidays, rituals, parades, and drama. This was not easy for them to accomplish in practice, though. For one thing, the Bolsheviks' advent to power was so recent that there had been no time for popular memory to accumulate. The actual process of revolution and civil war had been chaotic, and it was difficult to sum it up in presentations that would be understandable and appealing.

Nor had the supposedly sovereign workers and peasants yet been able to evolve their own stable forms of culture. A very serious attempt had been made, though, through the so-called Proletkults, working-class cultural associations that had been launched even before the October revolution. Their theorist was Aleksandr Bogdanov, who aimed to create a wholly new international proletarian culture, different in nature from the aristocratic and bourgeois cultures of the past, and reflecting the collective, machine-inspired spirit of the workers.[81]

In its early stages Proletkult proved tremendously popular among the workers, probably because it took their human dignity more seriously than any movement in tsarist Russia had done. They flocked to join drama groups, creative writing classes, choral societies, dance troupes, and painting workshops. They put on plays, designed posters, staged folk dance and folk song evenings; they sent performing groups to entertain Red Army soldiers at the front. There was little consistency about their styles: some groups were happy to learn from the folk culture or high culture of the past, while others considered such borrowing a betrayal of the revolutionary spirit, and demanded new forms of art. "In the name of our tomorrow we will burn the Raphaels, destroy the museums and trample on the flowers of art," wrote the Proletkult poet Vladimir Kirillov.[82]

What the more innovative Proletkult members had in mind was an art informed by a specifically proletarian view of the world, tough, muscular, assertively unrefined, collectivist, machinized, confident of creating a new world, international but also proudly Russian. Here is an example from a Proletkult poet in Saratov:

> Here they are, those calloused hands!
> These huge rakes,
> That pierce the depths of the earth
> With fingers of red steel!
>
> Here they are, those calloused hands!
> They will build a home
> For freedom, art and science
> With no room for pain or suffering.[83]

In his poem "Russia" Vladimir Kirillov combined these themes with a proud statement of universal mission:

> You, the renovated Russia,
> Take up the universal struggle
> As the sun-faced God-Messiah
> With proudly raised head . . .
> And the oppressed world looks
> At the refulgent East
> And with bright faith weaves
> A garland for you, Russia.[84]

In early 1918 the Bolsheviks announced a competition to design monuments that would replace the tsars and generals in the public squares and parks. The completed artefacts reflected an international, not a national, history—that of popular revolution: they included Brutus, Robert Owen, Robespierre, Marx, and Engels. In practice they were hurriedly erected and found little response among the public; some of them were vandalized or had graffiti scrawled on them, and most were subsequently dismantled. More success was enjoyed by the new public holidays, decreed, in the same spirit, to replace those of the church: January 1, January 22 (Bloody Sunday), March 12 (the overthrow of the autocracy), March 18 (the Paris Commune), May 1 (International Workers' Day), and November 7 (Bolshevik revolution). By contrast, some Saturdays—normally a rest day—were designated *subbotniki,* days of voluntary, unpaid labor, meant to symbolize the fact that under a workers' state manual labor was a form of creative freedom. The *subbotnik* held on May Day 1920, for example, was intended to clean up Petrograd from the rubble of civil war and to remove the last traces of the old regime.[85]

The Bolsheviks also staged a few mass spectacles to dramatize the providential role they were claiming for themselves in world history. On May Day 1920 the Red Army mounted the *Mystery of Liberated Labor* on the square before the stock exchange building in Petrograd. This was a massive, six-hour long presentation of the history of the international labor movement, from the Spartacus slave revolt in ancient Rome to the October Revolution. Similarly, the opening of the 1920 Comintern congress used what was becoming the symbolic center of the regime, Moscow's Kremlin, as a stage to depict the progress from the Paris Commune of 1871 to the future "world commune." The culmination had the following scenario: "A cannon volley heralds the breaking of the blockage of Soviet Russia and the victory of the world proletariat. The Red Army returns and is reviewed by the leaders of the Revolution in a ceremonial march. Kings' crowns are strewn at their feet. . . . In the sky flare greetings to the Congress in various languages: 'Long live the Third International!', 'Workers of the World, Unite!' A general triumphal celebration to the anthem of the world Commune, the *Internationale.*"[86]

There were thirty thousand spectators present, who joined in the singing at this point, but all the same, it cannot be said that such spectacles embodied popular creativity. They were carefully choreographed by leading theater directors, and they required the discipline of the Red Army to help the Proletkultists with their performances.[87] After 1921 public shows became more modest, then gradually evolved into the far more disciplined, minutely organized parades of the Stalin period.

By this time the party itself was becoming wary both of mass working-class spontaneity and of "proletarian culture." Lenin was decidedly not among those who wished to burn Raphaels; on the contrary, he believed that proletarian painters should study Raphael and other great painters of the past before trying out their own efforts. "For a start, we should be satisfied with real bourgeois culture," he wrote. He was as good as his word: the very day after the revolution he appointed commissars to oversee the protection of museums, art galleries, and fine public buildings from looting and destruction. *Izvestiia* informed the people that they had inherited "enormous cultural riches, buildings of rare beauty, museums full of rare and marvellous objects, libraries containing great intellectual treasures, things that enlighten and inspire."[88] He also regularly assisted Maksim Gorkii in his self-appointed task of finding rations to keep good writers alive, no matter what their ideological orientation.[89] Lenin regarded the task of Proletkult as being largely educational rather than creative. For that reason, and in order to gain more control over it, he wanted to see it subordinated to Narkompros (the People's Commissariat of Education). By 1922 he had his way, not least because the large-scale rundown of industry during the civil war had drastically cut Proletkult's membership and finances.[90] Therewith the crude but vibrant creativity of working-class culture faded.

The new regime's symbols looked back as well as forward: from the past they borrowed traditional elements to which people already felt some emotional attachment. The Soviet flag took the red banner that had for decades been the rallying point of European socialists and workers and placed on it the star of the Red Army and a hammer and sickle to denote the revolutionary alliance of workers and peasants. The socialist song, the "Internationale," became the new state anthem. An emblem was devised that combined the hammer and sickle with the slogan "Proletarians of All Countries, Unite!," a rising sun to point to the future, a wheatsheaf to denote abundance, and a classical scroll for less obvious purposes, probably to give elegance and unity to the composition.[91]

The ritual and emotional life of the Communist regime reached an early apogee in the ceremony devised to bury its founder. The regime had sponsored experiments in cremation, but Lenin's body was not incinerated. On the contrary, it was embalmed and exposed to public view in a manner that horrified Orthodox believers no less than cremation would have done. Anatolii Lunacharskii and Leonid Krasin, who played a major role in setting up the arrangements, had been so-called God-Builders before 1917. They believed socialism could not survive on a diet of scientific prediction and intellectual reasoning, but required its own ritual and sacral elements to bind ordinary people to the socialist vision and the socialist community. Lunacharskii and Krasin had both been attracted to the prerevolutionary thinker Nikolai Fedorov, who had preached that science would one day make possible the resurrection of all the dead. They may have been hoping to preserve Lenin for posterity, for possible resurrection.

At another funeral in 1921, Krasin said: "I am certain the time will come when science will become all-powerful, that it will be able to recreate a diseased organism. . . . The liberation of mankind, using all the might of science and technology, the strength and capacity of which we cannot imagine, will be able to resurrect great historical figures."[92]

Lenin's lying in state and his funeral procession were more or less traditional, with unspecific religious overtones, like those accorded to socialist heroes before 1917. The body was then laid to rest in a temporary sarcophagus, soon replaced by a dignified assemblage of cubes in red porphyry as a permanent mausoleum. This building became the focus of a popular cult, encouraged by the Communist leaders and taken up with enthusiasm by the population. In fact, Lenin's mausoleum established itself as the number one sacred space in the Soviet Union, permanently watched over by a guard of honor, an object of pilgrimage for the masses and a venue for the leaders to watch mass parades on festive occasions. Once dead, Lenin the founder could be safely identified with the socialist dream, unbesmirched by the imperfections of its subsequent realization. When later Communist leaders were in difficulties, they could always evoke the Lenin heritage.[93]

Right from the beginning, then, the Communist regime, though still bent on uprooting Russia's past, had begun to construct its own forms of memory and to celebrate them in rituals designed to have as much public appeal as possible. For the moment, however, their success was limited and uncertain. During 1917–1921 Russia's social structures and social memory had been destroyed on an unprecedented scale; an already ambiguous and fragmented national consciousness had been further attenuated. The attempt to create a new social order based on the Communist hierarchy and a new social myth based on the Communist worldview had barely had time to take shape.

# 3

# SOVIET NATIONALITY POLICY
# AND THE RUSSIANS

In the early 1920s a Chechen teenager, Abdurakhman Avtorkhanov, began to collect "infidel" books: Tolstoi, Gorkii, and the like. For this he was whipped by his pious Muslim father and expelled from the *mekhteb* (religious elementary school) in his village. He decided to leave home to find a secular school at which to study. Together with his cousin Mumad, who was carrying a revolver for protection, he set out over the mountains to the big city, Groznyi. On arrival they were both arrested, the revolver was confiscated, and they were interrogated as suspected members of a terrorist gang. When they denied the charge, the inspector retorted to Mumad, "Come on! What kind of Chechen are you, if you're not a thief, a bandit, and a murderer?" Mumad leaped at the inspector and punched his nose before being dragged away by guards. The next morning, to their great surprise, both were released. A check in their village had revealed their identity, and it was explained to them, "You are honest people, and the official who insulted the Chechen people has been punished."[1]

The two cousins had unknowingly become pawns in the complex interaction between ethnic groups and the new Soviet state. There were actually two governments in Groznyi at the time: a Russian municipal administration and a Chechen Soviet Executive Committee. The first had arrested them, the second released them.[2] The contretemps was just a tiny wrinkle in the patchwork ethnic mêlée of the North Caucasus region.

The Bolshevik leaders proclaimed that they were establishing an international republic. The *ABC of Communism* declared: "It is essential that the working-class should overcome all national prejudices and national enmities" in order to create a "unified world socialist republic."[3] But this goal was extraordinarily difficult to accomplish in a territory containing so many intermingled nationalities whose mutual relations had been embittered by the horrors of revolution and civil war.

Communists regarded nationalism as a kind of pubertal disorder of the human race, a necessary phase, but something to be got through as swiftly as possible. Lenin advocated national emancipation for oppressed peoples but always insisted that the international solidarity of the proletariat had absolute priority. Communist leaders themselves disavowed any national identity. Lenin wrote on his passport application "no nationality," and Trotskii, when asked if he was Jewish or Russian, replied: "Neither: I am a Social Democrat and an internationalist."[4]

At the time the Bolsheviks came to power they were confident that an international workers' state would soon be created. Fired by the Russian example, they believed, workers in other European countries would hasten to overthrow their imperialist governments and join their Russian comrades. In that way the national problem would quickly fade from the agenda. As time passed, the Soviet leaders came to realize that matters were not so simple, that the national "disease" could be protracted, messy, and dangerous. They also perceived, however, that it offered opportunities if exploited properly. The Bolshevik leaders believed the tsarist regime had mishandled the nationality problem by trying to Russify the non-Russians—a mistake symptomatic of the "prison-house of the peoples," and one they would not repeat. Writing to Sergo Ordzhonikidze, chairman of the party's Caucasian bureau, in April 1920, Lenin urged him to display "caution and maximum goodwill towards the Muslims, especially on advancing into Dagestan. Do everything to demonstrate, and in the most emphatic manner, our sympathy for the Muslims, their autonomy, independence, etc."[5]

In his anxiety not to replicate the high-handedness of the tsars, Lenin repeatedly railed against the "great power chauvinism" of the Russians and reiterated his determination to cut Russians down to size as one nationality among others. In the process, however, he perpetuated the error common among Russian intellectuals of assuming that the Russian people could automatically be identified with the Russian imperial state, that there was no difference between the Russian nation and the Russian Empire. Lunacharskii, cultural commissar for most of the 1920s, took the same approach: "We must educate people . . . so that they regard every-one, no matter what nationality they belong to, as their brothers, so that they love equally every inch of our common planet, and so that, if they have a prejudice in favor of Russian people, the Russian language, or the Russian countryside, they should recognize that that feeling is an irratio-nal prejudice."[6] Lunacharskii's task was to use educational and cultural policy to create a de-ethnicized international republic, first of all in the Soviet Union, later throughout the world.

If one considers the ethnic realities the Communists inherited, then it is obvious that to create even the makings of an international republic re-quired a complex and well-formulated policy. If matters were left to them-selves, the prospect was that in the course of modernization some of the non-Russians would gradually assimilate to the Russian language and culture, while others would reject Russia altogether and assert their own separate national identity. In neither case would internationalism be ad-vanced. So a clear-cut policy of "affirmative action" was required to pro-mote the national identity of non-Russians—a policy that in practice was bound to entail some discrimination *against* Russians. Bukharin accepted the logic of this situation, asserting that Russians would thus be given the opportunity "to purchase for themselves the genuine trust of the previ-ously oppressed peoples."[7]

Stalin, the Commissar for Nationalities, agreed with this policy in prin-ciple. He was uneasy, however, about making Russia just one national re-public alongside others. He had good reason. "Russia" had never existed as a discrete territory inside the Russian Empire. How should it be con-structed now? On this issue Stalin had serious differences with Lenin. As new Soviet republics took shape during the civil war, Stalin envisaged the Soviet state simply absorbing all of them to form a Russian Soviet Repub-lic, the direct territorial successor to the old Russian Empire. Lenin, how-ever, felt that such a "Soviet Russia" would merely revive the old imperial arrogance: at one point in discussions on the issue he burst out impa-tiently: "I declare war to the death on Great Russian chauvinism."[8] He recommended that, formally at least, Russia should not be an overarching state, but should enter a federal Soviet state on equal terms with the non-Russian republics. That overarching federal state would have no ethnic or geographic designation: it would simply be called the Union of Soviet So-cialist Republics.[9] As we know, that is what actually happened.

This solution did not address the fact that, whatever borders one assigned to the Russian republic within the USSR, it was bound to leave out a lot of Russians, and also to contain a large number of non-Russians, including many Muslims. One of the principal Muslim Communists, Mir-Said Sultan Galiev, proposed forestalling this problem by going even further than Lenin. He suggested that not only the larger non-Russian nationalities but also the smaller ethnic formations should no longer be subject to Russia, but should become full members of the USSR, on a par with Russia, Ukraine, and so on. Stalin's reply to Sultan Galiev highlighted sharply the dilemmas of situating Russia inside the new Soviet state structure. "Such a proposal," he argued, "means dissolving our federation into pieces and creating a Russian TsIK [Soviet Central Executive Committee]—not a *rossiiskii,* but a *russkii* TsIK. . . . Comrades, do we really need this?"[10] Stalin was indicating the danger of giving institutional embodiment to Russian ethnic sentiment inside the USSR. "Russia" was acceptable as a supranational entity, as a purified ghost of the old empire, and as a disembodied precursor of the coming proletarian international state—but not as an actual ethnos or nation-state. A real Russian ethnic-territorial state in the middle of the Soviet Union would be so large and powerful that it would either dominate the Union or render it unworkable.

In the end the constitution adopted in December 1922 was Leninist in form: that is to say, it was formally federal, and the new state, the Union of Soviet Socialist Republics, was not named after Russia. All the same, the content of the constitution was unmistakably Stalinist. The Russian republic, the RSFSR (the Russian Soviet Federal Socialist Republic), contained 90 percent of the land area and 72 percent of the population. Some two-thirds of Communist Party members were Russian.[11] Moreover, despite the federal costume in which the constitution was dressed, the party, the armed forces, and the economic administration were all tightly centralized. Given such a structure, very determined counteraction was needed to prevent the RSFSR and the Russians dominating the Union.

Initially such counteraction was forthcoming: to weaken the potential domination of Russians the Soviet leaders adopted a conscious policy of "indigenization," *korenizatsiia*—essentially affirmative action in favor of non-Russians. The 10th Party Congress in March 1921 proclaimed that "the party's task is to help the labouring masses of the non–Great Russian peoples to catch up with central Russia, which has forged ahead," by building their own state institutions, including courts and administrative and economic offices, staffed by their own people in the native languages, and "to develop their press, schools, theatres, recreation clubs and educational institutions generally, functioning in the native languages." *Likbez,* or the liquidation of illiteracy, was also to be carried out in the native languages.[12]

Now, in many regions of the Soviet Union the simplest policy would have been to send Russians in to develop the administration and promote economic development: they were usually better trained and more familiar with the workings of a modern economy than were non-Russians. Instead, under *korenizatsiia* the party deliberately decided to train local people to take over these jobs, providing them with education and experience that would equip them to run their own republics, which as a result effectively became temporary local nation-states, though under tight supervision from Moscow. Ethnographers were sent out into the regions to study local languages, customs, religions, economic life, tribal allegiances, and other factors affecting people's ethnic identity. The results were used in a program of what might be called "ethnic engineering," assembling new nations out of raw ethnic material and giving them their own republican institutions with boundaries that as far as possible reflected the ethnic composition of the population.[13]

The People's Commissariat of Nationalities (Narkomnats) was set up as a means of directing these nation-building programs from the center, and also as a forum in which the representatives of the various nationalities could articulate their difficulties and try to have them acknowledged, discussed, and overcome. Significantly, the only people not represented on Narkomnats were the Russians.[14]

In practice it was not possible to delineate ethnic territories tidily. For one thing, it was not clear what indicators of national identity one should adopt. Language, religion, dress, diet, everyday customs, economic activity, and self-identification were all possible markers. Moreover, people's national identity was evolving. The more backward groups were tending to assimilate to the more advanced, and in particular to adopt the Russian language. At this stage, however, ethnographers tended to interpret "Russification" as unnatural or forced, a hangover from the old regime, and to choose for their respondents an alternative nationality.[15] The main obstacle, though, was the complex intermingling of ethnic groups over much of Russia's old imperial territory. Not only in large cities but also in small towns and sometimes even in villages people of different ethnic origins lived side by side. Without massive population movements they could not just be assigned to a nation with unambiguous borders. The Communist leaders had studied the history of the national question in the old Habsburg Monarchy, where both Lenin and Stalin had lived for a time before 1914, and which had suffered from the same problem. They wanted to avoid the mistakes that had led to the Monarchy's disintegration. All the same, they did not take the advice of the Austrian Marxist thinkers who proposed what was probably the only workable solution for dealing with ethnic intermingling: personal cultural autonomy.[16] Such a solution would have implied a concept of individual human rights that Bolsheviks always dismissed as a bourgeois sham.

Since they rejected personal cultural autonomy, the Bolsheviks had a choice of two ways to tackle ethnic problems, both collective. Either they had to encourage minority ethnic groups to assimilate to the majority in their republic, or they had to be prepared to create very tiny ethnic-administrative territories. They chose the latter course. The result was a complex calibrated hierarchy of union republics, autonomous republics, autonomous regions, and so on, many of which survived to the end of the Soviet Union.[17] Within the Russian republic, the Bolsheviks favored a non-Russian nationality wherever possible. As a result, to take one example, the Mordovian Autonomous Soviet Socialist Republic, on the territory of the RSFSR, was called after the Mordovians, even though in 1926 Russians constituted 60 percent of the population there; similarly, Russians formed more than half the population in the Karelian and Buriat Autonomous Republics.[18]

Initially "national soviets" were created down to the very lowest levels, including individual villages, each with its own schools, law courts, and administrative offices, as a way of ensuring that minorities were not assimilated or forcibly incorporated into larger ethnic communities. Narkomnats was to adjudicate whenever conflicts arose. These national administrative units were probably the smallest ever created anywhere in the world. However small they were, though, there always remained a minority within a minority, feeling aggrieved that its national rights were not properly protected. So the system never eliminated ethnic friction altogether.[19]

The first republic to establish a fully calibrated system of national soviets was Ukraine, since it contained an unusual number of advanced and active ethnic groups who were not content simply to be ruled by Russians or Ukrainians: Poles, Germans, Jews, Armenians, Greeks, and Bulgarians. Wherever they had local minorities, even at the village level, these groups were awarded their own soviets, committed to full implementation of *korenizatsiia*, including promotion of the national language and culture and formation of national cadres. In this way, as one example, Jewish shtetls became full-fledged national soviets.[20] Only one nationality was left without any national soviets: the Russians. Had they been allowed them, whole cities like Kharkov and Donetsk would have become Russian administrative enclaves. The Russians were too powerful and numerous for their own good, and *korenizatsiia* therefore intentionally discriminated against them.

Inside the RSFSR, national soviets for non-Russians were numerous. In addition to the autonomous republics such as those mentioned above, by 1932 290 national districts *(raiony)* had been formed, along with some 7,000 national village soviets and some 10,000 national collective farms. About half of these were Ukrainian. Higher educational institutions in the RSFSR held places specially reserved for candidates from the minorities.[21]

In this way an imbalance was created, as a result of which Russians with good reason felt themselves disadvantaged. In Ukraine, for example, they were required to subscribe to Ukrainian-language newspapers and to send their children to Ukrainian-language schools, to be taught in what many of them considered a farmyard dialect. At an April 1926 session of the Central Executive Committee of the Soviets, Iurii Larin spoke of these grievances, raising "that part of the nationalities question which one must name the Russian question in Ukraine, for regrettably such a question does exist." According to the stenogram, his remarks provoked prolonged applause; evidently, he had tabled an issue about which delegates had strong unspoken feelings. His opponents reiterated the accepted view that "it is impossible to behave towards the Russians in Ukraine as a national minority."[22]

The following year Avel Enukidze repeated and expanded this criticism of the Ukrainians, charging that their practices led to the creation of "isolated little islands." Instead, he suggested, "our task is, in an ascending line, to lead national minorities towards the basic culture of their republic. That is for union republics. In relation to the USSR as a whole our task is different. Russian culture and Russian language is the main axis around which we should raise up all nationalities living in the USSR."[23] His remarks were greeted with indignation, even though his opponents acknowledged that he was voicing the sentiments of many Communists. He was asked to retract them but declined to do so. In effect, he had formulated an alternative nationality policy, that of proceeding by gradual assimilation to turn the Soviet Union into a Russian nation-state. That had been the policy of Mikhail Katkov and Konstantin Pobedonostsev under the tsars, but for Communists it was anathema.

One of the first examples of a policy that could be construed as anti-Russian was the campaign of terror conducted in 1919 against the Don Cossacks, who were thoroughly Russian both in descent and in outlook. Admittedly, the campaign was originally conceived as part of the class struggle. Among the staunchest supporters of the old regime, many—but certainly not all—Don Cossacks fought for the Whites during the civil war. As the Red Army occupied their territory in the early months of 1919, the Communist Party ordered a "merciless struggle with the entire Cossack elite by means of their total extermination," combined with confiscation of their grain and the reallocation of their lands to "outlanders," non-Cossack peasants and workers living in the region. "No compromises, no half-measures are permissible," the Orgburo circular of January 24, 1919, insisted. On the strength of these instructions, revolutionary tribunals tried and passed death sentences against arrested Cossacks: altogether, perhaps ten to twelve thousand were victims of this policy. Local Communists also wanted to abolish the Don Cossack Region as an administrative unit. Soon, however, a Cossack anti-Red rebellion gave them pause: with the front line still not far away, they could not afford to alienate all Cossacks by treating them indiscriminately as a single ethnic unit. As one local Communist proposed, the terror was reoriented and "conducted within the parameters of class struggle," and not as "an amorphous zoological struggle." "De-Cossackization" became more discriminating, using socioeconomic criteria to distinguish among Cossack households, welcoming some of them as allies rather than rejecting them all as enemies. "Be attentive, comrades, to the Don middle Cossack," as one instruction put it.[24]

It was not only in Ukraine and on the Don that Russians felt resentment at their treatment. Official policy came out against the many Russian and Ukrainian peasants, as well as Cossacks, who had settled in the North Caucasus region and in Turkestan in the decades before 1917. In the North Caucasus the newly formed Mountain Peoples' Autonomous

Soviet Socialist Republic (ASSR) launched its career in 1921 with the following command: "For the satisfaction of the desperate needs of landless
Mountain Peoples, begin immediately the planned expulsion of Cossack
settlements." Some fifteen thousand Cossacks were evicted and deported
in the course of this action.[25]

Similarly in Turkestan between 1920 and 1922, the new Soviet authorities carried out a land reform in favor of the indigenous peoples, in the
course of which many recent Slavic settlers were expropriated and driven
out, apparently on ethnic grounds, whether or not they were classified as
"kulaks." In places the policy was enforced with extreme harshness: peasant households would be given forty-eight hours to collect their movable
belongings and evacuate their homes and fields without any arrangement
for them to resettle elsewhere. In the village of Vysokoe near Chimkent,
for example, a Central Committee emissary later reported, "On April 16,
1921, policemen appeared and with the help of the army loaded the families onto trucks and transported them to the station of Abail on the
Semireche railway, where they sat in the open for three whole days in the
pouring rain. Most of the deportees were old men, women, and children,
including some small babies." Eventually they were offered new land in
the Golodnaia Step, but they declined it on the grounds that they were
too old to found a new settlement there. The victims of this operation
protested: "When 25 million people are starving in Russia, one should ensure that everyone sows as much grain as possible, but we are being deprived of a harvest which we have already sown. . . . Our 24 families are
being condemned to starvation. And not only us, but the families of our
children, who are serving in the Red Army. Why? What have we done,
simple peasants who eternally till the soil?"[26] A. A. Ioffe, emissary of the
RSFSR government, later reported visiting the region and seeing "abandoned Russian huts and abandoned vegetable plots, while alongside them
Kirgiz artels lived in their tents and neglected all this because they did not
know how to manage a Russian stove or cultivate a Russian market garden." In 1921 the Russian population of Turkestan fell from 2.7 to 2.2
million, and Russian arable landholdings from 3.3 million to 1.6 million
desiatinas.[27]

In Uzbekistan the authorities implemented *korenizatsiia* by favoring
Uzbeks in the labor market, in some cases laying off Slavs in order to em-
ploy them. At the Tashkent labor exchange in April 1927 unemployed
Russians complained: "What are the Russians supposed to do, or do they

not want to eat? Russians fought and won freedom for you devils, and now you say Uzbeks are the masters in Uzbekistan. There will come a time and we'll show you. We'll beat the hell out of you!" The Uzbeks responded in kind: "Just wait, it won't be long before we ask all you Europeans to go back to your homeland [*rodina*] and find work there." On a number of occasions serious brawls broke out as a result of such exchanges.[28]

The construction of the Turksib railway from Novosibirsk to Tashkent offered a stern test of *korenizatsiia,* for it was deliberately used by the Kazakh authorities, across whose territory it ran, to launch the creation of a Kazakh proletariat. In pursuit of this policy, Kazakh candidates for laboring jobs would often be given preference, even though Narkomput, the managers of the railway, preferred Russians, who were usually more skilled and easier to integrate into the workforce. The results were mixed. Quite a few Kazakhs did make it into long-term employment, breaking with their traditional nomadic background and overcoming management's prejudice against them. Sometimes their Russian colleagues would help them to adjust, though in the process they had to learn Russian as the language of their new life. Other times, however, the less skilled and unemployed Russians gave vent to bitter resentment by attacking Kazakh laborers. At Sergiupol in December 1928 a crowd of unemployed Europeans went on a rampage at the labor exchange and beat up every Kazakh job-seeker they could lay their hands on, then marched through the town and sacked the OGPU and party buildings. Some fifty Kazakhs were wounded in the brawls.[29]

Russians were slighted not only ethnically but also institutionally. Their republic, the RSFSR, had an insecure and humble status; it was the puny giant among the Soviet republics. It was certainly not "Russia" in the sense of being a potential nation-state. As we have seen, it was a patchwork of autonomous republics, regions, and so on. Besides, the leaders kept lopping chunks of territory off it. In 1924 the Uzbek and Turkmen Soviet Socialist Republics were created from inside the RSFSR (the Uzbek republic later divided to become the Uzbek and Tadjik republics). Vitebsk, Gomel, and (temporarily) Smolensk oblasti were transferred to the Belorussian republic. In 1936 a huge stretch of Central Asian steppe and desert—southern Siberia or northern Central Asia, according to taste— was reconstituted as the Kazakh SSR. A Karelo-Finnish SSR was carved out during the Winter War in 1940 but was returned to the RSFSR as an

autonomous republic in 1956. After the war the RSFSR gained the ex-
clave of Kaliningrad, beyond Belorussia on the Baltic coast, but lost the
Crimea to the Ukrainian SSR in 1954 as a good-will gesture during the
celebration of the 300th anniversary of the "reunion" of Ukraine and Russia. What these far-reaching but arbitrary transfers indicate is that the
RSFSR was never seen as a homeland for the Russian people, but rather as
a residual holding territory, to be adjusted and rearranged for administrative convenience.[30]

RSFSR ministries, though they had jurisdiction over the lion's share of
natural resources, were mostly subordinate to USSR ministries and dominated by them. Even more important, the RSFSR had no Communist
Party of its own with a Central Committee. Regional leaders in the
RSFSR felt they had no one to defend their interests in the highest eche-
lons of the party when it came to competition with other union republics, especially over economic policy. In 1926 Mikhail Kalinin was put
in charge of a special commission to examine "the construction of the
RSFSR, national republics and oblast organs within the RSFSR." The
commission worked for nine months and produced a report that was sent
to the Politburo, but no action was taken on it. With the first five-year
plan approaching, the authorities planned to augment the power of the
all-Union industrial ministries, not reduce it.[31]

In a sense, then, the Russians were the orphans of the Soviet Union.
They had no Communist Party, no capital city, no Academy of Sciences,
no national encyclopedia, no radio or television networks separate from
those of the Soviet Union as a whole. They had no means to defend their
own interests when they clashed with those of the other nationalities. Yet
at the same time those deprivations marked out Russians' supranational
status as the custodians of the USSR as a whole, their permanent role as
responsible "elder brother," whatever they might think of the other "prod-
igal sons." Yuri Slezkine has likened the Soviet Union to a communal
apartment in which each nationality had its own room except the Russians, who lived in the hallway, the corridor, the bathroom, and the
kitchen; they ran the place and got in everyone's way, but they had no secure space of their own.[32]

## Residual Russian National Feeling

Despite these formidable handicaps and for all the Bolsheviks' internationalism, from the outset countervailing factors made it inevitable that

some day the Soviet Union would take on a Russian coloring. The fact was, after all, that the international revolution *had* broken out in Russia, not in any other country. As Lenin himself explained to the Third All-Russian Congress of Soviets in January 1918, "Things have turned out *differently from what Marx and Engels expected,* and we, the Russian working and exploited classes, have been given the honor of being the vanguard of the international socialist revolution. We can now see clearly that the revolution will develop much further. The Russian began it—the German, the Frenchman, and the Englishman will complete it, and socialism will triumph."[33]

Lenin, then, still viewed the Russian contribution to revolution as only preliminary. However, military defeat at the hands of the Germans forced the Central Committee by February–March 1918 to take a fateful decision which cemented the relationship between socialist revolution and Russia. The young Soviet state had two alternatives: it could let the Germans invade and occupy the country, after which it would continue the war as an underground guerrilla campaign against the occupiers, while issuing clarion calls for the German workers to rise and overthrow their exploiters. Such a strategy would amount to a declaration of all-European class war: it would have been consistent with Lenin's policy through October 1917, and it was the strategy favored by the so-called Left Communists led by Nikolai Bukharin.[34] (It would certainly have embarrassed the Germans, who would have found it tricky to occupy effectively a country the size of Russia while still conducting a war in the West.) Alternatively Soviet Russia could surrender to the Germans and conclude a formal peace treaty, abandoning the prospect of immediate international revolution, and concentrate instead on saving what could be saved of sovereign Russian territory as a temporary bastion of socialism.

Lenin chose the latter course. By doing so, he turned Russia into the homeland of socialism, at least provisionally. He reformulated the immediate aims of the party, speaking of "our unbending determination to ensure that at any rate Russia [he used the archaic term *Rus*] ceases to be wretched and impotent and becomes mighty and abundant in the full meaning of those words. . . . Our natural wealth, our manpower, and the splendid impetus that the great revolution has given to the creative powers of the people are ample material to build a truly mighty and abundant Russia [again *Rus*]."[35] Here was the embryo of what later under Stalin would become Socialism in One Country.

These early, somewhat hesitant paeans to Russia focused on its working people. No Russian socialists had yet professed admiration for the Russian imperial state. Yet once the Reds won the civil war, they became the de facto inheritors of Imperial Russia and of most of its territories and peoples. Paradoxically, during 1917–1920 the Reds had proved themselves better able to ensure Russia's survival and integrity than had the tsarist regime, the Provisional Government, or the Whites. They had repelled foreign incursions which in some cases the Whites had actually supported, for all their imperial patriotism and their proclamations of "Russia One and Indivisible." When the Poles invaded Ukraine in the spring of 1920 the Reds set the seal on the temporary and improbable alliance between socialism and the ghost of Imperial Russia. Historically the Poles were national enemies who had for centuries disputed the western regions of what Russians considered their own territory. Resisting them was the duty of every patriotic Russian: or so the Reds now argued, for the first time combining revolutionary élan with Russian nationalism.

On May 8, 1920, Karl Radek—secretary of the Comintern, no less—appealed to White officers to join the Red Army for patriotic reasons. "The Soviet government, which defends the territorial integrity and independence of the country that is populated by Russians . . . is for honest White officers the government that defends Russian independence. . . . Our civil war was always national. It was a regathering of Russian lands in the hands of the dictator—the working class. It was always the struggle for independence from the yoke of foreign and native capitalism."[36] As we have seen, Brusilov and other old regime generals, most of whom had hitherto remained aloof from the Communists, responded positively to this appeal.

All the same, the two outlooks were far from identical. Brusilov still regarded Lenin as the Anti-Christ and considered Bolshevism a "temporary sickness," since "its philosophy of internationalism is fundamentally alien to the Russian people. . . . Communism is completely unintelligible to the millions of barely literate peasants, and it is doubtful that they will fight for it. If Christianity failed to unify the people in two thousand years, how can Communism hope to do so when most of the people had not even heard of it three years ago? Only the idea of Russia can do that."[37]

In essence Brusilov's outlook was the old-fashioned *rossiiskii* imperial attitude revamped for a particular occasion and purpose. It would nevertheless prove itself a powerful weapon. Thousands of officers *did* respond to the appeal and enlist in the Red Army, to an extent that surprised and even embarrassed the Soviet leaders. And the mood proved durable, out-lasting the war against Poland. For at least the first two decades of Soviet rule, Brusilov's kind of hybrid patriotism—inherited great-power imperialism plus instrumental accommodation with Communism—was common among Soviet Russia's professional strata, including its army officers, even though they now had no epaulettes.[38]

As censorship tightened inside the USSR, it became impossible to articulate Brusilov's outlook fully within the country. As so often in the next few decades, it fell to centers of Russian emigration to provide a fuller account of what was happening inside Russia itself and to formulate political conclusions in a trenchant and even provocative manner. The most innovative tendency was Eurasianism. First articulated in a collection of essays that appeared in Sofia in 1921, the movement posed a radical challenge to the whole orientation of Russian cultural life. Eurasianists proposed that Russia and the West were incompatible and that the policy of emulating the West, which had been pursued for the past two centuries by the bureaucracy and the intelligentsia, was misguided. Ordinary Russians were actually closer in their material and spiritual culture to Asiatic peoples, with whom they shared a common origin in the steppes of Eurasia. According to this view, the Bolsheviks had brought disaster to Russia because they had imposed yet another destructive ideology from Europe; but their very success would unleash the latent strength of the Russian people, who would finally sweep away the Western veneer overlaying their true instincts. A former colonized country itself, Russia would lead the emancipation of the other colonies from the domination of Western Europe and usher in an era of authoritarian rule, strong religious faith, and ethnic tolerance.[39]

Eurasianism was an abrupt and radical challenge to most of Russian thought, even to that of the socialists, who also rejected liberalism and capitalism. It offered an alternative way of being anti-Western. For the time being it remained an isolated émigré movement without echoes in the Soviet Union. Not till the 1980s, as we shall see, did it come to play an important part in Russians' self-identification. Of more immediate significance were those thinkers who saw in the Soviet Union a renewed Russian Empire.

The initial leader of this group was Nikolai Ustrialov, who had been chairman of the Kadet Party in the Russian Far East. He had fled to Manchuria after the Whites' final defeat, and from there to Prague, where he edited a collection of articles entitled *Smena Vekh* (Change of Landmarks), published in 1921.[40] It summed up the new mood, conciliatory toward the Communists, that was gaining ground among Imperial Russian patriots.

Its central thesis, expounded in Ustrialov's own article, "Patriotica," was that the Bolshevik revolution, despite appearances, was thoroughly Russian in spirit; the Soviet Union would now take over the traditional role of the Russian Empire as a great power, whether its leaders intended that outcome or not. Emigrés should therefore cooperate with the new government: "The anti-Bolshevik movement has become too closely associated with foreign elements and has thereby conferred on Bolshevism a certain nationalist halo. . . . The Soviet regime will strive in every possible way to reannex the peripheries—in the name of world revolution. Russian patriots will fight for the same goal—in the name of Russia, one and indivisible. For all the infinite difference in ideology, the practical way forward is the same." Ustrialov urged émigrés to accept that Russian culture needed to be renewed from within; at the moment, he asserted, only the Soviet leadership was capable of achieving such a renewal and at the same time of restoring Russia's great-power status: "As the power of the revolution— and at the moment only that power—is capable of restoring Russia's great-power status and her international standing, our duty in the name of Russian culture is to acknowledge its political authority."[41]

Ustrialov had completely turned his back on the liberal politics of the pre-1917 years. He believed that the authoritarian nature of the Russian state was a positive advantage in the new era: "Formal democracy is everywhere entering its twilight . . . History is striving to reproduce certain features of the enlightened absolutist state, though of course in a new form for a new era." It followed that Russia was well equipped to take the lead: "the new era will more than any previous one be marked by the influence of Russia and of Russian culture." Russia should be "powerful, great, and frightful to her enemies," for only a strong state could generate a great culture. It would be led by a "new aristocracy, in its own way both popular and progressive, an aristocracy of black bones and calloused hands." Ustrialov remained strongly Christian in outlook but held that Christianity was irrelevant to the conduct of politics.[42] In 1925 he demonstrated the sincerity of his beliefs by becoming an employee of the Soviet regime, as an official on the Manchurian railway.[43]

Another contributor to *Smena vekh,* the former Octobrist politician

Aleksandr Bobrishchev-Pushkin, was even more forthright in his praise of the Soviet state, both for its authoritarianism and for its messianism. He asserted that the greatest achievement of the Bolsheviks was that they redistributed property to the people, and thus created a stable social basis for their authority that the old regime had lacked.[44]

*Smena vekh* acknowledged, then, that the anti-Bolshevik movements had been defeated. In the words of one contributor, "We are going to Canossa. We recognize that we have lost, that we took the wrong road, that our activities and our assessments were mistaken." All the same, the implication of their way of admitting defeat was that the Bolsheviks had also miscalculated, since their revolution had generated not an international proletarian revolution but a renewed and strengthened Russian state. Bolshevism was "a disease, but at the same time a necessary, though unpleasant, stage of our country's evolution," from which it would emerge fortified and reinvigorated.[45]

The outlook of Ustrialov and his colleagues seemed to be confirmed by the developments of the early 1920s. The Soviet Union was finally consolidated on almost the same territory as the old Russian Empire, and it began to be tentatively accepted by other powers as the successor to it. By 1923 all other attempted European socialist revolutions had failed, while inside the USSR the New Economic Policy had been introduced, which meant, even in Russia, the temporary abandonment of the aim of immediately building socialism and the reintroduction of some forms of private economic activity. By 1925 Nikolai Bukharin was even exhorting peasants "Enrich yourselves!" as a contribution to the construction of socialism. In 1924, moreover, Stalin, now general secretary of the Communist Party, began to retreat from Lenin's vision of international revolution and to talk of the possibility of "socialism in one country."[46]

During these years the Soviet frontier had not yet become impermeable, and there was still a good deal of movement back and forth across it. Many émigrés had initially intended to return after the expected fall of the Soviet regime; now that it had not fallen, they began instead to hope that it might after all prove tolerable, so that they could go back to their homeland. The *Smena vekh* outlook was naturally congenial to them. Similarly, inside the Soviet Union many army officers, civil servants, and professional people were eager to continue serving their country and people, under whatever label, and they too hoped that the Soviet regime might prove to be simply Russia in a new guise.

Some writers clung to the same hope. In 1922, for example, Aleksei Tolstoi wrote: "If history has reason, and I believe that it has, everything that is happening in Russia is done for the sake of world salvation. . . . [One must] do everything to help the revolution develop in the direction of enrichment of Russian life, in the direction of the extraction of all good and all justice from the revolution . . . in the direction of strengthening Russia as a great power."[47] Tolstoi believed that Communism was Russia's national fate. In his novel *Peter the Great* he portrayed an earlier state-directed transformation, "combatting barbarism by barbaric means," as Lenin liked to say, while in *The Road to Calvary (Khozhdenie po mukam)*, he portrayed the transformation of an early-twentieth-century decadent intellectual into a true Communist believer.[48]

In the 1920s books and journals were sometimes published both in the Soviet Union and in emigration. One of the contributors to *Smena vekh*, Iu. V. Kliuchnikov (a former professor of law at Moscow University, a member of the Kadet Party, and a minister in Kolchak's government), founded a daily newspaper that was published in both Berlin and Moscow from 1922 to 1924. Called *Nakanune* (On the Eve), it was subsidized for a time by the Soviet government; it unreservedly endorsed the Soviet Union as a Russian state, entitled thanks to its internationalism to play a major role as a great power in the coming decades. Kliuchnikov called upon White émigrés to return and strengthen their homeland.[49] The monthly journal *Novaia Rossiia* (later simply *Rossiia*), edited by Isai Lezhnev, took a similar line and continued to publish Ustrialov after he was barred from the rest of the press—alongside the highly controversial prose writer and dramatist Mikhail Bulgakov.

Some émigrés did respond positively. Vladimir Vernadskii, one of the world's leading geologists, had struggled already before 1917 to persuade the tsarist regime to fund a Commission for the Study of Russia's Natural Resources, being convinced that a large-scale investigation of this kind was necessary to enable Russia to exploit its resources to the full, as was required to maintain great-power status. He failed then and emigrated after the civil war. In the West, however, he was no more successful in obtaining the large sums he considered necessary, and in 1926 he decided to return to the Soviet Union. He loathed the Communists but hoped nevertheless that, as Russian rulers eager to bolster their international status and with the resources of an unprecedently centralized state at their disposal, they would be able to assist him in a way nobody else could. He thought that Communism would prove ephemeral, while the state's devotion to science and economic development would endure. He was wrong on the first count but right on the second: the regime did in fact provide funding for his research.[50]

As for the Soviet leaders themselves, some gave conditional support to the *Smena vekh* line. Whatever the long-term future, in the short run the Soviet state had to be soundly run, both internally and externally, or the revolution would perish. It needed "bourgeois specialists" to take up the expert professional jobs, for which few Communists or workers were trained. If "bourgeois" thinkers were prepared for their own reasons to support the Soviet Union, they were worth accepting as temporary allies. That was the line taken by Lunacharskii, who claimed that the *Smena vekh* writers were "national liberals" who had realized that the Comintern "serves the interests of Russia as a great power, winning her friends both in the West and in the East among millions of oppressed people." Trotskii commented that they "approached not communism but at least the Soviet state through patriotic gates," having "come to the conclusion that . . . nobody can defend the unity of the Russian people and its independence from the external threat in contemporary historical conditions other than the Soviet state." He recommended that *Smena vekh* be circulated among the military.[51]

Other Soviet leaders were less well disposed toward *Smena vekh,* fearing that its supporters, should they become too numerous and powerful, might divert the revolutionary regime from its true purpose. Lenin gave *Smena vekh* a backhanded compliment when he admitted that its supporters were warning of dangers that might possibly materialize unless Communists acted to counter them.[52] Prominent among the opponents was Grigorii Zinovev, who as head of the Comintern spoke *ex officio* for the international dimension of the revolution. The writer Maksim Gorkii also warned against them: he loathed Russian peasants and worried that a resurgence of Russian nationalism might imply a willingness to give peasants a stranglehold on economic life. The leaders of the non-Russian republics likewise opposed the influence of *Smena vekh,* fearing that it would promote the interests of Russians to the detriment of their own peoples.[53]

Stalin, as so often, took up an intermediate position. At the 14th Party Congress in 1925 he was both accepting and wary:

Smenovekhism is the ideology of the new bourgeoisie, which is growing and gradually linking up with the kulaks and the working intelligentsia. . . . [It takes] the view that the Communist Party is bound to degenerate and the new bourgeoisie to consolidate itself, while it appears that, without ourselves noticing it, we Bolsheviks are certain to approach the threshold of the democratic republic, then to cross that threshold and finally, with the help of some "Caesar" who will come forward, perhaps a military man or perhaps a civilian, to find that we have become an ordinary bourgeois republic. . . . Ustrialov is the author of this ideology. He is in the transport service. It is said that he is working well. I think that, if he is working well, let him go on dreaming about the degeneration of our party. Dreaming is not prohibited in our country. . . . But let him know that, while dreaming about our degeneration, he must at the same time bring grist to our Bolshevik mill. Otherwise it will go badly for him.[54]

Stalin, then, was prepared to accept cooperation under sufferance and for limited tactical purposes—which is what Ustrialov had in mind too.

At the same time, Stalin was actually introducing a major modification of Leninism—though he was careful to present it as irreproachably orthodox. Lenin, and even more so Trotskii, had always insisted that the Russian revolution was the start of world revolution, and he had never seriously considered the question of what would become of the former if no Communist Party outside Russia managed to seize power. By 1924–1925, a full seven years after the October revolution, there was still no other European socialist state, and the question urgently needed tackling. According to Trotskii, Stalin acidly remarked, "Since there was no success yet in the West, the Russian revolution was left with the 'choice' either to wither on the vine or to degenerate into a bourgeois state." This was, he quipped, the theory of "permanent hopelessness." On the contrary, Stalin maintained —and this was a major turning point in the evolution of Russian socialism—that "socialism in one country" was wholly possible, given the will to succeed and the support of workers and socialists in other countries, which was certainly forthcoming.[55]

Already in the 1920s a fateful paradox was taking shape. The Soviet state was committed to an internationalist vision that implied active discrimination against the alleged "chauvinism" of the Russian people. It had created a Russian Republic that was the largest but also the weakest of all the union republics. Yet at the same time it was assuming a reluctant and instrumental—but nevertheless real—Russian imperial identity. This was a contradiction that could not last indefinitely. The "Russian question" was the concealed but mortally dangerous defect in the structure of the USSR. The Soviet leaders did not manage to eliminate it before it eliminated them.

# 4

# TWO RUSSIAS COLLIDE

In the late 1950s, after the death of his wife, to whom he had been married since 1895, the Old Believer Sergei Aleksandrovich Voronov dictated a brief autobiography to his son. The final page describes all the clothes his wife had sewn in the last months of her life for him and for their grandchildren, and it ends: "Altogether God's servant Evdokiia lived in this world eighty-one years and eight months. She lived together with me sixty-two years and five months. I, God's servant Sergii, have remained in this world alive in my body with my many sins and I ask forgiveness from the Lord God for my trespasses. God's servant Sergii."

The rock-steady piety of Voronov had become extremely rare by the time he told his story. It had borne him through a long life full of trials and misfortunes, the worst of which he recounted to his son:

In the winter of 1930 they dekulakized us. Our household was declared official property [*sdali v kaznu*], our lands were handed over to the *kommuna*. They ordered us to vacate our house. I was then fifty-five years old, my wife was fifty-three, my mother eighty, our sons seventeen, seven, and five, our daughters fifteen and thirteen. There were eight of us in all. In accordance with the order we left our house. We gathered what remained to us and moved to the house of our son Evsevii. In February 1930 my son and I were sent logging. We worked at that till April 15. Then we returned home. A village soviet official told us: "You have been given a horse and cow, and your son a horse. Here is your sowing plan." They assigned us land far from the village and in poor condition. The horse was one of ours, an elderly mare. We fulfilled the sowing plan and started to prepare the fallow. Then my old mare fell ill and died. They examined her and ordered me to take off the hide and deliver it as official property [*sdat v kaznu*]. The flesh was buried. That ended our task. Our household no longer existed, I had no job and no one to work for. I decided to move to acquaintances at Birokan station near Khabarovsk to seek work and somewhere to live.[1]

The dry, spare language of Voronov's account masks the enormity of what was happening to him: the destruction of his home, his family, his household economy, and his whole way of life. The devastation of rural Russia in the early 1930s was the climax of the collision between two Russias, that of the peasants and that of the new Communist ruling class. After the upheavals of revolution and civil war a brief normality had returned to the village for a few years under the New Economic Policy. But even that was overshadowed by foreboding. Communists and peasants had cooperated in the common aim of expropriating the landowners, but there was little else they could agree about. They lived in two utterly different mental worlds. Communists were optimistic, energetic, forward-looking, and confident of the future. Peasants were cautious, inclined to pessimism, and wary of "dark forces." They regarded time as a cyclical succession of good fortune and disaster.

Village time was measured in the recurring rhythms of night and day, the agricultural seasons, and the alternation of workdays and festivals. Apart from Christmas, Easter, Trinity (or Whit) Sunday, and Shrove Tuesday (Mardi Gras), they celebrated the holy days of their favorite saints, among whom would often be St. George, St. Mikhail, and the prophet Elijah. Just before festivals villagers would cook special meals and brew beer or samogon, so that on the day itself, after going to church, they could gather, drink together, and discuss the affairs of the village and the world. This was also an occasion for relatives and visitors from neighboring villages to take meals with families. Often at the end of the day there would be dancing and singing, and young people would meet and stroll together on the village street. Communists tried to ban festivals that fell on workdays and to discourage heavy drinking, which not infrequently led to hooliganism and violence or brought to a head feuds between village clans. Their exhortations had little effect, though: peasants regarded festival behavior as governed by special laws.[2]

The rural police force was greatly overstretched and simply could not cope with the illicit home-brew stills, the brawls, and the allegations of sexual misconduct which they were supposed to investigate. As for Communists, there were very few of them in the village: in Tver province, on average, there was only one party member for every five to seven settlements, and they were not usually peasants but rather schoolteachers or veterinary surgeons. Even if they were active and determined, they were cut off from the "real" Soviet Union by miles of mud-churned rural tracks and the uncertainties of the horse and cart. At this stage very few people had motor vehicles or telephones with which to conquer the remote desolation of the village.[3]

The new village soviet, which had briefly been a power in the countryside in 1917–1919, had yielded to the old village assembly, the *skhod,* which was now in its element. It could decide all village questions without interference from the landowner. As the village lapsed into the old routine, the older men elbowed out the women and younger men, who had played a serious role in the soviet during 1917–1919, and resumed their traditional authority. From the party's viewpoint, the *skhod* was an irritating remnant of the past, with its endless leisurely discussions on parish-pump issues, its blinkered focus on household and village, and its reluctance to innovate. Moreover, it symbolized the village as a unified structure led by its "best" families, rather than as a potential forum for class struggle with "poor peasants" against "kulaks."[4]

Exultant visions and dark forebodings remained as a hangover from the exhilarating but also horrifying period of revolution and civil war. In Vinnitsa district in Ukraine village folk talked about the last judgment and the resurrection of corpses. In Tyshtypskii raion in 1926 God was rumored to have spoken to a peasant, who promised that on June 19 he would communicate the divine message to the assembled people. Some three thousand gathered, and the peasant told them the world would end in forty-seven years if they believed in God, but in twenty-seven years if their hearts remained hard. A cross was erected on the spot, which for a few years was a pilgrimage site.[5]

Still, there was at least a brief period of normality. Viktor Petrovich Beliaev, who was born in 1923 in the village of Shileksha, in Kostroma guberniia, summed up the rural work patterns of his childhood in his memoirs. He saw the village as a complex organism linked to a wider world through much more than agriculture: "Returning from the spring-time timber floating, most peasants would begin sowing, while some would do carpentry till the haymaking; toward winter some would fell timber, while others would go carting, transporting loads. Some villagers would go to work in Kologriv [the nearest district town], Kostroma, Moscow, St. Petersburg, Nizhnii Novgorod. The men worked at the post office, in savings banks, in hospitals, private shops, or bakeries, while the girls usually found employment as chambermaids or servants."[6]

Handicraft *(kustarnyi)* industry was still widespread. Blacksmiths, stove-setters, and cobblers would both make and repair their goods for a few villages in the immediate neighborhood, while larger entrepreneurs would manufacture, say, spinning-wheels in their workshops and then distribute them over wide areas by railway and river. As a compromise between home-made artefacts and large-scale industrial products, these artisans were able to adapt the techniques of the industrial revolution to make rural life somewhat more comfortable and convenient. *Kustarnyi* manufacture reached its zenith in the first thirty years of the twentieth century.[7]

One Communist innovation did meet the approval of many villagers. In 1920 an Extraordinary Commission for the Struggle against Illiteracy launched a nationwide campaign under the snappy title *likbez.* Learning to read and write was declared the duty of everyone under fifty. Part of the task was handled by the growing network of primary schools, obligatory four-year study having been introduced for every child in 1923. For adults, literate people in the villages would be exhorted to open a *likpunkt,* often a "reading-hut" expropriated from a "kulak," where those who wished to learn to read could go in the evenings or during the winters. As one young peasant woman from Tambov province, Tamara Kuderina-Nasonova, described it, "On the tables were always laid out a great quantity of pamphlets, posters, little books with political content, which we devoured till they fell apart, and which greatly helped to open our eyes. . . . Often evenings of 'Questions and Answers' were arranged—a common way of organizing mass political work at the time. And lots of questions cropped up then. One had the impression that people had suddenly woken up, were rubbing their eyes and trying to understand where they were and how they got there."[8]

After everything they had been through since 1914, peasants, especially younger ones, naturally wanted to understand better the world in which they now lived. Revolution and civil war had taught them much, but they had not been a favorable environment for schooling, and many young people had lost time to make up. Most of them seized enthusiastically the new opportunity to make their way in the world, and the party used the occasion to spice elementary reading books with political propaganda. While learning the alphabet students also learned how the tsar had been overthrown, the landowners expropriated, and universal equality installed. They learned a great deal more, too, about how to lead a civilized life. When Theodore Dreiser visited Russia in the late 1920s, he reported that everywhere there were posters "urging (never really commanding) the people to do this and that, from combing their hair to swatting flies, washing out the stables and milk pails, cleaning the babies' milk bottles, opening the windows of sick rooms, ploughing with tractors, fertilizing with the right fertilizer, building with the right lumber, eating the right food."[9]

The census of 1939 showed that 87.4 percent of the population aged 9 to 49 could read (93.5 of men, 81.6 percent of women). That was a considerable achievement, given that in 1897 the comparable figures had been 28.4 percent (40.3 and 16.6), in 1920, 44.1 percent (57.6 and 32.3), and in 1926, 56.6 percent (71.5 and 42.7). The greatest advance, especially for women, came in the late 1920s and 1930s. Inevitably, though, many people, especially young men, used their new skills to escape from the village in that upheaval, so that in some ways even this advance made matters worse. Perhaps that is why the liquidators of illiteracy were among those attacked by peasants during collectivization: their instruction was seen as part of the general assault on village life.[10]

## Collectivization of Agriculture

The collectivization of agriculture meant the wholesale and deliberate destruction of the peasants' way of life. But it was for their own good, the Communists believed. Lev Kopelev recalled from his days as party activist in the countryside, "I was convinced that we were soldiers on an invisible front, waging war on kulak sabotage for the sake of bread the country needed for the five-year plan. For bread above all, but also for the souls of peasants whose attitudes had hardened through ignorance and low political consciousness, and who had succumbed to enemy propaganda, not grasping the great truth of communism."[11]

The centuries-old "village society," or commune, focus of the peasants' community life and decision-making, was abolished by a decree of July 30, 1930. Many of its authoritative householders—elders, judges, the "best people"—were labeled "kulaks" and deported. Markets and fairs that had served as forums for trade and sociability were likewise closed down, on the grounds that they served private capital. Perhaps most demoralizing of all, village churches were closed and either destroyed or turned over for secular use as warehouses, clubs, or cinemas. Clergymen were arrested—though many managed to flee, some to become clandestine "wandering" priests serving secret congregations in cellars, private apartments, or deep in the woods. Church closure was often accompanied by symbolic desecration. Icons were removed and, in one case, lined up against walls for "execution" by shooting, each with a superscription recording which saint had been sentenced to death for "resisting kolkhoz construction." The bells, whose peals were the village's celebrant voice and its protection against evil spirits, pestilence, and storms, were taken down—sometimes literally cast down from the belfry with a final harsh cacophony as they hit the ground—before being carted off to be melted down for the five-year plan.[12]

Not all the pressure for collectivization came from outside the village. The prospect offered new opportunities to poorer peasants, to younger sons, and to those who had political connections from the Red Army. Collective farming, Beliaev maintains, was at first not taken seriously by the villagers: "But quite a few young people from the village fell under the influence of Bolshevik propaganda. All the same, the decisive factor while the kolkhozy [collective farms] were being created was the authorities' direct pressure, the combination of persuasion and promises with downright sanctions against the opponents of kolkhozy."[13]

Sometimes peasants resisted passively, by sitting silently at meetings called to take the decision on collectivization or to identify "kulaks" for deportation. Or they would take the opposite stratagem and endlessly ask questions, or all shout at once to disrupt the orderly conduct of the meeting. If the church bell was still in place they would sound it as a tocsin so that villagers could shout "Fire!" and thus break up the meeting. Often it was women who seized the initiative: in the village of Taneevka in Tatariia, for example, they attacked and beat up members of the village soviet who were trying to close the church and take down the bell for recasting. Under the slogans "We won't give up the bell!" and "We don't need tractors or collective farms!" they even managed to form their own village government for a time.[14]

In March 1930 in the village of Bolshie Ialchiki, in the Central Black Earth region, someone broke into the church after it had been closed and rang the bells, summoning the villagers. They demanded the closure of the recently established kolkhoz, the reopening of the church, the return of the dekulakized, the restoration of property, and the reopening of communal woodlands. Part of the crowd broke away and forcibly evicted people occupying the homes of the dekulakized. Others armed with sticks threatened to beat up the chairman of the Young Communist League. They were held off by the threat of weapons until help arrived.[15]

For many households the greatest psychological blow came with the transfer of their animals to the collective. Especially painful was the loss of a horse: "I remember that parting with our horse was a dramatic event in the life of the family. We were losing not only the main producer in the household, but also a living being without whom we all felt orphaned. At first the horses assigned to the kolkhoz paddock would by force of habit return from the pastures back to their old owners. Our Peganko would canter up to our house during the day, since the pasture was nearby, and stick his head in at the open window; my mother would give him a slice of black bread sprinkled with salt."[16]

Anna Nikitichna Chernichenko, at that time a thirteen-year-old girl in a Siberian village, also recalled how their favorite horse, Zvezdochka, bolted back to the family from the collective paddock: "One of our neighbors called out, 'Hey, here comes your horse, just look at his eye!' I looked up, and saw Zvezdochka's eye dislocated and bloody, hanging by a thread. My mother fainted. She had always had a weak heart, but this was her first attack, and it was a serious one. . . . She was an invalid after that."[17]

Most damaging to the future of the village was the so-called dekulakization," the process by which the Bolsheviks rid the countryside of "wealthy" peasants. It began with the imposition of heavy taxes. One villager from Penza oblast recalls, "I remember how my father with tears in his eyes scraped together the last grains, intended for food and seed corn, from the barn. Once a peasant had paid off one tax demand, a little later another would arrive. And that could happen several times."[18]

When the taxes could no longer be paid, a "plenipotentiary" would arrive to conduct searches. One woman describes such a visit: "I remember three men came. One in a leather tunic tied with a leather belt—

the plenipotentiary from the town, the second a poor peasant from the Komsomol, the third from the village soviet. The plenipotentiary had a revolver at his hip. They had come to search for grain or bread. They looked under the stove and under the bed, where they found a small trunk improvised out of planks. That was my trunk with my 'finery.' They started to turf out my linen and dresses straight on to the floor. I was appalled—I thought they were going to take my clothes, so I rushed up to them, seized my trunk, and screamed at them to return everything."[19]

Sergei Voronov, whose narrative opened this chapter, was one of the "fortunate" kulaks who was not deported. Those who were suffered the further trauma of being transported in extremely harsh conditions and then resettled in a completely unfamiliar environment. According to one account, "We were loaded like cattle, forty to a truck. There were iron stoves inside. Inside everything was together, dining room, bedroom, and toilet: one did one's business through the open door while the train was moving. They curtained it off a bit with mats. The young girls were very embarrassed at having to use such a 'toilet.'. . . We ate what we had brought with us, but without liquid, and the small children suffered especially. At home they would be given milk from the cow, but now we were completely cut off from all that."[20]

From February to May 1930 alone more than 100,000 kulak families were deported, the largest numbers from the North Caucasus, Ukraine, Belorussia, the Central Black Earth region, and the Lower Volga—in general, the most fertile grain-producing zones. Many died in the course of transportation, of cold, hunger, dehydration, or untreated disease. Their corpses would simply be rolled out of the trucks during a halt. So great were the losses that one post-Soviet Russian historian has accused the Soviet authorities of "genocide."[21]

Such experiences were common. In 1933 the director of Siblag (Siberian Camp Complex) wrote to his superiors complaining that 3 to 4 percent of those transported died on the way. The reasons for the high mortality rate, he asserted, were that, contrary to instructions, many sick and elderly people were included, and insufficient food and water was supplied for the journey.[22]

When he arrived in Vologda region, the so-called kulak Anton Lisechko was separated from his wife and children, who were housed in a former monastery: "The place where my Kseniia and the children lived I can only call a death camp. How many children, old folk, and able-bodied people died there no one counted." Two of the children were later sent to live with relatives. Anton was transported further and detrained near a river: "Beside the river there were huts, or at least skeletons of huts. On the snow, without walls, stood beams and rafters about six meters high and eight meters wide. The roof was covered with a thin layer of straw hammered down. There we were left to get on with it. It was terribly cold. The hut was 18 meters long, and no matter how much you fed the two iron stoves with their iron flues, it didn't get warm. Everywhere it was draughty."[23]

The exiles' destinations were usually the far north, the Urals, Siberia, and Kazakhstan. They were not imprisoned there, but they had to report regularly to the local NKVD commandant. The intention was to put them to work in industries where labor was scarce: timber, fishing, mining, agriculture, and construction. Others were left to their own devices, to find chance employment in small-scale manufacture, the retail trade, domestic service, agriculture, or looking after animals.

One woman exiled to Kustanai oblast in northern Kazakhstan in early 1940 was dropped from a truck one evening in the snowy steppes. She thought she and her companions were being left to die in the void, until suddenly the director of the local sovkhoz (Soviet farm, a variant of the kolkhoz) showed up. He complained that there were too many old and sick people among them and not enough able-bodied workers. Then he dispatched them for the night to peasant huts that they had not noticed buried in the snowdrifts. They were ordered to report next morning to the sovkhoz office. "There," the woman recalls, "they told us they were not going to provide food or shelter for us—we would each have to take care of ourselves. We were detailed off to chop down trees (the saksaul, a hardwood that grows on the banks of large lakes and rivers) and to clean out the cattle stalls. For a piece of bread and some broth we worked like serfs from early morning to late evening. We had no suitable clothing and got tired easily. All February we suffered from cold and hunger. The older people fell sick and died."[24]

## Peasant Reactions to Collectivization

As early as December 1929, some peasants were already protesting against life in the new kolkhozy. From Minsk okrug a group of forty or so peasants wrote to Rykov, the chairman of Sovnarkom (in effect the prime minister), declaring:

> We never thought that the Soviet authorities would oppress us in this way. . . . They force us to enter collectives, and if some householder does not want to, then he is deprived of land. . . . If the Soviet authorities do not change course, things will get very bad, for peasants are starting to murder each other, and if we have to live together in collectives, it will be much worse. There will be mutual slaughter, because we're not used to barrack life. Everyone tries to work for himself, and now we have to hand everything over to the State, almost like returning to barshchina [labor dues, abolished in 1861]. We were very pleased when we were released from barshchina, and now the Soviet authorities are reimposing it. Is that just?[25]

Nearly everything about the kolkhozy was unfamiliar and repugnant to the peasants. They were used to having their own animals, their own household plots, and their own strips on the common fields, where they would work using their own tools and in their own time. Now their animals had been taken away, the status of their household plots was uncertain, and the fields were state property, where they were required to work under orders at specified times.

Peasants interpreted the outright assault on their way of life—indeed their lives—according to the cosmology they had inherited from their ancestors. Only a generation earlier they had been drawing up political programs and voting in parliamentary elections. Now they were plunged back into a world of medieval eschatology.[26] The imagery of the apocalypse seemed eminently realistic. "Soviet power is not of God, but of the Anti-Christ," went an oft-repeated slogan. Peasants who joined the kolkhozy voluntarily would, it was rumored, be stamped with the mark of the beast and picked out for damnation on judgment day. A chastushka warned:

> Oh brothers! oh sisters! Don't go into the kolkhoz . . .
> Antichrist will lay his mark upon you three times.
> Once on the hand,
> The second on the forehead for all to see,
> And the third on the breast.

> If you believe in God, don't join the kolkhoz . . .
> And if you're in the kolkhoz, oh sisters, leave . . .[27]

Official statements and the public media were utterly mendacious, so rumor resumed its sway, giving peasants a surrogate sense of community and identifying an enemy they should resist. A "St. Bartholomew's massacre" was prophesied in Ivanovo oblast, the Urals, and Chuvashia. Elsewhere people foretold a great peasant jacquerie, or a war in which the Soviet regime would be overthrown by—depending on the version—the British, the Poles, the Chinese, or the Japanese. "The Pope of Rome will come, the government will fall, and all Communists and collective farmers will be crushed," ran another prophecy. Yet other comments reflected the literal truth: "They take the last cow from a poor villager; this is not Soviet power, but the power of thieves and pillagers." "The kolkhoz is *barshchina,* a second serfdom." "We will be eternal slaves."

One prediction in the North Caucasus wove together several peasant nightmares:

> In the kolkhoz there will be a special branding iron, [they] will close all the churches, not allow prayer, dead people will be cremated, the christening of children will be forbidden, invalids and the elderly will be killed, there won't be any husbands or wives, [all] will sleep under a one-hundred-metre blanket. Beautiful men and women will be taken and brought to one place to produce beautiful people. Children will be taken from their parents, there will be wholesale incest: brothers will live with sisters, sons with mothers, fathers with daughters, etc. The kolkhoz—this means beasts in a single shed, people in a single barrack.[28]

A variety of motifs are blended here: the antireligious campaign, family reform, eugenics, sexual immorality, abolition of property, and loss of individuality. These were all direct or indirect reflections of policies the regime actually was pursuing. Communists dismissed such imaginings as the work of priests, kulaks, or "unenlightened womenfolk" *(nesoznatelnye baby).* But in their context the rumors were utterly realistic. Many of their premonitions were fully justified: famine, deportations, massacres, renewed serfdom. Moreover, they reflected the unquestionable fact that the upheaval was caused by a struggle perceived as one between absolute good and absolute evil. The wanderers, beggars, and *iurodivye* (fools in Christ) who retailed these rumors were people whose lives had been irreparably disrupted by the turmoil.

Women were the prime bearers of village memory and the protagonists of the "moral economy." They were also more likely than men to be regular churchgoers. Many of their menfolk had spent years away, fighting at the front or earning money in factories, whereas women were more likely to have spent their entire lives in or near the village, imbibing the lore of their own mothers and passing it on. They found the destruction of tradition even more intolerable than did their husbands and sons. Besides, they were less likely than men to be punished for their indiscipline, since the authorities (whatever they said about emancipating women) regarded women as inherently less "conscious," even apolitical. They found it expedient to write off opposition as coming from women, since to do so minimized the scale and significance of peasant resistance.[29]

One element of traditional peasant eschatology was, however, missing. No pretender made an appearance. Stalin may have been perceived as the agent of Anti-Christ, but there was no "genuine tsar" to oppose him and lead a popular rebellion. Why this was so one can only speculate. Perhaps the crucial element was the desacralization of the monarchy, which had been completed just over a decade earlier. No longer were peasants looking for a holy prince to restore the deposed dynasty: the Romanovs had been comprehensively discredited and were no longer regarded as bearers of God's grace.

Did the peasants really believe their own myths? We do not know, but at any rate the narratives of apocalypse were effective at mobilizing them to resist collectivization. Defiance often began when the local church was closed or the priest arrested. In the Mimry district, Moscow province, a priest gave a sermon warning that "the end of the world is approaching, Anti-Christ is come to earth. Come to the church. Tomorrow I will give my last sermon." The next day a large crowd duly showed up to obstruct his arrest.[30]

Sometimes peasant resistance was violent. Fighting usually started with the defense of "kulaks" earmarked for deportation, or of grain stores or animals. Since peasants were usually armed only with the most primitive weapons, they endeavored to avoid armed clashes. But they had one advantage: locally, they greatly outnumbered their opponents, who were not usually in a position to call up reinforcements. Often a warning or a threat was enough to induce officials to hide or even to withdraw temporarily. But if they persisted in their attempts to search for grain or to detain so-called kulaks, villagers might assemble in large numbers, equipped at least with pitchforks and stones, and perhaps the odd shotgun or hunting rifle. At the village of Cherepakha in the Middle Volga a crowd assembled in March 1930, demanded the return of all household property, ransacked the School of Kolkhoz Youth, and expelled poor peasants from requisitioned houses to return them to their owners. At Nachalovo in Astrakhan oblast in February 1930, a crowd armed with a few guns attacked the village soviet building, where local officials had barricaded themselves, broke in, and murdered at least half a dozen of them. At Salsk in the North Caucasus a crowd variously estimated at several hundred or several thousand stormed the soviet building and seized confiscated property; neighboring villages followed their example, and in the end Red Army units had to be dispatched to restore order. At Biisk in the Altai region insurgents actually managed to seize an arsenal and a police station, and to free all the local prisoners from jail. Here too troops had to be sent in to quell the disturbances.[31] In general, peasant resistance, though widespread and deeply felt, was ineffective, since it was unled, unarmed, and disorganized.

Confrontations were at an especially high level in Ukraine: in 1930 roughly 30 percent of "kulak" rebellions reported by the OGPU for the whole USSR took place in the Ukrainian SSR, and 45 percent in the worst month, March 1930. The other hardest hit areas included the North Caucasus (7.7 percent), the Central Black Earth region (10 percent), and the Lower Volga (7.3 percent). All three were in the RSFSR, but all three also bordered on Ukraine and contained substantial Ukrainian minorities.[32]

Worse still, from the regime's point of view, some of the rebels linked resistance to collectivization with nationalist demands. A leaflet from Shtrimbakh village, Krutianskii raion, for example, proclaimed: "Citizens, down with the bandit gangs, down with the villainous communards. Long live free Ukraine! Villagers, be prepared for the struggle against Bolshevism. Ukraine is defecting from Russia." A proclamation from Rogachi in Berdichev okrug added another target of ethnic hatred: "Brother peasants, we are all suffering under the oppression of the *panykommunisty* [Communist landlords]. They rob us. We are naked. . . .

Fight the Communist *zhidy* [Yids]. Throw him [*sic*] from power, don't believe him, he sits on your back, he drives you, he eats your bread!"[33]

Among the bitterest opponents of collectivization were the Kuban Cossacks. In the 1920s they had been granted national minority status because, though they lived on the territory of the RSFSR, they spoke a dialect closer to Ukrainian than to Russian. They were awarded Ukrainian-language schools and institutions of their own, which were then used by non-Cossack Ukrainians living in and near the North Caucasus. Many Communists had doubts about allowing them these concessions, not least because Kuban Cossacks had been prominent in the White movement during the civil war. The doubts had not been resolved when collectivization hit the region and generated bitter resistance. In February 1930, for example, the staff of the North Caucasian military district reported that as a result of "kulak agitation" in several districts "crowds of peasants of 2–300, sometimes up to 500 people, mainly women, wreck collectivization meetings, during the inventories of kulak property they beat up local authority representatives and activists, they break open stores of confiscated kulak property and hand it back to the kulaks, they set free detained kulaks, and so on."[34]

Ukraine and the North Caucasus were both regions where the civil war had been conducted with particular ferocity, and where many Cossacks had fought for the Whites or for Ukrainian separatists. It is not altogether surprising, then, that the Soviet leaders tended to interpret rural resistance there as a reversion to civil war, or as preparation for a Polish invasion. During the late summer and autumn of 1932, as grain requisitioning got under way, it transpired that there was a considerable shortfall from these regions. The Politburo reacted with fury, insisting there should be no concessions: requisition plans should be met in full, if necessary by the use of terror. As early as August Stalin wrote to Lazar Kaganovich, who had recently returned from leading the party in Kiev:

The *most important thing right now* is Ukraine. Things in Ukraine have hit rock bottom . . . Redens [head of the Ukrainian GPU] is not up to leading the fight with counter-revolution in such a large and distinctive republic. . . . Unless we begin to straighten out the situation in Ukraine, we may lose Ukraine. Keep in mind that Pilsudski is not day-dreaming, and his agents in Ukraine are many times stronger than Redens or Kosior [Ukrainian party first secretary] think. Keep in mind, too, that the Ukrainian Communist Party (500 *thousand* members, ha, ha!) includes quite a lot (yes, quite a lot!) of rotten elements, conscious and unconscious Petliura adherents, and finally direct agents of Pilsudski.[35]

Here we see an example of the mindset that a few years later was to generate the headlong terror of 1937–1938. A grain collection shortfall was interpreted as evidence, not of peasant self-preservation or reluctance to work on the collective farms, but rather of an intention to foment counter-revolution and assist a Polish invasion of Ukraine. In the following months the Politburo sent special commissions to chosen regions of Ukraine and the North Caucasus. Kaganovich oversaw a special meeting of the North Caucasus *kraikom,* where he warned against recent immigrants from Ukraine: "Without a doubt, among those arriving from Ukraine were organised groups, carrying out [counter-revolutionary] work, especially in the Kuban, where the Ukrainian language is spoken." The meeting decreed special economic and penal sanctions for failure to deliver the expected grain quota. As a warning, three large Cossack settlements *(stanitsy)* were placed on a black list, which entailed a total economic blockade and the arrest and deportation to the far north of much of the population. Then followed a purge of the Communist officials of the region, who were held to have been either weak or actively cooperating with the nationalist enemy.[36]

A number of problems had coalesced and come to a head in the Kuban grain-procurement crisis. Ukraine was the most sensitive republic for the operation of the Soviet Union as a multiethnic state. It was also important for the Soviet Union's international relations, since it bordered on Poland, Czechoslovakia, Hungary, and Romania. The region contained many of the Soviet Union's key industrial projects, and it was the Union's breadbasket, the arena for the struggle to feed the cities and the armed forces in the face of peasant defiance. There has been much controversy over the famine of 1933–1934, which killed some five million peasants, most of them Ukrainian. Some historians have suggested that the famine was deliberately induced as an act of genocide directed against the Ukrainian people.[37] Stephan Merl has contested this interpretation on the grounds that the famine did not embrace all of Ukraine but actually did affect some non-Ukrainian regions; and that the device of setting up road-

blocks to prevent peasants getting into towns to find food, or even sometimes crossing republican frontiers, was practiced in other areas besides
Ukraine.[38]

In actual fact, the most likely explanation seems to be that an ethnically
directed policy was not originally intended but emerged in the course
of the crisis. A Politburo decree of December 14, 1932, lambasted the
Ukrainian and North Caucasian leaders for having stood by and allowed
"kulaks, former officers, Petliurites and supporters of the Kuban *rada* to
penetrate the collective farm leadership" and for having provided "the
most evil enemies of the party, working class and kolkhoz peasantry, the
saboteurs of grain requisition, with party cards to put in their pockets."
The very next day another decree ended all Ukrainizing measures inside
the RSFSR, resulting in the loss of special Ukrainian status for several
thousand village soviets and collective farms. On January 24, 1933, a
Central Committee resolution stated that "the Party organs in Ukraine
have not succeeded in carrying out the Party tasks entrusted to them in
the areas of organization of grain storage and completion of the plan for
grain collection." The Ukrainian Communist Party leadership was thoroughly purged not once, but *twice,* first in 1933 and then in 1937, with
reliable outsiders being sent in both times to regain control.[39] There is
no question that Stalin regarded Ukraine as the key to gaining a grip on
the various problems that faced him in the 1930s. The result was that
Ukraine became the most oppressed and exploited of the republics (with
the possible exception of Kazakhstan) during those years, and considerable efforts were made to Russify it and subject it more tightly to Moscow.

## Life in the Kolkhozy

The face of the countryside was radically transformed by the upheavals of
1929–1933. Going back a few years later to take care of her sick sister,
Kuderina found her Tambov village almost unrecognizable:

> There were no threshing floors or courtyards anymore. The huts
> were neglected externally—they had not been painted or white-
> washed. But in almost all huts curtains had appeared at the win-
> dows, usually gauze, occasionally tulle. Only thatched roofs had re-
> mained, as I recall. Where there had been robust huts roofed with
> corrugated iron, only empty gaps remained with piles of old clay

wall plaster. These were the homes of the dekulakized, which had been dismantled and transported elsewhere. The church was closed and was falling apart. There was no fence around it. The roof had not been painted for a long time, and in places rust showed ominously through. The walls were dirty and stained with damp. The bell tower was densely occupied by the nests of jackdaws, which were flying around it.[40]

The disorganization and the demoralization of the peasants meant gross underproduction and eventually famine, especially in the most fertile grain-growing regions, such as Ukraine, the Kuban, west Siberia, and the Volga basin. In their new status as kolkhozniki, peasants sowed less grain than before, took far longer to do it, and tended the fields afterward less thoroughly, so that they became choked with weeds. When Viktor Kravchenko visited a village in Dnepropetrovsk oblast in 1932, he was shocked by the neglected condition of "implements and machinery which had once been cared for like so many jewels by their private owners." Horses were knee-deep in mud in their stalls, "reading newspapers," as a rural metaphor had it when they were idle and not being fed.[41]

Stalin sent instructions that grain collections were nevertheless to be rigidly enforced. Peasants reacted with sit-down strikes or deliberately negligent work. When they could, they would steal grain from the fields or at least leave it unharvested, to be gleaned later. They did not conceal what they were doing. At Petrovka, in Azov raion, they delivered an ultimatum: "When you give us bread then we will show up at work. If you don't, then bring in the harvest yourselves."[42]

Stalin reacted with cold fury; for him this was a renewal of the civil war, fought with different weapons. When the writer Mikhail Sholokhov warned him what was happening, he replied that "the grain-growers were waging what was virtually a 'quiet' war against Soviet power. A war of starvation, dear Comrade Sholokhov." Stalin reacted in kind, ordering that villages failing to deliver were to be cut off from all retail trade, while households hiding grain were to be punished by exile or up to ten years' imprisonment. A decree of August 7, 1932, actually prescribed the death penalty for thefts of "collective or cooperative property," that is, anything produced on the kolkhoz, which might be no more than a sheaf of corn. Blockades were not lifted until the first deaths from starvation had taken place. In March 1933 an official emissary in the North Caucasus noted that "cases are reported of edema and death from emaciation, of the consumption of dogs, rats and frogs, and even of cannibalism." In west Siberia a health inspector reported visiting a kolkhoz family at dinner time and seeing "on the table . . . gnawed bones from a dead horse," while elsewhere villagers were "grinding sunflower stems, flax and hemp seeds, chaff and dried potato peelings . . . People walk around like shadows, silent, vacant . . . One rarely sees an animal on the street (apparently the last ones have been eaten)."[43]

Unlike the famine of 1921–1922, this one remained strictly secret, in order to preserve the public image of a successful first five-year plan. Many starving peasants who tried to make for town to find food were turned back by roadblocks. All the same, quite a few got through. As Kuderina recalled, in Kharkov "one fine morning all the central streets of the towns were filled with crowds of incoming starving, swollen peasants. Whole families of them sat all along the sidewalks, including old people and children. Many were weeping, while others with a doomed look in their eyes stretched out their hands for 'alms.' Some were lying down, sick or dying. All of them had lice crawling over them. The sight of these desperately suffering people was intolerable, but there was no way one could help. Everyone walked silently past them, hanging their heads in unspoken sympathy." Not everyone was sympathetic, though. Some pushed the more persistent beggars away, frightened of their lice.[44]

In all, it has been estimated that some four to five million people died as a direct result of the famine.[45]

In a century of Russian tragedies, the wanton destruction of the peasant village was perhaps the most terrible. The poet Boris Pasternak made a "creative trip" to the Urals countryside in order to write a book on the new kolkhozy. When he returned, however, he never wrote it, so horrified was he by what he had witnessed: "Words do not have the power to express what I saw. It was such an inhuman, unimaginable catastrophe, such a terrible disaster that it became—if one can say such a thing—abstract and beyond rational apprehension. I fell ill. For an entire year I was unable to write."[46]

The tragedy was the product of two Russian traditions at war with each other, that of the socialist millenarians and that of the peasants. The socialists believed they were modernizing the village, bringing it into line with current industrial modes of production, technology, and social organization. They developed a whole barrage of new terminology to describe the labor processes of the new farms: *brigadir* (brigade leader), *trudoden* (labor-day: the unit of pay), *udarnik* (shock-worker), and most ominously *trudguzhpovinnost* (labor and cartage obligations).[47] The peasants, by contrast, saw themselves as being dragged back into a "second serfdom," a dependency from which their grandparents had been freed seventy years earlier.

The outcome of the confrontation was clear. The Soviet state and Communist Party were now the decisive forces in the life of the village: the power structure had been permanently altered. Ownership of the land, together with machinery and the larger animals, had been taken from individual households and vested in the kolkhoz as a whole; from that land the farm was obliged to deliver to the state a specific amount of assorted produce each year. This may look like a return to the land tenure system of the mir, but at the same time the strips were consolidated into large fields. In any case, the vital question was: Who decided how the land would be used? Whereas before 1930 such decisions had been in the hands of an assembly consisting of all heads of households, that assembly now became much larger and included all kolkhoz members: men, women, heads of households, and ordinary household members. In a purely formal sense, that assembly might be more democratic, but in practice authority rested with the kolkhoz chairman and the few professional people close to him. He was the representative of the party and the authority of the state, and his proposals regarding sowing, harvesting, the care of animals, or the upkeep of buildings were normally accepted.

Work organization also became collective. This was a complete innovation for the Russian village, where previously households had devised and implemented their own work patterns—admittedly in consultation with others when land was held in strips. Now they were organized in brigades of thirty or so, each headed by a brigade leader appointed by the chairman. He, in consultation with the chairman, would decide on their daily assignments, summon them at the beginning of the working day—sometimes using the bell confiscated from the church—supervise their labor, and keep a record of them for the purposes of later payment. Being subject to the equivalent of the factory whistle did not suit most peasants, and brigade leaders often had to go around to their homes in mid-morning knocking on doors to summon them to work. Or the opposite might happen, as Viktor Beliaev recalled from his village: "The sun stood high in the sky. Formerly the peasants would already long have been in the fields, but now the kolkhozniki were sitting on logs that someone had brought and waiting for the brigade leader to talk things over with the chairman and bring their various work assignments. They smoked and laughed themselves. All decisions were now being taken by the chairman, a towns-man."[48]

Their reluctance to work was explained partly by the system of pay. Their efforts were recorded in the form of "labor-days," notional units of work that were put down on their records and added up at the end of the year to determine their earnings. From the peasants' point of view there were two snags about this system. First, they were paid only after the kol-khoz's other financial obligations had been fully discharged, including de-liveries to the state, deductions for the kolkhoz capital fund, and repay-ment of loans to the State Bank. In bad years little or nothing remained, so that in effect they had reverted to the serflike practice of *barshchina* (corvée). Second, all pay was determined by the brigade's total work, not by that of each individual, which was too complicated to calculate, so that individual effort was not rewarded unless it was replicated by one's col-leagues. This was *krugovaia poruka* in a new guise. The result was that un-productive households might be expelled from the kolkhoz under pressure from their colleagues.[49]

The Communist victory was not quite complete. After the famine of 1932–1933 the Soviet authorities and peasant Russia dropped their con-frontation and reached a compromise. Peasants decided that continuing the struggle would destroy their villages and their children's future. The Communists could also see that full application of their plans would en-tail mass starvation, not only in the villages but in the towns too. They came to the conclusion that regular food supplies could be ensured only by leaving peasants some autonomy and some incentives to work hard. For that reason, it was decreed that each household could hold a small pri-vate plot, typically a third to half a hectare, on which it could keep chick-ens, graze a cow, and grow fruit and vegetables. Peasants were allowed to sell the produce from their plots for whatever prices they could fetch at designated markets in town (incongruously known as kolkhoz markets). In other words, a minimal private market in agricultural products was permitted. This private market became a crucial source of agricultural products for the towns. By 1950, for example, 47 percent of meat, 50 percent of milk, 61 percent of potatoes, and 74 percent of eggs sold on the market were being produced on these private plots. For everything except bread, in fact, townsfolk relied on private trade.[50]

Private sales constituted a tenuous link with the towns, but in other respects villages became both more isolated and less self-sustaining in their economic life. They lost the auxiliary economic activities that had provided essential services for villagers and kept them in touch with the towns:

> The authorities outlawed the small-scale village handicraft workers and craftsmen who made sheepskins and felt boots, sewed coats, manufactured carting equipment. . . . The owners and shareholders of little water mills, butter churneries, and beehives were declared kulaks, even though these tiny enterprises were essential to the village economy. . . . Tinkers stopped coming to the village to mend samovars, saucepans, and teapots, there was no longer anyone to solder buckets. The rag-and-bone merchants, the buyers of coarse cloth disappeared. There were no more carpenters' artels, as almost no one was building houses.

Even stove-setters, the most crucial village construction workers, would take on jobs only if they could prove that their earnings did not fall under the category of "nonlabor income."[51]

Taken together, these gross disruptions of the pattern of rural existence generated great bitterness and demoralization. One feature of prerevolutionary days that was *not* reproduced in the Soviet village of the 1930s was the myth of the "good tsar." Peasants hated everyone who was responsible for foisting the "second serfdom" on them—especially Stalin. A Finnish Communist who visited some villages in 1934 reported that "there were none of the paeans to the great Stalin that one heard in the cities"; "my first impression, which remained lasting, was that everyone was a counter-revolutionary, and that the whole countryside was in full revolt against Moscow and Stalin." Once the collective farms had settled down, there was little question of actual revolt, but in other respects materials that have recently come to light—as well as the general tendency to flee the countryside if possible—has confirmed his observation. Sheila Fitzpatrick, who has studied the evidence closely, sums it up: "The prevailing opinion, as expressed in rumors, was that Stalin, as the organizer of collectivization, was the peasants' inveterate enemy: they wished him dead, his regime overthrown, and collectivization undone, even at the cost of war and foreign occupation."[52]

Those who could leave the village did so, legally or illegally. Thousands of beggars and wanderers took to the roads, and many of them tried to settle down unnoticed in the towns. To stem the outflow the state introduced internal passports in December 1932, withholding them from kolkhozniki. Without a passport it was illegal to stay more than three nights anywhere but one's registered place of residence. That is not to say that no peasants did so, but the lack of a passport constituted a severe impediment to mobility. One needed the permission of the kolkhoz chairman to travel at all, let alone to resettle elsewhere.[53]

The devastation and demoralization of the villages was such that many families took the wrenching decision to abandon homes that had been in the family for generations. Some, the more far-sighted or those who already had urban connections or experience of life in the towns, left before collectivization gained momentum and while they could still sell their rural possessions. Others were caught up in the process itself, among them "kulaks" not deemed heinous enough to be deported, but deprived of house and home and left to their own devices. Later chaos, poverty, and famine drove out many who had initially decided to give the collectives a chance. One peasant from the Central Industrial Region wrote in May 1933: "Here on the collective farm I am living the life of a badly fed animal. I have been robbed of my grain and all my reserves. My cattle have also been taken . . . Therefore life here is impossible. I am going into the town to get a job as a workman, and there I will be fed."[54]

Much about the new life, including the restrictions on mobility, was reminiscent of serfdom. The overall social and ideological context was, however, quite different. All young men were now obliged to perform military service, while those with skills might be drafted under *orgnabor* (the state labor recruitment scheme) for one of many flagship industrial projects. They were caught up in a stream of social mobility that was part of the new life; but most women and older men were excluded from it. The 1930s saw the beginning of an exodus of young men that in time would reduce most villages to melancholy asylums for old people and unmarried women. Even those who stayed behind were beginning to acquire urban expectations. The state had assumed a much higher profile in their lives, and they came to expect that it—rather than their families—would provide for them in sickness and old age. If before 1861 they had looked to the *barin* to provide for life's shocks, they now transferred that expectation to the state. Having forcibly asserted its authority over the peasant way of life, the Soviet state had also created a new culture of dependency.[55]

## Ruralization of the Towns

During the first five-year plans millions of people left the countryside and streamed into the towns. Some of them were drawn by the attraction of training or a job in the city; some left what they felt to be intolerable conditions in the village—and a good many were motivated by both reasons. The results were startling. Between 1926 and 1939 the urban population of the Soviet Union more than doubled, from 26.3 million to 60.4 million, as did that of the RSFSR, from 16.7 to 33.7 million. Moscow grew to more than twice its size, to 4.54 million, Leningrad almost to 3.4 million. In some towns growth was even more remarkable: in Gorkii the population went from 222,000 to 644,000, in Sverdlovsk from 140,000 to 423,000.[56] Most of this growth was caused by immigration rather than the birth of children to existing townspeople; in fact the urban birth rate was declining by 1930, thanks to poor living conditions and the increased employment rate of women.

In the early years of industrialization, in the country as a whole the death rate increased as well as the birth rate, thanks to urban overcrowding, poor hygiene, and the uncertain food supply. Many people were living in cold, damp cellars or wooden barracks and hostels, poorly supplied with cooking, cleaning, and heating facilities.[57] Conditions were especially bad in 1932–1934, when the food supply was intermittent, and ration cards had to be introduced. Beginning in 1935 they improved somewhat, as the work of providing piped water, sewage works, and proper medical facilities advanced. Party-state officials and specially chosen workers began to escape from the communal apartments into newly constructed family units.

What peasants found when they reached the town was both exciting and bewildering—the tall buildings, the noise, the constant traffic, the huge number of unknown faces in the streets. The work of the factory was disorienting too: instead of working as long as necessary to complete a job, one had to clock in and out at certain times and do disconnected fragments of jobs, often using unfamiliar tools and equipment.

But for new immigrants there were some familiar features too. Many of them found lodging and work in a place where their fellow villagers had preceded them. They settled in a house as part of a *zemliachestvo,* an association of tenants from the same rural origin. Migration had been part of the pattern of peasant life well before 1917, and it redoubled now. Rural-dwellers would sometimes make use of connections or information networks that had been forged decades earlier. (In 1917–1921, after all, many city-dwellers had moved the other way, to escape poverty in the towns, sometimes after a decade or more of living there.) On the whole villagers made for a town not too far from their homeland, using invitations from relatives or at least people from their own rural area to help them find shelter, food, and a job in the early stages of relocation. One survey of Moscow construction workers showed that in the 1930s more than 80 percent of them had found their job through previous seasonal work or through information gained from village acquaintances. Migrants naturally trusted such contacts far more than the blandishments offered by officials from *orgnabor.*[58]

In a sense the new immigrants became urbanized, but it would be equally true to say that they ruralized the cities. Often the first dwelling place would be a communal barracks. Viktor Zamochin later described to oral historians the settlement he had lived in as a child at Medvedkovo, on the edge of Moscow:

It consisted of several single-storey long wooden *baraki,* with vegetable gardens all around. At one end of the *barak,* there was a communal kitchen and toilets. It had a central corridor with doors. Each family had its own door and window, but inside you could separate out the space as you wished. People put up partitions, but they were in a way—symbolic. Everyone knew everyone, everyone knew everything about everyone. You never locked the doors, of course, and no one would have taken a carrot or even a radish from your allotment, even if you hadn't put a fence round it. We children ran all over the place. Our mothers were at work all day, but they weren't worried: they knew there was no danger. It was like in the village; there was always someone left to look after us.

Some of the tenants kept a pig or chickens in a nearby shed, and in the spring and summer evenings everyone tended vegetables on the allotments, chatting to one another as they worked: "During the holidays, we cooked giant crocks full of stew and shared the food among us. Everyone brought a plate, someone played the accordion, and we sang and danced." Clearly the tenants were taking every opportunity to reproduce features of rural life, even though the living space was much more crowded and the arrangements far more communal than in the village.

After the barracks, the next stage for most immigrants was the communal apartment *(kommunalnaia kvartira).* The original intention of the Soviet regime was that people should live in *doma-kommuny,* where many family functions, such as cooking, laundry, and child-care, would be organized collectively, in order to relieve women of household chores and leave family members maximum freedom to lead their own lives together or apart, as they wished.[59]

The regime, however, never invested enough in the building and rebuilding required to establish such collectives as genuine models of social living. On the contrary, they became notorious for their squalor and lack of hygiene. They were just the kind of homes the new elite did *not* wish to have. In any case by the 1930s the official ideology had shifted back to regarding the family as the core unit of society, and such dwelling construction as did take place in those years was of family apartments. They were awarded to senior officials of party and state, to Stakhanovite workers, and to other specially favored groups. Ordinary people had to crowd into the existing, largely prerevolutionary, stock of dwelling space. Given the scale of immigration into the towns during the 1930s, providing adequate housing would have created problems in any circumstances, but the difficulties were exacerbated by the fact that construction of homes was not a priority of the first five-year plans. In most countries the result would have been shantytowns on the urban peripheries. Owing to the Soviet regime's egalitarian principles, however, together with its desire to administer and control social processes, shantytowns were unacceptable (though in extremis they sprang up too). Instead, as we have seen, as early as 1918 local soviets were decreeing *uplotnenie,* or "crowding together."[60]

To demarcate the unfamiliar, shrunken private spaces, tenants would erect plywood partitions: "Old rooms and hallways were partitioned and subdivided, creating weird angular spaces, with a window opening into a sunless back yard, or without any windows. Every tenant exercised her imagination in inventing curtains and screens to delineate their minimum privacy."[61]

The communal apartment fitted some of the outlook and practices of the village commune into the new structures of Soviet life. Since the former bourgeois members had been deprived of their wealth, everyone shared a kind of egalitarian poverty, and marked departures from the average were regarded with suspicion: the very poor because they were a burden to their neighbors, the affluent because their wealth suggested criminal behavior that could be disruptive. On the other hand, as in the village, a hierarchy of apartment-dwellers existed alongside the egalitarian features. At the top were the *kvartupolnomochennyi,* the appointed apartment supervisor, and also those who had good connections with the *domovoi komitet,* the house committee that managed the whole apartment block. At this level, too, were members of the "comrades' court," which adjudicated disputes with the local soviet or party committee, and with the police. Also near the top were those who had lived there longest, and therefore had the greatest commitment to the collective, as well as the most detailed knowledge of the apartment's "common law," the informal arrangements that had become legitimated by time. Most tenants had their billets in the apartment awarded by the institution for which they worked, so that their tenancy intensified their dependence on their employer.

Members of the apartment had to coexist somehow, and so they devised rules about how this could be done, in ways as far as possible acceptable to everyone. It is true that a statute law existed in the form of a 1935 circular entitled "On the Struggle with Hooliganism in Apartments." Among other things it prohibited "loutish behavior such as: arranging regular drinking sessions, accompanied by noise, brawling, and vulgar language; beating people up (especially women and children); making insults or threats of revenge; exploiting one's official or party rank; debauchery; ethnic victimization; personal abuse; the playing of malicious practical jokes (throwing other people's property out of kitchens or other public areas, spoiling food being cooked by other tenants, damaging property, groceries, etc)."[62] The circular presents a revealing checklist of practices that experience must have shown were common, but it offered no advice on how to deal with them, other than recourse to informal comrades' courts, which were structured rather like village courts.

Living in communal dwellings necessitated informal mutual consensus and decision-making, which required regular consultation, even if there was no mechanism resembling the *skhod.* Some rules, for example about the use of bathroom or telephone, or about paying for gas and electricity, were written and displayed in a prominent position. Most rules, though, were informal; they were mediated through kitchen gossip and perhaps tested through the occasional *skandal*—a row, scene, or shouting match conducted in public—in which the winner's version would be accepted as authoritative for the future.[63]

As in the village, the fortunes of families and individuals would fluctuate. Since they were all near the subsistence frontier, it was helpful if they could tide each other over during bad times. To some extent it was normal practice to keep an eye on one another's children, or use a neighbor's saucepan, sieve, matches, or salt, but all these instances of aid needed to be regulated by mutual agreement or convention. Lending money was more problematic but also generally expected where there were good relations. Besides, refusal to lend money might lead to theft, which always disturbed good relations and generated tension. Once a loan was made, the debtor would usually do his utmost to return the money on time, to keep up the relationship, even if he had shamefacedly to request another loan the next morning.[64]

In other respects the communal apartment was very different from the village, or even the *baraki*, where people shared a common background and outlook. Tenants did not usually engage in common activities, even on festival days. As one respondent put it, personal life was "bleached out," without a real sense of community being created to compensate. The boundaries of the private were far more porous, since private functions like washing were conducted in public rooms, and there was no buffer zone other than a flimsy door between family rooms and public spaces. Because several generations of one family usually lived in one room, the lack of privacy also meant that, as one respondent put it, "I had to take my trousers off in front of my mother-in-law."[65]

The kind of embarrassment that could result is exemplified in an incident Svetlana Boym recalls from her Leningrad childhood. Her mother was offering tea to foreign guests—unusual and exotic visitors in such surroundings—and discoursing on the cultural riches of the Hermitage and the Russian Museum, when an alcoholic neighbor slumped to the floor right outside their door: "A little yellow stream slowly made its way under the door into the room. Smelly, embarrassing, intrusive, it formed a little puddle right in front of the dinner table."[66] Nothing comparable could happen in the peasant hut, which by comparison was like a castle with a drawbridge.

Even going to the kitchen to make a cup of tea entailed being ready for a public encounter, possibly a *skandal*. This situation caused great distress to urbanized professional people and intellectuals, who needed long periods of privacy, peace of mind, and unbroken concentration for their work. It may be that the lack of privacy contributed to the relative frequency of paranoid mental disorders in the USSR; nearly every apartment had its mad person, like the "woman who was convinced that others were putting bits of glass in her soap, and that they wanted to poison her."[67]

The reduced privacy of the communal apartment was well suited to the needs of the surveillance state, especially given that the state owned all dwelling spaces and could reassign them at will. The sociologist Ekaterina Gerasimova has called the outcome "public privacy." Neighbors could supervise each other's behavior without any difficulty: the close proximity in which people lived ensured that major family events were known by everyone. Even ordinary conversations might well be overheard if they took place in the kitchen—the venue for general sociability—or in a family room with thin walls. Usually one or more members, perhaps the *upolnomochennyi* and one other, would be reporting regularly to the security police; so too would the *dvornik*, the janitor, cleaner, and handyman. Anyone could easily do so if they chose, merely by writing an anonymous denunciation. They might well do this in order to eliminate conflict, or in the hope of gaining extra living space or other forms of privilege.[68] Keeping up a sense of equality and fairness was even more crucial to collective harmony than in the village, and some tenants were always prepared to enforce that sense by turning to the authorities if they deemed it necessary. They did this with every feeling of justification, of sustaining a moral code, not violating it. That is one reason that denunciations became so common.

The greatest difference from the village commune, however, was the varied social background of the members. Usually a core of long-time urban-dwellers, some of them bourgeois in origin and relatively well educated, would find themselves sharing space with recent immigrants from the countryside. Their domestic habits, as well as their underlying views of life, were so different that collective norms were far harder to establish and maintain than in the village. (In this respect communal apartments also differed from shantytowns.) Long-time urbanites had expectations of privacy, hygiene, and courtesy that were not shared by the country cousins with whom they now had to live in close proximity. These discrepancies generated constant tension and conflict over dirt in the bathroom and toilet, over permissible behavior for visitors, over noise in the early morning or late evening, and over the disappearance of food and items of personal property. These conflicts, too, might provoke denunciations.[69]

From the late 1950s onward, as the regime undertook a huge program of domestic housing construction, many people left communal apartments to settle in private units. Usually they did so with great relief; some, however, reported that they felt uneasy in their new surroundings because of the lack of company and the feeling that there was no one to fall back on in difficulties.[70]

The communal apartment and (as we shall see) the Soviet enterprise ensured the continuation of what Daniel Bertaux has called the "communal" model of Russian life: equality, joint responsibility, discipline, and subjection to authorities, with enforced interdependence generating a certain reluctant solidarity. On the whole this was the social model fostered by the Orthodox Church too, though in the 1930s it was powerless to play any part in social life. The presiding patriarch was now Stalin. One way or another, everyone was permanently affected by the communal experience. As Svetlana Boym has commented, "Every communal apartment dweller is probably scarred for life by . . . symbolic 'joint responsibility,' a double bind of love and hatred, of envy and attachment, of secrecy and exhibitionism, of embarrassment and compromise."[71]

Daily life usually remained semirural too. To continue the full religious life of the village was impossible, but all the same, recent immigrants would continue to celebrate saints' days and other religious festivals, despite management's efforts to compel them to observe only the new secular holidays. The regime introduced a ten-day work week, but it never really caught on in many industrial enterprises, since the majority of workers would take Sunday off anyway. For several decades village customs coexisted alongside urban practices in a strange amalgam. Some recent immigrants, for example, hung both icons of saints and portraits of Lenin in their barracks or hostel rooms. Lenin was the deified figure in the society they now inhabited, and they wanted to invoke his intercessory powers to complement those of the more familiar saints. They would gather with friends in parks on church or Soviet holidays, gossip, and sometimes sing songs and dance—only now often with tunes they had heard over the radio or in the streets around them rather than those they had brought from the countryside. Former peasants who could afford to do so would dress in the latest urban fashions, to deflect the sneering condescension of more established townsfolk. A particular problem for recent urbanites was that their children almost invariably became more literate and far better educated than they themselves were; children learned the compulsory rhetoric of Soviet urban life and with it the skills required to manipulate the system, in a way that could leave their parents floundering in resentful incomprehension.[72]

Peasant culture gradually adapted itself to the urban scene, sometimes in the process bringing sharp rural skepticism to the inadequacies of city life, as in the following *chastushki* (ditties):

> Na verkakh oni zasedali
> I prozasedalisia.
> Magaziny opusteli,
> Bez shtanov ostalisia.

> They've held meetings at high levels;
> they've held meetings endlessly.
> Meanwhile the shops emptied,
> and we were left without pants.

> Priezzhali k nam uchenye,
> Chtoby zuby nam vstavliat,"
> A zachem nam ikh vstavliat,"
> Esli nechego zhevat."

> Scientists came to us
> To give us false teeth.
> But why give us false teeth,
> if there's nothing to chew on?[73]

Facilities for everyday life were usually inadequate, especially in the newly built industrial centers. One early recruit to the steel works at Magnitogorsk recalled getting out of the train at the (barely existent) railway station, staring out hopefully over the empty steppe and asking: "Is it far to the city?" "Two years," someone quipped in reply. Workers were living in tents, dugouts, or hastily thrown up barracks because finances assigned to building apartments was diverted to industrial needs. Even where an industrial town was raw and unwelcoming, though, many peasants flocked to it to escape the new-style rural destitution. In 1933 57 percent of new recruits in Magnitogorsk were peasants, most of whom had not come through *orgnabor*. Probably a third of them were illiterate and lacked elementary industrial skills. Labor turnover was enormous: in 1933, 53,000 workers were recruited in Magnitogorsk, but the same number quit.[74]

Many established townsfolk resented this flood of coarse and sometimes disorderly immigrants. In 1932 a Donbass worker—a keen upholder of law and order—wrote to the Central Executive Committee complaining that "at this time of intense struggle and selfless work, at a time of serious shortage of working hands, here—in the USSR—especially recently, the quantity of wandering, nonworking elements has increased, most of them from the countryside, people who have taken fright at the first difficulties of work on the kolkhoz. Crowds of them meander around the stations and city streets, committing robberies and murders." Moreover, he added, "in connection with occasional difficulties of a temporary nature with food supplies in some towns and with clothes and footwear in others many citizens have taken up speculation, exploiting the temporary difficulties of the toiling people. They should be apprehended as irreconcilable enemies of the proletarian toiling people, and the supreme measure of social defense should be applied to them: shooting without any abatement or amnesty."[75]

In the drive to create new industry at a super-fast tempo, technical norms were violated and nonindustrial needs slighted or ignored. A dammed lake intended for the water supply was built quickly but turned out too shallow and froze over in winter, so that it was utterly inadequate for its purpose. The official line, though, was that "what mattered was that the dam had been built—not only built but ahead of schedule—and in the process hundreds of youths had come of age as loyal partisans of the cause."[76]

The spirit of propaganda, gigantism, and record-breaking vitiated much of the planning and construction. There was no such thing as a small store or repair workshop that one could "pop around the corner" to. To buy food, clothing, or consumer goods, to get one's shoes repaired, even to make a bus journey to work, entailed long waits in line, where natural sociability generated a good deal of grumbling about the "system."

To the present day Russian urban life is still partly rural in texture. Intellectuals, at least of the older generation, cultivate a tradition of informal hospitability and sociability, usually in the kitchen. Manners are simple, and some might regard them as boorish, reflecting decades of living alongside imperfectly urbanized villagers. Most ordinary Russians now live in separate family apartments, but they still gather whenever they can, which is to say from early spring to late autumn, in courtyards and squares to sit on benches or improvised seats, where conditions allow them to do so. The men play dominoes or cards, the women gossip, and the children play nearby in sandpits and on swings.

## The Soviet Enterprise

The nature of the Soviet enterprise was severely distorted by the context in which it had been set up. In theory Gosplan (the state planning commission) assigned enterprises a set of annual production targets as part of the five-year plan. Their task was to fulfill those targets. In practice, however, managers could not just give orders; they found they had to concede to workers a good deal of control over the labor process. It was as if the artel had returned by the back door to determine matters such as the speed and organization of work and the quality of the finished product. Workers were scarce, and to retain them and secure at least their minimal cooperation, managers had to allow them a certain day-to-day autonomy, and also to turn a blind eye to lateness, drinking, periods of slack work, and insubordination. At the same time, given the ubiquitous shortages, workers depended on enterprise managers for many material benefits otherwise difficult to obtain, so they too had an interest in putting in enough serious work to fulfill the plan. This mutual "codependency" reproduced roughly the "joint responsibility" of the village commune, except that the link to the state was now much more direct and the element of state-supported patronage much greater.[77] Mutual supervision of the workforce was also much tighter, backed up by the party cell, the Cadres Department, and the NKVD/KGB.

Since there was no market economy to make demands on the productive system, the outcome of the encounter between these conflicting forces was a compromise between the demands of Gosplan, the enterprise managers, and the workers. The Soviet enterprise became an institution dedicated to fulfilling the needs of these three major participants. Gosplan required fulfillment of plan quotas. The managers and workers required a plan that was not too demanding; the job of the managers was to secure such a plan by negotiating with Gosplan, and then to create the framework within which the workers could formally fulfill it. In the absence of market disciplines, how they did this and the quality of the product turned out at the end was nobody's concern. The Soviet enterprise became ever poorer at generating the output that was its ostensible function and became instead an institution whose main aim was to satisfy the life needs of those who worked in it. Through the enterprise the workers received pay, housing, medical care, recreation, social security, and often staple food supplies—in fact the elementary requirements of life in a society of scarcity. The managers received those things too, and also status, security, and the habit of command. Managers and workers were dependent on each other for the continuation of this benign situation. An over-demanding manager was a threat to the workers' comfortable arrangements and would be met by strategies of resistance that in the end threatened to jeopardize *his* benefits. On the other hand, hopelessly lazy, drunken, or incompetent workers would not fulfill the plan and so would get him into serious trouble.[78] The whole situation is reminiscent of the communal village arrangements, which ensured subsistence by cooperation, ostensible deference to authority, and agreed traditional work practices, sustainable for those of average ability. Innovative technology, bringing with it new work practices, was a threat to these arrangements.

The result was an economy that produced a basic minimum to ensure a tolerable existence for those within the system, but that was hard on outsiders and insensitive to the needs of consumers or the demands of new technology. Soviet society was intended to be an egalitarian society based on abundance; it actually became a hierarchical society based on scarcity. The texture of the society can be found in the vertical and horizontal personal relationships necessary to get around the scarcity. Enterprise managers employed *tolkachi*, "pushers," to secure urgently needed materials, spare parts, and so on, in short supply: their job was to cultivate good personal relationships with potential suppliers. In everyday life ordinary people constantly came up against shortages or low-quality goods generated by this system of production. They would overcome the problems thus created by seeking alternative sources of supply, either through influence with superiors, or through personal relationships based on the mutual exchange of favors.[79] In either case, Soviet institutions had a certain *trompe l'oeil* quality: patron-client relationships or mutual personal networks offered the high road to survival. Those who were outside them were seriously disadvantaged; they did not, however, altogether form an underclass since the state provided minimal social security benefits to everyone. This was the beginning of a new kind of tacit agreement between the state and the mass of the people: the welfare compact. In this way Soviet Russia reached a compromise with traditional Russia.

This kind of informal economic system had the great advantage of simplifying the continued integration of non-Russians, especially those from the Caucasus and Central Asia. There the population, accustomed to the exchange of informal economic benefits through hierarchical extended families, was able to adjust fairly easily to the planned economy and to the nomenklatura appointments system, which generated its own "clans" in the form of personal dependency networks.[80]

So far we have been dealing with "normal" life. But as the son of a priest later recalled, "In this period reality evolved in two distinct dimensions. In one, stars were raised on the Kremlin, expeditions to the North Pole were achieved, young people took exams and danced to jazz. In the other, there were denunciations, arrests, prisons, illegalities."[81] It is to this other dimension, and its concentrated essence in the Gulag, that we must now turn.

## Gulag

The Gulag came into being at the intersection of the Bolsheviks' millennial dreams and their apocalyptic nightmares. Their hopes spawned consequences no less terrible than their fears. Russians had long dreamed of mobilizing the great mineral wealth that their geologists had prospected: gold, platinum, and nickel, not to speak of coal and oil, much of it buried in the frozen soil of the far north and Siberia. Before the revolution the great chemist Dmitrii Mendeleev had published a best-selling guide to Russia's riches, *Getting to Know Russia,* in which he had extolled his country's natural resources: "Our subsoil is rich in minerals, not to mention such monetary metals as gold and brass, of which we unquestionably have a much greater reserve than any other country. . . . We could flood the whole world with oil, we could not only supply ourselves with coal for all branches of industry, but also saturate many parts of Europe . . . Our ores could be turned into a quantity of iron and steel that would surpass not only England and Germany but the United States as well." (Among the resources he specifically mentions were iron ore in the Urals, at what later became Magnitogorsk, and coal at Ekibastuz in Kazakhstan, later extracted by forced labor.)[82]

Hitherto, however, the financial and human costs had simply seemed too burdensome for serious investment to be directed to the remote regions where most of these minerals were to be found. To lay down roads and railways, to build mines, factories, and homes, to fell timber, excavate minerals, and transport them to where they were in demand had seemed beyond the realms of economic practicality. Mendeleev had envisaged raising investment for the huge development costs by placing a high tariff wall around Russia and then promoting the growth of a network of both state and private banks.[83]

The Soviet state took a different path, replacing investment with coercion. In the late 1920s, as Gosplan reviewed its plans for industrial development, new possibilities opened up. It was difficult to attract wage laborers to move to these remote and inhospitable regions, but *zeki*—the inmates of prisons and concentration camps—could simply be sent there. A decree of March 26, 1928, envisioned "a series of economic projects with great savings in expenditure . . . by means of the widespread use of the labor of individuals sentenced to measures of social protection." To all intents and purposes they were to be turned into slaves. In 1930 Gosplan received instructions "to incorporate the work performed by those deprived of liberty into the planned economy of the country"; all prisoners sentenced to terms of three years or longer were to be transferred to labor camps, and a special department of the NKVD, Gulag (the Main Camp Administration), was set up to run these convict enterprises.[84]

In the early 1930s, accordingly, expeditions of prisoners and guards, together with geologists and mineralogists who somehow happened to have been recently arrested, penetrated these isolated landscapes by boat or even by horse and cart, hastily erected primitive huts, and began to dig, sometimes with just pick and shovel. Some of the early pioneers found nothing valuable they could prise from the frozen soil; they were then often abandoned to their fate. Others became the founders of huge prison empires bearing names like Sevlag (the Northern Camp Complex) and Ukhtpechlag (the Ukhta Camp Complex in the Pechora District), near Vorkuta in the Komi Republic of northern European Russia. Cut off as they were from civilization, they built their own brick works, electricity generators, warehouses, and hospitals. To train and civilize their uneducated, uprooted, and bewildered workers, the authorities provided apprentice workshops, cinemas, theaters, libraries, and, in one case at least, a so-called university.[85] Even in the depths of the Soviet inferno, its custodians did not entirely give up the hope of bringing a kind of culture and civilization to the victims.

What was at stake in these penal settlements can be seen from the history of the most formidable of all the penal empires, Dalstroi, the Far Eastern Construction Administration, in the Kolyma river basin of the Siberian far east, with its attached labor camp dependency, Sevostlag (the Northeastern Camp Complex), centered on the port city of Magadan, on the Sea of Okhotsk. In the 1920s Magadan had become a base for the provision of educational and medical services to the nomadic Evenki and Chukchi peoples of the region. With collectivization and sedentarization, however, the Soviet authorities established a more direct presence and used it to begin seeking out and exploiting the rich gold and platinum reserves of the region. In 1928–1930 the First Kolyma Geological Expedition under I. Iu. Bilibin confirmed and extended the findings of earlier prospectors. This was the signal for the Politburo to pour the resources of Gulag into the region.[86] Since the Kolyma basin is geologically related to the Yukon Territory and Klondike, on the other side of the Bering Straits, one might regard what followed as a grimmer, Soviet version of the "gold rush."

For its crash industrialization program the Soviet Union needed to buy advanced technology from Western countries, and Kolyma gold was to be its means of doing so. Hence mining in the region was supremely important, and Stalin gave it close attention. Reingold Berzin, an Old Bolshevik and Red Army commander during the civil war, was sent to head Dalstroi; he became the Grand Panjandrum of the whole region. Between August 1931 and March 1932 the Politburo discussed Kolyma no fewer than eleven times; Stalin demanded daily reports on the development of the gold industry and periodically summoned Dalstroi's managers to Moscow to brief him. In the settlement's early years, Berzin treated the inmates with what would later seem like relative humanity: they were given adequate food, warm clothing, and regular rest days. By 1936 they had built a whole port city, Magadan, of 15,000 people, together with the docks, roads, quarries, mines, warehouses, and apartment blocks needed to service it.[87]

The situation rapidly deteriorated, however, as first the dekulakization of 1929–1933, then the terror of 1936–1939 filled the labor camps with new, disoriented zeks branded as "enemies of the people." They had been stigmatized as, in Anthony Smith's words, "outsiders . . . who have no part in the sacred mission and its duties." They were therefore expendable, available to be worked to death if required for the success of the project. Their sentences were long—five years at the least, usually ten or even more—and to the victims they seemed interminable. There was no prospect of parole, so the only way to motivate them was through the goad of hunger. Those who fulfilled the daily planned output were rewarded with full rations, just about enough to keep a laborer going in the harsh climate. But those who failed to do so received a reduced ration, and through undernourishment became weaker and even less able to fulfill the plan. As Iurii Margolin, a former zek, later recalled, "We were never in a condition to do what was demanded of us to have enough to eat. The hungrier we were the worse we worked. The worse we worked the hungrier we became. From that vicious circle there was no escape."[88]

Solzhenitsyn maintains that even a full ration was not enough to nourish adequately a zek who carried out the planned work in full. Zeks therefore had to master the art of appearing to work zealously while not actually doing so, and then of disguising underproduction. This was what Solzhenitsyn called "the great principle of *tukhta*," or "padding the books," which enabled many to survive the Soviet penitentiary system. This tactic was easier than might appear. Let us suppose that the lumberjacks have deliberately exaggerated the amount of timber felled in a day, so as to ensure themselves an adequate ration. Those responsible for transporting the timber would have no interest in disclosing the shortfall, for the nonexistent surplus would help to feed them, too; the same was true at the sawmill downstream and on the freight trains taking the planks onward. Only at its ultimate destination, say a furniture works, would anyone be motivated to reveal the discrepancy—and by that time it would be too late to make up the deficiency and very difficult to find out who had been responsible for it.[89]

Whatever the potential for skiving, work had to be performed, and the incentive to do so was usually mediated through the work brigade. It was much easier for camp bosses to measure the output of a brigade of twenty or thirty people than that of each individual. If the brigade as a whole met its output target, then each member was properly fed, but not otherwise. This device made the guards' job of supervision much simpler: it was in the interest of each brigade member to make sure that all the others worked hard. Zeks policed themselves. As Ivan Denisovich, the hero of Solzhenitsyn's short labor camp novel, remarks, "The zek is kept up to the mark not by his bosses but by the others in his gang. Either everybody gets a bonus or else they all die together." The former Polish zek Gustaw Herling-Grudzinski confirms this account: "The most conscientious and fervent foremen were the prisoners themselves, for the norm was reckoned collectively by dividing the total output by the number of workers. Any feeling of mutual friendliness was completely abolished in favour of a race for percentages. . . . There was in all this something inhuman, mercilessly breaking the only natural bond between prisoners—their solidarity in face of their persecutors."[90]

This was the reaction of a Pole. Russians found the experience more familiar: it was a perverse variant of *krugovaia poruka*, the joint responsibility of the peasant commune, the artel, and the communal apartment. In this respect, as in others, the labor camp was a microcosm of Soviet society, which was taking shape through the osmotic absorption of Russian social memory.

Solzhenitsyn, only half ironically, maintains that the zeks formed a distinct *nation* in the shape of—to use Stalin's definition of a nation—"a historically formed community of people, with their own shared territory, language, common economic life, and a common psychological disposition manifested in their culture." Their territory was the archipelago, with its scattered but uniquely rigid boundaries marked by barbed wire and watchtowers. Their economic life was the slavelike fulfillment of the NKVD output plan. Their psychological disposition was determined by their enforced way of life: fatalistic, mistrustful, cunning, parsimonious in word and gesture, energetic only in struggling for the essentials of life. Their language was terse but pithy, often obscene, and scarcely employed the future tense of verbs, so uncertain and cheerless was their outlook. Their culture was of necessity oral but was rich in memories of a "golden age," a past way of life before arrest, now irrecoverably lost. Their folklore consisted of accounts of their masters' arbitrariness and their own wily ingenuity. They had no common religion but did have their own superstitions and irrational hopes, for example, the prospect of an Anglo-American invasion of the USSR or the expectation of an amnesty at each major Soviet festival, in May and November (never realized till after Stalin's death). In all these respects the zeks were a supranation. Whether they were Russian or non-Russian made no difference. They formed a grotesque subterranean parody of the ideal of the "Soviet people."[91]

After the Second World War, however, ethnic feeling did revive within the camps, as a result of wartime fighting and the deportation of nationalities. According to Solzhenitsyn, it began to manifest itself with the arrival of former soldiers of the OUN, the Ukrainian partisans who had fought against both the Germans and the Soviets. Unlike the cowed prewar prisoners, they would murder "trusties" in their midst and then cover up for one another.[92] Zeks began to form their own ethnic clans and mutual aid associations. Only the Russians had none: their ethnic solidarity was weak, and they were still divided either by ideology—Communists versus non-Communists—or by rodina, place of origin: Moscow, Leningrad, the Urals, Siberia.

The "zek nation" was a product of the downside of Russian messianism. Through the zeks' shared way of life their collective attitude, together with the Russian custom of *krugovaia poruka,* was disseminated to all the other Soviet peoples. Some of the zeks' characteristics became those of an entire Soviet generation, having been taken up and developed in analogous conditions of privation and austerity outside the camps. Anyone who visited the Soviet Union right up to the 1980s will recall how ferociously people would fight with their elbows to climb on to an already overcrowded bus or underground train, how they would jealously defend their hard-earned position in a line for *defitsitnye tovary* (goods in short supply). Even the grim, unsmiling expression of Soviet citizens going about their business on city streets bespoke experience gained, perhaps not in the penitentiary system itself, but in conditions not so very different, a determination to fight for rare opportunities or benefits as soon as they were available, but otherwise to have as little as possible to do with the public world and to reserve one's emotions for private life.

The terrible ordeal and the modes of survival could not help affecting the spiritual and cultural life of Soviet society right up to the end—not least because the memory of them was suppressed, so that when it surfaced, timidly in Solzhenitsyn's novel *Ivan Denisovich* in 1962 (fully in his *Gulag Archipelago* only in 1990), it burst forth with all the force of what Freud called the "return of the repressed." The questions the explosive revelations raised, the conflicts they engendered, formed yet another reason that even the Russians in the USSR could have no unified culture. In the 1950s, as zeks were released, Anna Akhmatova spoke of two Russias "eyeball to eyeball": those who had been in the camps, and those who had sent them there.[93]

The shadow of the Gulag hangs over even post-Soviet Russia. Here Russia's messianic crisis still casts its baleful shadow. For Germans to repent as a nation makes a certain sense, for under the Nazis most oppressors were German and most victims were non-German. For Russians, however, the issue is much more complicated and is fraught with mutual resentment. Russians were the oppressors, but they were also the victims. Non-Russians likewise. This reality does not excuse the failure of post-Soviet Russians to face up to the past, but it does help to explain their reluctance.

## Mass Terror

In the terror of the late 1930s Russian messianism reached its supreme crisis. Having fatally weakened the peasant community and nearly destroyed the Russian Orthodox Church, the men who had made the revolution went on to destroy one another. The Communist leaders were a tightly knit coterie of strong men who had come through the underground, revolution, and civil war together. Their shared experience had inculcated in them an extremely macho worldview, which valued determination, ruthlessness, and aggression. The mutual interdependence of life-and-death struggle imparted to their personal relationships a frenzied intensity: they valued small-group comradeship just as much as soldiers at the front line. The word "comrade" was not just a political affectation: it came absolutely naturally to them. They were carrying out the transformation of the country over which they ruled in a highly contested manner which overrode many of the traditions of the population. That is why they used the rhetoric of warfare to describe their achievements in normally unwarlike branches of the economy: "the breakthrough on the grain front," and similar expressions. Like crusaders in hostile occupied territory, they knew they had to stick by one another through thick and thin. The slightest wavering, the slightest breach of discipline, could be fatal to their whole enterprise.

The core of Stalin's leadership team consisted of what Gerald Easter calls the *komitetchiki,* the former local leaders who had kept the Bolshevik underground going between 1905 and 1917, then had become regional political commissars during the revolution and civil war. As he defeated the various "oppositions" in the late 1920s, Stalin promoted some of these men right to the top: Valerian Kuibyshev from the Volga region, Kaganovich from the Ukrainian underground, Ordzhonikidze from the Transcaucasus.[94] Naturally, they in turn brought with them the local subordinates whom they had learned to trust, thus forming a new layer of clients. The industrial ministries set up under the overlordship of Ordzhonikidze to run the five-year plans opened up a new and abundant source of patronage. In the absence of stable institutions and laws, personal pyramids of power were once again decisive, as they had been in tsarist Russia.

The *komitetchiki* were mostly of lower middle class, worker, or peasant origin. They had received a truncated education and had had to make their own way in life. Many of them were autodidacts, compensating for an inadequate education by voracious reading. They inherited the Russian intelligentsia's love for books, and so Soviet culture remained highly verbal and print-based right up to the end. About half the *komitetchiki* were Russian; the rest were Jewish, Latvian, Georgian, Armenian, or Polish. None of them considered ethnicity important, though: they had mostly broken with their family backgrounds and forged their most intense personal relations through the Red Army and the party. Party and army, in fact, had given them everything: their faith, their career, their friendships, and their marriages.[95]

Their comradeship revealed itself in their mode of life. They all had dachas just outside Moscow, in picturesque settings like Serebrianyi Bor, Kratovo, or Zubalovo, where a prerevolutionary oil magnate had built two walled estates, each with a mansion and several smaller cottages. Stalin and several other leaders shared the Zubalovo mansion and the cottages: their wives and children would spend the warmer months there, while they themselves came for weekends and summer evenings to escape the pressure of routine work. Stalin would clip roses and take his children for strolls in the woods. His daughter Svetlana milked cows, fed poultry, and felt in her element. In this relaxed atmosphere the leaders constantly visited each other, bringing presents for wives and children, and held long eating and drinking sessions, sometimes accompanied by music and dancing. Outwardly not much distinguished their gatherings from those that grace the plays of Turgenev and Chekhov.[96]

Yet at these cozy get-togethers grave matters of state were being discussed, the fates of millions decided. When plugged into the electric circuits of high politics, the comradely networks acquired an altogether weightier and more sinister character. For if friendship faltered, it turned immediately into the bitterest hostility. The comrades were borne aloft by a shared faith, and if any one of them showed the slightest sign of doubt, he was forthwith deemed untrustworthy, no longer a true comrade, and therefore objectively an enemy. These were the old traditions of Russian *kruzhkovshchina* (cliquishness) intensified by revolution and civil war.

Any group of people that has to work together over a long period to achieve its aim generates its own view of the world and its own style of discourse, which becomes more or less obligatory for all those involved. Anyone who adopts a different approach or a different language is either not really understood or, where issues are contentious, may be treated as a dangerous outsider. Moreover, groups in positions of power have a strong interest in preserving a facade of absolute and unshakeable unanimity, especially at times of crisis. The heavily monologic discourse is part of their repertoire of authority.[97]

These tendencies were hypertrophied in the case of the Communist leaders. They believed they possessed the key to world history, both to understanding it and to determining its future. They were fighting for absolute good against absolute evil, and anyone who claimed to perceive intermediate shades of grey had to be spurned as an apostate. During the civil war they had learned to treat all opponents and even waverers as deadly enemies who must be defeated and destroyed. Now, after 1933, they were faced with the threat of a German leader who proclaimed as his primary aim the invasion of the Soviet Union and the destruction of Communism. They knew they had to prepare the whole country for a serious and large-scale war.

Mentality and contingency thus combined to create a particularly embattled unanimity on all matters of doctrine and politics. The "general line," as enunciated by the Central Committee, and increasingly by Stalin himself, became compulsory in all its details. Fully elaborated in the Institute of Marxism-Leninism, it was disseminated by a huge and growing army of consultants, lecturers, agitators, and propagandists. Anyone who doubted or strayed from its formulaic prescriptions was considered no longer fully dependable. As the rhetoric escalated, the doubters became "oppositionists," then "deviationists," then people "with terrorist intentions," and finally "terrorists" or "spies" of capitalist powers, full-scale enemies to be exterminated.[98]

Stalin exemplified these traits to the extreme. He had a talent for friendship and could be extremely generous. When Anastas Mikoian first moved to Moscow to join the party Central Committee, Stalin lent him his own apartment; then, when Mikoian took a liking to it, he simply gave it to him and found another one for himself (admittedly not all that difficult for a top official). As general secretary of the party, he took care of the physical arrangements for his comrades, seeing that they all received the cars they wanted, and making up little *pakety* of extra money and holiday coupons when they needed it. Of course he was also building up his clientele, but the fact remains that he was good at it, and his comrades valued him for it. Yet, as Simon Sebag Montefiore has remarked, "his friendships, like teenage infatuations, meandered between love, admiration and venomous jealousy." If he was slighted or upstaged, or suspected that a "comrade" was trying to capture a close friend for himself, he became relentless and ruthless in his rancor, though he always remained patient, waiting for the best moment to strike. Stalin was also a good actor, continuing to simulate friendship up to the last moment. Some of his comrades did not cease loving him right up to their own violent deaths at his hands.[99]

The most poignant example of this dogged and incongruous devotion is the letter that Nikolai Bukharin wrote to Stalin from prison in December 1937. It lays bare the conflicting drives of comradeship, paranoia, and dedication to a great cause. Bukharin had not yet been tried as a member of a "Trotskyite-Rightist Bloc" accused of conspiring with foreign intelligence services to prepare the invasion of the USSR, but he already knew of the charges against him. His letter is full of conflicting emotions: terror at his probable fate, dedication to the party, devotion to Stalin: "If only there were some device which would have made it possible for you to see my soul flayed and ripped open! If only you could see how I am attached to you, body and soul, quite unlike certain people." He is tormented above all by the fear that Stalin might actually *believe* the grotesque accusations leveled against him. But he acknowledges that "*great* plans, *great* ideas and *great* interests take precedence over everything, and I know that it would be petty for me to place the question of my own person *on a par* with the *universal-historical* tasks, first and foremost, on your shoulders." Almost incredibly Bukharin ends by asking "one final time for your forgiveness (only in your heart, not otherwise)."[100] There could scarcely be more agonizing testimony to the mental world in which the Communist leaders lived.

The assumptions engendered by embattled unanimity seeped their poison into the most intimate family relationships, too. When Osip Piatnitskii, a leading Comintern official, was arrested in July 1937, the accusations against him aroused terrible doubts in the mind of his wife, Iuliia. She recalled that at times he had been gloomy and uncommunicative, that sometimes strange individuals had visited him. Could it be true that he had served in the tsarist secret police and still had connections with its agents, plotting to overthrow the Soviet regime? In her diary she applauded Nikolai Ezhov's drive to unmask spies and terrorists. The arrest of her elder son shook her faith in Ezhov, but even so, she continued to use the Stalinist rhetoric to reproach her younger son, Vovka, when he received a poor school report: "I reminded him that he was the son of an 'enemy of the people,' that he showed by his behavior he was the brother of an 'enemy,' and so on. Tears came to his eyes, and he said: 'Am I guilty that I am the son and brother of enemies? I don't want you to be my mother, I want to go into an orphanage.'"[101]

The drive to rhetorical unanimity clashed fatefully with the tendency to form personal patron-client networks. In one sense, the party-state mechanism was a single huge patron-client network, organized and directed through the nomenklatura appointments system. In fact, though, it did not function in a fully coordinated manner: intermediate and lower cells were not always easy to control from above. Local party secretaries knew their own people in a way no one at the center could. They would appoint their own enterprise directors, collective farm chairmen, school heads, and police chiefs, all of whom then had an interest in covering up for one another, throwing up joint smokescreens to obscure the view from above. Their secretiveness implied not political opposition but merely that they were unobtrusively enjoying the good things in life just like their superiors and wished to go on doing so. They were diverting funds to build themselves dachas, providing themselves with high-quality cars and chauffeurs, treating themselves to good wine and gourmet meals, pleasant summer holidays, or "rest-cures" on the Crimean coast, all at the expense of local populations who had to get by on cramped communal apartments and standing in line for inadequate food.

The Soviet Union had become a society of scarcity, and finding a rung on the patronage ladder, however low down, becoming the client of some patron, was by now the key to coping with its everyday problems. The trouble was, scarcity, hierarchy, and favoritism were not at all what the ideology envisaged, and the clash with reality, though not openly acknowledged, was obvious and painful.

The headlong industrialization, collectivization, and dekulakization had brought on one disaster after another. The top leadership knew about but steadfastly ignored the millions of deaths from starvation. The *komitet-chiki* supported the programs in general terms, but they knew from their regional contacts how much suffering and destruction they entailed. They would probably have preferred slower tempos, less use of coercion, and a more discriminating approach to the "kulaks." On the other hand, they had no alternative policies to propose, and in any case they and their protégés were drawn ineluctably into competition with one another to achieve ever higher tempos.[102]

At the 17th Party Congress in 1934 some of these leaders, worried about where Stalin was taking them, approached Kirov—who as the Leningrad first secretary was a senior figure—and asked him to stand against Stalin for the general secretaryship of the party. Kirov declined, but Stalin heard of the potential challenge and resented it, especially since in the subsequent ballot he received more than one hundred negative votes, while Kirov received only two. The published voting figures were falsified, and Stalin continued as general secretary.[103]

With Stalin's "general line" thus confirmed, how was one to explain the disasters? This is where the nature of Communism as a religion comes into question. Mature and well-developed religions all have a theodicy, that is, a way of explaining setbacks, failure, and suffering, learning from them, and renewing the faith in order to move on. Marxism-Leninism had no theodicy. If there were setbacks and failures, they could only be explained, as one would in a war, by assuming that the enemy was at work. If people died in a train crash or a coal mine explosion, or because poison gas had escaped at a chemical works, a commission would go down to investigate, but would invariably come up with the conclusion that "saboteurs," "diversionists," or "wreckers" were to blame.

In the attempt to root out "enemies" from within the party, Stalin ordered an "exchange of party cards"—that is, a screening process or "purge"—in 1933. Every party member had to appear before a commission, hand in his party membership card, and then be interrogated on his activities and beliefs before receiving a new one—or not, if the commission was not satisfied. Since the process had to be carried out at the grass roots, most local party secretaries, naturally enough, took the opportunity to get rid of rivals and opponents, and to confirm the membership of those they trusted. Stalin strongly suspected that, as a result, many "enemies" had remained ensconced in their positions. He decided he would have to bring in an independent force from outside the party to repeat the operation. That independent force was the NKVD.[104]

Thus from 1935 or so the secret police gained an independent purchase on inner-party intrigue. Since their professional obligation was to unmask and destroy "enemies," the process was to prove unprecedentedly destructive. The ratcheting up of operations began after the murder of Kirov—whether or not that was ordered by Stalin. Thereafter Kuibyshev died and Ordzhonikidze, the most powerful of the patrons, committed suicide after a confrontation with Stalin. Rival patron-client networks fought each other, using the blunt weapons of the secret police. Stalin determined who the individual victims were, but he never succeeded in eradicating the networks. Those who survived in the top leadership, and those who, slightly below, moved into senior and responsible positions over the dead bodies of their predecessors, were consequently all skilled and ruthless operators in the art of monopoly patronage politics, which thus, despite Stalin's best and bloody efforts, became the backbone of the new Russian-Soviet political system.

## Orthodox Church

Metropolitan Sergii had made his 1927 declaration of loyalty to the Soviet Union in order to ensure that the church, however much under siege, would survive as an organization able to run its own affairs. As we have seen, however, the regime did not fulfill its side of the bargain. It did not confine itself to legal restrictions on ecclesiastical activity. It was also pursuing a more positive strategy, trying to create a secular and scientific counterculture and to refute religious doctrine by means of antireligious propaganda. The regime set up a League of Militant Godless, which trained agitators to combat the claims of believers, to extol the virtues of science and atheism, and to denounce the church as an organization that extorted money from ordinary unenlightened people by means of false promises and bogus consolations. These efforts produced disappointing results. The atheists themselves were often too ignorant and rigid in their thinking to convince their opponents, and believers were suspicious of them as hirelings of the state.[105] Creating a positive atheist culture and way of life was beyond them.

In spite of its failure to offer an alternative to organized religion, the regime soon ceased to tolerate even weekly divine service. As we have seen, in the late 1920s and 1930s, during or soon after collectivization, the majority of parishes were closed and their church buildings turned into cinemas, clubs, or stores. The bells would be cast down from the tower, then carted off to be melted down for the five-year plan. In this way the two strongholds of traditional ethnic Russia, the church and the village commune, were destroyed simultaneously. In the process priests and servers, as well as active believers, were identified as especially dangerous "kulaks"— "the anti-Soviet active kulak groups of churchpeople and sectarians," to quote the OGPU directive of February 2, 1930.[106] That meant they were slated for deportation.

These operations did not always proceed smoothly. In the village of Olshanitsa in Briansk oblast, the village soviet sent a delegation to close the church and hand it over to the local seven-year school. The NKVD reported on what followed:

> It was envisaged that the churchwarden would give them the keys of the church. The warden refused to hand over the keys, and the priest of the church, who had by then been alerted, appeared in a drunken state accompanied by hysterical women. As a result a heated dispute arose over the handover of the church, during which two of the crowd who arrived with the priest, the woman KOLGANOVA and the old man DROZDOV in his seventies, climbed up the bell-tower and sounded the alarm. At the alarm call people ran in from the fields with sickles and stakes, up to 300–350 women, who drove away the representatives who had come to close the church.[107]

By 1939 all monasteries had been closed. Of 37,000 parish churches still active in 1930, only 8,302 were still officially registered as open. Many of them, however, were not functioning because there was no priest to officiate in them: it has been estimated that in Ukraine, only 1,116 of 4,487 churches were active. In Moscow a mere 15 churches out of 600 were still open; in Leningrad, 5 out of 300; and in the whole of Tambov diocese, 2 out of 110. In Odessa 1 church had been kept open at the personal request of Academician Filatov, Stalin's oculist. There was no officiating priest there, but each Sunday, so it was said, the congregation would gather, a priest would appear from among them, perform divine service, and at the end be arrested by the NKVD.[108]

In April 1939 Liubov Shaporina, wife of the composer, did not attend church in Leningrad at Easter for the first time in her life. She noted in her diary, "There are just three churches left in the city, and all are completely packed, so that there is no Easter procession, and you won't even hear the words 'Christ is risen' spoken on the streets."[109]

Of 163 bishops, only 4 were still at liberty in 1939 and able to perform some of their functions. One of them, Metropolitan Aleksii of Leningrad, was living in a cubbyhole in the belltower of the cathedral, in accommodation intended for the caretaker. Of the rest a few were retired, but the great majority were in prison, labor camp, or exile, and many of them had been killed. It is estimated that more than 40,000 ordained priests met a premature death between 1918 and the late 1930s. In 1941 there were officially reckoned to be 5,665 still active, which, including the renovationists, was only 5 percent of the 1930 figure. Fully 80 to 85 percent of priests had been imprisoned or executed.[110]

The most dramatic single incident in this wholesale persecution of the church was the blowing up of the huge Cathedral of Christ the Savior in central Moscow. The largest place of worship in Russia, the cathedral was built in the late nineteenth century to commemorate the Russians' victory over Napoleon. It had dominated the cityscape for decades, visible from a variety of vantage points. Preliminary removal of bells and structural features took nearly five months. The process was completed with high explosives on December 5, 1931. After two explosions the dome was still standing, and "believers in the crowd shouted that the Lord had heard their prayers and would not let the church be destroyed." However, a third explosion finally dashed their hopes.[111]

The regime intended the vacated site to be occupied by a Palace of Soviets, which was to be 415 meters high—taller than the recently completed Empire State Building in New York and far more massive in its lower floors—and topped with a 90-meter-high statue of Lenin, three times the size of New York's Statue of Liberty. The palace was to be approached by an avenue 250 meters wide, running right through the center of Moscow, along which columns of workers and soldiers would march. Inside, under a 100-meter dome would be a conference hall that seated 21,000 people, plus 17,000 square meters of oil paintings, 20,000 of bas reliefs, and 17,000 of frescoes and panels. When demolition was complete, however, an examination of the subsoil revealed that the high subterranean water table was likely to flood the foundations. The builders tried to harden the foundations by ramming into them hundreds of gravestones taken from local cemeteries. But even this expedient did not pre-

vent water seepage, and eventually the plans had to be abandoned altogether. A swimming pool was built instead. An empty space replaced what
should have been the symbolic heart of the entire new order.[112]

Many believers and some priests simply went underground. Priests
would work by day as hospital porters or cloakroom attendants, then in
the evening put on a cassock and conduct a secret service or visit the sick
and dying. There were even clandestine monasteries, some in the Siberian
forests, others within regular working institutions in the cities. Secret services and prayer meetings were held in the woods or in nonconsecrated
buildings. One woman described a catacomb Easter service:

> The little house where Father Serafim lived looked abandoned and
> uninhabited. But inside it was full of people who had come to cele-
> brate the joyous festival with their priest as they formerly did in
> church. The priest was busy fixing up the altar and iconostasis. . . .
> Before beginning divine service, the priest sent someone to check
> that the singing could not be heard in the street. Then Easter matins
> started, and the little house turned into a glowing temple, in which
> everyone was united by one incomparable feeling, the joy of Resur-
> rection. The procession of the cross took place inside the house, in
> the hall and the corridor.[113]

We cannot tell just how widespread such clandestine celebrations were.
What we do know is that in 1937 a census of the population revealed that
57 percent of Soviet adults still claimed to be believers. This cannot be an
overstatement, since both the census-takers and those questioned had an
interest in minimizing the true extent of religiosity. The figure was so
shocking that the census results were suppressed. Whatever the number of
believers, though, on the eve of the war the Orthodox Church was almost
destroyed as an institution. In May 1941, Sergii confessed to a visiting
priest: "Formerly they used to strangle us, but at least they fulfilled their
promises. Now they continue to strangle us, but they no longer fulfil the
promises they give while strangling us."[114]

## The Fate of a Priest

The story of one priest may help to clarify what servants of the church,
their families, and their congregations went through in these years. It is
recounted by the priest's younger son, Vasilii Ivanovich Sokolov, whose

papers are in the archive of the Russkaia Biblioteka Zarubezhia. Father Ioann was born in 1879 in Novospasskoe, Smolensk guberniia. After studying at a seminary, he worked for seven years as parish priest in a remote village, during which time he read widely in Russian theology and became convinced that Marxist socialism was an attempt to declare humanity divine, to create a Man-God, and that therefore it was a mortally dangerous doctrine. Any compromise with it, such as that proposed by the "renovationists" in the early 1920s, he rejected. Instead he believed it was necessary to rethink Christian doctrine by linking it more effectively with the church's care for its parishioners. He entered the Moscow Spiritual Academy, where Father Pavel Florenskii supervised his dissertation.[115]

Having completed his studies, Father Ioann was appointed as priest in charge of Nizhne-Nikolskaia church, the second most important church in Smolensk after the cathedral. He was arrested in 1923 as the author of a declaration in support of the recently arrested Patriarch Tikhon, but he was released when no copy of the paper was found among his possessions; his son, warned of the imminent search, had hastily removed them.[116]

There followed several years of relatively peaceful parish work. But life was becoming steadily more difficult for clergymen and their families. They belonged to the category of *lishentsy*, or "deprived people." These were members of "former" social classes—landowners, merchants, clergymen—stripped of civil rights. As Vasilii explained, "They could be conscripted at any time to fulfill menial tasks like cleaning toilets or mending roads, they could be arrested without a procurator's warrant, or taken as hostages, who were sometimes shot if the political situation got tense or even if it did not."[117] Many of them could not stand the pressure and left the clergy.

The plight of their families was agonizing. Father Ioann was once summoned to the GPU and warned to give up the priesthood because he was "ruining his children's future." If one's father was a priest, one needed to practice deception to join the party, to get a good job, or to enter specialized and higher education—unless, that is, one was prepared to forswear him publicly. Father Ioann's elder son did abandon the family. His daughter also disavowed him but kept up secret contacts, and she persuaded Vasilii to join her in Moscow, where he registered in the Institute of Chemical Engineering. He never forgot the sight of his father seeing him off at the railway station: "I was astonished and embarrassed to see my father with tears in his eyes as the train began to move. Ignoring everyone around him, he took off his hat and made the sign of the cross over me."[118]

Vasilii received no scholarship at the Institute because of the "dark places" in his biography. The director, who learned of his background, allowed him to stay on as long as he continued to gain good marks but advised him "to lose your birth certificate and not tell anyone about your father."[119]

In August 1936 what the whole family had been dreading finally happened. Father Ioann was arrested and sent into exile in Kazakhstan, where of course he was forbidden to exercise his priestly functions and had to perform manual labor. He did survive, however, till an incident took place in his former parish that allowed the authorities to apply to him the "highest penalty."

Some children playing in the ruins of a fort on the edge of Smolensk "discovered early one morning that from time to time an elderly or middle-aged woman would make her way to a nearby tower. They lay low and eventually saw a horse and cart driving up to the tower, out of which a very old man clambered, helped by the driver." Creeping right up to the tower, the children

saw an incredible spectacle: the old man, who had some kind of mantle over his shoulders and a black cap with a white cross on his head, was intoning something, while those present, mostly women, chanted quite engagingly and sometimes got down on their knees. . . . One woman hastily hung up a curtain and arranged a few icons on it, like an iconostasis, and then pulled an ordinary school desk out of a bush growing inside the tower and draped a towel with an embroidered cross over it, as a kind of lectern. Someone else took a pile of liturgical books out of a suitcase, and a third person heated up some coals and placed them in a homemade censer. An ordinary divine service began, with the censer swinging at the appropriate points, only with tar instead of incense.

The children related what they had seen to their parents, who reported it further. One day the service was raided in the middle, the priest and the old women were hauled away, and the books burned. As a result of this discovery in his former parish, Father Ioann, even though he was far away in exile, was re-arrested and this time was sentenced to "ten years' imprisonment without right of correspondence." Only when Vasilii investigated his file in the 1990s did he discover that in fact his father had then been shot.[120]

In the late 1930s, then, the Soviet Union was in the grip of a terrible and destructive sociopolitical psychosis, engendered by revolution, civil war, and the leaders' messianic struggle against the national church and against the traditions of the Russian people. In the face of the war against Germany which threatened, the leaders needed to do something to restore greater stability and social cohesion. But the task was daunting: Russians' social memory, already gravely damaged by revolution and civil war, was further fractured by their experience during the 1930s. There was little they could share because the social stratification was so extreme and the violence so damaging.

Yet, as we shall see in the next chapter, a new ruling class was emerging, drawing its recruits from all strata of Soviet society, but especially from the workers and peasants. It was creating not only its own monopoly patronage system, but also its own memory and its own myths. By exploiting the range of its own education and propaganda system, it was able to propagate them far down the social scale to the newly literate. At the grass roots, too, a reconfigured but not unrecognizable model of Russian social life was emerging, in the communal apartments and the workplaces, where the modified but familiar bonds of "joint responsibility" revived impecunious egalitarianism, mutual surveillance, and subjection to authority. In spite of all the conflicts, the outlines of a new kind of Russian society were forming, though they were not to be fully consolidated till after the Second World War. An incongruous but nevertheless workable symbiosis of Russian traditions and Communist practices was beginning to take shape.

# 5

## PROJECTING A NEW RUSSIA

From the late 1920s to the mid-1930s Soviet society was in turmoil. The institutions and myths of tsarist Russia were dead, and nothing stable had replaced them. Hitler had come to power in Germany, proclaiming his intention to invade the Soviet Union and destroy Bolshevism. Suddenly the country that Russian Marxists had always revered as their greatest hope had become their bitterest enemy. Unifying counterinfluences were sorely needed. Above all the Russians as the most numerous Soviet people needed a social memory, tales of achievement, and popular celebrations to heal the rifts and underpin the new society. The official history was still raw and unfamiliar: its heroes were not great men, but rather abstract social forces; its battles were the plodding and protracted engagements of the class struggle; its timeline was marked out not by kings and queens but by stages of socioeconomic development. Perhaps most important of all, its homeland was not Russia but the international working class and the ethnically anonymous Union of Soviet Socialist Republics.

One would have thought that tales of the revolution had a heroic potential and might have stirred the blood or stuck in the memory. Surveys conducted in Odessa schools in 1924 and 1927 suggested, however, that few children understood what Communism was, who led the Soviet government, or even what was the name of the country in which they lived. They knew about the revolution and civil war, but as memorized historical facts rather than as subjects on which they could answer questions or about which they felt deeply. As many as 20 percent of the respondents in

1927 did not even know who Lenin was. A wider survey conducted by the Pedagogical Section of Narkompros also revealed some startling ignorance about the Soviet Union and its institutions. One respondent thought the Komsomol was "an international organization of the homeless," another that Persia and China were about to enter the USSR, and a third that "imperialism is the best path to socialism."[1]

When Britain broke off diplomatic relations with the Soviet Union in 1927, the regime launched a series of stories in the press designed to arouse patriotic feeling. OGPU reports suggested that the popular response was indifferent or negative. A Russian from Krivoi Rog was reported as saying: "England is preparing to declare war on the USSR, but the Russians are tired of war and no one will go off to fight. Soviet Power for us is like a [bad] dream and a temporary phenomenon: sooner or later it will cease to exist and then there will be a Constituent Assembly." And a peasant from Moscow oblast: "Soon there will be a war and they will give weapons to us peasants and we'll turn them against Soviet Power; we do not need a workers' regime and we should overthrow it and smother the Communists." A question was asked at a public meeting: "Why can't we have Soviet power without the party?"[2] In case of an international crisis, the regime had good reason to question how much support it would receive from the public. Creating positive myths and memories had become an urgent priority.

## Ukraine and the Crisis of *Korenizatsiia*

The launch of the five-year plans and the collectivization of agriculture brought the problems of *korenizatsiia* to a head. By its very nature the planning and opening of technically up-to-date factories under tightly centralized control carried implicit Russifying overtones. The new enterprises were producing for an all-Union market whose predominant language was Russian. The commands, instructions, and specifications came from Gosplan and the Union industrial ministries in Russian. Most of the qualified staff, whether administrators, technical specialists, or workers, had received their training in Russian and, whatever their origin, spoke Russian on the job in preference to other languages; for many of them it was their only language. Kalinin, who sometimes blurted out what other Soviet leaders thought but kept quiet about, commented at (of all places) an Uzbek party congress in 1925 that "the national question is a purely peasant question. . . . The best way to eliminate nationality is a massive factory with thousands of workers . . . which like a millstone grinds up all nationalities and forges a new nationality. This nationality is the universal proletariat."[3] Inside the Soviet Union, that "universal proletariat" could only be Russian.

We have already seen that Ukraine was at the epicenter of the crisis over the collectivization of agriculture. The same was true of *korenizatsiia*, which was pursued as a flagship policy in Ukraine. By 1933, 89 percent of primary school children in the republic were studying in Ukrainian-language schools—impressive figures considering that Ukrainian-language instruction had been banned till 1905. The dramatic rise in literacy was accompanied by what might be called, following Benedict Anderson, a Ukrainian "print revolution": by the late 1920s the great majority of books, journals, and newspapers were in Ukrainian. Russians and Jews, compelled to scramble for places in the few remaining Russian-language schools, greatly resented these developments. Not even all Ukrainians were pleased. Viktor Kravchenko later recalled: "In theory we Ukrainians in the student body should have been pleased. In practice we were as distressed by the innovation as the non-Ukrainian minority. Even those who like myself had spoken Ukrainian from childhood were not accustomed to its use as a medium of study. Several of our best professors were utterly demoralized by the linguistic switch-over. Worst of all, our local tongue simply had not caught up with modern knowledge; its vocabulary was unsuited to the purposes of electrotechnics, chemistry, aerodynamics and most other sciences. . . . [We] suffered the new burden, referred to Russian textbooks on the sly and in private made fun of the *opera bouffe* nationalism."[4]

The Ukrainian "print revolution" meant that large-scale urbanization, when it came in the 1930s, took place in Ukrainian rather than Russian, as would have been the case a mere ten years earlier. For the first time ever, many cities on Ukrainian territory became mainly Ukrainian in language and culture. Even in the Donbass, traditional bastion of Russian workers, Ukrainians constituted 70 percent of coalminers by 1930, while 44 percent of the labor force in the region spoke Ukrainian as their native language. Mykola Skrypnyk, Commissar of Education, proclaimed proudly that "Ukrainian culture is now not only the culture of song, music, theatre, cooperatives and schoolteachers. It is now a culture of factories and enterprises, the culture of Dneprostroi and the Donbass."[5] This statement was somewhat premature: some cities in the east and south, like Kharkov,

Donetsk, and Odessa, remained mainly Russian in culture. It is also true that *korenizatsiia* was not Ukrainization in the full sense, but rather the adaptation of Ukraine to Soviet structures. All the same the changes were an unpleasant shock for Russians and those who were used to cultural and linguistic domination.

It was logical, then, that the crisis of *korenizatsiia* should come in Ukraine. It was the acid test case for a multiethnic state where Russians were the most numerous people. The Ukrainians' choice of national identity, along with that of the Belorussians, determined whether a united East Slav nationality would become overwhelmingly dominant in the USSR, or whether Great Russians would merely constitute a relative majority.

The Ukrainians also straddled a very sensitive international border: nearly five million of them lived in Poland. In the early 1920s, it had been confidently anticipated that Polish Ukrainians would wish to resettle in the USSR; in fact a Communist Party of Western Ukraine (KPZU) had been created specifically to make the Ukrainian SSR "a centre of attraction for the mass of discontented Ukrainians," by which was meant those living abroad. By the early 1930s, however, the Soviet Union began to look like a country one might wish to escape from rather than migrate to. Soviet leaders began to fear that Soviet Ukrainians might form a center of discontent, or even opt for Polish citizenship and emigrate. Josef Pilsudski's seizure of power in Poland in 1926, and his declared intention of working with Polish Ukrainians and Belorussians, had awakened fears of a new anti-Communist campaign exploiting ethnic conflicts against the USSR.

These fears were compounded by the effects of *korenizatsiia*. Some party members suspected that Ukrainization was proceeding too forcefully and taking on a dangerous life of its own. A great symbolic triumph for Ukrainian intellectuals was the return of Mykhailo Hrushevskyi from abroad in March 1924. Hrushevskyi had been chairman of the Ukrainian Central Rada during its fight for independence from Russia in 1917–1918, and therefore a key figure in the anti-Bolshevik movement. On his return he was elected chairman of the historical section of the Ukrainian Academy of Sciences. In spite of his past, though, he was now prepared to work with the Communists, like the Russian Change of Landmarks thinkers, and most Communists felt it advisable to return the compliment, in order to keep Ukrainian intellectuals aboard the Soviet ship.[6]

Hrushevskyi was the doyen of Ukrainian nationalist historians and author of a history of his country that minimized the role of Muscovite and Imperial Russia in its formation. He maintained that the prevalent Russian historiography, which saw Great Russians, Ukrainians, and Belorussians as a single nation, was defective because it concentrated too much on the state and ignored the peoples. In claiming Kievan Rus as the origin of the portmanteau "Russian" people, Hrushevskyi asserted, Russian historians were ignoring important ethnic distinctions: "We know that the Kievan state, its laws and culture, were the creation of one nationality, the Ukrainian-Rus, while the Volodimir-Moscow state was the creation of another nationality, the Great Russian." Moscow was, if you like, Gaul to Kiev's Rome. Kiev, in Hrushevskyi's view, had given birth to a quite different tradition, that of Galicia-Volynia in the thirteenth century, of Lithuania-Poland in the fourteenth to sixteenth centuries, and of the Ukrainian nation in the present day. The present Belorussian nation, on this interpretation, had also emerged from a parallel development, centering on the Grand Duchy of Lithuania. "There can be no 'all-Russian' [obshcherusskaia] history," Hrushevskyi asserted, "just as there is no 'all-Russian' nationality. There may be a history of all the 'Russian nationalities,' if anyone wishes to call it so, or a history of the East Slavs. It is this term that should take the place of what is currently known as 'Russian history.'"[7]

It may seem surprising that the reinterpretation of a distant past should prove so contentious, but in the fractured Soviet memory, it had explosive force. It challenged radically what had been an unspoken assumption of all the Soviet rulers, even in their anti-Russian moods: that for historical reasons the Russian people formed the underlying substance of the Soviet Union. This "cement" functioned far more effectively if Ukrainians and Belorussians were included as Russians, and this is precisely what Hrushevskyi denied.

Hrushevskyi's triumphal return was only the most striking example of a Ukrainian nationalist trend that worried the Soviet leaders, as well as many Russians, Jews, and other non-Ukrainians. Kaganovich, the party first secretary in Ukraine, feared in particular that the onward march of Ukrainization was threatening to engulf the large numbers of Russian urban workers living in Ukraine. As early as April 1926, acting on one of Kaganovich's reports, Stalin rebuked the Ukrainian Commissar of Education, Oleksandr Shumskyi, for his overbearing attitude: "We can and should, while observing the proper tempo, Ukrainize our party, state and other apparatus. But we must not Ukrainize the proletariat from above. We must not force Russian workers en masse to give up the Russian language and culture and declare their language and culture to be Ukrainian. This contradicts the principle of the free development of nationalities. This would not be national freedom, but a novel form of national oppression."[8]

Stalin's criticism provoked a furious controversy inside the Ukrainian Communist party (KPU) leadership. Unexpectedly it intersected with the Polish border question: in January 1928 the KPZU issued a statement in defense of Shumskyi, criticizing "the bureaucratic deformation of the process of Ukrainization" and "the denial of the need to Ukrainize the urban proletariat." This touched a raw nerve. The Comintern reacted with unprecedented ferocity by dissolving the KPZU and reconstituting it with an entirely new leadership, while the KPU denounced Shumskyi's line as "the theoretical formulation of Ukrainian fascism."[9] This was exceptionally strong language for comrades to be using about one another, and it reflected the increasing paranoia that by now marked the party's approach to all Ukrainian issues.

The same paranoia occasioned one of the most widely publicized show trials of the period, that of the Union for the Liberation of Ukraine, which was held in the Kharkov Opera Theater in March-April 1930. The defendants came from the Ukrainian Academy of Sciences, the Ukrainian Autocephalous Church, non-Communist Ukrainian political parties, and other public associations. They were accused of fomenting nationalist discontent within Ukraine in order to provoke a popular rising and facilitate foreign intervention.[10] The indictment was one of the first examples of the gross rhetorical overstatement that was soon to become characteristic of Soviet jurisprudence, conjuring "enemies," "spies," and "foreign agents" out of peaceful if discontented citizens, and forging "terrorist conspiracies" out of inconclusive gatherings or discussions.

Similar fears beset party leaders in relation to Belorussia, even though national consciousness was far weaker there. During the revolution and civil war, Belorussia had experienced only the briefest period of independence before being established as a Soviet republic in 1919. Even some local Bolsheviks had been opposed to its creation as an independent entity, on the grounds that Belorussia was not a nation, but Lenin was apparently very anxious to set up counterweights to "Great Russian chauvinism" by splitting the East Slavs.[11]

During the 1920s Belorussia had benefited, as had all non–Great Russian republics, from *korenizatsiia:* schools began to teach children in Belorussian for the first time. The peasants who made up the great majority of the population benefited first from the revolutionary land expropriation and then from the New Economic Policy. During the 1920s and 1930s a real social base for Belorussian national identity was being created, as newly educated peasant offspring moved into the towns, obtained urban jobs, and trained in the professions. A Belorussian-language press was taking root, and by the late 1930s nearly 90 percent of the population of Belorussia could read, though many of them did so in Russian.[12]

The specter of Belorussian nationalism so haunted the Soviet leaders that they mounted in Minsk a show trial very similar to the Ukrainian one. There was one major difference, however: among the defendants in the trial of the Union for the Liberation of Belorussia were four prominent leaders of the Belorussian Communist Party. Here, it was alleged, the nationalist danger had wormed its way into the party's very highest ranks. Vigilance obviously needed to be redoubled. Articles appeared in the party press declaring Belorussian nationalism the greatest political danger in the republic. "Belorussization"—the local variant of *korenizatsiia*—was never officially repudiated, but in the face of such official declarations it became a policy to be pursued only cautiously, if at all.[13]

Plunged back into the mindset of the civil war, Stalin and his colleagues had become convinced that most of the resistance to the "Great Socialist Offensive" was coming from non-Russians and especially from Ukrainians, who had shown themselves to be not only economically unreliable but also a prospective fifth column for the intrigues of a potential enemy, Poland. The Russians, by contrast, were proving themselves in the eyes of the party leaders to be not only the state-bearing people but also more reliable implementers of the party's economic plans.

## The Upgrading of Russia

The logic of the conflicts generated by the "Great Socialist Offensive," then, drove the Soviet leaders toward a pro-Russian posture. They were beginning to give due weight to the fact that the Russians were the bearers of the Soviet multiethnic idea. Russian was the official language of the Soviet state and the most widely used for interethnic communication. The Russians were the most numerous people and—along with the Ukrainians—the most geographically mobile, the most inclined to migrate beyond the borders of their own "homeland" republic. From the 1920s right through to the 1950s, despite *korenizatsiia,* they were desperately needed throughout the USSR as administrators, skilled workers, and technical specialists, especially where new branches of the economy were being developed. Outside the RSFSR they were concentrated mainly in the towns: by 1939, for example, Russians constituted 35.7 percent of the urban population of Azerbaijan, 35 percent in Uzbekistan, and in Kazakhstan a huge 58.4 percent. In dealing with the indigenous peoples, they normally expected Russian to be used, not the local language, which few of them bothered to learn.[14]

By now, the whole program of "grinding up all nationalities," as Kalinin had put it, was being taken off the agenda. On the contrary, nationalities were digging in for survival, and class war was being replaced by ethnic tension. During the 1930s class origin ceased to be the most important factor in determining one's fate, and was gradually replaced by ethnic identity. Formally the turning point was marked by the 1936 constitution, which proclaimed that socialism had now been constructed, and that as a result the class struggle had in the main been won. But as early as 1934 Stalin had warned that the national question presented the greatest threat to the moral-political unity of Soviet society.[15]

As a result of this change of approach, some of the "kulaks" only recently exiled found it possible to regain a certain acceptance in society. Since factories were short of labor, they could often find employment without questions asked. In 1936 their right to vote was restored. Their children were able to attend local schools and, at the age of sixteen, to receive a passport. Some kulaks "wrote off" their former status by volunteering for military service, and from 1941 this became a general practice. In that way exile status gradually became eroded, though the NKVD did its best to ensure that regulations were observed, residence permits regularly checked, passports withheld, and so on. Local officials became concerned that some *trudposelentsy* (labor exiles) were turning themselves back into kulaks. From Khabarovsk oblast it was reported that some of them had three to five cows, a horse, and a shotgun with which they went hunting. Others were said to be conducting "speculative" trade and making money out of local kolkhozniks.[16] They were acting as enterprising peasants have always done, trying to ensure survival and if possible prosperity by adapting to a harsh environment, to local economic conditions, and to prevailing social hierarchies.

Gradually the Soviet state was beginning to adopt the attitude that, though the Soviet Union was homeland for all social classes and for all peoples, it was especially so for workers and for Russians. Marx had stated that "the workers have no homeland." At a conference of industrial managers, however, Stalin adjusted this doctrine to bring it up to date. "In the past we did not have and could not have a fatherland," he proclaimed, but "now, since we have overthrown capitalism and power belongs to the working class, we *have* a fatherland and will defend its independence." By that time Hitler's accession to power in Germany had given a new dimension to the desire to defend what could now unself-consciously be called the "socialist fatherland." In March 1935 *Pravda* expatiated on this new doctrine: "Soviet patriotism is a burning feeling of boundless love, a selfless devotion to one's motherland and a profound responsibility for her fate and defence, which issue forth like mighty spring waters from the depth of our people." Only a year later *Pravda* was attributing to that Soviet patriotism an explicitly Russian core: "In the constellation of union republics, the RSFSR is the largest. And the Russian people are the first among equals."[17]

At a lunch with top officials of the Comintern, to celebrate the twentieth anniversary of the October revolution, Stalin ruminated publicly on his understanding of the Russian inheritance: "The Russian tsars did a great deal that was bad. . . . But they did one thing that was good—they amassed an enormous state, all the way to Kamchatka. We have inherited that state. And for the first time we, as Bolsheviks, have consolidated and strengthened it as a united and indivisible state, not in the interests of landowners and capitalists, but for the benefit of the workers, of all the peoples who make up that state." If any part of that state should be lost, he warned, it would "inevitably fall under foreign subjugation" and inflict damage on the cause of socialism: "Therefore, whoever attempts to destroy that unity of the socialist state, whoever seeks the separation of any of its parts or nationalities—that man is an enemy, a sworn enemy of the state and of the peoples of the USSR. And we will destroy each and every such enemy, even if he is an old Bolshevik."[18] In this way, the protection and defense of the neo–Russian Empire had become the Communists' top priority.

The rehabilitation of Russia soon found its reflection in policy. During the 1920s the Soviet leaders had begun Latinizing the various alphabets in use in the country. They had even considered Latinizing the Cyrillic

script, in order, as Lunacharskii said, "to give us maximum internationalism, link us both with the West and with the reformed East." A special
committee of Narkompros had been set up to prepare the changeover. It
declared Cyrillic "an alphabet of autocratic oppression, missionary propaganda and Great Russian national chauvinism . . . ideologically alien to
socialist construction." In July 1937, however, the committee was disbanded. The Latin alphabet was now dismissed as a product of "the bourgeois West." By the same token, the Union of Esperantists, which had
been attached to Narkompros, was closed in June 1938, on the grounds
that Esperanto was being used for espionage and counter-revolutionary
activity. Many of its activists, including its head, E. Drezen, were arrested.[19] In 1938 the teaching of Russian was made compulsory in the
non-Russian republics; in practice, though, its introduction was slow and
unsystematic: local soviets dragged their feet, head teachers resisted making room for it in crowded timetables, and the training of qualified teachers was haphazard.[20]

The Soviet Army was also turning into something more like the old
Russian Imperial army. Exemptions from service for certain non-Russians
were abolished, and territorial reserve units were phased out from 1935.
Members of these locally based units had done a few days' training every
month and had attended a summer camp each year. In regions of mixed
nationality the smaller formations of the regular army as well had generally been ethnically homogeneous, with training and command in the appropriate language. These ethnic formations were abolished from 1938.
Their abolition eliminated a locally based system of recruitment and
made mobilization much more cumbersome, as was catastrophically demonstrated in 1941. Russian was made the universal language of command,
and beginning in July 1940 instruction in Russian was provided for those
recruits who did not speak it.[21]

After the civil war, as we have seen, Cossack military formations had
been disbanded, and so also had Cossack administrative districts with
the attached privileges. Cossacks had lost their self-governing assemblies
headed by atamans and were reclassified, like other rural-dwellers, as
wealthy, middle, or poor peasants. From 1936, however, Cossack names
were given to five cavalry divisions and Cossack uniforms were restored;
Kuban and Don Cossack choirs reappeared and performed at the Bolshoi
Theater. These formations were not strictly Cossack in the old sense,
though, since recruits of all social and ethnic backgrounds were accepted,

including workers and Jews, long-time antagonists of the Cossacks. This was a synthetic, not a genuine, reanimation of tradition.[22]

The ethnic status of passport holders was also tightened up at this stage. When passports had originally been introduced in 1932, entry no. 5—nationality—was filled in on the basis of a citizen's simple declaration. Now, however, an NKVD circular of April 2, 1938, insisted that the nationality entry be substantiated by documents, such as a birth certificate, indicating the parents' nationality.[23] The designation of nationality was now essentially racial: one's nationality could only be "chosen" if one had parents of different ethnic origins, and then only at the age of sixteen on first receiving a passport. Thereafter it was unchangeable.

This was not quite racism in the Nazi sense. Although Soviet anthropologists took race seriously, they did not regard physiological characteristics as unalterable; nor did they reject particular races as inferior. On the contrary, they believed that intermarriage and racial mixing would contribute to progress and the evolution of higher human biological types. In any case, what interested the NKVD was not racial status but rather kinship and ethnic identity, and their implications for state security. If an ethnic group had a homeland abroad, then it was automatically suspect as potentially disloyal to the USSR. Similarly, having relatives abroad was becoming a reason for official doubt about one's total loyalty.[24]

The practice of surveying whole populations and collecting information about them, classifying subgroups on social, economic, ethnic, or racial criteria, and keeping track of every individual in huge filing systems had become a routine part of European politics since the outbreak of the First World War. Emerging social welfare systems depended on such data, as did industrial employment and military recruitment.[25] Information of this kind was especially useful to security forces. In the Soviet Union it became doubly potent as a political weapon, since classification was harnessed to a messianic ideology that aimed to create a perfect society and which divided human beings into comrades and enemies. In the words of Amir Weiner, "the Soviet purification drive . . . combined the modern European ethos of social engineering with Bolshevik Marxist eschatology. . . . The unprecedented increase in the capacities and aspirations of the state went hand in hand with the view of society as raw material to be molded into an ideal image."[26]

The new techniques of population control had initially been used for the purposes of class struggle, to aid in the exile of kulaks. But already in the early 1930s ethnic criteria were sometimes used to discriminate on the basis of social class. Thus in Ukraine dekulakization was applied with especial stringency to certain ethnic minorities, like Germans, Jews, and Poles. There was even a popular saying: *"Raz poliak, znachit kulak."* ("If he's a Pole, he must be a kulak.)[27]

Fears over the darkening international situation prompted the creation of frontier security zones in the west in 1934–1935. As the zones were delineated, the authorities undertook further deportations that had a more definite ethnic character than earlier. When some 8,300 families were moved eastward from the regions of Kiev and Vinnitsa oblasti bordering on Poland to other parts of Ukraine, more than half of those deported were Germans and Poles, though they formed only a tiny percentage of the population there. In January 1936 a further 15,000 German and Polish households were deported from the same region, this time to Kazakhstan, where they became "special settlers" like the kulaks who had preceded them.[28]

Thus deportations progressively became ethnicized. The first time the new techniques were applied to an entire nationality was the deportation of Koreans. In 1935 some 200,000 Koreans were living in various parts of Siberia, with a particular concentration in the Far East. Some of them had been resettled from the border regions when the Japanese occupied Manchuria in 1931. Then in 1937, because the Japanese had invaded China and posed a serious threat, Koreans—suspect because to local officials they looked like Japanese and might be suspected of spying for them—were deported from all Far Eastern oblasts plus Chita and the Buriat Mongol krai. They were packed into overcrowded and underheated freight cars and transported to various parts of Kazakhstan, Uzbekistan, Turkmeniia, and Kirgiziia, where they were "dumped in the middle of nowhere, with a few blankets and whatever they were able to bring along." Some found work on collective farms, in handicraft artels, or in the mines of Karaganda; others succumbed to cold, hunger, dysentery, malaria, or typhus. In those respects their fate was exactly like that of the kulaks. But an additional penalty was attached to ethnic deportation: those who eventually settled into Soviet institutions in their new homeland were not permitted to read Korean newspapers or send their children to Korean-language schools. Deportation was aimed at erasing their ethnic identity. The homes they had been forced to leave were occupied by incoming Red Army and NKVD personnel, to secure the frontier.[29]

Many non-Russians understandably saw deportation as Russification. They were wrong, though, for one of the deported ethnic groups was Russian. Until 1935 the Soviet Union owned and operated the Chinese Eastern Railway in Manchuria, on which most of the workers were Russian. After the line was sold to the Japanese, many of those railwaymen returned to the Soviet Union, where they immediately became the target of NKVD suspicion, since they had lived abroad and still had relatives there. Their fate prefigured that of the much larger number of returnees after the Second World War. Ethnic cleansing was a tool of imperial security, not of national, still less racial, prejudice.[30]

Reflecting on these developments after the end of the Soviet Union, Mikoian claimed: "Stalin's decision to deport entire nations had a depressing impact on me. I did not understand how one could accuse virtually entire nations of treason. After all, they had party organizations, Communists, lots of peasants, and a Soviet intelligentsia! Many had been mobilized into the army and had fought at the front. Quite a few representatives of these peoples were decorated as Heroes of the Soviet Union! . . . This was a deviation from the class approach to the solution of the nationality problem."[31] It certainly was. In fact henceforth ethnic policy largely replaced the class approach as the dominant mode of Soviet politics.

### Finding a "Usable Past"

On the face of it, the struggles and heroic deeds of the revolution should have offered the Soviet leaders ample material for a gripping foundation narrative. But a serious snag arose at precisely the wrong moment, in the mid-1930s: many of the heroes of that era were in the process of being unmasked as "wreckers," "terrorists," or "imperialist spies." A 1935 edition of *The History of the Civil War in the USSR* had to be withdrawn and reissued in a completely new edition in 1938, shorn of most of its photographs and with much of its text excised, because nearly half of the "heroes" mentioned in it had since become "unpersons." Schoolchildren found these tergiversations totally bewildering: "One day their pictures are on the walls in school and in the text-books. The next day, all of a sudden we were told they're enemies of the people." Liubov Shaporina, the composer's wife, reflected in her diary in June 1938: "People used to keep things and pass them down from generation to generation, archives were preserved and history was created. Now the present day denies the day that has passed, yesterday's leaders are shot today, everything that remains from the day before is destroyed in the minds of the young."[32]

Since much of the revolutionary narrative was unacceptable, the only alternative was to find a Russian past that could be safely evoked. If the workers now had a "socialist fatherland," what were its memories and symbols, the essential components of any vision of a fatherland?

In the schools the Central Committee and Narkompros decreed a retreat from the project-based vocational and labor-based teaching of the 1920s. Pupils were to return to their desks, study officially approved textbooks, and take exams. The class-struggle approach to history was also downgraded in favor of a simpler and more memorable narrative. At a special meeting of historians called in March 1934 Stalin complained: "My son asked me to explain what was written in this book. I took a look and I didn't get it either. . . . These textbooks are useless . . . What the hell is 'the feudal epoch,' 'the epoch of industrial capitalism,' 'the epoch of formations'? It's all epochs and no facts, no events, no people, no concrete information."[33] Young people needed a more patriotic and rousing narrative focusing on the Russian and Soviet state, which could guarantee the people's security in a dangerous world as no putative "international proletarian republic" could.

History teachers were instructed in a decree of May 1934: "On the teaching of civic history in the schools of the USSR," to avoid "abstract sociological schemes" and instead to employ "a chronological historical sequence . . . firmly fixing in the minds of pupils important events, personages and dates." Mikhail Pokrovskii, the doyen of socioeconomic historians, fell out of fashion; instead monarchs, dates, and battles were back in vogue, especially battles won by Russians. The expansion of the tsarist Russian state, oppressive and exploitative though it might have been, was projected as objectively beneficial and progressive, since it created the territory that was now the Soviet Union. In March 1936 *Pravda* commented: "To love one's great, free native land means also to know it, to take an interest in its past, to take pride in its bright, heroic pages and to hate its oppressors and tormentors."[34]

The task of making sense out of Russian and Soviet history was entrusted to a team at the Lenin Pedagogical Institute working under Professor A. V. Shestakov. Among the recommendations made by Andrei Zhdanov, the cultural commissar, were "explain better the cultural role of

Christianity"; "provide something on the progressive meaning of the centralization of state power"; and "strengthen the history of the individual peoples." In other words, he wanted religion, ethnicity, and the state to figure more prominently in the interpretation of history.[35]

The new textbook was published in September 1937 in an edition of no less than ten million copies. In many ways it re-established the historical orthodoxy of the late tsarist period. In implicit refutation of Hrushevskyi, it reasserted the unity of the Russian state, evoking an unbreakable tradition stretching from Kievan Rus through Muscovy to the Russian Empire and the Soviet Union. It presented the absorption of Ukraine in the seventeenth century as a liberation and "reunification." Russian imperial expansion and military victories were celebrated, and Ivan the Terrible, Peter the Great, and Alexander I extolled as great leaders. The non-Russian peoples were at the margin, brought in when Russian imperial expansion or Russian peasant revolts involved them. By putting the Russian state at the center of the picture, and presenting Ukrainians and Belorussians as part of the Russian people, the textbook projected a triune Russian nation as the focus of the Soviet Union.[36]

This was not simply a revival of pre-1917 Russian patriotism, though. Twenty years of *likbez* and mass primary education had transformed the situation: the narratives of nationhood were now able to reach a far wider audience than had previously been the case. Millions of Russians—all but the very elderly—had been taught to read and write their own language. They had come into the towns, had begun to read newspapers regularly, to listen to the radio, and to go to the cinema. They were thus drawn within the radius of conscious Soviet citizenship. This was the first Russian mass patriotism, and it took a Soviet statist form.

Since school resources were inadequate, however, many teachers were poorly qualified and children often distracted by other matters; students and the general public tended to oversimplify the historical doctrines being put before them. The new historiography was after all quite complex and difficult to understand. If tsarist Russia really had been a "prison of the peoples," then how could its expansion have been "progressive?" And how could the struggle of the revolutionary movement against it have been justified? A question at a Leningrad lecture summed up the dilemma. A student had just read about the late-eighteenth-century general Suvorov as a "people's hero"; "without doubt," he commented, "Suvorov was a brilliant military leader who never experienced defeat, but at the same time he was himself an instrument of tsarist policy, the Gendarme of Europe policy. So is it really right to call him a people's hero?"[37] Most children, and indeed most teachers, did not trouble with these quandaries: what they retained in their imaginations was a simple-minded Russian military and statist patriotism carried over from the tsarist to the Soviet state, without any of the sharp breaks or dialectical subtleties the new doctrine required.

One new element in Russian-Soviet patriotism was that it now delineated itself by contrast with the United States. Already in the 1920s Maiakovskii had written an ode to the Brooklyn Bridge, extolling its "steel-wrought mile" as a triumph of technology that Russia should emulate. He insisted, though, that Americans were brash, hypocritical, and obsessively mercenary. He evoked the imagined surprise of Americans at seeing Russians working enthusiastically to fulfill five-year plans without the driving force of money: "Gentlemen! You have long been used / To buying constructive energy with money. / You will never understand, plump gentlemen, / The roots of the zeal of our Communards. . . . / Your famous swift America / We shall catch up and overtake."[38]

"Catch up and overtake" became a universally understood cliché, even without its referent: it indicated one of the priorities of the regime. The formulation implied a respect for the United States that Stalin directly encouraged, recommending that Russian "revolutionary élan" be tempered by "American efficiency" if it was not to deteriorate into either daydreaming or an obsession with issuing decrees. "The combination of Russian revolutionary élan with American efficiency," he stated, "is the essence of Leninism in party work."[39] The new Russian-Soviet patriotism contained cells of Americanism encoded in its genetic structure, with both positive and negative signs. The United States was both opponent and model, with fateful implications for the future.

We should note that the rehabilitation of Russia was entirely imperial and statist, not ethnic. It was, if you like, neo-rossiiskii, not russkii. Stalin despised ethnic Russia, and during the 1930s he never ceased to pursue policies aimed at the destruction of its two most important citadels: the Orthodox Church and the village commune. In addition Russian literature, art, and music that did not conform to the new state-imposed canon was suppressed or at best subject to unpredictable persecution. Nor was korenizatsiia terminated altogether, even though its operation was modified to the benefit of Russians in the 1930s.

The new patriotism may have been statist, but that did not stop Russian people from responding warmly to it. They identified with the state because it defended them and because it symbolized the broad boundaries and the multiethnic solidarity they liked to think of as characteristic of their nation. Their reaction can be seen in the enthusiastic reception given to Sergei Eizenshtein's film *Aleksandr Nevskii,* released in 1938. The film evoked the thirteenth-century struggle of the people of Novgorod—presented straightforwardly as Russians—against the Teutonic Knights. Aleksandr Nevskii, their prince, was projected as cunning, humorous, resolute, heroic, able to inspire the mass of ordinary people against scheming and disloyal opponents. The Orthodox Church was much in evidence, but merely as a symbol of national identity, without any religious significance. At the very end, for instance, Aleksandr chooses the cathedral porch as the setting for his final peroration warning that "anyone who comes to Russia with the sword shall perish by the sword."

This film provided a reassuring linkage of historical symbols with a contemporary message. A Red Army officer commented, "The film touched me to the depths of my soul. It is a genuine masterpiece of Soviet cinematography. The unforgettable 'battle on the ice' characterizes the patriotism of the Russian people, their unwavering bravery and their deep love for their motherland." Or, as a metal worker put it: "The words of Aleksandr Nevskii, pronounced seven hundred years ago, are relevant even now. We will answer every blow of the enemy with a triple blow. The Russian people have [always] beaten their enemies, are beating them [now], and will continue to beat them."[40] One can imagine how comforting such declarations were to Russians facing what they already knew might be the most destructive invasion in their history. In this way even legends and historical episodes from seven hundred years earlier could be drawn on to inspire mass patriotism in the 1930s.

Were these changes both in national policy and in their popular resonance a tacit admission that the Change of Landmarks school had been right all along? Was this the "great retreat" they had anticipated?[41] Not really, because the messianic vision of the emancipation of humanity through an international proletarian movement had not been abandoned. But the process by which it was to be realized had been substantially reshaped. Now, rather than through international revolution, the goal was to be reached through the operations of the Soviet Union as a great power. This was certainly a change of direction, but it was not really a "great retreat." On the contrary, it coincided with and helped to generate the most frenzied crisis of Russian-Communist messianism, the "great terror" of the late 1930s.

## Russians and Jews

This new-style Russian mass patriotism was especially worrying for the Jews. In its early stages the Soviet project had been as much Jewish as Russian. The Jews, like the Russians, and perhaps even more so, had inherited from their past a messianic tradition that had found little sustenance in the everyday life of prerevolutionary Russia. The Jews were then the most oppressed nationality: the majority of them lived in the Pale of Settlement, in the towns and shtetls of Poland, Belorussia, Ukraine, and Novorossiia. A skilled, educated, or affluent minority lived (sometimes illegally) in the main cities of the empire, where they were first guild merchants, lawyers, doctors, bankers, professors, actors, musicians, and artists. Even before 1917, most of these urban Jews were becoming thoroughly Russified: they usually brought their children up in the Russian language and culture and drifted away from the synagogue.

We have seen that Jews had been prominent in the various wings of the Russian revolutionary movement, and that Trotskii was the most consistent internationalist among them. In April 1917 three of the nine members of the Bolshevik Central Committee were Jews, and in August six out of twenty-one were.[42] During the early years of the new regime Jews occupied several key positions: Trotskii was People's Commissar for Military Affairs; Sverdlov was chairman of the Central Executive Committee of the Congress of Soviets and also secretary of the Communist Party; Zinovev was chairman of the Comintern; and Kamenev and Zinovev headed the party committees of Moscow and Petrograd-Leningrad.

Jews were less well represented in the party as a whole: according to the 1922 membership census, there were 19,600 of them, just over 5 percent of members, and their share declined gradually thereafter, though it remained high in Ukraine, at around 12 percent, and especially in Belorussia, at 24 percent. In the government they remained prominent well into the 1930s: in 1936 six out of twenty people's commissars were Jews. Overall they held about 6 percent of senior administrative posts. In a sense they took over the position held by the Germans in the tsarist administration, that of an ethnic group influential well beyond their proportion in the population owing to their superior education and their strong attachment to the ruling system.[43]

The Soviet Union offered new and exciting opportunities to all Jews, not just those who aspired to high political positions. The Pale of Settlement was abolished, along with all other forms of anti-Jewish discrimination. As the most literate Soviet nationality, Jews seized their opportunities and flocked into educational institutions, especially at the higher and specialized levels. Between the mid-1920s and mid-1930s they formed 13 to 15 percent of the student body, while in 1934–1935, 18 percent of *aspiranty* (research students) were Jews. In Ukraine in 1923 they formed 47.4 percent of all students, nearly twice as many as the Ukrainians themselves. They went on from there to become prominent in the arts and in many of the professions, as managers, accountants, engineers, architects, agronomists, journalists, professors, and resarchers.[44]

The new opportunities attracted Jews in large numbers from the shtetls to the cities. These were mostly young Jews eager to escape from a relatively restrictive home environment and participate in the Soviet social construction project. Already by 1926 21 percent of Jewish marriages were to non-Jewish partners, a much higher level than before 1917. In 1926 nearly 25 percent of Soviet Jews declared their mother tongue to be Russian, and in 1939 the proportion had grown to 54.6 percent. Large numbers of Jews were, consciously or by inertia, breaking their ties with a synagogue-Yiddish background. While remaining aware of being Jewish, they were not only learning Russian (if it was not already their native language) but also assimilating to Russian culture.[45] As Vitalii Rubin, later a prominent Sinologist, put it, "All the Jews knew that they were Jewish but considered everything related to Jewishness as a thing of the past. . . . There was no active intention of renouncing one's Jewishness. The question simply did not exist."

He was exaggerating slightly, but among big-city Jews in the 1920s and 1930s such an outlook was common. It is summarized by one scientist, describing the situation in an Odessa school in the 1930s: "In my class, at least thirty out of thirty-five pupils were Jewish. Most knew some Yiddish. Although we spoke Russian among ourselves, our speech was sprinkled with many Yiddish words and expressions. I never experienced any anti-Semitism during all my school years. We did not feel separate from the rest of the 'Soviet people.' In school we did not study any Jewish history, but devoted a lot of time to Russian history and literature. We Jewish pupils perceived it as our history and literature, not realizing that we were strangers in the country. This was the paradox: we considered ourselves part of an indivisible Russian nation although we knew that we were Jews."[46]

This compound sense of national identity—feeling Jewish, Russian, and Soviet, and seeing no contradiction between them—was common among urbanized Jews in the 1930s. They were among the most convinced and goal-directed of Soviet citizens; they believed passionately in building an international socialist community in which ethnic distinctions would persist merely as colorful relics.

Even then, however, popular anti-Semitism sometimes broke into their consciousness. The journalist Viktor Perelman recalled that when he was a child in Moscow in the 1930s Russian teenagers would shout at him on the street, *"Eh, Abramchik, evrei!"* (Hey, Abramchick, you Jew!) Once he was attacked and had to defend himself with his fists. Significantly, however, he never told his mother what had happened: "Possibly I intuitively sensed that, however much she might love me, she would be as helpless as me in the face of these adolescent street bullies." Moreover, such incidents did not fit into his family's view of the world. Once, when he spoke in a way which implied that Jews were somehow distinct, his mother retorted: "You should be ashamed of yourself! What do you mean by 'us' and 'them'? I am Jewish by nationality, but I am proud to have grown up among the great Russian people. . . . As long as the party and the Soviet authorities exist, the Jewish people will not need anyone's protection."[47]

The fact that Jews were prominent in the Soviet administration meant that they were conspicuous in the OGPU, the militia, and the procuracy, which from the late 1920s onward played a leading role in collectivization and dekulakization, as well as in the closing of churches and arrest of priests. Of course many other nationalities worked in those organizations too, notably Russians, but the prejudiced and ill-inclined could always portray these destructive operations as part of a Jewish conspiracy. Popular resentment of the Communists could easily take anti-Semitic forms.

In the late 1930s some Jews were worried that the new Russophile party line would encourage such attitudes. During the terror many Jews were arrested, but not proportionately more than other nationalities. However, the fact that many high-profile defendants were accused of "Trotskyism" did provide an anti-Semitic "hidden transcript" to the show trials. In January 1939 V. I. Blium, a prominent theater critic, wrote to Stalin complaining that "the character of Soviet patriotism is being distorted . . . and starting to take on all the features of racist nationalism." The younger generation, he warned, had never seen bourgeois nationalism at work, still less the Jewish pogroms unleashed by the tsarist regime, and so they did not realize "that we cannot defeat the fascist enemy with his own weapon (racism) but only with a much better weapon, internationalist socialism."[48]

## Soviet Celebrations

With an acceptable history now in place, the present needed to be taken care of. How were the Soviet peoples, and especially the Russians, to regain a sense of their own community? We have seen that in the early years the Soviet leaders had difficulty devising celebrations which satisfied both popular feeling and the requirements of ideology. The effort to find such an effective combination continued for most of the 1920s and 1930s. On the whole during the 1920s emphasis was placed on relatively small-scale events, involving the workforce of a single enterprise or institution. Thus in 1922 the famous Putilov works in Petrograd were renamed "Red Putilov." Mass choral singing rang out as the old title was pulled down and the new erected; the workers then went in procession around the factory bearing torches, in a patent reference to the *krestnyi khod*, the procession of the cross around the Orthodox parish church. Life-cycle events were marked with new ceremonies, such as "Octobering" in place of baptism. Trotskii was a leading supporter of these experiments, and they were largely abandoned after his exile in 1927.[49]

Gradually celebrations took on more centralized and hierarchical forms. May Day and the anniversary of the revolution on November 7 would culminate in a parade through Red Square watched by the leaders from atop the Lenin Mausoleum, which had become the Soviet Union's most sacred space. They would line up, their order determined by an ever more rigid protocol, to take the salute. The sequence of the march defined the new social hierarchy: first came the armed forces, then industrial workers, then students, and finally collective farmers. The order in which the workers marched reflected the success of their enterprises in fulfilling and over-fulfilling the plan, with shock workers and Stakhanovites at the head.[50]

During the late 1920s and 1930s "Soviet time" gradually assumed a more settled form and challenged the ecclesiastical calendar. Harvest Day in October supplanted Pokrov (the festival of the Intercession), and May Day replaced Easter. Preparations for each began weeks in advance, highlighted in the local press. Instructions went out that production targets should be fulfilled in time for the festival, so that a new workshop or block of apartments could be solemnly handed over to the new owners during the celebration itself.

As late as the early 1930s, two-thirds of families in towns were celebrating religious festivals to the exclusion of Soviet ones. But this changed fairly rapidly thereafter, as churches were closed and industrial production schedules became tighter. Moreover, pleasurable public events, like soccer matches, film shows, music, and dancing were scheduled on Soviet festivals, to attract ordinary people to them. Special allocations of scarce goods and groceries would be sent to retail stores in the days preceding a festival, so that the public could rejoice on a full stomach, celebrate the new abundance, and feel gratitude to their leaders.[51]

Soviet festivals became occasions for rewarding success publicly by distributing certificates and medals. Beginning in 1936 festivals were decreed for certain favored professions: the railwaymen, naval and air force personnel, and athletes (fizkulturniki); after the war miners, radio personnel, artillery and tank soldiers were added. Soviet elections, since they contained no political competition, became public celebrations, accompanied by music, dancing, and merry-making in public places.[52]

The All-Union Physical Culture parades held periodically in Moscow were important in delineating the Soviet Union as a new kind of multinational collective. Not only did delegations from the Union republics pledge their loyalty to Stalin and demonstrate their physical fitness to undertake tasks of production or defense, according to the needs of the fatherland; but they also displayed aspects of their home culture or economy: the Uzbeks the construction of a canal to irrigate cotton production, the Georgians the harvesting of grapes and tea. They wore national costumes and performed folk dances, but only in a stylized and pre-approved form: the spontaneous merry-making, let alone the drunkenness, of folk festivals was not permitted. In July 1939 the delegation from the Russian Federation led the way, carrying a banner that read, "First among equals," confirming the current Pravda line on Russia's status within the USSR.[53]

For many participants the processions were most likely tedious and even embarrassing. Nonetheless, such feelings could give way to sudden elation at being identified with a huge collective. One Soviet student who later emigrated described his feelings: "Most of the participants—including Komsomol members—felt some inner resistance, something akin to embarrassment and humiliation, at the necessity of carrying 'Bolshevik icons.' . . . Sometimes one's sense of humiliation would suddenly give way to an opposite feeling—a sense of extreme pride and feverish enthusiasm." This was part of the Soviet drive to reforge the individual so that he would find his fulfillment in the collective.[54]

The new era also required its own heroes. One such figure widely promoted was the Donbass coalminer Aleksei Stakhanov, who achieved incredible output rates during ordinary work shifts. This acclaim was entirely in the consciousness-raising spirit of the regime, but its focus on the individual ran counter to established Russian labor patterns, which were collectivist. Stakhanovites' feats required the cooperation of colleagues to deliver materials and spare parts, keep the conveyer belt moving, lighting and heating working normally, and so on. Their monopoly of publicity and reward was resented by their colleagues, and some of them were physically assaulted.[55]

More widely applauded were the exploits of the aviationists and polar explorers, perhaps because they were *not* wholly planned, and certainly airmen and explorers were not exploiting ordinary workers. In 1932 Otto Shmidt led a crew of polar explorers in the ship *Cheliuskin,* which traversed the Arctic Sea route in one navigational season. But on a second voyage in 1933–1934 it was trapped by pack ice and then sank, leaving 104 people stranded on a remote ice floe. The hastily organized air rescue aroused genuine public concern, then rejoicing when it was successfully accomplished, and the whole narrative soon became a sacred text celebrating the heroism, resourcefulness, and technological sophistication of Soviet society. *Izvestiia* proclaimed, "Technology has conquered nature; man has conquered death." When the explorer Ivan Papanin landed at the North Pole and established a base camp there, he and his fellow explorers claimed that they did not feel alone in the icy wastes: "no distance can separate us, citizens of the USSR, from our country, the first socialist country in the world, from the Bolshevik Party, or from the warmth of our people."[56]

A couple of years later the record-breaking flights of Valerii Chkalov, first from Moscow to the Soviet far east, then across the North Pole to the United States, called forth comparable rejoicing. They provided a new opportunity to envisage not only the sheer size and diversity of the USSR but also the prospect that it would be made manageable by modern communications and transport systems. At the same time the hierarchy of place was preserved by the fact that Stalin welcomed the pioneers back and celebrated their feats in Red Square and the Kremlin. The Soviet Union was now being represented as a concentric space centered on Moscow, but with its brightest perspectives in the east: the immense frozen land of Siberia, which could be conquered only by the most up-to-date technology combined with heroism and high collective morale.[57]

A new song of 1936 summed up the motifs of size, diversity, freedom, and perpetual readiness for defense of the borders, while also suggesting that the Soviet Union was a huge family:

> Broad is my native land.
> It has many forests, fields and rivers.
> I don't know of any other country
> Where a man breathes so freely.
>
> From Moscow to the very borders,
> From the southern mountains to the northern seas,
> A man walks as the master
> of his immense motherland.
>
> But we will knit our brows severely,
> If the enemy wants to break us.
> We love the motherland as we would our bride.
> We protect her as we would our affectionate mother.[58]

The cities were becoming showcases of the new socialist way of life, and they also tacitly served to delineate its hierarchy—since collective farm workers, still the majority of the Russian population, were deprived of the passports needed to enter them. The cozy but ramshackle and semirural appearance of most Russian towns was giving way, not to rectilinear, functional glass buildings, as one might have expected in the 1920s, but to neo-Baroque palaces in stone and stucco. Moscow, as the pinnacle of the hierarchy, had its own General Plan for Reconstruction, approved only in 1935 but actually started some years earlier. The traders' stalls in Okhotnyi Riad gave way to the monumental edifices of Gosplan and the

Moskva Hotel, while the old Tverskaia Street was substantially widened and became Gorkii Street, a succession of voluptuous facades with arches, columns, and capitals, embellished with banners and statues of workers and soldiers. These were cities designed for massive celebratory parades converging on Red Square and the Kremlin at the center.[59]

The new architecture epitomized what Vladimir Paperny has called "Culture Two." Whereas early Soviet "Culture One" had been modernist, austere, antihierarchical, internationalist, and unspecific as to place, "Culture Two" was traditional, sensual, hierarchical, ethnically marked, and geographically specific. It answered the Soviet peoples' need for stability and a definite identity, a sense of place, time, and tradition.[60]

Perhaps the most extraordinary aspect of the new capital was its underground people's palaces. On the Moscow Metro, everyday mass travel was elevated into progress through an empyrean realm, a prefiguration of Communist abundance. Vast, democratic cavern-palaces were constructed, with baroque, classical, and avant-garde architectural motifs reassembled in new configurations and fulfilling new functions. Murals celebrated the history of the revolution, economic development, and the friendship of the Soviet peoples, like the series of friezes in the Kievskaia Station depicting scenes from the history of Russia's relationship with Ukraine. The ensembles were lit, not by the sun, but by evenly glowing arc-lights whose provenance was unclear, but which seemed to fulfill the promise both of the 1912 futurist opera by Burliuk and Kruchenykh, "Victory over the Sun," and of Lenin's declaration that "Communism = Soviet power plus electrification of the whole country."[61]

## Sport and "Physical Culture"

Public activities that had an element of genuine competition and unpredictability were the most popular. Hence the importance of sport. The Communist leaders had seen the potential value of sport from the outset, but its meaning subtly changed during the 1930s. The Third Komsomol Congress of 1920 had proclaimed that sport should help to create "harmoniously developed human beings, creative citizens of Communist society," specifically by preparing them for work and for defending their country. A Union-wide fitness program known as *fizkultura* was launched in 1931 under the slogan "Be Ready for Work and Defense."[62]

At this stage party sentiment still favored general physical development for everyone and opposed specialization, competition, or widespread spectator sports. By the mid-1930s, however, a different view became dominant: that watching, say, skilled soccer players was an excellent means to provide new townsfolk with a way of filling their leisure time, generating a kind of local patriotism—and perhaps also of getting out of cramped communal apartments. Like many other social facilities and welfare benefits, sports teams were formed at the workplace by the trade unions: in Moscow the Lokomotiv team represented railway workers; Spartak the producers' cooperatives; and Krasnoe Znamia the cotton textile workers. In Stalingrad, Traktor was drawn from the town's best-known factory; in Kharkov the team was drawn from Selmash (the agricultural machinery works). The armed forces also promoted sports: the Central House of the Red Army (TsDKA) sponsored one of the best Moscow teams, and another, Dinamo, was set up by the security police (though this identity was not widely publicized). Top players remained employees of their firms, while actually devoting most of their time to practice and exercise for the game: they became de facto professionals while remaining nominal amateurs.[63]

The organization of sport as mass spectacle had already begun in the 1920s and 1930s. As early as 1927 it was reported from the Donbass that "big games draw so many spectators that the mines are completely empty." By the late 1930s most major cities had reasonably capacious stadiums. In 1936 a national soccer league was set up to give structure to the competitions and to stimulate public interest, in line with the general tendency of the time to create regulated hierarchical structures geared toward publicly rewarding achievement. The teams were all from large towns: among the twenty-six in the first division, six were from Moscow, five from Leningrad, and two each from Kiev, Kharkov, and Tbilisi. Sports associations also took a leading part in organizing festival parades, to show off their progress and advertise their activities.[64]

By the early 1940s sport, whether played or watched, met the need for a mass urban occupation that gave people health, excitement, involvement, identification with a place, commitment to competitive excellence, and a hierarchy of achievement. Even at this stage, however, it did not encourage ethnic identification. The mass sports competitions, Spartakiads, were organized by towns and regions, not by republic, and the national sports team, when it began to enter international competitions after the war, represented the Soviet Union, not Russia or any other nationality.

## The Family

Social memory and social values are transmitted above all in the family. But, like all other Russian institutions, the family underwent such upheavals between 1914 and 1945 that it was seldom able to play that role effectively. It is not only that parents and grandparents died or were scattered and lost by the turmoil of those three decades; in addition, family fortunes were dispersed, and homes were expropriated or occupied by importunate outsiders. Books, tools and equipment, gardens and orchards— all the paraphernalia that enable children to learn skills from their parents—went missing, had to be sold, or were confiscated. Cultural and social capital was degraded on a huge scale.

On top of all that, the family as such came under legislative attack. During the 1920s the regime abolished nearly all inheritance and property rights associated with the family, erased the distinction between legitimate and illegitimate children, and simplified divorce to the point where one partner could achieve it simply by informing the other. Women were given greater freedom, for example, to obtain an abortion on demand, and their (scant remaining) property rights were equalized with those of men. The loosening of family relationships generated a sharp rise in the divorce rate, an even sharper escalation in the number of abortions, and a fall in the birth rate. Large numbers of orphans appeared on city streets: they would form bands and hang around markets and railways stations, begging or even attacking passers-by to obtain food, clothing, drink, or money. State orphanages could not cope and often became nurseries of crime and disease.[65] The orphans were the victims of social dislocation generally, but the state's family legislation certainly did not assist their reintegration into society. Women were supposed to be the beneficiaries of the new laws, but in practice many found that they were left shouldering family responsibilities by men who exploited the new freedom to abscond.

By the mid-1930s the regime had decided that unstable families and a low birth rate were endangering economic growth and weakening the country's defenses. Divorce was tightened and granted only after a court hearing. Men who fell short on their alimony payments were pursued. Abortion was prohibited except where childbirth would pose a serious health risk. Weddings, which had been conducted casually in dingy offices, were made more solemn and ceremonial; registration officials would pronounce short homilies to remind couples of their responsibilities. The right to inherit property was restored. In Soviet conditions property was modest, but significant because of the general scarcity: inheritance might, for example, include an urban apartment, in the circumstances a priceless acquisition. Since the offspring of unregistered unions had no such rights, the notion of "legitimacy" was tacitly reinstated.[66]

The regime's attitude to women was transformed. The state did not wholly abandon the ideal of giving them equal status with men but nevertheless began to regard them as having different functions. In 1936 Kaganovich addressed the wives of senior officials in the transport commissariat. He told them that "concern for [their] husbands" should be their priority. "Cook good food for them, don't cause them any stress, create a comfortable home and a good, relaxing family atmosphere." Galina Shtange, wife of a professor of railway engineering, commented in her diary, "If we have any strength left over, we can join in production work as well. He will not stand in our way if we do, but that is not what's important."[67]

A family's ability to transmit traditions, skills, and values to the younger generation hinged on whether one of its members had a professional specialism that could be adapted to the new society. Some qualifications, like those of lawyers or clergymen, were useless—or even dangerous—in the new circumstances. Others, like those of doctor, linguist, army officer, engineer, or scientist, could be adapted with little difficulty. Yet others, such as musician or journalist, might be turned to account with ingenuity, adaptability, and a capacity for compromise.[68]

Another way of preserving social capital was to obtain protection from someone influential in the new regime. Dmitrii Zhurnalistov had been a zemstvo statistician from a minor noble family in Chernigov oblast. He had known the revolutionaries Shchors and Podvoiskii, and in the early 1920s he used this acquaintance to keep the family home in Starodub from being communalized—though the cherry orchard in which it stood was expropriated and cut down, exactly as in Chekhov's famous play. Living in the old home ensured that there was private space for books, music, and games, and made it easier for the children to find marriage partners from similar backgrounds. Dmitrii's son Ivan, who trained in law and economics just before the revolution, was able to work as an administrator in construction trusts, and he eventually became a senior ministerial official, with a central Moscow apartment, a telephone, and a well-appointed dacha. From there Ivan was able to ensure that his own daughter received a good education, and he was able to place her in a promising first job.[69] In this way one family repositioned itself without losing all inherited cultural and social wealth.

The Arbat, the quarter where the Zhurnalistovs lived, lies just to the west of central Moscow. In the nineteenth century it was the home of several prominent writers and thinkers, and became a bastion of the Slavophile aristocracy and intelligentsia. Many of its tree-lined streets and pleasant, spacious buildings survived Moscow's redevelopment: one of them was Alexander Herzen's house, which became the headquarters of the Soviet Writers' Union. Its significance for the transmission of culture was celebrated in the 1960s in a much-performed guitar song by Bulat Okudzhava, himself the son of a prominent Soviet official. He calls Arbat his "calling," his "joy and sorrow," his "religion." "From love of you there is no cure, / Though one may love forty thousand other streets. / Ah, Arbat, my Arbat, / You are my fatherland, / Never shall I be able to get to know you to the end!"[70] Such was the importance of a stable and cultured environment for Russians: those who had it were able to recapture prerevolutionary traditions and re-create an enduring sense of national identity.

## The New Social Hierarchy

One result of the "great terror" was that prerevolutionary specialists and administrators were finally replaced by "Red specialists." A new society was forming. Officially the leading class was the working class, but actually the contours of the emerging hierarchy were determined by the nomenklatura system and its associated patron-client relations, by the passport system, and by the "hierarchy of consumption." One way to rise was through the Stakhanovite and "shock-worker" movements. Individuals who achieved record-breaking results on their shift were rewarded with higher pay, priority in the allocation of separate apartments, and the distinction of being marked out for promotion—eventually out of the working class into the Soviet "new class."

An important marker of social status was the award of certificates and medals. Just as Napoleon created his own hierarchy in postrevolutionary France through the *Légion d'Honneur,* so the Soviet leaders decreed the establishment of honors based on distinction in labor or on the battlefield.

The Order of the Red Banner was instituted in September 1918 for military feats, and it was followed in 1920 by the Order of the Red Banner of Labor. The highest civilian and military awards, the Order of Lenin and the Order of the Red Star, were decreed in 1930. Holders of medals were entitled to priority in receiving apartments, and sometimes to extra space and lower rent payments, as well as to higher pensions, some free travel, and free places in sanatoria and rest homes.[71] In this way the asperities and shortages of Soviet society were eased for them. They were also more likely than average workers to be elected to the Supreme Soviet or to local soviets, or promoted out of the working class into the nomenklatura hierarchy.

Crucial to social advancement was the art of filling in questionnaires, that is, of reconfiguring one's life story to conform with official expectations. In order to obtain any benefit—a job, an apartment, a place at a training establishment—one had to answer questions laid out on a form about one's social origin, education and training, political record, work record, and so on, and also obtain a reference *(kharakteristika)* from one's workplace. It was important at this stage to keep quiet about certain matters and to lay out others in the language of Soviet political correctness, in other words, to "speak Bolshevik," as Stephen Kotkin has put it. This was not just a matter of technique: one had to learn to think of one's life in certain ways and even to reshape it in order to do the kind of things that would look good on a questionnaire. Then one needed the protection of a powerful individual to secure the necessary *kharakteristika.*[72]

In the 1920s the ruling class still retained some of the characteristics of an idealistic underground movement of students or recently demobilized soldiers, accustomed to deprivation, hardship, and mutual aid. The lifestyle of many of them remained modest, even austere, and their behavior direct, unvarnished, as they liked to say, "proletarian," without the frills and euphemisms of an established high society. They remained inspired by the scientific certainty of ultimate victory, despite all setbacks on the way, and they were sustained by the brotherhood of those who have been through great ordeals together. For the first fifteen or so years after the revolution, the leather-jacketed commissar with a Mauser at his hip, rough, plain-spoken, vigilant, ready to coerce and be violent when necessary— that had been the ideal on which the party's first upwardly mobile young people had modeled themselves.[73]

During the mid- and late 1930s this model was gradually replaced by one that was altogether softer and less abrasive. The reshaped ruling class had acquired aspirations to comfort and a stylishly affluent lifestyle that the first generation had denounced as *meshchanstvo* (petty bourgeois mentality). The ideal taking shape was that of the *kulturnyi chelovek*—a term closer to "gentleman" in meaning than the "cultured person" which is its direct translation. But of course the aristocratic-bourgeois connotations of "gentleman" (as well as the exclusive gender) are misplaced. Lenin had always insisted that one of the main aims of the revolution was to create a new culture both of work and of leisure, in which people would behave toward each other with courtesy and tact, train themselves properly for their work, perform their duties conscientiously and punctually, and observe high standards of personal hygiene. All this meant raising ordinary people to new levels of consciousness, and this he felt was one of the most important tasks of the party, especially once it had accomplished the seizure of power.[74]

Many written genres were enlisted in the drive to improve standards of behavior. The simplest was the notice hung up in the communal apartment giving instructions on who was responsible for cleaning public places and when, forbidding spitting, walking the corridor with muddy boots, or making a noise during quiet hours. For factory walls the Central Institute of Labor, under Aleksei Gastev, produced posters on "How to Work" and a series of guides to the "scientific organization of labor." Pavel Kerzhentsev, a senior propaganda official, published three high-circulation brochures entitled *Organize Yourself!; The Fight for Time;* and *How to Read a Book.* As the titles implied, he gave advice on how to take a methodical and precise approach to work routines, how to avoid wasting time by smoking, gossiping, long tea breaks, or dawdling in the toilet, and how to engage in self-education by systematically perusing books, journals, and newspapers, taking notes, asking oneself questions, and discussing the contents with colleagues.[75]

Among Kerzhentsev's practical recommendations for reading we find the following: "If you aren't able to read in a library, find the best-lit and quietest corner that you can. Check whether the room needs airing. . . . It is best to read at a table, having selected a comfortable chair or bench. If you need to make extracts while reading, lay the paper or note book to the right of your book, and place the inkwell alongside. Have your dictionary of foreign words, your encyclopedia or other such reference books (which you may find helpful) on the left-hand side."[76] He seems to have in mind something not far short of a professor's private study; the tenant of an average communal apartment was more likely to have to snatch a few precious moments on a rickety table used mainly for eating meals and doing the ironing, without encyclopedias and probably with a radio blaring in one corner. This kind of discrepancy between the *kulturnyi* ideal and squalid everyday reality was to become one of the main sources of frustration in the life of the average urban Russian.

Expectations of a modicum of privacy and domestic comfort were sustained by a number of journals, especially those aimed at women, such as *Rabotnitsa, Krestianka, Obshchestvennitsa,* and *Sovetskaia zhenshchina.* Though containing much more overt political content, they had something in common with contemporary British journals like *Vogue* or *Homes and Gardens:* they offered tips on how to dress, how to cook tasty and nourishing meals, and how to keep an apartment clean, tidy, and attractive. Their precepts were less exotic and more functional but still provided information about cars, furniture, cosmetics, radio sets, and suitable toys for children. The advice was projected as advancing "the Soviet way of life," so it was accompanied by propaganda for the next elections and portraits of prize-winning milkmaids. But *The Book of Tasty and Nutritious Food,* published in 1939, was unrelenting in its concern for material well-being. It featured recipes for game, roast veal, hollandaise sauce, and carp stuffed with kasha, the ingredients for which—to put it mildly—would not normally be found in the average Soviet *Gastronom* (grocery). For most readers this book would fulfill the same function as an account of a $5,000 ocean-liner cruise: it was unashamedly aimed at those with access to privileged special stores.[77]

The discrepancy between these material aspirations and what was normally available intensified the drive toward blat, or patron-client networks, as a way of getting around the economy of shortage. It also generated a tension between admiration of Western standards of living, especially those of the United States, and rejection of the Western way of life.

The fractious and unwanted intimacy of the communal apartment did not resemble these idyllic scenes at all. Those townsfolk who could do so escaped to the nearby countryside in the summer, for weekends, or in the evenings. This relief was made possible by the dacha, the country shack, cottage, or mansion (according to status). The easiest way to rent or buy a dacha was through one's employer. Russians could build dachas themselves, but they still needed land, building materials, and skilled labor, resources that could only be obtained through their employers—or at great expense and some risk on the black market. So the dacha, symbol of freedom, civilized values, and personal choice, was yet another channel of subjection to a personalized hierarchy, another marker of the individual's standing or influence within it.[78]

## Creating a New Literary Canon

During and after the civil war the party did not attempt to impose an authoritative line in literature. Such had never been its aim, and anyway, it lacked a mechanism for doing so. Throughout the 1920s, for their part, writers divided into warring factions, each seeking the party's patronage by presenting themselves as the standard-bearers of the future and of true socialist culture. By the early 1930s, though, the party had decided that it ought to have a role in creating a unifying culture and in inducing writers to accept it. Creative artists, however, are not easy to organize or direct. The party tackled the problem by establishing a Union of Soviet Writers, membership in which would guarantee writers modest privileges—a pleasant apartment, good medical care, an agreeable vacation home—that shielded them from the grosser forms of the Soviet struggle for a minimal standard of living. The union was run by officials—often mediocre writers themselves—appointed under the nomenklatura system. Their manipulation of access to goods and services proved to be just as effective a means of administration in culture as in other walks of life.[79]

The new union aimed to present Soviet literature, not as the denial of the aristocratic and bourgeois heritage, but, on the contrary, as its culmination in a new, all-class mass culture. It was to be nationally inclusive, too. Several distinguished European writers were invited to the first congress—André Malraux, Louis Aragon, Theodor Plievier, Ernst Toller—to substantiate the claim that contemporary Russian literature was building on the best of European culture.[80] As in the field of architecture, modernism was spurned. The new literature was to be largely traditional and realist in form, but its realism was to be specifically "socialist," depicting Soviet society in the light of its great future, its "revolutionary development" ("socialist" rather than "proletarian" because class origin was already becoming less important than in the early years of the revolution).

Many Russian writers who were skeptical about Communist rule supported the initiative. Pasternak and Gorkii, for example, with support from Bukharin, now editor of *Izvestiia,* hoped to use the occasion to reorganize the Soviet literary world on a broad, nonsectarian basis, and to work with European anti-Fascist writers in resisting totalitarian regimes both at home and abroad.[81]

To symbolize its links with Russia's tradition of democratic writing, the new union was given "Herzen's House" on the Tverskoi Boulevard in Moscow, which also became the home of a kind of literary university, the Gorkii Institute of World Literature. Here aspiring young writers, whatever their social background—and there were workers and peasants among them—studied the classics of world literature, from Homer through Dante, Shakespeare, Voltaire, and Goethe, to Tolstoy and finally Gorkii himself. They composed their own first literary efforts, under the guidance of established writers, and had them discussed at seminars of their colleagues. At the pinnacle of the organization, initiating a kind of apostolic succession, was Maksim Gorkii himself. The graduates of the institute constituted a kind of roll-call of the mainstream of Soviet literature. They combined a high and consistent level of (usually rather traditional) literary technique with a desire to establish themselves in the society in which they were growing up and reaching maturity. Their efforts to fulfill the demands of party doctrine constituted "socialist realism" in practice.[82]

At the first Soviet Writers' Union congress, in August 1934, Andrei Zhdanov, the party's chief ideologist, laid down a set of theoretical requirements that writers were to fulfill, which included realism, *narodnost* (writing about the people in a manner accessible to them), and *partiinost* (writing in a "party-minded" spirit).[83] In practice, the ideological prescriptions were perhaps less important than the list of existing works that Zhdanov and others presented as models for the aspiring Soviet writer. This was the "canon," which differed from the biblical one only in that it was to be continually supplemented by the writings of Soviet authors. The archetypical socialist realist novel featured a hero who comes from among the people and draws strength from their simple though untutored wisdom. He encounters society's evils and at first reacts with primitive rage, which is impressive but fruitless. Then, however, with the help of an older, more experienced mentor from the party, he learns to understand and master himself, channel his anger more productively, and overcome weakness and doubt. Drawing on the party's ideology, he locates his place in the decisive historical struggle, keeping constantly in his mind the image of the Great Society of the future. The conflict within himself between "spontaneity" and "consciousness" provides the novels with their spiritual orientation, while the development of the action has many of the attractions of the adventure story.[84]

The socialist realist genre was similar in some ways to the *zhitie,* the traditional Russian saint's life. A far closer parallel, however, is the Puritan spiritual biography of the *Pilgrim's Progress* type. Its hero strives to reach the "magnificent city" by avoiding temptation, mastering his passions, and working within the community to confirm the good, extirpate the evil, and vindicate God's providence. The socialist realist hero is, though, always more closely bound up with his community, with ordinary workers and peasants, than is the Puritan prototype, who is more concerned with individual salvation. What the two heroes have in common is that they are following "a neo-religious doctrine of salvation and rebirth. . . . going beyond the this-worldly and mundane." In keeping with the new inclusiveness of Soviet society, this kind of novel was intended to reflect the consciousness of all social strata. In practice it appealed especially to the young, upwardly mobile members of the new elite of the 1930s to 1950s. This was the kind of self-image and social memory which they, as readers, liked to cultivate, while the authors, for their part, were also creating an ideal image of themselves.[85]

The party was endeavoring to mold not only a new kind of writer but also a new kind of reader. As a result of the loss of social memory, the audience's general culture or even sense of its own past could not be taken for granted. The poet Osip Mandelstam once remarked that the new era had "cast [people] out of their own biographies like balls out of billiard pockets"; the "person without a biography" had become the hero of the age. At any rate, the formation of the reader became one of the principal goals of cultural policy. As a Central Committee resolution of August 1931 stated, "a book should be a powerful means of educating, mobilizing, and organizing the masses toward the goal of economic and cultural construction."[86]

The process began in the schools and continued in the public libraries, which acted both as disseminators of the new culture and as a feedback mechanism to enable the cultural authorities to assess what they were achieving. These institutions now had a near monopoly on the distribution of literary culture: the last commercial publishers were closed during the first five-year plan, while all journals and newspapers were owned by official institutions of one kind or another. Many private libraries had been ransacked or dispersed during the revolution, while others had contracted in the process of *uplotnenie,* so that prerevolutionary books survived only in libraries and in a few reduced and endangered personal collections.

By the mid-1930s schools had stopped using literature as illustrations of sociological theories and had returned to teaching an accepted list of classics, Russian and foreign, intended to mold the aesthetic tastes of young readers. To these the new socialist realist classics were now added. Librarians were exhorted to do more than just hand books out to readers. They were recommended to keep records of each reader on index cards— yet another set of files—noting their interests and encouraging them to develop their tastes. They would hold periodic public discussions of popular works or form readers' circles, where excerpts would be read and evaluated. Reading was no longer a purely private activity: it was socially supported and interpreted, as was appropriate for a public still taking shape.[87]

One might have expected that a literature intended to be popular and accessible to ordinary readers would draw heavily on folklore. Gorkii had supported the idea in his speech to the first Writers' Union congress, claiming that the fundamental mission of folklore was "the striving of primitive working men to ease their own labour and increase its productivity." "The better we come to know the past," he urged, "the more easily, the more deeply and joyfully we shall understand the great significance of the present we are creating."[88] Following his call, anthologies of folklore were published and prerevolutionary collections reissued; performers were encouraged to refresh their memories by using them.

However, folk culture could not simply be carried over into socialist culture without considerable changes. Many Communists felt that folktales reflected a "kulak" mentality, a passive fatalism or superstition. Accordingly, folklorists were encouraged not so much to transmit old material as to reshape it and create their own. Folklore became written and textual rather than oral and improvised—which of course made it easier to censor. Epics were composed about Lenin, Stalin, the revolution, the civil war, and the five-year plans. Iurii Sokolov, the leading folklorist, told singers they should depict "the grandeur of their epoch, tell everyone of the huge gulf between the old and the new life, and show everyone what happiness it is to live in the Soviet Union." The remodeled epics were called *noviny,* "tales of the new," in contrast to the traditional *byliny,* or "tales of the past."[89] So the Soviet state even created its own synthetic folklore.

The prospect of a new mass culture helped to attract the émigré composer Sergei Prokofiev back to the Soviet Union. In 1935, after attending a concert of his own music in the Urals, he wrote in a newspaper article:

> I must say that the workers of Cheliabinsk have shown much more interest in the program than some sophisticated audiences in European and American cities. . . . What is needed above all is *great* music that would correspond both in form and content to the grandeur of the epoch. . . . At the same time, in turning his attention to serious, significant music, the composer must bear in mind that in the Soviet Union music is addressed to millions of people who formerly had little or no contact with music. It is this new mass audience that the modern Soviet composer must attempt to reach. . . . I believe the type of music needed is what one might call "light-serious" or "serious-light" music. . . . It is not the old simplicity that is needed, but a new kind of simplicity.[90]

On his return he composed perhaps the best-known example of the new-style folklore, *Peter and the Wolf.*

Russian was projected as the senior literary culture among the Soviet peoples, patron and protector of the others, which were to develop following the Russian model. The Pushkin celebrations of 1937 (the 100th anniversary of the poet's death) exemplified these themes. The imperial and multinational aspect of Pushkin's work was emphasized. His poem "Exegi monumentum" was much quoted, for it contained the lines, "Stories of me will spread all over Great Rus, and my name will be uttered in every one of its tongues, by the proud descendant of the Slavs and by the Finn, by the now still savage Tunguz, and by the Kalmyk, son of the steppes." The implication was both that Pushkin would be translated into all the Soviet languages, and also that non-Russians would learn Russian, and thus become full Soviet citizens, by reading him.[91] In co-opting Pushkin in this fashion, however, the regime was taking a risk: Pushkin—and other approved past writers, like Gogol, Tolstoi, and Chekhov—were figures too considerable to be forced into the Soviet mold. They remained awkward and irreducible heroes, subtly questioning the culture they were enlisted to endorse, and pointing back to a non-Soviet Russian past.

Pushkin was not the only poet celebrated in this way during the 1930s.

Rustaveli the Georgian and Shevchenko the Ukrainian had their own ju-
bilees, with public readings, discussions, and posters exhibited in schools.
These celebrations were conducted in the native language in Georgia and
Ukraine, in Russian in the RSFSR. Multinationalism and the "friendship
of peoples" were central to Soviet literature. The first Writers' Union congress was postponed for a year while leading Russian writers traveled to
non-Russian republics to acquaint themselves with "native" writers and
their texts. It was important to invite these non-Russians to the congress.
Vladimir Pozner, a French delegate to the congress, evoked their diversity
in his speech: "The representatives of 52 literatures, from Georgians, who
have fifteen centuries of cultural history behind them, to Yakuts, who before 1917 possessed only one book in their language, the Orthodox cate-
chism; from the Russians, who have given the world Pushkin and Tolstoi,
to the Lezgins of Dagestan represented in the congress by an illiterate bard
who sings poems he cannot write down—all these are united within a single Soviet literature by ties stronger than those of blood or language." The
Armenian writer Charents went even further, greeting the congress as an
arena "where we can see emerging before our eyes the image of a single
culture common to humanity."[92]

Russian literature, then, was reframed as *both* Russian *and* international, the culmination of world literature, but now couched in a form accessible to ordinary people, thanks to their schooling, and helping to prepare them for the great tasks of building socialism. The result was a
didactic and homogeneous, even monochrome, culture, which its critics
dismissed as monotonous. It was not primitive or undeveloped; nor did it
rely on vulgar, unformed taste. At one end there were no cheap romances
or thrillers, at the other no experimental, refined, or obscure aestheticism.
Soviet literature was what we might call "middlebrow." As Evgenii Dobrenko
comments, "the egalitarianism of Soviet culture lay not so much in primitive reliance on the 'undeveloped taste of the masses' as in a *comprehensive
strategy of averaging out* and devouring the enclaves of autonomy."[93]

Even artistic literature was written in a semi-bureaucratic style, devoid of semantic ambiguity or richness and bearing only one identifiable
meaning, which could be readily linked with the party's ideology. In
the long run this tendency proved self-defeating: people began reading
texts not for what they stated but for what they implied or even for what
they omitted. Readers became insensitive to the deadeningly omnipresent
norm and reacted only to fleeing aberrations. Cultural communication
became a treacherous quicksand of veiled hints or Aesopian allegories, in

which all but the well-informed reader were completely at sea. This undermining of the connection between printed text and reality meant a return to what Anna Akhmatova called the "pre-Gutenberg era," in which rumor and anecdote took the place of public culture.

For that reason the eventual rediscovery, decades later, of a Russian literature that connected with reality was to contribute significantly to the creation of a non-Soviet Russian identity. In the hidden niches of the Soviet cultural world, that creation was already beginning.

## A Hidden Countercanon

One of the most important functions of a national culture is to monitor memory, to ensure that representations of national life are not too distant from reality. A mendacious account of society cannot serve for very long as the basis of a national culture, for it causes resentment and grief to fester, deprived of outward expression, so that the nation becomes embittered and divided.[94] Yet in the USSR the new heroic, optimistic, forward-looking image projected by the various cultural unions and backed by the censorship suppressed all knowledge of the victims of the catastrophic social processes unfolding during the first five-year plans. It also ignored vital aspects of the mainstream of the Russian cultural tradition, notably Orthodox Christianity.

For those reasons a kind of hidden countercanon began to take shape— totally unknown to the general public—among writers who had been squeezed out of the official journals, who published only trivia there, or who had chosen not even to attempt publication in the stifling cultural atmosphere of the 1930s. I shall examine only three writers here: the novelists Andrei Platonov and Mikhail Bulgakov and the poet Anna Akhmatova. All of them shared with the official culture the messianic impulse and the apocalyptic fear, but they gave expression to these feelings in totally different forms and exposed different elements of Soviet reality. The rediscovery and publication of their most important work from the 1960s onward was a major formative influence on the renewed sense of Russian national identity which emerged at that time.

### Andrei Platonov

The hope and the despair of the ordinary Russian peasant and worker were expressed most adequately and poignantly in the work of Andrei

Platonov. Born in 1899, the son of a railway electrician, he was brought up in a working-class suburb of Voronezh, where he became accustomed to the half-urban, half-rural way of life lived by so many Russians in the late nineteenth and early twentieth century. Voronezh is close to the landscape border where the trees finally give out: south and east the steppes stretch away, apparently endlessly. Platonov's evocations of its immensity have sometimes a visionary and sometimes a despairing quality. He had to give up school at fourteen and take a job as a mechanic in the same locomotive depot as his father, but he continued to study part-time and later entered Voronezh Polytechnic. He became an electrical engineer, working on irrigation projects in the semi-arid steppes of his province, and helping to bring electricity to small towns and villages. Like Lenin, he was convinced that electrification would transform society and enable human beings to take charge of their own destiny, a belief he held tinged with Fedorov's mystic hope in the resurrection of the dead through technology.[95]

During the civil war Platonov was a military reporter for a Red newspaper and became a member of Proletkult, whose upbeat cosmic mysticism he shared. In 1921 he wrote in his newspaper, "The Russian people, in the person of its proletariat, will step forth like an armed machine and conquer the universe . . . The Russian muzhik feels constrained by his fields and has ridden out to plough up the stars."[96] His early stories concerned scientists, technicians, and artisans working on inventions intended to transform the future of humanity. In the course of time, however, the bright, open tones of the early works began to yield to darker perspectives, partly because the coming of NEP postponed indefinitely any hopes for a swift social transformation.

His best-known work, and the one that most effectively conveys his darker vision, was *The Foundation Pit (Kotlovan)*. It was written in 1929–1930, during the first winter of collectivization, but remained completely unpublished until it appeared in an émigré Russian journal in 1969. It was not published in Russia till 1987.[97] The novel's focus is an uncannily accurate anticipation of the real-life fiasco of the planned Palace of Soviets in Moscow—still in the future when he was writing. At its core is the project for an All-Proletarian Home, which is to rise in the center of the town and replace all the previous puny, fenced-off private dwellings: "In a year's time the entire proletariat would leave the old town and its petty properties and take possession of the monumental new home." Nor would it end there, for "in another decade or two, some other engineer would construct a tower, in the very center of the world, where the toiling masses of the whole earth would happily take up their eternal residence."[98]

In the event, the workmen discover in the soil a large number of coffins stored by nearby villagers who expect mass starvation as a result of collectivization. The workers become exhausted and demoralized at the excessive labor and the human cost their idealism demands: "They possessed the meaning of life, which is equivalent to eternal happiness," but "their faces were dour and thin, and instead of life's serenity they had emaciation."[99] The great edifice never rises beyond the foundations, and in the end the unfilled pit becomes a mass grave.

This novel is a *reductio ad absurdum* of the Soviet project of constructing a perfect world in the shape of an international proletarian republic. It builds on the biblical story of the tower of Babel, and also on Chernyshevskii's vision of the Crystal Palace (in his novel *What Is to Be Done?*), which had already been mocked by Dostoevskii and satirized by Evgenii Zamiatin. What is remarkable about Platonov is the way he allows the utopian imagination to take over his characters and saturate their being. Thought becomes action, and action is another form of thought. The abstract and the concrete are mingled incongruously. Voshchev, dismissed and evicted from the company hostel for "ongoing personal weakness and thoughtfulness amid the general tempo of labour," sleeps rough and is found by two workmen who ask him, "What are you doing coming and existing here?" He tells them, "I'm not existing here. . . . I'm only thinking here. . . . My body gets weak without truth, I can't just live on labour. I used to keep thinking at work and I got sacked."[100]

This strange, disjointed language is not just that of the characters but that of the narrator, too. Like his heroes, he feels abstract ideas in his body and translates them into the form of physical movement and effort. He reflects a society where the language of imagination has replaced reality and condemned everyone to the pursuit of mirages. As Joseph Brodsky commented, "Platonov speaks of a nation which in a sense has become the victim of its own language; or, to put it more accurately, he tells a story about this very language which turns out to be capable of generating a fictitious world, and then falls into grammatical dependence on it."[101] He is a writer who senses that utopia has become a prison, that his own greatest hopes have turned into meaningless abstractions, which have then acquired a frightening power over people's minds and actions.

The result is not a satire, whose author stands comfortably outside his subject matter and judges it confidently. Platonov is coming from inside, sharing the hopes of his characters, sharing too their bewilderment and discouragement that things have not turned out as anticipated. Now that we have from the archives so many letters written by ordinary Russians to *Pravda* and to Stalin, we can see that they often expressed themselves in a manner reminiscent of Platonov. He articulated the mood of workers and peasants, their frustrated and fearful utopianism, better than any other writer.

At any rate, in Platonov's vision peasants who simply wish to continue their own way of life become the victims of a giant implacable official machine, which herds them into bewildered and passive collectives. Enthusiasm and optimism cease to be genuine human feelings and become mere tools of power. The foundation pit never bears a great edifice, but it becomes the grave of an orphan girl, Nastia, who should have represented hope for the future, but who actually dies of neglect and disease. Voshchev stands over her and wonders "how Communism could ever come to exist if it didn't appear first of all in a child's feelings and sense of conviction. What use to him now was the meaning of life if there no longer existed a small, trusty being in whom truth would have become joy and movement?"[102]

We now know that Platonov originally intended the following ending: "Will the USSR die like Nastia, or will it grow into a whole person, a new historical society? This anxiety is what provided the theme of the book when the author wrote it. The author may have been mistaken in representing the death of Soviet society through the death of the little girl, but this mistake was occasioned only by excessive anxiety on behalf of something loved, something whose loss is equivalent to the destruction not only of the entire past, but of the future as well."[103]

## Mikhail Bulgakov

Mikhail Bulgakov's upbringing unfitted him for life in the USSR about as comprehensively as can be imagined. He was the son of a professor of theology at Kiev University who was a participant in the early-twentieth-century attempts to bring science, philosophy, and theology closer together. In his youth Mikhail read with enthusiasm the works of the neo-Kantian and idealist thinkers Nikolai Berdiaev, Semen Frank, Lev Shestov, and his own distant relative Sergei Bulgakov. He remained a Christian believer

misplaced in an atheist state and an old-fashioned Russian imperial nationalist stranded in first independent, then Soviet Ukraine. He was,
moreover, a maverick and rebel, a lover of drama in a land where bureaucratic conformity and a grey artistic mediocrity were increasingly de ri-
gueur.[104]

Bulgakov's intersection of utopia and reality takes place in a very different way from Platonov's. The action of his major novel *Master and
Margarita* is set in two cities where the history of humanity reaches a
turning point: Jerusalem at the time of Christ, and Moscow in the 1930s.
In this way the whole scheme of the novel reminds one that in the sixteenth century Moscow was known as the "second Jerusalem." Ironically,
however, the authorial technique transposes science and miracle: the holy
city, Jerusalem, is described with sober realism, and everything that happens there has its clearly identified secular cause, whereas Moscow, the
city of materialism, technology, and atheism, is evoked as a fantastic appa-
rition and becomes the stage for supernatural intervention. There people
suddenly disappear or die; fires break out without cause; material things
change their nature or vanish.

In Moscow the action focuses on literary life. Writers deal in spiritual
values, but without believing in them and for material reasons: for the
apartments they are awarded and the good food served up at the restau-
rant of the "Griboedov House," the Writers' Union headquarters. In one
of the fantasmagoric scenes, Woland awards dollars and fashionable foreign clothes to the audience of the Variety Theater; but after the show
these prizes vanish as magically as they had earlier appeared and audience
members have to travel home in their underwear.

The Master, the writer at the center of the novel, is a creative figure but
not a fighter. He is helpless in dealing with the dimension of power. He is
denounced by a neighbor who covets his apartment. When numerous articles appear criticizing a published extract from his novel, he becomes
anxious and depressed and burns the manuscript. He and his novel are
saved only by the intervention of Margarita, who combines the role of
Faust and Mephistopheles and concludes a pact with the Devil to save the
man she loves.

The Master's literary text on the crucifixion becomes the means for the
completion of the historical drama left incomplete (at least in Bulgakov's
interpretation) at Christ's death. In the Jerusalem chapters of Bulgakov's
novel, Pontius Pilate knows that his dialogues with Christ tell him impor-

tant truths, that they answer a need in himself. He is the cultured and cos-mopolitan urban skeptic who accepts power because it seems to be the dominant reality in this world, but he dimly perceives its emptiness. He delivers Jesus to the executioners because the High Priest and the people, whose support Rome needs, demand it. But he feels the need to complete his interrupted conversation with Jesus. The dialogue of power and love takes place only at the end of the novel in a dimension beyond both Mos-cow and Jerusalem, and thanks only to the mediation of Margarita, at the end of a cosmic ride that lifts Pilate beyond the empirical, power-ridden world of his imperial consulate.

*Master and Margarita* is permeated with apocalyptic imagery, especially that associated with horses. The last three chapters are an elaborate pas-tiche on the Book of Revelation. Moscow and its corrupt, materialistic, power-crazed temples are left behind to burn to the ground, while the Master and Margarita ride with the Four Horsemen of the Apocalypse through unlimited space and time, free Pilate, reunite him with Jesus, and simultaneously complete the Master's text.[105]

Bulgakov's imaginary world is both like Stalin's and the opposite of Sta-lin's. They both believe in absolute truths, in the salvation of humanity, and in the universal struggle between good and evil. Yet Bulgakov's hero will have nothing to do with power and is utterly incompetent in practical matters. His writings reveal truths that politicians cannot grasp and make possible the ultimate reconciliation of truth and power, but only beyond the bounds of this earth.

## Anna Akhmatova

The daughter of an aristocratic family living in Tsarskoe Selo, the imperial residence just outside St. Petersburg, Anna Akhmatova first made her name just before the revolution as the author of delicately crafted love po-etry, a convincing presenter of women's feelings in a literary world domi-nated by men.

After the revolution her kind of verse rapidly went out of fashion, and publishers soon turned away from her, even though she was still popular with the reading public—and even with one Bolshevik leader, the femi-nist Alexandra Kollontai, who called her verse "the poetic expression of the battle of a woman enslaved by bourgeois society." On the other hand, the critic Kornei Chukovskii, who also liked her work, called her "the last

poet of Orthodoxy," which was not calculated to win her favor in ruling
circles. In 1925 an unpublished circular banned further publication of her
works.[106]

Akhmatova hated the Bolshevik revolution, with its atheism and what
she saw as its disdain for culture, but she decided nevertheless to stay in
Russia, to do what she could to defend and maintain its culture. She did
not join the large number of her friends and literary colleagues who went
into emigration at this time:

> I am not with those who abandoned their land
> For enemies to tear apart.
> I do not heed their coarse flattery,
> And I shall not give them my songs.
>
> To me the exile is ever pitiful,
> Like a prisoner or someone ill.
> Dark is your path, oh wanderer,
> And alien bread reeks of wormwood.
>
> But here, in the murky fumes of the conflagration,
> Destroying the remains of our youth,
> We have not repelled a single blow,
> And we know that in the final reckoning,
> Every hour will be justified . . .
>
> But there is no people on earth less tearful,
> More arrogant and simple than us."[107]

It so happened that Akhmatova was living in an eighteenth-century
house on the banks of the Fontanka which had once been the home of the
aristocratic Sheremetev family. Her second husband, Vladimir Shileiko,
was an archeologist who had been tutor to the imperial family's last children, and the new regime allowed him to live there to watch over the
valuables. So symbolically Akhmatova played a part in preserving the
memory of the past. After she broke with Shileiko, she continued to live
in the Fontanka house with her next partner, the art critic Nikolai Punin;
but his ex-wife shared the same flat, so that her life was always disordered,
and she was often in great poverty, thanks to the banning of her work. She

was justified in saying, "We have not repelled a single blow," and her position as a woman made her life doubly difficult.[108]

The greatest test, though, came after 1935, when Punin and Akhmatova's son, Lev Gumilev, were both arrested. Over the next few years she spent countless hours standing in the lines outside the prisons, trying to find out the fate of her loved ones, or to hand over a parcel of food or clothes for them. The writer of exquisite love lyrics now became the bard of Russia's despair—and specifically the despair of women: "Oh cheerful sinner of Tsarskoe Selo, / What will happen to your life?" She found her calling in rescuing from oblivion the reality of their suffering (which otherwise left no mark whatsoever on the Soviet public media) and the memory of the time when "Leningrad dangled, a useless appendage, / Alongside its prisons." Akhmatova became the voice of these women, mandated by one of them, who "identified" her, even though she had long been unpublished, and asked her in a whisper, "'Can you describe *this?*' And I replied, 'I can.' Then something like a smile flitted across what had once been her face."

Her nonexile now became a profound and bitter fact: "No, not beneath a foreign sky, / Not sheltered by a foreign wing. / I was where my people were, / Where, alas, they had to be." She records her own suffering in counterpoint with the torments of the grey lines of women in the winter cold and the stifling heat of summer. Her voice is one "through which a hundred million people cry." Akhmatova compares herself with Mary the mother of Christ, but combines her personal fate with that of all her colleagues in distress: "I pray not only for myself / But for all those who stood with me / In savage cold and July heat / There, beneath that blind red wall." This was her answer to the optimistic, mendacious, and atheist culture of the Writers' Union.

To sustain her in her lonely self-appointed mission of people's tribune, Akhmatova tied her fate to that of Russia's past literature, and specifically to Pushkin's *Exegi Monumentum,* in the—otherwise arrogant—suggestion:

> If ever in this country
> They should think to erect a monument to me,
> I give my consent to that solemn deed,
> But only on condition it stands
> Not by the sea where I was born;

The last link with the sea is broken,
And not in the palace garden at the secret tree,
Where a disconsolate ghost awaits me still,
But here, where I stood for three hundred hours
And where no one unbolted the door.[109]

In this way Anna Akhmatova refashioned what had become a laborious and confused life in a manner precisely opposite to that required in a Soviet questionnaire. Defying the imperative to "speak Bolshevik," she became a witness to the suffering of her fellow women, a chronicler of the suppressed truth, and a custodian of the deeper Russian culture hidden under the official one.

The most important works of Platonov, Bulgakov, and Akhmatova were known only to a tiny circle of implicitly trusted friends. It was not till the late 1950s and early 1960s that they circulated among a somewhat wider audience, though even then still only in small coteries of scientific and cultural intellectuals prepared to entrust one another with what later became known as *samizdat*. Their acquaintance with these texts, and the long struggle for their publication, began the process of formalizing a countercanon that seemed to place the whole of Soviet "official" literature in doubt.

By 1941 an entire society was just beginning to recover from physical destruction and cultural amnesia, to construct a new social hierarchy and a new repertoire of myths, memories, celebrations, and practices. A new ruling class, mostly of very young people, was moving into the top positions in the party-state apparatus, the armed forces, and the professions. These leaders sponsored a new culture which bolstered their faith in their mission, but also suppressed much of reality as well as crucial elements of the Russian tradition. In spite of that, a Russian supra-ethnic patriotism was taking shape for the first time, colored—though not yet permeated—by the leaders' faith in the building of socialism and in the international mission of the Soviet Union. At the same time, everyone was shaken, even traumatized, by the upheavals from which they had scarcely begun to emerge; they were anxious to protect themselves and their families by seeking security in vertical and horizontal personal networks where they worked and where they lived. In this paradoxical and uncertain mood Russians suddenly faced the greatest peril in their history.[110]

# 6

# The Great Fatherland War

One day in 1950 the Russian-Jewish writer Emmanuil Kazakevich sat down to write a denunciation under the name of Citizen Unknown. Unlike most denunciations, it was to be addressed not to the secret police but "to the future." He intended to set down the truth about the decades through which he had lived as a kind of time capsule to float unseen over the ocean of Soviet censorship and wash up on some future shore of free speech. There, he hoped, it would be salvaged by readers eager to learn about a past they had been fortunate enough to miss. Once he settled down to work, though, he realized he had taken on a challenge beyond his powers: "To give an impression of the events of past decades, one would need to write a hundred volumes, with the many-sided realistic precision of *War and Peace* or *The Divine Comedy,* the outspokenness of Zola or Proust." He later burned the fragment of typescript.[1]

Kazakevich was right to feel overwhelmed by the demands made on his narrative abilities. The war which broke out with brutal suddenness on June 22, 1941, was the culmination of a quarter-century that had already included a world war, a revolution, a civil war, repeated famine, the collectivization of agriculture, the first five-year plans, tumultuous urbanization, and the great terror. If Kazakevich found it impossible to write about it all, then it is even more difficult for an outsider from a more sheltered country to comprehend what the Russians and the other Soviet peoples had been through in this time.

Any war faces a country's inhabitants with ordeals they never encounter in peacetime—and that is especially true of the war the Germans un-leashed, a race war, a frankly declared war of annihilation. War confronts everyone with the question of where their primary loyalties lie—in the twentieth century, above all which nation they belong to. The categories of citizenship and nationhood come together: one's rights and obligations depend as never before on the community to which one belongs. How people perceive their community depends, however, on a number of fac-tors: official propaganda, but also the cultural context and the recent life experience of the various social strata.[2]

The Soviet context was not promising. In the previous quarter-century national institutions and national memory had been destroyed, and the whole of society had been through upheavals that had pitched one class in bitter conflict against another, one nationality against another, ordinary people against the rulers and the privileged. The emerging neo-Russian imperial narrative had not yet had time to establish itself and take deep roots. The war, though anticipated in general terms, was nevertheless a great shock for nearly everyone when it actually began.

In the early months of the conflict, most Soviet people were mainly aware of disasters and privations and felt deep uncertainty and foreboding about the future. The fears, grievances, and doubts of the 1930s still hung over them. They were bewildered and resentful that the Soviet leaders had not prepared better. Many people concluded that they had been deceived yet again, that their army was inferior to the Germans', and that the So-viet Union would soon lose the war. Moreover, the collectivization of agri-culture and dekulakization, the terror and the devastation of the prewar officer corps had all left profound scars on Soviet society, while the Nazi-Soviet Pact had added a further residue of confusion and cynicism. In Moscow many young men refused to volunteer and conscripts failed to report for duty. In Arkhangelsk oblast the NKVD reported workers and peasants as saying, "Everyone said we would defeat the enemy on his own territory. It turns out the other way around . . . For two years our govern-ment has been feeding the Germans; they would have done better to stock supplies for their own army and people. Now we all face starvation." In Kaluga oblast a miner commented in July 1941 that he would go to the front and defend the Soviet land, but not those sitting in the Kremlin.[3]

In August 1941 the official in charge of evacuating Machine Tractor Stations (state-owned institutions that rented heavy agricultural machin-ery to the collective farms) from Kalinin oblast wrote to Stalin complain-

ing that retreating soldiers were sowing panic in the rear. They were seizing cars and gasoline from Soviet offices in order to get further from the
front. Some party and Soviet officials were beginning to do the same. Rumors spread that Marshal Timoshenko had been dismissed and had fled
abroad. One source reported: "There is no discipline in the rear. Everyone
does what he wants. Is this as it should be? Everyone is indignant, but says
nothing." From Beliaevka and Ovidiopol in the south it was also reported
that local officials "are sitting on their suitcases," i.e. ready for departure at
a moment's notice.[4]

By November 1941, as the siege closed around Leningrad, many of its
inhabitants felt it would make sense to rebel against Communist leadership and surrender the city to the Germans in order to be fed.[5] The
NKVD reported a factory worker as declaring, "If the Germans come, we
shall have enough to eat, but if Soviet power remains, we shall all starve to
death." An economist from the local branch of Gosplan commented,
"Our army is doomed to constant defeats because the Russian people have
lost any ideal worth fighting for. The peasant does not want to fight for
the kolkhozy, as the ideal of collective farming has failed." In Moscow
also, as the Wehrmacht approached, the NKVD reported a female factory
worker as complaining, "We don't have a firm and united home front.
People are embittered, and inside the country there will be conflicts that
will complicate matters. The war will be bloody and debilitating."[6]

Pessimism was not the only reaction, however. Some, especially in the
armed forces and in the nomenklatura elite, where the official ideology
was more pervasive, were much more confident. From the mid-1920s
military propaganda teams had been offering their recruits political education programs that encouraged individual soldiers to locate their own
*rodina* (home town or village and surrounding district) on a map and to
see it as part of a broader territory, a Union Republic, the USSR, and
finally the international proletarian community that the USSR would one
day emancipate. Soviet citizens were taught to think of themselves as surrounded by enemies, the imperialists of all countries, who would crush
them if they could. For that reason the Soviet military doctrine anticipated a major war, but expected it to be a relatively brief class war fought
mainly on enemy territory, with few casualties *(maloi kroviu)*, since the
proletariat of the enemy nations would rise, overthrow their rulers, and
welcome the Soviet Army. True, in the late 1930s, as the Japanese and
German threats mounted, military strategists were starting to take a more

somber view and to prepare for a protracted war fought by huge forces, possibly partly on Soviet territory.[7] Little of this debate reached even most of the nomenklatura elite, however, let alone a broader public. Most "ideologically conscious" people remained confident of a swift victory.

Moscow factory workers reportedly expressed incredulity at the Germans' rashness: "Who do they think they're attacking? Have they gone out of their minds? . . . Of course, the German workers will support us, and all other peoples will rise up . . . It will all be over in a week." Even a sophisticated intellectual like Lev Kopelev was prone to such illusions. As he remarked in 1979 in a conversation with the German writer Heinrich Böll, "When the first reports of the war came in on June 22, 1941, I must admit honestly, I was so stupid that I was delighted. I thought, 'This is the holy war, now the German proletariat will support us, and Hitler will be overthrown immediately.'"[8]

The actual war was very different. It took a while for the unforeseen to sink in. Initially many people held to the illusion that the Soviet Union was fighting an international class war. Frontline soldiers also took some time to realize what had hit them. One noted in his diary on July 20, 1941, after destroying a German tank and capturing the crew: "What naive philanthropists we were! In our interrogation we tried to get them to express class solidarity. We thought talking to us would make them see the light, and they would shout 'Rot Front!' . . . But they guzzled our kasha from our mess-tins, had a smoke from our freely offered tobacco pouches, then looked at us insolently and belched in our faces 'Heil Hitler!'"[9]

In the western part of the Soviet Union, and especially in the recently annexed regions, many people initially greeted the Germans as deliverers from Stalin. When they saw how the Germans behaved, however, they quickly changed their mood. A Russian watchmaker in Kiev, himself a devout Orthodox believer, recalled later how he and others had initially welcomed the Germans with bread and salt, but soon turned against them: "If we had to be under masters, then we preferred to have our own masters, not foreign ones." A west Belorussian peasant who actually fought for a time in the German Army felt the same: "better Russian slavery than German slavery."[10]

This minimal nationalism gradually became the dominant sentiment. Then, as the war unfolded, it blossomed into convinced patriotism. The overbearing ruthlessness and cruelty of the Germans and the doctrine they preached and practiced, of murdering Jews and enslaving Slavs as

Untermenschen, ensured that most Soviet citizens, whatever their previous views, also came to see the war as a national one, to be fought to the bitter end. A letter from a Red Army soldier to *Komsomolskaia Pravda* illustrates the way in which this German pressure soldered Russian and Soviet patriotism together. It was written in October 1942, at a very low point in the war, but when the reconquest of some occupied territory had demonstrated beyond doubt the atrocities the Germans were committing: "The Aryan-blooded Fascist Ober-vermin wants to enslave our freedom-loving hearts. That will never be! Never will those monstrous vampires gain a hold on our hearts, which are filled with freedom, pride, and infinite devotion to our beloved and long-suffering Homeland. Russian hearts, forged in the Bolshevik smithy, will never yield to the German scum."[11] The overheated rhetoric well represented the common ground the regime shared by this time with most ordinary Russians.

Even though the Soviet state remained committed in principle to internationalism, then, most of its citizens came to see the struggle as one, not between imperialists and toilers, but between Russians and Germans. In ordinary parlance the terms "Fascist" and "Hitlerite" were used less than simply "German." In contrast with the First World War, when Russian soldiers had regarded their enemy as human, they now used metaphors that suggested the Germans were wild beasts or vermin. The reaction of the Russian-Jewish novelist and war correspondent Ilia Erenburg is indicative of this new attitude. In 1936–1939 he had reported from the International Brigade in the Spanish Civil War, which he had portrayed as an internationalist crusade of the toilers against the imperialists. But he realized in the first days of the new war that this was going to be a wholly different kind of struggle, and that Jews like himself had to identify with Russia: "I suddenly felt that there was something very important and tenacious—the soil. I was sitting on a Moscow boulevard. Beside me sat a sad, unattractive woman with a child. Her features seemed infinitely familiar to me, as she said, 'Petenka, don't be naughty, take pity on me!' I realized that she was a member of my family [*chto ona rodnaia*], that one could die for Petenka."[12]

This feeling of being a large family, not divided by class origins, was articulated by Stalin in his first wartime broadcast to the Soviet peoples, on July 3, 1941, when he supplemented the accustomed Communist mode of address, "Comrades," and the neutral civic term "Citizens" with the words "Brothers and sisters!" There was even perhaps here an echo of the greeting given by the Orthodox priest to his parishioners. This was no ordinary war, Stalin emphasized: "This is a great war of the entire Soviet people against the German-fascist armies." But, he added, they would have powerful allies, Britain and the United States (who were, of course, "imperialists," though he did not say so). He called on all "the peoples of the Soviet Union" to rise *en masse* to defend their "soil" and their "homeland" against a "vicious and perfidious enemy." He reminded everyone of the eventual Russian success in driving out the Mongols, the Swedes under Charles XII, and the French under Napoleon.[13]

Erenburg became the most vehement exponent of the new view of the war as a national struggle to the death between Russians and brutish Germans. He wrote in *Pravda*, "If you haven't killed a German in the course of a day, then your day has been wasted. . . . If you have killed one German, kill another. Nothing gives us so much joy as the sight of German corpses." As a Jew, Erenburg had double reasons for hating the Germans, but the Russian poet Konstantin Simonov expressed very similar sentiments in his poem "Kill him!" published in *Pravda* in 1942: "If your home is dear to you where you were nursed as a Russian, . . . / If your mother is dear to you, and you cannot bear the thought of a German slapping her wrinkled face. . . . / If you do not want to give away all that you call your Homeland, / Then kill a German, so that he, / Not you, should lie in the earth. . . . Kill a German every time you see one!"[14]

In this atmosphere the idea of the *rodina*—the homeland, the small town or village where the family feels at home—became all-important. It had been downgraded in the 1920s and 1930s as a concept that belonged to the past, used by sentimental, old-fashioned poets like Sergei Esenin. Now the Leningrad poet Olga Berggolts, who was already thoroughly disillusioned with Communism by 1941, welcomed its rehabilitation: "It is wonderful that the concept of the Homeland *(Rodina)* has come so much closer to the ordinary person, has become so immediate: to save the life of one's friend in combat—that means to fight for one's Homeland."[15]

Similarly *byt*, everyday routine, had been despised as something soon to be transformed in the new way of life that science and technology were constructing under the inspiration of party ideology. That all changed. Thoughts of home and family life became especially treasured, precisely because they were now under such a terrible threat. Although by the mid-1930s the leaders had abandoned the intention of undermining the family, it remained true that before the war official propaganda had subordinated home and hearth to public meeting places and public duties. Courtship and conjugal love had been valued, not for their own sake, but rather as part of the process of building socialism. Now, by contrast, Simonov's lyric poem *Zhdi menia i ia vernus'* (*Wait for Me and I Will Return*) extolled the act of simply waiting for one's beloved as the supreme human duty. Published in *Pravda* and frontline newspapers in January 1942, it was an instant success. Soldiers would cut it out and send it to their sweethearts at home, and some of the improvised replies were also published.[16] One woman, a communications worker at the front, wrote to Simonov, "You who do not know me are helping me to live. . . . There have been no letters from my husband for a long time. I was already starting to lose hope. Then suddenly 'Wait for Me.' It reached me on our wedding anniversary. It was as if Iura had written those lines himself, for that is just what he would have said if he could have got in touch. I had been wanting to cry, but after that I felt really good. And I sent a radio-letter to him, a long one in verse."[17]

Individual love was now officially approved both for its own sake and as part of the life of the traditional community. Most soldiers carried in inside pockets or around their necks a photograph of home, of family members, or of a sweetheart, both as a reminder and as a form of protection. The long-established life cycle, the village community, and the influence of ancestors were evoked in literature in a manner gently provocative to Soviet atheism, as in another very popular poem of Simonov, "Do You Remember, Alesha, the Lanes of Smolensk?": "As if, around every Russian village, / Protecting the living by crossing their arms / And gathering in assembly, our ancestors prayed / For their grandchildren who no longer believed in God."[18]

Since it was the Soviet Army that was defending these values, Russian national feeling and Soviet military pride coalesced. As Lisa Kirschenbaum has put it, "*Rodina*, home and family emerged as key constituents of Soviet patriotism."[19]

The demands of war added a new dimension to the integration of women into the community. Of course in Marxist-Leninist theory women were considered the equal of men. In practice, too, they already had the vote, enjoyed the same civil and political rights as Soviet men, and were able to enter any profession. Now their contribution became even more crucial, and their status was correspondingly raised. In factories women took over work of all kinds, including the most physically demanding, to replace men who had left for the front. By August 1941 they already constituted 90 percent of the labor force in the Kirov Works in Leningrad. Half of all doctors and virtually all nurses in the armed forces were women. The army now had women's units, and they were among the defenders of Kiev and Odessa in the autumn of 1941. Male prejudice did not altogether evaporate, though: unkind quips about "powder-puff regiments" continued, and some commanders apparently considered pregnancy a breach of military discipline.[20]

In wartime public discourse, however, women figured largely as defenders of hearth, home, and family. Take, for instance, a letter sent from Cheliabinsk to the front and published in *Komsomolskaia pravda* in November 1941: "My beloved! Now during the long nights and evenings I sit for a long while near the cradle with our little one and think of you. . . . Where are you now? One thousand kilometres away is the city about which the whole world is thinking [presumably Moscow]. And you must be there now with your artillery men. Probably you're sleeping very little. And sharing *makhorka* [shag, coarse tobacco] with your friends and remembering us—me, your little boy, your ChTZ [Cheliabinsk Tractor Works]." It is impossible to know whether this letter was genuine or whether it was composed in the editorial offices of *Komsomolskaia pravda*. But the very appearance of such letters confirmed a new official mood, and it is quite certain they were popular with the public. Home and hearth now validated the war, and vice versa. One of the most popular war posters showed a middle-aged woman holding out a military draft form and summoning the hesitant to enlist.[21]

The heightened sense of community, military and civilian, male and female, was accompanied by a new acceptance of what had already before the war been a highly authoritarian and militarist style of leadership. Even at MIFLI (the Moscow Institute of Philology, Literature, and History), bastion of cosmopolitan, free-thinking intellectuals, collectivism and discipline were now welcomed. As a former student later recalled, "We all wanted to be together, not to struggle alone with our bewilderment, and we wanted someone firm, intelligent, aware to tell us what to do, to organize and direct us . . . That is how, incidentally, the party acquired such authority in Russia, because it could direct the mass of people in the desired direction." Similarly, Viktor Nekrasov, author of popular war novels and an inveterate nonconformist, later confessed, "We forgave Stalin everything, collectivization, 1937 [the terror], his revenge on his comrades. . . . And we, lads from intelligentsia families, became soldiers and believed the whole myth with a clear conscience. With open hearts we joined the party of Lenin and Stalin."[22]

One finds the opposite reaction, too. The historian M. Ia. Gefter, who was a young Jewish intellectual in 1941, asserts that a kind of "spontaneous de-Stalinization" took place as a result of the defeats of the war's first months. And looking back decades later, the former frontline soldier Viacheslav Kondratev declared, "There was one strange thing about the war: we felt ourselves freer than in peacetime . . . If you were lucky and you got to the enemy's trenches, then you had to show that you could think for yourself. There no one commanded you and much was in your own hands . . . In a sense you even felt you had Russia's fate in your hands: it was a real, genuine feeling of being a citizen, responsible for the Fatherland."[23]

These apparently contradictory sentiments can perhaps be reconciled. Feeling oneself free and a citizen was compatible during a terrible war with a strong sense of community and a desire to be firmly led. One woman, interviewed in the 1990s by Catherine Merridale, expressed it by contrast with later times: "We knew our motherland, we knew Stalin, we knew where we were going." At the front line such emotions were felt with even greater intensity, along with the binding power of soldierly comradeship, which remained the strongest memory of most Soviet Army men who survived the experience. As one of them wrote in December 1945 to the fiancée of his fallen comrade: "Life at the front brings people together very quickly. It's enough to spend one or two days with someone, and you know all his characteristics and all his feelings in a way you would never know them in peacetime, even after a whole year. There is nothing stronger than front-line friendship, and nothing can break it, not even death."[24]

Not everyone welcomed the new comradeship or accepted the need for authoritarian leadership. Aleksandr Stolpovskii, who had graduated with distinction from an agricultural institute in Omsk, wrote to his parents in September 1941: "In army conditions only people of a certain type can flourish: those who are rude and overbearing . . . I have no wish to learn how to kill people, and I cannot forget my special knowledge, which I acquired with such labor and enthusiasm."[25]

In the 1930s the official rehabilitation of Russia had been entirely statist. Now the regime found that it needed to revive certain civic and ethnic aspects of the Russian heritage as well. One example was the tacit authorization of private trading. On a rail journey from Murmansk to Moscow, Alexander Werth reported seeing peasant women trading on platforms and "soldiers bartering little pieces of soap or tiny packets of tobacco or boxes of matches for milk and eggs. . . . The militia appear to be fairly tolerant of these 'barter markets,' as they enable the peasants to obtain a bare minimum of essential goods with which the state is no longer able to supply them."[26]

Through such small-scale commerce peasants acquired nonagricultural goods and nonpeasants food they could longer buy elsewhere. The loss of most able-bodied young men to the armed forces meant that the agricultural workforce consisted mainly of middle-aged and old men, women, and children. Furthermore, a great deal of fertile land was lost to the invaders for much of the war. So the demands on agriculture were much greater than before 1941, but its resources much smaller. To face this problem, on the one hand, the regime raised the compulsory minimum of labor-days that each collective farmer had to work, including adolescents. Those who failed to achieve the minimum without good reason were tried and sentenced to up to six months' compulsory corrective labor.[27]

On the other hand, contrary to Bolshevik policy during the civil war, the Soviet leaders also turned a blind eye to the "misuse" of kolkhoz land for private cultivation and to the sale of the resultant produce on the open market. Farm workers were excluded from the rationing system, so they used their discreetly enlarged plots for subsistence, but also sold a good deal to hungry townsfolk. The private plots were known as "subsidiary plots," but actually their production was the principal life support of villagers, enabling them, as well as some townspeople, to survive. During 1942–1945 private production of milk increased 2.5 times, of potatoes 3.5 times, of vegetables 4.8 times. Prices rose very steeply, fueled by inflation: a liter of milk that before the war would have cost 2 rubles, 28 kopeks, now cost 38 rubles, while a kilogram of rye rose from 1 ruble, 88 kopeks, to 53 rubles, 80 kopeks.[28] In some regions the *zveno*, or "link" system, was widely adopted, under which a dozen or so collective farmers, usually with a family as nucleus, would take complete responsibility for a plot of land throughout the year, decide what to grow, deliver a proportion of the yield to the state, and consume the rest or sell it for profit on the private market.[29]

By 1945 quite a few peasants seriously hoped that the continued toleration of private trade would lead to the abolition of the kolkhozy. The party's information department reported that in Pskov, Penza, Voronezh, Rostov, and Dnepropetrovsk oblasti "provocative rumors about the alleged abolition of the kolkhozy have intensified"; while in San Francisco, Molotov was said to have offered to reopen churches, abolish the kolkhozy, and permit free trade in order to avoid war with the United States. On a number of Pskov oblast farms kolkhozniki declined to put their signatures to a traditional greetings letter to Stalin. They explained their refusal in traditional patriarchal style: "This letter has a hidden meaning, as comrade Stalin asked the people to put up with the kolkhozy for another seven years, while the local bosses are determined not to dissolve the kolkhozy and are now collecting the signatures of kolkhozniki. If we do sign the letter, the kolkhozy will not be abolished."[30] These were clear examples of rumors as wish-fulfillment, since there was no evidence for any of the assertions.

Media policy became more enlightened during the war. Censorship for military security was of course tightened, but in other respects a lighter touch was adopted. This did not happen immediately. In the opening days of the war rumor replaced information. The Soviet media agency Sovinformbiuro reported evasively on the defeats, but this aroused only mistrust, since the slightest geographical knowledge indicated that the combat locations were moving ever further east. One Moscow letter-writer commented: "Fear of facts . . . is one of the factors that aid the spread of unofficial information and rumors." Stalin's acknowledgment on July 3 that the Soviet Union had lost Lithuania, western Belorussia, and most of western Ukraine actually caused relief, since many of the rumors had been even more luridly catastrophic.[31]

Sovinformbiuro gradually learned, then, that it was important in all-out war to gain the trust of the population. On the radio unscripted live talk shows and live reporting, which had been banned in 1937, were resumed in autumn 1941. Unit commanders were instructed to provide facilities for war correspondents. Sometimes they reported directly from the front, with noises of battle in the background. A series of daily broadcasts, Letters from the Front and Letters from the Rear, helped to keep soldiers and civilians in touch; many people listened regularly to such programs in the hope of hearing news of a relative or friend with whom they had lost contact.[32] This kind of concern for relationships of family and friendship helped to cement feelings of community under stress.

In *Pravda* also the emphasis shifted from preaching ideology, leader-ship, and party discipline to reporting directly on the lives and feelings of ordinary citizens, evoking their personal motivation to fight for their fam-ilies, friends, and native land. The skill, initiative, and conviction of ordi-nary soldiers and workers were praised as much as the quality of military and political leadership. In the army newspaper *Krasnaia zvezda* Erenburg claimed as early as October 1941 that "all distinctions between Bolsheviks and non-party people, between believers and Marxists, has been obliter-ated . . . They pray for the Red Army in old churches, the domes of which have been darkened so that they should not attract German pilots. Muftis and rabbis pray for the Red Army."[33] Such political and religious eclecti-cism would have been unthinkable before the war.

## The Russian Orthodox Church

In the spring of 1941 the plight of the church seemed desperate. Metro-politan Sergii, who had seen all his attempted compromises bring no re-wards, remarked bitterly, "We are living through the last days of the Rus-sian Orthodox Church." The war, however, transformed the situation. From the outset the church committed itself to the Soviet cause as the em-bodiment of Russia. Metropolitan Sergii issued appeals to the faithful to fight for the fatherland, and prayers were regularly said in all churches for the victory of the Red Army. Parishioners collected money and ob-jects such as warm clothing for the war effort, and the State Bank opened a special account to receive them, in a tacit acknowledgment that the church was once more a single structure and a juridical person. One Le-ningrad parish offered to set up, run, and finance a field hospital; others collected money to create a special tank column called after Dmitrii Donskoi. In November 1941 Metropolitan Nikolai of Kiev was appointed to a State Committee of Enquiry into Nazi crimes in occupied territory. Nothing much came of the committee, but it was a significant appoint-ment, for it was the first time a clergyman had been invited to join any Soviet institution.[34]

Official persecution of religion was unobtrusively dropped, and the Soviet leaders gradually sanctioned the reopening of parish churches. In a national war, in which the Germans were reopening churches on the territory they occupied, there was perhaps no choice. In September 1943, however, Stalin went much further. He suddenly invited the three highest-ranking prelates of the Orthodox Church, Sergii, Metropolitan Nikolai of Krutitsy (Moscow), and Metropolitan Aleksii of Leningrad, to an interview in the Kremlin, at which he announced his intention to restore the patriarchate and permit a more generous approach to the reopening of parishes. How long would it take, he asked them, to convene a bishops' conference to formalize the re-establishment of the patriarchate? They thought about a month. "Could one not apply Bolshevik tempos?" Stalin asked. With the help of government air transport, it turned out, one could indeed. A mere four days later, the bishops had been flown in. Most of them looked unkempt and bewildered, straight from labor camps, but the conference duly took place and elected Sergii as patriarch.

Stalin's main motive was not the encouragement of Russian patriotism, as is often assumed. The timing is indicative of the purpose. The Red Army had just won the Battle of Kursk, and with that success it became realistic to begin planning for ultimate victory and for postwar Europe. If Stalin wanted to ensure the security of the USSR by establishing a cordon sanitaire of allied states in Eastern Europe, then the help of the Orthodox Church would be very useful to him. His major concessions to the church, then, were motivated not by the desire for popular support, which he already enjoyed, but to secure the USSR's great-power position after the war.

Accordingly, for the first time since 1918, the church was allowed to set up a central administration (installed in the former residence of the German ambassador). The patriarchal cathedral in Moscow was restored to the church, together with the Monastery of the Trinity and St. Sergii in Zagorsk, complete with sacred vessels returned from the local museum. It was supplied with foreign currency to open and maintain missions abroad (Stalin's special priority). It was permitted to publish its own journal (subject to Soviet censorship) and to open a theological academy and three seminaries for the training of priests. The three highest prelates received chauffeured cars and the right to supplies at state (not market) prices. A few weeks after being virtual outcasts the senior clergy had become part of the privileged nomenklatura elite.[35]

The church accepted those benefits at the price of strict subordination to the state. The patriarchate was placed under the supervision of a Council for Affairs of the Russian Orthodox Church, whose first head, G. G. Karpov, was simultaneously head of a special NKVD department responsible for "struggle with ecclesiastical and sectarian counter-revolution."

The council was to advise on the appointment of all bishops, and for that purpose kept up-to-date files on the careers of all potential appointees, in authentic nomenklatura style. For religious zeal they received black marks; for services to the peace movement they were praised. The council had its delegates in each diocese to liaise with local authorities and to ensure that the laws on religion were observed; they also had a team of inspectors to keep an eye on *them*.[36]

Permission to revive parishes and reopen churches was given grudgingly, even after Stalin met with Sergii and his colleagues. Many local officials, aghast at what they were being asked to countenance, obstructed the process as long as they could. Reports from all over the country show that members of the League of Militant Godless were bewildered and resentful, even outraged. Some people linked the new policy with the restoration of military ranks and insignia. One soldier commented: "Epaulettes have reappeared, and now the churches are open. It only remains for chains and whips to return and we really will have the old regime back!"[37]

The new policy was not simply a concession to traditional Russian patriotism. Mosques were also reopened and Islamic organizations were given new powers. Three new Muftiyats (Muslim administrative boards) were created in addition to the existing one in Ufa: they were in Dagestan, in Baku, and in Tashkent. In May 1942 Muslims were permitted to hold a conference in Ufa, which sent greetings to Stalin and called on all Muslims to support the war effort. The Central Asian republics received many evacuees, mostly Slav, from the European part of the Soviet Union, along with numerous new industrial enterprises transferred from there. Recruits from the Muslim regions were called up on the same basis as elsewhere and made their contribution at the front—in fact, perhaps for political reasons, they received more battle honors per capita than did the Slavs.[38] Unlike in the First World War, the Muslims shouldered their full share of the war burden.

These concessions to traditional religion did much to sustain social solidarity among a population undergoing terrible ordeals. The constant fear and uncertainty, the grieving for fallen comrades and family members, generated a lively and unashamed revival of religious feeling, especially among women and older people, but also among soldiers at the front. For the latter, any kind of open worship was impossible, but many Red Army men carried a secret cross or talisman of some kind and would pray discreetly before going into battle.[39]

All the same, compromise with religion entailed a radical change in Soviet spirituality, which had hitherto combined socialist messianism with atheism. These concessions were extremely unsettling for Communist true believers, who had been confident that the old faiths had been or soon would be thoroughly discredited and supplanted. When Christian believers petitioned for the reopening of their churches they evoked by contrast a solidarity that was archaic, traditionally Russian, and inclusive of all social classes: "The open churches in Moscow and other towns are conducting services in unison and offering prayers for victory over the enemy. Therefore why shouldn't our church and we the labouring kolkhozniki be part of that unison?" Or, even more succinctly: "The internal battle is over. Our people of All Rus are united."[40] The Communist Party needed the support of such sentiment now. Under the pressure of war the regime was moving decisively away from messianic universalist atheism toward a traditional, pragmatic great-power outlook based on neo-*rossiiskii* imperialism.

## Russian Culture

War could not be conducted on the basis of lies and enforced silence. In his novel *Doctor Zhivago,* Boris Pasternak recalled: "When war flared up, its real horrors and real dangers, the threat of a real death, were a blessing compared to the inhuman reign of fantasy, and they brought relief by limiting the magic power of the dead letter." It cannot be said that the "dead letter" disappeared entirely. Still, the common struggle for survival did conjure up a sense of community where previously there had been fear, suspicion, and discord. Pasternak himself worked for a time in the fire watch service: his task was to dislodge incendiary bombs from the roof of the twelve-story apartment building where he lived and throw them into an empty lot. Some of his work was published again, and he celebrated the reunion with his public through a series of poems entitled *On Early Trains:* "Through the mutations of the past / And the years of war and poverty, / Silently I came to recognize / Russia's inimitable features."[41]

Nowhere was the revived sense of community felt more keenly than in Leningrad, which for much of the 1930s had been, in Akhmatova's words, "a useless appendage to its prisons." As we have seen, before the war Akhmatova had been almost an outcast. She had made her choice to stay in Russia, however, and accepted the consequences. The outbreak of war, for all its horrors, gave her a new reason for living. At the beginning of the fighting she resisted being evacuated from Leningrad, even as the Germans were approaching, and she joined the Civil Defense. Olga Berggolts recalled her sewing sandbags for the trenches and taking fire watch duty, "her face at once severe and angry, a gas mask thrown over her shoulder, she took on the fire watch like a regular soldier."[42] Despite her long exclusion from public culture, the authorities knew that Akhmatova was a popular figure. Now for the first time she was treated with honor, as a full citizen of the country in which she had decided to remain. At last she was allowed to publish, and she brought out a collection called *From Six Books:* the title perhaps reflected her tacit protest against the fact that the six books had been so long unpublished, and even now were appearing only in fragments.

Akhmatova was invited to speak on the radio to boost the spirits of Leningraders, and this she did with conviction: "The city of Peter, the city of Lenin, the city of Pushkin, Dostoevskii and Blok, this great city of culture and labour, is threatened by the enemy with shame and death. My heart, like those of all the women of Leningrad, sinks at the mere thought that our city, my city, could be destroyed. . . . I, like all of you at this moment, live only in the unshakeable belief that Leningrad will never fall to the fascists . . . We know that the whole of our country, all its people, are behind us. We feel their alarm for our sakes, their love and help."[43]

Akhmatova had her own war aim, which was also her reason for staying in Russia when so many friends had left. She summed it up in her poem "Courage":

> We know what lies in the balance right now,
> And what fate is being decided.
> The hour of courage has struck on our clocks,
> And courage will not desert us.
> We're not frightened to die under bullets,
> Nor daunted at losing our home.
> For we will defend you, Russian language,
> The great Russian word!
> We will carry you forth free and pure,
> To pass on to our heirs, saved from servitude
> For ever![44]

Akhmatova, then, had sacrificed everything for the preservation both of genuine memory and of cultural tradition at a time when both were under mortal threat. Her version of Russian national identity as consisting above all in language and culture had powerful resonance among her educated fellow citizens.

The composer Dmitrii Shostakovich, previously prolific, had also fallen silent in the late 1930s. He had been publicly attacked in 1936 for his opera *Lady Macbeth of Mtsensk,* and he never dared to perform his Fourth Symphony, which faithfully reflected the terror and despair of the time. It climaxes with one of the most ferocious unresolved dissonances in the entire orchestral repertoire, and then collapses, to fade out on an uneasy, repetitive rhythm, like a patient on a life-support machine. This was not music to inspire the workers as they toiled to fulfill the five-year plan. Now Shostakovich, too, was not only rehabilitated but celebrated.

Initially he applied to be sent to the front but instead was detailed off to dig trenches; then, like Pasternak, he was assigned to fire watch duty on the Conservatory roof. He took part in the same broadcast as Akhmatova, announcing that he had completed the first two movements of his Seventh Symphony. This was Shostakovich's great contribution to the war effort, but, like much of his work, its implications were ambiguous. The obsessive and brutal march theme of its first movement could be interpreted as either anti-Nazi or anti-Soviet. Less than any other art form can music be tied down to a specific interpretation, though in the context of the time only one reading was possible. The symphony was first performed in Kuibyshev, but the great event was the Leningrad premiere on August 9, 1942, for which musicians had to be brought out of retirement or even from the trenches and given special rations. The score was flown to the city, and a team of copyists worked day and night to transcribe the orchestral parts. The performance was, not surprisingly, far from perfect, but it was relayed on loudspeakers to hushed, expectant crowds in the streets, and it did much to boost morale.[45]

As war correspondent for the army newspaper *Krasnaia zvezda,* Vasilii Grossman witnessed the catastrophic defeats and the headlong retreats of 1941–1942. He covered the battle of Stalingrad, where his colleague Semen Lipkin recalls him "in a greatcoat drenched in petrol and spattered with dirt." His frontline reportage, vivid and honest, was very popular with readers. Stalingrad also gave him the theme for his greatest literary work, the first part of which, *For a Just Cause,* was written in 1945–1949 and published in *Novyi mir* in 1952. It was a remarkable achievement for a Jew to publish a closely observed account of the war at a time of maxi-

mum official anti-Semitism, and he only achieved it after several rewrit-
ings, undertaken to satisfy editorial demands.[46]

This was nothing, however, compared to the tribulations of the novel's
second part, entitled *Life and Fate*. By the 1950s, when Grossman spent
nearly a decade writing it, he had come to believe that the line between
good and evil runs, not between Communism and Nazism, or between
Russia and Germany, but, as Dostoevskii once put it, through every human heart. He portrays the Soviet and Nazi systems as oppressive and inhuman twins and presents parallel scenes from the Gulag and from German concentration camps. The armies of both sides are authoritarian
automata, from which, paradoxically, the soldiers escape into the intense
camaraderie of the small frontline unit. This feature of war is seen at its
most intense in "House 6/1," an isolated observation point and fortified
outpost behind the German lines, which can only be accessed by night in
a covered trench. Its commander, Grekov, is fiercely independent; he cares
only for creating a warm, friendly atmosphere among his men. They discuss political matters quite openly, including collectivization and the terror, knowing that no political commissar can overhear their conversation.
Grekov refuses to send in reports to his superiors, commenting tartly, "I'll
settle my paperwork with the Germans alone." His men are devoted to
him, and their fighting spirit holds off the Germans. House 6/1 symbol-
izes for Grossman the reason for the eventual victory at Stalingrad.[47]

It took Grossman many years after the war to come to his own personal
understanding of the struggle between good and evil. When he did, it
contradicted 100 percent the official mythology. Without perhaps fully
realizing it, he was monitoring the nation's memory in grand confrontational style. In the early 1960s he was almost alone among Soviet intellectuals in taking such a negative view of the regime. By the late 1980s
this attitude was commonplace and prepared the way for the delight
with which many of them greeted the dismantling of Communist rule.
Mikhail Suslov, the regime's ideological guardian, saw the text and is said
to have exclaimed, "This cannot see the light of day for at least two hundred years!" If indeed Suslov did make this statement, it was a recognition
both of the novel's significance and of its explosive nature. Perhaps on
Suslov's instructions, the book suffered the most devastating fate to which
any literary text has ever been submitted. It was "arrested" by the KGB: all
copies of the text were confiscated from the editorial offices of *Znamia*
and from Grossman's home, together with rough drafts, and even car-

bon paper and typewriter ribbons used for its composition.[48] Such was the fate of a remarkable Jewish-Russian writer who was inspired by his wartime experience to attempt a fundamental reinterpretation of the Soviet Union's messianic mission.

## The All-Slav Committee

The war compelled the Soviet leaders to mobilize public opinion and mass sentiment in completely new, untried ways. One strategy was to stimulate Russian and Slav solidarity not just inside but also outside the Soviet Union. Many of the countries occupied by the Germans were Slav: the Belorussians and Ukrainians inside the USSR, the Poles, Czechs, Slovaks, Slovenes, Serbs, Croats, and Bulgarians abroad. Moreover, sizeable Slav communities lived in emigration in the United States, Britain, and elsewhere in the world; since the late 1920s the USSR had spurned them as politically suspect, and Soviet citizens had suffered for any contact with them. In wartime, though, every source of potential aid had to be investigated and encouraged.

The All-Slav Committee was formed in August 1941 from among Slavic cultural and political leaders who happened to find themselves in the USSR. It was placed under the umbrella of Sovinformbiuro, in whose elegant Moscow mansion it was housed. This arrangement was logical, since the bureau coordinated Soviet news and propaganda broadcasting, including to the countries of occupied Europe. Its head was General A. S. Gundorov, director of the Military-Engineering Academy, who was also in charge of Moscow's anti-aircraft defenses in the autumn of 1941. The All-Slav Committee was one of a number of public anti-Fascist committees formed at around that time to mobilize patriotic sentiment. Others included the Women's Committee, the Youth Committee, the Scholars' Committee, and the best-known, the Jewish Anti-Fascist Committee. These groups were set up at the initiative of A. S. Shcherbakov, who was head of both Sovinformbiuro and Agitprop, and were associated with the party's drive to enroll new members and also to gain more popularity among the general public by bringing the concerns of civilians to the attention of the rulers.[49]

According to the Yugoslav Communist and partisan leader Milovan Djilas, however, the committee was merely "an anti-German facade for Soviet patronage over the Slavic peoples outside the USSR," and it appealed especially to the Communists among them, to whom it offered the prospect of coming to power after the war.[50] Not all Slavs present at its founding congress accepted its mandate: the Polish General Anders, for example, attended but did not take part. He refused to join the committee because he did not recognize the legitimacy of the Soviet annexation of western Ukraine and western Belorussia, and because he (correctly) suspected the Soviet authorities of having organized the mass murder of Polish officers in Katyn Forest.

The committee's main job was to propagandize the anti-German cause among Slav audiences all over the world, and to try to raise material or financial support from those living outside German rule. Through its journal, *Slaviane,* and its radio broadcasts it reported the course of the war, stressing the heroic efforts of Russians, Ukrainians, and Belorussians in fighting at the front and in keeping the home fires burning. It also painted a heartening picture of partisan resistance from Slavs under occupation. The committee's overriding message was that the Slav peoples had been conquered and enslaved in the past as a result of their disunity, and that they now urgently needed to unite to face the gravest threat in their history.

In many Western countries these efforts met with considerable success. In the United States, for example, Committees for Aid to the USSR were set up which sent food, clothing, and other items, worth $16 million in 1943 and $22.7 million in 1944. Some Slavs abroad remained irreconcilable, either because of hostility to Communism or because of specific grievances. By contrast, some former Whites felt that the Nazi threat to their homeland justified a reconciliation with their former Red enemies.[51]

The committee's name and much of its propaganda inevitably evoked the memory of the nineteenth-century Panslavists, who had tried to persuade the government to intervene more actively in support of Slav peoples in the Habsburg and Ottoman Empires. The opening congress, however, explicitly disavowed this heritage as a "thoroughly reactionary tendency, exploited by Russian tsarism for its own political purposes, and deeply hostile to the exalted goal of equality of peoples and the national development of all states."[52]

All the same, the All-Slav propaganda was sometimes consciously archaic, redolent of the 1870s. Take, for example, the proclamation to the Bulgarian people of January 1944: "Dear brother Bulgarians! The Russian [N.B.: not Soviet] people is inflicting incurable wounds on Hitlerism, is cleansing the holy Russian lands from the foe, is preparing the ultimate defeat of Hitler's Germany and bringing liberation to the enslaved Slav peoples. . . . Bulgarian quislings [are] taking from the peasant everything he has obtained by his toil, they help the Germans to destroy the centuries-old Bulgarian culture. With their approval the Teutons besmirch your national shrines and mock your national honor." Then followed an appeal to priests: "Servitors of the Bulgarian Orthodox Church. Let the call resound in your churches for the struggle against Hitler, and let the prayer be heard for the speedy liberation of your people from the power of the German foe."[53] Almost every word of this appeal could have been written by the Panslavs seventy years earlier. Especially striking is the word used for "foe" at the end: *supostaty.* This is an archaic and rhetorical term confined almost entirely to religious usage; it carries the idea, not only of enemy, but also of "evil spirits," the enemy in the sense of the devil.

This kind of focused rhetoric worked, or so at least Gundorov reported at the end of the war, maintaining that "the nongovernmental [*obshchestvennyi*] nature of the committee and the popularity of its slogans enabled our propaganda to gain acceptance among foreign circles that would not have been possible for official Soviet propaganda organs, and attracted to our work people of diverse political convictions."[54]

## Russian National Identity

If one had asked a Red Army soldier at the time what he meant by Russia, he might well have pointed to the extraordinarily popular narrative poem by Aleksandr Tvardovskii, *Vasilii Terkin,* which had been appearing in installments in frontline newspapers. The image of Russian patriotism projected in the poem differed markedly from what would have been expected before the war. Terkin is a very ordinary soldier, a simple peasant lad, with minimal education and no interest in science, technology, or industry. He is completely apolitical: the text contains no mention of the Communist Party nor even of Stalin. Terkin's attachment to his country centers on his *rodina,* his home province of Smolensk: at one points he has a friendly spat with a soldier from Tambov, who boasts that the feats of Smolensk people cannot match those of the Tambovtsy. Yet Terkin is also proud of the fact that he is fighting to save Russia, which, like all his countrymen, he straightforwardly equates with the Soviet Union: "The hour has come,

/ Our fate has caught us. / Today we answer for Russia, / For the people, / For everything in the world. From Ivan to Foma, / Dead and alive, / We together are we, / The people, Russia . . ."[55] He has no family of his own but feels his unit to be a family, and he connects to Russian villagers as to a larger family, epitomized by the elderly couple for whom he mends a clock as his unit passes their home. After he has done so, he drinks with the husband, who is a veteran of the First World War, and thus renews the symbolic link with Russia's previous wars.

Viewed in the light of prewar proletarian internationalism, even in its neo-*rossiiskii* phase, Terkin is a strange and archaic figure, closer to the fantasies of the nineteenth-century *narodniki* than to anything Lenin or Stalin might have conceived. Yet this was the hero Soviet soldiers liked to read about in their spare time, and Tvardovskii's book was a familiar object in their knapsacks. The censorship occasionally demurred to some minor aspect of the text, but in general it was given the green light because of its obvious popularity.[56] Besides, the work was in no sense anti-Soviet; it simply re-emphasized aspects of Russian national identity that had been obscured or downplayed in the public discourse of the interwar years. Terkin represented, in fact, for the first time since 1917, the honorable re-emergence of the *russkii*.

Cumulatively, the wartime changes of policy consolidated the feeling, held by most Russians and non-Russians of whatever social class, that they belonged to a society whose nature was determined by its Russianness. Rogers Brubaker has suggested that national identity can take shape quite suddenly. Indeed, he speaks of "nationness" rather than of national identity, and characterizes it as "something that suddenly crystallises rather than gradually develops, as a contingent, conjuncturally fluctuating and precarious frame of vision and basis for individual and collective action."[57] We may say that during 1941–1945 "Russianness" crystallized in that way, as an ethnic and imperial amalgam, a blend of *russkii, rossiiskii,* and Soviet elements. In 1945 the USSR was closer to being a compound neo-*rossiiskii* nation-state than ever before—or, as it turned out, ever after.

As if to give symbolic form to this neo-*rossiiskii* identity, in 1943 the Soviet state reintroduced the full panoply of military ranks as they had been in the tsarist army, with gold braid and shoulder straps to match, and a series of new decorations for officers, including the Orders of Aleksandr Nevskii and Mikhail Kutuzov. It also dissolved the Comintern, institutional embodiment of the old proletarian internationalism. This step worried and distressed many Communists, as the party's information department reported. In one Moscow factory, very understandably, an engineer wanted to know: "What will happen to the slogan 'Workers of the world, unite'? What is going to replace it?"[58] What indeed?

In place of the "International," a new national anthem was adopted whose opening words celebrated in archaic language the concept of Russia as the heart of the USSR: "An unshakeable union of free republics / Has been united by Great Rus. / Long live the country founded by the people's will, / The united, mighty Soviet Union."[59] The same concept was confirmed by Stalin when he spoke at a Kremlin banquet of Red Army commanders on May 24, 1945: "I drink above all to the health of the Russian people, because it is the outstanding nation among all the nations which make up the Soviet Union. I drink to the health of the Russian people because in this war it has deserved general recognition as the driving force among the peoples of the Soviet Union."[60]

## POWs and Returnees

Within half a century the Soviet Union had fallen apart and the non-Russian republics had declared their independence of both Russia and Communism. One is bound, therefore, to ask: What happened to this spirit of Russian-led solidarity?

One answer is that, even during the war, but especially afterward, the regime continued to undermine the ethnic and civic aspects of nationhood, both Russian and non-Russian. Its leaders still saw themselves primarily as the rulers of a great power, not of a nation. Although, being more intelligent than Hitler, they were prepared to compromise wherever necessary with the Russians and other peoples, they never really identified with them, and always safeguarded their right to rule over them regardless of cost.

This mindset is well illustrated in the state's attitude toward Soviet prisoners of war in enemy captivity: they were simply abandoned to their fate. The Soviet regime refused to give the International Red Cross any help or information to make possible the delivery of food parcels or correspondence to them. As a result most Soviet prisoners suffered extreme neglect, especially during the early months of the war. A commissioner of the German Ostministerium described the conditions in a POW camp in Poland in the autumn of 1941: "The camp was completely surrounded by barbed wire and guarded by sentinels with machine guns. There were several huts for the camp administration, but the prisoners lived in dugouts and slept on the bare earth. The weather was cold and wet, and all the dugouts were leaking, but 40 percent of the prisoners were without greatcoats, tunics, or sometimes even footwear. . . . Morning and evening each prisoner received a mug of hot water, for (so-called) dinner a liter of thin soup, and a slice of bread a day. . . . Half-clothed, grimy, exhausted, with unshaven faces, they were in complete despair. No one was concerned about their fate; they had been declared outlaws by their own government."[61]

As a result of these appalling conditions, only 2.4 million of the 5.7 million POWs captured by the Germans in the course of the war survived to the end. The remainder, roughly 57 percent, died in captivity. Especially dreadful were the first six months of the war, when large Soviet armies were defeated and encircled, and the Germans had still not decided what to do with prisoners. At that stage POW camps were almost literally extermination centers. Thereafter it occurred to the Germans that Soviet prisoners could be exploited as manual labor rather than being left to rot. This entailed feeding them well enough to have the strength for work, so the survival rate after the spring of 1942 was higher than earlier. During the war as a whole, some 9 to 10 million Soviet citizens were captured or deported to occupied territory at one time or another, and barely half of them survived till the end of the war.[62]

The original intention of the Soviet government had not necessarily been to abandon its own citizens in this manner. From the outset, however, it declared that it would observe international conventions on the conduct of war only insofar as the Germans did the same. Faced with evidence of the racism and extreme brutality of the Germans in the areas they occupied, the Soviets refused in August 1941 to supply the Red Cross with information about the identity of German prisoners in their hands. Foreign Minister Molotov stated that "in view of the systematic violation by Hitlerite Germany of international agreements and conventions, the Soviet government shall observe with respect to Germany the [Hague and Geneva] treaties and conventions only insofar as they are observed by Germany."[63]

At first sight there might seem a certain logic to that position. In practice, though, it meant that the Soviet leaders adopted Nazi moral standards, even Nazi racist policies, as their own, and disowned citizens who had suffered no more than a normal misfortune of war. A deeper motive was at work as well. As we have seen, during the 1930s the Soviet regime had come to view its frontier with the hostile outside world not as offering opportunities but rather as posing a threat. Anyone who had lived beyond it knew things that no Soviet citizen ought to know and might be a spy for a hostile power. Now, suddenly, as the result of war, millions of Soviet citizens were in that situation, mostly through no fault of their own. To the regime, all the same, they were a menace. For that reason being taken prisoner was construed as an act of cowardice or even deliberate betrayal. Encircled units were instructed to fight to the last man. A Stavka decree of August 16, 1941, proclaimed that "cowards and deserters must be annihilated" and ordered that "commanders and political workers who during battle tear up their insignia and desert to the rear or give themselves up as prisoners should be considered malicious deserters, and their families are subject to arrest as families of deserters, who violated their oath and betrayed their homeland. Higher-ranking commanders must shoot out of hand such deserters among the commanding officers."[64] This decree was read out in units but not published. Although strictly it applied only to officers and political commissars, in practice the Soviet regime construed it as applying to all servicemen. In 1943, in reply to a papal inquiry about Soviet prisoners of war, the Soviet ambassador in Turkey told the nuncio that the Soviet government ignored all information about them, since it regarded them as traitors. The government also withdrew from the families of POWs the supplementary rations normally given to the families of serving soldiers.[65]

One way the Soviet POWs could be fed and clothed was by volunteering to serve in the German armed forces. Most such volunteers were assigned as auxiliaries to units under German commanders, since Hitler was determined not to allow the creation of Russian national formations, even anti-Communist ones. Some of his officers, though, reckoned that the Germans' chances of winning the war would be greatly enhanced if they had Russians fighting on their side for patriotic reasons and from anti-Communist conviction. In the summer of 1942 they recruited to their cause General Andrei Vlasov, who had been captured during the encirclement of his unit on the northern front. They encouraged Vlasov to believe that he might become the leader of a Russian national liberation army, enjoying the backing of Germany in overthrowing Stalin and the Communist system.

Vlasov is a kind of touchstone for the dilemmas of Russian patriotism during the Second World War. In December 1942 he issued the Smolensk Declaration, which set out a political program for a free Russia independent of Communism, or, as Vlasov himself put it, "a new Russia without Bolsheviks and Capitalists"—since he believed that the British and the Americans were ganging up with Stalin to exploit the Russians. It is revealing, then, that Vlasov accepted many of the aims of Communism: the ideal of social justice, protection from exploitation, the right to work, education, leisure, and a secure old age. His declaration also promised the unrealized civil rights guaranteed in the 1936 Soviet constitution, such as freedom of speech, conscience, assembly, and so on. On the other hand it also called for an end to terror and forced labor, the abolition of the collective farms, and the re-legalization of private manufacture and trade. Remarkably for a political program published under Nazi sponsorship, it contained no trace of anti-Semitism. We cannot tell for certain, but it seems likely that such a program resembled more closely the aspirations of Russians at the time than the policies of the Communist Party. At any rate, the Second World War Russian émigrés interviewed at Harvard in the late 1940s, certainly not pro-Soviet in their general outlook, expressed similar appreciation of Soviet welfare programs while criticizing precisely the aspects of Soviet rule that Vlasov proposed to abolish. His political vision also seems to have provoked a positive response in the few occupied towns he visited in the spring of 1943, Smolensk, Mogilev, Bobruisk, and Pskov, though some of his listeners are reported to have accused him of collaborating with an occupation regime that was enslaving Russians.[66]

They were right. Politically Vlasov was in an impossible situation. There was never any real hope that Hitler would allow him to form a Russian army—not, at least, until the final months of the war, when its mission was already hopeless. His Smolensk Declaration contained patently untrue statements, such as: "Germany is waging war not against the Russian people and their *Rodina*, but only against Bolshevism," or "Germany does not wish to encroach on the living space of the Russian people or on their national and political liberties." Those joining Vlasov's movement were required to take an oath of loyalty not only "to the Russian people" but also "to Hitler as the supreme commander of all anti-Bolshevik forces."[67]

Few Soviet officers from the POW camps were prepared to join him, partly because they had no desire to take such an oath, and partly because they could see that his cause was doomed. Some 250,000 Soviet citizens, including 165–170,000 POWs, served at one time or another in the German armed forces, and perhaps 800,000 if one adds in Vlasovite units and the police. This represents about 8 percent of the total number of Soviet citizens who fell under enemy control during the war—a remarkably low proportion, considering the appalling alternatives.[68] The project of a non-Communist Russian patriotic movement was a hopeless dream, crushed between the millstones of Stalinism and Nazism.

All the same, the regime reacted with extreme distrust toward all Soviet citizens returning from captivity or from occupied territory. One British sailor described their reception from his own viewpoint: "When we brought the Russians to Odessa, we unloaded the steamer from six in the morning till four in the afternoon, but no one was there to greet them. . . . After the unloading, NKVD officials lined up the men and marched them off somewhere for interrogation. The women and children stayed behind and, if they had heavy luggage, had to sit all night in the open waiting for trucks to come."[69]

We now know where the men were being marched off to. As early as the Finnish war, special NKVD filtration camps had been set up to receive and investigate returnees before deciding on their further status. In December 1941, as soon as the Soviet Army began to reconquer occupied territory, those camps were reactivated, and their number greatly increased during 1943–1945, when large swathes of territory were being recovered. Conditions in them resembled those of strict regime labor camps. Many of them were located in industrial and mining areas, and detainees were often required to perform heavy manual labor.[70]

One inmate, Sergei Terpilovskii, recalled the Stalinogorsk camp in Tula oblast, where he worked in a coalmine: "Barracks, poor food, work. They would summon you to the investigators in the evening, or in the daytime if you were working the evening shift. There were lots of questions: how were you captured or did you surrender? Why didn't you shoot yourself? Why did you work in a military factory?—as if I went there voluntarily rather than with a machine-gun at my back. It all came down to one thing: a guilty verdict as soon as possible." In the west of Russia Evgenii Murshel lived in tents and had to transport stones and surface asphalt roads. There

everyone was registered according to their specialty: mechanic, metalworker, lathe operator, and so on. The specialists were distributed among the military units. But most, like me, had no specialty. During our stay in the camp we were detailed off to surface roads, lugging stones around (just like in occupied Simferopol). The junior officers supervising us sometimes behaved no better than Germans: they chivied us, shouted at us. There was one incident when someone from our brigade climbed onto a trailer conveying stones for another platoon and began to throw some of them out. Their commanding officer galloped up on his horse and struck him a fearful blow with his riding crop, as a result of which he had a heart attack.[71]

Later Murshel was transferred to a camp near Perm, where he was required to fell timber in -30 to -40 degree temperatures in ragged clothing, with worn footwear and without proper mittens. His pay depended on his output. Eventually the investigations began:

A raw young man in uniform came and started to fill in questionnaires. We were taken one by one to see this official. Everyone returned from seeing him either very downcast or barely containing their anger. At last it was my turn. And what do you think? It was some kind of madman filling in those questionnaires. He kept on twitching. What was the use of talking to him? I said I had been captured when my regiment ceased its existence. The Germans had pulled me out of a swamp in the Udai basin somewhere near Piriatino. "We know all about that," he shouted. I should think you do, I thought, it's your lot that destroyed the army. "I can see through you," he shouted. "You're a spy!" He seized me by the hair, pulled my head back, and gazed into my eyes.[72]

Eventually, when he received news that his father had died in Kazakhstan, Murshel was allowed to go and settle with his mother there, but only as a *spetsposelenets,* a political exile.

By December 1946, 5.4 million returnees had been through filtration camps, 1.8 million military personnel and 3.6 million civilians. Investigations were conducted by the NKVD, the NKGB, the military procuracy, and a new counterintelligence organization called SMERSH (short for *smert shpionam,* "death to spies"), set up to detect agents infiltrated into the USSR by foreign intelligence services. Their work sometimes took several years, and for some of the investigated the end result was execution or long prison sentences. In other cases, already before the return home, former POWs were gathered at meetings where, as one soldier recalled, a political officer "told us that we had committed a grave offense before the motherland and our people, and proposed that we sign on voluntarily for five years' construction work in the Urals as the only way to atone for our guilt."[73]

An especially remarkable case was that of Lieutenant General I. A. Laskin, who had received the capitulation of Field Marshal Paulus in Stalingrad in 1943, and had been decorated by both the Soviets and the Americans. In August 1941, when still a colonel, he had been surrounded near Uman, captured, and interrogated by a German noncommissioned officer. After a few hours he had succeeded in escaping and rejoining his unit. Knowing about the NKVD investigations, he had decided to conceal his brief period in captivity. The fact came out, however, in 1943, and he was arrested. The investigation of his case took nine years, and in 1952 he was sentenced to fifteen years' corrective labor.[74]

Of those interrogated, some 340,000—those who had served in the German army, the Vlasov army, or the police—were handed over to the NKVD. Some were shot as traitors, some were sent to strict regime labor camps, and some were treated like deported peoples, sent to "special settlements" where they lived in exile. Roughly 600,000 were assigned to hard labor battalions working in places like the Donbass coalmines or felling timber in the far north. Just over a million were sent for further service in the Red Army. Even those not mobilized or subjected to criminal penalties suffered discrimination thereafter, in many cases to the end of their lives. Any documents they had at the time of repatriation were confiscated, and they received a "temporary certificate," which recorded their sojourn under occupation, assigned them to a particular region (not necessarily where they had previously lived), and enabled them to apply there for a residence permit, but did not guarantee them one. In other words, it left them with a permanent black mark on their identity documents, and at the mercy of the local police and party officials.[75]

Aleksandra Fedorovna Lychagina, for example, had been deported to Germany to work as a farm laborer. In summer 1945 it took her two months to return, via various displaced person camps, to her home in Michurinsk, near Moscow. There she discovered that her husband, Mikhail, a major in the army, whom she had married only just before the outbreak of war, was now stationed in the Far East, and that her parents had

sold their joint home and moved elsewhere. She crowded in with her poverty-stricken elder sister, the sister's husband (who had returned from the
war minus one leg), and their children, and she reported to the local
MVD (as the NKVD had now been renamed). There, as she reports in
her diary, the station chief warned that "until I undergo an investigation
and receive identity papers I have no right to leave the town. If I ignore
his warning, I will be arrested and imprisoned for five years." Unable to
visit either her parents or her husband, she appealed to the town council,
where she was even more harshly received. The secretary of the party cell,
she recalled, said "I ought to be exiled to Kazakhstan for having been in
captivity in Germany. There is no place for me here." Six months later, after many fruitless visits to the MVD, and an equally fruitless letter to
President Kalinin, she noted in her diary: "I don't live a normal human
life. I have no passport, no right to life, which a person should have in his
own country. *I really regret I didn't die during the war!*"

Aleksandra's marriage fell apart, since she could not get to see Mikhail,
and she took up with another man, Kostia, whom she had known at
school. But Kostia's brother advised him not to marry her "because there
was a shadow over me. Kostia told me that, and we separated." Later she
discovered that Mikhail had married again, but that the marriage had not
worked out: he had committed suicide by throwing himself under a train,
having sent his wife a telegram saying, "Your husband has been killed."[76]
One cannot say for certain that the stigmatizing of those who returned
from captivity ruined her marriage, but it clearly deprived her of any serious opportunity to save it.

As a lingering token of mistrust, right up to the end of the Soviet
Union all citizens applying for a job, education, or a living permit had to
fill in a questionnaire that asked, among other things, "Were you or any of
your relatives in captivity or on occupied territory?" This question was
finally deleted only in 1992.[77]

The regime's distrust extended to the partisans, that is, to the Soviet
Union's most staunch defenders, those who fought for its cause behind
the German lines. The Soviet leaders had not anticipated fighting a partisan war and had made no preparations for one, partly because they anticipated an offensive war, and partly because they distrusted their own population. Although Stalin's radio address of July 3, 1941, called for the
development of partisan combat in occupied territory, in practice the Soviet leaders were cautious about encouraging such activities during the

early phase of the war, for they were worried about sanctioning the formation of armed bands beyond their control. The first partisans were young men in occupied territory who wished to avoid German labor conscription. In response, to exert some control over them, the Soviet authorities created a network of underground party and NKVD cells, and emphasized that partisan units should be formed under the personal supervision of responsible leaders from those cells.

Soviet officials found, however, that local people and scattered Red Army units deep in the German rear were improvising their own fighting detachments with or without supervision, and so they hastened to equip those units as far as was practical, in order to gain some influence over them. A Central Staff of the Partisan Movement was set up, attached to the Red Army. It had its own representatives in each army front, who were supposed to keep in radio contact with partisan detachments behind the lines in their area. The Central Staff was led by the Belorussian Communist Party first secretary, P. K. Ponomarenko: command was thus vested in the most prominent nomenklatura figure from the republic with the greatest number of partisans. The NKVD had its own *osobyi otdel* (special department) in each partisan detachment, partly to provide security against enemy infiltration, but also undoubtedly to keep an eye on the partisans themselves and on local people. For the same reason political commissars were appointed to each detachment; they were kept on with full powers even after their equivalents had been downgraded in the Soviet Army in October 1942.[78]

In the summer of 1942 there were probably some 150,000 partisans active in the German rear, especially concentrated in Belorussia and northern Ukraine, where the swampy, wooded terrain favored their activity. Their numbers grew progressively thereafter, and the effectiveness of their operations is undeniable: parts of Belorussia were more or less under their control, and even elsewhere the movement of German troops and supplies was under constant threat. The Wehrmacht had to divert some 10 percent of its men from frontline duty to guard supply depots and communications deep in the rear. All the same at the end of the war most partisans had to undergo filtration by the Soviet authorities, and unless they could demonstrate their unbroken loyalty—obviously difficult to do in the confused circumstances—they could suffer discrimination or even criminal penalties. This was a strange reward for what might have been considered a sterling demonstration of courage and patriotism.

On the other hand, there was good reason for the authorities' suspicions: although many Ukrainians were willing to become citizens of the Soviet Union, some were irreconcilably hostile to it. Remembering the state-imposed famine and terror of the 1930s and the brutal annexation of western Ukraine in 1939–1941, they were determined to prevent the reimposition of Soviet authority after the war. The UPA (Ukrainian Insurgent Army), established in 1943, fought against the Soviets as well as the Germans, and kept up the struggle even after the end of the war. They were only finally rooted out in the early to mid-1950s.[79]

The upshot, though, was that many of those who had fought against the Germans most resolutely and in the most adverse circumstances were denied full integration into the patriotic community after the war.

If there was any prospect of a cohesive Russian-led Soviet Union, then it was destroyed by the deportations carried out in 1939–1941 and 1944–1947. These took place in the Baltic republics, western Belorussia, western Ukraine, Moldavia, and the north Caucasus. The story is by now well known and does not need to be expounded here.[80] But certain aspects of it should be emphasized. The deportations aimed not just to rid sensitive territory of potentially unreliable people but often actually to annihilate the ethnic groups involved. In the Baltic republics "only" some 1.5 to 4 percent of the population was deported in 1940–1941, but they were intellectuals and professional people, all those who might lead anti-Soviet political parties or independence movements; a further 3 percent or so were deported after 1945, mostly "kulaks" victimized during collectivization. After the occupation of western Ukraine and Belorussia in 1939, some 900,000 people were deported, about half as prisoners and half as "special settlers" (spetsposelentsy), technically not in confinement but required to live in certain locations and to report regularly to the police. Of these, some 52 percent were Poles, 30 percent Jews, and 18 percent Ukrainians and Belorussians. In Moldavia there were some 90,000 victims in the wave of arrests and deportations that immediately followed the annexation of 1940, and even more in the dekulakization and famine of 1946–1947: probably some 115,000 peasants starved and some 16,000 families were transported to Siberia and Kazakhstan. In all these regions, moreover, agriculture was collectivized, industry was nationalized, and culture and education were brought under Communist control and censorship in the established Soviet pattern, without any consideration for the specific features of the peoples involved.[81]

In other cases entire peoples were deported: the Germans, Crimean Tatars, Meskhetians, Kalmyks, Chechens, Ingushes, Balkars, and Kara-chais. They were moved without any concern for their health during the journey, so that many died of cold, hunger, and untreated disease. Those who survived were resettled in regions wholly unfamiliar to them—for example, the Caucasian mountain people in the semi-arid plains of Kazakhstan—so that it was difficult for them to re-establish their economic life. Moreover, they were deprived of education or any public media in their own language. In essence the policy was attempted genocide through physical mortality and cultural deprivation.[82]

These peoples, understandably, reacted with extreme anti-Russian and anti-Communist embitterment and also a sense of collective victimization that rendered them irreconcilable to continued Soviet rule. They brought a new mood to the postwar labor camps. Whereas prewar inmates had cringed before the guards and criminal "trusties," these new contingents imported a feeling of ethnic solidarity and moral outrage that made them impossible to infiltrate or manipulate. In fact, they began to organize the murder of informers in their midst. Aleksandr Solzhenitsyn records that in the camp where he was confined everyone feared informers until former soldiers of the Ukrainian Insurgent Army arrived and made short work of them: "Other forms of human association now bound people more closely than the work teams artificially put together by the administration. Most important were national ties. National groups—Ukrainians, United Muslims, Estonians, Lithuanians—which informers could not penetrate, were born and flourished. No one elected the leadership, but its composition so justly satisfied the claims of seniority, wisdom and suffering that no one disputed its authority over its own nation."[83]

In that way new, specifically anti-Soviet forms of social solidarity were generated during and after the war. Later, after Stalin's death, the policies of national victimization were revoked, and many of the deported were allowed to return to their homelands. Nonetheless, the memory of attempted genocide left an enduring legacy of bitter resentment. These peoples became and remained profoundly unreconciled to both Soviet and Russian domination. In the end they made a major contribution to the eventual collapse of the Soviet Union: as we shall see, the Baltic republics were the first to declare their secession from it, and the outcome of the Ukrainian referendum of December 1991, heavily influenced by west Ukrainian attitudes, was its final death knell. Last but not least, the

Chechens have given post-Soviet Russia its most protracted and insoluble internal conflict. All these developments are legacies of mistakes—indeed terrible crimes—committed by the Soviet leaders before, during, and immediately after the war.

As for the Russians themselves, the war had for a time given them a sense of shared purpose with their leaders. It had offered the opportunity to bridge the gap between elites and masses, to consolidate and confirm the patriotic narrative that the party had deployed during the 1930s, and to give it a broad popular resonance. *Rodina,* home, family life, and conjugal love had been revalidated, acknowledged as valuable for their own sake. It is of such materials that nations are constructed. But the mindset engendered by enduring nomenklatura domination fatally impeded the process. The incipient civil institutions granted to Russians during the war—a free agricultural market, the reopening of churches, relaxed cultural censorship, the somewhat freer and more spontaneous media—were withdrawn or emasculated after it. Especially damaging to the forging of civic solidarity among former soldiers was the policy of either banning regimental and veterans' associations or subjecting them to strict party control.[84] Furthermore, Stalin indicated in 1946 that it would be inadvisable to publish memoirs on the war, because it was too early to take an objective view of it. That statement was in effect a prohibition of them, which lasted some ten years. Even after the ban was lifted, memoirs were heavily edited and censored.[85] Memories of the war were to be strictly rationed and shaped to the purposes of the regime, not articulated as part of authentic social memory.

Where memory is not validated in the public media, where it cannot be periodically reinforced by the spontaneous exchange of personal recollections in the community, then it becomes fragmented, insubstantial, and cannot function as an underpinning of national identity. That was an especially serious matter in a country where there were so many deaths to be mourned and so much suffering to be assimilated. In the Soviet Union, memory became instead part of the official narrative, deployed to celebrate and bolster the regime, and otherwise to be treated with extreme suspicion. As a result, Soviet patriotism remained in large part that of a ruling elite, manipulated for purposes of political rule, and therefore resonating uncertainly and in distorted fashion among ordinary people.

In one sense, the outcome of the war did confirm the millennial outlook of the Communist Party's convinced believers. True, the perfect society had not been built, and there was no prospect of its being built any time soon. But on the other hand, the Soviet Union *had* averted the apocalypse, in the form of Nazi victory, and had saved Europe from it, too. That was not a bad second best, a genuine international mission accomplished against enormous odds. But that very success had a strange effect on Communist millenarianism. The center of gravity of the symbolic life of the Soviet state, and therefore of Soviet society too, shifted from the future to the past, from anticipation of the distant triumph of socialism to remembrance of the very real and undeniable victory of Soviet arms in what everyone could agree in calling "the Great Patriotic War." This fixation on the past combined with the fracturing of national identity, *russkii, rossiiskii,* and *sovetskii,* to hollow out the spiritual life of the Soviet peoples and to undermine their sense of community. In that way the Soviet regime gradually negated its own greatest triumph, weakened its bond with the Russian people, and prepared the way for its own eventual downfall.

# 7

# THE SWEET AND BITTER
# FRUITS OF VICTORY

May 9, 1945, was the greatest day in Russian history. Alexander Werth, the British journalist, was in Moscow for the victory celebrations and reported: "The spontaneous joy of the two or three million people who thronged Red Square that evening—and the Moscow River embankment, and Gorkii Street all the way up to the Belorussian Station—was of a quality and a depth I had never yet seen in Moscow before. They danced and sang in the streets; every soldier and officer was hugged and kissed; outside the US Embassy the crowds shouted 'Hooray for Roosevelt!' (even though he had died a month before); they were so happy they did not even have to get drunk, and under the tolerant gaze of the militia, young men even urinated against the walls of the Moskva Hotel, flooding the wide pavement. Nothing like *this* had ever happened in Moscow before."[1]

There was ample reason for their rapturous informality, their patriotism, and their spontaneous internationalism. As we have seen, at a Kremlin reception for Red Army commanders on May 24, Stalin had raised a special toast to the Soviet people and, above all, to the Russian people, "the most outstanding of all the nations that make up the Soviet Union . . . the directing force among all the peoples of our country . . . [for their] clear mind, staunch character, and patience." He admitted that the government had made mistakes. "Another people might have said to its Government: 'You have let us down. Get out and we will put in place another Government, which will conclude peace with Germany and ensure us a quiet life.' But the Russian people did not do that, for they had faith in the correctness of their government's policies, and they accepted sacrifices to make certain of Germany's defeat. That faith of the Russian people in the Soviet Government was the decisive force which guaranteed victory over the enemy of humanity—fascism."[2]

We may presume that Stalin was being sincere on this occasion. What he said was a pretty clear statement of the reasons that after 1945 the regime made Russian patriotism a central plank of its policy. He had never before so wholeheartedly praised the Russian *people*—as distinct from the Russian state tradition. He abandoned the rather contemptuous attitudes of Lenin and Bukharin toward the Russian people and explicitly recast Russians as the central pillar of the Soviet multiethnic polity. But the terms in which he praised them are revealing: he implied that he valued them because they were patient and accepting, unlikely to cause trouble, raw material at the regime's disposal for its policies, however mistaken. This was a subliminal warning not to expect a genuine constitution or democratic elections.

The warning was needed, for the victory aroused the greatest expectations. A people who had achieved such a signal triumph expected to be treated at least with respect. Such treatment was incompatible with, among other things, the current condition of the kolkhozy, as an anonymous correspondent complained to Stalin: "Have the people of Siberia really deserved to be condemned to slow starvation? After all this is a heroic people, a people of great warriors *(narod-bogatyr)* . . . Don't send your answer to me. Reply to the Russian people. They want to know if they are valued by the state or just an unnecessary burden."[3]

Stalin's exaltation of the Russian people was, then, conditional on their docility; it was still subordinated to the needs of the state. There were two distinctive features about the public mood on which this official patriotism rested. First, conscious national pride was much more widely felt and supported than ever before. During the 1920s and 1930s nearly all Russians, male and female, except the very elderly, had learned to read and write in their own language and had absorbed much of the history and culture of their own country. Many of them had been urbanized, integrated into social security systems, and undergone other changes of the kind envisaged by Karl Deutsch, Ernest Gellner, Benedict Anderson, and others as fortifying national consciousness. During the war they had read newspapers and listened to radio bulletins with greater attention than ever before. In addition, the young men had gone through the binding experience of combat in the great national war between Russians and Germans. Russian patriotism was thus now for the first time ever a mass phenomenon, and it had become so partly as a result of Soviet policies—even if that had not originally been the intention of the Soviet leaders themselves.

Second, the *russkii* and the *rossiiskii* had largely coalesced, and that coalescence took the form of the *sovetskii*. Russians accepted as never before the right of the state to interfere in their lives, indeed to determine completely many aspects of it. Many non-Russians (though, as we shall see, not all) also accepted the legitimacy of a Soviet state that was led mainly by Russians and transmitted its values through Russian language, history, and culture. People from all nationalities, especially the young and upwardly mobile—and there were plenty of those after the wartime destruction—saw that legitimacy as grounded in the recent victory, in the USSR's resulting superpower status, and in the momentous project of building Communism, not just for the Soviet peoples, but ultimately for the exploited and oppressed of the whole world.[4]

This patriotism was articulated in both positive and negative ways in the postwar years. Many people drew the lesson that no imperialist power could be trusted, and so they were ready to make sacrifices for the sake of improving defense against the United States. A woman from Leningrad wrote in October 1950 to Kliment Voroshilov, Deputy Chairman of the Council of Ministers: "Our government and Comrade Stalin should know that we want our army and our Soviet Union to be very strong. If it's necessary for the army, let food become dearer, raise a new loan, do whatever is needed. . . . Forgive me for interfering, but the Soviet Union belongs to all of us, and the army too. My husband was in the war, and my son will go to fight."[5]

Russians assumed that they were entitled to the leadership role in the Soviet Union, not just because they were numerically the largest nationality, but also because, as a Russian engineer put it, "Russians are not nationality-minded, but state-minded." He expressed the view that, if an Armenian or Ukrainian on Russian territory were asked who he was he would reply, "a Russian." Russians, he felt, also had the highest culture, and so other nationalities readily looked up to them without belittling their own culture. A Ukrainian engineer commented that Russians were not nationalistic but felt "patriotism for the socialistic state of Russia, which has to destroy the capitalistic system the world over." He added, "I am Ukrainian, but my fatherland is the Soviet Union."[6]

Moreover, the consciousness of an international mission, extending beyond the borders of the USSR, reached a new height. Looking back on that time decades later, the Russian-Jewish historian Mikhail Gefter commented, "What we had then was our own, *russkoe, rossiiskoe, sovetskoe,* but we also belonged to the World."[7] It is significant that a Jew expressed this sentiment: many non-Russians, but especially the Jews, were more than ready to acknowledge Russian primacy at this juncture, precisely because of the international and messianic mission of the USSR.

Of course, the Russians' missionary nationalism could be looked at from the other end of the telescope. One Ukrainian, interviewed in emigration after the war, poured out a flood of invective against the Russians: they regarded themselves as a "chosen people," they rode roughshod over local traditions and spoke their own language everywhere, refusing to learn the native language. Other Soviet peoples, by contrast, he felt, were more open and more likely to help each other out, regardless of ethnic distinctions. A young Russian army officer indirectly confirmed this view of his own people when he commented that Ukrainians were "always dreaming of their independence. . . . They consider themselves insulted, but that will gain them nothing, especially in the struggle with Bolshevism."[8]

Wise leadership might have conserved both Russian patriotism and the Russian leadership and cemented a more harmonious and united Soviet Union. But wise leadership was not forthcoming. Instead the nomenklatura elite, fortified by the war, moved to consolidate its grip on an uprooted and insecure postwar population, of which it had always been suspicious.

The suspicion was mutual. Many people of all ranks, Russians and non-Russians, continued to distrust the Soviet regime and to hope that it would be forced by the wartime allies to make concessions to its own peoples. The distrust found an outlet in rumors. According to a mathematics teacher from Voronezh, "Intellectuals. . . thought that after the war Stalin would have to make concessions to Roosevelt and Churchill . . . that there would be a new NEP, that the monopoly of foreign trade would be changed, and that ties—both cultural and material—with the West and especially with America would be improved and increased. I heard a lot being said about it from different sorts of people."[9] This was the kind of wishful thinking generated by the absence of open public media.

## Origin of the Cold War

It was both paradoxical and frustrating that, at the very moment of its greatest victory, the USSR should be confronted with a danger potentially more threatening than any it had yet faced: the atomic bomb. The Americans' "successful" bombing of Hiroshima and Nagasaki in August 1945 gave notice that a new era in warfare had opened, in which the multimillion-strong Red Army and its recent sweeping territorial gains suddenly looked almost irrelevant. As the British ambassador, Sir Archibald Clark Kerr, put it, "Russia was balked by the west when everything seemed to be within her grasp. The three hundred divisions were shorn of much of their value."[10]

If the Soviet Union was to remain true to its self-appointed task of spreading socialism around the world, then it could do so only as a great power capable of tackling the United States as the ringleader of imperialism. So at least Stalin saw it, and the logic was that the Soviet Union must, like the United States, have the atomic bomb. The country's political structure and its war mentality made it possible to prioritize resources in such a way as to gather the necessary scientific and technical expertise, and build laboratories, factories, and testing grounds at maximum speed. Slave labor was even available from the NKVD for the dirty and dangerous work, such as digging uranium ore in Central Asian mines or erecting a nuclear reactor near Cheliabinsk. The prisoners were inadequately protected against radiation, and most of them died fairly quickly. Even the ordinary population was not much better protected. Near the Cheliabinsk reactor radiation sickness was reported in 1949, and in 1951 it was discovered—though of course not reported in the media—that the Tobol River system was contaminated by nuclear waste. Thousands of people were evacuated and the affected watercourses were sealed off.[11]

The rivalry with the United States was of a kind Russia had never experienced before. Russians were used to enemies who threatened their borders directly. The United States was an ocean away and had no territorial claims on the USSR whatsoever. The confrontation was ideological. In some respects the two countries resembled each other: both were partly European, partly non-European, both had grown out of visions of the perfect society generated by the eighteenth-century Enlightenment, and both aimed to spread their particular version of it around the world. The new Soviet-Russian national identity stressed science, technology, urban growth, and a high-quality mass culture—and in all these areas the United States led the world. For that reason even convinced Soviet Communists in many ways admired the United States. The upshot was that the United States became the Soviet Union's defining "other." Throughout the period of their confrontation, Soviet citizens retained the tendency to judge their own society through a prism of what they knew about the United States. The unceasing rhetoric of confrontation sowed in them the latent assumption that, if things went seriously wrong at home, then at least the United States might know how to put it right. This tendency was to prove fateful when the USSR finally collapsed.

For the moment, however, the United States was international enemy number one, abhorred for its gross social inequalities, its ethnic conflicts, its uninhibited flaunting of power. If it succeeded in spreading its gospel around the world, then the USSR was doomed. The opposite was also true, so that, in spite of the absence of territorial disputes, the two became deadly adversaries. The formation of the North Atlantic Treaty Organization (NATO) in 1949, headed by the United States, confirmed this enmity. For each the other became the focal and defining influence in foreign and military policy.

In postwar Europe the USSR had the advantage of being a powerful neighbor. To consolidate that advantage, in 1944–1948 it built an "outer empire," a cordon sanitaire of Central and East European states whose social and political structure was similar to that of the Soviet Union itself. Single ruling Communist parties were installed, economic enterprises were nationalized and subjected to planning, farmers were expropriated and herded into collective farms, and education, culture, and the mass media were brought under strict political control.[12]

As in the USSR itself, these changes brought benefits to true socialist believers, and also to the officials who ran the new institutions. Most people, however, regarded with distrust and with lasting resentment the imposition of an alien and repugnant way of life. Furthermore, though the Second World War had been destructive, it had not obliterated social memory in the way revolution and civil war had done in Russia. National identity in Poland, Hungary, Czechoslovakia, Romania, and Bulgaria remained strong and now became generally, though to varying degrees, anti-Russian and anti-Communist. This was something Russians themselves could never understand. Had they not made huge sacrifices to liberate those peoples from Nazism? Had they not provided them with economic aid and advice at a time when Russians themselves were in desperate straits?

From the outset, then, the benefits of the outer empire were reduced or even nullified by the sullen hostility of most of its population. Over the decades that mood evolved into resigned acquiescence, but it never disappeared. The Soviet bloc provided territorial depth, but that was increasingly irrelevant in the age of ballistic missiles. It was also a perpetual source of security worries and heretical ideas. That was part of the cost of converting messianic Russia into a superpower.

## The Official Ideology

Russian-Soviet patriotism was articulated in the years after 1945 more fully and discursively than any previous form of Russian nationalism. It remained, with periodic slight modifications, the hegemonic ideology till the end of the Soviet Union, and it has strongly colored the outlook of post–Soviet Russian nationalists. The new patriotism established its dominance not only because it was officially proclaimed throughout the media, but also because it was congenial to the Russian-led multiethnic ruling class, and also to upwardly mobile war survivors moving into their first responsible jobs—the "new bourgeoisie" with which, as Vera Dunham first perceived, the regime concluded a "Big Deal."[13] It also provided a clear and unambiguous role for the USSR in the "cold war" with its former allies.

The ideology amalgamated the revolution and the Second World War as the "sacred past" of a new form of messianic, Russian-led internationalism. According to its tenets, Russia had played the key role in providing the inspiration and leadership for world socialism. The Soviet Union, with the Russian people at its heart, so the message ran, was leading the workers, peasants, and colonized peoples of the world toward victory in the great struggle with imperialism. As an official commentary put it, "Leninism, which was born in Russia and was closely associated with the revolutionary movement of the Russian *(rossiiskogo)* working class, was able to draw upon the achievements of progressive Russian *(russkoi)* culture and to use them in the interests of the workers' revolutionary movement. For that reason Leninism was rightly considered the highest achievement of Russian culture." At the same time Leninism "drew on the achievements of the culture of all peoples, saved them from falsification by bourgeois reactionaries and opportunists, critically refashioned the most valuable achievements of humanity in science and culture, and placed them at the service of the proletarian revolution."[14] This was "missionary nationalism" in its purest form.

The standard textbook on historical materialism issued by the Institute of Philosophy of the Soviet Academy of Sciences claimed that "the Russian people, led by the Russian working class, have offered and continue to offer generous and wide-ranging help in economics, politics, and culture to all the peoples of the USSR, so that they can build and develop socialist industry, a national and socialist state system, and a culture national in form and socialist in content. Thanks to the Soviet socialist system many of the peoples of the USSR—the Uzbeks, the Tadjiks, the Kirgiz, the Turkmens, the Kazakhs, and others—have completed a major historical leap from the ancient ox-plough to the tractor, from sickle and scythe to combine harvester, from the traveling smithy to the huge machine-building works." As Stalin put it, "Soviet patriotism combines harmoniously the national traditions of the peoples with the vital interests of all the toilers of the Soviet Union. Soviet patriotism does not divide but on the contrary unites all the nations and nationalities [*natsii i narodnosti*] of our country into a single brotherly family."[15]

To the possible objection that most socialists—including Lenin and his comrades—had hitherto considered patriotism a bourgeois ideology, a booklet published in half a million copies by the State Publishing House retorted: "It is not the bourgeoisie but the working class that today is the authentic spokesman and defender of the national interests of the peoples. It is the leading patriotic force of Soviet society, the most staunch and consistent champion of the cause of the motherland *(rodina)*." True patriotism was impossible in bourgeois society: "Private property limits patriotism by dividing people and acting as a source of enmity between them, but social property, as consolidated in the USSR, on the contrary unites people, blends their vital interests, aspirations, and actions. . . . The Soviet Union is the fatherland of the toilers of the whole world."[16]

Patriotism was now a thoroughly respectable sentiment, then. "Overcoming national prejudices," which *The ABC of Communism* had recommended as a prime duty of Communists, was now stigmatized as "cosmopolitanism." This meant "indifference to one's own homeland *(rodina)*, to one's fatherland *(otechestvo)*, to national culture and national traditions." Cosmopolitanism "endeavors to eradicate peoples' concepts of national honor, to blunt their patriotic feelings, and thus to undermine their will to struggle for independence and national liberation. . . . It runs counter to the national and international interests of the toilers."[17] As we shall see, cosmopolitanism was identified primarily with the Jews.

In 1947 Stalin summoned the writers Aleksandr Fadeev and Konstantin Simonov and warned them: "There is a very important theme . . . which writers should take up. That is the theme of our Soviet patriotism. If you take our average intelligentsia . . . professors, doctors, say, they have an inadequately developed sense of Soviet patriotism. They display unjustified reverence for foreign culture. . . . They still feel immature, . . . they've got used to being eternal pupils." Stalin put his reflections in historical perspective: "This is an outdated tradition and it can be traced back to Peter the Great. Peter had some good ideas, but too many Germans soon established themselves; this was a period of groveling to the Germans."[18]

Victory in the Second World War was held to demonstrate "the superiority of the Soviet system" and "its unconquerable strength. . . . By defeating the German and Japanese aggressors, the Soviet people saved the peoples of Europe and Asia from fascist tyranny, and that great service to humanity inspires in the hearts of Soviet people a legitimate feeling of national pride."[19] The threat was far from over, however: the international working class faced a new and dangerous enemy in the shape of world imperialism, led by the United States and embodied in NATO.

At the height of the "anti-groveling" propaganda, Russians were credited with having invented the steam engine, the electric light bulb, the radio, and the aircraft, while the eighteenth-century polymath Mikhail Lomonosov was lauded as the founder of modern science. A textbook on the history of science claimed: "In the history of discovery and exploration the Russian people justifiably occupy the number-one spot. . . . The Russian nation has always been a nation of discoverers. Courage and perseverance in pursuing their goals, endurance and an indestructible desire for discovery have been characteristic of its sons through the centuries-long history of Russia."[20] A vestigial inferiority complex remained, all the same, and with it the tendency to evaluate all Soviet achievements in the light of the experience of "bourgeois" societies.

Until the final years of the Soviet Union, this Soviet-Russian patriotism served as the basis for the civic education of the population, especially its young people. It reminded Isaiah Berlin, who in the late 1940s worked in the British Embassy in Moscow, of "public school religion, actively believed by a small minority, passively held by the rest."[21] In its full form it was meticulously worked out and articulated. Like the Hanlin Academy in Imperial China, the Institute of Marxism-Leninism preserved the sacred texts, periodically reviewing them, interpreting them, offering commentaries on them, and imposing authoritative interpretations in contentious cases. Whole institutions, headed by the Soviet Academy of Sciences, the Higher Party Schools, and the Central Committee's Academy of Social Sciences elaborated, explained, and construed the doctrine. Beneath them departments of ideology, propaganda, and culture, professional and creative unions, and whole armies of ideological workers—lecturers, consultants, agitators, and propagandists—disseminated Soviet-Russian patriotism through the mass media and at all levels of the educational system. Even more than before 1941 ideas possessed a unique importance in Soviet society. The life of the compliant intellectual was, though not affluent, more secure and stable than anywhere else in the world.

No student could gain a university degree without passing courses in Marxism-Leninism, the History of the CPSU, Political Economy, Scientific Atheism, and the like. In the Komsomol, DOSAAF (the Voluntary Society of the Army and Navy), and schools at all levels efforts were made to inculcate patriotism through making listeners aware of their home town, their district, their republic, the Soviet Union, and finally the international proletariat. In this way a compound identity was created: one was an inhabitant of Riga, a Latvian, a Soviet citizen, hence an honorary Russian *(rossiiskii)*, and also a member of the world's toiling classes.[22] Even for non-Slav peoples, the history and culture of Russia formed a compulsory paradigm.

In the case of Ukraine and Belorussia another level was implied or openly stated: in addition to being Ukrainian-Belorussian and Soviet, one could also be Russian *(russkii)*, a member of the triune Russian nation. For the first time in many centuries all the peoples of Ukrainian and Belorussian identity were united in their own states and bound by the closest ties with Russia (a brief prelude in 1939–1941 had been rudely interrupted by the German invasion). The relationship was not an easy one. As a direct result of Soviet policies Ukrainians and Belorussians had experienced dekulakization, the destruction of many productive farms, in Ukraine's case a disastrous famine, then terror, and the repeated purge of their political leaders, followed by the loss of their entire territory to the Germans. After the war Sovietization meant the ruthless imposition of collectivized agriculture, the planned economy, and Russian-Soviet culture in the newly integrated regions. Guerrilla fighters were crushed; political opponents were arrested and deported.[23]

A nationally conscious Ukrainian or Belorussian might well conclude that the Soviet leaders should not be entrusted with the fate of their country; that indeed was the conviction of those who joined the Organization of Ukrainian Nationalists (ONU) and fought in its guerrilla armies, first against the Germans, then against the returning Red Army. Similar partisan groups operated in the Belorussian marshes and forests. Their outlook was a natural though extreme result of the ethnicization of Soviet policies, intensified by the firsthand experience of Nazi ideology. The ONU demanded outright independence, and considered anyone who did not favor an ethnically pure sovereign Ukraine as an enemy, to be expelled or destroyed. They fought wars of national exclusion by turns against the Germans, the Poles, and the returning Russians. Their views reflected the general twentieth-century obsession with labeling and classifying, and, like the Nazis, they aimed at an ethnically cleansed population.[24]

The evidence suggests, though, that most Ukrainians and Belorussians were prepared to forget the crimes committed against them, to abandon the struggle for ethnic purity, and to settle down to rebuild their country as part of the multiethnic Soviet Union. This attitude was partly acceptance of the inevitable: once it was clear that the Germans were defeated and that the United States and Britain were not going to fight the USSR, there was no alternative. More was involved than fatalism, though. Stalin had not only united the territories of Ukraine and Belorussia but also persuaded the founders of the United Nations that both countries should have seats in its General Assembly, alongside the USSR. This move was a neat way of ensuring three votes for the USSR and at the same time celebrating the revived triune East Slav nation.

More important was the fact that Ukraine and Belorussia *were* united for the first time, and that the Ukrainian and Belorussian languages were the medium of instruction in most primary schools. The war had obscured memories of previous evils with a layer of fresh and horrifying impressions. Above all, Soviet citizens had little choice but to pick up the pieces and try to make their way in the new world. That process entailed filling out forms and presenting one's life story in the most favorable light possible, omitting mention of a kulak or Jewish background, eliding or distorting dubious behavior under German occupation, and emphasizing periods of Red Army service or partisan affiliation. The only way to survive was by "forgetting" unusable elements of one's past while playing up those that fitted into the now compulsory worldview. The war provided people with a myth that allowed them to re-evaluate their past and present themselves as patriotic Ukrainian, Belorussian, and Russian (the two were not mutually exclusive) Soviet citizens.[25]

One of the great strengths of the Soviet-Russian patriotic ideology was that it could be absorbed and understood on different levels. Rare indeed were the Soviet citizens who, once they had finished their exams, continued to take an interest in the whole complex and highly academic doctrine. Most Soviet citizens utilized the ideology in a much more workaday fashion, as justification for their routine actions and attitudes. At this level, shorn of its sophisticated superstructure, it resembled much more closely a crude and unreflective neo-Russian imperialism: the assumption that the Soviet Union was one of the world's two superpowers, leader in the struggle of good against evil, and that the Russians were the principal protagonists in this struggle, encouraging, inspiring, and helping the other Soviet peoples and the other nations of the socialist bloc to play their part in it. Victory in the Second World War confirmed the rightness of this view and inspired a renewal of the revolutionary faith of the early 1920s, short-lived though it proved in practice.[26]

This working ideology offered an assured position in society to the nomenklatura elite in party and state, in the military and the security services, in the economy, and in the major professions. They could all claim that they were making their contribution, in one way or another, to the power, the prestige, and the ideals of the Soviet state.

A backhanded compliment to this complex of ideas and sentiments was paid by the few underground opposition groups that existed in the postwar years. They consisted of young people who had been through the Soviet higher-education system and had thoroughly internalized its practices and its ideological messages. They formed secret circles with the paraphernalia familiar to them from the Komsomol: statutes, programs, party cards, or badges. They articulated their opposition to the system in Marxist terms, calling it "state capitalist" or "imperialist." They drew their inspiration from the wartime patriotic upsurge, whose ideals they believed their parents' generation was now betraying.[27]

In Voronezh, for example, seventeen- and eighteen-year-old schoolboys created a "Communist Youth Party" (CYP) which at one stage numbered more than fifty members. Their main aim, laid out in their party program, was "the construction of a Communist society throughout the world." Their intended technique was to infiltrate Soviet institutions and reorient them toward "genuine socialism." Like the CPSU, the CYP had its own Central Committee and its own Voronezh obkom. It was structured in cells of five, in each of which only one member knew any member outside the cell: this was a conspiratorial principle they would have read about in their history textbooks. New members took an oath in a blacked-out room: "I swear to keep the sacred secret of the CYP. I swear to fight to my last breath and to bear the banner of Leninism aloft until the final victory!"[28] At this stage even the opposition was inspired by the Soviet messianic mission.

## The Postwar Soviet Union

The end of the war confronted the Soviet peoples with a terrible paradox. They had just won the greatest war in history, yet at the same time their country was devastated and they mourned untold millions of dead. Soldiers being demobilized did not expect to find a flourishing country when they returned home. Even so, it was unsettling and dispiriting to see whole cities and villages reduced to jagged ruins, people living in dugouts and cellars or crowded together in the few surviving habitable buildings. The population of Voronezh had been reduced to 20 percent of its prewar size, that of Stalingrad to little over 10 percent. The British journalist Alexander Werth reported a Red Army soldier saying to him: "There's nothing left of Stalingrad, not a thing. If I had any say in the matter, I'd rebuild Stalingrad somewhere else: it would save a lot of trouble. And I'd leave this place as a museum."[29]

Factories, schools, farms, agricultural equipment, railway stations and rolling stock, gas, electricity, and water systems had been seriously damaged or destroyed, so that normal life was virtually impossible in much of European Russia. From the occupied regions some two and a half million people had been deported to forced labor in Germany or its satellites, leaving old men, women, and young people as the only surviving local workforce.[30]

Electoral meetings in January 1946 reflected the difficulties the population faced, their weariness, their worry about the future, and also a certain injured pride, an expectant patriotism combined with a gnawing distrust of the regime. Like the serfs who had not been freed after the Napoleonic war, they felt themselves cheated of a just reward for their sacrifices. In Sverdlovsk and Vologda they asked: "The war ended six months ago. Why are there constant shortages of matches, salt, and paraffin?" In Rostov-on-Don: "Why don't they release workers who were mobilized for emergency factory duty till the end of the war?" Elsewhere: "When will the citizens of Novgorod be moved from dugouts and cellars into houses?" "In Troitsk the water supply has not worked for two months. Nor has the electricity in schools and hospitals, not to mention private apartments. There is no-where to buy firewood or coal."[31] Such questions reflected weariness, dis-appointment, unrealistic hopes, and the general expectation that the state should provide for its citizens.

Some people complained about the electoral process itself. According to a party report from Penza oblast, a lathe operator (and party candidate) blurted out: "The elections are a fraud, a mere formality. The deputies are not the people's choice but the puppets of our rulers." A land surveyor complained: "Too much money and energy is being spent on preparations for the election to the Supreme Soviet. It's all just a formality, the confir-mation of a candidate already chosen." A stable-hand alleged: "These up-coming elections won't give us anything. Now, if they were held as in other countries, that would be another matter. In Russia there were free elections only under Kerenskii; the Communists will do their electing without consulting us."[32] Russians were aware of their own past and of what was going on in other countries, and the war had inspired many of them with the feeling that they deserved better from their own rulers.

They were also sensitive to inequality and unfairness. As Sonya Rose pointed out in her study of wartime Britain, patriotism makes people acutely conscious of the way burdens are shared out and doubly indignant at injustice. "Equality of sacrifice" becomes a crucial concept. In March 1947 a Moscow party agitator wrote to Stalin asking how he should an-swer embarrassing questions posed by ordinary people during the election campaign. Why were food prices higher than before the war, and why did the better-paid have access to special stores where goods were cheap, while most people had to make do with poorly stocked state shops or markets where prices were very high? From Molotov [Perm] a worker wrote to the Council of Ministers inquiring sarcastically if society was divided into the "super-competent" and the "worthless." "The super-competent live in luxury, they have their personal automobiles, their dachas, their holiday resorts, their huge salaries. But the 'worthless' (the great majority) mostly can't even feed themselves, no matter how hard they work. . . . Earlier we had 'depersonalization' (obezlichka) of people and labor. Now we have 'super-personalization' *(slishkom perelichka).* One person receives 4,000 rubles pay, another 250. How can you live on 250? Yet the 'cheap' person is a person too. He works and wants to eat. He also has children. And they want to eat too."[33]

Money was not the only decisive factor in determining how individuals fared. People lived largely on entitlements, to which they had to prove their right with documents handed out by officials of one sort and another. So everyone was dependent either on employers or on bureaucrats who could grant the appropriate vouchers. Those unable to establish any rights would crowd around markets and railway stations, hawking pathetic personal possessions or looking for opportunities to steal. Petty crime became universal, and former soldiers who had retained their weapons had more opportunities than most. When one returned soldier requested replacement of his lost party card, the investigation revealed that he had lost it while participating in an armed raid on a train! By contrast, a report from Saratov in October 1945 revealed that an officer had arrived back from Berlin, having served right through the war, only to be stabbed in the back on the main street. People wrote to newspapers complaining that "bandit gangs roam the cities with impunity, terrorizing the population. When darkness falls, citizens are afraid to go out on the streets. Workers do not show up for evening and night shifts. Party propagandists cannot do their job of visiting people in their homes. In some towns (Saratov, Arkhangelsk, etc.) the cinemas and theaters are empty, major political and cultural events are cancelled."[34]

Many frontline soldiers returned, inevitably, to find their homes destroyed or their families dispersed or fractured. Some wives had not withstood the long separation and had paired up with other men. Lives had been casually ravaged beyond repair. All this was unavoidable: returning soldiers were confronted with similar grim realities in all combatant nations. What was worse was the moral shock of finding that qualities valued at the front—courage, boldness, determination, devotion to comrades—were not required at home, indeed were positively dysfunctional in trying to get help from civilian officials. Aleksei Tarasov, a former frontline soldier, discovered when he returned home to Moscow that all his furniture had been sold and that his wife and three children had been evicted from their flat and were living in someone's bathroom. When he wrote to his factory committee asking for an overcoat for his wife and clothes for his eldest daughter, they assigned him one pair of lady's overshoes. When his daughter was invited to a celebration of the twenty-eighth anniversary of the Red Army, she burst into tears because she had no suitable clothes for the event. In February 1946, despairing of local officials, Tarasov went to the very top. He wrote to Molotov appealing for help. It worked: Molotov instructed V. Liubimov, People's Commissar for Trade, to look into his case and help him out.[35] Local bosses were helpless or obstructive, and only recourse to the very top would work—two characteristics that were to persist long after the war. The party-state elite had tightened its grip over society during the war and was not about to relax that grip at its moment of triumph.

Perhaps most shocking was the official treatment of soldiers who were permanently disabled in the war. These men were given the status of "invalids first class," but the benefits they received in the general economic stringency were meager. In Moscow disabled students lived in unheated, overcrowded hostels along with everyone else, and they were expected to get to their classes on trams and buses. In April 1946 two such students gave up the struggle and committed suicide. In October 1948 the Procurator-General reported that enterprises were not fulfilling their quotas for employing handicapped people or making adjustments to equipment and facilities to enable them to work usefully. As for the most seriously maimed, they would crouch at street corners and in outdoor markets begging or hawking their possessions. Someone in Kiev reported seeing a young lad without legs in military uniform hunched against the wall begging for bread or money. Then in 1947 the persistent beggars suddenly disappeared; they had been rounded up and dispatched to "special colonies" in the far north.[36]

When at last a Soviet Committee of War Veterans was permitted in 1956, one of the issues it raised immediately was the mistreatment of those who had been permanently disabled in the war. One speaker at the first meeting of the section of frontline soldiers reported seeing a disabled old soldier come into an office of a Leningrad raikom asking for help, whereupon he was sent packing with the words *"Mnogo vas takikh zdes khodiat"* ("There's no shortage of people like you around here.") The speaker complained that he had written several times to Zhukov about this matter but had received no reply. When he went to the reception room of the Ministry of Defense he had been given the brush-off.[37]

People who complained at being ignored by bureaucrats might easily find themselves accused of "slanderous assertions about Soviet and party

organs" and of taking an "antiparty line." As one official in the coal industry lamented in a letter to the Central Committee, most party, trade
union, and economic organizations considered domestic problems "of
secondary importance. . . . During the war the authorities had gotten used
to working with POWs, with people repatriated, interned, imprisoned,
encircled, mobilized . . . and they continue to behave toward workers as
they did toward people under armed escort."[38] Having won a great war,
the nomenklatura ruling class was digging in and constructing new pyramids of patron-client dependency. The habit of classifying, labeling, commanding, threatening, punishing, and granting or withholding benefits
helped them to consolidate their dominance.

## The Countryside after 1945

Nowhere were the costs of war and of the subsequent armed peace so protracted and so distressingly apparent as in the villages. When the war
ended hopes were high that the collective farms might be abolished. In
Pskov oblast one party worker was asked, "Will they dissolve the kolkhozy
soon? If they didn't exist, we would live better and bring the state more
benefit." In Penza oblast peasants were reported as saying: "The real victory will come when the kolkhozy are dissolved. Otherwise the situation there is hopeless: people receive no more than a hundred grams of
bread per labor-day. The Allies will force [our leaders] to break up the
kolkhozy."[39]

Contrary to their hopes, not only were the collective farms retained,
but the relative freedom of agricultural trade allowed during the war was
ended. Collective farmers were required to make high compulsory deliveries to the state, not only from the collective sector (as during the war), but
also from their private plots; the prices paid were low, sometimes not sufficient to cover the cost of production. From Penza oblast in May 1946
came the following complaint: "We went to war so our life should improve, but on the contrary it gets worse. Now they demand taxes [i.e.,
compulsory deliveries] twice as high as we paid in the war." From Riazan
oblast: "In Korostovo life is impossible, because they levy very high taxes:
300 liters of milk, 40 kilograms of meat, 75 eggs, and 1,500 rubles in
cash. Where can I raise all that, when I'm half dead myself and eat only
starch. We're all starved, walking around barefoot and half-naked." From
Stavropol region in June 1946: "Soldiers return from the army, but they

soon leave again, so there are only children to do the work, and they're hungry. There are no meals for those working in the steppe, and the women refuse to go out there. Only the second brigade is working, on the others' fields everything is choked by weeds."[40]

The poet Olga Berggolts visited a village in Novgorod oblast in May 1949 and noted in her diary: "The spring sowing has been turned into drudgery, almost forced labor. The authorities want a large area plowed urgently, but there is nothing to plow with—there are no horses (14 of them for a farm with 240 households) and just two tractors. So women with mattocks and spades are turning the soil over *by hand* ready for wheat."[41]

Villagers were also compelled from time to time to perform heavy manual work felling trees, lifting peat, or repairing roads. As before the war, payment to collective farmers for their work on the collective fields, their "labor days," was made only when all the farm's other financial obligations—taxes, compulsory deliveries, paying back loans to the State Bank—had been met. Quite a few kolkhozy paid their members little or nothing; yet at the same time prices increased for the produce villagers purchased from outside. Under a draconian law of June 1948, any farmers "maliciously avoiding work and leading an antisocial, parasitic way of life" were to be exiled to "distant regions." By 1953 some 33,000 people had suffered this fate, including old people, invalids, and adolescents.[42]

In 1946–1947 wartime devastation compounded by agricultural underproduction triggered a famine, which struck with particular force in the grain-growing regions. The Kaluga party obkom, for example, reported that "the kolkhoznitsa Tsareva Evdokiia, whose husband died at the front and who has three children, earned 300 labor-days but received no grain [for them]. She has no cattle, and the bread and potatoes in her household have all been consumed. She and her children are all ill from undernourishment." Similar scenes were played out over large areas of Russia and Ukraine. The leading historian of the famine estimates that in the USSR as a whole some 100 million people were undernourished and some two million died prematurely as a result, at least half a million of them in Russia, while perhaps two million more became long-term disabled as a result of malnourishment and eating noxious surrogates.[43]

Those who could do so reacted by emigrating from the village. Men who were fortunate enough to return from the war often departed almost before arriving. Far from founding new peacetime households, they were closing down existing ones: between 1945 and 1958 the number of households in collective farms fell by 20 percent, and by 25 to 30 percent in the north and non–black earth zones. Between 1950 and 1958 in those regions the number of active men fell from 1.9 to 1.7 million and the number of women from 3.9 to 2.7 million, so that the excess of women was reduced only slightly as the effects of war faded. The number of old people remained stable at 1.9 to 2 million, but, ominously for the future, the number of adolescents aged 12 to 15 fell sharply, from 1.2 million to 500,000: this was the stage when young people were departing for secondary education and vocational training, from which few returned permanently. The shortage of young people meant a decline in the number of children, from 3.5 million to 2.5 million.[44]

## Commemoration of the War

The question of how many Soviet citizens lost their lives as a result of the war remained taboo for a long time. The figure was difficult to calculate and terrible to contemplate. The Soviet leaders, whose mistakes had been partly responsible for the extent of the casualties, preferred not to make the effort. Khrushchev once surmised publicly a figure of twenty million, but he also remarked that "no one was keeping count." Not until the end of the USSR was it possible to make better grounded calculations. Now the number of those killed by enemy action or by war-generated hunger and disease is generally accepted to be about 27 million (though this figure must include some who died at Soviet hands, for example in the labor camps). Of these, roughly 8.7 million were combat deaths. The full demographic loss to the Soviet peoples was even greater: since a high proportion of those killed were young men of child-begetting age, the postwar Soviet population was 45 to 50 million smaller than post-1939 projections would have led one to expect (178.5 million in 1950 as opposed to 225 to 230 million). Of this "shadow" demographic loss the Russians, Ukrainians, and Belorussians bore a disproportionate share.[45]

It was not only a matter of absolute losses. Family structures were distorted by the disproportion of men and women. In 1959 (the first postwar census) there were 825 men for every 1,000 women (in the RSFSR the number was 814). For some age groups the discrepancy was even more marked. For every 1,000 people aged 35 to 39 (hence 17 to 21 in 1941), 385 were men and 615 were women. At aged 40 to 44 (22 to 26), the numbers were 401 and 599, respectively; at 45 to 49 (27 to 31), 399 and 601; at 50 to 54 (32 to 36), 381 and 619. Altogether there were only 600 to 700 men aged 30 to 50 for every 1,000 women of the same age. For many women the discrepancy meant either having no children or bringing them up without a permanent male partner. For children it meant having no father. Instead, "the New Socialist Man . . . was being raised by a legion of grandmothers," with the result that many children received a more archaic moral upbringing than would have been the case in a "normal" family.[46] This pattern may help to account for the generally traditional, unrevolutionary moral outlook of Soviet citizens who were children in the 1940s and 1950s. The dislocations of war were compounded by the disruption of continuity within the family and the absence of a male role model for many children. This factor helps explain the unprecedentedly unstable family life of Russians during the later Soviet decades, and therefore their demographic decline.

Few Soviet families were left unaffected by slaughter on this scale. Nearly all survivors had someone to mourn, someone either dead or left permanently disabled by the war. Yet the regime deliberately obstructed the cultivation of memory. An appropriate way of maintaining both Russian and Soviet national consciousness might have been to encourage community celebration and commemoration of the war, and to institute rituals of mourning for the huge losses. In practice, the opposite policy was followed. In 1947 May 9, Victory Day, was made into an ordinary working day, which it remained till 1964. Moreover, in a 1946 memorandum Stalin advised against the publication of war memoirs, indicating that it was too early to be objective about the war. (As if the function of memoirs was to be objective!) Probably he feared that memoirs would deflect attention from his role as personal leader of an impersonal machine—the retrospective wartime narrative he was then constructing. Stalin's "advice" was of course a binding command, so that war memoirs were in effect prohibited, at least till after his death.[47]

Military commemoration in the form of regimental parades was permitted and indeed encouraged. But the formation of veterans' associations was barred till 1956, even at the highest level. In May 1945 Semen Lozovskii, head of the Sovinformbiuro, proposed that two elite veterans' associations be set up—one a Council of Marshals chaired by Stalin, the other a Society of Heroes of the Soviet Union. His proposal was rejected. Even (perhaps especially) at such an august level Stalin was not willing to sanction gatherings of people who might in their cups get around to criticizing him. At the lower levels of society such associations were unthinkable. Instead, veterans would meet unofficially to drown their sorrows in cafes and bars, popularly known as "Blue Danubes." The writer Emmanuil Kazakevich noted in his diary on May 9, 1950: "Victory Day . . . I dropped into the bar *(pivnuiu)*. Two handicapped veterans and a plumber . . . were drinking beer and remembering the war. One of them was weeping, and then he said 'If there's another war, I'll volunteer again.'"[48]

## The All-Slav Committee

With the end of the war the whole purpose and nature of the Slav movement changed radically. The various Slav leaders returned to their countries and became influential figures there; the Slav Committee branches in those countries became more self-reliant, and it was much harder for Soviet leaders to monitor them, still less control what they were doing.

This decentralization placed the Ccmmittee's leaders in an awkward position. They had always been uneasily aware that it was counterproductive to address Slovak partisans or Canadian Dukhobors in the wooden language of Soviet bureaucracy, and that each audience required its own specific approach. But there was little they could do about it, since every dispatch had to be approved at the very top. Now after the war, far from easing, censorship tightened. Lozovskii, reproaching a correspondent on behalf of Sovinformbiuro for willfulness in interpreting Soviet foreign policy, had to explain: "We cannot organize the same kind of contribution as those made in the English press by journalists, scholars, and public figures, who put forward their own personal views on international politics. That is not our way of doing things." By "way of doing things" he meant, of course, political guidance and censorship. The Slav Committee secretary V. V. Mochalov protested with a picturesque mixed metaphor: "If you've given us the job, let us get on with it. If we overstep the mark, then rein us in, but to hold our coat-tails and stop us going anywhere—that is intolerable."[49]

The intention of the committee's leaders had been to convene an All-Slav Congress in Belgrade in May 1946 to coordinate the work and discuss the differences and disagreements that were increasingly impeding their activities. The congress was postponed, however, because the Soviet delegation felt they had not been given a sufficiently strong position in the organizing committee. The congress finally met in December 1946. Tensions were immediately apparent between the Soviet delegation and the others. Most participants wanted to revive and celebrate their national cultures and to assert their political autonomy, whereas the Soviet participants envisaged a more unified and disciplined common approach designed to secure peace and strengthen the socialist bloc.

With the hardening of the Cold War in the following year or so, those differences came fully out into the open. It had been agreed that a second congress should be held in Prague in June 1948. The Soviet Slav Committee had initially accepted this decision, but began to rethink it as it became evident that the Czechs were planning to use the opportunity to celebrate the centenary of the first Slav Congress, also held in Prague, in June 1848. The Soviets had no wish to recall nationalist triumphs of the past; on the contrary, they wanted to bolster socialist international solidarity for the future. At a preparatory meeting in summer 1947 the Soviet delegation insisted that the next congress "must not look back to the past, but should be dedicated to the present and future, and should arm the Slav peoples for the struggle for urgent contemporary issues, against the danger of a revival of fascism, and against those who would unleash a new war."[50] The Soviets brought strong pressure to bear on the Czechs to postpone the congress till later in 1948, so that it would no longer be seen mainly as a centenary celebration.

In the event, the congress was not destined to meet at all. Before it could do so, a fatal rift took place within the movement. Yugoslavia was expelled from the Cominform, the successor to the Comintern. This was the first unambiguous sign that the overbearing nature of Russian-Soviet imperialism was undermining solidarity in the outer empire. The split occurred because the Yugoslav leader, Marshal Tito, wanted to pursue a more ambitious plan of industrial development and collectivization of agriculture than Stalin considered expedient. The Yugoslav Communists, having liberated their country themselves, were not prepared to follow the Soviet line as abjectly as most of their East European colleagues. This rupture proved to be a mortal blow to the idea of Slav solidarity. The Cold War fronts had hardened, and Yugoslavia was now on the wrong side of them; one of the major Slav nations was in the enemy camp. By the same token, several non-Slav nations were on the correct side: Albania, Romania, and Hungary. The lineup in the Cold War was socioeconomic and political, not ethnic. Panslavism had become inexpedient. The international Slav Committee atrophied and was replaced in some of its functions by the foundation of the Council for Mutual Economic Aid in 1949. The Soviet Slav Committee was reduced in size and budget, and became in effect merely a department of the Soviet peace movement.[51]

The fate of the Slav Committee demonstrates yet again that the social and public initiatives supported by the Soviet government during and after the war were intended exclusively to protect and advance the USSR's great-power position. As soon as the committee's activities clashed with that imperative, it was downgraded. The rupture between Soviet citizens and émigrés became even more rigid than before the war. There was to be no mutual contact between émigré Russians or Ukrainians and their fellow countrymen in the Soviet Union, such as existed between Israelis and Jews of the diaspora, or even under Communist rule between Chinese émigrés and their counterparts in the People's Republic. There was no sense whatsoever of a world-wide community of Russians, independent of political regime.

## The Russian Orthodox Church

At the end of the war Stalin had ambitious plans for the Russian Orthodox Church. As always, these plans reflected great-power imperatives. Evidence suggests that his intention was for the church to establish itself as the leader among Orthodox churches and as the focus of faith for Orthodox believers all over the world. Having abolished the Communist International, he was now aiming to establish a kind of Orthodox International, headed by the Moscow Patriarch, as a rival to the Vatican. In his conception, such an ecclesiastical International would strengthen the standing of the Soviet Union, especially in Eastern Europe and the Middle East.

The process began with the abolition of the Uniate Church on the territories of Ukraine and Belorussia that had been annexed in 1939. The *Journal of the Moscow Patriarchate* celebrated the occasion as the final defeat of the "Polonizing and Latinizing tendencies" that had been dominant there since the sixteenth century. The Russian church had "demonstrated its universal mission by reuniting the whole Orthodox world and all the Slav peoples under a common ecclesiastical and national rallying call, as originally conceived by the immortal Saints Cyril and Methodius.

'Moscow the Third Rome' remains the symbol of this universal all-inclusive concept, a counterweight to the papacy, with its drive to spiritual tyranny, episcopal aristocracy, and its manic dreams of earthly power."[52]

In January-February 1945, for only the second time since 1700, a National Council *(pomestnyi sobor)* of the Russian church was convened in Moscow, with a number of foreign Orthodox dignitaries present. As Patriarch Sergii had died by that time, the council's main business was to elect a successor, Metropolitan Aleksii of Leningrad. Stalin ensured that the occasion was lavishly financed, with 65 meters of silk for the hangings and 35 meters of carpeting for dignitaries arriving at the assembly. Ecclesiastical valuables were returned from the State Historical Museum, and generous gifts were presented to foreign guests—everything possible to impress delegates with the standing of the Russian church and the support of its own government.[53]

Russia's prelates followed up the council by visiting their counterparts in the Balkans and Middle East, while Patriarch Aleksii sent out invitations to a Pre-Conciliar Consultation to be held in 1947. Metropolitan Nikolai visited church leaders in the Balkans and Middle East to solicit their support, sometimes with financial inducements. Initially he was extremely successful. The Karlovci Church had lost ground among émigrés for supporting Hitler. In addition to Nikolai's outgoing personality, his persuasive rhetoric and his evident erudition won over many doubters.[54]

The Pre-Conciliar Consultation was intended to clear up controversial issues such as the church calendar, the date of Easter, and relations with other Christian churches. It would thus prepare the ground for the Orthodox Church's highest international gathering, an Ecumenical Council. By 1947, however, the Cold War was beginning to take hold, and the Vatican and the American Protestant churches were activating their own diplomacy. Only the churches in the new people's democracies accepted Aleksii's invitation. The Patriarchs of Jerusalem and Alexandria declined, on the grounds that the consultation would better be held in Jerusalem or on Mount Athos, "where we should be free from the great commotion of this earthly life, and from any political interference or pressure." Archbishop Leontii of Cyprus, probably deliberately, misunderstood the invitation and answered as if he were being summoned already to an Ecumenical Council, which, he objected, could be convened only by the Ecumenical Patriarch of Constantinople.[55]

In the end, then, there was no proper consultative assembly, let alone an Ecumenical Council. The church had in effect let Stalin down, and he treated it henceforth with less consideration, keeping it in reserve mainly as a tool of international diplomacy. After autumn 1947 very few parishes were opened, and none after March 1948. In fact, some churches that had been reopened under German occupation were closed again. The local soviet would claim the buildings were urgently needed for grain storage or some other purpose; in a few cases the closure was carried out during a service, with insulting language and behavior.[56]

Even where parishes had been opened, strict limits were placed on what they could do. Their principal business was the weekly conduct of divine service in an approved building. They were allowed to ring bells to summon the faithful to prayer, but in practice very few churches still possessed bells after the depredations of recent years, and casting new ones from scrap metal was forbidden. In all other respects the prohibitions of the 1929 Law on Religious Associations remained in force. After 1948 religious processions in public were restricted to the immediate vicinity of the church.[57]

The authorities had good reason to be concerned. Religious feeling was at a high level among Russians, Ukrainians, and Belorussians, especially in the western regions that had been under Polish rule till 1939, then under German occupation. There was plenty of evidence of religious activity elsewhere too. In 1946 the Council for Orthodox Church Affairs reported that in Stalingrad at Easter eight thousand people tried to attend the service in one church, and six thousand each in two others. In Ulianovsk some ten thousand worshippers came to celebrate the festival of Nicholas the Wonder-Worker, and there were mass prayers in front of his icon. In Kalinin oblast the rural population was celebrating religious festivals whether or not there was an active church; in the village of Okovtsy, where there was none, believers gathered by a holy spring to say their prayers. In Kirov oblast priests were going out to the fields to pray for rain, while in Pskov oblast priests were reported to be making money by "going on tour," visiting churchless parishes and performing sacraments requested by the local people. The secular authorities were not above exploiting these sentiments: in Dnepropetrovsk they actually asked priests to preach to the farmers on the value of hard work and care of collective property, and in several regions it was common to ask the church to help with the sick and handicapped.[58]

The motive for religious activity was often worry or grief over those lost in the war. In the town of Kimry, Kalinin oblast, a blind man would sing in the streets and people would give him money to go into the churches and pray for their dead and missing loved ones. In Novosibirsk oblast a twenty-one-year-old sailor from the navy had himself baptized because his ship had been mined, he had lost most of his colleagues, and he himself, while struggling in the water, had taken an oath to be baptized.[59]

The Council for Orthodox Church Affairs received a large number of petitions to reopen churches. There would often ensue a long delay, during which initiative groups of believers would occupy empty church buildings and began to use them for services without permission. In Central Russia by 1948 there were perhaps two to three times as many unofficial prayer houses as legally active churches. In the village of Riazantsy in Moscow oblast villagers declared that, if their church was not reopened for services, they would stop working in the kolkhoz, while at a village near Volokolamsk they threatened to write to a foreign embassy and reveal the truth about "freedom of religion" in the USSR.[60]

Karpov warned the government that refusing parishes only stimulated religious fanaticism, and thus played into the hands of enemies of Soviet power. He suggested that his council, rather than the local soviet, should have power to decide about reopening churches, but his request was turned down.[61]

Even the church hierarchy itself became nervous at the unrestrained revival of religious life and the reaction to it of excitable and minimally trained priests. When in 1947 Archbishop Luka tried to organize Sunday schools in Tambov diocese, Patriarch Aleksii wrote to him warning: "Suppose the impossible happened and Sunday schools were permitted. How many pretexts would they offer for accusations of counter-revolutionary deviations, of anti-Soviet activities and so on! How many new victims would there be! So it is just as well that servants of the cult are spared that danger."[62]

The hazards that popular religiosity posed for church-state relations were demonstrated in Saratov at Epiphany 1949. Some 10,000 people took part in a cross-bearing procession around the cathedral; they then went down to the Volga River bank to commemorate Christ's baptism in the River Jordan by receiving a blessing from a crucifix steeped in the water. Several hundred participants were not content with this perfunctory sacrament, and after the service they broke through a police cordon and insisted on taking their blessing in the archaic form of full immersion in the river. This massive unauthorized religious spectacle was precisely the kind of thing the regime was allergic to. Karpov tried to defend the church authorities. "Such bathings," he commented, "are not an ecclesiastical ritual. On the contrary, according to the Deputy Patriarch Metropolitan Nikolai, it is an ancient, probably pagan tendency, and in any case incorrigibly fanatical. The clergy did not encourage the bathing. . . . It was the duty of the local administrative organs to prevent such violations of public order." A satirical article on the "Saratov bathings" was published in *Pravda,* and the Patriarch reprimanded the local clergy for failing to foresee and prevent the disorders. He forbade any further "pilgrimages to the River Jordan" and ordered that future Epiphany blessings must take place within the precincts of the church.[63]

Church and state thus cooperated in the curtailment of unauthorized religious activity. The "satisfaction of religious needs" was henceforth to remain separated from the rest of social life, as if the church were a hermetically sealed premises where addicts of a forbidden drug could satisfy their cravings. No kind of civic engagement was permitted; nor was the kind of charitable or educational work that underpins the fellowship of a congregation. The church was to remain without any kind of social dimension, and worship was only to be performed by consenting and registered adults in private. It is difficult to exaggerate the importance of this stunting of the congregational life of Orthodox believers. A religion that has no social dimension cannot nourish the spiritual life of the community, nor can it sustain and develop a national identity—not even a church so closely identified with nationhood as the Orthodox.

## The Leningrad Affair

In 1949–1951 a purge was carried out in Leningrad which affected some two thousand senior officials, effectively breaking up the Leningrad party-state leadership and far outstripping any other high-level purge of the post-1945 period. Altogether some 220 senior officials were tried and sentenced to death or various terms of imprisonment. The reasons for the purge have remained obscure, though most commentators have linked it with the attempt by Beria and Malenkov to reclaim the power positions they had temporarily lost to Zhdanov and A. A. Kuznetsov, the Leningrad party secretaries respectively during and after the war.[64]

Stalin had reason to react with deep suspicion to any hint of trouble in

Leningrad. The city had its own revolutionary traditions, it had already been the center of a party opposition movement in the 1920s, and for much of the war it had been cut off from the rest of the USSR, as a result of which it now had its own heroic myth.

But the situation was more complex than that. Many years later, Molotov recalled that in the Leningrad affair there was "a hint of Russian nationalism," though he linked it mainly to the idea, approved by N. A. Voznesenksii (head of Gosplan and deputy chairman of the Council of Ministers), of convening a Russian trade fair in Leningrad on the model of the pre-1914 fairs in Nizhnii Novgorod. Since Zhdanov had been first secretary in Nizhnii/Gorkii before moving to Leningrad, he probably sponsored the plan. According to Molotov, the Gorkii and Leningrad party people got together and drew up the idea without consulting Stalin. Beria then reported them to Stalin, who was furious.[65]

Most likely, however, the explanation for the ferocity of the Leningrad affair lies deeper than a trade fair. In the indictment that the chief military procurator presented at the trial in September 1950, one of the accused, P. G. Lazutin (former first secretary of the Leningrad obkom), is reported to have said, "Revealing a chauvinist outlook, Kuznetsov, Popkov [former chair of the Leningrad City Executive Committee], Kapustin [second secretary of the Leningrad obkom], and I slanderously declared that the Central Committee did not show the necessary concern for the RSFSR, and gave more attention to the other national republics of the USSR." Kuznetsov was said to have been even more specific: "We several times with hostile intent [s vrazheskikh pozitsii] discussed the necessity of creating a Russian Communist Party (Bolshevik) [RCP (B)] and the desirability of transferring the capital of the RSFSR to Leningrad. In private conversations among ourselves Popkov and Kapustin talked of me as the future secretary of the RCP (B), and I was already rejoicing in my heart and imagining myself as the leader of the Communists of the Russian Federation."[66]

This notion seems to be the heart of the matter. If the Leningraders had any serious plan to create a Russian Communist Party or to transfer the capital of Russia to Leningrad (leaving the capital of the USSR in Moscow), then they were proposing a structural revolution inside the party-state apparatus against which both Lenin and Stalin had expressly warned. If Russia was to have a serious institutional presence in the Soviet state or (especially) in the Communist Party, then it could not help challenging the power of the top Soviet leadership. (And indeed, when both events took place in 1990, they signaled that the Soviet Union was nearing its end.)

Admittedly, the accusation concerning the potential Russian Communist Party and the transfer of the Russian capital occupies only one and a half of the thirty-seven pages in the indictment, and very little further documentary evidence has ever come to light to demonstrate that such plans were being seriously considered.[67] Most of the evidence in the indictment concerns other matters: creating an "antiparty group," displaying "lack of respect for the central party and soviet organs," criticizing their decisions, and plotting to have Voznesenskii promoted to Soviet Prime Minister. The accused were also said to have placed their own protégés in key positions in Leningrad and elsewhere in the RSFSR, and to have kept them in line by means of bribery, deception, and coercion. Much of the evidence concerned corruption and nepotism among members of the Leningrad party and soviet apparatus—holding "banquets" and "collective booze-ups" [kollektivnye p'ianki] while Leningrad starved, receiving expensive stolen goods (in one case, a silver chalice), embezzling municipal funds, and building themselves luxury dachas. Voznesenskii was said to have protected these shenanigans, diverting funds to Leningrad, "practicing nepotism and krugovaia poruka in USSR Gosplan, and encouraging a dishonest approach to the cardinal state function of planning the national economy."[68]

Bureaucratic rivalry was, then, clearly a major component of the Leningrad affair. All the same, one cannot dismiss the purge as nothing more. The behavior of which the Leningraders were accused was absolutely normal in the nomenklatura elite by this time, and it was conducted more openly and confidently after victory in the war. Usually by now Stalin simply tolerated it as something he could manipulate to his advantage. But in Leningrad such behavior was potentially much more serious. If Leningrad became the core of a patron-client network that could possibly infiltrate the entire RSFSR, then it would represent a very formidable challenge to the leaders of the USSR and to the Central Committee of the Soviet Communist Party. Stalin, who wanted absolute control over all high-ranking personnel questions, would be bound to regard the very possibility as a serious threat, even if it never moved beyond being the subject of casual conversations.[69]

Moreover, some credible evidence exists that party officials in Leningrad were concerned with the idea of raising Russia's status. The discrepancy between the ostensible standing of the Russian people as "elder brother" and the continuing abject poverty of small towns and villages in the RSFSR was too blatant to be ignored at a time of pro-Russian propaganda. According to Khrushchev, Zhdanov raised the matter with him after the war. Each republic, he said, had its own Central Committee, which could consult with regional and lower party organizations, and then make representations on economic, political, or cultural matters to the All-Union Central Committee or the Council of Ministers of the USSR. Only the Russian party organizations lacked their own Central Committee, and as a result "each oblast stews in its own juice," not having the status to raise matters at so high a level.

Khrushchev agreed with him: "That's true. The Russian Federation is handicapped, and its interests suffer as a result." On the other hand, he pointed out, Lenin had warned that, if the Russian Federation was to have its own Central Committee, it would become overbearing, because of the weight of the Russian population, industry, and agriculture. "We would have two Central Committees in Moscow at the same time: one inter-republican, the other for the RSFSR." To avoid destructive rivalry at the top, Zhdanov therefore proposed the creation, not of a separate Russian Communist Party, but of a Russian bureau attached to the Central Committee of the All-Union Communist Party, such as had existed for a time in the 1930s.[70]

As far as Khrushchev was concerned, the matter rested with that conversation, for Zhdanov died shortly after; only later did he hear complaints from Malenkov and Beria about "Russian nationalism." However, a specific proposal was actually made for the creation of a Russian bureau. It came not from Zhdanov, but from a protégé of his (also from Gorkii), M. I. Rodionov, then chairman of the Council of Ministers of the RSFSR. In a letter to Stalin of September 27, 1947, he made the proposal, which he called "necessary for the preliminary examination of problems of the RSFSR before they are presented to the Central Committee of the VKP(b) and the Union Government." Such a bureau, he stated, would enable local party and soviet organizations to make better use of their facilities to fulfill the five-year plans, especially in the areas of municipal and road construction, agriculture, local industry, education, culture, and propaganda.[71] The fate of this proposal is not known, but it is significant that Rodionov, though not associated with Leningrad, was one of the highest-ranking officials accused in the subsequent trial.

It is interesting to note that a Central Committee Bureau for RSFSR Affairs had actually existed for just under a year in 1936–1937. To judge by its archive, it was set up to improve party supervision of nonpriority sectors of the economy, which were generally recognized to be in a deplorable condition at that time. During its brief existence it endeavored to supervise such matters as the timber and construction industries, housing, consumer goods, agriculture, and the local government service sector. Its papers show that it was embroiled in constant demarcation disputes over which economic ministries should come under its purview, and which should remain under the supervision of the All-Union Communist Party. Perhaps that tedious in-fighting explains why the bureau was closed, though no reasons appear in its papers.[72] At no stage did it deal with issues of crucial concern to the leaders, such as security, heavy industry, or military affairs. It looks then as if any explicitly Russian body in the Communist Party had to be given a totally innocuous agenda.

The most likely explanation for the Leningrad affair, then, is that there were at least discussions among Zhdanov's protégés of the possibility of creating a Russian Communist Party and of making Leningrad the capital of Russia. These discussions were probably never minuted but sprouted rumors suitable for use in a political trial. It is important to stress that the issue at hand concerned not ethnic Russian nationalism but rather the project of giving Russia institutional status inside the Soviet Union, and possibly also of strengthening the appeal of the party by attaching it more explicitly to *rossiiskii* patriotism.[73]

An important subsidiary reason for the purge was that Zhdanov and the Leningrad party organization were quite closely identified with the Yugoslav Communist leaders. In January 1948 a Yugoslav delegation led by Milovan Djilas had visited Leningrad and had gotten along well with party leaders there; they had received information from the Leningraders about Soviet internal politics, a leak that had annoyed Stalin. The idea of Leningrad's pursuing any kind of independent line in foreign policy was absolute anathema. Yugoslavia's expulsion from the Cominform was a severe defeat for Zhdanov, and the meeting at which it was decreed was his last public appearance. Two months later he died of a heart attack caused at least partly by heavy drinking.[74]

The break with Yugoslavia provided another weapon with which to attack Leningrad. Together with the "failure" of the Russian Orthodox Church and of the All-Slav Committee, it also meant a sharp loss of Soviet influence in the Balkans, an area of traditional Russian interest, and certainly must have helped Beria and Malenkov to turn the tables on their Leningrad-based opponents in the apparatus. Communism in Europe had by now become and was to remain a facet of Soviet great-power pretensions, with Russian language, culture, and history as its quiescent instrument, but with the RSFSR still a reduced and stunted republic and with the Russian people, if anything, disadvantaged among the Soviet peoples.

## Culture and Science

By 1948 the Cold War had become the main consideration in politics. Potential cells of civil society had shriveled under the impact of renewed nomenklatura domination, and Russianness was once again manipulated as an instrument of imperial control, now in the doubly harsh climate of great-power confrontation. As in the late 1930s, the system worked by means of traditionally Russian hierarchical patron-client networks, only with one vital difference. In the 1930s Stalin had tried to destroy those networks by means of terror; now he was more restrained, realizing just how destructive terror could be. Instead, he used corrupt patronage relationships for his own ends, to divide and dominate his subordinates. His underlings, however, had also learned from both the 1930s terror and the war. Members of the ruling elite, not only those in the party-state apparatus, but also those in the professions, were much more experienced, determined to keep their positions and privileges and better able to resist the supreme leader. One of the skills they had learned was how to deploy the rhetoric, the compulsory "Bolshevik-speak" in order to protect their own networks and wherever possible advance their interests.

This system consolidated itself in the cultural world. During the late 1940s official positions were allocated in the main creative unions and their control of patronage finally put in place. The secretaries of the Unions of Writers, Artists, and Composers distributed favors at their disposal, including publication of books, performance of musical works, studios, apartments, dachas, "creative retreats," cures in sanatoria, and so on—all inestimable benefits in the bleak, poverty-stricken postwar Soviet

Union. They lobbied party-state leaders for higher pay, higher print-runs, better concert halls and practice facilities, the construction of new apartment blocks—and even for improved nails, light bulbs, and toilet seats in those apartments![75]

The new power of the literary barons implied victims, however. Mediocrities feared real talents, and the need for truth was less pressing in peacetime than it had been during the war. The relative cultural freedom that had seemed necessary in war yielded to the consolidation of the new patronage networks. The blow fell heaviest on Anna Akhmatova and on the short story writer Mikhail Zoshchenko, who was known for the verbal inventiveness with which he pointed up the discrepancy between the soaring aims of official Soviet rhetoric and the petty squalor of Soviet reality. In August 1946 both writers were attacked in a Central Committee resolution, together with the journals *Zvezda* and *Leningrad,* for "groveling to everything foreign." Zoshchenko was accused of preaching "a rotten ideological nihilism . . . designed to lead our youth astray and poison its consciousness," while Akhmatova was stigmatized as "imbued with the spirit of pessimism, decadence . . . and bourgeois-aristocratic aestheticism." Neither was arrested, but they were both expelled from the Writers' Union, a penalty that amounted to a kind of civil death sentence, since they were barred from publication and lost their ration cards. Akhmatova burned most of her manuscripts. Both had to live from hand to mouth or depend on the help of friends, among them Boris Pasternak. Akhmatova's son, Lev Gumilev, was once again arrested.[76]

Akhmatova's ostracism was preceded by a remarkable meeting—one that delighted her, but to which she attributed her subsequent disgrace. The poet was visited in her flat by Isaiah Berlin, first secretary in the British Embassy. Berlin was a Russian Jew, born in Riga in 1909 and now in emigration in Britain, where he had made his name as a scholar with a book on Karl Marx. While on a visit to Leningrad, he discovered that Akhmatova, some of whose poems he had read and admired, was alive and living there. During a rapt conversation that lasted some twelve hours, right through the night, he talked to her about Western literature and about her friends in emigration, from whom she had been sundered for more than two decades. She described her life to him and read him her two major unpublished works, *Poema bez geroia* (Epic without a Hero) and *Rekviem* (Requiem), which he recognized as remarkable and wanted to transcribe immediately. For Akhmatova, Berlin's visit was like a temporary but glorious release from an intellectual and spiritual prison. With the return of peacetime, she had been feeling strongly the loss of the exciting and cultured milieu destroyed in 1914. As Berlin recalls, she told him that "Leningrad after the war was for her nothing but a vast cemetery, the graveyard of her friends." His visit was a cosmic event, a gift of God: "In a world become mute for all time, / There are only two voices, yours and mine." She saw in Berlin the world culture for which she yearned; she also experienced a reunion with her youth and with the Russian culture of emigration, from which she had been cut off. Such was her sense by now of being engaged in a lonely struggle with the regime that she actually attributed the outbreak of the Cold War to this meeting.[77]

Scientists, like writers, were learning to defend themselves through their institutes in the Soviet Academy of Sciences. Each institute had its own director, its own "scientific council," and was developing its own authoritative repertoire of doctrines and practices. The links between the director and his staff were partly personal, based on long acquaintance and possibly trust, and partly rooted in a common intellectual approach to the discipline. In the manipulation of these links the director, vested with the authority of party and state, could act in a more or less autocratic manner. His opponents would be summoned to attend meetings billed as "discussions" of various kinds, some of which were more open-ended than others. A *diskussiia*, for example, was intended to clarify differences of opinion on which no binding decision had been taken. An *obsuzhdenie*, by contrast, usually meant discussion of an authoritative decree or text, and on such occasions the conclusions were fore-ordained. Opponents would probably then be required to exercise "self-criticism" and to undergo a rebuke, demotion, or even dismissal. However, the practice of purging and arresting them, common in the 1930s, had lapsed. Sometimes, indeed, opponents might be relegated to a lower-status college or laboratory but then later revive and reconquer lost territory. Most academic issues were politically insignificant and did not require the imposition of rigid ideological unity.[78]

These practices helped to socialize new members of the academic community and to reaffirm the predominant political, social, and intellectual hierarchy without terminally destructive consequences for science and learning. They conformed to Russian communal traditions in combining strong leadership with formally democratic procedures and a hefty dose of "joint responsibility."

During the war, Soviet science had enjoyed considerable prestige. The State Defense Committee had set up a special scientific council including major figures like the physicists Abram Ioffe and Petr Kapitsa and the biologist Sergei Vavilov to oversee the strategic direction of scientific research. Effectiveness was paramount, and so it was accepted that Soviet science was merely part of a "single world science." Throughout the war leading Soviet scientists had been able to correspond with their colleagues abroad, to visit them, and even to elect them to the Academy. The Bulletin of the Academy of Sciences had included a regular section summarizing foreign scientific research.[79]

With the intensification of the Cold War, this situation changed completely, and international contact became grounds for official suspicion. The turning point came in 1946. Two Soviet scientists, Nina Kliueva and Grigorii Roskin, had been working on a cure for cancer in close consultation with American colleagues and had published a book on their research in the United States. In June 1946 they were visited by the U.S. ambassador, Walter Bedell Smith, who had helped them procure necessary cultures from his homeland. He proposed a joint U.S.–Soviet research project, with the United States providing finance, facilities, and materials. This proposal provoked a major showdown: Soviet political leaders had been taking a close interest in the work of Kliueva and Roskin, but they were now beginning to think of it as more than a promising piece of international science. Rather they were hoping that curing cancer might become a Soviet speciality, a showpiece in international propaganda, and even perhaps be deployed as a bargaining tool when negotiating with the United States over atomic weapons. Science, in other words, was no longer a field for international collaboration: it had become an instrument in great-power diplomacy.[80]

Yet in dealing with wayward, internationally minded scientists, the Soviet authorities did not simply return to the brutal methods of the late 1930s. They tried, instead, to induce scientists to engage in self-policing. With this in mind, an "honor court" was set up in Kliueva and Roskin's institute. This was a revival of an institution that had existed among nobles and army officers in tsarist Russia. "Honor courts" had been tried again in the Red Army in 1939 and were extended to the civil service in 1947 under a decree that defined their aim as being "to re-educate workers of state institutions in the spirit of Soviet patriotism and devotion to the interests of the Soviet state."[81] These courts could reprimand offenders without undermining the professions—as arrests in the 1930s had done—but on the contrary uphold and reassert professional pride. The device suggests that the political leadership was looking for ways to impel scientists and professional people to police themselves, without the vicious reprisals of the 1930s, and in a way that would promote both professionalism and patriotism. This was another variant of "joint responsibility."

Before the honor court Roskin admitted he had been wrong in making American contacts. "Having assumed that there is civilian science and military science," he stated, "I had thought that [what we were doing] was civilian science. But after the war all sciences became military, every science is used against us, cancer included." The last sentence might stand as the watchword for postwar Soviet scientific policy. Every institute, every laboratory, was assessed in the light of its contribution to the Soviet position in the great-power standoff. The court publicly reprimanded Kliueva and Roskin for antipatriotic acts, endangering state secrets, and servile behavior toward Western science. But they were not arrested and were allowed to continue their work in a smaller laboratory.[82]

After the court hearing the Central Committee sent a letter to party cells in government agencies and academic institutes denouncing servility toward the West in scientific matters, and instructing them to hold meetings and report on how they proposed to root out this tendency.[83]

A few scientific issues did have direct political significance. The most famous ideologically loaded case was that of Lysenko, whose research suggested that characteristics acquired from the environment could perpetuate themselves in living organisms by hereditary means. This finding implied that social and environmental changes could actually imprint themselves on plant and animal species and even on human biology. It seemed to follow that both agricultural productivity and the evolution of humanity might be genetically assisted: Lysenko's assertions raised the possibility that "genetically modified Communism" would be more rapid and self-reinforcing than conventional genetics. Lysenko boasted that his doctrine was authentically Russian and promised the victory of Russian, socialist science over cosmopolitan, Western, bourgeois science. His followers triumphed in the Agricultural Academy elections of August 1948. A wave of purges of scientific institutes followed, in which scientists exercised "self-criticism," accusing themselves of servility toward the West, and promised to reorient their work along "Michurinist" lines—whatever that might mean in their individual branches of learning.[84]

The case of linguistics also reveals much about the way official Soviet attitudes were changing. In the 1930s the field had been taken over by the followers of Nikolai Marr, according to whom at one time, from Asia Minor and the Caucasus to the Pyrenees, a family of languages known as the Japhetic had been spoken. The Japhetic had subsequently been supplanted by the Indo-European languages and was now discernible only in a few isolated cases such as Georgian, Albanian, and Basque. Japhetic languages and cultures, he proclaimed, formed the "ethnic substratum" of the Mediterranean world, "or indeed the very foundation of the Mediterranean culture, the historic source of world civilisation." At a wave of Marr's wand the primacy of the Indo-European languages was thus swept aside, while formerly neglected and colonized peoples were awarded new dignity. Indeed, he maintained that the later incursion of Indo-European had engendered "confusion . . . hybridization, the emergence of new mixed linguistic types and the end of mutual comprehension."[85]

This theory chimed well with anti-imperialist, internationalist, and class-based Marxism. So did another of Marr's hypotheses, according to which languages pass through various stages closely connected with the economic and material evolution of society. Early communication, he maintained, is mostly by gesture and mimicry, but spoken sounds gradually become more complex and semantically richer and then evolve into complete languages. These in turn tend to cross-fertilize each other, phonological-semantic elements transferring themselves from one to another, creating higher-order languages more suitable for international communication. This doctrine had supplanted both classical Indo-European linguistics and modern structuralism to establish itself as the one genuinely Marxist linguistics in a debate in the Communist Academy in 1929.[86]

Marr died in 1934, but his "new doctrine on language" continued to be taught and disseminated from his academic bastion, the Institute of Language and Thought of the Academy of Sciences. His followers never managed to establish a monopoly, however; indeed, they suffered in the indiscriminate terror of the late 1930s. But they mounted a comeback, and by 1949 seemed to have gained total victory, when the Presidium of the Academy of Sciences adopted a decree denouncing their opponents. Then, unexpectedly, in June 1950, came an attack on them from the highest of all sources, Stalin himself. In *Pravda* he denounced Marr's errors and accused his followers of running "an Arakcheev regime in linguistics." From the theoretical viewpoint, Stalin's most important assertion was that language was not part of the "base" or the "superstructure" of society, and therefore did not vary in line with social changes. The Russian language, for example, was in its grammatical and syntactical forms essentially the same as that which Pushkin had used, in spite of the far-reaching social changes which had taken place in Russia since his time and especially since the October Revolution. "[Language] is created not just by one particular social class," Stalin maintained, "but by the whole society, by all classes of society, by the efforts of hundreds of generations. . . . It is created as a single all-national language for the whole society and for all the members of the society." As a result of Stalin's intervention the Academy's decree of July 1949 was annulled, and the Institute of Language and Thought was amalgamated with the Institute of Russian Language and placed under the directorship of Marr's leading opponent, Viktor Vinogradov.[87]

What motivated this abrupt reversal of policy? On this matter no direct evidence exists, but one may hypothesize that the change was a delayed aspect of the move away from a class-based and internationalist approach to the building of socialism toward a Russian cultural and imperial one. Marr's doctrine had implied that there might ultimately be an international language of the proletariat, generated by cross-fertilization of existing languages but distinct from any of them. Stalin, however, clearly believed by now that the appropriate international proletarian language was and would remain Russian. World socialism was to be an infinitely extended Russian-Soviet empire, at least until the ultimate triumph over imperialism.[88]

## Anti-Semitism

The Second World War radically changed the situation of Soviet Jews, first, of course, because Nazi genocide exterminated almost half of them, most of those who lived in the shtetls and former Pale of Settlement.[89] Thereafter nearly all surviving Soviet Jews were urbanized and the great majority Russified too. The proportion who still spoke Yiddish or regularly attended the synagogue was relatively small. Second, the war intensified national and ethnic feelings of all kinds, including the popular anti-Semitism that had never disappeared, especially in the west of Russia. Rumors spread—completely unjustified by the evidence—that Jews were not pulling their weight in the fighting, that they were poor frontline soldiers and sought "comfy" posts in the rear services or in trade, where they were alleged to be responsible for the high prices actually caused by wartime. In 1942 there were physical assaults on Jews evacuated with other administrative staff from central Russia to Uzbekistan and Kazakhstan, where, like many other evacuees, they lived by petty trade or found jobs in the local supply organizations.[90]

At this stage ordinary Russians, Ukrainians, and Belorussians harbored a number of—mutually inconsistent—stereotypes of Jews. The Harvard émigré interview project, which in the early 1950s interviewed recent émigrés from the USSR, found that many believed Jews:

> were a purely urban and trading people who stuck together: when one
>    Jew landed a good job, he brought in all his friends and relatives,
>    and they excluded everyone else;
> had lots of jobs sewn up in the party-state apparatus, especially in the
>    police and security services, so they were responsible for all the di-
>    sasters which had befallen the Orthodox peasantry and ordinary
>    working people;
> were cowards who during the war did everything possible to avoid
>    frontline combat duties; so they monopolized the rear services; in
>    fact many of them sat out the war making money in distant places
>    like Tashkent;
> were disloyal or even traitors; many of them wanted to emigrate to
>    Palestine (one respondent reviled them as "Palestine Cossacks").[91]

Much of this characterization was displaced scapegoating. These stereotypes represented what most of the population resented about the party-state apparatus, of whose behavior (except on the last point) they gave a far more accurate picture. All the same, the regime took over these stereotypes and manipulated them as a propaganda tool to reinforce Russian-Soviet patriotism. The Jews were a convenient target on which the sins of corruption and self-serving careerism, combined with excessive internationalism—cosmopolitanism and kowtowing—could be unloaded.

During the war official attitudes toward the Jews had been ambivalent. On the one hand, as with the Slavs, the Soviet government did its best to cultivate Jewish connections in other parts of the world for the war effort. As we have seen, it established a Jewish Anti-Fascist Committee (EAK). At its first public rally the Jewish writer Ilia Erenburg declared: "I grew up in a Russian city. My mother tongue is Russian. I am a Russian writer.

Like all Russians, I am now defending my homeland. But the Nazis have reminded me of something else: my mother's name was Hannah. I am a Jew. I say this proudly. Hitler hates us more than anything, and this makes us proud."[92]

The committee's chairman was the writer Solomon Mikhoels. The EAK published a Yiddish newspaper, *Einikait,* whose articles were syndicated for publication all over the world. It carried regular information on Jewish themes, including the Nazi extermination program—information suppressed inside the USSR itself. Lozovskii, the deputy chief of Sovinformbiuro, was himself one of the chief figures in the EAK. In August 1941 he asked Jewish writers to collect information about the fate of Soviet Jews under German occupation—but none of the findings were ever published in the USSR, even though Soviet propaganda disseminated abroad described Nazi anti-Jewish policy in detail. Members of the committee traveled the world, forming links with Jewish and other anti-Fascist organizations, giving lectures, meeting people, and collecting money. Mikhoels, Itsik Fefer, and others had an especially successful visit to the United States in June 1943, where they addressed massive public gatherings and were lionized along with such stars as Paul Robeson, Yehudi Menuhin, and Charlie Chaplin.[93]

At the very same time the opposite policy was being pursued at home. Concerted official action was being taken to reduce the number of Jews in top jobs. In August 1942 Agitprop began to complain about the large number of non-Russians engaged in administering Russian cultural institutions, such as the Moscow and Leningrad Conservatoires, and the distinguished Jewish pianist A. B. Goldenveizer was dismissed from his directorship of the former. An official of the state cinema committee complained about the well-known actress Faina Ranevskaia being given a leading role in Eizenshtein's film *Ivan the Terrible* on the grounds that "Ranevskaia's Semitic features are very prominent, especially in close-ups."[94]

Once the war was safely over, Stalin asked G. F. Aleksandrov, head of Agitprop, to investigate Sovinformbiuro. Aleksandrov reported that many of its reporters were substandard, that cadres were selected "through personal and family ties," and that there was an "excessive concentration of Jews" working there. Lozovskii was accused of weak budgetary control and irresponsibility: "There cannot be another such string-pulling organization in the whole Soviet Union, a milch cow for all kinds of correspondents and editors. It is a malignant tumor on a healthy body." Lozovskii was dismissed both as Deputy Foreign Minister and as head of Sovinformbiuro, and many of the staff there, mostly Jews, were also let go.[95]

The creation of the state of Israel in 1948 exacerbated the anti-Jewish mood in the Soviet leadership, even though the USSR had actually supported the campaign to establish a Jewish national homeland in Palestine. The Soviet government offered aid to the *yishuv*, spoke consistently in favor of Israel in the United Nations, and voted for the admission of the new state in May 1949. Stalin seems to have hoped that Israel, as a socialist state of a kind, might play a role similar to the People's Democracies of Central and Eastern Europe and act as a bastion of Soviet influence in the Middle East. He was swiftly disillusioned. Almost from the outset Israel took up a pro-American position; at the stage the Cold War had reached by 1949, that had to mean an anti-Soviet stance. Moreover, the very existence of Israel exacerbated the anomaly of the Jews' status in the Soviet Union: not only did they have no national territory there (if one ignores the failed republic of Birobidzhan on the Chinese border), but they now *did* have an alternative national homeland abroad—an increasingly successful one, too.

That is the context in which we must view the intensified anti-Semitism of Stalin's final years. He may have wanted Israel as an outpost of Soviet great-power influence, but he certainly never intended to encourage Soviet Jews to seek their home there. Despite supporting the creation of Israel, the Soviet Union had never supported Zionism as a political movement, nor had it issued passports to Soviet Jews who wished to emigrate to Israel. Soviet Jews were treated, in other words, as if they were a distinct ethnos with no relationship to the new Jewish state in the Middle East: they were simply Soviet citizens, to be assimilated to a generalized Soviet-Russian identity.[96]

In November 1948 the Jewish Anti-Fascist Committee was closed down as "a center of anti-Soviet propaganda" that "regularly provides anti-Soviet information to foreign intelligence services." In the following months most of its leading activists were arrested. During their protracted interrogation, they were closely questioned on the trips some of them had made to the United States during the war, and their attempts to bring welfare help from abroad to Soviet Jews. In July 1952 fifteen of them, including Lozovskii, were tried in a secret hearing before the Military Collegium of the Supreme Soviet; they were all convicted of treason, and fourteen were sentenced to death.[97]

While their trial was being laboriously prepared, a broad campaign was gaining momentum, directed at Jewish organizations of all kinds. Jewish cultural institutes, museums, theaters, journals, and newspapers were closed down in Moscow, Leningrad, and numerous provincial centers. Even many of the leaders of Birobidzhan were arrested, which finally ended any hope of turning that territory into a Jewish national homeland. Significantly, though, synagogues and the Jewish religion were left in relative peace during this time, like other "official" religions.[98] What alarmed the Soviet authorities was not the traditional Jewish faith but evidence of a dynamic new secular Jewish national consciousness, Zionism, wholly independent of the Soviet Union and its neo-Russian official ideology, indeed a rival to it.

For the same reason the Soviet leaders deliberately suppressed information about the Holocaust inside the USSR, so that the Soviet public either remained ignorant of the scale of the mass murder of the Jews or was aware of it only through inference and rumor. In 1946 two distinguished Soviet Jewish writers, Ilia Erenburg and Vasilii Grossman, proposed bringing out their *Black Book,* originally commissioned by the Sovinformbiuro. It detailed the atrocities committed by the German occupying forces against Soviet Jews and was to be published simultaneously in the USSR, the United States, and Palestine. The Soviet authorities delayed and eventually vetoed publication and broke up the type.[99]

A new escalation of the anti-Jewish campaign appeared imminent with the accusation, published in a communiqué from TASS on January 13, 1953, that a conspiracy had been discovered among senior medical staff to murder high party officials. Like many elderly people, Stalin cherished a chronic distrust of doctors. In 1952 he discovered evidence that Zhdanov had suffered an infarction which had been ignored by the doctors, and that their neglect had probably contributed to Zhdanov's death. He became convinced that there was a medical conspiracy directed against the top Soviet leaders. He ordered arrests of physicians from leading medical institutes and from the Kremlin Medical Administration. Most of those arrested had Jewish-sounding surnames. Gradually the security services wove a web of alleged treachery involving dishonest medics with Zionism, the Jewish international charity Joint, and U.S. and British intelligence (including Isaiah Berlin).[100] Immediately after the death of Stalin in March 1953, however, the charges were dropped and those imprisoned were released. The climax of the anti-Jewish campaign never happened.

*       *       *

By the early 1950s to be Russian meant to be the leading people of a great multiethnic state that had won a remarkable victory in the war, and that now claimed to stand for the oppressed and exploited peoples of the world against their great common enemy, the United States and the countries of NATO. This view of international affairs committed the Soviet peoples—but especially the Russians—to a highly ambitious geopolitical role that entailed massive rearmament, spearheaded by nuclear weapons, and to creating a large and penetrative security apparatus. As two contemporary scholars have commented, "The Stalinist legacy . . . included a distribution of resources skewed towards arms production and heavy industry, a bipolar world locked in mutual suspicion and conflict, and a role for informers and security agents who were not 'afraid of soiling themselves.'" Stalin also reinforced the "traditional desire in Russia for a tough, powerful leader, who could show the way forward and save the country and the political order from itself."[101] That is why, when Stalin died, millions of people flocked to Moscow to see his funeral, and why they stood weeping as the cortège passed by. Whatever his crimes, Stalin had been their leader and father-figure at the time of the greatest peril in their history. He was the embodiment of their Russian-Soviet fatherland, the man who had saved them from slavery.

The requirements of the huge military-industrial complex needed to sustain this superpower role determined the shape of the Soviet economy, and in many ways of society too, in the following decades. By the mid-1980s the complex consumed some 20 percent of gross national product.[102] Its output was secret, unknown even to those working within it, but its peremptory claims determined the hierarchies of supply and finance within Gosplan. Its dominance in the economy ensured that the supply of consumer goods was insufficient and of poor quality, and that the income of the great majority of Soviet people remained low. Given the secrecy the military-industrial complex demanded, there was no chance of public pressure being brought to bear on those priorities—indeed there was not in any meaningful sense a public at all. The majority of Soviet people remained poor—though not indigent, for the Soviet state was now beginning to guarantee basic necessities for the urban poor—without the means to articulate their political input, dependent on hierarchical patron-client networks or the more informal and egalitarian *blat* for material and other benefits, including social security.

A yawning gap remained between the ostensible greatness of the Russian-led Soviet Union and the actual poverty of much of the Russian people, the demoralization of their villages, their relative demographic decline, their inability to develop their own culture freely, and the abject state of their national church. Superpower status was purchased at the cost of national degradation. The stage was set for even patriotic Russians to become disenchanted with the Soviet Union.

# 8

# THE RELAUNCH OF UTOPIA

Stalin bequeathed his successors, and the Soviet peoples, a paradoxical and in most respects baleful legacy. He had raised the Soviet Union to the status of a superpower, mightier than any Russian state had ever been before. To keep it there, though, he had committed the country to huge expenditures and a massive leeching of talent and resources into the military field, leaving most of society poverty-stricken and demoralized. He had created a security state also unmatched in Russian history, insulated from the outside world, enclosed in a cocoon of narrow-minded ideological dogma, cut off from its own past—even from much of the Soviet past. And he left a heritage of Russian imperial chauvinism and ethnic hatred—resented by the Baltic peoples, many west Belorussians and Ukrainians, many north Caucasian Muslims, and an increasing number of Jews—which was to poison later attempts to preserve the Soviet Union as a multinational state.

Stalin's appalling crimes against the Soviet peoples posed his successors a terrible dilemma. On the one hand, to keep silent about them meant leaving a perfect weapon for a future political opponent to use. It also meant incurring the danger of another, as yet unrecognized, Stalin arising in their midst to destroy them all. On the other hand, to denounce Stalin and reveal his atrocities meant dethroning the great wartime hero, undermining the founding ideology, and besmirching the shared social memory that had been built up during "socialist construction" and the war.

The new party first secretary, Nikita Khrushchev, decided all the same that Stalin's crimes could no longer remain completely hidden. He grasped the nettle at the 20th Party Congress of February 1956. He did so in a so-called secret speech, which took place not in the public sessions but at a special closed session held afterward, to which delegates were admitted by a special pass. They were instructed to brief colleagues back at home in closed meetings, but otherwise not to disclose the contents of the speech outside the party. The speech itself was bitter in tone, but strictly limited in its attacks on Stalin. It was directed almost entirely against the terror waves of 1935–1939 and 1949–1953. Khrushchev gave detailed accounts of many individual victims and the humiliations visited on them, but his enumeration of arrests and executions was far from complete: the only victims he named were senior members of the nomenklatura elite. Apart from a mention of the deportations of the late 1930s and 1940s, he ignored the sufferings of ordinary people. He thereby implied that ordinary people were expendable, and that all Stalin's other brutalities had been acceptable, even correct: the outlawing of the various opposition groups within the party in the 1920s, the whole collectivization and dekulakization program, the closure of churches, and the arrest and murder of priests.

Khrushchev made out that Stalin's crimes had been the result of a temporary "cult of personality," that they had been limited in time and scope. He implied that the party had somehow led a separate existence throughout, struggling to uphold order, legality, and the "Leninist norms of party life," even while Stalin was perversely creating havoc in their midst. He gave his audience to understand that party and people had shared a common fate in suffering Stalin's illegalities. He was attempting, in other words, to maintain the party's aura of unique rectitude and its myth of a special link with the people. If one took his words at face value, both Soviet institutions and public memory were still valid, the great project of building socialism had not been fatally defiled by the passing aberrations of one leader, and the party could now purge itself of its errors and resume the advance toward Communism.[1]

For all his attempts to limit the damage, however, Khrushchev had radically devalued the regime's own hallowed memories. He had torn the veil away from the inner sanctum and revealed a blood-stained torture-chamber. The self-understanding of all the Soviet peoples, but especially the Russians, was placed under question.

The secret speech was fatal to the party as a faith-based movement of true believers. Some of its own members began publicly to question its right to a monopoly of politics. At a Leningrad meeting a questioner asked: "Is the cult of personality not furthered by the one-party system and the almost complete amalgamation of government and party organs?" In Molotov (Perm) a responsible party member complained: "When party committees are being elected, the lists for the secret ballot are discussed with lightning speed—God forbid that anyone should put forward an unwanted candidate!" In Kuibyshev (Samara) an undaunted participant at a party conference asserted: "It is difficult to imagine that one man could impose his will on six million party members . . . That became possible because of the incorrect upbringing of party members, because of cowardice, servility, and toadying. Irresponsible party bosses have appeared, answerable to no one, who have several apartments, dachas, who are provided with unlimited supplies of food and consumer goods, who have become isolated from the party masses and forgotten their needs."[2]

The leaders reacted with panic and fury at the irreverent questions they themselves had provoked. People who questioned the party's sacrosanct rights were expelled and excoriated in the media as "rotten elements."[3] To limit the damage Agitprop had hastily to erect a countervailing myth that an unbroken succession led from the founder, Lenin, to the present generation of leaders, mysteriously bypassing Stalin. The propaganda machine began to turn out multiple portraits and statues of Lenin, as well as books and articles commemorating him, while Khrushchev and his successors permitted themselves only a very modest allowance of glorification.

Russia's successive empires have been rendered vulnerable by the fact that many of its "colonies" were more advanced than the metropolis, and had vibrant, semi-suppressed civil societies of their own. The shock wave touched off by the secret speech provoked both intellectual dissent and popular revolts against Communist rule in Poland and Hungary in the summer and autumn of 1956. The trouble spread to the Baltic republics, where protest was not only anti-Communist but also anti-Russian. In November 1956 Lithuanians held demonstrations demanding freedom for the Catholic Church; they chanted: "Let's follow Hungary's example" and "Russians, get out of Lithuania!" In Estonia young people paraded with placards reading: "Down with our Russian rulers!" and "Death to the Russian occupiers!" Those gathered for a student meeting were told: "We could solve the housing problem in Tartu by evicting all the Russians."[4]

Because its meetings were less formal than those of the party itself, the

Komsomol was the scene of some of the most serious debates in 1956. At a meeting in Leningrad University, for example, participants discussed lifting the ban on Akhmatova and Zoshchenko and ending the practice of compulsory applause after all Khrushchev's speeches. One delegate asserted: "We young citizens of the USSR, students and Komsomol members, we want to hear firsthand—from our press—the truth about what is going on right now in Poland and Hungary."[5] The Komsomol leaders became alarmed at such frank and guileless demands and tried to steer the meeting toward more harmless subjects like "Physics or Lyrics?" or "Friendship, Comradeship, and Love."

Those determined to explore serious issues took themselves elsewhere—to gatherings on Maiakovskii Square in Moscow, for example, where a statue to the poet was unveiled in 1958. For protesters Maiakovskii had the advantage of being a legitimate figure in the party's eyes, but all the same a model of youthful irreverence and rebellion. The meetings began as public readings of his verse. Gradually, however, speakers began to take up controversial issues, and the gatherings threatened to turn into an open-air club, something like Speakers' Corner in Hyde Park, when the KGB intervened and broke them up. The young Vladimir Bukovskii was taken to a police station, beaten up, and warned: "Don't ever go to Maiakovskii Square again. Next time we'll kill you!"[6]

Others sought informal or underground forums in which to exchange information and ideas. Some inscribed their opinions on wall-newspapers in university corridors, which were then torn down by the authorities. Some joined in discussion circles with trusted friends, at which they would read Hegel, the early Marx, the less-known works of Lenin, and sources on Soviet history not mentioned in Stalin's *Short Course*. Or they would piece together what news they had managed to learn about events in Poland, Hungary, and Yugoslavia. These young people were not anti-Soviet, but they did want to discover the truth about the present and recent past, so that they could discuss possible ways forward. Their aims were both intellectual and practical, and well within the bounds of the repertoire of socialism.[7]

A new mode of articulating nonconformist ideas was suggested by Boris Pasternak. By now the doyen of Russian poets along with Akhmatova, he could look back on a literary career stretching back more than forty years since his involvement in the prerevolutionary Futurist movement. After the war, responding to what for a time felt like a freer cultural atmosphere, he embarked on a long novel, *Doctor Zhivago,* which reassessed the early Soviet years from the viewpoint of a doctor and poet, whose rambling, inconsequential life was as distant from the ideal of the "positive hero" as could be imagined. In 1956, after the "secret speech," Pasternak submitted the novel to *Novyi mir,* but the editors rejected it as a rampantly individualist work that denied the value of politics and the importance of the collective. While *Novyi mir* was still considering the text, Pasternak offered a draft script to a visiting Italian, to give to the Milan Communist publisher, Feltrinelli. Like many of Pasternak's acts, this seems to have been an impulsive, unreflective gesture, though he was not wholly unaware of its significance: he remarked to his visitor, "You're now invited to attend my execution."[8] At any rate Feltrinelli published it in 1957. Its appearance and the subsequent award of the Nobel Prize for literature provoked a storm of official abuse directed against Pasternak. He was castigated as "Judas," "a literary Vlasov," and "a pig who fouls his own sty," and he was expelled from the Soviet Writers' Union.[9]

Pasternak was a loner. He belonged to no underground organizations, and he did not himself circulate his typescripts among acquaintances. Nevertheless, *Doctor Zhivago* appeared in the private apartments of Soviet writers and scholars. In addition, the text was read over foreign radio stations, and the Feltrinelli edition was smuggled into the country. Both the content of the novel and the mode of its dissemination suggested new ways of thinking about the Soviet Union and new methods of spreading unacceptable ideas. Within a year or two the first underground literary journals had begun to appear, with names like *Syntax, Phoenix,* and *Boomerang,* clumsily typed in multiple copies and passed from hand to hand. They contained the verse of young poets, but also the first "republications" of poetry long banned, of Akhmatova, Mandelstam, and Pasternak. This was not just the dissemination of suppressed culture: knowledge of these texts constituted a badge of membership for a new form of sociability: "One had only to quote a few lines of favorite poets, and people of like mind recognized each other."[10] Consequently, "Whereas Tsarist detectives had had to study socialist treatises in order to infiltrate the youth of their time, our KGB agents were willy-nilly obliged to become devotees of poetry."[11]

Such was the thirst for free creativity and authentic memory that even the austere, obscure, and determinedly nonpolitical verse of the Jewish poet Osip Mandelstam could become a symbol of Russian cultural self-distancing from the Soviet regime. Akhmatova's *Requiem,* because of its elegiac and subversive content, became an especially evocative entry ticket to the counterculture. A new form of the dissemination of letters was born, gratefully evoked by Vladimir Bukovskii: "I would erect a monument to the typewriter . . . It brought forth a new form of publishing, *samizdat* or self-publishing: write myself, edit myself, censor myself, publish myself, distribute myself, go to jail for it myself."[12] Samizdat was not just an individual enterprise, however: retyping, redistributing, and sometimes reading the texts was a collective endeavor, in which everyone ran the risk of being discovered. This was "joint responsibility" in creative mode, re-establishing a Russian cultural community that had been lost in the Soviet "creative" institutions.

Even Soviet citizens who had no access to samizdat were beginning to have alternative sources of information. They heard a non-Soviet version of events on the newly popular short-wave radio sets. They could tune into faint and crackly Russian-language broadcasts from the BBC, the Voice of America, and Deutsche Welle, where "enemy voices" swelled and faded like a demented harmonica. In the West, they learned, many people who had hitherto been convinced Communists had quit the party in disillusionment over Khrushchev's revelations and his brutal suppression of working-class people in Central Europe. Communism, at least in its Soviet guise, was ceasing to be a worldwide movement enjoying the fervent support of intellectuals with freedom of conscience.

## Refashioning the Future

The post-Stalin leaders were aware that they were losing credibility both inside and outside the USSR. In the era of "peaceful coexistence" that followed the first stage of the Cold War they needed urgently to establish a principle of order and legitimacy to replace millennial terror combined with Russian-Soviet chauvinism, both of which were now counterproductive. Their strategy was to intimate that the basic goal remained the same, the building of Communism, combined with "catching up and overtaking" the United States. In a completely new departure, they announced a date for the completion of these accomplishments, 1980. They also indicated that, having condemned the "cult of personality," they would proceed in a more systematic, orderly, and above all legal manner. The Soviet leaders were now committed to "socialist democracy" in action. Ordinary people were to be given a much greater right of participation in the process, and also more tangible benefits from it.

These ideas had been germinating inside the party apparatus since the immediate postwar period.[13] But they were adopted as official policy only in the mid- and late 1950s as part of the post-Stalin relaunching of the Soviet project. In its fullest form the resumption of the march toward utopia was set out in Khrushchev's report to the 22nd Party Congress in 1961. Since socialism had already been built (theoretically as long ago as 1936), Khrushchev argued, the Soviet state no longer needed to exercise a "dictatorship of the proletariat"; it had already become the "state of the whole people." The stage was being set for what Marx had called the "withering away of the state," to be completed with the full construction of Communism. In the meantime the masses would play a much greater part in running the country. Nationwide discussions would be held before major laws were passed. Ordinary nonparty people would sit on commissions monitoring the performance of official bodies. Organs of state power would be democratically elected and would gradually be transformed into instruments of "social self-administration," a process in which the Communist Party would play a "leading and guiding role." To ensure that the party also became more democratic, its leading officials were henceforth to serve for only a limited period and were to be replaced by properly conducted elections with secret ballot.[14]

If there was to be a new relationship between state, party, and people, then there must be a new, more stable, and impartial concept of law. Khrushchev introduced what he called "socialist legality," which differed from bourgeois law but recognized some of the same general principles. A reform of the criminal law in 1958 stipulated that an accused person could be convicted of a criminal offense only by a properly constituted court on the basis of serious evidence other than personal confession, and only for violating a specific article of a published law. No longer could people be imprisoned by emergency or military courts on the basis of secret instructions or for vaguely worded offenses like "terrorist intentions" or "counter-revolutionary activity." No longer could they suffer penalties merely for belonging to a particular social class or ethnic group.[15]

A more democratic politics required that the mass of the people should enjoy better living standards and thus have an incentive other than fear to support the regime. The post-Stalin leaders launched a massive program for the production of consumer goods, which continued with some success right through the 1960s and 1970s. The most noticeable change was in the provision of housing. From the mid-1950s visitors to the Soviet Union could see that any large town was surrounded by a forest of tall cranes and a broad moat of muddy building sites, as enormous new apartment blocks were erected. For many townsfolk their construction meant long-awaited emancipation from the communal apartment and a move into separate family accommodations, not spacious perhaps, but equipped with all modern conveniences. Between 1955 and 1964 alone, the urban domestic housing stock of the USSR nearly doubled, from 640 to 1,182 million square meters, and by 1980 it nearly doubled again, to 2,202 million.[16]

This new housing was a dramatic improvement in people's lives, and it affected above all the Russians and Ukrainians, who formed the bulk of the population in the largest cities. They could now rearrange their lives on a more private basis and conduct their conversations away from the ever-alert ears of potential police informers. They no longer had to frequent the public baths to wash properly, and they found the sociability of public meetings less alluring. Instead, ordinary townsfolk cultivated their private lives, gradually acquiring a radio, a television set, more presentable furniture, elegant china in glass cupboards, and their own collections of books. They could invite guests home—though not too many, owing to the modest dimensions of most apartments—and, given mutual confidence, they could discuss whatever they wanted to openly and uninhibitedly. They were creating for themselves a modest level of private comfort and a sociable culture outside the party-dominated public arena. Now, though, they had to make careful choices about whom they trusted; the result was greater cliquishness and a more marked divide between public and private spheres. This situation was very different from the 1930s and the decade or so after the war, when almost every aspect of daily life had been conducted in at least a semi-public context.

The house-building program also created new forms of stratification in Soviet society. Most people rented their apartments cheaply from a local authority or from the economic enterprise in which they worked. A tiny group of nomenklatura appointees at the very top received more opulent apartments (the degree of luxury calibrated according to rank) from the state at a low rent. In the middle a new stratum appeared: professional people or skilled workers who through their employers or trade unions could purchase an apartment with a deposit of 30 to 40 percent, with the balance to be paid at a low interest rate over a period of up to twenty years. Such "cooperative apartments" were mostly found in large towns, were usually somewhat larger and better appointed than local authority ones, and could be passed on to heirs—an appreciable benefit in a country still suffering from a housing shortage. A small but significant class of modest property-owners was being created.[17]

Social security benefits were improved and made more widely available. Men with a twenty-five-year work record could draw a pension at age sixty; women with a twenty-year work record at fifty-five. This rate was generous but reflected the needs of a population that had suffered heavily during the war. It was one of the legislative initiatives that underwent popular discussion in the press and at meetings.[18] People were being given a stake in the community through free education, health care, pensions, and social security benefits. Ostensibly they were being encouraged to broaden their dependency beyond the patron-client links at the workplace. Most benefits were modest, however, and since (apart from pensions) they were allocated by the trade unions, they were available in practice only to people with a stable employment record, and they thus reinforced dependency on the patron-client networks of the statized economy. Moreover, in one sense, welfare benefits also accentuated social polarization: kolkhozniki were not entitled to them till 1965 and did not receive their own passports till 1974, an exclusion that reinforced their inferior social status.

## Sport

In the two decades after the war sport developed rapidly, both as spectacle and as mass involvement. It became a kind of substitute for the *rodina* in the homogenized large-town setting. It offered an excellent replacement for civic identification: players and spectators could be loyal to the Soviet system while also subverting its authoritarian and monolithic aspects. The soccer league established itself again as the object of eager public attention. The best-known teams drew huge crowds, which clogged up roads and transport systems for hours before and after major matches.[19] One passionate fan was the composer Dmitrii Shostakovich, who had a season ticket for the Leningrad Dinamo team, and on match days would schedule his classes early at the conservatory so that he could get to the stadium.[20]

The bogus amateurism and the system of rewards in sport enhanced the importance of the ubiquitous Soviet patronage system. Firms were quite literally patrons to the players in their teams. Factory directors would urge particular tactics and line-ups, dismiss coaches, and even bribe referees to obtain good results. They were not allowed to pay their players directly, but they could retain the best ones by offering them separate apartments, access to special grocery stores, and other privileges otherwise available only to the nomenklatura elite. When in 1975 the Uzbek Sports Committee asked players in the leading Tashkent soccer team what would help them play better, none of them mentioned improved training: instead, "it turned out that one player needed a better apartment, another needed a telephone installed, and still others wanted scarce consumer goods."[21]

Mass involvement in active sport was slower to develop, not least because creating the facilities for it was expensive. However, physical education was given new prominence in school curricula after the war. By 1956 it proved possible to mount a Spartakiad of the Peoples of the USSR, a kind of inner-Soviet Olympic Games, in all the major outdoor sports. Collectives from every district, region, city, and republic were encouraged to hold qualifying contests. The finals were held in the Luzhniki Stadium in Moscow before party leaders and eminent foreign guests, including the president of the international Olympic Committee, Avery Brundage. Torch-bearers, running in one-kilometer laps, brought a flame to the stadium from the tomb of the Unknown Warrior, outside the Kremlin. The games began and ended with huge gymnastics displays, featuring the slogans "Ready for labour and defense," "Glory to the Fatherland," and "Success to the Communist Party." Moscow came first overall in the team chart, followed by the RSFSR, and then Leningrad—a result that well reflected the ethnic and propiska (residence permit) hierarchy now becoming consolidated.[22] Spartakiads were held every fourth year thereafter, with participation from all regions and peoples. In 1971 Sergei Pavlov, chairman of the State Committee on Physical Culture and Sport, called it "a true festival of fraternal friendship of the peoples of our multi-national country." But the top prizes continued to go to Moscow, Leningrad, the Russian Republic, Ukraine, and Belorussia.[23]

The regime also decided to begin competing seriously in international sports. Like most countries, the USSR wanted to raise its standing in international affairs and bolster its prestige in the eyes of its own citizens by winning sports events. It had a greater stake than most countries in success, though. Its explicit aim was "to ensure top performance by Soviet athletes as a means of widely publicising our attainments in building communism and in promoting physical culture and sport."[24] Soviet leaders were initially cautious where success did not seem guaranteed: in 1948, though invited, the USSR did not enter the Olympic Games, since Stalin was advised his country might not do well. All the same, from 1946 Soviet sports associations began to affiliate with their international counterparts, beginning with soccer, basketball, skiing, and weight-lifting. As early as 1945 the Moscow Dinamo soccer team visited Britain to play against Arsenal, Chelsea, Cardiff City, and the Glasgow Rangers: they won two matches and drew two. In 1947 a Soviet basketball team, including five Russians, two Lithuanians, two Estonians, and two Georgians, won the European championship in Prague.[25]

From the outset, in fact, Soviet "professional amateurs" had good chances of success in the Olympic Games against genuine amateurs from other competing nations. In the seven Olympics held between 1952 and 1976, the Soviet Union finished first six times in both the summer and the winter games, and was second on the remaining occasion in each. Its successes were well distributed in all forms of sport. When the highly centralized Soviet system concentrated resources and organizational efforts into a particular campaign, it could produce results at the highest international levels: as in the production of nuclear weapons, missiles, and the conduct of space exploration, so also in sport. The priority given to sport overrode even the normal arthritic sluggishness of the bureaucracy. One report cites the case "of a soccer player who was suddenly required for [the Rest of the World against an All-England side]. He was summoned and rushed by air from the resort where he was on holiday, approved by all departments, including the visa section, delivered from Moscow to England, driven straight from the airport to the stadium, and all this within twenty-four hours."[26]

By the 1960s sport fulfilled the same function in the USSR as in most Western societies, but even more hinged on it, owing to the paucity of other forms of civic identity. It simultaneously satisfied two contradictory drives: it offered a form of collective identification when political collectivism was in decline; and it also presented incentives for competition and the individual drive to succeed. Furthermore, sport provided a relatively painless way for the USSR to prove its great-power credentials when it was faltering in the political and economic spheres. One point should be noted, however: unlike in the United Kingdom, where English teams compete in world sport, fans from the dominant ethnos identified with the USSR, not Russia, which did not have its own international team.

## Persecution of Religion

The relaunch of militant messianic socialism necessarily entailed a renewed assault on religion. Since 1941 there had been a powerful revival of religious belief, especially within the established churches. By the late 1950s congregations were very different from the cowed remnants of the 1930s. The war had profoundly affected everybody's perception of their country and had resulted in universal concern for home and family. Most people had experienced extremes of fear, worry, despair, hope, and grief. A whole new generation of young people had grown up who, though not socialized into religion as children, had heard about their parents' and grandparents' experience, and were anxious about the fate of their people and eager to learn within a generally patriotic framework. A considerable minority found Russian Orthodoxy attractive because it linked them to the past and provided them with a tried source of spiritual sustenance.

The few surviving, battered, and increasingly frail prerevolutionary priests and bishops were now at last able to hand over to a new generation of clergy, products of the seminaries that had reopened in the 1940s. Given that the church was anything but a cushy career, these younger clergymen were perforce men of strong convictions, some of whom had undergone a conversion experience that had changed their lives. They were more likely than their predecessors to take time and care to explain the faith to congregations who had inherited a culture of religious ignorance. The preaching of sermons had become much more common for the same reason; and some priests held *besedy*—informal dialogues—to elucidate the church's beliefs and practices.[27] Other churchmen went even further. Bishop Arsenii of Kostroma, for example, preached openly anti-Marxist sermons, allowed services to be held outside closed churches, and encouraged pilgrimages to shrines in his diocese. On May 15, 1956, while his Council of Religious Affairs (CRA) commissioner was absent owing to illness, he conducted a mass open-air service.[28]

Alarmed by such revivalism and the public's strong response, the Central Committee tried to boost its own, competing message. In October

1958 it issued a statement entitled "Shortcomings in Scientific-Atheist Propaganda," which warned that, thanks to a "deformation of the ecclesiastical policy of the socialist state," opportunities had been created for the dissemination of "reactionary ideology" and for "open and hidden enemies of Soviet power to become more active."[29] As always, the religious revival was interpreted in military terms as part of the struggle between good and evil.

Seeing the clouds darkening, Patriarch Aleksii tried but failed to obtain a private audience with Khrushchev to discuss the situation. Then, in February 1960, he took the offensive himself. At a disarmament conference held in the Kremlin he reminded an international audience that the Bible was "the source of the idea of universal peace," for which all the delegates were assembled, and that the Orthodox Church represented millions of Soviet citizens. Moreover, the church had, he asserted, played a cardinal role in the creation of the Russian state. "At the dawn of Russian statehood," he said, the church had "helped to instil civic order in Russia . . . strengthened the legal foundations of the family, asserted the woman's position as a legal person, condemned usury and slavery, developed the sense of duty and responsibility in man and often, with the help of its own canons, filled in the gaps of state law." The church had "created wonderful monuments enriching Russian culture that still remain the object of national pride of our people." It had helped to forge a fragmented land into one whole, "defending Moscow's significance as the sole ecclesiastic and civic focus of the Russian land." It had led and inspired the Russian people during foreign invasions, right up to recent memory: "It remained with the nation during world war two, helping it by all means possible to win the war and to achieve peace."[30]

This speech was nothing less than an attempt to seize the ideological initiative. By positioning the church at the center of both Russian national identity and the international peace movement, Aleksii was tacitly challenging the party in two of its chosen ideological fortresses. The author of Aleksii's speech was Metropolitan Nikolai, who after the war had led the campaign to make the Russian church the leader of world Orthodoxy. His words provoked bitter attacks from the floor: "You make out that the whole of Russian culture was created by the church, that we owe everything to it, but that is not true!"[31]

The party responded forcefully. In the next few months Nikolai was dismissed as head of the church's foreign affairs department and removed from his metropolitanate in Moscow, despite a personal appeal to Khrush-chev. Not long after, he died suddenly, from what was reported to be a heart attack. Karpov was replaced as head of the CRA by V. A. Kuroedov, who repositioned the office not as the church's intercessor with the state but rather as the state's plenipotentiary within the church. As recently re-leased archival documents show, Karpov had endeavored to be even-handed and to ensure that the church could genuinely function within the narrow limits imposed by Soviet law.[32] Under his successor's pressure its already truncated autonomy was even more severely circumscribed. Kuroedov convened a synod of bishops in July 1961 which agreed under pressure to reform parishes so that priests lost most of their power. Hence-forth all secular parish business, up to and including the closure of the church, was to be decided by an elected executive committee of three. The priest was to become merely their employee, charged with looking after the parish's spiritual affairs. The new structure made it much easier for party activists to infiltrate parish councils, run them in a way acceptable to the local soviet, and sooner or later decide by "democratic" decision that the church was superfluous to society's needs and could be closed.[33]

The administrative measures were accompanied by intensified cam-paigns of "scientific atheist" education. A new journal, *Science and Reli-gion (Nauka i religiia)*, was founded in 1959, and atheist propaganda was stepped up through public meetings, lectures, and films. Young people known to attend church were summoned for "special chats." Five of the eight seminaries were closed and entry to the remainder restricted, so as to impede the preparation of a further generation of clergy.[34] The 22nd Party Congress in 1961, which launched the program to build Communism by 1980, was a natural forum for attacks on the church. O. P. Kolchina, sec-ond secretary of the Moscow oblast party committee, warned: "We can-not help noticing that some amongst us, including the young, have been caught up in the snares of the clergy and sectarians, who have stepped up their activity of late . . . It should be added that, as a result of compla-cency, some comrades by their actions create for the clergy conditions conducive to the revival of religious beliefs and the observance of religious holidays."[35]

The effects were soon felt. By 1965 Orthodox cathedrals had been closed in cities as large as Riga, Orel, Briansk, and Chernigov, while 43 percent of parish churches still open in 1958 had been closed (a reduction from 13,430 to 7,560). In Kiev only 8 churches remained out of 25, in

Odessa 9 out of 23, in Rostov-on-Don 4 out of 12. In some large towns and regions, such as Kaliningrad and Kamchatka, no churches were left at all. Many of the closures were in western Russia, Belorussia, and Ukraine, where churches had remained open at annexation in 1939 or had been re-opened during the German occupation. The figures varied markedly from one diocese to another, suggesting that much depended on the zeal of local CRA commissioners and their interaction with the clergy and the local soviets.[36] The campaign was accompanied in places by the disruption of services and meetings. In one town a group of young people invaded a service, bearing aloft a naked girl. When they tried to break through the iconostasis to place her on the table used for preparing the Eucharist, members of the congregation intervened, and a general fistfight ensued.[37] In some churches icons and other sacred objects were removed and some-times destroyed, and worshippers were harassed and assaulted, amounting in a few cases to rape or even murder. In some regions local soviets de-manded custody of children whose parents were believers, claiming the latter were mentally ill. Clergymen (including Archbishops Iov of Kazan and Andrei of Chernigov) and believers were arrested and charged with "parasitism" or embezzlement of church funds.[38]

Monasteries suffered even more. Their number fell from ninety or so to fewer than twenty. They were most likely targeted because of their sig-nificance as nurseries of religious culture and memory. They were centers where pilgrims could stay when visiting shrines, where parishioners could come on retreat to read and meditate, and where priests could use librar-ies, chapels, and the counsel of elders to refresh their spiritual life. The closures were sometimes carried out with extreme abruptness: monks and nuns were offered no alternative accommodation but simply advised to go to relatives or apply for a place in an old people's home. In a few cases be-lievers would mount a twenty-four-hour vigil, armed with sticks, stones, and pitchforks, and actual fighting took place before the closure order could be enforced. Among the monasteries closed was the Kiev Monastery of the Caves, the first of the Orthodox monasteries of ancient Rus and the heartland of Russian Christianity.[39]

Ultimately, the renewed persecution served to harden the effects of pre-war religious policy. Once again the half-hearted and the careerists with-drew, while the utterly convinced retreated into a rigid defense of a sim-plified version of their faith. The number of committed believers seems to have been directly related to the number of churches within an area, as is suggested by a survey undertaken in 1988. It showed that in Lvov oblast, where there had always been a fairly large number of working churches, the number of people considering themselves believers was many times higher than in Kemerovo oblast in Siberia, where there had been almost no working churches for decades.[40]

Above all, the church remained dependent on the state for everything it did. Its senior clergy were part of the nomenklatura hierarchy, regularly reported on and assessed for their service to party and state, not the church. Zeal in conducting services or expounding church doctrine earned them black marks, while conformity to the state's restrictions and energetic work in the peace movement brought praise.[41] Concessions made during and after the war were finally withdrawn, so that any kind of public religious activity once again became impossible. The church remained a closed community dedicated to weekly performance of the liturgy. It is true that outsiders could attend services, and some did so, but they were drawn to the liturgy as a fascinating and mysterious spectacle that sparked their curiosity but remained largely beyond their comprehension.

## Returning from the Gulag

In his "secret speech" revealing Stalin's crimes, Khrushchev implied that those unjustly sentenced should be allowed to return from prisons and labor camps and obtain a full rehabilitation. The process began even before the speech and speeded up during the mid-1950s. Millions of zeks were suddenly granted what they had cherished as an impossible dream for years: they were free, they could return home, they had the prospect of being exonerated from unjust accusations and of being able to play a full part in society.

In practice, their fate was less happy than they had anticipated. Evgeniia Ginzburg, on finally being released after ten years in Kolyma, took her certificate of release to a special office, where, she had been told, she would be given Form A, the first step toward applying for an internal passport. She recalled: "The window through which documents were handed out was so deeply recessed that looking at the man sitting there was like peering through binoculars from the wrong end." When he asked for her hand, she thought he wanted to shake it, as a sign that wrongful imprisonment was over and that she was now accepted as a legitimate

member of society. She was rudely disabused: "You've done ten years inside, and still you don't know the ropes!" he barked at her, pointing to an
ink-pad on which she was to press her finger. "I'd been imagining I was
free. All my release meant was that I could come and go without escort for
the time being. I was stuck with jailers for life. Even now, after ten years as
a prisoner, they wanted my fingerprints all over again, they wanted to harass and persecute me to my dying day."[42]

Her experience was emblematic. It was rare for former zeks to return
to normal life and be accepted as full members of their society. True,
there was a procedure by which the illegality of their internment could
be established in court and they could be rehabilitated, but only a minority of zeks completed the process. It has been estimated that some 4 million prisoners were released between 1953 and 1958. Of these, between
250,000 and 750,000 were fully rehabilitated between 1954 and 1963.
Then a curtain descended, and only a few hundred more managed it in
the next twenty years. During perestroika in 1987–1989, 840,000 further
rehabilitations were granted. In 1991 nearly 2 million applications were
still outstanding, of which 500,000 had been granted by 1993, but by
that time a further backlog was building up, nearly forty years after the
abolition of the Gulag and the closure of most of the camps.[43]

The truth was that most Soviet officials, whether consciously or not,
considered everyone who had been "inside" residually guilty, and did not
wish to see them return to society as citizens with full rights. Evgenii
Eduardovich Gagen, a journalist who had been "sitting" (that is, imprisoned) for fourteen years, was fully rehabilitated in 1955, but even so he
had great difficulty obtaining even temporary registration in Moscow, let
alone a proper passport. When he complained, an official retorted: "So
what? This is Moscow, not the countryside!" A potential employer made it
clear that he could never put his camp experience behind him: "Even though
I was rehabilitated, in his eyes I was still a person with a dark past."[44]

In the worst case, those who had fabricated denunciations were terrified
of confrontation with their victims. As Anna Akhmatova commented in
1956, "Now all the prisoners will return and two Russias will be eyeball to
eyeball: those who were sent to prison and those who sent them there."[45]
Even without individual confrontations, a swift general rehabilitation for
all those unjustly accused would, as Anastasii Mikoian later admitted,
make it "clear that the country was being run not by a legal government,
but by a band of gangsters."[46]

To have one's property and social status restored was often impossible.

Former apartments were now inhabited by someone else, and amid a serious housing shortage there was little prospect of acquiring anything remotely comparable. Some former zeks tried to have medals and awards reinstated, but they ran up against insuperable obstacles: of 73,000 citizens stripped of awards between 1938 and 1953, only just over 2,000 managed to reclaim them by 1958. Of those who requested readmittance to the Communist Party, only about half had their claim satisfied.[47] People's life situations, their pride in their social standing, and therewith their allegiance to the existing order had been ripped to shreds by Stalin's meat grinder and could not simply be patched together.

Zeks' families did not always welcome them back, either. In many cases too much time—up to twenty years—had elapsed. Few families could simply return to the starting point after such a long absence. Life had moved on: spouses had made other arrangements, found other jobs, other places to live, brought up children alone or with other partners. In any case imprisonment bore a stigma. One little girl was told by her mother that her father had died in the war, and she had always slept with his photo under her pillow, her childhood hero. Then out of the blue in the mid-1950s she received a letter from him: he told her that he had just been released from labor camp and that the thought of his daughter was the only thing that had kept him alive for so many years. The girl's mother froze when she heard about the letter: "Yes, it's from your father. He's been in prison. He's an enemy of the people." Since she was used to respecting her mother's feelings, the girl wrote back to her father saying: "I do not want to know you."[48] A man was deprived of his family, and a little girl of her hero. Thus the shadows of the past and its paranoid images continued to claim their victims.

Even those who were able to return to their families found it difficult to talk of their camp experiences. Like soldiers who return from war having witnessed atrocities, they found that ordinary civilian life was simply too different from what they had experienced. They could find no narrative framework into which to fit their memories without, as they feared, traumatizing their listeners. Working through painful memories with a sympathetic listener is the best way to overcome the past, but sympathetic listening requires a certain shared background and some common assumptions.[49] One woman met her mother, from whom she had been parted thirteen years before, at the age of eight: "We were the closest possible people, mother and daughter, and yet we were strangers, we spoke of irrelevancies, mostly crying and remaining silent."[50]

Other barriers had to be overcome, too. Some zeks had signed documents on release promising not to reveal anything about life in the camps; they were afraid that breaking their promise might land them back there. Some simply did not want to dwell on a past that seemed eminently worth forgetting. Others, on the contrary, were so obsessed by their experience that it haunted every aspect of their lives, causing them to wake in bed screaming from nightmares. Some had bells removed from their front doors, because their journey through hell had started with the doorbell ringing. Some went through long spells of anxiety or depression, which Soviet psychiatry was ill equipped to treat. Such people were difficult for any family to cope with, and sometimes new separations resulted.[51]

Perhaps uncertainty and insecurity derived from the past contributed to the energy, even frenzy, that some Russians put into seeking a better collective future. The historian Catherine Merridale, whose study of death and grief penetrates deep into Russians' social psychology, hypothesized that many Russians never re-established a personal equilibrium, but instead tried to lose themselves in the collective. Writing in the 1990s, she observed that "Russians really do seem to have lived with their histories of unspeakable loss by working, singing and waving the red flag. Some laugh about it now, but almost everyone is nostalgic for a collectivism and common purpose that have been lost."[52] However one interprets their reaction, it seems clear that the releases did little if anything to heal the wounds of the past and restore a more genuinely cohesive Russian or Soviet civic community. Instead, old forms of division and discord were replaced by new ones, papered over by artificial displays of unanimity.

## The Technological Dream

The most persuasive element of Khrushchev's relaunch of utopia was the space program. Its origin lay in the utopian thinking of the early twentieth century. It developed from the visionary impulse of Konstantin Tsiolkovskii (1857–1935), who was a pioneer in the fields of aviation and rocketry. He had always dreamed of making space flight possible, so that human beings could apply energy from the sun to colonize the solar system and erect space cities. He had nourished vague hopes of making contact with superior, more intelligent beings from elsewhere in the cosmos, and thereby overcoming death. He was impelled by a vitalist pantheism similar to that of Fedorov. "Death is one of the illusions of a weak human mind," he once asserted. "There is no death, for the existence of an atom in inorganic matter is not marked by memory and time—it is as if the latter did not exist at all."[53]

Tsiolkovskii worked out many of the basic principles later applied in space flight, including liquid fuel and successive-stage rockets. These were developed further with the encouragement of Marshal Tukhachevskii. In the 1930s, however, Tsiolkovskii died and Tukhachevskii was arrested; thereafter the research program lacked institutional support and fizzled out. It resumed after World War II, but in a completely different context: not for space colonization but as part of the lavishly financed program to achieve military parity with the United States by devising long-range missiles capable of delivering destructive weapons. This was the second stage of the military revolution that Stalin had started by initiating the creation of the atomic bomb. The book *Military Strategy* (1962) by Chief of the General Staff Marshal V. V. Sokolovskii showed that the USSR had moved away from reliance on huge land forces toward a global aggressive capacity based on intercontinental missiles with nuclear warheads.[54] In accordance with this strategy, in the late 1950s Khrushchev cut the land forces and set up a new branch of the armed services, the Strategic Missile Forces. The space program thus eventually took shape as an exuberant offshoot of the grimly unattractive military-industrial complex.

But it was effective. On October 4, 1957, an SS-6 rocket, developed from the German V2, launched the world's first artificial satellite, Sputnik 1, into orbit around the earth, provoking disbelief and consternation in the United States. It was soon followed by another satellite containing Laika, a black-and-white fox terrier, who thus became the first living being in space. She was attached to instruments that transmitted to earth a detailed account of her biological reactions to the strains of cosmic flight. In October 1959 the Soviets launched two more satellites, which took photographs of both sides of the moon.[55]

Khrushchev took advantage of these achievements to point out not only the scientific but also the military significance of Sputnik: "We can now send a missile to any point on the globe, carrying, if necessary, a hydrogen warhead. Our announcement to this effect was greeted with disbelief and regarded as an attempt by the Soviet leaders to instill confidence in their own people and intimidate the Western governments. But then the Soviet Union, using the inter-continental ballistic missile, launched an artificial earth satellite, and when it started circling the globe, and when everyone—unless he was blind—could see it by looking up at the sky, our opponents fell silent."[56] These were the words of a leader overcompensating for an inferiority complex by ostentatiously reasserting the status of his own country as one of the world's two superpowers.

The climax of the Soviet space program came on April 12, 1961, when the test pilot Iurii Gagarin took off from the cosmodrome in Tiuratam (Baikonur) on the semi-arid steppes of Kazakhstan east of the Aral Sea, to become the first human being ever to enter cosmic space. Equally important, Gagarin accomplished the return an hour and a half later without being consumed in the intense heat of re-entry into the atmosphere, and touched down very close to the planned landing ground near the Volga.[57] He was awarded the title of Hero of the Soviet Union and was personally received by Khrushchev in Red Square. The pioneering triumphs of the 1930s had been repeated on an even grander scale, and for a time the Soviet sacred narrative seemed to have been successfully renewed, even taken to new heights. *Pravda* wrote that Gagarin's flight "has convincingly demonstrated to the whole world the great superiority of the new socialist system over capitalism."[58] The writer Nikolai Gribachev pointed to the lesson for the Great Other, the United States: "We still haven't taken down our posters saying 'Let us catch up with America!' Now the Americans will have to put up posters saying 'Let us catch up with the Soviet Union!'"[59]

The second cosmonaut, German Titov, a more educated and urbane figure than Gagarin, reported from space in terms reminiscent of the Cosmist poets or of the Suprematist paintings of Malevich or Kandinskii: "The terrible, intense brightness of the sun contrasts with the inky blackness of the planet's shadow with huge stars above glittering like diamonds, while a lovely powder-blue halo surrounds the planet."[60] For a time it seemed as if the visionary impulse of Tsiolkovskii was being fulfilled.

## The Cuban Missile Crisis

Unexpected reinforcement for the Soviet utopian vision came when Fidel Castro seized power in Cuba in January 1959. He provided the Soviet Union with both an ideological and a strategic opportunity. He offered a model of a socialist revolution independent of Moscow and transferable to countries in the Third World, especially in Latin America; he renewed the international impetus of socialism and a memory of the hopes of the early 1920s.

In the strategic arena the potential gains for the USSR were no less significant. Cuba was a potential bridgehead for Soviet missiles. The Soviet Union had only just begun to build intercontinental missiles capable of hitting the United States from launchpads on Soviet soil. But on Cuba the Soviet Union could place intermediate-range missiles, of which it had a much greater number, capable of reaching targets from Dallas, Texas, to Washington, D.C. As Khrushchev said at a meeting of the Defense Council, "The Americans have surrounded our country with military bases and threatened us with nuclear weapons, and now they will learn just what it feels like to have enemy missiles pointing at you . . . The USA is now not at such an unattainable distance from the Soviet Union as formerly. Figuratively speaking, if need be, Soviet artillerymen can support the Cuban people with their rocket fire should the aggressive forces in the Pentagon dare to start intervention against Cuba." When Castro's guerrillas were successful, the KGB symbolically changed the name of its file on Cuba from *Iuntsy* (youngsters) to *Avanpost* (bridgehead or outpost).[61]

Precisely for those reasons, of course, U.S. President Kennedy was determined to eliminate Castro and bring Cuba back under U.S. hegemony. To that end he sent a force to invade Cuba at the Bay of Pigs in April 1961 and continued covert military preparations after the assault failed. When Khrushchev responded by shipping missiles and nuclear warheads to Cuba in September-October 1962, he was aiming both to defend Cuba from a U.S. attack and to overcome the nuclear and missile imbalance currently working to the disadvantage of the USSR.

Khrushchev's initiative was a huge gamble. When the CIA discovered the missiles and Kennedy challenged the Soviet leader over them, he had no real choice but to concede defeat: the alternative was to risk a massively destructive nuclear conflict, for he could see that the United States had local military superiority in the Caribbean.[62] Khrushchev backed down and withdrew the missiles. His decision tore the veil from the bluff he had felt was necessary to sustain the Soviet Union's position as superpower. Clearly, after all it was still not the genuine equal of the United States.

His capitulation seriously weakened the Soviet claim, hitherto scarcely contested, to lead the world socialist movement. The Chinese leaders received a golden opportunity to pour scorn on Soviet pretensions. Castro was furious to find that he had been first manipulated as a frontline pawn in a great-power game, then abandoned with no weapons more effective than a verbal promise from Kennedy not to attack him. Other East European leaders were anxious to be reassured that the USSR would support *them* in a future crisis.[63]

Khrushchev's successors were determined never to find themselves in a similar plight. As Adam Ulam has remarked, in geostrategic matters the Cuban missile crisis represented "the collapse of the most comprehensive and far-reaching policy design effected in the Soviet Union since the end of world war two; it was now necessary to pick up the pieces and rethink the whole problem."[64] While continuing to expand nuclear weapons programs, the Soviets also returned to massive conventional rearmament, including surface and underwater naval capacity, so as to project Soviet power throughout the world, wherever an international crisis might arise. Soviet citizens—and especially Russians and Ukrainians—were condemned to further decades of austerity and squalor to finance this expansion of conventional rearmament. Such was the cost of superpower status.

## Agriculture, the Food Supply, and Social Unrest

By the time of Stalin's death, nearly a generation had passed since the collectivization of agriculture. The impoverishment and demoralization of the village had become an established fact. So too, as a result, was the chronic insufficiency of food supplies. Urban state food shops usually presented a dismal spectacle to the potential purchaser: a few withered cabbages, some wrinkled potatoes and carrots, and a pyramid of dusty tins that never moved from one month to the next. Anyone who wanted good food could find it, but only through restricted supplies at work, or for much higher prices at the misleadingly named "kolkhoz market," where peasants sold produce they had grown on their small private plots.

The party leaders had to grapple with this problem. If the urban workers, allegedly the leading class, could not be properly fed, the party would lose all legitimacy. Moreover, the underproductivity of agriculture and the low morale of the farm-workers not only jeopardized the urban diet but also undermined Russians' perception of themselves as a people with strong roots in the village.

Khrushchev made a few short-lived concessions to private farming, but the central thrust of his program was the cultivation of so-called virgin lands, former nomadic pastures in north Kazakhstan and western Siberia. They were not quite virgin, since "Stolypin peasants" had settled there in the early years of the twentieth century, but they had been branded "ku-

laks" and deported in the 1930s, and much of the land had been neglected ever since. Now it was slated to become the main source of grain
for Soviet bakeries, while the traditional grain-producing soil of Ukraine
and the black earth was to be turned over to maize to provide cattle-feed
and revive the Soviet Union's lagging meat and dairy sector. To help expe-
dite the program, Komsomol volunteers were mobilized and sent to provide working hands till the new farms could establish themselves. Their
enthusiasm was displayed in the newspapers and in propaganda films,
along with pictures of rows of combine harvesters advancing through
huge fields, ears of wheat rippling in the breeze as far as the eye could see.

From the outset, though, the initiative was vitiated by defects inherent in the Soviet order. Like the five-year plans, the virgin lands program was run like a military campaign, conducted with maximum speed
and accompanied by the incessant trumpeting of "victories." Khrushchev
pressed ahead without waiting for scientific reports on the nature of the
soil or taking any precautions to prevent its deterioration. For a few years
cultivation worked well, state procurements rose substantially, and the
danger of famine seemed permanently averted. But without extensive irrigation, the planting of trees and hedges, and the use of crop rotation or
fertilizer, the soil proved vulnerable in prolonged dry weather. Between
1960 and 1965, in a series of dust storms, much of the topsoil was blown
away. Some land was rendered arid, and the fertility of much more was seriously degraded. The output of grain once again declined.[65]

In the 1950s, then, Kazakhstan became a key republic for the development of the USSR. The space program and the virgin lands campaign
that were at the center of the relaunch of utopia were both situated there.
Yet there too the optimism and social dynamism generated by Khrushchev among young people came up against the road blocks left over from
the Stalin tyranny. Since the 1930s Kazakhstan had been used as a dump-
ing ground for the Soviet penal system. It was suitable for the purpose because of its immense size, its harsh climate, and the need to develop an in-
frastructure where wage-laborers would not freely go. The manual work
for the large industrial projects was performed by zeks, *spetsposelentsy,* and
stigmatized peoples deported from their homelands. It has been estimated
that fully one-eighth of the inhabitants of Kazakhstan were such "suppressed" victims of the Soviet state. The concentration was especially high
in and around the raw industrial town of Karaganda, where a large new
metallurgical complex was being constructed, sometimes referred to as a

"second Magnitogorsk."[66] Heavy drinking, hooliganism, gang fights, and other kinds of casual violence were common, and the local police were used to dealing with rowdies in a brusque and often brutal manner.

The influx of young workers to the new industrial sites and of Komsomol volunteers to the virgin lands brought a strongly contrasting spirit to the region. These were ambitious, well-educated, often idealistic youngsters, imbued with the aims and the spirit of official propaganda, keen to "build socialism" as well as to start making careers for themselves. They were confronted with living conditions more primitive than most of them had ever experienced, as well as with uncouth and recalcitrant locals whose attitude both to work and to the authorities was quite different from their own. Unemployed youths recently released from labor camps and either held in exile or awaiting return home gave their time to heavy drinking, gambling, fighting, and stealing. Komsomol youths were often their victims. Faced with inadequate provisions, lack of organization, and suspicion or even hostility from the local population, the newcomers provided their own self-organization in time-honored Russian style. They improvised self-defense groups with their own elected leaders bound by "joint responsibility."[67]

In the summer of 1959, in addition to the virgin lands activists, some two thousand Komsomol volunteers between the ages of seventeen and twenty arrived at the Karaganda Metal Works in the suburb of Temirtau. This was one of the largest industrial projects of the epoch, the pride of Kazakhstan. In spite of that, the newcomers were accommodated in large communal tents, which were torn and leaky and did not have proper facilities for taking baths or washing and drying clothes. The young Nursultan Nazarbaev (future president of post-Soviet Kazakhstan) was one of them: "After a short time in damp and dirty basement accommodation, we were moved to an unheated dormitory, where we kept warm by sleeping in twos on iron cots covered with mattresses. There was no place even to hang out our clothes to dry. . . . There were no recreational facilities—the only entertainment that people had was big fights. Murders and other serious crimes were rife."[68] There was no radio, and newspapers arrived only sporadically. On the building site equipment often arrived late or was in disrepair, so that for long periods normal work was impossible. Worst of all, the food supply was intermittent and the water was often contaminated. The conditions were calculated to turn idealism into embitterment and bloody-mindedness.[69]

On August 1, 1959, workers returned from the building site to one of the tent settlements to find there was no water for drinking or washing. Such shortages were common enough, but on this occasion tempers flared, and the young people raided a cafeteria, beat up a night watchman, and stole food and drink from inside. The police eventually arrived and arrested two participants, selected for no obvious reason. The volunteers responded by displaying group solidarity and marching on the police station to free their comrades. As most of the policemen were still at the cafeteria, the crowd was able to break into the police station and smash equipment there, though apparently without managing to free the prisoners. The next evening, the police agreed to release them, but by that time soldiers had arrived and the conflict reached flashpoint. Crowds of young people attacked and destroyed the police station and tried to do the same to a department store and the administration building of the metal works. At this point the soldiers used their firearms, and 16 people were killed or fatally wounded, while a further 27 received nonfatal wounds. The fighting was serious: 109 soldiers and officers were wounded, and 190 people were arrested, including 75 Komsomol volunteers.[70]

The whole incident showed up very poor crowd control on the part of the Kazakh police and the Soviet army. It also suggested a rather panicky response from Soviet leaders. Khrushchev and his colleagues were still understandably highly nervous about public reaction to the revelations about Stalin. They had, moreover, just announced their ambitious economic development program at the 21st Party Congress, intended to enable the Soviet Union to overtake the material standards of the United States by 1980. They could not afford to let news of serious social tensions and economic failures reach the West or even their own public. Temirtau, like all conflicts inside Soviet society, was never mentioned in the Soviet media.

Minor incidents of working-class unrest were quite common during the years 1955–1963. They resulted from resentments that had built up since the end of the war, especially over continuing inequality and injustice, from the sometimes panicky and aggressive behavior of the militia, and from expectations aroused by the criticism of Stalin and the move to "socialist legality." Workers led to believe they were the ruling class had been disillusioned twice: once after the end of the war, a second time after the "secret speech."[71]

The most serious outbreak was the rising in the southern city of

Novocherkassk in June 1962. By this time, following the dustbowls in the virgin lands, the food supply situation had deteriorated again. There were serious shortages in the towns, and lines of indignant townsfolk had ample opportunity to discuss the shortcomings of the economic system. As often happens, indignation was especially strong because people had experienced several years of reliable food supplies and had not expected to be faced again with shortages. Workers by this time took it for granted that the state, through the enterprise that employed them, was obliged to provide a basic living in return for regular work. So their complaints were not just about working conditions and pay but also about housing, food supplies, urban facilities, and the behavior of the police. From Kuibyshev a pensioner wrote to Khrushchev: "On the placard that talks of poverty and unemployment in capitalist countries and of the improvement of life in our country the headings should be the other way around." Another wrote: "The radio keeps boasting that we are approaching communism. We'll starve before we get there. You, of course, have your own communism, but what we have is hungerism and expensivism."[72]

At the Budennyi Locomotive Works in Novocherkassk, by especially crass bad timing, wage rates were lowered on May 31, and increases in food prices were announced on June 1. The Budennyi Works was a typical Soviet enterprise of the period, and conditions there illuminate the way many urban Russians lived. It had a good reputation, but it had suffered from a recent lack of investment. Technical equipment was out of date and heavy manual labor still very common, while facilities for eating, washing, and resting were poor. The administrative building, however, had recently been rebuilt to a high standard. Many employees had lived for years in barracks, and some even in tents. Turnover among laborers was high, and the management was often compelled to hire unsatisfactory employees to plug gaps, including candidates with criminal records— though the criminal activity might have been no more than casual pilfering from work, a more or less universal practice. In the city food supplies were especially poor: people were forced to stand in line for hours to buy potatoes, let alone butter or meat, which was often not available.[73]

According to KGB reports, popular reaction to the price increases was that the *tolstopuzye* (fat-bellied) bosses should take a pay cut instead. One elderly and respected worker, when told that the price rises were temporary and that "the time would come when everyone would live well," replied: "I have waited forty years for such a day, and, while I wait, life on

the contrary gets worse." Another opinion was that "we should stop helping under-developed socialist countries"; "the Soviet government 'feeds'
other states but does not provide for its own workers."[74] These complaints
indicated that ordinary Russians were losing their internationalist sentiments, beginning to prefer acceptable living conditions at home to com-
mitments abroad, the consumer society to revolution.

By noon on June 1 a crowd had gathered in front of the factory administration building, exchanging sentiments such as these. The factory director rebuked the "slackers" and added flippantly: "If they haven't enough
money for meat and sausages, let them eat liver pasties *(pirozhki)*."[75]

This tactless pastiche of Marie Antoinette was probably the spark that
ignited the conflagration. One of the workers present, a former Komsomol activist and virgin lands volunteer, now living in a small room with
a pregnant wife—broke away in fury and set off the factory siren. This
sound, the twentieth-century version of the alarm bell that used to summon peasants to emergency village meetings, provoked many more workers to down tools, quit the shop floor, and congregate in the courtyard, all
of them agitated over the wage cuts and price rises. Some of them decided
to stop a train passing on the main Saratov-Rostov Railway just a hundred yards away. They did so in the way they had seen in numerous
films on the 1905 and 1917 revolutions: by erecting a barricade out of
broken fencing and planting a red flag on top. On the stationary locomotive they then hung a placard: "Cut up Khrushchev for sausages!" Others
tore down a portrait of Khrushchev and broke into the administration
building, where they smashed windows and destroyed furniture and telephones. Kurochkin and the first secretary of the Rostov obkom, A. V.
Basov, tried to appear on the balcony and address the crowd, but they
were driven back with stones and bottles and cries of "You need to tell us
how we are going to live when norms [wages] are lowered and prices
raised."[76]

By this stage the crowd, thoroughly roused and angry, was responsive to
inflammatory appeals, even from individuals who were drunk. A popular
Russian saying has it that "what the sober have on their mind, the drunk
have on their tongue," or, in the language of contemporary sociology,
James Scott's "hidden transcripts" were suddenly made public. During the
night the disorders spread to other parts of the town, with the aid of the
factory siren. Early next morning a large delegation of Budennyi employees marched into town, breaking through a military cordon on a bridge,

and assembled on the main square, where they were joined by workers from other factories and many ordinary citizens as well. Some of them carried red banners and portraits of Lenin alongside placards reading: "Bread, meat and a pay rise."[77]

Already overnight the crisis had alarmed the leaders in Moscow, and several members of the CPSU Presidium had come down to take charge. As the situation grew more threatening they ordered all roads and railway lines leading into Novocherkassk to be sealed off, and they gave permission for tanks to be brought in, one of which crushed a demonstrator.

Now the workers found themselves in a confrontation that was familiar to them from propaganda films: workers facing tanks. Only now the plus and minus signs had been reversed: the tanks were on the wrong side. Moreover, the workers lacked any consistent leadership, organization, or purpose. Some of those who shouted rallying cries were drunk. There were calls for Mikoian, the senior Presidium official present, to come out and negotiate with them. Mikoian was reportedly willing to try but was dissuaded by his colleagues; it would have been difficult for him to achieve much, since the workers had no leaders with whom he could talk nor coherent demands to negotiate. All the same, the refusal infuriated the crowd. Breakaway groups began to storm the city party headquarters on one side of the square. One of them appeared on the balcony with a bottle of vodka and two dishes piled high with cheese and sausages: "Look at what they eat!"[78]

At this point the senior military officer present used a megaphone to order the crowd to disperse. When his words had no effect, the troops drawn up around the square began to shoot, at first in the air, then at the crowd itself. There are indications that the first fatal shots were actually fired by MVD internal troops stationed on the roofs or inside nearby buildings, even as the Red Army soldiers were still firing warning shots. At first the crowd hesitated, aghast and not believing that troops of their own army could actually try to kill them. Then they began to flee in panic, but because the square was so tightly packed, they had difficulty getting away, while the shooting continued relentlessly behind them. Sixteen people were killed on the square, and five more as soldiers cleared the party headquarters. Some seventy people were seriously injured, and an unknown number incurred minor injuries. Some of the wounded did not report to hospital for fear of being arrested.[79]

The deaths divided the demonstrators. The majority preferred to desist in order to avoid further bloodshed, but a minority used the accumulated fear and outrage to whip up feelings further. During the following night a curfew was declared, and mass arrests followed. Next morning Frol Kozlov, from the Presidium, made a speech over the radio, accusing "hooligan elements" of having provoked the violence. He did not speak of revoking the price increases but promised to look into workers' grievances.[80]

The authorities fabricated an indictment against those they considered "ringleaders," accusing them of "organizing mass disorders" and "offering armed resistance to the authorities." They decided not to publicize the trial throughout the Soviet Union, but it was open to invited representatives of the "public" in Novocherkassk itself, where it was manipulated as a warning and a propaganda lesson. The sentences, including seven death sentences and prison terms of ten to fifteen years, were greeted with applause.[81]

The whole tragedy demonstrated how completely the art of ordinary politics had been lost in Russia and how the political stage was monopolized by extreme and paranoid imaginings. The workers acted in accordance with assumptions they had inherited unquestioningly from both Russian and Soviet culture: that the distribution of resources should be egalitarian, that wealth and luxury were iniquitous, that there was a tacit "social contract" under which the authorities take the decisions but have a duty to provide for their protégés, and finally that the tsar/first secretary was just, the custodian of the truth, but that his local officials were corrupt and deceitful. In striking contrast to Poland in the same period, there was no contact whatsoever between workers and intellectuals: they lived in different intellectual and moral universes.

Moreover, although the workers shared most of the declared aims of the Soviet state, they had no means of defending their interests and expressing their grievances until they became so overwhelming that the slightest incident could provoke large-scale violence. Soldiers and internal troops without serious training in crowd control were let loose on an unarmed (though angry and undisciplined) crowd of civilians. The Soviet leaders in Moscow also overreacted. The frightening abruptness and speed with which events developed put them on notice that their party and police apparatus, in appearance so strong, could suddenly and without warning lose control of a major industrial city. They knew from their studies of the history of the CPSU that working-class unrest, once successful in one center, could rapidly spread to others. They were determined never to find themselves in such a situation again.

But then, to ignore or suppress workers' protests was no longer possible without reverting to full-scale Stalinist methods. Khrushchev instead took the critical decision to neutralize them by using precious foreign currency to buy grain on foreign markets, and thus keep the price of bread down. This was the greatest possible humiliation. The much-derided tsarist regime had exported grain; the Soviet one was now having to import it. In a policy field that he had made his specialty and where he had promised so much, Khrushchev had demonstrated a lack of even basic competence. Inevitably his failings were identified with the party of which he was first secretary: far from leading the people to the broad uplands of Communism, the party, it seemed, could not even feed them properly.

The regime learned several lessons: to keep food prices low, at the cost of making support payments that soon became what one economist called the "highest food-and-agriculture subsidy in history."[82] Between 1965 and 1985 subsidies on basic foodstuffs rose more than sixteenfold, from 3.5 billion rubles to 58.8 billion. They rose especially sharply in 1971, 1976, and 1980, after workers' unrest in Poland, also arising from food prices, reminded Soviet leaders of the dangers. In 1980 this subsidy consumed 11 percent of the state budget expenditure, and it continued to rise thereafter.[83] This huge sum represented the cost of no longer resorting to massive terror and of fulfilling the "social contract" with the urban workers, keeping their food prices low while offering high enough payments to farms to stem the poverty and demoralization of the villages and offer some incentives to skilled workers to stay there. The excessive subsidy was, in short, an absolute necessity if the contradictions of Soviet policy were not finally to destroy traditional Russia.

The cost of the subsidy could not be absorbed easily, since the authorities were simultaneously spending huge sums to project Soviet power all over the world by massive rearmament. The only way to square the circle was to allow ordinary workers a modest share in corruption by turning a blind eye to shoddy work and to the "black economy." This was Leonid Brezhnev's tacit social contract: "they pretend to pay us, and we pretend to work." For those in regular employment this formula generated an easy-paced way of life, in which most people were guaranteed life's minimal benefits in one form or another, no matter how slovenly their work. It also guaranteed a more stable society: from 1969 to 1977 far fewer outbreaks of public disorder were recorded.[84] But it was a way of life in which only the bosses could prosper, in which squalor, shoddy goods, and mutual back-scratching became the norm. It was incompatible with the drive to create a more humane society, let alone build Communism, and it could not indefinitely sustain great-power status. On both grounds the tacit contract eroded the popular faith which in the 1960s was still alive, as is evident from the slogans and appeals that fueled the unrest of that decade. In those circumstances either ethnic or consumer aspirations replaced international socialist ones.

## Ethnic Unrest

The post-Stalin leaders' policy on nationality issues was less crudely russifying than Stalin's. They called off the anti-Jewish Doctors' Plot investigation and released those arrested. They allowed somewhat more cultural and economic autonomy to the non-Russian republics. On the other hand, they continued to operate on the assumption that the Soviet Union was a predominantly Russian state and that international socialism should have a Russian face. They also took for granted that the national question had been settled, that ethnic conflicts were a thing of the past, anomalous if they flared up now. Khrushchev told the 22nd Party Congress in 1961 that "the party has solved one of the most complex of problems, which has plagued mankind for ages and remains acute in the world of capitalism to this day—the problem of relations between nations." The congress resolution claimed that the nationalities of the USSR were "all united into one family by common vital interests and are advancing together toward a single goal—Communism."[85]

The keyword now was *sliianie,* the "merging" of nationalities. It was meant to denote the creation of harmonious interethnic relations and the gradual emergence of a supraethnic working-class community. A major step toward this goal was taken in the language reform of 1958, which made Russian a compulsory subject of study in all Soviet schools, while non-Russian languages became optional. The explicit objective of the law was to make Russian the "second native language" of all non-Russians.[86] Its greatest novelty was that parents received the right to choose whether to send their children to a Russian-language school or a native-language one. In most republics—even those where Russians were most resented, as in the Baltics—a high proportion of parents chose the Russian-language schools, so that their children would have better chances in education, job hunting, and promotion throughout the USSR. Contrary to its intention, though, the law raised tension by arousing new fears among all ethnic groups. It alarmed the non-Russians, who suspected it meant the submerging of their national existence in Russia. Russians, paradoxically, also felt threatened, fearful that in "merging" they too would lose their identity through the creation of a homogenized international culture, probably dominated, like most of the world, by the ubiquitous "other," the United States.[87]

Open ethnic conflict became more frequent in the 1950s. Now that there were fewer labor camp inmates and the danger of war seemed less imminent, soldiers were often used to carry out labor-intensive construction projects, such as the construction of roads, railways, and large buildings. These battalions were a milieu that tended to generate ethnic tension. Senior officers would often send to them men who were poor soldiers, undisciplined, weaklings, or prone to heavy drinking. Since the discipline was less strict on the building site than in the barracks and living facilities were often inadequate, construction troops would form their own spontaneous bands to steal or trade on the black market. They tended to drink and then harass local citizens or beat up traders who they thought had cheated them. The result would sometimes be gang fighting on city streets, or incidents in which soldiers attacked policemen who tried to restrain or arrest them. Sometimes there was an ethnic element to the mutual hostility. In Klimovsk (Moscow oblast) in May 1955, for example, three Azerbaijani construction soldiers were beaten during a brawl. When their comrades tried to take revenge, local young men attacked their dormitory, shouting: "Beat up the Chuchmeki! They are for Beria!"[88] This slogan combined two especially negative ethnic stereotypes. "Chuchmeki" is an insulting portmanteau term used by Russians to stigmatize people of Central Asian or Caucasian origin. Russians suspected them of rigging the black market, yet also, illogically, of being especially closely associated with the security police, probably because for many years it was run by Beria, who was a Georgian.

Even more serious and sustained ethnic conflict was generated by the attempt to rectify the injustice of Stalin's deportation of nationalities. In 1954–1956 the civil rights of deported peoples were gradually restored, and in January 1957 the Chechen-Ingush ASSR was restored (in its 1944 boundaries, except for the loss of Prigorod district to the North Ossetian

ASSR). The authorities were prepared to permit a gradual return of those Chechen and Ingush who wished to do so, but they wanted time to organize and channel the influx properly. Many Chechens and Ingush were not prepared to wait, and they returned before homes had been assigned to them. They found, naturally enough, that Russians, Avars, and others were now living in their old homes. The returnees tried to have the "interlopers" evicted. Their attempts provoked lasting resentment and a number of violent incidents.[89]

Of these the most serious occurred in Groznyi, the capital of the Chechen Ingush ASSR. The city had been multinational ever since its founding, numerous Russians had always lived there, and Chechens had never constituted a majority of the population. However, the returning Chechens demanded the restoration of their former houses and apartments. On August 23, 1958, after a drunken brawl in Groznyi, a Russian worker from a chemical factory was stabbed to death by Chechens. His colleagues displayed the coffin in front of the home of his fiancée, in the area of town where most of the chemical workers lived. The "lying-in-state" turned into a protest meeting. An elderly chemical worker, L. Miakinin, made a speech. Miakinin was widely respected as a civil war veteran who had worked in the chemical industry all his life and had received the Order of Lenin in 1955. He called on those present to act: "Chechens are killing Russians. They do not want to live in peace. We must write a collective letter in the name of the Russian people, gather signatures and designate a person to carry the letter to Moscow with a request for a commission to be sent to Groznyi, and if the commission is not formed, then let Comrade Khrushchev come himself in order to investigate on the spot."[90] This procedure was an old Russian way of expressing a grievance: drawing up a collective petition, then sending a delegate *(khodok)* to the ruler with a request for his personal intervention to restore justice.

The funeral procession turned into an anti-Chechen demonstration. The petition, when drawn up, called for the expulsion of Chechens from Groznyi, and this demand attracted the support of townspeople who had nothing to do with the funeral. They were further worked up by the speech of an elderly man who had served in the Special Troops (ChON) as long ago as 1922, and had been a long-time Komsomol and party member before being expelled. He recounted outrages that he alleged had been committed by Chechens and demanded their expulsion from the

city, accusing the present Communist leaders of not being true Communists. He added that "Great Rus is waking up," and called for a strike if
the protesters' demands were not met. On the evening of the procession a
crowd attacked and occupied the headquarters of the regional party committee, and the police eventually arrested some twenty people in order to
clear it. The next morning, a crowd gathered outside to demand their release. As a result of the mêlée the military were brought in. Soldiers managed to bring the rioting to an end without using their firearms (which argues considerable skill). All the same, as a result of the disturbances, two
people died and thirty-two were injured. Many of the latter were police
and party officials, which suggests that violence was directed against them
as much as against Chechens.[91]

It is symptomatic that in these clashes the two most fiery speeches were
made by true-believing veterans of the 1920s. Their message, in crude
and subversive form, was a version of what Khrushchev was currently
preaching, a return to the revolutionary idealism of the early years of
the Soviet state. Now, however, the message was both adulterated and re-
energized by reactive Russian nationalism. The rebels' perception of the
authorities was also traditional, only it belonged to an older, prerevolutionary tradition of the "good tsar." Local Communist leaders were
seen as "false Communists," accused of maladministration and of ignoring the interests of the people, but justice was expected from the supreme comrades in the sacred city of Moscow. The internationalism of
the 1920s was now absent. On the contrary, ethnic stereotyping was
marked: Russians seemed to hope that the Central Committee would save
them from the "evil Chechens." Their aspirations were formulated in
a resolution composed by a retired Russian engineer of the Gudermes
state farm and presented to the local party committee. It called for all
"privileges" of the Chechens and Ingushes (that is, their right to return) to
be revoked, and the Chechen-Ingush ASSR to be renamed Groznyi
oblast, or even made into a multinational Soviet Socialist Republic, in
which the Chechen-Ingush population would not be allowed to exceed 10
percent.[92]

Obviously this principle, if widely imitated elsewhere in the Soviet
Union, would put an end to its viability as a multinational great power.
The creeping ethnicization of the country was beginning to take its toll.

## The Significance of Khrushchev's Fall

Khrushchev was by now unpopular not only with the public. Senior party officials were becoming more and more disillusioned and alarmed at seeing their privileges and tenure of office eroded, and at the leader's disruption of the patron-client networks by which they sustained their power. In October 1964 Khrushchev was summoned to a plenary session of the Central Committee, where the principal ideological secretary, Mikhail Suslov, read out what amounted to an indictment of the leader. He was accused of gross mistakes in agricultural administration, of erratic conduct of foreign affairs, of obsession with reorganizations inside the party, of nepotism (though all party secretaries had their protégés, whose careers they promoted, and of "crude violations of Leninist norms of party leadership."[93]

Khrushchev's period of rule marked the last attempt to combine neo-Russian empire with millennial socialism. Once it had failed, the most persuasive argument for Russia's imperial mission finally faded with it. Other than as partners in a great power, non-Russians had little reason to go on accepting Russian domination. In those circumstances Russians became just one ethnos among many others in the USSR; they were the largest, but they were also faced with handicaps from which other ethnic groups did not suffer. Over the next quarter-century, even Russians began to wonder whether the Soviet Union was really good for them.

# 9

# THE REDISCOVERY OF RUSSIA

By the mid-1960s the Soviet Union had become a stable, hierarchical, and conservative society—and after the upheavals of recent decades, most people were content to see it that way. At the apex of the pyramid was Moscow, and in Moscow the Kremlin and *Staraia Ploshchad* (Old Square), the building of the Central Committee of the CPSU. From that focal point tentacles of appointment, control, and supplies extended outward to the Russian provinces and to the non-Russian republics. Every enterprise and institution had its place in the hierarchy, according to whether its work was deemed to be of "all-Union significance," of "republican significance," or lower. The salaries and perks of its managers and employees depended on that rating. The positioning of each town on the ladder would depend on the status of its enterprises, and on that in turn would depend the quality of its facilities and the supplies of its shops. Villages stood on the lowest rung.

Individual citizens seeking to rise in the world would apply first for education and then for employment in a town of higher standing, if possible Moscow or Leningrad, or, failing that, one of the Union Republic capitals. Whether they received a propiska in the town of their choice would depend on a number of factors: their proposed training or employment, their ethnic origin, their military service, their standing in the party, and whether or not a patron or protector was prepared to intervene on their behalf. In this way the hierarchy was maintained and supervised by superiors deriving their authority ultimately from Old Square. The only way to circumvent the uphill obstacle course was to marry someone of "higher" rating; that practice was widespread, as common as financial marriages in bourgeois society.

The ethnic configuration of the ruling class had crystallized by the mid-1960s and remained fairly stable thereafter. The Slavs, and especially the Russians, were dominant, but not overwhelmingly so. For example, in the CPSU Central Committee of 1981, Slavs constituted 86 percent of members, and Russians alone 67 percent, compared with their 52 percent share of the population. By contrast, the peoples of the Muslim union republics formed 5.4 percent of the Central Committee membership, compared with 11.6 percent of the population.[1] In the union republics the first secretary was normally a local, but the second secretary, the commander of the military district, and the head of the KGB would normally be Slavs—in effect Russians, since Ukrainians and Belorussians outside their home republics were generally regarded as Russians. The same was true of directors of enterprises "of all-Union significance," military enterprises, and secret "postbox" research institutes.[2]

In spite of the Slavic "minders" the non-Russian union republics were dominated by their own ethnic elites. When seeking the good things of life, membership in the republican titular nationality was a decided advantage. According to Mikhail Gorbachev, who should know, there was a kind of "gentlemen's agreement" between Brezhnev and local party secretaries, under which he left them free to manage their own affairs in return for their continual support and praise. In Azerbaijan, for example, the Aliev family and the Nakhichevan clan dominated political decision-making and the distribution of economic benefits. If a delegation was sent down from Moscow to investigate possible abuses, the republican bosses would receive it with lavish hospitality and a dazzling display of local color, while drawing a veil over corrupt practices that non-Azeri speakers had little chance of penetrating anyway. The "government inspectors" would return to Old Square with a hangover and little to report.[3]

Maintaining superpower status was of paramount importance in the Brezhnev era, and accordingly the military-industrial complex occupied the center of the power network. More than half the members of the CPSU Central Committee had worked at one time or another either in the armed forces or in the military branches of industry. In 1950 military expenditure accounted for nearly a quarter of gross domestic product (GDP). It fell thereafter, but in 1955 it still consumed nearly half of all industrial investment. When Gorbachev became general secretary in 1985 and at last was permitted to see the figures (to which he had not had access even as an ordinary member of the Politburo!), military expenditure constituted some 40 percent of the state budget and about 20 percent of GDP. As Gorbachev noted in his memoirs, "in virtually all branches of the economy military expenditure sapped the vital juices," so that, for example, one and the same factory might be turning out the latest tanks alongside the most primitive tractors.[4]

The military-industrial complex was largely a Russian, or at least a Slavic, monopoly. The language of command was Russian, and the traditions and symbolism of fighting men also derived from Russian history and culture. The great majority—about 75 percent—of military-industrial research and production facilities were situated in the RSFSR, with a further 15 percent in Ukraine. In addition, some 7 percent of the territory of Kazakhstan, mainly in the north (where most of the Russians of Kazakhstan lived), was occupied with testing sites for the nuclear industry, missile systems, and space satellites. The greatest concentration of military production was in and around Moscow and Leningrad, in the Volga basin, Siberia, and the Urals. The greatest number of defense industry employees were found in Sverdlovsk, Leningrad, Moscow, Gorkii, Moscow oblast, Perm, Kuibyshev, and Novosibirsk (all Russian cities with a considerable majority of Russians living in them), as well as in Tatarstan (where in 1989 43.2 percent of the population was Russian) and in Udmurtiia (58.8 percent Russian). Some cities and regions were especially dependent on the defense sector: in Udmurtiia, for example, the defense industry accounted for 85 percent of output and 60 percent of employment.[5]

The RSFSR contained half of all industrial enterprises, both military and nonmilitary, and produced two-thirds of industrial output, that is, heavy industry was especially concentrated there. In the late 1980s, 69 percent of Russian output was of "all-Union significance" (in Ukraine it was 58 percent, in Estonia, 28.5 percent), and 51 percent of the RSFSR population—58 percent in the towns—worked in industry, construction, transport, and communications, a higher figure than for any other republic. But output was not matched by income: per capita, Russia was in tenth place among the republics. Some other republics, notably the Baltic ones, were more advanced technologically and incomes were markedly higher.[6] Russians, then, were not earning a fair share from their productive activity.

Many of the cities associated with the military were closed to a greater or lesser degree. In the late 1970s and early 1980s, there were about four hundred "installations" and associated "special regime" towns, with three levels of secrecy. At the lowest level were anonymous factories, designated merely by zip code, in otherwise open towns; at the second level were enterprises in cities closed to all foreigners; the third level consisted of special settlements isolated even from Soviet citizens and known by codenames: Arzamas-16 (built on the site of the monastery of St. Serafim of Sarov in Kursk oblast), Cheliabinsk-40, Penza-19, Krasnoiarsk-26, and so on.[7]

These production complexes were guarded by Interior Ministry troops and situated on compounds some distance from the town whose name they bore. Those living and working there needed official approval to leave; they had to present letters to the outside world for official censorship; they were unable to invite friends and relatives to visit them; and they were blocked from the Soviet telephone network. On the other hand, they had priority for the supply of food and consumer goods, so that the shops were always well stocked, and they received high pay and generous retirement packages. Above all employees of these special complexes enjoyed high prestige, the feeling that they were working on a crucial mission for which they were respected and rewarded. They believed they were fulfilling an essential and urgent patriotic duty, necessary to guarantee the defense of their homeland and to preserve world peace by putting up a counterbalance to the military might of the imperialist powers. The closed settlements had no difficulty attracting the best graduates from the relevant technological faculties of universities, partly because of the prestige of the job and partly because new well-qualified arrivals were provided with a separate apartment, good child-care facilities, and good schools for a later stage in their children's lives.[8]

However secret they were, the "installations" and the surrounding settlements did attract the attention of the ordinary populations living nearby. In some cases this was because radio-active waste was escaping and causing ill health, especially in the early years, before proper nuclear-safety standards were established. In August 1956 an anonymous letter was sent from Cheliabinsk oblast to Bulganin, then prime minister, complaining that "the health of thousands of people in the Urals and Siberia is suffering." The letter continued: "It is no secret that there exists a certain Cheliabinsk-40. Its extensive territory is surrounded by barbed wire. What goes on there we ordinary mortals do not know, and we don't want to know. But we all feel its bad breath." The writer commented, "It is prov-

ing possible to cut the army, so couldn't we cut these factories as well?"
Bulganin's secretariat appended a commentary to the letter for the prime
minister's information, admitting that one of the factories in Cheliabinsk-
40 regularly discharged (nuclear) waste into the nearby River Techa.[9]

Many Russians accepted these privations as sacrifices necessary to maintain their country's superpower status. A military career enjoyed the highest prestige. The daughter of an officer in the army engineers recalled that
her father entered a military college in 1951 because it was the best way to
escape the poverty and hunger of village life. Later he came to feel that his
was the noblest calling as well as the most secure: "If my father were a religious person, he would pray for the Army, because for him the Army is
like a mother who gave him food, clothing, stability and a middle-class
living standard that was very good for Russia." To put this perception in
perspective, she explains what a "middle-class living standard" meant in
an army that provided almost all living requirements: "Often when they
had to change their residence from one town to another, they took with
them only simple beds, chairs and a couple of suitcases. That was all the
furniture they had. But they also had good prospects: Army officers were
treated with great respect."[10] In the later Soviet decades taking pride in the
armed forces and the country's defense facilities was an important part of
being Russian; but so also was ambivalence and suppressed resentment at
the privation they imposed on ordinary people.

### Continued Urbanization

During the 1950s a historic change had taken place in the Russian population: it was becoming mainly urbanized. According to the 1959 census
52 percent of Russians lived in towns in the RSFSR, and 58 percent in
other republics. By 1979 the proportion was 69 percent in the RSFSR,
and 74 percent elsewhere.[11] Large towns grew faster than small ones, and
fastest of all was Moscow, whose population in the 1970s alone rose by 13
percent, according to official figures. In reality the growth was probably
greater, since many employers desperate for labor would hire so-called
*limitchiki,* employees permitted to live in Moscow (or another large city)
for a limited period; in practice, many of them stayed on illegally afterward. It was becoming almost impossible to obtain a propiska in Moscow,
so that immigrants tended to settle in the large towns just beyond the city
Ring Road, such as Liubertsy, Mytishchi, and Odintsovo. As a result the

towns of Moscow oblast expanded even more markedly than the capital city, by 21 percent, and those within fifty kilometers of the capital by 27 percent.[12]

The propiska system actually encouraged people to stay who might otherwise have left: a Moscow propiska, once lost, could be regained only with the greatest difficulty. A one-room Moscow apartment was worth a two-room apartment in Gorkii, Kharkov, or Sverdlovsk, a three-room apartment in a medium-sized provincial town, and a mansion in the countryside. The only other Russian towns to experience growth comparable to Moscow's were sites of major new industrial developments, such as Toliatti on the Volga, where cars were produced, or Naberezhnye Chelny on the Kama River in the Urals, where the Kamaz truck was manufactured.[13]

The reason for this growth was clear: large cities, and Moscow in particular, offered a wide choice of jobs, educational opportunities, consumer goods, entertainments, and human contacts in general. Young people were attracted by the absence of parental supervision, which was still felt in small towns and villages. So much was true of capital cities all over the world in the late twentieth century. What was distinctive about Moscow was that the Soviet "hierarchy of consumption" was especially marked and especially rigid. A disproportionate growth of conurbations and over-crowded housing are normal effects of modernization, but Soviet social policies and the nomenklatura appointments system exaggerated their effect by increasing both the relative rewards of living in large towns and the costs of staying in a small-town or rural environment.[14]

Yet in many ways the large cities were unattractive places to live. In spite of the huge domestic construction program, many people still had to crowd into communal apartments. They also had to suffer the consequences of heavy industrial pollution. When the Soviet media at last began to admit to the problem, a report on Sterlitamak noted: "Immense chimneys belching out clouds of smoke into the sky and a blue-grey pall of poisonous smog creeping over the horizon—thus awakens the second largest city of Bashkiria, where 270,000 people live." This situation was not untypical. In the far north nine-tenths of the inhabitants of Nikel, which as its name suggests contained nickel smelters, were reported to be suffering from respiratory ailments. In Nizhnevartovsk, in western Siberia, with its oil and gas refineries, particulates were concentrated in the air at six times the permitted maximum level; in Bratsk, thanks to its alumi-

num smelter, the air contained seventeen times the permitted concentration of benzopyrene. Even in the capital, in Izmailovskii Park, where Muscovites love to stroll on summer evenings, there were notices warning
"No Admission," indicating danger of chemical and radioactive emissions
from a landfill site of the 1950s.[15]

The rural environment was suffering too. Hydroelectric projects and irrigation schemes had so reduced the flow of the Volga that, in the words
of one commentator, "[it] has virtually ceased to be a river: it has become
a chain of reservoirs." In the Volga and many other rivers the diminished
water flow was heavily polluted by untreated sewage, factory discharges,
and fertilizer and pesticides washed off fields. The supply of fish had fallen
so drastically that people feared for the sturgeon, source of Russians' beloved caviar.[16]

Overcrowded, polluted cities were not good places for children. Beginning in the 1960s the birth rate of the most urbanized peoples fell drastically, especially the Baltic nationalities and the Russians. The new non-
communal apartments were at least private, but they were cramped. In
any case the tall housing blocks offered a poor environment in which to
bring up children, who had little space of their own and nowhere to meet
neighbors' children and play in the open air while under parental supervision. (In the less tall apartment blocks built until the mid-1960s—five
stories or less—they could still play in courtyards while their mothers
chatted or their fathers played dominoes not far away.)

As early as 1972 the demographer Viktor Perevedentsev warned that
the Russian population was not reproducing itself.[17] To keep the population stable, he calculated, each couple would have to have an average of
2.65 children; the actual average for the USSR as a whole was 2.4, and in
Moscow it was as low as 1.6. Forty-three percent of Muscovite women
stated in answer to a questionnaire that they wanted no more than one
child. There were a number of reasons for this situation, associated with
modern Soviet urban life. Modern health care ensured that the great majority of children survived into adulthood, so that one child now provided
security into old age; nor were children needed to sustain the family economy, as had been the case in small towns and villages fifty years earlier. Besides, far more people had higher education, were building professional
careers, and therefore married later. Women were taking paid employment for a number of reasons: to supplement the family income, to use
their professional training, or to have an independent role and status in

society.[18] As a result they had less time to look after children. Typically both parents worked but also had to spend time standing in line for scarce food supplies or deficient services, so that they had little spare time or energy. As one mother reported, "In the shops after work there are lines. It's true that in the supermarket you can find any groceries you want in a quarter of an hour, but it takes half an hour to get there, and as long as that again standing in line at the check-out. . . . The kindergarten works only while 'mother is at work.' God forbid you arrive quarter of an hour late to pick up Vovochka. But yesterday I had to wait twenty minutes for a bus."[19]

Relatively few men were prepared to take on their share of these burdens, so that women were in effect bearing a "double burden," holding down a full-time job while also taking care of home and family. The divorce rate was rising rapidly: by the early 1970s in Russia every tenth marriage fell apart within a year, and a further tenth ended in the first five years. Fatigue and lack of leisure time figured high among the causal factors, along with heavy drinking by men. Besides, marriage was increasingly seen as a personal choice, and therefore revocable, rather than as part of the stable relationship of extended families.[20]

Meanwhile in the Caucasus and Central Asia, by contrast, fewer women were employed and more people stayed in traditional village or small-town housing. There were fewer modern conveniences there but more space and usually a courtyard just outside the dwelling place, and relatives nearby, so that families were willing to have more children and the birth rate remained much higher than in Russia.[21] As a result, in the later Soviet decades the population of the Caucasus and Central Asia was gradually growing relative to that of the European republics, especially among the young, which meant that they formed a larger percentage of recruits to the armed services.

The landscape of the new industrial towns, or the new suburbs of older towns, looked similar, wherever they were constructed. Massive apartment blocks went up, first in yellow-pink brick, then from the 1970s in prefabricated concrete panels and blocks, which could be assembled quickly, using mass-produced industrial methods. Visiting the Siberian city of Bratsk, the American journalist Hedrick Smith commented: "To me what was most depressing was the naked, Orwellian monotony of row upon row of identical grey prefab apartment blocks."[22] They were gathered in *mikroraiony,* huge housing estates, which looked impressive as cardboard mock-ups for bureaucrats and political patrons, but were often shoddily constructed and situated a long way from employment opportunities. They tended to become dormitory beehives from which stoic tenants would commute long distances to work on overcrowded public transportation.[23]

These huge housing blocks were no longer always grouped around courtyards, and, when they were, those courtyards were now so large and open that they were often penetrated by high winds, and had none of the coziness needed for informal human contact. It was not a favorable environment for the traditional Russian custom of casual socializing. Heating was provided for a whole estate, and often for a factory or two as well, by area power stations belching out smoke. Their delivery pipes, often lagged with asbestos, ran alongside roads and railways, arching over obstacles.

Public spaces, by contrast with housing estates, formed part of the symbolic geography and were more attractively laid out. Transport thoroughfares would be lined with trees and sometimes planted with flowers as well. They were broad and spacious, not to accommodate large numbers of cars—few people owned a car in the 1960s, though their numbers grew quickly thereafter—but rather to serve as the setting for public parades on special occasions. Boulevards, wherever possible, would converge on a main square that contained a statue of Lenin, a war memorial, and perhaps a stand for announcing local achievements, as well as grand buildings with classical columns housing the municipal soviet, the party committee, or the local university. These urban spaces told a story of a great (recent) past and prefigured the progress toward an even greater future. The war memorials, on the other hand, did not usually list individual names. Russian grief was represented in large, impersonal, monolithic slabs, not as the aggregate of individuals' grief.

Behind public buildings, or just around the corner, a totally different scene usually presented itself: construction firms seldom landscaped a site after completing their building work, so that for years afterward the immediate neighborhood of apartment blocks was disfigured by unsightly rubble, abandoned breeze blocks, sawed-off metal pipes, and concrete slabs with rusty metal rods poking out of them. Public splendor and public squalor coexisted side by side.

By the 1960s in most Russian towns it was becoming difficult or impossible to discern any traces of the past. The novelist Alan Sillitoe, who visited the USSR in 1964, commented, "All over Moscow they are ripping out the past like rotten teeth."[24] Older buildings had been torn down, while churches had been destroyed or at best had the crosses removed from their domes; they were then converted into cinemas, warehouses, or palaces of culture. Monolithic high-rise blocks, dual carriageways, and sprawling factory complexes had obliterated most relics of previous settlement, of ancient fields and pathways. As they went about their daily business, most Russians saw little to remind them of their history or of their national culture.

## Youth Culture

Many of the social features that generated a specific youth culture in the West—relative affluence, a long period of "latency" between childhood and adult life—were missing in the Soviet Union right up to the 1960s. Or rather they were present only among the privileged nomenklatura strata, high state and party officials, and top professional people in the large cities. Already by the early 1950s these privileged few lived in an ambiance which was relatively secure and opulent, and where young people could take years over study and choosing a career. It was in this milieu that the first signs of a youth culture emerged. Soviet diplomats, and then party officials, adopted Western-style clothing and life-styles, complete with cocktail cabinets, gin-and-tonics (rather than vodka), and the foxtrot. Their offspring became fascinated with these borrowed artifacts for their own sake, and took their practices to extremes, violating official taboos and relying on "Papa" for protection in difficulties. These were the *stiliagi*. They took up jazz, still disapproved in the 1950s as a "bourgeois fashion," and then rock-and-roll. Through their connections they obtained Western designer clothes, perfumes, and later, short-wave radios, cassette recorders, and other items of conspicuous consumption before they reached the general population.[25]

The 6th World Festival of Youth and Students was held in Moscow in 1957, and it spread images of modern Western youth culture much more widely. At the same time, in more acceptable Soviet style, Komsomol volunteer groups were taking part in construction work and bringing new soil under the plow in the virgin lands of Kazakhstan. Others were going on geological expeditions or standing guard over nature conservation sites to prevent poaching or unauthorized logging. Such groups would improvise their own forms of entertainment in the evenings, with little more than a guitar or tape recorder around a camp fire or in a temporary barracks.[26]

By the 1970s the meaning of youth had changed in Soviet society. Hitherto young people had always been at the frontline or in the vanguard of socialist construction, urgently needed for the tasks of war or peace. Now they were more affluent and better educated, but partly as a result their itch for better things was stronger too, and they knew far more about life in the "West" (which the USSR was still trying to "catch up and overtake"). Moreover, college graduates were no longer automatically finding high-status jobs on completing their studies; often their way was blocked by far less qualified incumbents from a previous generation, hanging on to the perks of office. Condemned to boring work that they considered beneath their dignity, such young people gravitated to alternative modes of self-assertion. They would meet in *tusovki,* informal gatherings, well away from the eye of the Komsomol, in the open air in summer, in basements at other times of year, to dance to their own kind of music, drink, take drugs, perhaps engage in casual sex. *Rokery, bitniki, panki, metallisty,* and other epigones of Western musical fashion made their appearance. Soccer teams would attract fan clubs that traveled around with their heroes, wearing their colors and taunting and sometimes attacking the fans of rival teams. Some experimented with drugs or, going in a completely different direction, would cultivate eastern modes of spirituality through meditation or yoga. Hippies preached a doctrine of reconciliation and universal love that, while not threatening to anyone, was utterly at odds with the official ideology of class struggle.[27]

By the 1980s, then, youth culture had definitely established itself as a discrete social category, and it took a great variety of forms, some of them more or less acceptable to the Komsomol and assimilable into it, others completely contrary both to Russian tradition and to the proclaimed ideals of Soviet society. In the face of a communal ethos much more tightly defined than was usual in the West, the attraction of transgression was all the more alluring.

## The Russian Countryside

From the mid-1960s, the collective farms were given higher priority and more generous and stable investment than in earlier decades. By then, however, it turned out that their productive capacities had been so eroded that they were not capable of making good use of the new resources. Besides, in some ways the investment deepened and accelerated the "depeasantization" of village life. The party was determined to "liquidate the difference between town and countryside." This meant enlarging kolkhozy and wherever possible turning them into sovkhozy, state farms, whose land was owned by the state and whose workforce was paid a wage and received social security benefits, like industrial workers. It also meant abandoning small rural settlements—now officially known as "villages without a future" (neperspektivnye derevni)—as unviable and concentrating rural-dwellers in larger centers, where multistory apartment blocks were built to receive them.

In many ways this policy was humane: it eliminated extreme rural poverty and enabled the provision of more satisfactory educational, medical, and social facilities, not to speak of lighting, heating, and running water. But it also obliterated many of the distinctive features of village life, which most Russians—even, perhaps especially, those who had fled it—still considered an indispensable part of their heritage. It was difficult for people living on the fifth floor to look after a cow or to give attention to a garden plot that might be some distance away. Besides, abandoning the familiar village or hamlet entailed weakening kinship or neighborly ties, and perhaps disrupting ancestral bonds by leaving family graves without regular care.[28]

The concentration of farms and villages did not, moreover, prove very productive. Building apartment blocks, laying water pipes, providing sanitation, and constructing tarmac roads was relatively expensive for the rural sector, and the improved yield of grain, fruit, or vegetables did not always justify the expenditure. Prices paid by the state for specialized or industrial crops, like cotton in Central Asia, or citrus fruits, tea, and grapes in the Caucasus, were quite high. But for the grain, vegetables, apples, and pears of Russia, Ukraine, and Belorussia, procurement prices fluctuated but generally remained low, sometimes lower than the costs of production.[29]

It was not only low pay that drove away the young and energetic, but also the general conditions of the village. Communications were very unreliable: they depended on rutted cart tracks, which could become impassable with mud during the spring thaw or the autumn rains. Village shops often lacked even basic consumer supplies: whereas in the 1920s most households had still been capable of making their own clothes, footwear, and furniture, by the 1960s that was no longer the case. People had to find some way of going into town to obtain these essentials.

Plenty of tractor drivers and mechanics were being trained in agro-technical colleges. But the great majority of them were using their special skills to get a job in town. The account of one such worker helps to explain why: "They assigned me to the sovkhoz 'Zaraiskii,' where my parents live. They had asked the college for tractor drivers. When I and my comrades arrived, instead of tractors they handed us pitchforks and shovels to fill sacks with hay and straw. We requested work in accordance with our specialty, but the answer was always: 'We've no tractors.' Why had we gone to college? You can load sacks without any training."[30]

In 1981 a farmer wrote from Tula oblast to the newspaper *Selskaia zhizn:* "In the cowsheds, where milk is poured off, there is mud up to one's knees. There are no overalls. Sometimes there is no lighting to work by. Cows get milked only every other day, and sometimes there is no one at all to do the milking. Labor accounting is badly handled, and the pay is low. As a result people leave the kolkhoz. That's the kind of bad management we have, a mere 100 kilometers from Moscow." Lack of facilities was legendary. As a popular *chastushka* had it, "Ia i baba i muzhik. / Ia i loshad', ia i byk. / Ia i seiu, ia i zhnu, / Na sebe drova vozhu. ("I am both woman and man. / I am both horse and ox. / I both sow and reap, / and I carry firewood on my back."[31]

Social facilities in the village were minimal. Large villages would have a club, which might be the former parish church. In one village in Vologda oblast it was reported that "the church was a fine brick building with a lot of icons. After they arrested Father Sergii it was turned into a club. Some of the icons were destroyed, others were stolen, and only bare walls remained."[32] Eventually it was painted and decorated as a venue for showing films, holding dances, playing chess and checkers, or reading newspapers. Most smaller villages, though, were without social facilities. Such conditions, accepted for centuries, now seemed intolerable to mid- and late-twentieth-century villagers.

Most important of all perhaps for people of child-bearing age, many village schools, housed in dilapidated wooden buildings, heated by wood or coal stoves and without running water or a sewage system, were not in a position to provide an adequate education. Teachers were reluctant to work in such conditions; many of those who did were poorly qualified, and important subjects might remain untaught for months. To bring up a

child in the village was to condemn him or her to a lifetime of under-
achievement and demeaning jobs. There was no easy solution to the problem of rural education. Many villages were not in a position to support a
general-education school. Larger villages that could were distant from the
more remote settlements, and there were seldom buses to transport children back and forth.[33]

Emigration from Russian villages was especially marked during the late
1950s and 1960s, when exciting and much-publicized economic projects
beckoned workers to the cities and other parts of the Soviet Union. Kolkhoz chairmen were under heavy pressure from the party to hand over
passports to villagers volunteering for them. Between 1959 and 1973 the
number of rural inhabitants in their twenties fell by two-thirds. Between
1959 and 1964 alone, the able-bodied rural population of the kolkhozy of
Pskov oblast fell from 200,000 to 110,000. I. S. Gustov, the local party
secretary, warned at a Central Committee plenum in 1965: "If the decline
in the able-bodied workforce continues at the present rate, then in ten
years' time there will be no one capable of working in the kolkhozy."[34]

Actually the emigration rate eased off in the 1970s and 1980s, as there
were fewer young people left to emigrate, and urban employers became
less willing to take on unskilled workers. All the same the loss of rural
population in the non–black earth oblasti between 1959 and 1989 was
everywhere between 40 and 60 percent. By 1974 people aged sixty and
over constituted 45 percent of the agricultural workforce in Novgorod
oblast, and 40 percent in Pskov. They could not cope with the heavy work
during harvesting and potato picking time, and so students were brought
in from local colleges to help out.[35]

As a result of the exodus of young people, marriages in the village became rare, and consequently so did the birth of children. In the largely rural oblast of Vologda, for example, births, which were 42,155 in 1940 and
23,651 in 1959, had fallen to 9,647 by 1967.[36] Since villagers traditionally had far more children than townsfolk, this decline, as we have seen,
affected the entire Russian population.

The demoralization of village life was such that many of the men took
to regular heavy drinking. Because of state fiscal policy, vodka was one
consumer item normally available in village shops; and if it was not, peasants would concoct home-made *samogon* (moonshine) instead. As one
woman complained in Orel oblast in 1969, "They get drunk at public
meetings, in the dairy farm, and even in the 'red corner' [the center for

propaganda in the village, usually in the club]. Instead of propaganda pamphlets what do we see on the table? Half a liter. The carters sit and drink with the dairymen, swearing at each other. The chairman and the livestock man take no notice, as if all this were normal."[37]

It was. The sale of alcohol had risen six times between 1940 and 1965, and doubled again by 1975, the figures for the RSFSR being throughout slightly higher than the Soviet average. Family budget studies showed that in 1967–1968 in the towns 8 to 9 percent of families were spending 40 percent or more of their budget on alcohol, while for the collective farms the proportion was 10 to 11 percent. These figures represent only sales in state shops, and do not include substantial expenditure on *samogon*. According to a confidential study in the 1970s, nearly 11 to 12 percent of the adult population were "heavy drinkers" or alcoholics; a similar number passed through the "drying-out stations" at least once a year. Comparison with other countries is difficult, but these figures certainly place the USSR in general and Russia in particular among the world's greatest consumers of alcohol.[38] Among males of working age the most common cause of death was alcohol poisoning or accidents and traumas resulting from drunkenness. Such deaths were more frequent in villages than in towns, where they were common enough. Chronic alcoholism was also higher in the countryside: in 1991, the figure for Russia, Ukraine, Moldavia, and Latvia was 152 cases per 100,000 people as against an average of 123 for the population of those republics as a whole.[39]

For those not condemned to live in the village permanently, there was still something touching and reassuring about rural existence. Liudmila Selezneva, for example, a university teacher born in 1956, recalled being sent each summer to stay with her grandmother as a child in the 1960s: "Life in the villages was much as it had been forty, fifty or even seventy years before. There were no conveniences. People lived in small houses with two or three rooms. . . . When we visited my grandmother, we used to help her by carrying water in two buckets from a pond to the kitchen. This was the only source of water. There was no gas, no petrol. People used ancient stoves built of stone. To cook and to heat the house they had to have wood, so one of their main tasks was gathering enough wood to last for the whole winter." One of the children's jobs was to help grandmother look after the kitchen garden on which the household's food supply depended, apart from the bread they bought from the collective farm. "This was a good way to bring up children," Selezneva noted, "by having us participate in a job, and we liked it very much. But from an economic point of view it was hopelessly inefficient. This was typical. So my grand-mother produced for her family—she and her husband and his sister all lived together—potatoes, onions, beets, cabbage, carrots, corn, cherries, apples and plums."[40] Some Russians attribute the human warmth of their culture and their remarkable capacity for survival in adversity to the vil-lage upbringing that, till very recently, most of them experienced.

It was a dying way of life, though. When Viktor Beliaev visited his home village of Shileksha in 1984, the spectacle he encountered was ut-terly demoralizing:

> There were eight homes standing—still quite robust, and not boarded up, as people usually do when they go on a long journey, but simply abandoned. The doors were not locked, one or two were even wide open, and on the porch of the one nearest the river stood a samovar. I looked inside—one could have lived there. The huge Russian stove was still undamaged, and so were the windows, the door, the floor. Outside was a large yard. The village streets were covered with grass, and the former garden plots were wildly overgrown with nettles and burdock. The field where twenty-eight kolkhozniki had sown oats after plowing up the virgin soil was now overgrown with trees and bushes. The other fields were abandoned. The magnificent meadows on which four villages used to mow hay the year round was water-logged and covered with sedge.[41]

## Migration

Even though the whirlwind social change of the 1930s and the upheavals of war were over, the continual growth of industry, the ambitious pro-grams of technological development, and the improvements in transpor-tation and communications from the late 1940s right through to the 1970s brought Russians and Ukrainians (Belorussians less so) into motion in unprecedented numbers. Inside Russia itself, as we have seen, people were leaving the small towns, villages, and central regions for the large towns and also for peripheral regions that offered either employment op-portunities or a better climate. Certain regions of Russia, though, experi-enced serious population loss: the Volga-Viatka basin, western Siberia, the northwest, and the black-earth agricultural region. By 1989 more than half of all Russians had made at least one major move—out of their home town or oblast into another part of the country—at some time in their lives.

The same was true of the Baltic peoples, but the equivalent figure was one-third for Georgians, one-quarter for Kirgiz, and one-seventh for Uzbeks.[42]

The republics that underwent the greatest Russian influx from the 1940s to the 1960s were Ukraine, especially the east and south, whose towns became largely Russian in language and culture; Kazakhstan, especially the north; Uzbekistan; Estonia; and Latvia. A lot of elite Russians also lived in the Crimea, which in 1954 was transferred to Ukraine. Until the 1960s Russians formed the backbone of the skilled working class and the technical staff almost everywhere in the USSR. This was especially true in the Central Asian republics, Azerbaijan, and Moldavia, where most of the indigenous population was occupied in agriculture, handicrafts, and the retail trade. Russians dominated heavy industry in these republics right through to the 1980s. They could also be found at the lowest end of the social scale, as semi-skilled and unskilled laborers in mining and industrial operations, especially in Ukraine and in the Baltic republics. An abiding peculiarity of Russian labor patterns is that women were employed in roughly the same posts as men, including heavy manual labor, which non-Russian women, especially Muslims, spurned as inappropriate or even shaming for women.[43]

Up to the 1960s Russians were also prominent in managerial and professional posts, especially in enterprises concerned with production of "all-Union significance," where it paid to have good contacts in Gosplan and the Moscow ministries. These were what one might call "all-Union Russians," who treated their location as a fortuitous part of their homeland, where they happened to be working. Few of them learned the local language beyond what was needed to buy bread, cheese, and melons at the market, and they had only vague conceptions of the history and culture of the indigenous population. One Russian in Baku, when asked whether he spoke Azeri, replied: "Only to swear."[44]

The outmigration of Slavs from their own republics resulted in many mixed marriages during these decades. In fact nearly all mixed marriages (97 percent) involved at least one Slav partner. The proportion of such marriages reached its high point in the 1960s and declined thereafter (though unevenly), especially in Central Asia and Kazakhstan. In the RSFSR the children of ethnically mixed couples, when applying for their first passport, tended to choose Russian as their nationality. If they lived in one of the non-Russian union republics, then they would usually choose the titular nationality, except in Ukraine and Belorussia, where Russian was often preferred.[45]

A striking feature of these marriages is that more of them joined a Slav woman with a non-Slav man than the other way around. This is probably because Russians, especially those living outside Russia, felt fewer religious or customary inhibitions to such marriages than did other nationalities, inhibitions that would particularly restrain women. In this respect Russians represented "secularity" and "modernity" throughout the USSR. Among Russians the social control exercised by families had become weaker than among many non-Russians, especially the peoples of the Caucasus and Central Asia, more of whom tended to stay at home in village or small town. Since such control was stronger over the marriage choices of young women than of young men, women from those regions generally acted according to the expectations of their kith and kin, and therefore chose husbands from among their own people.[46]

A turning point came in the 1970s, when inter-republican migration flows began to go into reverse. For the first time the RSFSR experienced a net growth in population, while Kazakhstan, Kirgiziia, Turkmeniia, and Moldavia suffered a net loss. Some of those leaving were non-Slavs with high skill levels seeking opportunities in Russia's fast-growing cities. Others, however, were Russians, who were discouraged to find that their language, culture, and education no longer guaranteed them a head-start in the competition for good jobs, superior housing, and other privileges reserved for the elite. Local nationals tended, for example, to be preferred for entry to higher education and in the competition for high-status jobs, especially in Central Asia and Kazakhstan.[47] Before the late 1980s this deterioration in Russians' life-chances did not lead to large-scale emigration from the non-Russian republics. Even where the number of Russians outside Russia continued to rise, though, their proportion in the population was declining, because their birth rate was lower than that of locals. During the 1970s, then, overall the prospect of a "single Soviet people" faltered and then began gradually to recede. The tendency grew for people to regroup in their national homelands, especially in Central Asia and the Transcaucasus.[48] (See Table A.1, p. 412.)

## Languages

The tendency toward ethnic distinctiveness, beginning to be clearly marked in the 1960s, did not mean that non-Russians were ceasing to learn Russian. Modernization of the Soviet Union generated two distinct and at first sight contradictory linguistic tendencies. On the one hand the use of the Russian language increased; on the other, so did that of the main Union republics, with the exception of Ukraine and Belorussia.[49] Actually, of course, this is not difficult to explain: many non-Russians were learning Russian for instrumental reasons, to make themselves available on the job market throughout the USSR. Similarly, in the non-Russian union republics, locals speaking dialects or minority languages were learning the republican language as an aid to social mobility. For that reason, modernization strengthened both the all-Union language and the major republican national languages. Ukrainian and Belorussian formed the exceptions because they were so close linguistically to Russian. Upwardly mobile Ukrainians and Belorussians found it easy to adapt to the all-Union language and preferred to do so.

The increased use of Russian was caused by a number of factors, first of all the migration of Russians to non-Russian republics, where, as we have seen, they did not usually learn the local language. Second, non-Russians were increasing their life-chances through military promotion or higher education, which in the natural and technical sciences was conducted in Russian almost everywhere. Third, the flow of paperwork generated by the center tended to increase, and all of it was in Russian.[50]

The drift toward Russian was accelerated by the language reform of 1958, whose objective was to make Russian the "second native language" of all non-Russians, though this was done not in order to Russify but in order to Sovietize.[51] Offered the choice of Russian-language or non-Russian instruction, a high proportion of parents in most republics chose the Russian option, so that their children might have better life chances throughout the USSR. That was true even in the Baltic republics and Georgia, where many people were opposed to Russians on principle; parents with anti-Russian convictions could still calculate that their children would benefit from a good knowledge of the Russian language. On the other hand, the tendency was weaker in the Central Asian republics, where social mobility was less prized.

Parents chose Russian-language schools especially frequently in Ukraine and Belorussia, where educated people in any case spoke Russian without difficulty, and often did so even at home.[52] Thus in 1955 in Ukraine 73 percent of children enrolled in Ukrainian-language schools, but in 1967 the figure had fallen to 62 percent, while in primary schools it was estimated that the proportion of children receiving their lessons in Russian doubled between 1953 and 1973. In Belorussia in 1959 slightly more than half the urban population spoke Belorussian as their native language, but thereafter the proportion began to decline. In 1959 60 percent of newspapers in the republic were in Belorussian, but by 1970 that proportion had fallen to 36 percent.[53] Urbanization, which had begun by boosting Belorussian, was now downgrading it in favor of Russian. Many Ukrainians and Belorussians were naturally alarmed by this tendency, fearing that their national identity was gradually being erased. As for the Union as a whole, by 1974–1975 64 percent of day-school pupils were being taught in Russian-language schools, while the proportion of the population claiming some fluency in Russian rose from 49 percent in 1970 to 62 percent in 1979.[54]

Non-Russians were ready to accept Russian as a means of personal advancement but not as an instrument of rule. In 1978 proposals to make Russian an official language of Georgia, of equal status with Georgian, provoked a massive student demonstration in Tbilisi. What Georgians feared was that Russian, though theoretically equal, would soon in practice replace Georgian in most spheres of life. Such was Moscow's fear of upsetting Georgians that the proposal was withdrawn.[55] Similarly, in autumn 1980 Estonian secondary-school students took to the streets of Tallinn to call for an end to what they called "Russian rule." Their protest provoked open letters from high-ranking Estonian intellectuals objecting to the increasing number of Russian workers coming in for large industrial projects, and showing how Russian was increasingly being used for official business and was gradually squeezing out Estonian in the schools and in book publication.[56]

A spontaneous differentiation of linguistic functions was taking place, with Russian being used for industry, science, technology, military service, wholesale trade, and administration involving the center, while the local language—republican or regional—was used for agriculture, the service sector, retail trade, the humanities, and local administration. Russians were seldom employed in the latter spheres outside their own republic, and so they refrained from learning the local language. Most of the Russians who *did* take the trouble to learn a second language were women, many of them probably women who had married into a non-Russian family. In any case women were more likely than men to be involved with the spheres of life in which the local language was regularly employed.[57]

Ukraine was in an especially problematic situation. It was the second most populous republic, home to the Soviet Union's most productive agriculture and much of its major industry. Yet its language and national culture were fading in the face of the Russian linguistic onslaught. In the towns of the east and south, Russian was the most commonly spoken language, though with an admixture of Ukrainian vocabulary, pronunciation, and syntax. In the 1980s three-quarters of the population of Odessa spoke Russian as a native language; less than one-quarter spoke Ukrainian, even then with Russian words mixed in. Most Odessites considered Ukrainian a low-status dialect for country bumpkins. In the Donbass most people knew Ukrainian from school—though less so after 1958—but spoke Russian among themselves at home. In the Dovzhenko film studio in Kiev a strange situation arose. Most of the actors did not know Ukrainian, so their soundtracks were dubbed in Ukrainian for showing to audiences in the home republic. Then, however, for wider circulation in the USSR, they had to be redubbed in Russian, the first language of most of the actors![58]

Incongruities of this kind led some Ukrainian intellectuals to claim that their country was being deliberately Russified by the Soviet authorities. In 1979 the Ukrainian Helsinki Group circulated a samizdat letter by Iurii Badzio complaining that scientific works and foreign classics were being published in Russian rather than Ukrainian, that the Kiev Operetta Theater staged its shows in Russian, and that television and radio broadcasts in Kiev were largely Russian. Even in the Ukrainian-language schools, "teachers . . . converse with each other and with the pupils in Russian, thereby instilling children with a contemptuous attitude towards the Ukrainian language and culture." Ukraine, Badzio concluded, was being transformed into a border region of the Russian state. The literary critic Ivan Dziuba lamented that Ukrainian cities had become "gigantic Russifying mincing-machines" and noted ironically that "there can be a kind of Ukrainophobia that springs from a great love of the Ukraine as the 'pearl' of Russia."[59]

## Rituals

The antireligious campaign of the early 1960s had outlawed many venerable customs and thus posed with renewed urgency the question of giving Soviet citizens a viable set of rituals through which they could make sense of their lives. Since the mid-1920s the holiest shrine in Soviet ritual life had been Lenin's mausoleum, and Red Square in front of it the principal sacred space. When the leaders stood on the mausoleum and saluted the march-past on May 1 and November 7 each year, they received, as it were, a fresh injection of his charisma and passed it on to the soldiers, workers, and young people who were parading below, exhibiting the productivity, energy, and military might of their country. Soldiers would visit the mausoleum at the start of their military service. Young newlyweds would go there to dedicate their marriage and their future family. They would usually then proceed around the corner to the Kremlin wall, to stand before the Monument to the Unknown Soldier and recall those who had died to defend the Soviet Union.[60]

Alarmed at the declining birth rate, the authorities tried from the late 1950s to restore some of the solemn symbolic elements of marriage in order to deepen the meaning of family life, both for the couple and for society as a whole. Municipalities built or adapted special Wedding Palaces, to which young couples would come with their friends and relatives to hear a short homily on wedded love before exchanging rings and signing the civil register. Music would be played, possibly by a band, more likely on a phonograph. In the best-appointed palaces there was an eternal flame, from which the bridegroom would light a torch. The master of ceremonies would exhort the couple: "Take this torch with the holy fire. Let it be your family keepsake. And through all your life carry the flame of love and devotion to our Motherland, the fire of the hearts of the heroes who have defended its freedom and independence."[61] Thus the ceremony attempted to forge a link between the Motherland, the memory of the war dead, the building of socialism, conjugal love, and the creation of a new family.

Ceremonies were also introduced for other life-cycle events, such as a child's first entry into civic life, when he or she joined the Young Pioneers. The entrant would receive a new red scarf and, before donning it, would solemnly pronounce an oath: "I, a young Pioneer of the Soviet Union, in front of my comrades solemnly promise to warmly love my Soviet Motherland, to live, learn and struggle as bequeathed to us by the great Lenin, and as the Communist Party teaches." Once a year all Pioneers would parade before a local war memorial, salute their banner, and present wreaths, while a reader proclaimed the words of the anthem "Eternal Glory to the Heroes." Similarly, on the first day of their schooling, children would arrive in new clothes, line up, and march into the assembly hall to place flowers before a bust of Lenin, after which the star pupils of the previous year would present them with their first textbooks.[62]

Russians' attitude to the very beginning of life was, however, more traditional. Even during the harshest periods of persecution of the church, many parents—or grandparents—would try to have their children baptized. This was true even of some nonbelievers: they were continuing popular tradition as a kind of insurance policy for their children, to give them the best chance of health and success in life.[63]

The regime did not ignore the past. It endeavored to adapt rituals from Christian or even pagan festivals already widely popular before the revolution. But such celebrations were no longer organized by the *skhod;* they no longer represented the initiative of village people and were disconnected from any religious festival. One example was the start of the harvest, originally St. Ilia's Day in July. One of the older kolkhoz women would begin the scything, bind the first sheaf, decorate it with flowers and ribbons, and bear it to the Dom Kultury, accompanied by songs from the local folklore group. The harvest festival on the second Sunday of October was replaced by the All-Union Day of Agricultural Workers, when banners and prizes would be awarded to brigades held to have performed well. Similarly *maslenitsa,* Shrove Tuesday, was shorn of its religious associations and replaced by the ceremony of Farewell to Winter, which included the season's last ice-skating competitions, as well as horse-riding, singing, and dancing. These rituals tended to fade with the depopulation of the countryside. When revived in the towns, they were unmistakably synthetic and belonged to the same category of entertainment as going to the theater. People enjoyed them without necessarily attributing deep meaning to them.[64]

Death faced the Communist regime with its most formidable challenge, partly because Soviet policies caused so many premature deaths, and partly because it is difficult to be positive about death when one no longer believes in a life after it. The official Soviet handbook to civil ceremonial, published in 1977, omitted funerals entirely. For a consistent materialist the only sensible course was to dispose of the corpse as swiftly and hygienically as possible. The regime did experiment with cremation from the outset, but it was slow to catch on. In this symbolic realm the population remained faithful longer than in any other to Orthodox prescriptions, which forbade cremation (since it made impossible the resurrection of the body). From the 1950s, however, it gradually became habitual in the large towns, where the closure of churches often meant the destruction and "redevelopment" of cemeteries.[65]

In practice, though, for this most solemn of rituals, the people rejected materialism and stuck to familiar practices as far as they could, whatever the authorities might think. Religious ritual, even without priests, was more tenacious in funerals than in any other ceremonial practice. In the village of Viriatino, in Tambov oblast, one study showed that in the five years between 1952 and 1956, all but three funerals had been religious: villagers themselves had recited what they could recall of the sacred texts over the body of the dead. It was still customary there on Shrovetide for older women to place the first batch of cooked pancakes beneath an icon, in order to remind families of their departed relatives.[66]

Even official funerals, though without religious rites, preserved as much of the traditional ceremonial as was compatible with atheism. The body would be washed, placed in the coffin with the lid open, then displayed with a photograph and medals, usually in a funeral pavilion or House of Civic Funerals. An official would pronounce a dedication containing such words as "Citizen of the RSFSR . . . has concluded his life's journey. The Motherland takes leave of her son/daughter. May a good memory of him/her be preserved eternally in our hearts." Relatives would then accompany the deceased to the cemetery, where a solemn burial would take place, with mourners casting earth on the coffin. Then they would adjourn for a shared meal, with speeches and recollections of the recently departed. Often memorial meetings *(pominki)* would be held on the ninth, twentieth, and/or fortieth day after the death.[67]

The funerals of well-known people had powerful public resonance, especially if the deceased had had an uneasy relationship with the regime. When Boris Pasternak was buried in May 1960, his coffin was carried from his dacha to the Peredelkino cemetery by a relay of prominent writers, published and unpublished. The philosopher Valentin Asmus made a speech over the grave, openly blaming official persecution for hastening Pasternak's death.[68] Such funerals seemed to endow people both with civic courage and with a certain impunity, perhaps because they suggested a dimension of existence that even the most powerful state could not control. They bore witness to a spiritual life in which it seemed cheap and unworthy to mouth platitudes or untruths.

In the late 1970s the British sociologist Christel Lane concluded that the most successful Soviet rituals were those which marked a moment of passage in life, especially those involving young people and those commemorating the Second World War. The ceremonies that replaced former religious or seasonal festivals were less successful, probably because they were synthetic, imposed from above, and bore a clearly marked, relatively narrow official meaning rather than a spontaneously generated symbolic one. All the same, people participated in them, probably because the old rituals had faded away, and because they offered the opportunity for variety, social contact, and a solemn, festive mood that made their community life somewhat more meaningful. Their participation generated "a diffuse kind of identification with the political system."[69]

The one festival that was unambiguously popular as well as officially approved was the celebration of Victory Day on May 9. As a chance acquaintance told the principal American historian of war commemoration in 1985, "Victory Day is the only real holiday, the only one that means anything. As for *their* holidays—*their* May Day, *their* anniversary of the revolution—you can send them all to hell! But Victory Day . . . Can you imagine: twenty million dead? So much suffering . . . I always cry on Victory Day!" Its reinstatement in 1965 as a public holiday was a major turning point in the evolution of the regime's symbolism. People would dress in their best clothes, veterans would pin on their medals, and everyone would go to visit the local cemetery to remember deceased friends and relatives—not only those killed in the war—with a picnic and a glass of vodka at the graveside. Veterans would gather in public parks with their former colleagues to discuss their regimental memories, recall lost comrades, and reflect sadly on the decadence of contemporary youth. Then they would gather in one another's apartments, watch on television the parade from Red Square, and eat what for many was the greatest feast of the year, swapping stories of the past. This was the Russians' greatest annual celebration of memory, when they would attempt together to link their past and present into some kind of continuing narrative.[70] In some ways Victory Day replaced all the festivals Russians had lost along with their rural way of life, their national religion, and any agreed version of their national history.

In the later decades of the USSR war memorials became the main sites of public memory and the focus of many public rituals. They symbolized what the authorities and the great majority of Russians could agree on. They reminded the people why they were making such great sacrifices to guarantee their country's military security. They augmented the pride of Red Army officers, gave meaning to the grim lives of conscripts, and legitimated and glorified the toil and privations of millions. True, they embodied forgetting as well as remembering. The giant aluminium female figure holding aloft a sword and shield on the banks of the River Dnieper in Kiev both recalled and suppressed memory. Dedicated by Brezhnev in 1980, she called to mind the huge losses of soldiers and civilians in the battles for Kiev in 1941 and 1943. Yet at the same time, she stood above the Monastery of the Caves, the most ancient site of the Russian Orthodox Church, whose golden domes featured in some of her photographs, but which had been closed to the public for two decades. She consigned to oblivion the fact that many Ukrainians had welcomed the departure of the Soviet forces in 1941 and that some had never become fully reconciled to their later return. She drew a veil over the millions of wartime deaths that resulted from Soviet policies rather than from the German invasion. The memorial, moreover, lists no names of the dead. As Michael Ignatieff has commented, Soviet war memorials "convey the heroic and the grandiose, never the humble and particular."[71]

## Stagnation

By the end of the 1960s the relaunch of utopia had already blown itself out. Khrushchev had fallen into disgrace. In 1968 the Warsaw Pact occupation of Czechoslovakia brought an end to hopes of a pluralist form of socialism, or "socialism with a human face." In 1969 the United States landed the first man on the moon and thus invalidated the Soviet claim to leadership in the exploration of the cosmos: not a disaster, but a symbolic defeat on territory where the Soviet Union had asserted pioneer rights.

The year 1980, once billed as the target date for entry into full Communism, gradually faded from the media. The regime no longer promised the present generation that it would "live in Communism": blander, more noncommittal red banners appeared instead. Political propaganda focused more and more on the past, on what had already been achieved, on the great-power status of the Soviet Union, on the defense of the "socialist bloc," and above all on the great, undeniable victory in the Second World War. Public life centered around the celebration of anniversaries of past events, sometimes quite artificial ones, like the 175th anniversary of Pushkin's birth in 1974. The process began with one anniversary that at least was a round figure, the 100th anniversary of Lenin's birth in April 1970, for which "preparation" started in the media nearly two years in advance. By the time the date was at last reached, "hundredth anniversary fever" had been diagnosed as an acute form of boredom: *nam ostoiubileilo.*[72]

The contrast can be seen in two literary works that appeared only a decade apart, in 1965 and 1976, on the same subject, the construction of the Bratsk hydroelectric power station on the Angara River in Siberia. The earlier work, by Evgenii Evtushenko, *Bratskii GES,* was a lengthy ode to the building of the future. It celebrated the new dam as the culmination, first of an age-old tradition of monumental construction going back to the Egyptian pyramids, and second, of the Russian revolutionary heritage that began with the seventeenth-century Cossack rebel Stenka Razin, who freed slaves like those who had toiled on the pyramids. At the beginning Evtushenko appeals to the Russian poets of the past—Pushkin, Lermontov, Nekrasov, Pasternak—to assist him in his task. At the end they return to observe the completion both of the dam and of the ode, while Evtushenko evokes cardinal elements of the Russian tradition: literature, rebellion, motherhood:

> And, as if bearing Russia's own command
> Not to barter ideas for mere words,
> Pushkin, Tolstoi, and Lenin looked down
> And Stenka's daredevil spirit.
> I am glad that I was born in Russia
> With Stenka's daredevil spirit.
> In the Bratsk GES I dimly make out
> Russia, your maternal image.[73]

Eleven years later came the novel by the Irkutsk writer Valentin Rasputin, *Proshchanie s Materoi* (Farewell to Matera), the story of an island village due to be submerged by the Angara during the construction of the Bratsk dam. Here the atmosphere is entirely different. There is no celebration of man's free creativity, no expectation of a great future. On the contrary, the destruction of the village is seen as an irreplaceable loss, because it violates the villagers' bonds with their ancestors, and also with a way of life that has lasted for centuries. In place of Evtushenko's upbeat, declamatory rhetoric, we have Rasputin's subdued and elegiac tones, evoking lovingly the cyclical rhythms of the seasons and the details of everyday life in the doomed village. Daria, the old woman who is the last to leave the island, believes that human attempts to transform nature bear witness, not to man's self-emancipation, but on the contrary to his subjection to a new form of slavery: "Man thinks he's master of life, but he lost that mastery lo-o-ong ago. . . . Life has got the better of him, has climbed on to his back and demands what she wants of him."[74]

By 1976 Rasputin was much more in tune with the mood of the reading public than Evtushenko. This reorientation of Soviet cultural life along with the regime's doctrinal impasse set severe limits on the extent to which Soviet society could change, or to which people could even put forward ideas on how it should change. But that very deadlock meant that debate had to seek new directions, even if it could not do so publicly. It went forward among the elite in confidential memos, and among intellectuals in samizdat and in semi-clandestine discussion groups and study circles based in scientific institutes. Oblique reflections of these discreet polemics sometimes surfaced in literary journals, now as in the nineteenth century the bearer of ideas too controversial for a proper public airing.

## "Joint Responsibility" Triumphant

Messianic socialism, then, was dead by the 1970s as a belief and value system directed toward the future. But the sense of a special mission had survived as (1) the basis of a claim to be a world power; (2) a belief and value system deriving its impetus from the past, especially from wartime victory; (3) the ideological ballast of a society that had become rigid, hierarchical, and conservative. This was, if you like, petrified messianism. By now, though, unlike the 1930s, the Soviet Union did have its own established social structure, its own hierarchy, and its own social memory, which rested on a Russian substratum. The attempt to create a self-regulating "state of all the people" brought out and consolidated certain features of this substratum. As we have seen, the basic principle of self-regulation to which Russians were accustomed was *krugovaia poruka*. It continued to serve now in a somewhat modified form.

The most penetrating, if at times erratic, analyst of Soviet society at this stage was Aleksandr Zinoviev, a mathematical logician at the Institute of Philosophy in Moscow. The title of his first book, *Yawning Heights* (*Ziiaiushchie vysoty*, 1976)—not, of course, published in the USSR—evokes in a verbal pun the haunting absence of the messianic vision. Zinoviev maintained that Soviet society was organized and regulated not from above but from below, by the collectives, or "communes," which constituted its units. These collectives were workplaces—factories (or individual shops within them), farms, transport depots, schools, hospitals, research institutes, branches of professional unions, and so on. The communes constituted the setting where individuals conducted the fundamental business of their lives: "At the level of the primary collective people not only work, they spend time in the company of people they know well. They swap news, amuse themselves, do all kinds of things to preserve and improve their position, have contacts with other people on whom their well-being depends, go to innumerable meetings, get their vacation vouchers, living space and supplementary foodstuffs."[75] According to Zinoviev, the commune was the battlefield on which the Hobbesian war of each individual against every other was played out; but its members were also vitally interested in its preservation. The resulting interplay of individual and collective motives made up the texture of everyday life within it. The ostensible economic purpose of the commune—production of some commodity or service for society—was secondary to these social functions.

Existence outside a commune was more or less impossible: in a society of shortages the commune guaranteed access to a basic minimum. It offered the setting within which individuals exchanged goods and services they could not obtain through the official economy.[76] In any case, those who attempted life outside were either in the criminal underground or could at any time be arrested and indicted for "dronery." Life within the commune, by contrast, was in many ways easy. Members did not have to work hard: pilfering, *tukhta* (padding the figures), mutual cover-ups, and the absence of a market ensured that everyone would get by, no matter how deficient the output of the collective. On the other hand, talented or unusual people inside a commune found life extremely difficult. To ensure the survival of the commune, its members would take action against individuals whose behavior might threaten its existence through nonconformity with the prevailing ideology and social norms. For that reason, the secret police and the Communist Party's panoply of disciplinary measures were almost superfluous: communes could be relied on to police themselves and to discipline or even expel members who did not submit to the will of the collective. Mutual surveillance remained, as always, a paramount function of the collective bound by *krugovaia poruka*. The "cadres department" and the secret police were, then, no more than a "concentrated essence" of Soviet society.[77]

The commune was the indispensable basic unit of the system, then, yet crucially it also subverted the system. Its productive inefficiency in the long run undermined the economy and hence the USSR's claim to great-power status. It also offered opportunities for getting around the official rationing of information and ideas: through gossip exchanged at work one could learn a great deal that was not reported in the mass media, and one had the chance to try out one's own assessments and have them informally criticized. (Anyone who tried to conduct genuine business in a Soviet workplace will have observed with what reluctance employees broke off the endless conversations that were the real content of their day.) The risk of denunciation for political heresy was ever present, though relatively slight where group cohesion was strong; the greater danger in such discussions was violation of the group's norms.

The line was another social "institution"—ubiquitous in a society of shortages—which fulfilled the same function. In lines people were forced to spend hours in each other's company, their minds of necessity focused on the economy's deficiencies, and with nothing to do but discuss them. Men at a loose end would often gather in threes, contribute a ruble each for a bottle of vodka, and drink it together while engaging in unrestrained gossip.

Khrushchev's campaign to involve ordinary people in the law and to make Soviet society self-governing increased the power of primary collectives over their members. Laws dating from the time of revolutionary zeal in the early 1920s were revived. Local soviets, trade union cells, and house committees were empowered to set up so-called comrades' courts, consisting of judges chosen from their own members, to try minor offenses and impose noncustodial sentences, which might be a small fine, a reprimand, corrective labor, or in more serious cases dismissal from work. In the same spirit, and in order to reduce the population of prisons, criminal courts now sometimes dealt with minor offenders by "binding them over in surety" (peredat na poruki) to labor collectives, whose task was to monitor their behavior and report on it periodically to the court.[78]

One task of comrades' courts was to expose and shame heavy drinkers or people illegally brewing samogon. Another was to examine the way of life of individuals who seemed to have more money or property than their working income would suggest. Yet another was to identify "drones," people doing no socially useful work. If within a certain period they did not find regular employment, the comrades could hand them over to the authorities for a criminal indictment. This provision could prove very awkward for professional or creative individuals who were working informally and did not belong to an accredited union.[79]

Under its terms the poet Iosif Brodskii was indicted for dronery in a district court in 1964. Aged twenty-three at the time, he had been writing and translating poetry for some years, much of it nonconformist from the regime's viewpoint, and without joining any officially recognized literary association. At the time of his trial the newspaper *Vechernii Leningrad* accused him of quitting a beginners' study circle at the local Palace of Culture in order "to scramble up Mount Parnassus on his own . . . He continues to lead a parasitic lifestyle. The healthy twenty-six-year-old [sic] lad has done no socially useful work for four years. He lives on casual earnings, and in an emergency his father lets him have a small sum. . . . It is high time for Brodskii to pull himself together, start doing some work, and stop being a drone at the expense of his parents and society."[80]

This is the language of envious insiders expelling an unusual and talented individual. Brodskii's altercation with the judge offers a classic insight into this particular collision of two mental worlds:

JUDGE: What is your specialty?

BRODSKII: I am a poet—a poet and translator.

JUDGE: So who recognizes you as a poet? Who certified your status as a poet?

BRODSKII: Nobody. [Undefiantly] Who certified my status as a human being?

JUDGE: But have you received training?

BRODSKII: For what?

JUDGE: For being a poet. Haven't you tried taking a training course in . . . where they teach you to . . .

BRODSKII: I didn't think it required training.

JUDGE: Well, how do you become a poet, then?

BRODSKII: I think it . . . [lost for words] . . . comes from God.[81]

The judge was unconvinced, and she sentenced Brodskii to five years of internal exile for "dronery." Altogether, then, the courts reinforced the mutual surveillance and compulsory egalitarianism of traditional Russian institutions.

Each collective had its own leadership group, known as the *aktiv. Aktiv* members were the people who embodied in themselves the norms of the collective and so were looked up to by the other members—a kind of collective starosta, in fact. They had personal links to the external authority world, the cadres department, the trade union, the local police station, and the local party cell, and could call on their backing for dealing with the most difficult or intractable cases. From the 1960s the authorities came increasingly to rely on such *aktivy* in prisons and labor camps.[82]

Soviet officials also utilized *aktivy* in the armed forces, with results that proved extremely damaging. During the 1950s, as Khrushchev shifted his priorities toward the missile forces, a large number of officers in conventional formations were laid off, a measure that degraded the prestige and morale of the officer corps as a whole. At the same time the social composition of the army was changing: there were fewer relatively docile peasant recruits and more urban ones. These were more versed in the ways of the world, but also more affected by urban problems like alcoholism, drugs, and gang warfare, and more likely to bridle at commands they considered unreasonable. Such changes destabilized barracks discipline and rendered NCOs, notoriously the weak link in the Russian and Soviet army, even more vulnerable. They would often react by leaving discipline to be enforced on the most recent recruits by second- and third-year conscripts.

The result of this casual approach was the spread of heavy drinking and drug-taking and the establishment of "do-it-yourself" discipline. Here the aggressively masculine mores of young soldiers living without women overcame the puritan and conservative features of traditional Russian collectives, and turned army units into vicious parodies of joint responsibility, dedicated to male bonding through drink, drugs, and the humiliation of juniors. The elders (*dedy*, or "grandfathers") would take charge of the barracks in off-duty periods and compel recent recruits to perform the menial tasks: clean their weapons, polish their boots, launder their clothes, and clean out the latrines. Any recalcitrance, the slightest violation of accepted practices, would be punished, sometimes extremely brutally, by ritual humiliations, beatings, even rape. This was *dedovshchina*, or "grandfathers' rule." NCOs would be reluctant to interfere, and might even support such treatment as an aid to discipline. Officers who were aware of *dedovshchina* would be reluctant to report it, since it would reflect badly on their own leadership qualities. For that reason such practices, once established, were extremely difficult to restrain, let alone eliminate.

As national identities became more pronounced and ethnic tensions mounted, *dedovshchina* often took on an ethnic coloring. Recruits from the Caucasus or Central Asia would sometimes refuse to perform menial labor on the grounds that it was women's work. Young soldiers from those regions and from the Baltics would be singled out for mistreatment; then their co-nationals from neighboring barracks, linked informally by their own *zemliachestvo* (regional association), would exact retaliation. The result could be extended feuds, with vicious brawls involving dozens of soldiers, some of whom would be seriously injured or even killed.[83]

The growth of *dedovshchina* was disastrous not just for the armed forces but also for Soviet society as a whole. After 1945 the army had been the pride of the country. It had not simply enjoyed an extremely high reputation among ordinary Soviet citizens; it had also been a success story in terms of the integration of ethnic minorities. Brezhnev called it "a school of internationalism." By the 1970s it had deteriorated into the very opposite: an Augean stables of alcoholism, drug abuse, and vice, and an arena for interethnic feuds. Rumors of barrack-room incidents, sometimes rendered more lurid in the telling, spread widely, so that young men and their parents, especially non-Slavs, would go to almost any lengths to avoid military service. One recruit, on reporting for service, said he had heard stories from old soldiers from which he imagined the army to be "a prison where people are beaten, humiliated, and insulted."[84]

The degradation of the army undermined the Russian-Soviet patriotism and the sense of international mission which had underlain the attitudes of many ordinary Russians. By 1985 soldiers' mothers were writing to the Soviet leaders pleading for withdrawal from Afghanistan: "International duty? In the name of what? Do the Afghanis themselves want it? Is it worth the lives of our children, who do not understand why they were sent there, what they are fighting for, killing old people and children?"[85] Within a few years soldiers' mothers had set up their own pressure group, "Mother's Heart," to monitor abuse, noncombat injury and death, and to lobby for guaranteed soldiers' rights. It had branches all over Russia, and agitated against using the Soviet Army to suppress national liberation movements inside the USSR, organizing large demonstrations, for example, when the army occupied Baku in January 1990.[86] The mothers' movement offered clear testimony that Russians were losing the will to go on paying the cost in young men's lives which empires demand in order to subjugate the subordinate peoples.

*Dedovshchina* was an especially injurious stigma, because it sullied the reputation of the Soviet Union precisely where it had been highest: in military strength and in the cultivation of interethnic cooperation. It undermined the attempt to forge a new cohesive identity for the country after "building Communism" had faded as an ideal.

Between the mid-1960s and the mid-1980s, then, the Soviet Union was unmistakably becoming ethnicized: that is to say, ethnic identity was becoming the primary marker of social and political status. This development was hard on the nationality that on principle was pan-Soviet, the Russians. They were beginning to find that the Soviet diaspora did not bring them the life-chances they had been taught to expect, that the increasingly self-aware local ethnic patron-client networks excluded them. Yet the so-called Russian Republic was not a promising homeland for them either. Its cities were crowded and polluted, not conducive to having families and bringing up children, while its villages were under-populated, under-productive, and demoralized. The Soviet Army, which had offered a prestigious and satisfying career, was no longer the proud showpiece of a secure multiethnic society. It began to look as if the Soviet Union was not achieving its professed ideals, but in the attempt to do so was undermining Russia's own culture, economy, and identity. The stage was set for the Russian question to become the nemesis of the Soviet Union.

# 10

# THE RETURN OF POLITICS

The rediscovery of a "Russia" separate from the Soviet Union began in the very heart of the Soviet establishment: not among the released prisoners of the Gulag, not among the deported nationalities, not among the victimized peasants, not even among the working class that had so obviously been cheated of its role as "leading class." In fact Russia began its rebirth among writers and scientists, people who accepted at least passively the tenets of the ideology, and who worked in institutes, associations, and on journals created and maintained by the Soviet authorities themselves.

This reawakening was inherent in the nature of Soviet society. From the very outset the official ideology and the published constitution had coexisted uneasily with informal and personalized structures which were needed to ensure that the country functioned at all. At all levels and in all walks of life individuals were cushioned from the harshness and inefficiency of the system by their primary collectives; and in the post-Stalin period these collectives had been given new responsibilities for society's self-regulation.

Informal collectives played as vital a role outside the official sphere as within it. As the fear of denunciation abated during the 1950s, as domestic construction accelerated and people moved out of communal apartments into their own private spaces, it became easier for like-minded people, wherever they worked or lived, to gather casually in one another's homes and chat about whatever concerned them. The new apartments were not spacious, and one room often fulfilled several functions, so that the natural venue for such gatherings was the kitchen, where food and vodka could be produced from the fridge and tea from the kettle on the stove. With the rapid growth of higher education in the 1960s and 1970s, more people than ever before developed intellectual interests and had ideas to exchange. The attraction of forbidden fruit, and the long-standing obsession with the United States, meant that most of those ideas came from the West.

Joseph Brodskii called this younger generation "the most bookish in the history of Russia"; "This was the only generation for whom Giotto and Mandelstam were more imperative than their own personal destinies. Poorly dressed but somehow still elegant, shuffled by the dumb hands of their immediate masters . . . they still retained their love for the non-existent (or existing only in their balding heads) thing called 'civilization.' Hopelessly cut off from the rest of the world, they thought at least that world was like themselves."[1]

There was a certain rural coziness about the coteries in which they would gather. All the same, in the larger towns these circles attracted people of high intellectual distinction and ability, who in the real (as distinct from the imagined) West would have been overwhelmed with professional and administrative work, but who in the Soviet Union were distrusted by the authorities and hence largely free of responsibility. Some of them, moreover, were not able to publish regularly because of cultural censorship. So they had time on their hands and a desire to communicate and exchange ideas. In Stalin's time they might well have been denounced as "enemies of the people" for their nonconformist ideas. Now they were relatively free and able to express their thoughts unhindered—at least in oral form, and provided they trusted their interlocutors. The question of whom to trust once again became crucial.

This was the natural milieu for dissent. In the 1950s and 1960s many participants in such gatherings were intellectuals who had once enthusiastically supported the Communist project, only to see it tarnished, first in the 1930s terror, then in the petty infighting that followed Khrushchev's "secret speech." They were by now the most embittered and articulate opponents of Communism, both in theory and in practice. If they were non-Russian—and especially if they were Jewish—they had an additional, national reason for despising and condemning the existing regime. Such milieux generated the first underground poetry, later works of fiction, and eventually political, philosophical, and religious treatises.[2]

"Why did the Soviet authorities create their own gravedigger—Soviet culture?" asked a literary critic after the fall of the USSR.[3] They did so because the Communist Party continued to depend on ideology for its legitimacy, and this overriding political need bestowed high status on those whose business was ideas. The regime paid them to generate and propagate those ideas, and it offered relatively high salaries and privileges to those on whose work it particularly depended—among them the scientists who elaborated new technologies and the writers and journalists who gave ideas popular currency. At the very least, even the most modestly placed intellectuals had security of employment and a guaranteed minimum income. With the dismantling of indiscriminate terror, the "joint responsibility" structure of professional organizations—designed in the 1930s to subject professional people to party authority—now began, paradoxically, sometimes to work the other way around and to offer little oases of security for independent thinking. These factors applied especially in academic and cultural institutions: there circles of like-minded intellectuals could find a refuge, as well as support from colleagues, to study and discuss themes not envisaged in the official curriculum.

The Academy of Sciences discreetly protected some of the principal nonconformists. The distinguished Russian physicist Petr Kapitsa once remarked: "To be able to maintain democracy and legality it is absolutely essential for a country to have an independent institution to serve as an arbiter in constitutional problems. In the United States this role is reserved for the Supreme Court, and in Britain for the House of Lords. It looks as if in the Soviet Union that function falls morally on the Academy of Sciences."[4]

In science and the arts, then, the primary collectives formed tiny bridgeheads of freedom of speech. They did so because their function was in implicit tension with the official ideology. Science at the highest level requires the freedom to think, facilities for keeping up with the latest international research, and opportunities to discuss ideas with leading foreign colleagues; the regime thus had no choice but to provide these resources, even if on a tightly rationed basis. Soviet officials also recognized the importance of the arts and especially of literature, both for the education of young people and for maintaining the cultural prestige of the Soviet Union in the world at large. In particular, the reputation of nineteenth-century Russian literature conferred on its mid-twentieth-century inheritors a moral status given to few others in Soviet society.

Literature played the role of the Greek classics in the formation of the Victorian Christian gentleman: it introduced an element of tolerated, even revered, ideological unorthodoxy inherited from an officially approved past. If your parents were cultured people, or you had access to a good library, you could read the thoroughly heretical and antisocialist Dostoevskii. His unacknowledged closeness to the imperial aspects of the official doctrine made him a kind of "shadow" ideologist of the Soviet period. But even the more "acceptable" Tolstoi encouraged a strict conscience, truth-telling, and extreme suspicion of the state. Reading them was a revelation for many young Russians. A teacher at Moscow's School no. 2 in the 1960s, for example, later told a Western scholar: "Reading Tolstoi, I realised I was an enemy of the [Soviet] system . . . My spiritual conscience [was formed] through Russian literature."[5] It was not uncommon for readers to discover a religious significance even in writers who were far from mainstream Orthodoxy: in a completely nondenominational sense, literature fed the spiritual life of educated Russians.[6] In this milieu the rediscovery of Akhmatova, Mandelstam, Bulgakov, and Platonov—some of whose works were now at last being laboriously negotiated through Soviet publishers, others of which circulated in samizdat—was a revelation of a Russian identity most people thought had long ago been buried under the Soviet monolith.

## Aleksandr Tvardovskii and *Novyi mir*

The literary figure who made greatest use of these opportunities, both as author and as editor, was Aleksandr Tvardovskii. He was a complex personality who reflected in his own character many of the contradictions of contemporary Russian consciousness. He was born the son of a peasant in Smolensk province. His father had been dekulakized in the early 1930s, just as Tvardovskii was starting out on his literary career, and for a time he kept his distance from his family while making his way as a young poet. As we have seen, during the war he created the most popular emblem of simple Russianness, the fictional soldier Vasilii Terkin. As editor of *Novyi mir* from 1950 to 1954 and from 1958 to 1970, he was entrusted with the country's most prestigious literary monthly. From 1961 to 1966, moreover, he was a member of the Central Committee of the CPSU, and hence one of the two hundred highest-ranking officials in the Soviet political pecking order.

As principal editor of the number-one journal of the Soviet Writers' Union, Tvardovskii implemented the official doctrine of "socialist realism," but he gave it a twist that ultimately undermined it. He repudiated the aesthetic of the heroic rejection of *byt* (routine everyday life) in the name of the future. For him "socialism" meant something more prosaic: the effort to improve people's lives so that they would be properly fed, clothed, housed, and educated; "realism" meant publishing works that gave a frank picture of Soviet social life and of the history of the Soviet peoples; "narodnost" meant focusing on the life of ordinary people, using their language and concepts.

Tvardovskii specifically disavowed the "positive hero" who had been the staple figure of Stalin-period fiction. He complained that "exalting the personality of the principal character . . . inevitably meant despising the 'ordinary masses.'"[7] A persistent theme of *Novyi mir* was that peasants lacked the feeling of being a *khoziain,* a word that implies both "master" and "owner," so that it could be interpreted as meaning that peasants suffered either because they lacked their own property or because they had no control over their own fate—probably both. In the Russian tradition generally the categories of ownership and political power tend to be fused, so that a hybrid reading of the word is legitimate.

It might well be argued that Tvardovskii—whether he thought of it in this way or not—was attempting to revive the two ideals of pre-1930 peasant communities, *mir* and *pravda*. One of his watchwords was *pravda zhizni*, "life's truth." "The failing of many of our books," he claimed, "is above all the lack of *pravda zhizni*." He specifically did not mean truth as expounded by official ideologists, but something more like truth as taught by the experience of life itself, as lived by ordinary people in their communities—which in Russia till recently had still been peasant communities.[8] For most of his life he believed in the basic virtues of the Soviet system, but he understood them in a different way from the official ideologists, in the light of the moral precepts learned from peasant culture.[9]

Tvardovskii was reviving another Russian tradition, too, that of the "thick journal." He was guided by the example of Nikolai Nekrasov, who, like himself, was both the editor of a major journal and a poet depicting the life of the ordinary Russian people. *Novyi mir* proclaimed on its masthead that it was a "belletristic and sociopolitical journal," and Tvardovskii took both aspects extremely seriously. He believed that in Russia the "thick journal" had an altogether broader function than the specialized literary journals of the West: it had a cognitive and civic role, helping to form an educated public. "The second half of that masthead is no mere accidental formality," he declared. "The editors know that many of our subscribers and readers do not always have access to specialist journals, and therefore we do our utmost to satisfy their interest in problems of contemporary politics and science, problems of the struggle for peace, problems of the economy, culture, art, education, and so on."[10]

To fulfill its civic role, Tvardovskii believed that a serious journal should have its own recognizable *napravlenie* (civic and aesthetic position, tendency, or identity). It should publish writers and critics who were kindred spirits, and not only publish them but draw them into its work and into contact with its readers. A journal should become a focus for the intellectual and spiritual life of like-minded people, committed to the same humane ideals—which were those of the party, though they were not always promoted by the party. As one scholar has commented, "One must imagine the *Novyi mir* editorial offices—at least under Tvardovskii—as not merely the offices and desks of editors and their staff, but also as the meeting place for a fringe of active, interested writers and intellectuals, who would drop in to talk, to discuss matters of mutual interest, to bring manuscripts which they considered worthwhile, or just to share the camaraderie."[11] *Novyi mir* was a normal cell of Soviet society, like many others, but it was also the haven for a counterculture that would eventually undermine the official Soviet culture.

In fulfillment of its editorial aims, *Novyi mir* published works of fiction that reported in a realist style—and as far as possible frankly (this was the subject of continual battles with the censorship and the officials of the Writers' Union)—the history of ordinary people during the critical junctures of Soviet history: the civil war, the collectivization of agriculture, the first five-year plans, and the Second World War.[12] It published numerous *ocherki,* a characteristic Russian genre of semi-fiction and semi-reportage that described the contemporary lives of ordinary people in farm, factory, and office. As Tvardovskii pointed out, the *ocherk* lay on the boundary between the journal's two functions, "belletristic" and "sociopolitical," and its aim was to express *pravda zhizni.*[13]

*Novyi mir* also began the key task of publishing works that had been suppressed from the 1930s to the 1950s: Akhmatova, Pasternak, Bulgakov, and others.[14] It brought out memoirs, diaries, and other documents that reflected the past directly. Thus *Novyi mir* fulfilled the function of monitoring memory, which Barbara Misztal has identified as crucial in sustaining a viable national identity. This monitoring involved correcting mistaken impressions, rehabilitating the forgotten or suppressed, and initiating a dialogue in place of a monologue. In the early 1960s the public eagerly devoured the memoirs of Ilia Erenburg, who, as a participant in the European cultural life of the 1920s, had personally known many major artistic figures whose names had long been under a veil: Akhmatova, Babel, Tatlin, Malevich, Gide, Malraux. Readers could discover with pride the great and innovative contribution Russia had made to Europe's cultural life in the early decades of the twentieth century.[15]

Tvardovskii's most celebrated contribution to both politics and literature was the publication in 1962 of Aleksandr Solzhenitsyn's novel *A Day in the Life of Ivan Denisovich*. At the time Solzhenitsyn was a completely unknown figure. While serving in the Red Army in 1945 he had been arrested for writing a letter critical of Stalin; after nine years in prisons and labor camps, then in exile in Kazakhstan, he was now an obscure schoolteacher in Riazan. Yet *Ivan Denisovich* was a path-breaking work in several respects. It was the first frank account of what life had been like in Stalin's labor camps. It also challenged the dominant Soviet mentality by pioneering a new and unfamiliar narrative standpoint. In place of the omniscient narrator who sees history unfold and understands the place of every character and every action in its texture, in place of the dauntless hero leading waverers and doubters along the tough and battle-strewn road to socialism, Solzhenitsyn employed the discourse of a character from the *narod*, using the language of village, army, building site, and labor camp. He accepted all the limitations such a discourse implied: little education, no politically informed outlook, no superior knowledge of events or personalities. The action led to no particular achievement, no breakthrough to higher knowledge; indeed, the narration implied that time was cyclical rather than unilinear. This was the viewpoint of Russians as victims of the upheavals of their era.

The publication of *Ivan Denisovich* unleashed a flood of memories, an extraordinary "return of the repressed," poured out in letters to the editors and to Solzhenitsyn himself. The rediscovery of memory provoked feelings ranging from proud civic consciousness to suicidal impulses: "Now I read and weep, but when I was imprisoned in Ukhta for ten years I did not shed a tear"; "After reading it the only thing left to do is to knock a nail in the wall, tie a knot and hang oneself"; "Although I wept when I read it, I felt myself a citizen with full rights among other people."[16]

Tvardovskii in his personality and activity tried to encompass several contradictory worlds. Son of a "kulak," he attempted to become a thoroughly loyal poet; later a senior member of the nomenklatura elite (and in the Central Committee for four years), he sponsored the journal that did more than any other to corrode that elite's belief system. Overall he was trying to achieve the same thing as Dostoevskii, though by completely different means: to reconcile peasant pravda and collectivism with the empire and great power that was the Soviet Union. The two were not reconcilable. Tvardovskii was torn apart by the contradiction between them— which probably explains why at times he drank heavily.

Tvardovskii's heritage was sufficiently flexible and all-embracing that it could be taken up by both "Russianist" and "cosmopolitan" wings of the literary world. His dedication to high-quality literature and to freedom of speech, his championing of authors in political difficulties, his exposure of the seamy side of Soviet life, and his battles with the censors and the cultural authorities all placed him in the camp of the "liberals." Yet at the same time, his dedication to Russian civic-literary traditions, which he considered "holy," his determination to depict the true story of the Russian *narod,* and especially the peasantry, in a literary language close to their colloquial speech, placed him close to the Russian nationalists.[17] After he lost his editorial post in 1970, Tvardovskii's collective of authors moved in both directions. Most of the village writers (though not all) went to *Nash sovremennik,* which embodied the nationalist tendency.[18] Most other authors either went to *Druzhba narodov* (Friendship of the Peoples), whose very title proclaimed the liberal tendency, or actually emigrated, feeling that an open-minded literature was no longer possible in the Soviet Union itself.

## The Formation of a Russian Party

The ethnicization of the Soviet Union left both intellectuals and Communist Party leaders in the RSFSR in an anomalous and unhappy position. The non-Russian party bosses were now able discreetly to seek political and cultural support from nationalists within their own republics. They were able to build a tolerated culture of ethnic distinctiveness attractive to non-Russian intellectuals, which took the sting out of their feelings of national humiliation and relative deprivation in the USSR.[19]

Russians, however, whether party bosses or intellectuals, did not have the fallback position of cultivating Russian distinctiveness. There was no "homeland" nationalism in which they could take refuge. Moreover, the attempt to create one would defeat its own ends, since Russians' national identity was bound up with the Soviet Union as a whole. To "liberate" Russia from the Soviet Union would destroy the Soviet Union and hence Russia too.

So what kind of Russian identity should they cultivate? History was an uncertain and ambivalent guide, for Russians had a multiplicity of national ideals. Several different models were available for "Russia," and in crucial respects they contradicted one another:

1. The Stalinist state victorious in the Second World War;
2. The tsarist Russian Empire;
3. The peasant commune and the associated Russian tradition of collective solidarity and consensus decision-making;
4. The Russian Orthodox Church.

The first model was in many ways the easiest and most obvious one to adopt. Nineteen forty-five had been a moment of mass support for the Soviet regime, and the historical apogee of Russian national consciousness. It was still fresh in the memories of many people, and it was the road through which the current party-state leadership had consolidated its power. For those reasons the Stalinist outlook had enduring attraction and staying power in the late Soviet decades. All the same, those who adopted it had to face serious questions. Stalin had been responsible, not just for winning the war, but also for bringing the Soviet Union close to defeat, and therefore for the length and cost of the war. He had unleashed the terror and caused the deaths of millions of innocent people, many of them Russians. He had destroyed or attempted to destroy cardinal elements of the Russian social and cultural tradition: the Orthodox Church, the village commune, much of the best art, literature, and music. After Khrushchev's "secret speech" and the return of millions from the Gulag, these crimes were on many people's minds, even if they were not fully illuminated in the media. How could one seriously take Stalin as a Russian national hero?

As for the tsarist state, it could not serve on its own as a satisfactory model. There was no question of restoring the monarchy. But Communists could save some of the tsarist heritage by linking it with the Soviet Union as the bearer of Russian statehood: this was the theory of the "single stream" *(edinyi potok)*, outlined by Shestakov in his prewar textbook.

The authoritarianism of both could be held up as a more appropriate political form for Russians than Western liberal democracy. But if a Communist accepted those premises, how was he to explain why Lenin had supported the overthrow of tsarism? Had the February and October revolutions, the murder of the royal family and of millions of "former people" been merely monumental historical misunderstandings?

The peasant commune was not in itself a practical ideal, but in modified form it had considerable attractions. One could argue that Russians practiced community consensus and mutual aid, whereas the West was succumbing to ever more rampant individualism, hedonism, and mercenary materialism. Communism, in this theory, was a modified version of the Russian tradition.

The Orthodox Church was a more viable option, at least for some of the oppositional intelligentsia, since it had—just—survived the upheavals of the Soviet decades in recognizable form. But its long cohabitation with the regime rendered it an uncertain harbor for those seeking spiritual security and independence in a stormy world. The fundamental question remained: Had Sergii's compromise of 1927 been a betrayal of the faith or a measure regrettable but necessary for a greater good, the survival of the church? And what should people think about those prelates who had made themselves servants of an atheist regime and collaborated with a murderous secret police?

One could argue that the Orthodox Church exemplified the old Russian spirit of community continued in the Communist Party—but only if one were prepared to ignore decades of atheist propaganda and official persecution of the church.

The Soviet Union was an indissoluble part of Russian history, yet it had destroyed much of Russia. The Soviet model had succeeded in certain ways: it had educated the masses; it had created modern industry, science, and technology; and it had defeated the Germans at war. Yet it had also precipitated a Russian demographic disaster, devastated Russian agriculture, destroyed the Russian peasantry, undermined the Russian church, and paralyzed Russian culture. It was both Russian and anti-Russian. That was the fundamental dilemma.

## Russian Nationalism

The tensions between "Russia" and the Soviet Union are reflected in the memoirs of Stanislav Kuniaev, the chief editor of *Nash sovremennik* in the

1990s. Kuniaev was a Russian from Kaluga who studied at Moscow University and then worked for a time in the editorial offices of the literary journal *Znamia*, before moving on to *Nash sovremennik*. He claims even in his youth to have felt a sense of foreboding about Russia's future: "I saw the still bleeding gash, only partly healed, between Russia's past history and the Soviet epoch. I realized that we could not have a fully viable [*polnotsennyi*] future without reviving everything durable and flourishing that had been created before the revolution. But how could we launch that revival without destroying the real historical life of the last seventy years? How could we reconcile the Whites and Reds? Bunin and Esenin? Sholokhov and Solzhenitsyn? The Russian and the Soviet?"[20]

One way to evade these paradoxes was to ascribe all the "bad" results of Soviet rule to the Jews. This was the Dostoevskian temptation in a new form, and it was the stratagem adopted by Kuniaev. It especially appealed to young writers like him from provincial Russia who were struggling to make their way in the highly cultured literary world of Moscow or Leningrad. The difficulties of the early stages of his career he put down to Jewish domination of the literary world. He caricatured the "arrogant expressions," the "thrusting chins and lower jaws" of established Jewish authors. According to his version, Jewish writers had flourished while their Russian colleagues were being arrested and murdered by "the fellow tribesmen of the Odessans Agranov and Iagoda"—that is, the supposedly Jewish-run NKVD.[21] (This is to ignore the fate of Mandelstam and Babel, to name only the most prominent Jewish literary victims of the NKVD.)

Literary life—like all forms of Soviet life—compelled people to band together with like-minded colleagues to fight for what they believed in. Everyone felt they belonged to a besieged minority condemned to struggle against great odds, while the "others"—the "opponents," "they"—enjoyed official favor without lifting a finger. The "Russian party" was no exception, even though its members were securely ensconced in the official journals and publishing houses that formed the well-barricaded fortresses of the literary battlefield. Many of them had been students at Moscow University in the early 1950s, and they had imbibed the Soviet-Russian anti-Semitic patriotism of the late Stalin era. When they later studied at the Gorkii Literary Institute, in the late 1950s and early 1960s, though, they encountered a very different atmosphere: the tone was being set by the "thaw," whose eponymous work had been written by a Jew, Ilia Erenburg (albeit one who in his time had been a protagonist of the most monolithic Soviet-Russian patriotism).

Russianists felt themselves outnumbered and disadvantaged. They became uneasily aware that, by comparison with the champions of the "thaw," they were making little impact on the reading public and had no following whatsoever outside the Soviet Union. In their eyes, their neglect simply demonstrated that there was an international conspiracy against genuine Russian values. The young poet Evgenii Evtushenko was filling stadiums with his declamatory verse, delivered in a dramatized, even bombastic manner, which irritated his rivals, especially when he deployed it to attack anti-Semitism, to evoke the ghosts of Babii Iar, and to warn that the "Heirs of Stalin" were planning a comeback. He identified himself with Dreyfus, with Anne Frank, with the victims of the Bialystok pogrom and the Babii Iar massacre: "In their callous rage, all anti-Semites / Must hate me now as a Jew. / For that reason / I am a true Russian!"[22] One anti-Semite, a certain A. Markov, proved Evtushenko right by dedicating to him a poem entitled "What kind of true Russian are you?"[23]

The conflict between "Russian" and "cosmopolitan" literary figures was an extremely serious one—indeed, for all anyone knew at the time, it was a matter of life and death. Each side accused the other of complicity in the denunciations of the recent past—denunciations which for some had been equivalent to a prepackaged death sentence. The Moscow branch of the Writers' Union was a stronghold of "liberals." In 1953 nearly one-third of its members were Jews, and most of the rest, like Evtushenko, considered anti-Semitism repugnant and redolent of Stalinism.[24] They mounted a campaign to uncover the truth about the recent past, especially the story of those arrested or murdered for their part in the Jewish Anti-Fascist Committee: Which writers had denounced their Jewish or "cosmopolitan" colleagues? The events had taken place only a decade or so earlier, yet those responsible had not been dismissed, let alone punished; nor had anti-Semitism been officially condemned. There was no guarantee whatsoever that similar murderous campaigns might not resume at any moment.[25] Hence the bitterness with which accusations were advanced and rebutted. Although Khrushchev's "secret speech" made these accusations a subject of legitimate debate, it offered no resolution to them.

Those who were under suspicion decided to defend themselves by organizational methods. Profiting from the Soviet leaders' reaction against the "excesses" unleashed by the "secret speech," they obtained permission in 1957 to set up a Union of Writers of the *RSFSR* as a counterweight to the dominant influence of the Moscow branch of the Union of Writers of the

*Soviet Union.* This was a momentous step. After all, as we have seen, Soviet leaders were very reluctant to create Russian institutions of any kind: in the Communist Party, in the academic world, in the mass media. Yet here was a Russian institution in the most sensitive cultural sphere of all. The new union was intended to give greater weight to Russian writers living in provincial towns and in villages as opposed to those of Moscow and Leningrad. Its newspaper *Literaturnaia Rossiia* and its journals *Nash sovremennik* and *Literaturnai i zhizn'* became influential forums for the "Russian" point of view, and not only in literature. Unions of Russian composers and artists were created at the same time.[26]

## Village Prose

Between the mid-1960s and the mid-1980s many of the most widely read works of fiction were written by a unique generation of Russian novelists: graduates of the Gorkii Institute who in their youth had been peasant lads. They combined real literary skill with genuine knowledge of village life. Born between the 1910s and the 1930s, these writers had witnessed or at least heard their parents evoke the last years of traditional peasant agriculture and the creation of the collective farms. They were in a unique position to portray in artistic terms the great sociological and psychological split at the heart of their generation: between the gentle, cyclical rhythms of traditional rural life, oriented toward the past, and the hectic, forward-thrusting tempo of modern urban life, directed in unilinear fashion toward the future.

Their first task was documentary, to compile a kind of oral history, to assemble memory and make it available before it disappeared. As one village prose writer, the Siberian Sergei Zalygin, noted: "I feel that the roots of my nation are . . . in the village, in the ploughed field, in daily bread. Furthermore it seems to me that our generation will have been the last to see with its own eyes the thousand-year-old way of life in which each of us grew up. If we do not write about it and about its radical transformation in a short space of time [a reference to collectivization], then who will?"[27]

The village writers were chroniclers, then, but they were also moralists. It is no accident that their works began to be published just at the time when the urge toward creating a better future no longer seemed convincing. Narrating past customs was no longer of merely antiquarian interest: it had become a moral quest. Many Russians had left the village with relief and moved to the town in search of superior chances. Now they began to ask themselves what they had gained and what they had lost. A number of stories in this mode began with the narrator or hero returning to the village of his childhood, which he had not visited for decades, seeing the churchyard, the familiar family home, dilapidated but still standing, the bathhouse, the samovar, "a world he thought had long ceased to exist."[28]

This self-questioning mode was well exemplified in a story by the Vologda writer Vasilii Belov, "That's the Way Things Are" (*Privychnoe delo*). It was published in 1966 in *Sever*, a hitherto little-read journal of the Arkhangelsk branch of the Writers' Union. The story is a simple one. It concerns Ivan Afrikanovich, his wife Katerina, and their nine children. Ivan cannot earn enough from his labor on the kolkhoz to feed and clothe them all. His brother-in-law persuades him that he would do better to leave for the city, earn some money, and resettle his whole family there. Against his better judgment Ivan is persuaded to go, but as soon as he leaves the village he finds life so bewildering that he is unable to cope. He does not even get as far as the city, but is thrown off the train for traveling without a ticket. Struggling back home, he finds that Katerina, exhausted by years of drudgery and the strain of parting, has had a heart attack and died.

In this work the village is a universe of seasonal rhythms and work patterns, where men, women, children, and animals share the same way of life. (Symptomatically, one of the chapters is the autobiography of the family cow.) If they work conscientiously and help one another out in difficulties—in other words, if they observe traditional "joint responsibility"—they survive physically and flourish morally. But in Belov's portrayal urban modes of exploitation have invaded this pristine microcosm, taking the shape of the kolkhoz, with its high-handed officials, its restrictive regulations, and its compulsory grain deliveries. Thus alienated from the primeval Eden, Ivan brings destruction on himself and his family.[29]

In a variety of forms, this moral universe was replicated in other village prose works. It was of course the reverse of the socialist realist morality. Its setting was the village, the peaceful, unchanging, yet threatened *rodina*, not the *otechestvo*, where great transformations were taking place. The life experience evoked was often childhood, the time of direct, unmediated feeling and spontaneous integrity. Its ideal world was found in the past, not the future; its version of time was cyclical not unilinear; its content was pessimistic not optimistic; its principal characters, and usually the narrator too, were uneducated, colloquial in their language, and limited in their outlook: they did not understand the grand movements of history. These rambling, easy-going novels evoked a "non-Soviet" past that could easily be presented as a model of Russian national existence, destroyed by the irruption of the Westernizing or Jewish (according to your taste) ideology of Marxism. That model had the potential to become, in the words of Anthony Smith, "an idealised golden age and heroic past that could serve as exemplars for collective regeneration in the present."[30]

## Human Rights and Conscience

The questioning of the 1960s also generated a completely different view of morality from the one implied by "joint responsibility," one that could not be claimed as intrinsically Russian but which nonetheless also had deep roots in Russia's intellectual tradition: pursuing all-human ideals, and linking up with international institutions that embodied them. This trend was one possible interpretation of the official ideology. Ten of the twelve points of the "Moral Code of the Builder of Communism" were all-human ones, that is, not specific to socialist or Communist movements. Besides, the 1961 party program asserted that "Communist morality includes the fundamental all-human moral norms which were worked out by the popular masses in the course of the thousand-year struggle with social oppression and moral vices."[31]

The leading exponent of human rights and conscience was someone at the heart of the Soviet Union's most destructive research establishment, the nuclear physicist Academician Andrei Sakharov. Science had an honored place in the school curriculum, and scientists were members of the Soviet pantheon of glory. But the qualities and practices that were required for real achievement in science—skepticism, rational thinking, constant questioning of accepted notions, keeping up with the latest ideas and information, and regular contact with foreign colleagues—were contrary to those fostered by the Soviet system. Science requires a culture of trust, for no scientist can replicate all the experiments and measurements he would need to be sure of his facts. He must be able to trust his colleagues to do their work honestly and conscientiously.[32] By the same token, he must be in a position to send and receive ideas across frontiers, and to evaluate and discuss them openly. Hence there was a paradox at the heart of the official Soviet adulation of science: a closed society was extolling an open system of cognition.

Sakharov began his career attracted by what he considered "superb science." But he also felt that the Soviet Union had to stand up to the United States. To defend again what had so nearly been lost in the Second World War, and to create at least a balance of international terror, the Soviet Union could not allow the United States to hold its monopoly on nuclear weapons. Evaluating himself critically later, Sakharov felt that he had been gripped by a "war psychology," but those were his genuine feelings at the time.[33]

Once he and his colleagues succeeded in producing a working Soviet hydrogen bomb, however, he realized with horror that the atmospheric testing of such bombs would inevitably, through radiation, cause the deaths of an unknown but potentially very large number of people. He also realized that he had put terrible weapons in the hands of politicians who were capable and energetic, but who would take decisions on criteria quite different from his own. Even his own colleagues, he discovered to his dismay, did not share his concerns: "During the 1950s I had come to regard testing in the atmosphere as a crime against humanity, no different from secretly pouring disease-producing microbes into a city's water supply. But my views were not shared by my associates, and I saw how easy it is for people to adapt their thinking to what they regard as their own best interest."[34]

He tried but failed to persuade Khrushchev not to resume atmospheric testing in 1961. This was a turning point in the physicist's life. "It was the ultimate defeat for me," he recalled. "A terrible crime was about to be committed, and I could do nothing to prevent it. . . . That was probably the most terrible lesson of my life: you can't sit on two chairs at once. I decided that I would devote myself to ending biologically harmful tests."[35]

Sakharov's spiritual crisis was paradigmatic. He was torn between different and ultimately incompatible ideals of the Soviet system. He resolved to pursue some of them single-mindedly—internationalism, humanitarianism, devotion to science—while rejecting others with equal determination: utopianism, class struggle, great-power status. He condemned Soviet messianism along with "delusions as to the uniqueness of a society . . . dogmatism, adventurousness and aggression."[36] In his memorandum "Reflections on Progress, Peaceful Coexistence, and Intellectual Freedom" he projected the image of a world run on scientific principles, that is, by methods "based on the deep study of facts, theories, and opinions, and assuming open discussion, unprejudiced and dispassionate in its findings." He warned that the present disunity of humankind threatened

it with complete annihilation, that human beings must try much harder
to live together in peace and mutual tolerance, and that for this purpose
they needed intellectual freedom and the ability to choose their own governments. He spelled out the dangers posed by nuclear war, famine, and
environmental degradation, but also by closed societies and tyrannical political systems that violated the law and were unresponsive to the aspirations of their own peoples. He proposed that statesmen should aim to dis-
mantle the barriers which divided them, cooperate to tackle the problems
which could only be solved by common effort, and ensure the rule of law
and democracy in their own countries. He called specifically on the Soviet
leaders to reverse the trend of the late 1960s to impose sanctions on nonconformist thinkers who tried to disseminate their views, and to undertake a complete re-examination of Stalin's crimes, with a view to making
the results public.[37]

Like Lenin's colleagues a half-century earlier, Sakharov was a convinced
internationalist, but of a completely different kind. Although he still occasionally referred to "socialism," the source of his ideals was something else
entirely. He was a prime example of the way in which contact with the
West had transformed the outlook of many Soviet intellectuals. He was
inspired by the principles on which the United Nations was founded, and
which in theory the USSR had endorsed. Sakharov explicitly recommended the convergence of socialist and nonsocialist systems, not their
continuing struggle. In later years Sakharov referred repeatedly to U.N.
documents in appealing for the rule of law inside the Soviet Union, especially after the USSR signed the final act of the Helsinki Conference in
1975. Thenceforth, international agreements endorsed by the USSR in
pursuit of peaceful coexistence became a major source of both concepts
and inspiration for a generation of human rights activists, among whom
Sakharov was the leading but far from the only figure.

The principal organ of the human rights movement was the samizdat
journal *Chronicle of Current Events*. Each issue bore on its masthead a
quotation from article 19 of the United Nations Declaration of Human
Rights of 1948 guaranteeing freedom of speech. The journal's text carried
no political commentary; it simply enumerated cases in which the Soviet
authorities had violated their own laws in proceeding against Soviet citizens. This bald, unadorned presentation was deliberate: it was intended to
elevate the rule of law to the supreme principle of social life. The channels
through which information was collected (in one direction) and the jour-

nal was discreetly disseminated (in the other) constituted a durable network of alternative opinion.[38]

The problem with this stance was that it was easily represented as subversive, drawing on Western "bourgeois" ideals. Moreover, since human rights activists could not publish their materials in the Soviet media, they were compelled to have recourse to foreign publications and radio stations for their publicity, a practice that their opponents stigmatized as at best disloyalty, at worst treason.

The ideal that had perhaps the broadest resonance among the nonconformist intelligentsia, even broader than human rights, was "conscience." The word had different meanings for different people, but it was acceptable to Orthodox believers, Western liberals, and reformed Marxists alike. Even the regime could not object to it. One of the prescribed norms of the "Moral Code of the Builder of Communism" was "honesty and truthfulness, moral purity, modesty, and unpretentiousness in social and private life," which was a kind of itemization of the qualities of a good conscience.[39]

Taking "conscience" as an absolute seemed especially appropriate: the ruthless violence of the early Soviet decades had convinced many people that the notion of a relative morality was suspect. The proposition that one should not vest one's conscience in the state or in any political movement—perhaps any collective movement at all—was both appealing and persuasive. The ideal also had secure roots in Russian culture. Before the revolution writers had felt obliged by their literary calling to speak out for the oppressed and deprived *narod*, and in their works to promote enlightenment, morality, good conscience, and creative freedom.[40] Furthermore, in Russian émigré philosophy *sovest* and *lichnost* (conscience and personality) had been key concepts, precisely as a reaction against the statization of both in the Soviet Union. In the late 1950s and 1960s intellectuals were discovering that already well before 1917 some Russian socialists had turned against Marxism because it left no room for free personality and belief in transcendental ideals. They began avidly reading the 1909 neo-Kantian symposium *Vekhi*, along with the philosophers Soloviev, Berdiaev, Bulgakov, and Frank, and then through their prism returned to Dostoevskii and discovered new meanings in him. Some of them converted to the Orthodox Church and rejected socialism outright.[41] So the idea of conscience came to be connected with that of personality as a fundamental value in the discourse of Russians who otherwise held many diverse convictions. From the 1960s to the 1990s, Russian intellectuals believed in "personality" and "conscience" more steadfastly and eloquently than the great majority of Western intellectuals to whom they looked as a model.

The imperative of reviving good conscience was stated at its starkest by Solzhenitsyn, in a widely circulated samizdat letter he wrote just before he was expelled from the USSR in 1974. Sweeping aside the excuses of helplessness in the face of power that most people made to themselves for not resisting spiritual and ideological oppression, he declared: "It is not 'they' who are guilty of everything, it is *we ourselves* and only we! . . . Violence has nothing with which to cover its nakedness save the lie, and the lie can sustain itself only through violence. . . . This is where the simplest and most direct key lies to our self-emancipation: *personal nonparticipation in the lie!* All right, lies blanket everything, hold everyone in their grip . . . but *not through me!. . . The way ahead is never consciously to uphold the lie.*" According to this recipe, Soviet citizens should never write anything they did not hold to be true; they should not hold up placards with slogans they did not believe in; they should walk out of meetings where the speaker mouthed official untruths to general applause.[42]

## The Environment

The Soviet Union's role as a great power and its commitment to modernization entailed a ruthless attitude toward the environment. From the 1920s to the 1950s the requirements of industrialization, military power, and economic growth had absolute priority: nature was there to be "conquered," in Bolshevik-speak. Heedless gigantism was the order of the day, as ministries vied with one another in the ambition of their projects: huge hydroelectric power schemes, chemical and armaments factories belching smoke and discharging toxic waste.

Yet even at the height of these preoccupations a few small and insecure islands still existed within the establishment where people were dedicated to the defense of the environment. These were in the Academy of Sciences and certain RSFSR ministries, where people worked to preserve *zapovedniki,* reservations where flora and fauna could develop in their own way, protected from pollution. For others what mattered was rescuing an indispensable element in Russia's history and culture, ensuring that its ancient buildings (many of them churches), its forests, lakes, and rivers survived for the appreciation and edification of later generations.[43]

Eventually, during the "thaw" in the 1960s the environment became a political issue. The first major campaign concerned a question close to the heart of all Russians: What was to become of their capital city? Moscow symbolized Russian identity, and up to the early 1930s it had retained much of its nineteenth-century character as a rambling semi-rural city, loosely clustered around its ancient Kremlin. As we have seen, however, in the 1930s the regime had begun to demolish and rebuild extensively, under the terms of a "general plan" that was never submitted to public discussion. The plan envisaged destroying most of the low-rise nineteenth-century buildings near the center and replacing them with more monumental constructions. Khrushchev was an enthusiastic supporter of this concept, and he was notorious for his contempt for old churches, which he used to refer to sarcastically as *Spasy na iaitsakh* ("the savior of the bollocks").[44]

The main opposition to this destruction came from P. D. Baranovskii, an architect and restorer with experience going back before the revolution. In the late 1950s he set up an initiative group to organize petitions for the preservation of threatened buildings. When unsuccessful, he would photograph and record every detail of a building before demolition. Members of his group would meet on Wednesday evenings in his apartment in the Novodevichii Monastery to discuss their work and to hear lectures and papers on architectural history. Baranovskii lobbied organizations like the Soviet Peace Committee, the Academy of Arts, and the Moscow branch of the Union of Artists, with growing success, and he gained the support of the writer Vladimir Soloukhin, the sculptor Sergei Konenkov, and the painter Ilia Glazunov. The club's work was singled out for praise at the December 1965 Komsomol plenum.[45]

In 1962 a group of architects, engineers, and artists published a letter in the journal *Moskva*, protesting the continuing destruction of Moscow's old buildings. Their appeal combined arguments of aesthetics and historical tradition with protest against undemocratic procedures. These acts of vandalism had been carried out without any public discussion, the writers accused, even though architecture was an art that belonged to the people, and love of one's home town was a vital part of patriotism. The Moscow "master plan," a matter affecting every Muscovite, had remained secret: "It is time to end the situation when Muscovites see only *faits accomplis* and the magical formula 'This has already been decided' cuts short any further discussion of the issue."[46]

Moscow was not the only threatened city. Many young people brought up in Russian towns in the 1950s and 1960s, with new buildings all around them after wartime destruction, had very little idea of the way the urban landscape had changed and knew nothing of old Russian architecture. In 1964 students from the Chemical-Technological Institute in Moscow made a bus trip to Pereiaslavl, Rostov, and Uglich, centers of medieval church architecture. They were so surprised and impressed by what they saw that they met with Baranovskii and began to organize *subbotniki*—a Communist practice of donating unpaid labor to society— cleaning up the sites of old buildings, such as the Krutitskoe Podvore (headquarters of the Moscow Patriarchate). They set up a club, Rodina, dedicated to the preservation of old buildings. Its board of trustees *(obshchestvennyi sovet)* included leading Russian writers, such as Leonid Leonov and Vladimir Soloukhin, as well as Komsomol officials.[47]

In July 1965 the RSFSR (*not* the Soviet) Council of Ministers announced that it was sponsoring an organization to promote preservation, VOOPIK, the All-Russian Society for the Preservation of Historical and Cultural Monuments. Its foundation undoubtedly reflected growing concern about the destruction of old buildings, especially old churches, which was still going on at the time. VOOPIK became what in Britain might be called a "quango"; that is, though legally a nongovernmental organization, it was actually staffed largely by senior RSFSR officials. Its huge membership numbers—seven million by 1972, fifteen million by 1985—suggested not that its main strength was enthusiastic volunteers, but that it was a front organization like the Soviet Peace Committee. Probably it represented a bid by the RSFSR government to strengthen its position in the Soviet hierarchy by drawing on widespread Russian national feeling and outrage at the destruction of old buildings.[48]

This is not the whole story, though. The society promoted tourism in what became known as the "golden ring" of old Russian towns to the north and east of Moscow; it published brochures and guidebooks to make old buildings and sites of memory more accessible to ordinary people. It sponsored the revival of folksongs and folk dancing and the celebration of significant Russian dates, such as the 600th anniversary of the Battle of Kulikovo in 1980. It fought battles in public over the threatened demolition of more old buildings. Reportedly, for example, it had a sausage factory ejected from a monastery in Smolensk and compelled the Kalinin town soviet to make good damage it had caused to two old houses. It mobilized students to carry out voluntary restoration work at the monastery of St. Kirill of Belozersk and at Solovki.[49]

The headquarters of VOOPIK, in the dilapidated but still habitable Petrovskii Monastery in Moscow, hosted weekly meetings of what became known as the "Russian Club," usually chaired by either the literary critic Petr Palievskii or the historian Sergei Semanov. Here, at first cautiously, but with increasing boldness, participants raised questions about religious art, the physical condition of Russian churches, non-Marxist Russian philosophy, Zionism, and the state of Israel. For those involved it was a course of self-education in Russian national culture. Many of these themes were taken up, more cautiously, in the pages of journals such as *Molodaia gvardiia* and *Nash Sovremennik*.[50]

Young people were beginning to mobilize to resist the heedless exploitation of nature. One unexpected fruit of Khrushchev's experiment with the *druzhina*, or popular militia, was the creation of a student nature-protection service. High party-state officials were in the habit of building themselves country cottages in remote and beautiful locations, and inviting colleagues and guests to hunting parties to shoot animals, some of which were already endangered species. In some universities, including the Biological Faculty of Moscow University, student *druzhiny* were formed in the early 1960s. They would patrol stretches of country popular with hunters and check the papers of anyone found shooting. Those unauthorized they would denounce as poachers to their workplace.[51]

Attempts were made to initiate a gentler and more rational exploitation of the environment. Students of the Leningrad Forestry Academy, led by Sergei Shipunov, announced that they aimed to protect a tract of forest in the Altai containing many Siberian stone pine *(sibirskii kedr)* trees, and to undertake sustainable harvesting and marketing of their nuts, as well as timber and furs. This so-called Kedrograd experiment had the support of officials both from the RSFSR government and from the Altai region. All the same the students soon came up against loggers from the timber industry who simply wanted to fell large numbers of trees for their wood. The long struggle that ensued became a *cause célèbre*. The preservationists' principal champion in the national press was Vladimir Chivilikhin of *Komsomolskaia pravda*. At one stage Iurii Gagarin took up their cause and selected wood from the stone pine for the handle of the controls in his space module. By 1963 the project was making a profit from nuts, timber, sable, and squirrel fur. Nonetheless, in the end the students lost out to their rivals. The RSFSR Main Forest Administration sent loggers into their tract and forced the activists to relocate to a less favorable site.[52]

Chivilikhin was a Siberian, born in the coalmining region of Kuzbass, who studied at Moscow University. In his youth he was strongly influenced by Leonid Leonov's novel *Russian Forest (Russkii les)*, published in 1953, which warned against excessive exploitation of timber resources at a time when it was highly unfashionable to hint that Russia's resources might not be limitless. The fate of the Kedrograd project confirmed Chivilikhin's views and turned him into a convinced campaigner on environmental issues, which he raised frequently in the Komsomol over the next thirty years, as well as writing a regular series called *Memory* in the monthly journal *Nash sovremennik*.

For Chivilikhin protection of the environment was indissolubly linked with defense of the nation's cultural memory. He called the link "the ecology of culture": "The natural environment creates what, poetically, we call the soul of the people and in reality determines the salient characteristics of national culture. . . . The Russian character is impossible to imagine without expanses of forest." Like Solzhenitsyn, Chivilikhin viewed Siberia as containing the essence of Russia: it had not known foreign conquest and occupation; and its inhabitants, who had never lived as serfs, had on their own efforts and skills built a viable economy despite the severe climate. "Almost every summer I come down with an attack of 'Siberian longing' and travel to my homeland," Chivilikhin said, to the land of "strong characters and uncorrupted language."[53]

It is natural, then, that Chivilikhin was among the first to take up what became the most important environmental battle of the late Soviet decades, that concerning Lake Baikal. As the largest fresh-water lake in the world, Baikal was unquestionably a unique resource, the focus of an ecosystem containing fish and plants not found elsewhere in the world. By the early 1960s the lake was threatened by two developments: heedless timber felling near its shores and the planned construction of two factories to produce a special cellulose cord for aircraft tires. Scientists had already protested to the ministries involved, held conferences, and published open letters, but Chivilikhin was the first to seize the public imagination, with an article entitled "The Bright Eye of Siberia," published in April 1963. His article provoked a flood of letters from concerned readers, all of them echoing his alarm at what the planners had in mind. In the next few years he was joined by other writers, including Mikhail Sholokhov, who at the 23rd CPSU Congress in 1966 exclaimed: "Our descendants will not forgive us if we do not preserve this glorious lake, this sacred Baikal!" For the first time the country's best-known writers joined with its top scientists to launch a united and coordinated protest campaign.[54]

Formally the campaign was defeated. In 1966 the cellulose factories started production without the elaborate purification equipment that the campaigners wanted to see installed. But the defeat had remarkable consequences for Russian national identity. A well-informed public opinion had taken shape, even if initially over only one issue. It had identified a nodal point where the imperatives of maintaining great-power status clashed not only with environmental priorities but also with strongly held convictions about what it meant to be Russian. It was a warning that being Russian might sometimes mean being opposed to the Soviet Union, or at least to the policies of its leaders.

## Official Russian Nationalism

Both the human rights movement and the revival of Russian nationalism presented the top party leaders with an uncomfortable dilemma. They wanted to mobilize public opinion in support of the Soviet state and its drive to superpower status, and they wanted to retain the hierarchical and conservative society they had inherited from Stalin and rescued from Khrushchev. At the same time they regarded law as an instrument of the state, not as an autonomous value system. And they were aware that the uninhibited promotion of Russian traditional values—and even more, of Russian institutions—might tear the Soviet Union apart; it would certainly alienate both non-Russians within the USSR and world opinion outside it.

Accordingly the leaders adopted a compromise. They upheld Marxism-Leninism as the official ideology, but they tolerated simple-minded Russian imperial nationalism as a kind of "working ideology," a routine everyday outlook, especially in the armed forces and in the medium and lower levels of the apparatus. They appointed RSFSR obkom secretaries to many of the top posts in the Central Committee.[55] They gave preference to the RSFSR in budgetary allocations for military industry (most of which was in the RSFSR and Ukraine), subsidies for agriculture, and programs to rescue the economy of the non–black earth regions. They were not unswerving in their support for the various Russian nationalist groups, but for most of the period 1965–1985 they found it expedient to allow Russian nationalist journals high print-runs and to award their au-

thors lucrative contracts and state prizes. This is what the scholar Yitzhak
Brudny has called "the politics of inclusion," which was intended to give
Russian nationalists a real stake in the system without yielding fully to
their demands.[56]

The Russianists themselves wanted this unacknowledged "shadow" ideology to be converted into the official ideology of the Soviet state. In the
higher levels of the apparatus, the Russianist outlook had the strongest
support in the Komsomol. This was natural, since Komsomol members
were acutely aware that the official ideology was losing its power to act as
a magnet for the loyalty of young people. They also realized that, after the
"secret speech," the suppression of the Hungarian revolution, and even
more so after the crushing of the "Prague spring," Soviet Communism no
longer attracted the hopes of socialists throughout the world, as it had
once done. Isolation and demoralization threatened. The most obvious
way to combat them was to write off Western public opinion and promote the kind of Russian patriotism that had proved so effective during
the Second World War. Sergei Pavlov, Komsomol first secretary, complained at the December 1965 plenum of the Komsomol Central Committee of the "unpatriotic" nature of the youth journal *Iunost*. Other
speakers accused writers of undermining national morale if they dwelt on
the horrors of Stalin's labor camps or recalled the neglect of Soviet prisoners of war. The congress resolution warned of the dangers posed by Western media, which was attempting to undermine the morale of Soviet
youth by preaching "pacifism, abstract humanism . . . and peaceful co-ex-
istence in the realm of ideology." The resolution specifically resurrected
the Stalinist bogy of "groveling" *(nizkopoklonstvo)* and called for more effective patriotic propaganda and military training for young people.[57]

In terms of reaching the public, Pavlov's most important allies were in
the world of literature and publishing, notably the periodicals of the
RSFSR Writers' Union. The Komsomol monthly *Molodaia gvardiia*—its
name evoking the heroic Red Youth detachments of the revolution and
civil war—and its associated publishing house took the lead in promoting
the outlook articulated in the Komsomol resolution. Nineteen sixty-five
was a key year for them, since for the first time the anniversary of the victory in the Second World War, May 9, was celebrated as a public holiday. Pavlov hoped to use the occasion to encourage schoolchildren and
youth groups to visit the sites of victorious battles, to take care of graves,
to seek out documentation of the war and its heroes, and to take oral tes-

timony from former Red Army soldiers. At the highest level, Pavlov's groups found support from Politburo member Aleksandr Shelepin and from Aleksei Epishev, head of the army's Chief Political Administration. The *Molodaia Gvardiia* publishing house issued the memoirs of several W.W. II generals, sometimes ghost-written by its in-house editors.[58]

In the late 1960s in a series of articles the journal *Molodaia gvardiia*, under its editor Anatolii Nikonov, tried to construct a coherent Russian national identity that could underpin the status of the Soviet Union as a great power. Each month the journal ran a feature under the rubric "Preserve our Sacred Heritage" [*Beregite nashu sviatyniu*]. According to its contributors, what distinguished Russian culture was that it was rooted in the collective life of the ordinary people yet also exhibited lofty moral values and universal, all-human concerns which justified the USSR's engagement in international affairs. This argument portrayed Russian national pride as fully compatible with the national identity of the Soviet non-Russian peoples. Viktor Chalmaev remarked on a "deeply Russian characteristic: to sympathize with others' sufferings to the point of forgetting one's own. Today's Russian, who has borne much in his time, who participated actively in the struggle against fascism, cannot watch unconcernedly the sufferings of a distant Congolese. . . . After the destruction of fascism is it possible that evil and criminality are not eradicated from the world? That is the question the Soviet warrior-citizen asks himself when he hears about the atrocities of reaction in various parts of the planet."[59]

Some authors tried to bolster their moral claims in a different way, by evoking, not proletarian solidarity, but the Orthodox Church. They did so not by extolling religious belief or even the church as an institution—neither would have been acceptable to the censorship—but by portraying the church as part of the popular heritage, which should be protected. They protested against the continued neglect and destruction of church buildings, contending that church architecture, icons, and frescoes were fine examples of popular art and reflected mass protest against the ruling class's abuse of power. The writer Dmitrii Balashov commented that "in religious buildings the architect was able to express in an exalted and pure form the ideas of the unity of all the people, to reflect the people's spirit and character. . . . In the midst of a gloomy and cruel reality, the maestro could express ideals of justice, goodness, and humanism." The painter Ilia Glazunov wrote that Andrei Rublev's *Trinity* icon "reflected the collective traits of the Russian people during the epoch when Russians began to realize that victory comes to those who are united and morally exalted. . . . [It] will always remain as an appeal to eternal peace and to the brotherly unity of our nation."[60]

The writer Vladimir Soloukhin breached a long-standing taboo by condemning Stalin's destruction of the Cathedral of Christ the Savior, "the tallest and most majestic building in Moscow, visible from all over the city," built by Muscovites to commemorate the Russian people's great victory over Napoleon in 1812 and to give thanks for the survival of their city in spite of the great fire of that year. It had been blown up, Soloukhin pointed out sardonically, to build a swimming pool.[61]

The new Russian patriots praised Russia's continuing tradition of authoritarian statehood and military might: "For centuries the Russian people asserted and defended both Russia as a state and its own remarkable moral dignity, not by prayers, but with weapons, with the support of a painstakingly created, mighty, organized state and an integrated patriotic philosophy. . . . Sergii of Radonezh did not deny the warrior Dmitrii Donskoi, nor did Pushkin the state-builder Peter the First, nor Sergei Esenin the great revolutionary Lenin! That is the greatness of the Russian character, that it has been embodied in very different historical figures, from Avvakum to Chekhov, from Chaadaev to Kirov."[62]

Chalmaev took the opportunity to attack the Soviet Union's Other, the United States. Russian patriotism, he asserted, was quite different from the soulless international consumer culture prevalent in the West, the "patriotism of cars and refrigerators," accompanied by "standardization of ways of life, consumer items, work conditions, and the leveling of human character, the disintegration of religious, community, and family bonds," which turned the notion of the Homeland into an "overblown abstraction." He asserted that "money, which, as is well known, has no smell and no homeland, does not tolerate any feeling for homeland in those who fall under its domination."[63] Mikhail Lobanov warned that "many profound Russian minds have gone through the disease of wanting to replace Russia's spiritual and cultural distinctiveness, its unique national way of life, with a new 'Europeanized,' standardized Russia, like the countries of the West. Either Russia will be distinctive (samobytnoi) and give the world its own message, or it will be bourgeois and faceless on the Western model."[64] In this reading, the Soviet revolution was a logical development of earlier Russian history, not its negation.

Altogether, then, the Molodaia gvardiia writers now depicted Russia as an age-old great power, thanks to the church and the tsars; as a champion of all-human values, a nonmaterialist faith, and a social solidarity resting on long-established peasant institutions. Their message recalled Patriarch Aleksii's spirited defense of the church in 1960, and it was certainly a long way from the revolutionary, future-oriented, atheist, proletarian rhetoric with which the Soviet Union had launched itself on the world scene several decades earlier.[65]

These implications were picked up by *Novyi mir,* which became the main opposition forum to the new Russian nationalism. In one article *Novyi mir* editor Aleksandr Demeniev accused Chalmaev of speaking the language of "Slavophile messianism," of admiring not Russia's revolutionary traditions but, on the contrary, the conservative, patriarchal, and mystical ones. He was rehabilitating Orthodox obscurantism, racism, and Stalinism. The struggle against the West was not national, Dementiev maintained, but socioeconomic, in fact a class struggle. The CPSU program "requires us to conduct a resolute struggle against any kind of nationalism and chauvinism," Dementiev reminded his opponent.[66]

Soon Dementiev's article itself came under attack for undermining Soviet security by weakening vigilance against Western "bourgeois" ideas. In an unprecedented display of "Russianist" solidarity, eleven writers and editors wrote a letter to the weekly journal *Ogonek* attacking *Novyi mir.* In February 1970 the Soviet Writers' Union accepted their protest and dismissed most of Tvardovskii's colleagues on the editorial board of *Novyi mir.* With his own position thus made intolerable, Tvardovskii himself resigned. Ironically, his journal had suffered, not for its oppositional stance, but for an article defending party orthodoxy. A few months later, as if to balance his removal, the Soviet Writers' Union also dismissed Anatolii Nikonov.[67] The Central Committee of the CPSU was reserving for itself the right to determine the doses of Russian nationalism to be administered to the sick Soviet patient.

Thereafter, until the early 1980s, Russian nationalism was preached in a less systematic, more fragmentary way, both in official journals and more outspokenly in samizdat outlets such as *Veche,* which appeared sporadically and was distributed through the mail between 1971 and 1974. *Veche* voiced Russians' widely shared concern about growing crime, alcoholism, individualism, the instability of the family, and a low birth rate. Its line was that the Russian people needed to rediscover their traditional collective morality by returning to Orthodox Christianity.[68]

Solzhenitsyn made his own idiosyncratic contribution to the debate. His "Letter to the Leaders of the Soviet Union" of 1973 also pleaded for a revival of Russian national values, but unlike the *Molodaia gvardiia* authors he argued that class struggle and international revolution did not strengthen those values but undermined them. He urged the Soviet leaders to abandon their ideology, because it had inflicted on Russia such enormous damage: its collectivized agriculture was unproductive, its air and water were polluted, its industry had become gigantomanic and perverted for military needs, its schools drummed empty ideological slogans into bored children, and its cities had lost their old two-story buildings and green spaces in favor of soulless modern concrete boxes in which people lived cooped up on top of one another. Depressed and demoralized, men had become drunkards, drawing on the one consumer item regularly available in the shops, while women performed unfeminine and degrading manual labor and had no time for their children. Solzhenitsyn attributed all these evils to the One True Ideology, which ignored genuine national interests in favor of invented international ones; altogether, so he claimed, it had cost Russia the lives of sixty-six million people. Russia was not ready for Western-style democracy, so the soviets, he thought, might be kept, but as the backbone of a system in which people could influence their own fate, not as the bearers of party dictatorship.[69]

If Russia was to recover, then in Solzhenitsyn's view it must renounce all international ambitions and stop financing revolutionary parties all over the world. It must also avoid the Western illusion of endless material progress taken over lock, stock, and barrel by Marxism. Instead Russians should devote themselves to creating a sustainable nongrowing economy by developing the one resource they still had in unspoiled abundance, land. They should open up the vast spaces of their northeast, of Siberia, which Solzhenitsyn described in a vivid if inelegant image as "our hope and our settling tank," the territory where the material and spiritual pollution of life under the Ideology might be cleansed and national convalescence initiated.[70]

Solzhenitsyn was far from being a typical Russian nationalist. The great virtue of his exposé was that it distinguished, as no one else had, between the Russian people and the Russian-Soviet state. His Russianist critics failed to see the distinction between *russkii* and *rossiiskii;* they were assuming that Russian national feeling automatically takes imperial forms and has the right to do so. Russian liberals also ignored the distinction: they simply assumed that the values they espoused were universal, and they were largely uninterested in ethnic characteristics. Solzhenitsyn's vision here was clearer, but he could also be accused of the opposite failing, of not acknowledging that Russian national feeling, even though distinct from Russian imperialism, is indeed attracted by universal "missionary" ideals and therefore does tend to assume the right to hegemony over other nations. Socialism may have come to Russia from the West, but messianic socialism is a distinctively Russian version of it.

## Official Westernizers

Russian nationalists did not have everything their own way at the party's highest level. Liberal and Westernizing tendencies also had their defenders, under the cautious patronage of Iurii Andropov, head of the KGB. They were especially strong in the International Department of the CPSU Central Committee, which was a kind of successor to the Comintern and hence to the party's internationalist traditions. The department's function was to advise the Soviet leaders on events abroad and to liaise with non-Soviet Communist parties. The working atmosphere that prevailed there was different from that of most Central Committee departments, and by some officials it was regarded with suspicion as a "white crow." Its members were genuine professionals, people who had worked hard to study the languages and cultures of the countries for which they were responsible. They were widely read, had seen a great deal of the modern world, and knew a lot of people outside the USSR. They were "cosmopolitans" in the best sense of that misused word. They valued the Soviet Union's great-power status—without which most of them would have been without a job—but they were not thoughtless chauvinists. They knew that capitalism, in its revised Keynesian variant, had improved workers' living standards more effectively than the Soviet planned economy. Many of them favored some kind of evolution toward European social democracy or even liberalism. Others merely wanted a gradual and gentle reformism within the Soviet mold, and they regarded Russian nationalism with concern because they associated it with Stalin: this was Andropov's own position.[71]

The approach of the International Department received strong and well-informed backing from the Central Committee's policy studies think tanks, such as the Institute for the Study of the United States and Canada, run for many years by Georgii Arbatov, and the Institute of the World Economy and International Relations (IMEMO), under N. N. Inozemtsev and from 1983 Aleksandr Iakovlev. In 1981 Mikhail Suslov was sufficiently worried by the "subversive" advice coming out of these think-tanks to propose closing IMEMO, but he was outvoted in the Politburo. The cosmopolitan eggheads had their value for the leaders, both for their expertise and for the ammunition they provided in the ideological battle against China.[72]

For twenty years, then, from the mid-1960s to the mid-1980s, there was a tense stand-off, both among the Soviet leaders and also among the unofficial intelligentsia, over the path that the Soviet Union should take to renew its ideological appeal and improve the effectiveness of its social and economic system. Marxism-Leninism was still unchallenged as the official ideology, but it was beginning to split into its Russian and Western components. One current of thought wanted to attach the Soviet Union more securely to the Russian statist tradition, the other to return to the West European roots of Marxism and rediscover the main road from which Stalin—or, some whispered, Lenin—had gone astray. Gorbachev's perestroika represented a final, brief surge of this Westernized Marxism, combined with missionary Communism returning to first base: humanism (all-human values), the Enlightenment, the "all-European home."[73]

The conflict was serious, but the front lines were never clear and unambiguous. The issues were complex, as we have seen, and individuals wavered in their interpretation of them, aligning themselves with different individuals and groups according to the subtleties of each contentious issue.

## Lev Gumilev and the Eurasianists

Russianists' ideas received a new impetus in the early 1980s. It stemmed indirectly from the émigré movement of the Eurasianists, as extended and reinterpreted by Lev Gumilev, the son of Anna Akhmatova. He had spent many years in the labor camps, where he had met the last survivor of the Eurasianists, Petr Savitskii, and afterward conducted a long correspondence with him. Gumilev's ideas on ethnic identity generally and on the fate of Russia in particular provoked strong disagreement among official ethnographers, and his work remained largely unpublished. All the same, he managed eventually to defend and deposit his thesis in Leningrad.[74]

Gumilev believed that the driving force in human history was "ethnogenesis," the rise and decline of peoples, which he saw as determined partly by geography, landscape, and climate, partly by the forces of the cosmos and the biosphere (here he drew on the ideas of Vladimir Vernadskii), and partly by the leadership of "passionary" *(passionarnye)* personalities, imbued with great energy and determination to achieve collective goals. Neighboring ethnoses sometimes combined to form a "superethnos," and when this happened a whole epoch of world civilization was launched. But ethnoses from wholly different backgrounds or, as Gumilev put it, from different "galaxies," should not try to mix, for the result would be destructive wars. This had happened in the thirteenth century, when Catholic and Orthodox Christians had tried to combine against the Saracens, but found they were incompatible and fought each other instead.[75]

Applying his theory to Russia, Gumilev asserted that it was one of the world's great superethnoses, wholly different from Western Europe and North America. Of course, in a sense this idea was familiar from the nineteenth-century Slavophiles. But Gumilev made his claim in a far more radical sense than they. Russia, he contended, was "Eurasian," that is, it derived its way of life from the nomads of the Eurasian steppes, and from the Finno-Ugrian and Turkic peoples, a statement that would have horrified the Slavophiles—and indeed horrified more conventional Russian nationalists.[76] The Russian Empire and the Soviet Union were the heirs of the great medieval empire of the Mongols. Its superethnos was characterized, according to Gumilev, by a collective ethos, religious tolerance, nondestructive use of the environment, and acceptance of authoritarian rule. Gumilev drew from his claims the lesson that Russians should not try to adopt forms of life derived from Western Europe or North America, where the dominant ethic was individualist and politics were constitutional and parliamentary. Any attempt to do so would be disastrous.[77]

In the 1970s Gumilev was unable to publish his ideas in social science journals, but he found an outlet in geographical and natural science publications at Leningrad University. His articles circulated unofficially among scholars during the 1970s, and exerted such influence that in 1974 the prominent ethnologist V. I. Kozlov issued a rebuttal, claiming that Gumilev's theories "impeded a true scientific understanding" of ethnic development, discouraged interethnic contact, failed to explain the "emergence of a new historical community, the Soviet people," and "justified cruel conquests and bloody interethnic conflicts."[78]

The idea that Russia was a distinct Eurasian superethnos assumed a new importance in the final decade of the Soviet Union, as its internal crisis became ever sharper. The deputy editor of *Nash sovremennik,* Iurii Seleznev, an expert on Dostoevskii, took the initiative in propagating the idea when he was responsible for a special number of the journal that appeared in November 1981.

The most important article in the issue was by the literary critic Vadim Kozhinov. He denied that Russia's culture came mainly from the West and quoted Dostoevskii's view of Russia as "all-human." "The genius of the Russian soul is perhaps more capable than any other nation of assimilating the idea of all-human unity.," he said. "A Russian understands equally well the social pathos of the Frenchman, the practical activity of the Englishman, the misty philosophy of the German." Russia, Kozhinov asserted, should not simply take over Western social structures or cultural attitudes. Most important, Russia was multinational and devoid of the national egoism that disfigured European peoples and led them to exploit other cultures, treating them as objects. Hence the extra spiritual dimension in Russian literature; hence also Russians' enhanced capacity to adopt Bakhtin's "aesthetic of the dialogue."[79]

Kozhinov called for a reassessment of the Russian attitude to Asia, something Dostoevskii had pointed toward in his later writings. Hitherto virtually all Russian intellectuals had simply mimicked the European arrogance toward Asia. In actual fact, compared with Europeans, Asians had a superior capacity for tolerance and mutual understanding, which enabled Russians to interact fruitfully with them. Here Kozhinov quoted with approval the work of Lev Gumilev, and he drew on his scholarship to reinterpret the battle of Kulikovo (the great stem battle of the Russians) as a struggle not against the Tatars but against a cosmopolitan slave-owning plutocracy with its center in Genoa, which happened at that time to be allied with the Tatar breakaway, Mamai.[80]

Kozhinov's conception was a kind of "Occidentalism" (that is, the converse of Edward Said's "Orientalism"). He was laying the groundwork for a new geopolitical conception which was to assume greater importance with the collapse of the Soviet Union: that Russia should seek its future not in a bloc with the West, which was bound to exploit and undermine it, but rather as a Eurasian power.

The mathematician Igor Shafarevich, widely read in samizdat in the 1980s, sculpted the most fully crafted "enemy image" against which Russians could define themselves. He asserted that socialism was a dangerous mirage which had tempted human beings throughout history, but had always proved in practice to entrench the absolute power of a small elite.[81] In recent centuries of European history he identified this tendency with a "minor people" *(malyi narod)* whose purpose was to undermine and destroy established ways of life. As examples he pointed to the Calvinists in seventeenth-century England, to the Jacobins in the French revolution, and to the left Hegelians in 1840s Germany. The natural habitat of such people was clubs, academies, and masonic lodges. They rejected the prevailing norms and traditions of the society in which they lived, its religion, its monarchy, its folk customs, in favor of abstract ideas about society that they had dreamed up in their studies. They infiltrated institutions or seized power by violence in order to put their ideas into practice, displaying nothing but contempt for the outlook of ordinary people and those who loved their nation's inherited way of life.[82]

Today's "minor people" Shafarevich identified directly with the Jews, and he accused them of deliberately spreading "Russophobia," of painting Russians as a servile people addicted to tyranny: "Almost foaming at the mouth they demonstrate to us that Western democracy is absolutely alien to the spirit and history of our people, and in the same breath insist just as forcefully that we should adopt that very political system." They got excited about human rights—but "the fate of the Crimean Tatars attracts much more attention than that of the Ukrainians, and the fate of the Ukrainians far more than that of the Russians." Jews did not wish to share the fate of a people they considered "servile," but instead demanded the right of emigration "to a distant tropical country . . . to which they are attracted, not by the icons to which their fathers and grandfathers used to pray, but by a Temple destroyed almost two thousand years ago!" Their real aim was "the complete destruction of the religious and national principles of life," as a result of which the Russian people would cease to exist.[83]

By the mid-1980s, then, Russianists were developing their own distinct ideology. Their reformulated nationalism taught that the great conflicts in world history were not socioeconomic but ethnic; that Russia had its own distinct role to play as a superethnos with its own collectivist mentality and authoritarian politics, exemplified by both the tsarist and the Soviet states; and that Russia should not attempt to follow Western precepts in solving its current crisis.

# 11

# AN UNANTICIPATED CREATION: THE RUSSIAN FEDERATION

Paradoxical though it may seem, it was Russia that destroyed the Soviet Union. In the words of one political scientist, "What distinguishes the terminal phase of the Soviet empire from most of its [twentieth-century] counterparts was the remarkable and quite rapid transformation of Russian national identity from imperial to separatist."[1] That outcome is all the more remarkable in that few Russians, of whatever persuasion, intended it. Rather, Russia's anomalous and unsatisfactory status within the Soviet Union had never been solved, and, when a serious crisis developed, that anomaly became ever more serious and began to dictate the political struggle.

The begetter of that crisis was Mikhail Gorbachev. The program of perestroika and glasnost that he launched soon after becoming CPSU general secretary in 1985 presented all Russians with a new and unfamiliar situation which challenged many of their habitual assumptions and with which they were ill equipped to cope. Perestroika legalized private firms, including those that had long flourished on the black market. Their newfound freedom of operation enabled them to outperform state firms, sucking goods out of the state sector of the economy, on which most ordinary people still relied. As a Saratov worker complained to *Pravda,* "In the shops everything has vanished, but in the private markets there is more and more. How does it get there? You have to pay 250 to 300 rubles for a pair of women's boots. My daughter needs some, but she earns only 115 rubles a month."[2] The mechanisms of blat and patronage, which had enabled most employees to keep their heads above water, began to unravel, threatening their subsistence. The cozy if claustrophobic "communes" of late Soviet Russia could not survive in a market economy.

The market was not only in commodities. Glasnost created for the first time an incipient free market in public ideas and initiatives. In 1986 the RSFSR Ministry of Justice issued a set of "Regulations on Amateur Associations," which made it possible for people to open clubs or societies without applying for official sanction, merely by following the rules. Up to then, even a stamp-collectors' club had required permission, so this was a major new departure. A variety of *neformaly*, or informal clubs, movements, and associations, sprang up in the major cities, mostly in the fields of culture, sport, and hobbies. A few, however, had civic implications, like the Leningrad group that campaigned to save the Hotel Angleterre, an old building where the much-loved Russian poet Sergei Esenin had committed suicide. In Moscow the residents of the outsize high-rise Brateevo estate banded together to protest the construction of a toxic heavy industrial plant opposite their front doors, and in the process took over much of the day-to-day running of their estate.[3]

Most members of such associations were young people under thirty, and they drew on the experience of unofficial youth movements: they were lively, casual, disorganized, and often relied on the inspiration and energy of one person. The participants were not dissidents or human rights activists, but they did want to carve out some social field in which they could exercise initiative. Some of them were sponsored by local soviets or Komsomol organizations that welcomed public support or wanted to pursue certain local aims. As political pressures eased, civic associations began to seek one another out, exchanging correspondence, or meeting in conferences to swap ideas and plan wider activities. One such association representing twelve cities met in Moscow in August 1987.[4]

Many students and scholars were eager to use their special knowledge to discuss serious social issues and then do something effective about them. Discussions held in 1987 on the new economic reforms at the Central Economic-Mathematical Institute in Moscow led to the creation of specialized action groups, for instance, to protect legal rights or to tackle environmental problems.[5]

One of these groups proved especially significant. "Memorial" began life as a petition campaign calling for a monument to be erected to Stalin's victims. The demand was a shrewd and well-conceived one. It was permissible from the party viewpoint, since Khrushchev's condemnation of the "cult of personality" had never been explicitly revoked; the idea of a monument was in fact approved by a CPSU conference in the summer of 1988. Yet the monument campaign also spoke to the profound feelings of numerous Soviet citizens who wanted social memory to be restored and their suffering and grief over loved ones acknowledged in a dignified manner. In November 1988 Memorial held a "week of conscience." A "wall of memory" was constructed, exhibiting photographs of those arrested under Stalin. People peered intently at it, seeking out relatives they had lost, and leaving notes of the kind, "Does anyone know my father?"[6]

Memorial was an umbrella movement, the first receptacle for the long unexpressed hopes and fears of Soviet citizens from a great variety of backgrounds. Its significance reflected the crucial importance of suppressed memory for both Russians and non-Russians. The movement had to take on an almost insupportable diversity of functions. One of the founders, the historian Iurii Afanasiev, summed up its meaning at the initial conference:

> The most important task of Memorial is to restore to this country its past. But the past is alive in the present. Therefore Memorial is a political movement, insofar as today has not yet settled accounts with yesterday. Our problem is the human being in history. But for us history is not just politics projected into the past, for man's historical habitat is culture. Therefore Memorial is also a cultural movement. By talking about terror and lawlessness, we help to form a notion of legality in the public mind. Therefore Memorial is also a movement concerned with the rule of law *(pravovoe dvizhenie)*.[7]

Memorial also promoted networks where none had existed before. It brought together for the first time young "informals" with former dissidents and human rights activists, as well as with leading figures from the Academy of Sciences and the cultural world: its Public Council, elected by popular vote on the street, included Sakharov and Solzhenitsyn, the writers Evgenii Evtushenko and Bulat Okudzhava, the literary scholar Dmitrii Likhachev, the actor Mikhail Ulianov (famous for his portrayal of his namesake, Lenin), and Boris Yeltsin, recently expelled from the CPSU Politburo for demanding more radical reform. An alliance of such figures would have been inconceivable up to a year earlier. From Memorial's success came the confidence that it was possible to organize outside the party, even on occasions against it, with the support of prestigious personalities.[8]

This confidence in turn helped to generate genuine political debate over issues and personalities. Political influence now emanated not only from the hushed and discreet cabinets of Staraia Ploshchad, but also from noisy public meeting halls, on television, and in electoral campaigns which were becoming increasingly frank and heated. The "democrats" created informal campaigning movements and "popular fronts to support perestroika" which caught the public's imagination and effectively contested the Communist Party's political monopoly under a slogan it had itself approved. Young people were taking to the streets with slogans and banners not decorously fashioned in the local party bureaus but in boisterous public meetings.

In Iaroslavl, for example, a popular front was formed at a public meeting in June 1988 to protest the automatic dispatch of the long-standing oblast first secretary, F. I. Loshchenkov, to the 19th Party Conference, without any consultation with ordinary party members. This had been normal procedure for decades, but Loshchenkov was unpopular because he had backed the construction of a chemical works in the town. The Popular Front meeting demanded his recall and open, unrigged elections for a successor. In the long run, using the weapons of glasnost, they were successful. They moved on from their victory to hold meetings in the soccer stadium and agitate on other local issues, including the abolition of privileged stores for the nomenklatura elite, a grievance that had never been publicly aired before. It was not officially acceptable even now. The editor of the local party newspaper refused to publish their materials, falling back on familiar authority mechanisms: "I answer to the party. If they tell me to publish this, I will. But they haven't, so I won't."[9]

The party's defense mechanisms no longer worked automatically, however. In the March 1989 elections to the new Congress of People's Deputies, the popular fronts did manage to score sensational victories over apparatus nominees in a few constituencies. Their greatest success was the election of Boris Yeltsin in Moscow. In a situation of rapid political change, a key figure is one who breaks away from a dominant elite in order to stand up for that elite's own traduced values. That was what Yeltsin had done. He had made his name by speaking out publicly against the privileged and corrupt life-style of the nomenklatura hierarchs—the very grievance that the public most resented—and he had been thrown out of the Politburo for his impatience and forthrightness. With his electoral success in March 1989 he became a popular tribune, a spokesman for the many long-suppressed—and not always compatible—aspirations of the Russian people.

Alarmingly for Russians, the opening up of politics was proceeding faster in some of the non-Russian republics, especially the Baltics and Georgia, where opposition candidates swept the field. In Moldavia, too, and a little later Ukraine, "popular fronts" with various names demanded greater autonomy for the titular peoples and sometimes turned upon Russians as "occupiers," "aliens," or "immigrants." Russians, who had long felt themselves increasingly marginalized in everyday life and in economic exchanges, now found political agitation directed against them as well.

The First Congress of People's Deputies, held in May-June 1989, transformed the political situation. It was televised live in its entirety, and something like three-quarters of the urban population stayed home to watch it. What they saw amounted to a crash course in Soviet political reality. Deputies openly questioned whether Marx's hundred-year-old writings were still relevant, attacked the KGB for "crimes unknown in the history of humanity," called for an end to the Communist Party monopoly, and demanded that Lenin be removed from the mausoleum. Many had individual horror stories to tell to illustrate their accusations.[10] When the congress was over, few Soviet citizens can have had many illusions about the system under which they had lived for seventy years. But in many ways the revelations were too diverse and too overwhelming: it was difficult to disentangle from them coherent proposals about what should be done, especially since the economic situation was fast deteriorating and seemed to require emergency solutions. Most people entrenched themselves in the political attitudes that had been forming gradually over the previous decades. Among Russians there were broadly three tendencies: Western liberal-democrat, Russianist imperial, and labor-based economic—the last being the reaction of Russian workers to their long exploitation by the apparatus and the military-industrial complex. Much depended on what allies this third tendency would seek.[11]

There was another problem too. The congress offered a forum for the first outbreaks of publicly expressed ethnic hatred. Russians were horrified to discover that the oppression they attributed to Communism was identified by Balts, Georgians, and Armenians as being the result of Russian arrogance. Their attacks provoked the writer Valentin Rasputin to comment sardonically, "Perhaps it is Russia that should secede from the Union, since you accuse her of all your misfortunes and since her backwardness and awkwardness obstruct your progressive aspirations? . . . We could then pronounce the word 'Russian' without fear of being rebuked for nationalism, we could talk openly about our national identity. We could set up at last our own Academy of Sciences. . . . Believe me, we're fed up with being scapegoats, with being mocked and spat upon."[12] Rasputin's sour witticism was probably intended ironically, but it highlighted Russia's anomalous position in a country where ethnic identity had become paramount. Many a true word is spoken in jest.

In order to offer a constructive alternative to interethnic quarrels and to reaffirm the joint struggle against the Communist apparatus, Yeltsin gathered around himself an "Interregional Group of Deputies," consisting of both Russians and non-Russians, committed to "the transition of the country from totalitarianism to democracy," and to "the economic independence of the republics and regions."[13] These rather vague aspirations implied that the non-Russian nationalities should be able to determine their own future, if they wished outside the USSR. In this way Russian liberals, for tactical reasons, become allied with movements whose implicit—soon explicit—aim was the break-up of the USSR.

The first mass association of Russian liberals was Democratic Russia. It was hastily patched together in January 1990 from a large number of informal movements in order to organize a political campaign for the non-party candidates in the republican Soviet elections due in March. Symptomatically, it did not succeed in holding a founding congress till much later. Democratic Russia never ceased to be a loose patchwork of personalized political groups with vague, ambitious, and partly contradictory aims, held together by little more than anti-Communism. The movement aimed to propagate "the ideas of Andrei Sakharov" (who had just died), meaning a commitment to "liberty, democracy, the rights of man, a multi-party system, free elections and a market economy." The movement's most obvious political model was Polish Solidarity of ten years earlier, a movement of anti-Communist national revival. Among Democratic Russia's specific goals were the ending of the party political monopoly, the subjection of the KGB to parliamentary supervision, the creation of a "regulated market economy," and the declaration of sovereignty for the RSFSR.[14] But Russia was a very different political entity from Poland.

Sovereignty of the RSFSR was a key demand. It was borrowed from the

Russianists and indirectly from the Baltic popular fronts. It is not clear how seriously anyone took the idea at this stage, or even if people understood what it implied. Sakharov, and all Russian liberals hitherto, had always assumed that the reforms they envisaged would apply to the USSR as a whole. They had never considered ethnic identity important and had not grappled seriously with the national question. The two words "Democratic" and "Russia" had hardly ever been used together before, and it took people some time to realize that when inscribed together on a banner, they implied the dissolution of the Soviet Union, which was neither democratic nor Russia.

The liberals performed extraordinarily well in the republican soviet elections of March 1990. They took control of Moscow, Leningrad, and a number of other large Russian industrial cities, defeating party nominees and installing their own chairmen in the municipal councils. However, they did not do well enough to outnumber the party-nominated candidates in the RSFSR Supreme Soviet, the people whom Iurii Afanasiev in another context called "the aggressively silent majority." In the attempt to complete the job and end Communist Party rule, the liberals took two important steps: they tightened their alliance with Yeltsin, and they pressed the slogan of "Russian sovereignty" into service as a political weapon.

### Russianists

Unlike their liberal counterparts, who were spontaneously united by informal sociability and by their dislike of Communism, the Russianists were slow to mobilize and combine, partly because they were accustomed to protection from above and partly because they came from contradictory backgrounds. How could people who had in their homes portraits of Nicholas II and his reforming prime minister, Petr Stolypin, ally themselves with those whose portraits were of Marx and Lenin? How were Vasilii Belov or Valentin Rasputin, who in their novels had outspokenly and vividly condemned Stalin's collectivization of agriculture, to find common ground with neo-Stalinists like Egor Ligachev or military enthusiasts like Aleksandr Prokhanov, sometimes known as the "nightingale of the General Staff" for his paeans to the Soviet war effort in Afghanistan? And how could the Stalinists embrace the prelates of the Russian Orthodox Church, which their hero had spent much of his life trying to destroy?

Nevertheless, those who believed in "Russia"—whatever they meant by it—did in the end contrive a kind of cooperation for one simple reason: they discovered that the dangers facing all of them together were more serious than the issues which had divided them. During the autumn and winter of 1989–1990 political developments challenged everything they held dear. The fall of the Berlin Wall, the winding-up of Comecon and the Warsaw Pact, and the collapse of Communist governments brought the "outer empire" to an end and threatened the "inner empire" too. Germany, the ancient enemy, long divided and held down, was on the way to being reunited. In February 1990 the Communist Party of the Soviet Union surrendered its political monopoly, leaving the way open for even more fiercely contested elections and the "politics of the street" to become universal. In March 1990 Lithuania declared its secession from the USSR; Latvia and Estonia announced their intention to follow suit.

Russianists realized that what they faced was the disintegration of the Soviet Union—and hence, as they all understood it, of Russia. In the Russian writers' newspaper *Literaturnaia Rossiia*, Aleksandr Prokhanov drew a terrifying picture of the collapse of the Soviet state, which he contended would lead to a civil war, conducted "with all the ruthlessness of the last war, compounded by new nightmarish components added by military-technological civilization." He predicted that "the world will look with horror at our blood-torn expanses, belching nuclear and chemical fumes into the atmosphere and the oceans," and would intervene to try to stabilize the situation.[15]

Less apocalyptic but still threatening was the specter of Westernization, which some Russianists considered almost as destructive as war. The incursion of pop music, pornography, mass culture, a sensationalist media, and a market economy oriented toward the maximization of profit seemed to them to undermine the whole Russian way of life. Writers were the first to sound the alarm, at the USSR Writers' Union Congress of April 1987. Vladimir Krupin, editor of the journal *Moskva*, declared that "Elvis Presley, soft rock, then hard rock, then punk rock—these are all species of narcotics." Iurii Bondarev, a prominent war novelist, drew on his wartime memories to dramatize his point: "I would define the present situation in Russian literature as that of July 1941 . . . when the progressive forces, showing unorganized resistance, retreated before the battering onslaught of civilized barbarians . . . If this retreat should continue and the time of Stalingrad not come, then it will end with our national values and everything that represents the spiritual pride of our people being toppled into the abyss."[16]

Some Russianists began to perceive that their long, tacit alliance with the Soviet authorities was now actually a source of weakness. The Fellowship of Russian Artists, formed in autumn 1988, said in its founding document, "It has become common to identify the will of the administrative-bureaucratic apparatus with the view of the Russian people, whereas it is precisely Russia that is in the most critical position, close to collapse. And the collapse of Russia will inevitably lead to the loss of the unity of the political and state system of the whole country."[17]

The first constituency the Russianists attempted to mobilize was the industrial workers. This strategy reflected the dominance of Russians in industry throughout the USSR, especially in the military-industrial complex and in enterprises of all-Union significance; and it spoke to Russian workers' sense of grievance over their lowly social status in some of the non-Russian republics. The creation of workers' protest movements began in the Baltic republics in the winter of 1988–1989: Interfront in Latvia, Interdvizhenie and the Council of Labor Collectives in Estonia, Edinstvo (Unity) in Lithuania. Significantly, their names reflected internationalist aspirations, not ethnic ones: at this stage Russianists still saw themselves as speaking for the entire Soviet population. They protested against the Baltic governments' plans to restrict immigration and to institute language tests which, they claimed, would discriminate against Russians and threaten the integrity of the Soviet Union as a whole. In March 1989 some fifty thousand workers marched through Tallinn, carrying banners warning of "creeping counter-revolution undermining socialism in Estonia" and demanding: "Give Russian the status of an official language."[18]

In July 1989 a United Workers' Front was founded in Leningrad, and it held its first congress in Sverdlovsk in September. Anatolii Salutskii, a journalist from *Literaturnaia Rossiia,* warned that for all their internationalism Russians would now have to defend their own interests: "The Russian people has shown in deeds its unbending adherence to socialist internationalism. But this does not contradict a Russian's considering it his patriotic duty to do everything possible to strengthen the economic life of Russia and bring about a rebirth of her historical and cultural values."[19]

However, even industrial workers turned out to be unreliable allies for the Russianists. Most of them did not want the electoral process to be squeezed back into the party cabinets. The most serious expression of working-class militancy was the wave of strikes in the coal-mining industry in the summer of 1989. Though many participants were Russians living in non-Russian republics (Ukraine, Kazakhstan), the strikes were directed not against the local non-Russian peoples but against the party-state apparatus, which condemned miners to low pay, squalid and dangerous working conditions, cramped housing, and uncertain food supplies. The strikers actually favored Gorbachev's reforms but wanted them taken further. They called for an end to the party's political monopoly and for the right to emancipate their mines from the dictates of Gosplan, as well as to sell their coal on the open market.[20] The strikes fizzled out, though, since in the era of economic reform the miners were even more dependent on their employers than they had been earlier.

The first political organization to articulate the Russianist approach for a broader constituency was the United Council of Russia (*Obedinennyi sovet Rossii*), founded in September 1989. Among its constituent members were cultural societies, environmental associations, military-patriotic organizations, workers' fronts from Russian cities, and "international fronts" from the Baltic republics and Moldavia. The council also received advice and administrative support from local CPSU committees; this was the moment when Communists stopped regarding Russian nationalists as raw material to be exploited instrumentally and started to accept them as allies.[21] The council's principal aims were to preserve the "state sovereignty of the USSR as a voluntary union of republics" and to "assist the development of the sovereignty of the RSFSR and its international status as a full member of the United Nations." These two goals were potentially contradictory: as both Lenin and Stalin had seen, the achievement of the latter would lethally weaken the former. However, the demand for Russian sovereignty sounded patriotically Russian, and it reflected the popularity of democratic political movements at the time. It was fateful, as it was soon taken over by Yeltsin and used against the Russianists.

During the winter of 1989–1990 the United Council of Russia drew under its wing a bloc of other Russianist organizations including VOOPIK, the United Workers' Front, the Association of Russian Artists, and the All-Russian Cultural Fund. Together they launched a "Patriotic Bloc" manifesto ready for the republican soviet elections of March 1990. It warned of the destruction of "established administrative and economic structures" and their replacement by "an uncontrolled market mechanism." It reproached the CPSU for adopting an approach of compliant passivity in the face of these dangers, "progressively yielding to a bloc of separatists and 'left radicals' who are ready to dismember the USSR and to sell out our national wealth to Western 'partners.'" As a countermeasure the bloc recommended that Russia demand its full rights as a member of the Soviet Union and create its own system of economic administration and its own Russian Communist Party, followed by a separate Russian Academy of Sciences, which would work out a specifically Russian economic development program. Russia would stop making payments into the Union budget to subsidize other republics and would demand rent from all-Union institutions that wished to locate on Russian territory.[22]

Coming from people who insisted on the unity of the USSR, this program was a breathtaking departure. It was also contradictory: it aimed to strengthen the Soviet Union, yet it withdrew the Russian leadership and financial support that made that Union possible. It reflected the frustration and alarm of Russians who saw their primacy in the USSR challenged and who were faced with the possibility of not even being able to assert the modest but tangible rights belonging to other nationalities. This was the dilemma of a hitherto dominant ethnicity compelled to defend itself in real politics.

Russians themselves, however, responded coolly to the Russianists' public appeal. In the republican soviet elections of March 1990 the Patriotic Bloc performed disastrously. In the first round not one of its sixty-one candidates gained the 50 percent needed to win outright; only sixteen survived till the second round, and they were all defeated at that stage. Accordingly, Russianists switched back to operating through the existing power structure. In order both to save the Communist party and to Russianize it, in June 1990 they set up a Russian Communist Party, officially as part of the CPSU, but actually in opposition to it, or at least to its current leadership. This was a step of decisive importance. Both Lenin and Stalin had explicitly warned against any such move on the grounds that it would endanger the cohesion of the USSR. As late as November 1989 Iurii Manaenkov, a Central Committee secretary, had warned: "The formation of a Russian Communist Party . . . could strengthen the centrifugal forces in the CPSU and, obviously, in the country as well."[23] Yet, ironically, it was now the protagonists of the USSR who were forming a Russian party, in order to give weight to their opposition to Gorbachev's reforms. For both sides the identity of Russia had become an instrument of power politics.

## Yeltsin and Russian Sovereignty

Before 1990 there is little evidence that Yeltsin regarded Russian sovereignty as a major issue. He was well-liked among Russians because he symbolized their resentment at the domination of the nomenklatura elite and because he seemed to embody the one aspect of Communist policy which remained very popular: its declared aspiration to social justice. That appeal and the support of the informal democrats helped him to his electoral success in Moscow in March 1989.

Once he had clinched his political comeback, though, Yeltsin soon realized that Russian sovereignty could be used as an instrument in his struggle against Gorbachev. He took it up in the election campaign of 1990, during which, stimulated by the recent Lithuanian declaration of sovereignty, he warned that Russia could no longer continue as an "appendage of the center," and that "as a Union Republic, it is also entitled to leave the Union, and this is not only a formal right."[24] Eventually Russian autonomy became his principal weapon, and he steered a "declaration of sovereignty" through the Russian Congress of People's Deputies on June 12, 1990. Both Russianist deputies and democrats voted for it, though for completely different reasons.

By then Yeltsin's assumptions were widely shared: in an opinion poll of September 1990, 48 percent of the RSFSR population stated that their republic should have the right to revoke decisions of the Soviet government on RSFSR territory; only 22 percent thought not.[25] In the campaign for chairmanship of the RSFSR Congress of People's Deputies, Yeltsin's main opponent, Aleksandr Vlasov, backed by Gorbachev, also supported a declaration stating that Russia suffered from "a rapacious Soviet government 'even more than the others,'" and calling for Russia to regain control of its natural resources and industrial wealth. Yeltsin criticized "the long-standing policy of the center"—implying that Russia was not the center and that Russians were victims, not the leading nationality, of the USSR. At this stage Yeltsin seems to have envisaged Russia, not as a seceded state, but as a self-governing republic in some kind of confederal USSR. He may have hoped Russian sovereignty would impart new strength at the heart of the Soviet system and make possible the negotiation of a new union treaty. His use of the words "sovereign" and "independent," like everyone else's, was capaciously ambiguous.[26]

By the end of 1990, legitimated and even pressured by the Russian decision, all the Union republics and most autonomous ones had issued declarations of sovereignty and stated that their own laws took precedence on their own territories.[27] By this time the leading apparatchiks in the non-Russian republics had begun to appropriate the independence agenda for themselves, seeking alliances with their own nationalists to replace the faltering support from Moscow. They had common ground on which they could work together: to nationalists "sovereignty" meant democracy and national self-determination, while to republican apparatchiks it meant an end at last to interference from Moscow.

Over the next year Yeltsin turned Russian sovereignty from a symbolic statement into a reality. His main motive was to gain economic and administrative freedom of action. In the summer and autumn of 1990 Russian liberals contemplated an alliance with Gorbachev, under which economic reform would speed and reinforce republican autonomy, though still within the framework of a restructured USSR. They also hoped to obtain Western financial support for the plan: at this stage most Russian liberals still held a highly idealistic view of the West as genuinely democratic, genuinely civilized, and allied with them in a common struggle against totalitarianism. This conception was embodied in a plan proposed by the economist Stanislav Shatalin, which called for a market economy to be introduced within 500 days. The plan was predicated on support from the United States and international financial institutions. It also devolved most economic decisions to the republics. The RSFSR legislature accepted the Shatalin plan, but the International Monetary Fund was highly critical of it, and shortly afterward Gorbachev decided to reject it. Thereafter Yeltsin became more confrontational. Only if Russian sovereignty meant something could he carry out the market economic reforms he and his advisers were planning. As we have seen, owing to Russia's dominance in the military-industrial complex, many of the enterprises on RSFSR territory were all-Union ones, under the aegis of USSR ministries.[28] Gaining control over them was a key to Yeltsin's strategy.

Gorbachev hoped to overcome the divisions by negotiating a new union treaty that would give the republics much more autonomy. His disagreement with Yeltsin made these negotiations much harder to conduct. In fact, under pressure from both Russianists and "democrats" led by Yeltsin, Gorbachev was increasingly losing control of events. In the Baltic republics Russianists and imperial Communists combined to create "National Salvation Committees," which in January 1991 announced they were assuming power there to "avert an economic collapse" and prevent the establishment of a "bourgeois dictatorship." Paratroopers and Ministry of the Interior troops tried to seize strategic buildings in Vilnius and Riga but were thwarted by large crowds. After a tense stand-off they backed down. The "center" had already lost its firm grip on the periphery.

At around this point some of the leading figures in Democratic Russia at last woke up to the fact that the alliance of Russian liberals and non-Russian nationalists against the Communist Party was endangering the Soviet Union. This was a situation scarcely any of them had consciously intended: they had all assumed that their planned reforms would be carried out within a more democratic Soviet Union. Nikolai Travkin, Viktor Aksiuchits, and Mikhail Astafiev formed a temporary alliance, the People's Accord *(Narodnoe soglasie),* to try to revive liberals' support for the union treaty.[29] But by this stage Gorbachev was already too weak to help them, while Yeltsin's trajectory was carrying him ineluctably along the line of destroying the Union. Unable to prevent the collapse of the Union, Astafiev and Aksiuchits later drifted into the Russianist camp by joining the National Salvation Front.

All the same, by March 1991, Gorbachev had prepared the draft of a new union treaty, which he put to a referendum. Both in the USSR as a whole and in Russia the voters gave their approval, somewhat contradictorily, both to sovereignty for their own republics and to membership in a reformed USSR. Yeltsin profited by the occasion to insert a clause on the creation of a Russian presidency, to give him enhanced legitimacy. Therewith the demands of Russian liberals finally coalesced fully with the demand for Russian sovereignty.[30] The wording of the referendum was ambiguous, and some republics adopted slightly different versions. Significantly, Yeltsin used the civic term *rossiiskie* rather than the ethnic *russkie.* He considered all those who lived in the RSFSR to be "Russians," regardless of ethnicity, and he had no policy for ethnic Russians living outside Russia. On this basis, on June 12, 1991, Yeltsin became the first democratically elected leader in the history of Russia.

## The End of the Soviet Union

All this still did not mean the final disintegration of the USSR. What precipitated the end, ironically, was the action of its most convinced supporters. On August 19, 1991, a so-called State Committee for the Emergency, consisting of senior ministers and the head of the KGB, seized power in Moscow, warning that "extremist forces have embarked on a course toward liquidating the Soviet Union, destroying the state, and seizing power at any cost." The committee claimed that it aimed to "overcome the profound and comprehensive crisis, political, ethnic, and civil strife, chaos,

and anarchy that threaten the lives and security of the citizens of the Soviet Union." The putschists prepared to arrest Yeltsin and, if necessary,
storm the White House, the seat of the Russian Supreme Soviet.[31] Significantly, their public statement made no mention of defending Communism: it was devoted to preserving the USSR, preventing economic break-
down, and maintaining public order.

The coup failed partly because of sheer incompetence. The coup leaders were used to senior positions in a smoothly running state machine.
They had always had underlings to handle the details, and they did not
foresee the consequences if even a few of their subordinates declined to
obey orders. For that reason, Yeltsin managed to elude arrest, fax and telephone lines remained open, and oppositionists were able to publicize their
views in newssheets and even on television.

Even more important, the coup foundered on its own internal contradictions. There was something incongruous about the prime minister, the
defense minister, the interior minister, and the head of the KGB mounting a coup. As General Aleksandr Lebed, deputy commander of the paratroopers and by no means a democrat, remarked, "How could these people seize power? They were already the very embodiment of authority."[32]
But that was the point. The coup leaders were reacting to the very contingency every Soviet leader since Lenin had done his utmost to avoid: Russia's becoming a serious political actor. Worse still from their viewpoint,
Yeltsin was an elected head of state, which they were not. Even under the
Soviet constitution, that fact gave him a legitimacy which they lacked. It
enabled him to scramble dramatically and photogenically onto one of the
tanks sent to assault the White House, to denounce the coup as "a state
crime" directed against "the legally elected authorities of the Russian Republic," and to warn that those who supported it would be indicted under
the Russian criminal code.[33]

That warning was enough to paralyze the intended military repression:
no commander wished to give the order to fire on civilians if his action
might later be denounced as illegal. Thousands of Russians came to sur-
round and defend the White House, emboldened by the well-publicized
arrival of Mstislav Rostropovich, the famous cellist, who had flown in
post-haste from Paris through the still open Moscow airport. For a few
brief, heady days it seemed as if Russian civil society was not only alive
but could triumph over anybody.

The Emergency Committee's action was, then, a coup of the Soviet

Union against Russia. Once it failed, the Soviet Union was doomed, even though Gorbachev continued for several months to try to hold it together by renegotiating his union treaty. The very day after the coup collapsed, Yeltsin ritually humiliated Gorbachev before the Russian Supreme Soviet by forcing him to sign a decree suspending all CPSU activity on Russian soil. The parliament went on to decree a new Russian flag—red, blue and white—which from December was flown above the Kremlin.[34] This was great theater, but it did not offer a strong institutional basis for Russian politics to build on.

On December 1, 1991, the population of Ukraine in a referendum voted overwhelmingly for independence. Once more Ukraine demonstrated its key position: without it, as Gorbachev had warned, there could be no Soviet Union, even on a reduced basis. Without the Union, though, how could Ukraine and Russia continue to coexist? A new umbrella structure was urgently needed that would include both without infringing the sovereignty of either. This is what Yeltsin tried to achieve when he met with the leaders of Ukraine and Belorussia in Belaia Vezha on December 8. Together they created the Commonwealth of Independent States, which was to coordinate—though not direct—the economic, foreign, and military policies of those former Soviet states that wished to join it.[35]

This step was ratified by the RSFSR Supreme Soviet on December 12, so it was, strictly speaking, constitutional—despite later attempts to argue the contrary. At the same time, it was a hasty device, adopted without much forethought, and its results were meager. During the following years the Commonwealth of Independent States achieved very little in the way of effective coordination of policy. What was happening was that not just the Soviet Union but a Russian Empire going back to the sixteenth century was being dismantled. Russia, Ukraine, and Belorussia—and therefore the remaining republics of the USSR, which were not even consulted—were restarting life as nation states from the flimsiest of foundations. It is scarcely surprising that the Russianists regarded the process as an act of conscious betrayal. They, however, were also to blame: the idea of Russian sovereignty was originally theirs, and they did not lift a finger to help Gorbachev, whom they loathed, when he was trying to save the Union to which they were devoted.

Overall, then, the way in which politics had revived in Russia in the late 1980s and early 1990s bore the marks of the system out of which it grew. For decades the party had occupied the political stage with its own ersatz institutions, and had monopolized all political communications from above, through persons at the apex of each power network. For that reason it proved very difficult for concerned citizens now to create genuine institutions or horizontal communications. The new political associations began in the role of *neformaly* and retained many of their "informal" characteristics right through to the creation of the Russian Federation. Nearly all political movements were dominated by individual personalities, proclaimed very general ideologies, and found no framework of institutions and laws within which to operate. All their activities were conducted either on a very limited and local basis or on a huge and unstructured political stage. For the same reason, they were unable to articulate the interests of specific groups of the population: nearly all political movements tried to speak for everyone.[36] All this made the construction of an ordered contestatory democracy extremely difficult.

These problems were aggravated by the institutional setup. With the end of the Soviet Union, Russia had gained its freedom but lost its birthright. As a political entity, Russia came into being as a negative: "not-the-USSR." There was no founding election, no constituent assembly, and no new constitution. The Russian Supreme Soviet continued to exercise the mandate it had inherited from the USSR; as Yeltsin's partner in victory over the Emergency Committee, it could scarcely be dissolved. Yet the majority of deputies were CPSU nomenklatura nominees, whose names had been put forward before opposition parties had had a chance to organize themselves. So there was no symbolic moment when Russia broke with the Soviet past and created its own institutions. The CPSU was banned, but there was no investigation of its crimes or trial of those responsible for its abuses. Since the CPSU had been the de facto executive branch of government in the USSR, its elimination left gaping holes in the administrative transmission system.

"Russia" was an amorphous and undefined entity, the repository of the hopes of innumerable individuals and movements, many of them incompatible with one another. Above it floated the rather undefined figure of Boris Yeltsin, as a kind of father to the Russian nation in its painful birth. Because Russia emerged at a time of deep crisis, immediately after the August coup, it was generally accepted that he should rule by emergency decree.

The institutions of the new Russia took shape, then, in an uncoordinated and piecemeal manner. As the scholar Liliia Shevtsova observed at the time, "What has arisen is a completely chaotic accumulation of separate power blocs, which not only belong to different periods of social development but even to different social systems."[37] On the whole they assumed a modified but unmistakable Soviet form because there was no other framework into which to fit them, no alternative memories of political practice. In accepted nomenklatura tradition, Yeltsin brought some of his former associates from Sverdlovsk to Moscow to assume responsible posts in the executive, combining them with leaders of the anti-Communist movements. Many members of Democratic Russia were now in the Supreme Soviet and in the various city soviets, but it soon turned out that their parliamentary discipline was weak. As one observer wrote, "vote after vote would be suspended for lack of a quorum while deputies sipped tea in the buffet or jawed with one another outside the legislative chamber."[38] The habits of cozy oppositional conversations in kitchens proved difficult to shake, especially when in any case the president ruled by decree. Yeltsin largely ignored the deputies; he never cultivated regular contacts with parliamentary leaders, as any constitutional president has to do. His decree powers, coupled with the shapeless state of Russia's institutions, enabled him to act independently of the Supreme Soviet more or less as Communist Party first secretaries had always done.

By now he had a vision of Russia's future that intersected only partly with that of the democrats, and he held it with ruthless intolerance. He had converted to "democracy" and "the free market" at the crisis of his career, after his expulsion from the Politburo in late 1987. Having found that it brought him popular support and a weapon with which to destroy the party that had rejected him, he now clung to it with all the missionary tenacity of the convert.[39] To put the vision into effect, he appointed a team of bright young economists from academic institutes, men without any practical experience of politics, but brimming with ideas and convictions derived from their study of Hayek, Friedman, and the Chicago school of economics. Like Yeltsin, they were determined to destroy the Communist system root and branch, since they believed it was utterly pernicious. They were confident that a market economy, by contrast, would generate both prosperity and freedom. Anatolii Chubais, one of their leaders, liked to quote Hayek: "A market economy is the guarantee not just of the effective use of financial and natural resources . . . but also of a free society and of the citizen's independence."[40] Egor Gaidar, Yeltsin's

deputy prime minister with responsibility for the economic reform, believed, like all his reformist colleagues, that the world was divided into
two camps, and that Russia should move decisively from one to the other.
Alternatively, as one of them put it, Russia must "return from the twilight
of 'beyond the looking-glass' to the real world."[41] The Soviet economy
had failed, so it seemed to follow that the great "Other," the United
States, must provide the only viable alternative.

Ideas of "genuine democracy" and "a normal society" had a magic ring
after decades of Communist rule; they were seen as connoting a prosper-
ous, civilized, and cultured society where individuals were free to fulfill
themselves in their own way, protected by the rule of law and guaranteed
a basic minimum by the welfare system. This, of course, is the ideal imagined by most Westerners too, but they know their own society is some
distance from it. It was difficult for Russian democrats to admit the possibility of imperfection for themselves, so compelling was the notion of
escaping from Communist domination. In that way a kind of reverse
messianism was at work, the ideal of struggling for absolute good with
support from the democratic, economically advanced West. This mood
ensured that in the first year or two of post-Soviet Russia there was widespread support for market reforms: as late as April 1993 a popular referendum specifically confirmed the population's approval of Yeltsin's social and
economic policies.

The new rulers called themselves "democrats," and they had some support from the population. All the same, these "boys in pink pants" (as
their opponents dubbed them) had no clear mandate for reform from the
Russian Supreme Soviet, which was divided on economic issues. They depended on Yeltsin's emergency powers. They were not fazed by the situation, since they knew that they did indeed face an emergency: the distor-
tions of perestroika had caused a serious food-supply shortage. Region was
ceasing to trade with region, and towns were threatened with starvation:
shops demanded proof of residence before they would sell bread, potatoes,
or cheese. A highly distorted market economy already existed; the reformers felt their task was to convert it into a proper one.

They faced a practical difficulty: it was not possible to reform everything at once, but doing so piecemeal created destructive strains and dis-
tortions. By choosing to prioritize the freeing of prices and the privatiza-
tion of firms, the reformers revived trade but provoked hyperinflation,
which wiped out the savings of a potential middle class. They also en-

abled the nomenklatura bosses to convert their administrative power into the ownership of assets. In these circumstances the basic units of the still essentially Soviet system (Zinoviev's "communes") functioned as one might expect. Instead of trying to negotiate a favorable plan target from Gosplan, as in the old days, industrial bosses now used their personal connections to privatize their firms and receive government contracts, or, if they could not achieve that, to demand subsidies, pile up debts, and trade by barter in order to avoid bankruptcy. In this way, they could line their own pockets but also continue to shoulder the social responsibilities they had traditionally borne on behalf of their employees. Even Gaidar was not prepared to insist on pure market remedies for them, which would have entailed massive bankruptcies and unemployment affecting the entire population of large cities like Sverdlovsk and Gorkii (Ekaterinburg and Nizhnii Novgorod, as they were now called, in a return to their pre-Soviet names). Full-scale "shock therapy" was not really an option, then, but Gaidar's adaptation of it actually reinforced some of the most unmarket-like structures of Soviet society.[42]

There was an international dimension to these paradoxical developments, too. Yeltsin continued Gorbachev's line of seeking Soviet/Russian security through cooperation with international institutions, which meant with the leading Western powers. From Yeltsin's standpoint, the support of financial institutions such as the IMF and the G-7 was especially vital. They gave it with what was by now their usual conditionalities: with the collapse of Soviet Communism, the U.S. government had become even more convinced that its own economic system was a model for the entire world. All this chimed nicely with the Gaidar reforms. But in sending their advisers to help with reform, the IMF and the U.S. Treasury actually intensified the operation of nomenklatura cliques by insisting on colluding only with Chubais and his associates, dismissing all other potential allies as unsound and refusing even to consult with them.[43] In that way, U.S. financial messianism augmented post-Soviet Russian radicalism, to the detriment of the living standards of most of the population.

Meanwhile, in the Russian Supreme Soviet, some deputies were learning the same lessons as the economic bosses, and acting in the way Soviet parliamentary deputies had always done. They were taking advantage of their position to forge personal contacts, make deals, and secure their portion of the gravy train. Under the Soviet system, the benefits that could be acquired that way had been modest, but as Russia privatized, the opportunities for corruption and quick profits were breathtaking. Being at the center of things and having the right contacts made possible gains that were unimaginable just a few years before. Sidelined by Yeltsin's "boys in pink pants," the Supreme Soviet was in any case given little to do in the economic sphere.

The new leaders carried out economic reform in a radical and ruthless manner because they wished to eliminate every vestige of the old power structure. But in doing so they also dismantled both the formal and informal protections that Soviet society had offered ordinary people: the official welfare system and the patronage extended by state firms. Blat continued to operate but became much more dependent on money, and hence unavailable to many people.[44]

The result was a serious deterioration in medical provision and a rise in the death rate. Between 1992 and 2000 the population of the Russian Federation declined by 2.8 million, or nearly 2 percent. Men were worse affected than women: their life expectancy, which had reached 64 by the 1980s, fell to 57 in 1994, a staggering drop in such a short time.[45] The effects of a lifetime of drinking, smoking, and working in a polluted environment were now exacerbated by a sharply reduced pension and a health care system difficult to access without money. The worst sufferers were those who had spent their teenage years and early adulthood in the war and now reached retirement age with minimal expectations for the future. It was a poor reward for the generation that had done the most to deserve the support of their fellow citizens. Such people could be seen lined up outside Moscow Metro stations, selling anything they could spare—old clothes, ornaments, books, flowers, even their wartime medals. Not surprisingly, many Russians came to identify "democracy" with poverty and degradation.

## The Refugee Crisis

The disintegration of the Soviet Union raised urgently the question of what was to happen to the 25 million Russians who lived outside the newly formed Russian Federation. Initially the Yeltsin government, notably his foreign minister, Andrei Kozyrev, took a purely civic view of the obligations of the Russian state: those who lived within its boundaries were *Rossiane,* citizens of Russia, whatever their ethnic origin. Those who lived outside it were citizens of other states, even if they were ethnic Russians, and should look to the rule of law in those states, or to international institutions like the Conference on Security and Cooperation in Europe, to defend their interests.

This position soon became untenable. Ethnic conflict and local discrimination against Russians escalated sharply in the late 1980s and early 1990s. Russian emigration from the Caucasus and Central Asia, which had been a steady trickle, turned into a flood and became a critical political issue. Russians in particular and Slavs in general were increasingly identified as "outsiders," "aliens," or even "occupiers." Economic reform meant upheavals in everyone's way of life, but Russians and Ukrainians, long somewhat disadvantaged in competition with indigenous ethnic networks, now found themselves especially marginalized and impoverished. Large enterprises of "all-Union significance," with their considerable Russian and Ukrainian workforces, were often the first to close in the course of reform programs.

Violent ethnic conflict broke out in some republics; Russians were not often direct targets—though they were in Moldavia and Azerbaijan—but the degradation and unpredictability of the social environment, the prospect of becoming chance victims of other people's bloody clashes, gave them additional motives to leave. Finally, as republics declared their own sovereignty and the primacy of their own legislation, many of them passed laws that reduced the civil rights of nontitular peoples, or at least demanded a good knowledge of the local language for full citizenship rights and certain types of employment. Few Russians had troubled to learn the local language, and, in the competitive market economy, they found their property rights and civic status seriously jeopardized.[46]

It took the government of the RSFSR and then the Russian Federation a long time to recognize the seriousness of the refugees' plight. Most of them arrived having lost nearly all their property and without jobs or education for their children. They would be temporarily housed in hostels and barracks, but were typically given only two months to find a job and alternative accommodations—difficult to achieve in a country with a housing shortage, a faltering economy, and daunting official hurdles to surmount. In any case, as the wave of refugees mounted, even that emergency provision was discontinued.[47]

In January 1990, alarmed by the violence in her home town of Baku, a Russian woman wrote a desperate letter to *Literaturnaia Rossiia:*

The problem of leaving and finding work in Russia is incredibly complicated. I have made enquiries in Saratov, Lipetsk, Smolensk

and towns around Moscow. Nothing doing. It is impossible to exchange our apartment for one in those towns: nobody is interested. I
can't settle in the countryside: I haven't got the right training. I have
no money to buy a house. I am astonished at the indifference that
we, Russians from other republics, encounter in Russian towns. Although they need specialists, they will not issue a propiska or even a
promise of a propiska, nor put one down on the housing list. After
all, I could hand over our Baku flat to the state. Are we really unwanted by our historic Homeland?[48]

The answer to that question, it seemed, was "yes." The Russian government offered refugees, most of them ethnic Russians, no civil status which
even guaranteed them the right to live in Russia, let alone to obtain work
or welfare benefits. They relied on chance employment, on relatives' help,
and on the care and kindness of ordinary people in order to survive. This
neglect is especially striking when one considers the very different reaction
of the Federal German parliament nearly half a century earlier to the
floods of refugees reaching western Germany from the eastern territories
and the Soviet occupation zone. In 1951 the parliament had passed a law
entitled "the Equalization of Burdens," making the provision of help for
refugees a duty of the West German taxpayer. The Russian parliament,
and Yeltsin's government, it seems, felt so little solidarity with their cona-
tionals returning from "the near abroad" (as the ex-USSR became known)
that they never took such a step.

A political movement was formed specifically to defend the interests of
the Russian diaspora: the Congress of Russian Communities (CRC). Its
leader, Dmitrii Rogozin, had a much broader definition of Russia than
Kozyrev:

We are convinced that Russia is not contained within the borders
that have been assigned to it today. Russia is a special, unique civilization, uniting the most diverse peoples and ethnic groups. The
CRC considers Russians *(Rossiiane)* to be all those who recognize
that they belong to this civilization, value its history, care about the
development of its culture, and believe in the future of Russia. In the
struggle for survival, several tasks stand before the Russian *(russkii)*
people. Without a revival of the Russian National Idea it will not be
possible to return to the age-old bases of Russian spirituality and
Russian *(rossiiskii)* Statehood.[49]

Under the influence of such ideas, the Russian Supreme Soviet passed a motion in summer 1993 declaring that Sevastopol in the Crimea—base of the Imperial and Soviet Black Sea Fleets—was a Russian *(rossiiskii)* city. This declaration that "Russia" existed well outside the borders of the Russian Federation was one of the main reasons Yeltsin dissolved the Supreme Soviet in September 1993 and announced new parliamentary elections, to be followed by new presidential elections. This was a fateful decision. Some members of the Supreme Soviet denounced the dissolution as illegal and led an armed uprising against it. Yeltsin sent in tanks to crush the rebellion: in the course of the operation, according to official figures, 187 people were killed and 437 wounded.[50]

The dissolution of the Supreme Soviet was meant to mark the final end of Soviet Russia. It should have been an occasion for rejoicing, national unity, and a new democratic beginning. Instead it was a time of terrible bloodshed, in which new hatreds were ignited and a new authoritarian spirit was generated. Its symbolism was destructive: Yeltsin had fired on the very building, the White House, that had been his own bastion of democracy two years earlier. The birth of the new Russia was tainted and desecrated.

In any case, after the conflict, Yeltsin felt bound to move much closer to the Supreme Soviet's viewpoint. At New Year 1994 he addressed diaspora Russians: "Dear compatriots! You are inseparable from us and we are inseparable from you. We were and will be together. On the basis of law and solidarity we defend and will defend you and our common interests."[51] The Russian Federation pledged to use its influence in the new states and within international organizations to defend the interests of ethnic Russians and Russian speakers, wherever they lived. This was an important moment in the evolution of Russian national consciousness, for the Soviet Union had never seen itself in the role of interceding for Russian émigrés.

Evidently realizing that building a market economy and Western-style democratic institutions had ceased to attract much loyalty among Russians, Yeltsin also, after his re-election in July 1996, instructed his advisers to formulate a new "national idea." The official newspaper *Rossiiskaia gazeta* advertised a competition: the person who devised the best "national idea" would win a prize of ten million rubles. Symptomatically, however, though many correspondents sent in proposals, no winner was identified and the prize remained unawarded.[52] There was absolutely no consensus on what "Russia" was.

## The New Russianist Synthesis

There was, then, ample fuel for a Russianist reaction. Remarkably, however, racist Russian nationalism was relatively insignificant. True, in the late 1980s a party of anti-Semitic blackshirts had hijacked the name *Pamiat* (Memory) for their Russian supremacist demonstrations. But they never attracted much public support, and soon they split into squabbling factions and faded away, though a splinter group under Aleksandr Barkashov played a role in the anti-Yeltsin armed rising of October 1993.

Another figure who could be accused of racism is Vladimir Zhirinovskii, whose misnamed Liberal Democratic Party performed well in the presidential elections of June 1991 and the parliamentary elections of December 1993. Zhirinovskii was a truculent politician with a penchant for terse, cutting soundbites that played well on television. Some of his remarks implied that he sought supremacy for Russians within a reconstituted Soviet Union. But his ideas were inconsistent, and his party's program was imperial rather than racist, seeking to reinstate the Soviet Union's (and the Russian Empire's) great-power status with Russians playing an integrative rather than a dominating role. In other words, behind the aggressive buffoonery, he held a rather traditional view of Russia as multiethnic empire.[53]

The mainstream of the Russianist reaction lay elsewhere. Eurasianism, geopolitics, the perception of "Russophobia," and the synthetic patriotism of *Molodaia gvardiia* combined to provide the ideological underpinning for the new Russian Communist Party, founded in 1990. Its principal spokesperson and later its leader, Gennadii Ziuganov, emphasized Russia's distance from the West. Russia, in his interpretation, was a distinct civilization "whose fundamental values are collectivism, *sobornost,* statehood, and striving for the embodiment of the highest ideals of goodness and justice." Contemporary Western civilization, on the contrary, "is based in the last analysis on an atomized, mechanical picture of the world. . . . Market individualism has become the basic human disposition. . . . Hence the absolutization of the rights of the individual, which in the nationality sphere has justified the welding of tiny peoples into nations; hence the 'war of all against all' in the social arena." Russian statehood, by contrast, whether tsarist or Soviet, was well equipped to absorb non-Russian peoples without undermining their identity. Russia he defined as "a state based on the indissoluble fraternal union of the Great Russians, the Little

Russians, and the White Russians, and also all the tribes and nationalities that voluntarily wish to join that union."[54] This was inclusive, statist nationalism as opposed to exclusive, ethnic nationalism.

On this basis, Ziuganov presented a "single-stream" vision of Russian history, arguing that Orthodoxy and Communism were merely different expressions of one basic Russian ideal:

If we look at our thousand-year-long history, it becomes clear that the moral-ethical principles of Orthodox Christianity and socialist ideas coincide in many respects. There have been two core tendencies that have shaped world development. One is private-egotistical, and the other is social-collectivistic. The private-egotistical tendency has been expressed variously through fascism and war, between generations and across continents. . . . We are a communal nation, brought up on a thousand years of experience in mutual support and patriotic feeling. And the West is trying to impose on us their individualism and Protestant egotism.[55]

Like Gumilev and Shafarevich, Ziuganov viewed the Jews as the vanguard of the Western project. He asserted that "the Jewish diaspora, which has traditionally controlled the financial life of the continent," was now becoming the "controlling shareholder" in the Western economy as a whole, and making its bid for "leadership of the world."[56]

For a Communist, the greatest volte-face was the new acceptance of the Orthodox Church. According to Ziuganov, the church had played a decisive role in the creation and sustenance of the Russian state: "A politician cannot understand Russia if he does not understand the central role of religion in the process of developing and establishing our statehood and culture. . . . By baptising Russian a millennium ago, the grand prince St. Vladimir laid the foundation of our unity. Without this Rus would not have overcome the Tatar invasion or survived the Time of Troubles. During the Great Patriotic War the Orthodox Church called upon the people to defend our native land."[57] This declaration was a virtual replay of Patriarch Aleksii's 1960 speech, which had incensed so many Communists at the time.

It annoyed many even now. Ziuganov's position required Communists to de-emphasize or drop altogether the elements in their ideology that had to do with atheism, dialectical materialism, and proletarian internation-

ism. Class struggle remained, though in shadowy form as the conflict between nations with a collectivist principle and those with an individualist
principle. These omissions, combined with the new acceptance of Orthodoxy, alienated many former members of the CPSU. The resulting disagreements and splits weakened the Russian Communist Party's appeal to
the electorate at this critical time.[58]

There was much in common between Ziuganov's outlook and the post-
1945 Soviet official ideology, including its anti-Semitism. Ziuganov was
prepared to rehabilitate Stalin, who, he claimed, "understood as no one
else the need for an updated worldview within the framework of the new
geopolitical form, the USSR. He understood the urgent need for a con-
gruence of the new realities with age-old Russian traditions. The result of
his understanding was a radical change in the official ideology of the Soviet Union in 1945–1953."[59]

Some Orthodox believers were ready to support this anti-Western ideological amalgam. One party in the church, led by Metropolitan Ioann of
St. Petersburg, combined geopolitical conceptions with anti-Semitism.
Ioann drew a picture of Rus and Russia as a nation constantly under threat
from cunning and malicious foreigners. He quoted the words of Alexander
III: "Russia has no friends. Everyone fears our immensity." Russia had been
able to survive only thanks to the staunchness of its Orthodox faith, the
firmness of its autocratic leaders, and its readiness to sacrifice everything in
defense of the homeland. The twentieth-century form of this threat Ioann
saw as embodied in the Protocols of the Elders of Zion. He compared the
post-Soviet evolution of Russia with the alleged plans of the "elders":
domination of Russia through the power of international finance and
the media, undermining the national faith, the family, and traditional
morality.[60]

This view was far from universal among clerics. The Orthodox Church
had benefited both politically and symbolically from the revival of Russia.
Since 1988 it had reopened many of its parishes and restored many of its
buildings, culminating in the reconsecration of Moscow's Cathedral of
Christ the Savior. But the condition of the church, though outwardly
flourishing, reflected the confusion over Russian nationhood. In questionnaires as many as 80 percent of Russians described themselves as "Orthodox," but this self-identification did not translate into religious belief or
practice. Only 6 to 7 percent of Russians attended church at least once a

month, while 18 percent claimed belief in a living God, and 24 percent believed in life after death. Quite a few Russians who professed themselves Orthodox believed in phenomena explicitly disavowed by the church, such as extrasensory perception and the migration of souls.[61]

In actual fact, identification with Orthodoxy was more a statement about national feeling than a reflection of religious belief. Most church hierarchs also emphasized this aspect of the church, preaching loyalty to the Russian state, the development of national traditions, and the preservation of national unity as much as they dealt with personal salvation or moral issues. This approach continued the role of the church as it had been under the tsars and, with modifications, in the later Soviet decades, as the spiritual extension of the state.

The church was defensive in outlook, in spite of its obvious external success in reviving parish life, creating choirs, and restoring buildings. It remained sensitive to the charge that many of its clergymen had cooperated with the Soviet secret police. Many urban Russians found their spiritual needs better met in the Protestant churches, especially the Baptist and Pentecostalist, both by now well established in Russia. With the stunted congregational life and weakly developed pastoral experience it had inherited from the Soviet Union, the Orthodox Church felt disadvantaged when faced by the open competition of other denominations, especially Christian ones financed from abroad. In 1997, after a long campaign, it persuaded the State Duma to pass a law restricting the activity of "nontraditional" churches and sects.

There were three main factions within the Orthodox clergy. The imperial nationalists, led by Metropolitan Ioann (quoted above), were left with no obvious leader when Ioann died in 1995. The relatively small number of reformists and ecumenists, mostly in the big cities, welcomed contact with other Christians and wanted to reform their own church from within, for example, by increasing the use of the Russian language within services and allowing a greater role for lay people in running parish affairs. But by far the greatest number of clergymen belonged to what we might call the "institutionalists," who simply emphasized restoring canonical structures and practices within the church, re-establishing the full range of educational activities, and overcoming the long deficit of the Soviet period.[62] Most likely their aims will have to be achieved before the church can decide exactly where it is going.

## An Emerging Nation State?

What did most Russians think of the headlong developments of the early 1990s, about the country they had lost and the one they had gained? Their attitudes were revealed in a survey conducted by Iurii Levada and the All-Russian Center for the Study of Public Opinion in 1991–1992. Levada found that Russians were still predominantly imperial or supranational in their outlook, and that they considered ethnic characteristics relatively unimportant—though when the supranational state failed in its functions, they did often blame ethnic factors. They viewed Russia as a distinctive and exceptional country, whether or not they considered that a good thing. They identified with the USSR as a whole, and with a *malaia rodina,* a home town or rural region, rather than with the RSFSR or the Russian Federation. (Non-Russians, by contrast, tended to identify with their individual republic.) Russians were also more likely to define their sense of themselves by opposition to "others," whether those "others" be Jews, Muslims, or "the West." They took a paternalist view of the state: they felt it should be present in all spheres of social life, should provide social and economic benefits for everyone, and should offer a safety net when needed. They expected society to be hierarchical, for example in access to information and material benefits, but they viewed hierarchy in moral terms and resented "undeserved" superior status. They valued "simplicity," believing that human beings should not aspire to more than the satisfaction of basic needs. Strikingly, the survey found no objective evidence of "collectivism," even though many Russians believed themselves to be oriented to the collective rather than the individual: Levada concluded that the Soviet state had prevented the formation of civil associations and had "atomized" society.[63]

The ambiguities and uncertainties that plagued the formation of post-Soviet Russia were soon reflected in the choice of symbols for the new state. Even its official name caused difficulties: deputies eventually settled for "Russian Federation (Russia)," an awkward concoction which implied that the Federation was not really Russia. No law was ever passed abolishing the symbols of the Soviet Union, and the Russian army continued to bear a red banner with a star, though without a hammer and sickle. Many Russians, including Yeltsin, felt that it was time to remove Lenin from the mausoleum and give him a normal burial, but Yeltsin never did so, since he knew that such a move would mortally offend the substantial minority of Communists in the electorate. So there was no symbolic dissociation from the USSR. The white, red, and blue tricolor was chosen as the new national flag, but only over the objections of those who identified it with the tsarist regime, for which it had been the symbol of the merchant navy, or, worse still, with the Vlasovite anti-Soviet movement. The adoption of the imperial double eagle, with St. George spearing the dragon, as a national emblem was even more contentious, since it was not only tsarist but also explicitly Orthodox.[64]

The national anthem aroused more controversy still. Yeltsin scrapped the Soviet anthem and adopted a melody by the nineteenth-century composer Glinka, which remained without words, however, because the Duma would not ratify them. At the 2000 Olympic Games Russian athletes complained that they were made to look foolish on the victors' podium, having no words to sing when their anthem was played, unlike any other nation. The new president, Vladimir Putin, then took a major symbolic decision, to bring back the Soviet anthem, with new words by the aged poet Sergei Mikhalkov—who, by an exquisite irony, had composed the original Soviet words fifty years earlier.[65] This compromise seemed to reflect perfectly Russia's dual identity, both attached to and dissociated from the Soviet Union.

On July 18, 1998, a remarkable ceremony took place in the church of the Peter-Paul Fortress in St. Petersburg. The remains of Nicholas II and his family, recovered from the woods north of Ekaterinburg and positively identified after DNA testing, were finally laid to rest in a special service conducted by the local parish priest, exactly eighty years after their brutal murder in the Ipatev House. What was most striking about the occasion was the absence of most of Russia's political establishment. The service was boycotted by the entire Communist and Russianist wing of the State Duma; the patriarch and senior prelates of the Orthodox Church did not attend either; even President Yeltsin decided to be present only at the last moment. What might have been a moment of national reconciliation, a coming to terms with at least one of Russia's great tragedies, became instead a further symbol of the disagreements that still divided Russians on the most fundamental questions of their national identity. Many Communists did not wish to honor the imperial family in any form. Others were kept away by their insistence that Nicholas II had been murdered in a "Jewish-masonic plot," and the bodies then burned in a cover-up. For those who gave credence to this version, "the killing of the tsar's family is the most terrible and sinister crime of the twentieth century. This is where the greatest catastrophes of our country and the world had their origin— Bolshevism and Fascism, mass murders. . . . The Gulag system began in the Ipatiev House, and without the Gulag it is impossible to understand Hitler's camps."[66] Not all Orthodox clergymen accepted this view, but enough did so to divide the church hierarchy and prevent any bishop from attending. In this way the shadows of the great battle between good and evil continued to cast their gloom over the young Russian nation state.

Today Russia's identity is still unsettled, and there are several forms it might take.[67] They reduce, however, to two fundamental alternatives: it can become a Russian nation state or it can remain a modified empire. In the former case, Russia accepts its status as one among a large number of nation states in the world, with a special responsibility to speak for Russians, wherever they may be. In the latter case, it tries to preserve its role as a great power, with dominant interests throughout the former Soviet Union and a worldwide mission.

So far, Russia has vacillated between the two concepts. It has accepted the breakup of the Soviet Union, including the existence of a separate Ukrainian nation state (a very hard pill for Russians to swallow); it has withdrawn its troops from the former Soviet bloc and from its own former Baltic republics, accepting, with some reluctance, that the European Union and even NATO can move into those regions. On the other hand, it has continued to take on imperial responsibilities and assert imperial influence around the old Soviet Union, including in the defense of the Tadjik frontier and a continuing military presence in Moldavia, Central Asia, and the Transcaucasus. In Chechnia more than anywhere else it has behaved in the most overbearing imperial traditions, seeking military rather than political solutions to complex problems, bombarding cities and forcing their inhabitants to become refugees. In its coercive policy, it has treated Russians living in Chechnia just as badly as Chechens. As one recent commentator has put it, "The problem of Chechnia lies between two models of Russian statehood, and, like a spanner thrown into a machine, it blocks a much-needed transitional phase."[68]

Of all the forms which "Russia" might take, it appears that a modified imperial identity is likely to prove dominant. The threat of international terrorism has augmented that tendency, since it provides a persuasive justification for Russia to operate beyond its borders without international mandate, and to emulate—not for the first time—the United States. Most Russians accept that the Soviet Union is gone forever, but they believe nevertheless that Russia has a supranational role in the post-Soviet space, which is officially designated as the "near abroad"—in tacit distinction to the "full-scale" abroad. It is normal for a postimperial power to seek continuing association with its former colonies: the British still have their Commonwealth, and the French the Lomé Convention. Russia has the additional motive of concerns about security in countries adjacent to its borders. So its interest in the post-Soviet space is wholly legitimate, even if its methods are sometimes questionable. Driven by considerations such as these, it seems likely that for some time to come, Russia will be a residual empire rather than a nation state.

# CONCLUSION

Russia is a formidable problem for theorists of national identity, especially for those who believe nations are the product of modernity, like Karl Deutsch, Ernest Gellner, and John Breuilly.[1] They are faced with the paradox that modernization seems to have impeded rather than advanced Russian nationhood. When Peter the Great consciously promoted an ambitious modernizing agenda in the early eighteenth century, he did so by borrowing a foreign culture and by reinforcing an authority system that rested on archaic social structures of "joint responsibility" rather than on institutions and laws.[2]

It now looks as if the Soviet project of modernization was carried out in similar abrupt and headstrong fashion, and with comparable results. According to Breuilly, the nation is "a modern political and ideological formation which developed in close conjuncture with the emergence of the modern, territorial, sovereign and participatory state."[3] Furthermore, "the process which created the modern idea of the state in its earliest form also gave rise to the political concept of the nation." That is because the powers which the modern state needs to govern effectively, such as taxation, military recruitment, and law enforcement, could only be achieved "through a process of negotiation between the ruler and the political community of the core territory under his sway."[4] That process not only strengthened the ruler but also consolidated the political community and gave it firmer outline—created, in effect, a potential nation.

In the Soviet Union, however, this was not at all what happened. Although the Soviet state assumed and performed many of the functions of a modern state, it did so without generating a political community. The Communist Party functioned as a substitute for such a community, and its conduits of power were largely directed from above through personal channels. At the lower levels, at the workplace and in domestic life (the "communal apartments"), social units reemerged resting on the archaic practices of *krugovaia poruka*. "Urbanization" really meant ruralization of the cities. The trust of ordinary people was placed in patron-client hierarchies and mutual aid networks rather than in institutions and laws. The Soviet modernization project did not advance but rather obstructed the formation of a Russian nation, especially in the civic sense. The most pernicious product of this paradox was Stalin's terror, which resulted from a confluence of frustrated messianism, personalized power structures, and "joint responsibility."

In appearance, it is true, the Soviet Union did create many of the characteristics of a modern nation: large industrial cities, a mass education system, a penetrative network of communications and public media, a centralized welfare system, and universal military service for young adult males. The language employed as the cement of the system was Russian, the common history, myths, and memories evoked in education and the media were mainly Russian; the Soviet state also did much to overcome the split between elite and popular Russian culture. But the potential nation thus promoted was not Russia; it was "the Soviet people." Russians were the state-bearers of the Soviet Union, but they were also rendered anonymous by it. "Their" republic, the RSFSR, was a puny and somnolent giant, a glaring anomaly that, if awoken, had the potential to destroy the Soviet Union.

Benedict Anderson has talked of "print capitalism" as a vital motive force in the generation of nations.[5] In some ways "print socialism" operated in a similar manner; but once again the "nation" thus constructed was Soviet, not Russian. It is true that it drew much of its symbolic repertoire from Russian culture, but as an instrument of Sovietization, not as an expression of growing Russian national consciousness. In any case, "print socialism" generated a "language of wood" which was so distant from reality that it actually obstructed communication. Instead, information and opinion were conveyed largely through gossip, rumor, and anecdote. Moreover, the Soviet authorities were never able to generate either a narrative or a commemoration of the past which would enable the Soviet peoples to feel themselves members of the same community, whether Russian or not. Nation-building, when it came, articulated itself in opposition to the Soviet multiethnic community, and therefore usually also against its apparent bearers, the Russians.

All the same, the Soviet Union was in a real sense Russian. Bolshevism revived elements of the inherited system of Russian myths and symbols dating right back to the sixteenth century: the idea that Russia has a special mission in the world, to practice and disseminate Truth and Justice (Pravda) based on egalitarianism and the frugal way of life of ordinary toiling people. This was *krugovaia poruka* in modern dress, if you like. By virtue of this special mission, so the assumption went, Russians were entitled to exercise patronage or protection over less developed people, and also to speak for the poor and oppressed in the developed or "capitalist" world; this was a form of service to them, what one might call "the Russian's burden." Such an outlook was fully compatible with Soviet Communism, and it constituted the practical, working ideology of many Russians employed by the Soviet state.[6]

Actually, then, the Soviet Union represented Russia's crisis of messianism. It was the state form in which the Russians' sense of being a chosen people worked itself out in reality. It is true that the deity doing the choosing was not God but rather history itself. It is also true that the messianic impulse was not uniquely Russian, but also Jewish. The Soviet Union in its energetic early phases was a Russian-Jewish enterprise, and the later exclusion of the Jews from its roll of honor profoundly changed its nature.

Russians entered the USSR with a national identity that was itself split, into imperial and ethnic elements. Those Russians who felt the messianic urge of their culture were also divided, into mutually hostile Orthodox and socialist tendencies, both of which overlapped partly, but incompletely, with the peasants' outlook. The Soviet project was an experiment conducted not only *by* Russians, but also *on* Russians, by the rulers against the ruled, by socialists against Christians, by townspeople against peasants. Only during the Second World War did imperial and ethnic, socialist and Orthodox Russians really pull together, united for the defeat of a mortally dangerous external enemy. As the war receded, they drifted apart again.

The international mission was in one sense a Russian idea. All the same, it ran counter to the needs and customs of ordinary Russian people.

As a modern Russian scholar has put it, "Bolshevism's exploitation of the Russian mytho-symbolic system had ambiguous consequences. On the one hand it ensured that the Communist ideology was convincing, it imparted immense dynamism to all spheres of social life and guaranteed the legitimacy of the new state and its sociopolitical institutions. On the other hand, the glaring contradiction between the new reality and the *ethnic* interests of Russians in the long run weakened the mobilizational potential of the Soviet mythologems and degraded the imperial mythology."[7]

The contradiction was deepened by the way Russians' historical memory was uprooted and fragmented between 1917 and 1921 by revolution and civil war. The monarchy, the keystone that had held ethnic and imperial Russia together, was destroyed and discredited. The Orthodox Church survived, but in a reduced and jeopardized condition that rendered it incapable of contributing to the social and cultural life of the Russian people. The public media operated in a defective and mendacious fashion that made serious facts and opinions a field for rumor and gossip. The Soviet state's attempts to create new rituals and ceremonies was partly successful, but did not compensate for the loss of an organic link with the past.

Victory in the Second World War did restore a sense of national pride to the Russians as "first among equals" of the Soviet nationalities. It also provided a heroic narrative and an array of compelling symbols to which to attach Russian national identity and Soviet citizenship. Yet at the same time, the regime's treatment of returnees, its brutal social reforms in the new western republics, its deportation of whole nationalities, and its anti-Semitic campaigns both weakened Russian national feeling and undermined Russian leadership of the Soviet Union.

In the second half of the Soviet Union's existence the messianic impulse took a different form. In part, it became backward-looking, fixated on the great victory achieved in the past. In its attitude to the future it crystallized around the ambition to become a great world power, the equal of the United States and the leader of peoples who rejected the American version of capitalism and democracy. The United States had always been a preoccupation of Soviet idealists. Now it became the great Other, a model to be imitated but also rejected, aspired to but also reacted against.

The huge effort of mobilization, especially military mobilization, required to sustain this ambition turned the USSR into a militarist society whose resources were monopolized by the priorities of the armed forces.

Many of the cities of the RSFSR and Ukraine became centers of military industry, with the majority of their workforce directly or indirectly employed by the military-industrial complex. They lived in cramped but serviceable newly built apartments in nondescript high-rise blocks. They were poorly paid and owed most of their goods, amenities, and services to the enterprises where they worked. All young men were in principle required to perform military service, and to be an officer in the armed forces was to enjoy special respect among the population. Ordinary people grumbled at the heavy burdens imposed on them and the often squalid conditions in which they lived, but they appreciated the basic services provided by the socialist state and took pride in their country's great-power status—a pride of which they became fully conscious only when that status was lost.

This military mobilization was accomplished at the cost of all nonmilitary aspects of society, especially in the three Slavic republics. The villages and small towns of Russia, Belorussia, and Ukraine, especially those in the non–black earth regions, became demoralized and decayed, among the most abject and poverty-stricken regions in the entire Soviet Union, forsaken by all who had any choice about where to live. Thus the maintenance of a neo-Russian empire meant the abandonment of a core aspect of ethnic Russia. Similarly, the continued preaching of the international socialist ideology entailed the strict limitation and supervision of the Orthodox Church, the Russian people's ancient and long-standing religious faith. It gradually became obvious, moreover, that the urbanized, militarized life-style of the core republics was leading to a decline in the birth rate of the Slavic peoples.

For intellectuals and professional people, the nomenklatura domination needed to sustain great-power status was doubly irksome. The ideological system did accord intellectuals a status they would not have enjoyed in a more commercially oriented society. On the other hand, it also imposed on them forms of self-limitation that severely hampered their freedom of thought and creativity. This applied especially to scientists and people working in the arts and humanities. It was they who produced the solubles that eventually loosened the cement of the Soviet system. Their challenge to Soviet institutions and attitudes packed a punch because it came from deep within Russian value systems long despised and suppressed by the Soviet state. It had appeal and credibility because of what the Russians, not least among the Soviet peoples, had suffered under Stalin, and because the past criminality had never been properly disclosed and purged.

In the end, the Russians destroyed the Soviet Union, not because they wished to—very few of them did—but because of the logic of their republic's position in the country's institutional structure. As it acquired tangible powers under perestroika, the anomalous position of the RSFSR was exploited by the liberals to weaken the over-centralized CPSU and Soviet state, and by conservatives and Russian nationalists to attack Gorbachev. They agreed on nothing else, but because they both used the RSFSR as a tactical instrument, they worked in unintended alliance to undermine the USSR.

Most Russians would agree that the disintegration of the Soviet Union was a disaster, not because they are inveterate Stalinists, but because it was "their" country. Unlike the other Soviet nationalities, they experienced independence not as liberation but as deprivation. They are now building a nation state few of them wished for. They have no choice, though. As President Putin has commented, "He who does not regret the break-up of the Soviet Union has no heart; he who wants to revive it in its previous form has no head."[8]

Russians have great resources, economic, political and cultural above all, to bring to this reluctant nation-building enterprise. They are beginning to piece together, from the Soviet and non-Soviet past, a coherent identity and the institutions of a modern nation. Yet, because the overhang of the imperial and messianic past is so strong, much of what they create feels to Russians themselves makeshift and unworthy. Like the English, they have lost an empire and still not found a role. There is still a long way to go before we can feel certain what kind of community Russia has become.

# Appendix: Tables

Table A.1  Russians in Union republics, 1959-1989, in thousands (with percentage of total republican population)

| | 1959 | | 1970 | | 1979 | | 1989 | |
|---|---|---|---|---|---|---|---|---|
| | Total | Urban | Total | Urban | Total | Urban | Total | Urban |
| Armenia | 56 3.2% | 40 4.5% | 66 2.7% | 52 3.8% | 70 2.3% | n/a | 52 1.6% | 44 1.5% |
| Azerbaijan | 501 13.6% | 439 25% | 510 10% | 470 18.3% | 475 7.9% | n/a | 392 5.6% | 372 9.8% |
| Georgia | 408 10.1% | 327 19.1% | 397 8.5% | 328 14.6% | 372 7.4% | n/a | 341 6.3% | 264 8.7% |
| Kazakhstan | 3,974 42.7% | 2,343 59% | 5,522 42.4% | 3,818 59.3% | 5,991 40.8% | n/a | 6,228 37.7% | 4,823 50.1% |
| Kirgiziia | 624 30.2% | 360 51.7% | 856 29.2% | 564 51.4% | 912 25.9% | n/a | 917 21.4% | 641 39.1% |
| Tadjikistan | 263 13.3% | 228 35.3% | 344 11.9% | 323 30% | 395 10.4% | n/a | 388 9.6% | 365 21.9% |
| Turkmeniia | 263 17.3% | 248 34.9% | 313 14.5% | 300 29% | 349 12.6% | n/a | 334 9.5% | 326 20.3% |
| Uzbekistan | 1,091 13.5% | 913 33.5% | 1,474 12.5% | 1,312 30.6% | 1,666 10.8% | n/a | 1,653 8.3% | 1,567 19.3% |

*Table A.2   Russians as percentage of population in RSFSR Autonomous republics*

| Republic | 1926 | 1939 | 1959 | 1970 | 1979 | 1989 |
|---|---|---|---|---|---|---|
| Bashkiria | 39.8 | 40.6 | 42.4 | 40.5 | 40.3 | 39.3 |
| Buriatia | 52.7 | 72.0 | 74.6 | 73.5 | 72.0 | 66.7 |
| Chechen-Ingushetia | 2.6 | 28.8 | 49.0 | 34.5 | 29.6 | 23.1 |
| Chuvashia | 20.0 | 22.4 | 24.0 | 24.5 | 26.0 | 26.7 |
| Dagestan | 12.5 | 14.3 | 20.1 | 14.7 | 11.6 | 9.2 |
| Kabardino-Balkaria | 7.5 | 35.9 | 38.7 | 37.2 | 35.1 | 31.9 |
| Kalmykia | 10.7 | 45.7 | 55.9 | 45.8 | 42.6 | 37.8 |
| Karelia | 57.1 | 63.2 | 63.4 | 68.1 | 71.3 | 73.6 |
| Komi | 6.6 | 22.0 | 48.6 | 53.1 | 56.7 | 57.7 |
| Mari | 43.6 | 46.1 | 47.8 | 46.9 | 47.5 | 47.5 |
| Mordovia | 59.2 | 60.5 | 59.1 | 58.9 | 59.7 | 60.8 |
| N. Ossetia | 6.6 | 37.2 | 39.6 | 39.6 | 33.9 | 29.9 |
| Tataria | 43.1 | 42.9 | 43.9 | 42.4 | 44.0 | 43.3 |
| Tuva | n/a | n/a | 40.1 | 38.3 | 36.2 | 32.0 |
| Udmurtia | 43.3 | 55.7 | 56.8 | 58.3 | 58.3 | 58.9 |
| Yakutiia | 10.4 | 35.5 | 44.2 | 47.3 | 50.4 | 50.3 |

*Source:* Viktor Kozlov, *The Peoples of the Soviet Union* (London: Hutchinson, 1988), 80–81; Robert J. Kaiser, *The Geography of Nationalism in Russia and the USSR* (Princeton: Princeton University Press, 1994), 118,174–175.

*Table A.3*    *Russians as percentage of population in Union republics*

| Republic | 1926 | 1939 | 1959 | 1970 | 1979 | 1989 |
|---|---|---|---|---|---|---|
| Armenia | 2.2 | 4.0 | 3.2 | 2.7 | 2.3 | 1.6 |
| Azerbaijan | 9.5 | 16.5 | 13.6 | 10.0 | 7.9 | 5.6 |
| Belorussia | 7.7 | 6.5 | 8.2 | 10.4 | 11.9 | 13.2 |
| Estonia | n/a | n/a | 20.1 | 24.7 | 27.9 | 30.3 |
| Georgia | 3.6 | 8.7 | 10.1 | 8.5 | 7.4 | 6.3 |
| Kazakhstan | 19.7 | 40.3 | 42.7 | 42.4 | 40.8 | 37.8 |
| Kirgiziia | 11.7 | 20.8 | 30.2 | 29.2 | 25.9 | 21.5 |
| Latvia | n/a | n/a | 26.6 | 29.8 | 32.8 | 34.0 |
| Lithuania | n/a | n/a | 8.5 | 8.6 | 8.9 | 9.4 |
| Moldavia | 8.5 | 10.2 | 10.1 | 11.6 | 12.8 | 13.0 |
| Tadjikistan | 0.7 | 9.1 | 13.3 | 11.9 | 10.4 | 9.6 |
| Turkmeniia | 8.2 | 18.6 | 17.3 | 14.5 | 12.6 | 9.5 |
| Ukraine | 9.2 | 12.9 | 16.9 | 19.4 | 21.1 | 22.1 |
| Uzbekistan | 25.4 | 11.5 | 13.5 | 12.5 | 10.8 | 8.3 |

*Source:* Viktor Kozlov, *The Peoples of the Soviet Union* (London: Hutchinson, 1988), 81–82; Robert J. Kaiser, *The Geography of Nationalism in Russia and the USSR* (Princeton: Princeton University Press, 1994), 174–175.

# NOTES

## Preface

1. I offered an introduction to the village prose writers in my article "The Russian Peasant Rediscovered: 'Village Prose' of the 1960s," *Slavic Review* 32 (1973), 705–724, and in my book *Beyond Socialist Realism: Soviet Fiction since Ivan Denisovich* (New York: Holmes and Meier, 1980).

## Introduction

1. Vladimir Zhirinovsky, *My Struggle: The Explosive Views of Russia's Most Controversial Political Figure* (New York: Barricade Books, 1996), 15, 17.

2. Edward Allworth, ed., *Ethnic Russia in the USSR: The Dilemma of Dominance* (New York: Pergamon, 1980), 156.

3. Irina Kantor, "Ashche zabudu tebe, Ierusalime," *Vestnik russkogo khristianskogo dvizheniia*, no. 144 (1985), 209–210.

4. Irina Ratushinskaia, *Stikhi* (Ann Arbor: Ermitazh, 1984), 9–12, 22.

5. For a recent study that highlights such groups see Eric Hoffmann, ed., *Rethinking Ethnicity: Majority Groups and Dominant Minorities* (London: Routledge, 2004).

6. Clifford Longley, *Chosen People: The Big Idea That Shaped England and America* (London: Hodder and Stoughton, 2002).

7. Anthony D. Smith, "Ethnic Election and National Destiny: Some Religious Origins of Nationalist Ideals," *Nations and Nationalism* 5, part 3 (July 1999), 332, 335–336; see also his *Myths and Memories of the Nation* (Oxford: Oxford University Press, 1999), chap. 4.

8. Smith, "Ethnic Election," 336–337.

9. Krishan Kumar, *The Making of English National Identity* (Cambridge: Cambridge University Press, 2003), 31, 34; Kumar compares English with Austrian, Ottoman, and

Russian consciousness in "Nation and Empire: English and British National Identity in Comparative Perspective," *Theory and Society* 29, no. 5 (2000), 575–608.

10. Anthony D. Smith, *Chosen Peoples: Sacred Sources of National Identity* (Oxford: Oxford University Press, 2003), 96.

11. Eric P. Kaufmann, "Dominant Ethnicity: From Background to Foreground," in Kaufmann, ed., *Rethinking Ethnicity,* 1–14.

12. N. A. Berdiaev, *Russkaia ideia* (Paris: YMCA Press, 1946), 12.

13. Ibid., 250–251.

14. Ibid., 12.

15. I have argued this point at length in Geoffrey Hosking, *Russia: People and Empire, 1552–1917* (Cambridge, Mass.: Harvard University Press, 1997).

16. This point is discussed at length in Tim McDaniel, *The Agony of the Russian Idea* (Princeton: Princeton University Press, 1996), 24–29.

## 1. Marxism and the Crisis of Russian Messianism

1. These matters are more fully explored in Geoffrey Hosking, *Russia: People and Empire, 1552–1917* (Cambridge, Mass.: Harvard University Press, 1997), 5–8, 64–74.

2. Adrian Hastings, *The Construction of Nationhood: Ethnicity, Religion and Nationalism* (Cambridge: Cambridge University Press, 1997), chap. 1.

3. Susan Reynolds, *Kingdoms and Communities in Western Europe, 900–1300* (Oxford: Clarendon Press, 1984), 115–116, 149; Hilton L. Root, *Peasants and King in Burgundy: Agrarian Foundations of French Absolutism* (Berkeley: University of California Press, 1987).

4. Jerome Blum, "The Internal Structure and Polity of the European Village Community from the Fifteenth to the Nineteenth Century," *Journal of Modern History* 43 (1971), 543–576.

5. H. Dewey and A. Kleimola, "From Kinship Group to Every Man His Brother's Keeper: Collective Responsibility in Pre-Petrine Russia," *Jahrbücher für Geschichte Osteuropas* 30 (1982), 321–335.

6. P. Czap, "Peasant Class Courts and Peasant Customary Justice in Russia, 1861–1912," *Journal of Social History* 1 (1967), 149–178; L. V. Danilova and V. P. Danilov, "Krest'ianskaia mental'nost' i obshchina," in V. P. Danilov and L. V. Milov, eds., *Mentalitet i agrarnoe razvitie v Rossii (xix–xx vv.)* (Moscow: Rosspen, 1996), 22–39; L. S. Prokop'eva, *Krest'ianskaia obshchina v Rossii vo vtoroi polovine xviii–pervoi polovine xix veka* (Leningrad: Nauka, 1981), chap. 4.

7. *Poslovitsy russkogo naroda: sbornik V. Dalia* (Moscow: Khudozhestvennaia Literatura, 1984), 22, 26.

8. B. N. Mironov, *Sotsial'naia istoriia Rossii perioda imperii* 1 (St. Petersburg: Dmitrii Bulanin, 1999), 330; T. K. Dennison and W. W. Carus, "The Invention of the Russian Rural Commune: Haxthausen and the Evidence," *Historical Journal* 46 (2003), 561–582, argues that Russian peasants acted in a less egalitarian and collective spirit than is usually thought. However, the article takes its evidence from only one village and concerns practices rather than attitudes.

9. Danilov and Danilova, "Krest'ianskaia mental'nost'"; L. V. Milov, *Velikorusskii pakhar' i osobennosti rossiiskogo istoricheskogo protsessa* (Moscow: Rosspen, 1998), 418–423.

10. M. M. Gromyko, *Traditsionnye normy povedeniia i formy obshcheniia russkikh krest'ian xix veka* (Moscow: Nauka, 1986), chap. 1.

11. C. A. Frierson, "Razdel: The Peasant Family Divided," *Russian Review* 46 (1987), 35–51; C. D. Worobec, *Peasant Russia: Family and Community in the Post-Emancipation Period* (Princeton: Princeton University Press, 1991), chap. 6.

12. Geroid Tanquary Robinson, *Rural Russia under the Old Regime: A History of the Landlord-Peasant World and a Prologue to the Peasant Revolution of 1917* (New York: The Macmillan Company, 1932), 34–35; Robert Edelman, *Proletarian Peasants: The Revolution of 1905 in Russia's Southwest* (Ithaca: Cornell University Press, 1987), 61–62.

13. Andreas Kappeler, "The Ukrainians of the Russian Empire, 1860–1914," in Kappeler, ed., *The Formation of National Elites* (New York: New York University Press, 1992), 106; Jan Zaprudnik, *Belarus: At a Crossroads in History* (Boulder, Colo.: Westview Press, 1993), 62.

14. Alexei Miller, "Shaping Russian and Ukrainian Identities in the Russian Empire during the Nineteenth Century: Some Methodological Remarks," *Jahrbücher für Osteuropäische Geschichte* 49 (2001), 257.

15. M. K. Lemke, *Epokha tsenzurnykh reform, 1859–1865* (St. Petersburg, 1904), 303; David Saunders, "Russia and Ukraine under Alexander II: The Valuev Edict of 1863," *International History Review* 57 (1995), 31.

16. Zaprudnik, *Belarus,* 63–65.

17. Kappeler, "The Ukrainians," 105–131.

18. Peter Gatrell, *A Whole Empire Walking: Refugees in Russia during World War I* (Bloomington: Indiana University Press, 1999), 165–168.

19. Mark von Hagen, "The Great War and the Mobilisation of Ethnicity," in Barnett R. Rubin and Jack Snyder, eds., *The Post-Soviet Political Order: Conflict and State-Building* (London: Routledge, 1998), 34–57.

20. Wolodymyr Stoiko, "Ukrainian National Aspirations and the Russian Provisional Government," in Taras Hunczak, ed., *The Ukraine, 1917–1921: A Study in Revolution* (Cambridge, Mass.: Harvard University Press, 1977), 4–32.

21. Geoff Eley, "Remapping the Nation: War, Revolutionary Upheaval and State Formation in Eastern Europe, 1914–1923," in P. J. Potichnyj and Howard Aster, eds., *Ukrainian-Jewish Relations in Historical Perspective* (Edmonton: Canadian Institute of Ukrainian Studies, 1988), 240.

22. S. L. Guthier, "The Popular Base of Ukrainian Nationalism in 1917," *Slavic Review* 38 (1979), 30–47; Andrew Wilson, "Ukraine: Between Eurasia and the West," in Seamus Dunn and T. G. Fraser, eds., *Europe and Ethnicity: World War I and Contemporary Ethnic Conflict* (London: Routledge, 1996), 110–137.

23. Zaprudnik, *Belarus,* 63–65; Nicholas P. Vakar, *Belorussia: The Making of a Nation* (Cambridge, Mass.: Harvard University Press, 1956), 87–92; Steven L. Guthier, "The Belorussians: National Identification and Assimilation, 1897–1970," *Soviet Studies* 19 (1977), 37–61; Andrew Wilson, "Myths of National History in Belarus and Ukraine," in Geoffrey Hosking and George Schöpflin, eds., *Myths and Nationhood* (New York:

Routledge, 1997), 186–194; Grigory Ioffe, "Understanding Belarus: Belarusan Identity," *Europe-Asia Studies* (2003), 1241–1249.

24. Robert Service, *Lenin: A Political Life,* vol. 3: *The Iron Ring* (Basingstoke, England: Macmillan, 1995), 92–94.

25. Hosking, *People and Empire,* 271–275.

26. N. Riasanovsky, *Russia and the West in the Teachings of the Slavophiles: A Study of Romantic Ideology* (Cambridge, Mass.: Harvard University Press, 1952), 135.

27. Hosking, *People and Empire,* part 4, chap. 2.

28. Jay Bergman, "The Image of Jesus in the Russian Revolutionary Movement: The Case of Marxism," *International Review of Social History* 35 (1990), 223–224.

29. David McLellan, ed., *Karl Marx: Selected Writings* (Oxford: Oxford University Press, 1977), 576–577.

30. Peter J. S. Duncan, *Russian Messianism: Third Rome, Revolution, Communism and After* (London: Routledge, 2000), 50.

31. Erich Haberer, *Jews and Revolution in Nineteenth-Century Russia* (Cambridge: Cambridge University Press, 1995), 253–272; quotations on pp. 270, 260.

32. Duncan, *Russian Messianism,* 51; Baruch Knei-Paz, *The Social and Political Thought of Leon Trotsky* (Oxford: Clarendon Press, 1978), chap. 4 and pp. 308–310.

33. Daniel Field, "Peasants and Propagandists in the Russian Movement to the People of 1874," *Journal of Modern History* 59 (1987), 415–438.

34. A. I. Klibanov, *Istoriia religioznogo sektantstva v Rossii (60-gody xix veka-1917g)* (Moscow: Nauka, 1965), 39–49; A. A. Panchenko, *Khristovshchina i skopchestvo: fol'klor i traditsionnaia kul'tura russkikh misticheskikh sekt* (Moscow: OGI, 2002), chaps. 2–3.

35. A. S. Prugavin, *Staroobriadchestvo vo vtoroi polovine XIX veka* (Moscow, 1904), 7–23; Roy R. Robson, *Old Believers in Modern Russia* (DeKalb: Northern Illinois University Press, 1995), 20–21.

36. Frederick C. Conybeare, *Russian Dissenters* (Cambridge, Mass.: Harvard University Press, 1921), 245.

37. "Ispoved' V. I. Kel'sieva," *Literaturnoe nasledstvo* 41–42 (1941), 319.

38. Pierre Pascal, *The Religion of the Russian People,* trans. Rowan Williams (London: Mowbrays, 1976); A. A. Panchenko, *Narodnoe pravoslavie* (St. Petersburg: Aleteia, 1998), especially chap. 2.

39. Vera Shevzov, *Russian Orthodoxy on the Eve of Revolution* (Oxford: Oxford University Press, 2004).

40. John Meyendorff, "Russian Bishops and Church Reform in 1905," Robert L. Nichols and Theofanis G. Stavrou, eds., *Russian Orthodoxy under the Old Regime* (Minneapolis: University of Minnesota Press, 1978), 170–182.

41. J. Y. Cunningham, *A Vanquished Hope: The Movement for Church Renewal in Russia, 1905–1906* (Crestwood, N.Y.: St. Vladimir's Seminary Press, 1981), 133–162.

42. Edward E. Roslof, *Red Priests: Renovationism, Russian Orthodoxy, and Revolution, 1905–1946* (Bloomington: Indiana University Press, 2002), 7.

43. Geoffrey Hosking, *Russia and the Russians: A History* (Cambridge, Mass.: Harvard University Press, 2001), 381–382.

44. Prot. Ioann Vostorgov, *Rech' v den' prazdovaniia kazanskoi ikony Bozhiei Materi* (Moscow, 1909), 4–6, quoted in Shevzov, *Russian Orthodoxy,* 245.

45. F. M. Dostoevskii, *Polnoe sobranie sochinenii,* vol. 23 (Leningrad: Nauka, 1981), 41.

46. Ibid., vol. 25 (1983), 17.

47. "Dnevnik pisatelia," April 1877, ibid., p. 100.

48. Ibid., vol. 25, p. 85.

49. David I. Goldstein, *Dostoevsky and the Jews* (Austin: University of Texas Press, 1981), 160–163.

50. Richard Wortman, *Scenarios of Power: Myth and Ceremony in Russian monarchy,* vol. 1 (Princeton: Princeton University Press, 1995), 49–50.

51. This is my own interpretation, but it rests in part on V. M. Zhivov and B. A. Uspenskii, "Tsar' i Bog: semioticheskie aspekty sakralizatsii monarkha v Rossii," in B. A. Uspenskii, ed., *Iazyki kul'tury i problemy perevodimosti* (Moscow: Nauka, 1987), 47–153.

52. Abraham Ascher, *The Revolution of 1905,* vol. 1, *Russia in Disarray* (Stanford: Stanford University Press, 1988), 92–98, 164.

53. Mark D. Steinberg, "Workers on the Cross: Religious Imagination in the Writings of Russian Workers, 1910–1924," *Russian Review* 53 (1994), 213–239; quotations on pp. 220, 223.

54. L. T. Senchakova, *Prigovory i nakazy rossiiskogo krest'ianstva, 1905–1907gg* (Moscow: Institut Rossiiskoi Istorii RAN, 1994), 133.

55. Oskar Anweiler, *The Soviets: The Russian Workers', Peasants', and Soldiers' Councils, 1905–1921* (New York: Pantheon Books, 1974), esp. 40–43, 51–55.

56. Peter Holquist, *Making War, Forging Revolution: Russia's Continuum of Crisis, 1914–1921* (Cambridge, Mass.: Harvard University Press, 2002), chap. 1.

57. William G. Rosenberg, *Liberals in the Russian Revolution: The Constitutional Democratic Party, 1917–1921* (Princeton: Princeton University Press, 1974), 142–144, 170–175; Oliver H. Radkey, *The Agrarian Foes of Bolshevism* (New York: Columbia University Press, 1958), 274–278, 473–484.

58. John Channon, "The Bolsheviks and the Peasantry: The Land Question during the First Eight Months of Soviet Rule," *Slavonic and East European Review* 66 (1988), 593–624.

59. Hosking, *People and Empire,* part 4, chap. 6. The best overall account of the 1917 revolution is Orlando Figes, *A People's Tragedy: The Russian Revolution, 1891–1924* (London: Jonathan Cape, 1996).

60. Figes, *People's Tragedy,* 523–524, 529.

61. Konstantin Paustovsky, *Story of a Life,* vol. 3: *In That Dawn* (London: Harvill Press, 1967), 18.

62. Figes, *People's Tragedy,* 531–532, 462–463.

63. A. D. Maliavskii, *Krest'ianskoe dvizhenie v Rossii v 1917g, mart-oktiabr'* (Moscow: Nauka, 1981), 343–346.

64. Lev Kopelev, *I sotvoril sebe kumira* (Ann Arbor, Mich.: Ardis, 1978), 112.

65. This view of the revolution is well set out in Figes, *People's Tragedy.*

66. Aleksandr Blok, *Polnoe sobranie sochinenii i pisem,* vol. 5 (Moscow: Nauka, 1999), 20.

67. Avril Pyman, *The Life of Alexander Blok,* vol. 2 (Oxford: Oxford University Press, 1980), 365; John Garrard, "The Twelve: Blok's Apocalypse," *Religion and Literature* 35, no. 1 (Spring 2003), 45–72.

68. Anatolii Lunacharskii, "Revoliutsiia i iskusstvo," in Lunacharskii, *Sobranie sochinenii,* vol. 7 (Moscow: Khudozhestvennaia Literatura, 1963–1968), 484.

69. Lunacharskii, "Novyi russkii chelovek," in Lunacharskii, *Sobranie sochinenii,* vol. 7, pp. 303–308, quotation on p. 305.

70. Peter Kenez, "A Profile of the Pre-Revolutionary Russian Officer Corps," *California Slavic Studies,* no. 7 (1973), 121–158.

## 2. The Effects of Revolution and Civil War

1. Andrzej Walicki, *Marxism and the Leap to the Kingdom of Freedom* (Stanford: Stanford University Press, 1995), chap. 4, "Leninism: From 'Scientific Socialism' to Totalitarian Communism."

2. V. I. Lenin, *Polnoe sobranie sochinenii,* 5th ed., vol. 35 (Moscow: Gospolitizdat, 1962), 67 (hereafter Lenin, *PSS*).

3. Walicki, *Marxism,* 361.

4. N. Buharin and E. Preobrazhensky, *The ABC of Communism: A Popular Explanation of the Program of the Communist Party of Russia,* trans. Eden Paul and Cedar Paul (London: Communist Party of Great Britain, 1922), 69–75; quotation on p. 72.

5. Ibid., 198, 203, 200.

6. Ibid., 140.

7. Trotsky, *Literature and Revolution* (Ann Arbor: University of Michigan Press, 1960), 256.

8. Jane Degras, ed., *The Communist International, 1919–1943: Documents,* vol. 1 (London: Oxford University Press, 1956), 43, 46; Adam Ulam, *Expansion and Coexistence: The History of Soviet Foreign Policy, 1917–1967* (New York: Praeger, 1968), 115–116.

9. Lynn Viola, *Peasant Rebels under Stalin: Collectivization and the Culture of Peasant Resistance* (New York: Oxford University Press, 1996).

10. Emma Goldman, *My Disillusionment in Russia* (London: Heinemann, 1923), 11–12.

11. D. R. Brower, "'The City in Danger': The Civil War and the Russian Urban Population," in Diane P. Koenker, William G. Rosenberg, and Ronald Grigor Suny, eds., *Party, State, and Society in the Russian Civil War: Explorations in Social History* (Bloomington: Indiana University Press, 1989), 75.

12. Orlando Figes, *A People's Tragedy: The Russian Revolution, 1891–1924* (London: Jonathan Cape, 1996), 603.

13. M. M. Prishvin, *Dnevniki, 1918–1919* (Moscow: Moskovskii rabochii, 1994), 169.

14. *Time of Troubles: The Diary of Iurii Vladimirovich Got'e,* trans., ed., and with an introduction by Terence Emmons (London: I. B. Tauris and Co., 1988), 233.

15. Sofia Volkonskaia, "The Way of Bitterness," in Sheila Fitzpatrick and Yuri Slezkine, eds., *In the Shadow of Revolution: Life Stories of Russian Women from 1917 to the Second World War* (Princeton: Princeton University Press, 2000), 156.

16. *Time of Troubles,* 246–248, 262, 269, 258.

17. D. Berto [Berteaux], "Transmissii sotsial'nogo statusa v ekstremal'noi situatsii," in

V. Semenova and E. Foteeva, eds., *Sud'by liudei: Rossiia XX vek. Biografiia semei kak ob"ekt sotsiologicheskogo issledovaniia* (Moscow: Institut sotsiologii RAN, 1996), 213–214.

18. Igor' Narskii, *Zhizn' v katastrofe: budni naseleniia Urala v 1917–1922gg* (Moscow: Rosspen, 2001), 392.

19. Figes, *Tragedy,* 529.

20. Goldman, *Disillusionment,* 16–17.

21. Figes, *Tragedy,* 610–611.

22. On towns in the civil war, see Brower, "'The City in Danger,'" 58–80.

23. Narskii, *Zhizn' v katastrofe,* 261–262.

24. Ibid., 231.

25. Ibid., 281.

26. Lars Lih, *Bread and Authority in Russia, 1914–1921* (Berkeley: University of California Press, 1990), 135.

27. Russkaia Biblioteka-Fond Zarubezh'ia (hereafter RBZ), fond R 243 (Kuderina-Nasonova), list'ia (henceforth ll.) 57–58.

28. Figes, *Tragedy,* 524; Lenin, *PSS,* 5th ed., vol. 35, p. 204.

29. Narskii, *Zhizn' v katastrofe,* 235–236.

30. *Naselenie Rossii v XX veke: istoricheskie ocherki,* vol. 1 (1900–1939) (Moscow: Rosspen, 2000), 78–81. See also Iu.A. Poliakov, *Sovetskaia strana posle okonchaniia grazhdanskoi voiny: territoriia i naselenie* (Moscow: Nauka, 1986), 92–128.

31. *Naselenie Rossii,* 95–96.

32. Ibid., 105–106, 113.

33. Barbara Evans Clements, "The Effects of Civil War on Women and Family Relations," in Koenker et al., *Party, State, and Society,* 105–122.

34. Barbara Misztal, *Trust in Modern Societies* (London: Polity Press, 1996), 139.

35. Maurice Halbwachs, *On Collective Memory,* ed., trans., and with an introduction by Lewis A. Coser (Chicago: University of Chicago Press, 1992), 40; Jan Assmann, *Das kulturelle Gedächtnis: Schrift, Erinnerung und politische Identität in frühen Hochkulturen* (Munich: Verlag C. H. Beck, 1992), 35–49.

36. Assmann, *Kulturelle Gedächtnis,* 77.

37. Misztal, *Trust,* 195.

38. Hans-Joachim Neubauer, *The Rumour: A Cultural History,* trans. Christian Braun (London: Free Association Books, 1999), 90.

39. Ibid., 4, 116; Francis Fukuyama, *The Great Disruption: Human Nature and the Reconstitution of Social Order* (London: Profile Books, 1999), chap. 9.

40. Neubauer, *Rumour,* 94–101.

41. James C. Scott, *Domination and the Arts of Resistance: Hidden Transcripts* (New Haven: Yale University Press, 1990), 144.

42. Nadezhda Mandelstam, *Hope Abandoned,* trans. Max Hayward (Harmondsworth: Penguin Books, 1976), 20.

43. This is the basic thesis of Joshua A. Sanborn, *Drafting the Russian Nation: Military Conscription, Total War, and Mass Politics, 1905–1925* (DeKalb: Northern Illinois University Press, 2003).

44. Ibid., 122–131, chaps. 4 and 5; Elena Dubrovskaia, "'Shkola muzhestva'—for-

mirovanie novykh tsennostei v armeiskoi i flotskoi srede v 1920-ye gody," in *Normy i tsennosti povsednevnoi zhizni: stanovlenie sotsialisticheskogo obraza zhizni v Rossii v 20–30 gody* (St. Petersburg: Institut Finliandii, 2000), 317–346.

45. Stefan Plaggenborg, "Gewalt und Militanz in Sowjetrussland, 1917–1930," *Jahrbücher für Geschichte Osteuropas,* vol. 44 (1996), 409–429.

46. Sheila Fitzpatrick, "The Legacy of the Civil War," in Koenker et al., *Party, State, and Society,* 385–398; Eric Naiman, *Sex in Public: The Incarnation of Early Soviet Ideology* (Princeton: Princeton University Press, 1997).

47. Gerald M. Easter, *Reconstructing the State: Personal Networks and Elite Identity in Soviet Russia* (Cambridge: Cambridge University Press, 2000).

48. Fitzpatrick, "The Legacy of the Civil War," 385–398; quotation on p. 393.

49. Sanborn, however, does: see, e.g., *Drafting,* 207.

50. Figes, *Tragedy,* 696–699.

51. Sanborn, *Drafting,* 82–91.

52. Peter Holquist, "'Information Is the Alpha and Omega of Our Work': Bolshevik Surveillance in Its Pan-European Context," *Journal of Modern History,* vol. 69 (1997), 415–450; quotation on p. 419.

53. Ibid., esp. 422, 431.

54. Peter Holquist, "What Is So Revolutionary about the Russian Revolution? State Practices and New-Style Politics, 1914–21," in David L. Hoffmann and Yanni Kotsonis, eds., *Russian Modernity: Politics, Knowledge, Practices* (London: Macmillan, 2000), 87–111.

55. Peter Kenez, *The Birth of the Propaganda State: Soviet Methods of Mass Mobilisation, 1917–1929* (Cambridge University Press, 1985), 253.

56. Igal Halfin, *From Darkness to Light: Class, Consciousness, and Salvation in Revolutionary Russia* (Pittsburgh: University of Pittsburgh Press, 2000), 156, chap. 4.

57. Ibid., 286–287.

58. Figes, *Tragedy,* 756.

59. Oliver H. Radkey, *The Unknown Civil War in Soviet Russia: A Study of the Green Movement in Tambov Region, 1920–1921* (Stanford, Calif.: Hoover Institution Press, 1976).

60. Jonathan Aves, *Workers against Lenin: Labour Protest and the Bolshevik Dictatorship* (London: Tauris, 1996), 112–130.

61. Figes, *Tragedy,* 761.

62. *Rossiia XX vek: Kronstadt 1921* (Moscow: Mezhdunarodnyi Fond "Demokratiia," 1997), 50–51.

63. *Desiatyi s"ezd RKP(b), mart 1921: stenograficheskii otchet* (Moscow: Politizdat, 1963), 34.

64. Edward E. Roslof, *Red Priests: Renovationism, Russian Orthodoxy, and Revolution, 1905–1946* (Bloomington: Indiana University Press, 2002), 20.

65. Paul B. Anderson, *People, Church and State in Modern Russia,* 2nd ed. (London: SCM Press, 1944), 53–55.

66. Ibid., 59–60.

67. Roslof, *Red Priests,* 47.

68. Anatolii Levitin and Vadim Shavrov, *Ocherki po istorii russkoi tserkovnoi smuty,* vol. 1 (Küsnacht: Glaube in der Dritten Welt, 1978), 11–14.

69. Robert Service, *Lenin: A Political Life*, vol. 3 (London: Macmillan, 1995), 246.

70. RBZ, fond R 254 (Sokolov, Vasilii Ivanovich), ll. 97–101.

71. Gregory Freeze, "Counter-Reformation in Russian Orthodoxy: Popular Response to Religious Innovation, 1922–1925," *Slavic Review* 54 (1995), 305–339.

72. Roslof, *Red Priests*, 63, 147, 152–153.

73. Levitin and Shavrov, *Ocherki*, vol. 1, 180–181.

74. Roslof, *Red Priests*, 33.

75. *Russkaia Pravoslavnaia Tserkov' i kommunisticheskoe gosudarstvo, 1917–1941: dokumenty i fotografii* (Moscow: Bibleisko-Bogoslovskii Institut, 1996), 203–206. The whole text is on 224–228.

76. Mikhail Shkarovskii, *Iosiflianstvo: techenie v Russkoi Pravoslavnoi Tserkvi* (Moscow: Memorial, 1999), 12–14, 15–16, 19.

77. Ibid., 15–16.

78. Dimitry Pospielovsky, *The Russian Church under the Soviet Regime, 1917–1982*, vol. 1 (New York: St. Vladimir's Seminary Press, 1984), 164–166.

79. Prot. Nikolai Balashov, *Na puti k liturgicheskomu vozrozhdeniiu* (Moscow: Dukhovnaia Biblioteka, 2001), 6, quoted in Roslof, *Red Priests*, 204.

80. *Perepis' naseleniia 1937g: kratkie itogi* (Moscow: Nauka, 1991), 106–107.

81. Zenovia A. Sochor, *Revolution and Culture: The Bogdanov-Lenin Controversy* (Ithaca: Cornell University Press, 1988).

82. Lynn Mally, *Culture of the Future: The Proletkult Movement in Revolutionary Russia* (Ithaca: Cornell University Press 1990), 131.

83. Ibid., 140.

84. L. M. Farber, *Sovetskaia literatura pervykh let revoliutsii, 1917–1920* (Moscow: Vysshaia Shkola, 1966), 81.

85. James von Geldern, *Bolshevik Festivals, 1917–1920* (Berkeley: University of California Press, 1993), 82–85, 122–125.

86. Ibid., 156–162, 180–187, 200–207.

87. Richard Stites, *Revolutionary Dreams: Utopian Vision and Experimental Life in the Russian Revolution* (New York: Oxford University Press, 1989), 94–95.

88. Ibid., 76–78.

89. Figes, *Tragedy*, 606–607.

90. Mally, *Culture of the Future*, chap. 7.

91. Stites, *Revolutionary Dreams*, 86–87.

92. Nina Tumarkin, *Lenin Lives: The Lenin Cult in Soviet Russia* (Cambridge, Mass.: Harvard University Press, 1983), 178–182; Jay Bergman, "The Image of Jesus in the Russian Revolutionary Movement: The Case of Marxism," *International Review of Social History* 35 (1990), 242.

93. Tumarkin, *Lenin Lives*, chap. 6.

## 3. Soviet Nationality Policy and the Russians

1. Abdurakhman Avtorkhanov, *Memuary* (Frankfurt am Main: Posev, 1983), 71–83.

2. Ibid., 83.

3. N. Buharin and E. Preobrazhensky, *The ABC of Communism: A Popular Explana-*

*tion of the Program of the Communist Party of Russia* (London: Communist Party of Great Britain, 1922), 201.

4. A. I. Vdovin, V. Iu. Zorin, and A. V. Nikonov, *Russkii narod v natsional'noi politike: xx vek* (Moscow: Russkii mir, 1998), 87; Baruch Knei-Paz, *The Social and Political Thought of Leon Trotsky* (Oxford: Clarendon Press, 1978), 536.

5. Mary Holdsworth, "Lenin and the Nationalities Question," in Leonard Schapiro and Peter Reddaway, eds., *Lenin: The Man, the Theorist, the Leader—A Reappraisal* (London: Pall Mall Press, 1967), 265–294, 287.

6. Vdovin et al., *Russkii narod,* 103.

7. Ibid., 91.

8. Holdsworth, "Lenin," 292.

9. Robert Service, *Lenin: A Political Life,* vol. 3: *The Iron Ring* (London: Macmillan, 1995), 92–97; Eric van Ree, "Stalin and the National Question," *Revolutionary Russia,* no. 7 (1994), 214–238.

10. *Natsional'nyi vopros na perekrestke mnenii: 20-ye gody. Dokumenty i materialy* (Moscow: Nauka, 1992), 114.

11. Gerhard Simon, *Nationalism and Policy toward the Nationalities in the Soviet Union* (Boulder, Colo.: Westview Press, 1991), 415.

12. Jeremy Smith, *The Bolsheviks and the National Question, 1917–1923* (London: Macmillan, 1999), 26.

13. Ibid., chap. 4; Valerii Tishkov, *Ethnicity, Nationalism and Conflict in and after the Soviet Union: The Mind Aflame* (London: Sage, 1997), chap. 2; Terry Martin, *The Affirmative Action Empire: Nations and Nationalism in the Soviet Union, 1923–1939* (Ithaca: Cornell University Press, 2001), chap. 1.

14. Smith, *Bolsheviks and the National Question,* 30–34, 40–41.

15. Francine Hirsch, *Empire of Nations: Ethnographic Knowledge and the Making of the Soviet Union* (Ithaca: Cornell University Press, 2005), chap. 3, esp. 120.

16. T. Bottomore and P. Goode, eds., *Austro-Marxism* (Oxford: Clarendon Press, 1978), 114–117; Andreas Kappeler, *Russland als Vielvölkerreich: Entstehung, Geschichte, Zerfall* (Munich: C. H. Beck, 1992), 300–302.

17. Smith, *Bolsheviks and the National Question,* 29–65.

18. V. Kabuzan, *Russkie v mire* (St. Petersburg: Blits, 1996), 249–250; Robert Kaiser, *The Geography of Nationalism in Russia and the USSR* (Princeton: Princeton University Press, 1994), 118.

19. Terry Martin, "Borders and Ethnic Conflict: The Soviet Experiment in Ethno-Territorial Proliferation," *Jahrbücher für Osteuropäische Geschichte* 47 (1999), 538–555.

20. Martin, *Affirmative Action Empire,* 33–48; Martin, "Borders," 540.

21. Martin, "The Russification of the RSFSR," *Cahiers du Monde Russe* 39 (1998), 103–104.

22. Martin, *Affirmative Action Empire,* 38–39.

23. Ibid., 45–46.

24. Peter Holquist, *Making War, Forging Revolution: Russia's Continuum of Crisis, 1914–1921* (Cambridge, Mass.: Harvard University Press, 2002), 180, 188–202; quotations on pp. 195, 199.

25. Martin, *Affirmative Action Empire,* 60–61; N. Bugai amd A. M. Gonov, *Kavkaz:*

*narody v eshelonakh* (Moscow: Insan, 1998), 83–91; Peter Holquist, "'Conduct Merciless Mass Terror': Decossackization on the Don," *Cahiers du Monde Russe,* 38 (1997), 127–162.

26. V. L. Genis, "Deportatsiia russkikh iz Turkestana v 1921 godu (delo Safarova)," *Voprosy istorii,* no. 1 (1998), 46–47.

27. Ibid., 57; a desiatina is 1.09 hectares or 2.7 acres.

28. Martin, *Affirmative Action Empire,* 148–149.

29. Matt Payne, "The Forge of the Kazakh Proletariat? The Turksib, Nativization and Industrialization during Stalin's First Five-Year Plan," in Ronald Grigor Suny and Terry Martin, eds., *A State of Nations: Empire and Nation-Making in the Age of Lenin and Stalin* (Oxford: Oxford University Press, 2001), 223–252.

30. Robert Service, *Russia: Experiment with a People* (London: Macmillan, 2002), 34–38; Yuri Slezkine, "The USSR as Communal Apartment, or How a Socialist State Promoted Ethnic Particularism," *Slavic Review* 53 (1994), 414–452.

31. Martin, *Affirmative Action Empire,* 400–401.

32. Slezkine, "The USSR as Communal Apartment."

33. Lenin, *PSS,* 5th ed., vol. 35, p. 279.

34. Stephen Cohen, *Bukharin and the Bolshevik Revolution: A Political Biography, 1888–1938* (New York: Vintage Books, 1975), chap. 3.

35. Lenin, *PSS,* 5th ed., vol. 36, pp. 79–80.

36. Mikhail Agursky, *The Third Rome: National Bolshevism in the USSR* (Boulder, Colo.: Westview, 1987), 217–218.

37. Orlando Figes, *A People's Tragedy: The Russian Revolution, 1891–1924* (London: Jonathan Cape, 1996), 696–699.

38. Jeremy R. Azrael, *Managerial Power and Soviet Politics* (Cambridge, Mass.: Harvard University Press, 1966), 38–39, 59–61.

39. Nicholas V. Riasanovsky, "The Emergence of Eurasianism," *California Slavic Studies* 4 (1967), 39–72.

40. E. Oberländer, "Nationalbolschewistische Tendenzen in der russischen Intelligenz: die Smenavekh-diskussion," *Jahrbücher für Geschichte Osteuropas* 16 (1968), 195.

41. N. V. Ustrialov, "Patriotica," *Smena vekh* (Prague, 1921), 52–71; quotations on pp. 59, 57.

42. N. V. Ustrialov, "Krizis sovremennoi demokratii," in his *Pod znakom revoliutsii* (Kharbin, 1925), 248–264; quotations on pp. 250, 252, 254; Agursky, *Third Rome,* 243–246. The old aristocracy was sometimes called "the aristocracy of white bones"; hence the reference to "black bones."

43. Oberländer, "Nationalbolschewistische Tendenzen," 203.

44. A. V. Bobrishchev-Pushkin, "Novaia vera," *Smena vekh,* 91–149, esp. 130.

45. S. S. Chakhotin, "V Kanossu!," *Smena vekh,* 150–166; quotations on pp. 161, 159.

46. J. V. Stalin, "October and Trotskii's Theory of Permanent Revolution," in Stalin, *Works,* vol. 6 (Moscow: Foreign Languages Publishing House, 1953), 378–397.

47. Agursky, *Third Rome,* 251–252.

48. Jürgen Rühle, *Literatur und Revolution: die Schriftsteller und der Kommunismus* (Munich: Knaur, 1963), 95–101.

49. Oberländer, "Nationalbolschewistische Tendenzen," 194–211.

50. Kendall Bailes, *Science and Russian Culture in an Age of Revolutions: V. I. Vernadsky and His Scientific School, 1863–1945* (Bloomington: Indiana University Press, 1990), esp. 160–164; Gennadii Aksenov, *Vernadskii* (Moscow: Molodaia Gvardiia, 2001).

51. Agursky, *Third Rome,* 260–261.

52. Oberländer, "Nationalbolschewistische Tendenzen," 206.

53. Agursky, *Third Rome,* 261–266.

54. I. V. Stalin, *Sochineniia,* vol. 7 (Moscow: OGIZ, 1947), 341–342.

55. Stalin, "Oktiabr'skaia revoliutsiia i taktika russkikh kommunistov," *Sochineniia,* vol. 6, pp. 358–401 (quotation p. 377), and "K voprosam leninizma," vol. 8, pp. 13–90.

## 4. Two Russias Collide

1. RBZ, fond R-168 (S. A. Voronov), ll. 17, 22.

2. Helmut Altrichter, *Die Bauern von Tver: vom Leben auf dem russischen Dorfe zwischen Revolution und Kollektivierung* (Munich: R. Oldenbourg Verlag, 1984), 100–108.

3. Neil Weissman, "Policing the NEP Countryside," in Sheila Fitzpatrick, Alexander Rabinowitch, and Richard Stites, eds., *Russia in the Era of NEP: Explorations in Soviet Society and Culture* (Bloomington: Indiana University Press, 1991), 174–191; Altrichter, *Tver,* 154–159.

4. Altrichter, *Tver,* 92–100.

5. Lynn Viola, *Peasant Rebels under Stalin: Collectivization and the Culture of Peasant Resistance* (New York: Oxford University Press, 1996), 54.

6. RBZ, R-385 (V. P. Beliaev), ll. 7, 7ob.

7. Roger Pethybridge, *The Social Prelude to Stalinism* (London: Macmillan, 1974), 229–235.

8. RBZ, R-243 (T. G. Kuderina-Nasonova), ll. 77–78.

9. Theodore Dreiser, *Dreiser Looks at Russia* (London: Constable, 1928), 90.

10. *Narodnoe khoziaistvo, 1922–1982 gg* (Moscow: Finansy i Statistika, 1982), 41. For a general account of the *likbez* campaign, see Pethybridge, *Social Prelude,* chap. 4.

11. Lev Kopelev, *I sotvoril sebe kumira* (Ann Arbor: Ardis, 1978), 249.

12. Lynne Viola, *Peasant Rebels,* 38–41; Richard Hernandez, "Sacred Sound and Sacred Substance: Church Bells and the Auditory Culture of Russian Villages during the Bolshevik Velikii Perelom," *American Historical Review* 109, no. 5 (Dec. 2004), 1475–1504.

13. RBZ, R-385, ll. 7ob-8.

14. Viola, *Peasant Rebels,* 147–150, 194–195.

15. Hernandez, "Sacred Sound," 1502.

16. RBZ, R-385, l. 8.

17. RBZ, R-464 (Anna Nikitichna Chernichenko), ll. 4–5.

18. RBZ, R-211 (N.I. Kuznetsova), l. 6.

19. RBZ, R-211, l. 6.

20. RBZ, R-206 (Anton Savel'evich Lisechko), l. 5. This excerpt is from the diary of a

peasant from Dnepropetrovsk oblast, which was found by his daughter after his death in 1973.

21. *Tragediia sovetskoi derevni: kollektivizatsiia i raskulachivanie. Dokumenty i materialy, 1927–1939,* vol. 2 (noiabr' 1929–dekabr' 1930) (Moscow: Rosspen, 2000), 704–705; N. A. Ivnitskii, *Kollektivizatsiia i raskulachivanie nachala 30-kh godov* (Moscow: Magistr, 1996), 139–140, 203; Jörg Baberowski, "Die Kulakendeportation," *Jahrbücher für Geschichte Osteuropas* 46 (1998), 572–595. For an NKVD progress report on the deportation of kulaks, see Diane Koenker and Ronald Bachman, *Revelations from the Russian Archives: Documents in English translation* (Washington, D.C.: Library of Congress, 1997), 384–387; and also the account by Ivan Tvardovskii, brother of the well-known poet, in *Iunost,* no. 3 (1988), 10–32.

22. V. N. Zemskov, "Kulatskaia ssylka v 30-ye gody," *Sotsiologicheskie issledovaniia,* no. 10 (1991), 6.

23. RBZ, R-206, ll. 6–8.

24. RBZ, R-331 (Diliia Abbas-ogly), l. 63.

25. *Pis'ma vo vlast', 1928–1939: zaiavleniia, zhaloby, donosy, pis'ma v gosudarstvennye struktury i sovetskim vozhdiam* (Moscow: Rosspen, 2002), 104–105.

26. I owe this perception to Professor Claudio Ingerflom.

27. Viola, *Peasant Rebels,* 63.

28. Ibid., 57–60, 62, 59.

29. Ibid., chap. 6.

30. Ibid., 145.

31. Ibid., 161–163, 165, 168.

32. Figures in ibid., 138–139; Andrea Graziosi, "Collectivisation et révoltes paysannes en Ukraine," *Cahiers du Monde Russe* 35 (1994), 599–628; *Tragediia sovetskoi derevni,* 801, 191–194; 405–409; 430–432; 710–722; 787–808.

33. Viola, *Peasant Rebels,* 120–121.

34. *Tragediia sovetskoi derevni,* vol. 2, p. 191; Ivnitskii, *Kollektivizatsiia,* 92, 156–157.

35. Terry Martin, *The Affirmative Action Empire: Nations and Nationalism in the Soviet Union, 1923–1939* (Ithaca: Cornell University Press, 2001), 296; R. W. Davies et al, eds., *The Stalin-Kaganovich Correspondence, 1931–1936* (New Haven: Yale University Press, 2003), 180.

36. Martin, *Affirmative Action Empire,* 301; Nobuo Shimotomai, "A Note on the Kuban Affair (1932–3)," *Acta Slavica Iaponica* 1 (1983), 39–56.

37. Notably Robert Conquest, *The Harvest of Sorrow: Soviet Collectivisation and the Terror Famine* (London: Hutchinson, 1986), and James Mace, *Famine in the Soviet Ukraine, 1931–33* (Cambridge, Mass.: Harvard Ukrainian Institute, 1986).

38. Stephan Merl, "War die Hungersnot von 1932–33 eine Folge der Zwangskollektivierung der Landwirtschaft oder wurde sie bewusst im Rahmen der Nationalitätenpolitik herbeigeführt?" in Guido Hausmann and Andreas Kappeler, eds., *Ukraine: Gegenwart und Geschichte eines neuen Staaates* (Baden-Baden: Nomos Verlag, 1993), 145–166.

39. Martin, *Affirmative Action Empire,* 302; Terry Martin, "The Russification of the RSFSR," *Cahiers du Monde Russe* 39 (1998), 99–118, esp. 104, 107; Robert Conquest, *The Great Terror: Stalin's Purge of the Thirties* (London: Macmillan, 1968), 251–259.

40. RBZ, R-243 (T. G. Kuderina-Nasonova), l. 144.

41. Viktor Kravchenko, *I Chose Freedom: The Personal and Political Life of a Soviet Official* (London: Robert Hale, 1947), 99.

42. D'Ann R. Penner, "Stalin and the Ital'ianka," *Cahiers du Monde Russe* 39 (1998), 27–39; quotation on p. 39.

43. Conquest, *Harvest of Sorrow,* 232; Penner, "Stalin and the Ital'ianka," 40–45, quotation on p. 45; Koenker and Bachman, *Revelations,* 363.

44. RBZ, R-243, l. 141.

45. Ivnitskii, *Kollektivizatsiia,* 203–225; R. W. Davies and S. G. Wheatcroft, eds., *The Economic Transformation of the Soviet Union, 1913–1935* (Cambridge: Cambridge University Press, 1994), 74–76; Conquest, *Harvest of Sorrow,* 249–253.

46. Lazar Fleishman, *Boris Pasternak v tridtsatye gody,* Jerusalem: Magnes Press of the Hebrew University, 1984, 81.

47. Sheila Fitzpatrick, *Stalin's Peasants: Resistance and Survival in the Russian Village after Collectivization* (New York: Oxford University Press, 1994), 128.

48. RBZ, R-385, l. 8.

49. Fitzpatrick, *Stalin's Peasants,* 114–115, 145–147.

50. Karl-Eugen Wädekin, *Privatproduzenten in der sowjetischen Landwirtschaft* (Cologne: Verlag Wissenschaft und Politik, 1967), 96.

51. R-385, ll. 9–9ob.

52. Arvo Tuominen, *The Bells of the Kremlin* (Hanover: University of New England Press, 1983), 113; Fitzpatrick, *Stalin's Peasants,* 288.

53. Fitzpatrick, *Stalin's Peasants,* 92–102; Gijs Kessler, "The Passport System and State Control over Population Flows in the Soviet Union, 1932–40," *Cahiers du Monde Russe* 42 (2001), 477–504.

54. Quoted in David L. Hoffmann, *Peasant Metropolis: Social Identities in Moscow, 1929–1941* (Ithaca: Cornell University Press, 1994), 40.

55. The best summary of kolkhoz life is Fitzpatrick, *Stalin's Peasants,* especially chaps. 4–5.

56. See the analysis of the reasons for moving to Leningrad in Maria Vitukhnovskaia, "'Starye' i 'novye' gorozhane: migranty v Leningrade 30-kh godov," in Timo Vihavainen, ed., *Normy i tsennosti povsednevnoi zhizni: 1920–30e gody* (St. Petersburg: Neva, 2000), 106–114. Statistics from *Naselenie SSSR 1973: statisticheskii sbornik* (Moscow: Statistika, 1975), 14–15, 26–33.

57. *Naselenie Rossii v xx-om veke: istoricheskie ocherki,* vol. 1 (1900–1939) (Moscow: Rosspen, 2000), 235–242.

58. Hoffmann, *Peasant Metropolis,* 54–63.

59. Daniel Bertaux, in collaboration with Marina Malysheva, "The Cultural Model of the Russian Popular Classes and the Transition to a Market Economy," in Daniel Bertaux, Paul Thompson, and Anna Rotkirch, eds., *On Living through Soviet Russia* (London: Routledge, 2004), 28; E. Iu. Gerasimova, "Sovetskaia kommunal'naia kvartira," *Sotsiologicheskii zhurnal,* nos. 1–2 (1998), 224–242.

60. Gerasimova, "Sovetskaia kommunal'naia kvartira."

61. Svetlana Boym, *Common Places: Mythologies of Everyday Life in Russia* (Cam-

bridge, Mass.: Harvard University Press, 1994), 146. Boym spent her childhood in a Leningrad communal apartment.

62. E. Iu. Gerasimova, "Sovetskaia kommunal'naia kvartira kak sotsial'nyi institut" (candidate's thesis, Institute of Sociology, Russian Academy of Sciences, St. Petersburg branch, 2000), 91. I am grateful to Ekaterina Gerasimova for sending me her thesis.

63. Il'ia Utekhin, *Ocherki kommunal'nogo byta* (Moscow: OGI, 2001), 95–100.

64. Ibid., 129.

65. Victoria Semenova, "Equality in Poverty: The Symbolic Meaning of *Kommunalki* in the 1930s-1950s," in Bertaux et al., *On Living,* 64; Gerasimova, "Sovetskaia kommunal'naia kvartira," 239.

66. Boym, *Common Places,* 121.

67. Sheila Fitzpatrick, *Everyday Stalinism: Ordinary Life in Extraordinary Times—Soviet Russia in the 1930s* (New York: Oxford University Press, 1999), 48; Utekhin, *Ocherki,* 131–140.

68. Gerasimova, "Sovetskaia kommunal'naia kvartira kak sotsial'nyi institut," candidate's thesis, 80, 91–93; Utekhin, *Ocherki,* 100–104.

69. Gerasmova, "Sovetskaia kommunal'naia kvartira."

70. Utekhin, *Ocherki,* 122n.

71. Bertaux, "Cultural Model," 44; Alena Ledeneva, "The Genealogy of *Krugovaia Poruka:* Forced Trust as a Feature of Russian Political Culture," in Ivana Markova, ed., *Trust and Democratic Transition in Post-Communist Europe* (Oxford University Press for the British Academy, 2004), 85–108, esp. 99–104; Boym, *Common Places,* 123–124.

72. Hoffmann, *Peasant Metropolis,* 182–189.

73. Ibid., 169–177, 182–189.

74. Stephen Kotkin, *Magnetic Mountain: Stalinism as a Civilization* (Berkeley: University of California Press, 1995), 106, 85.

75. *Pis'ma vo vlast',' 1928–1939,* 185–186.

76. Kotkin, *Magnetic Mountain,* 91–92, 95–96.

77. Hiroaki Kuromiya, "Workers' Artels and Soviet Production Relations," in Fitzpatrick et al., *Russia in the Era of NEP,* 78–82; Donald Filtzer, *Soviet Workers and Stalinist Industrialisation: The Formation of Modern Soviet Production Relations, 1928–1941* (London: Pluto Press, 1986), chap. 6 and pp. 256–257; Kotkin, *Magnetic Mountain,* 223–225.

78. Fitzpatrick, *Everyday Stalinism,* 49, 56–57.

79. J. S. Berliner, *Factory and Manager in the USSR* (Cambridge, Mass.: Harvard University Press, 1957), chap. 12; Alena V. Ledeneva, *Russia's Economy of Favours: Blat, Networking and Informal Exchange* (Cambridge: Cambridge University Press, 1998); Fitzpatrick, *Everyday Stalinism,* chap. 2.

80. See, for example, Tamara Dragadze, *Rural Families in Soviet Georgia: A Case Study in Ratcha Province* (London: Routledge, 1988).

81. RBZ, R-254 Sokolov, Vasilii Ivanovich, "Papka pandory" (Moscow, 1994), l. 222.

82. D. Mendeleev, *K poznaniiu Rossii,* 6th ed. (St. Petersburg: A. S. Suvorin, 1907), 79–80.

83. Ibid., 100–104.

84. Anne Applebaum, *Gulag: A History* (London: Allen Lane, 2003), chap. 3; G. M. Ivanova, *Gulag v sisteme totalitarnogo gosudarstva* (Moscow: Moskovskii Obshchestvennyi Nauchnyi Fond, 1997), 31.

85. Applebaum, *Gulag,* 73–84.

86. David J. Nordlander, "Origins of a Gulag Capital: Magadan and Stalinist Control in the Early 1930s," *Slavic Review* 57 (1998), 791–796.

87. Applebaum, *Gulag,* 84–91; Nordlander, "Origins," 797–808; David Nordlander, "Magadan and the Evolution of the Dal'stroi Bosses," *Cahiers du Monde Russe* 42, 2–4 (April 2001), 649–665.

88. Anthony D. Smith, "Ethnic Election and National Destiny: Some Religious Origins of Nationalist Ideals," *Nations and Nationalism,* vol. 5, part 3 (July 1999), 336–337; Iurii Margolin, *Puteshestvie v stranu ze-ka* (New York: Izdatel'stvo imeni Chekhova, 1952), 48.

89. Aleksandr Solzhenitsyn, *Arkhipelag Gulag, 1918–1956: opyt khudozhestvennogo issledovaniia,* vol. 2 (Paris: YMCA, 1974), 158–160.

90. Alexander Solzhenitsyn, *A Day in the Life of Ivan Denisovich,* trans. H. T. Willetts (London: Harvill, 1991), 48–49; Gustaw Herling-Grudzinski, *A World Apart,* trans. Andrzej Ciolkosz (Oxford: Oxford University Press, 1987), 37; for Solzhenitsyn on the brigade system, see *Arkhipelag,* vol. 2, 155–157.

91. Solzhenitsyn, *Arkhipelag,* vol. 2, 489–520. James Scott, *Domination and the Arts of Resistance: The Hidden Transcripts* (New Haven: Yale University Press, 1990), chaps. 5–6, describes how rumor generates shared fantasies of wish fulfillment.

92. Alexander Solzhenitsyn, *The Gulag Archipelago,* vol. 3, trans. H. T. Willetts (London: Collins and Harvill, 1978), 235–236.

93. Lidiia Chukovskaia, *Zapiski ob Anne Akhmatovoi,* vol. 2 (Paris: YMCA Press, 1980), 137.

94. Gerald M. Easter, *Reconstructing the State: Personal Networks and Elite Identity in Soviet Russia* (Cambridge: Cambridge University Press, 1999), chap. 4.

95. Ibid., chaps. 2–3.

96. Simon Sebag-Montefiore, *Stalin: The Court of the Red Tsar* (London: Weidenfeld and Nicolson, 2003), 57–61; Stephen Lovell, *Summerfolk: A History of the Dacha, 1700–2000* (Ithaca: Cornell University Press, 2003), 131–132.

97. James C. Scott, *Domination and the Arts of Resistance,* 55–58.

98. The process is well examined in the introduction to J. Arch Getty and Oleg V. Naumov, eds., *The Road to Terror: Stalin and the Self-Destruction of the Bolsheviks, 1932–1939* (New Haven: Yale University Press, 1999).

99. Sebag-Montefiore, *Stalin,* 44–45, 135; Robert Service, *Stalin: A Biography* (Basingstoke: Macmillan, 2004), chaps. 30–31.

100. Getty and Naumov, *Road to Terror,* 556–560.

101. Iuliia Piatnitskaia, *Dnevnik zheny bol'shevika* (Benson, Vt.: Chalidze Publications, 1987), 88, 117–120, 75–76.

102. Easter, *Reconstructing,* chap. 6.

103. Sebag-Montefiore, *Stalin,* 114–115; Robert D. Tucker, *Stalin in Power: The Revolution from Above* (New York: Norton, 1990), 247–252, 260–264; Service, *Stalin,* 312–

315. Even with the Central Committee archives open, these events remain shrouded in uncertainty. For a recent treatment by Russian historians, see E. G. Plimak and V. S. Antonov, "1-oe dekabria 1934g: tragediia Kirova i tragediia Sovetskoi Rossii," *Otechestvennaia istoriia,* no 6 (2004), 31–45.

104. Getty and Naumov, *The Road to Terror,* 119–134.

105. Glennys Young, *Power and the Sacred in Revolutionary Russia: Religious Activists in the Village* (University Park: Pennsylvania State University Press, 1997), 92–100, 135–146.

106. Felix Corley, ed., *Religion in the Soviet Union: An Archival Reader* (London: Macmillan, 1996), 86–87.

107. Ibid., 82.

108. M. V. Shkarovskii, *Russkaia pravoslavnaia tserkov' pri Staline i Khrushcheve* (Moscow: Krutitskoe Patriarshee Podvor'e, 1999), 98–99; Pospielovsky, *Russian Church,* vol. 1, 173–175.

109. Veronique Garros, Natalia Korenevskaia, and Thomas Lahusen, eds., *Intimacy and Terror: Soviet Diaries of the 1930s* (New York: The New Press, 1995), 368.

110. Testimony of Anatolii Krasnov-Levitin, quoted in Michael Bourdeaux, *Patriarch and Prophets: Persecution of the Russian Orthodox Church Today* (London: Macmillan, 1969), 291; Pospielovsky, *Russian Church,* vol. 1, 174–177.

111. Timothy Colton, *Moscow: Governing the Socialist Metropolis* (Cambridge, Mass.: Belknap Press of Harvard University Press, 1995), 260–264.

112. Igor Golomshtok, *Totalitarian Art* (London: Collins Harvill, 1990), 274–275; Colton, *Moscow,* 331–334.

113. Pospielovsky, *Russian Church,* vol. 1, 180–181; Mark Popovskii, *Zhizn' i zhitie Voino-Iasenetskogo, arkhiepiskopa i khirurga* (Paris: YMCA Press, 1979), 356–357.

114. *Vsesoiuznaia perepis' naseleniia 1937g: kratkie itogi* (Moscow: Nauka, 1991), 106–107; Catherine Merridale, "The 1937 Census and the Limits of Stalinist Rule," *Historical Journal* 39 (1996), 225–240; Pospielovsky, *Russian Church,* vol. 1, p. 191.

115. RBZ, R-254 (Vasilii Ivanovich Sokolov), ll. 17–28.

116. RBZ, R-254, ll. 78–86.

117. RBZ, R-254, l. 142

118. RBZ, R-254, ll. 147, 155.

119. RBZ, R-254, ll. 221–222.

120. RBZ, R-254, ll. 222–228, 238–240, 249–250, 262.

## 5. Projecting a New Russia

1. Anne E. Gorsuch, *Youth in Revolutionary Russia: Enthusiasts, Bohemians, Delinquents* (Bloomington: Indiana University Press, 2000), 76–77; Larry E. Holmes, *The Kremlin and the Schoolhouse: Reforming Education in Soviet Russia* (Bloomington: Indiana University Press, 1991), 60–61.

2. David Brandenberger, *National Bolshevism: Stalinist Mass Culture and the Formation of Modern Russian National Identity, 1931–1956* (Cambridge, Mass.: Harvard University Press, 2002), 20–24.

3. Terry Martin, *The Affirmative Action Empire: Nations and Nationalism in the Soviet Union, 1923–1939* (Ithaca: Cornell University Press, 2001), 147.

4. Victor Kravchenko, *I Chose Freedom: The Personal and Political Life of a Soviet Official* (London: Robert Hale, 1947), 63–64.

5. George Liber, *Soviet Nationality Policy, Urban Growth, and Identity Change in the Ukrainian SSR, 1923–1934* (Cambridge: Cambridge University Press, 1992), 111–118; quotation on p. 118; Bohdan Krawchenko, *Social Change and National Consciousness in Twentieth-Century Ukraine* (London: Macmillan, 1985), chap. 2.

6. Norman Davies, *God's Playground: A History of Poland,* vol. 2 (New York: Columbia University Press, 1982), 405–406; Martin, *Affirmative Action Empire,* 225, 222–223.

7. Mychailo Hrushevskyi, "The Traditional Scheme of 'Russian' History and the Problem of a Rational Organization of the History of the Eastern Slavs," in *From Kievan Rus' to Modern Ukraine: Formation of the Ukrainian Nation* (Cambridge, Mass.: Harvard University Ukrainian Studies Fund, 1984), 356–357, 363.

8. Martin, *Affirmative Action Empire,* 214.

9. Ibid., 218–219.

10. Ibid., 250–254.

11. Robert Service, *Lenin: A Political Life,* vol. 3: *The Iron Ring* (London: Macmillan, 1995), 92–94.

12. Steven L. Guthier, "The Belorussians: National Identification and Assimilation, 1897–1970," *Soviet Studies* 29 (1977), 59–61.

13. Martin, *Affirmative Action Empire,* 265–268.

14. Robert J. Kaiser, *The Geography of Nationalism in Russia and the USSR* (Princeton: Princeton University Press, 1994), 113–124; V. I. Kozlov, "Russkie v novom zarubezh'e (statistiko-geograficheskii obzor)," in *Russkie v sovremennom mire* (Moscow: Institut etnologii i antropologii, 1998), 14–47.

15. J. V. Stalin, *Works,* vol. 13 (Moscow: Foreign Languages Publishing House, 1955), 368–370.

16. V. N. Zemskov, "Kulatskaia ssylka v 30-ye gody," *Sotsiologicheskie issledovaniia,* no. 10 (1991), 18–20.

17. I. V. Stalin, *Voprosy Leninizma* (Moscow: Gospolitizdat, 1952), 362; Brandenberger, *National Bolshevism,* 28; G. V. Kostyrchenko, *Tainaia politika Stalina: vlast' i antisemitizm* (Moscow: Mezhdunarodnye otnosheniia, 2001), 163.

18. *The Diary of Georgi Dimitrov, 1933–1949,* ed. and with an introduction by Ivo Banac (New Haven: Yale University Press, 2003), 65.

19. Martin, *Affirmative Action Empire,* 194–203, quotation on p. 197; Kostyrchenko, *Tainaia politika,* 165, 167–168. Varlam Shalamov wrote a story about the Esperantists, "Esperanto": see Shalamov, *Sobranie sochinenii v 4-kh tomakh,* vol. 1 (Moscow: Khudozhestvennaia Literatura, 1998), 311–316.

20. Peter A. Blitstein, "Nation-Building or Russification: Obligatory Russian Instruction in the Soviet Non-Russian School, 1938–1953," Ronald Grigor Suny and Terry Martin, eds., *A State of Nations: Empire and Nation-Making in the Age of Lenin and Stalin* (Oxford: Oxford University Press, 2001), 260; Gerhard Simon, *Nationalism and Policy toward the Nationalities in the Soviet Union: From Totalitarian Dictatorship to Post-Stalinist Society* (Boulder, Colo.: Westview Press, 1991), 149–152; Y. Bilinsky, "Education of the Non-

Russian Peoples, 1917–67," *Slavic Review* 27 (1968), 418. Both Simon and Bilinsky interpet these measures unhesitatingly as Russification.

21. Roger R. Reese, *Stalin's Reluctant Soldiers: A Social History of the Red Army, 1924–1941* (Lawrence: University of Kansas Press, 1996), 26–27, 32–33, 39–40.

22. Philip Longworth, *The Cossacks* (London: Constable, 1969), 321–328.

23. Kostyrchenko, *Tainaia politika,* 206–207.

24. Francine Hirsch, "Race without the Practice of Racial Politics," *Slavic Review* 61 (2002), 30–43; Terry Martin, "The Origins of Ethnic Cleansing in the Soviet Union," *Journal of Modern History* 70 (1998), 829.

25. Peter Holquist, "'Information is the Alpha and Omega of Our Work': Bolshevik Surveillance in Its Pan-European Context," *Journal of Modern History* 69 (1997), 415–450; also his "To Count, to Extract, to Exterminate: Population Statistics and Population Politics in Late Imperial and Soviet Russia," in Suny and Martin, eds., *A State of Nations,* 111–144; Stephen Kotkin, "The Soviet Union and the Interwar Conjuncture," *Kritika* 2, no. 1 (Winter 2001), 111–164.

26. Amir Weiner, "Nature, Nurture, and Memory in a Socialist Utopia: Delineating the Soviet Socio-Ethnic Body in the Age of Socialism," *American Historical Review* 104 (1999), 1116.

27. Terry Martin, "The Origins of Soviet Ethnic Cleansing," *Journal of Modern History* 70 (1998), 837.

28. Martin, *Affirmative Action Empire,* 329–330.

29. Michael Gelb, "An Early Soviet Ethnic Deportation: The Far Eastern Koreans," *Russian Review* 54 (1995), 389–412; quotation 400–401. It could be argued that Red policy toward the Don Cossacks in 1919 amounted to ethnic cleansing. It was short-lived, however, and was soon abandoned because it did not fit with normal Leninist theory and practice. See Peter Holquist, "Conduct Merciless, Mass Terror: Decossackization on the Don, 1919," *Cahiers du Monde Russe* 38 (1997), 127–162.

30. Martin, *Affirmative Action Empire,* 343.

31. Anastas Mikoian, *Tak bylo: razmyshleniia o minuvshem* (Moscow: Vagrius, 1999), 514.

32. Brandenberger, *National Bolshevism,* 39–41; Veronique Garros, Natalia Korenevskaia, and Thomas Lahusen, eds., *Intimacy and Terror: Soviet Diaries of the 1930s* (New York: The New Press, 1995), 362.

33. Brandenberger, *National Bolshevism,* 34.

34. Maureen Perrie, *The Cult of Ivan the Terrible in Stalin's Russia* (Basingstoke: Palgrave, 2001), 29.

35. Brandenberger, *National Bolshevism,* 51–52.

36. A. V. Shestakov, ed., *Kratkii kurs istorii SSSR: uchebnik dlia 3-ego i 4-ogo klassov* (Moscow: Gosudarstvennoe Uchebo-pedagogicheskoe Izdatel'stvo, 1937); Brandenberger, *National Bolshevism,* 51–55.

37. Brandenberger, *National Bolshevism,* 99.

38. V. V. Maiakovskii, *Sochineniia,* vol. 2 (Moscow: Khudozhestvennaia literatura, 1965), 424–425; Alan M. Ball, *Imagining America: Influence and Images in Twentieth-Century Russia* (Lanham, Md.: Rowman and Littlefield, 2003), 47–51.

39. I. V. Stalin, *Voprosy Leninizma* (Moscow: Ogiz, 1939), 75–77.

40. Brandenberger, *National Bolshevism*, 101–103.

41. The term was also used by the historian Nikolai Timasheff in his celebrated book *The Great Retreat: The Growth and Decline of Communism in Russia* (New York: Dutton, 1946).

42. Benjamin Pinkus, *The Jews of the Soviet Union: The History of a National Minority* (Cambridge: Cambridge University Press, 1988), 78–79.

43. Ibid., 83–87.

44. Ibid., 96–98, 111–127.

45. Ibid., 136–137.

46. Ludmilla Tsigelman, "The Impact of Ideological Changes in the USSR on Different Generations of the Soviet Jewish Intelligentsia," in Yaacov Ro'i and Avi Becker, eds., *Jewish Culture and Identity in the Soviet Union* (New York: New York University Press, 1991), 44–45.

47. Viktor Perel'man, *Pokinutaia Rossiia*, vol. 1 (Tel Aviv: Vremia i My, 1976–1977), 34–35.

48. D. Brandenberger and K. Petrone, "'Vse cherty rasovogo natsionalizma . . .': internatsionalist zhaluetsia Stalinu (ianvar' 1939g)," *Oktiabr'*, no. 1 (2000), 130–131.

49. Christopher A. P. Binns, "The Changing Face of Power: Revolution and Accommodation in the Development of the Soviet Ceremonial System," *Man* 14 (1979), 593.

50. Karen Petrone, *Life Has Become More Joyous, Comrades: Celebrations in the Time of Stalin* (Bloomington: Indiana University Press, 2000), 25, 28–29.

51. Malte Rolf, "Constructing a Soviet Time: Bolshevik Festivals and Their Rivals during the First Five Year Plans," *Kritika* 1 (2000), 447–473; Jeffrey Brooks, *Thank You, Comrade Stalin! Soviet Public Culture from Revolution to Cold War* (Princeton: Princeton University Press, 2000), chap. 4.

52. Binns, "Changing Face," 602–604.

53. Petrone, *Life Has Become More Joyous*, 35–45.

54. H. G. Friese, "Student Life in a Soviet University," in George Kline, ed., *Soviet Education* (New York: Columbia University Press, 1957), 61–62; "Interviews with Igal Halfin and Jochen Hellbeck," *Ab Imperio*, no. 3 (2002), 217–260. Halfin and Hellbeck have been at the forefront of scholars seeking to understand the relationship between individual and collective in the 1920s and 1930s Soviet Union.

55. Stephen Kotkin, *Magnetic Mountain: Stalinism as a Civilization* (Berkeley: University of California Press, 1995), 207–214; Lewis H. Siegelbaum, *Stakhanovism and the Politics of Productivity in the USSR, 1935–1941* (Cambridge: Cambridge University Press, 1988).

56. Petrone, *Life Has Become More Joyous*, 48; John McCannon, "Tabula Rasa in the North: The Soviet Arctic and Mythic Landscapes in Stalinist Popular Culture," in Evgenii Dobrenko and Eric Naiman, eds., *The Landscape of Stalinism: The Art and Ideology of Soviet Space* (Seattle: University of Washington Press, 2003), 243, 255.

57. Petrone, *Life Has Become More Joyous*, chap. 3; James von Geldern, "The Centre and the Periphery: Cultural and Social Geography in the Mass Culture of the 1930s," in Stephen White, ed., *New Directions in Soviet History* (Cambridge: Cambridge University Press, 1992), 62–80.

58. Petrone, *Life*, 54.

59. Igor Golomstock, *Totalitarian Art in the Soviet Union, the Third Reich, Fascist Italy and the People's Republic of China*, trans. Robert Chandler (New York: Icon Editions, 1990), chap. 7; Vladimir Paperny, "Moscow in the 1930s and the Emergence of a New City," in Hans Günther, ed., *The Culture of the Stalin Period* (London: Macmillan, 1990), 229–239.

60. Vladimir Papernyi, *Kul'tura Dva* (Ann Arbor, Mich.: Ardis Press, 1985); see also his "Men, Women and Living Space," in William Craft Brumfield and Blair A. Ruble, eds., *Russian Housing in the Modern Age: Design and Social History* (Cambridge: Cambridge University Press, 1993), 149–170.

61. Boris Groys, "The Art of Totality," in Dobrenko and Naiman, *Landscape*, 117–120.

62. James Riordan, *Sport, Politics and Communism* (Manchester: Manchester University Press, 1991), 24–29.

63. Robert Edelman, *Serious Fun: A History of Spectator Sports in the USSR* (New York: Oxford University Press, 1993), chap. 3.

64. Ibid., 55; James Riordan, *Sport in Soviet Society: Development and Physical Education in Russia and the USSR* (Cambridge: Cambridge University Press, 1977), 122–128, 136.

65. Wendy Z. Goldman, *Women, the State and Revolution: Soviet Family Policy and Social Life, 1917–1936* (Cambridge: Cambridge University Press, 1993), chaps. 1, 6, 2, pp. 105–109, 288–291, 304–310.

66. Ibid., chap. 8.

67. Garros et al., *Intimacy and Terror*, 184–185.

68. Daniel Berteaux, "Révolution et mobilité sociale en Russie soviétique," *Cahiers Internationaux de Sociologie* 46 (1994), 77–97.

69. V. Semenova, "Iz istorii sovetskoi intelligentsii: semeinaia khronika Zhurnalistovykh," in V. Semenova and E. Foteeva, eds., *Sud'by liudei: Rossiia xx vek. Biografiia semei kak ob"ekt sotsiologicheskogo issledovaniia* (Moscow: Institut sotsiologii RAM, 1996), 151–156.

70. Bulat Okudzhava, *Arbat, moi Arbat* (Moscow: Sovetskii Pisatel', 1976), 21.

71. *Bol'shaia sovetskaia entsiklopediia*, vol. 18 (Moscow: Izdatel'stvo "Sovetskaia entsiklopediia," 1974), 492; O. S. Smyslov, *Zagadki sovetskikh nagrad, 1918–1991 gg.* (Moscow: Veche, 2005), 10–11, 51–56.

72. Kotkin, *Magnetic Mountain*, 215–223.

73. It is well described in the early chapters of Simon Sebag Montefiore, *Stalin: The Court of the Red Tsar* (London: Weidenfeld and Nicolson, 2003).

74. Catriona Kelly and Vadim Volkov, "Directed Desires: *Kul'turnost'* and Consumption," in Catriona Kelly and David Shepherd, eds., *Constructing Russian Culture in the Age of Revolution, 1881–1940* (Oxford: Oxford University Press, 1998), 291–313; Robert C. Tucker, *Political Culture and Leadership in Soviet Russia* (Brighton: Wheatsheaf Books, 1987), chap. 3.

75. Catriona Kelly, *Refining Russia: Advice literature, Polite Culture and Gender from Catherine to Yeltsin* (Oxford: Oxford University Press, 2001), 260–265, 270–278.

76. Ibid., 271.

77. Ibid., 284–285.

78. Stephen Lovell, *Summerfolk: A History of the Dacha, 1700–2000* (Ithaca: Cornell University Press, 2003), chap. 5, esp. 159–162.

79. Geoffrey A. Hosking, "The Institutionalisation of Soviet Literature," in Geoffrey A. Hosking and George F. Cushing, eds., *Perspectives on Literature and Society in Eastern and Western Europe* (London: Macmillan, 1989).

80. On the congress and the doctrine proclaimed at it, see Régine Robin, *Socialist Realism: An Impossible Aesthetic,* trans. Cathy Porter (Stanford: Stanford University Press, 1992), chaps. 1–2.

81. Lazar' Fleishman, *Boris Pasternak v tridtsatye gody* (Jerusalem: Magnes Press of the Hebrew University, 1984), 201–204; Stephen F. Cohen, *Bukharin and the Bolshevik Revolution: A Political Biography, 1888–1938* (New York: Vintage Books, 1975), 355–364.

82. Hans Günther, *Die Verstaatlichung der Literatur: Funktion und Entstehungsweise des sozialistisch-realistischen Kanons in der sowjetischen Literatur der 30-er Jahre* (Stuttgart: Metzler Verlagsbuchhandlung, 1984); Evgeny Dobrenko, *The Making of the State Writer: Social and Aesthetic Origins of Soviet Literary Culture* (Stanford: Stanford University Press, 2001), 340–365; Hosking, "The Institutionalisation of Soviet Literature," 55–75.

83. The doctrine is conveniently presented and analyzed in C. Vaughan James, *Soviet Socialist Realism: Origins and Theory* (London: Macmillan, 1973).

84. Katerina Clark, *The Soviet Novel: History as Ritual* (Chicago: University of Chicago Press, 1981).

85. Ibid., 151; Geoffrey Hosking, *Beyond Socialist Realism: Soviet Fiction since Ivan Denisovich* (London: Granada Publishing, 1980), 13–19; Gunther, *Verstaatlichung,* 11–12; Vera Dunham, *In Stalin's Time: Middleclass Values in Soviet Fiction* (Cambridge: Cambridge University Press, 1976).

86. Osip Mandelshtam, "Konets romana," in his *Sochineniia v 2-kh tomakh,* vol. 2 (Moscow: Khudozhestvennaia Literatura, 1990), 303–304; Evgeny Dobrenko, *The Making of the State Reader: Social and Aesthetic Contexts of the Reception of Soviet Literature,* trans. Jesse M. Savage (Stanford: Stanford University Press, 1997), 163.

87. Dobrenko, *Reader,* chaps. 4, 6, 7.

88. *Soviet Writers' Congress 1934* (London: Lawrence and Wishart, 1977), 29–30.

89. Frank J. Miller, *Folklore for Stalin: Russian Folklore and Pseudofolklore of the Stalin Era* (Armonk, N.Y.: M. E. Sharpe, 1990), 9.

90. David Nice, *Prokofiev: A Biography from Russia to the West, 1891–1935* (New Haven: Yale University Press, 2003), 320–321, 326.

91. Petrone, *Life Has Become More Joyous,* 126–131; Wendy Slater, "The Patriots' Pushkin," *Slavic Review* 58 (1999), 407–427.

92. Robin, *Socialist Realism,* 31, 34.

93. Stephen Lovell, *The Russian Reading Revolution: Print Culture in the Soviet and Post-Soviet Eras* (London: Macmillan, 2000), 34; Dobrenko, *Reader,* 143; italics in original.

94. Barbara Misztal, *Trust in Modern Societies* (Cambridge: Polity Press, 1996), 140–144.

95. Ayleen Teskey, *Platonov and Fyodorov: The Influence of Christian Philosophy on a Soviet Writer* (Trowbridge: Avebury Publishing Co., 1982), 22–29.

96. Quoted in Viktor Chalmaev, *Andrei Platonov* (Moscow: Sovetskii Pisatel', 1989), 83.

97. *Grani*, no. 70 (1969), 3–107; *Novyi mir*, no. 6 (1987), 50–123.

98. Andrey Platonov, *The Foundation Pit*, trans. Robert Chandler and Geoffrey Smith (London: Harvill Press, 1996), 26. I have modified the translation in a few places.

99. Ibid., 14.

100. Ibid., 1, 13.

101. Joseph Brodsky, *Less Than One* (New York: Farrar, Straus and Giroux, 1986), 290.

102. Platonov, *Foundation Pit*, 160.

103. Ibid., xx. My interpretation of the novel derives in part from Mikhail Geller, *Andrei Platonov v poiskakh schast'ia* (Paris: YMCA Press, 1979), 253–272.

104. Elendea Proffer, *Bulgakov: Life and Work* (Ann Arbor, Mich.: Ardis, 1984), esp. chap. 1.

105. David Bethea, *The Shape of Apocalypse in Modern Russian Fiction* (Princeton: Princeton University Press, 1989), 221–229.

106. Roberta Reeder, *Anna Akhmatova: Poet and Prophet* (London: Allison and Busby, 1995), 169–174.

107. Anna Akhmatova, *Stikhotvoreniia i poemy* (Leningrad: Sovetskii Pisatel', 1976), 152.

108. Orlando Figes, *Natasha's Dance: A Cultural History of Russia* (London: Allen Lane, 2002), chap. 7.

109. Anna Akhmatova, *Sochineniia v dvukh tomakh*, vol. 1 (Moscow: Tsitadel', 1996), 196–198, 196, 202–203.

110. The mood is well described in E. S. Seniavskaia, *Psikhologiia voiny v xx veke: istoricheskii opyt Rossii* (Moscow: Rosspen, 1999), 174–179.

## 6. The Great Fatherland War

1. Emmanuil Kazakevich, *Slushaia vremia: dnevniki, zapisnye knizhki, pis'ma* (Moscow: Sovetskii pisatel', 1990), 30.

2. See the remarks of Sonya O. Rose, *Which People's War? National Identity and Citizenship in Britain, 1939–1945* (Oxford: Oxford University Press, 2003), chap. 1, esp. 13–14.

3. V. F. Zima, *Mentalitet narodov Rossii v voine 1941–1945gg* (Moscow: Institut Rossiiskoi Istorii, 2000), 113–114; *Moskva voennaia, 1941–1945: memyary i arkhivnye dokumenty* (Moscow: Mosgorarkhiv, 1995), 50–55; *Istoriia Rossii, XX vek: materialy i dokumenty dlia shkol'nikov i postupaiushchikh v vuzy* (Moscow: Drofa, 1999), 302–303.

4. *Sovetskaia povsednevnost' i massovoe soznanie, 1939–1945* (Moscow: Rosspen, 2003), 308–310. At this time Timoshenko was deputy defense minister and commander of the western front. (Much of the material in this book comes from the monthly reports of the "information and organization" department of the Central Committee, among the best sources we have for studying the popular mood.)

5. N. A. Lomagin, *V tiskakh goloda: blokada Leningrada v dokumentakh germanskikh spetssluzhb i NKVD* (St. Petersburg: Evropeiskii Dom, 2000), 147–148, 157, 165. Security police reports would, of course, tend to exaggerate such rumors: that is what their authors are paid to do.

6. M. M. Gorinov, "Budni osazhdennoi stolitsy: zhizn' i nastroenie moskvichei (1941–2gg)," *Otechestvennaia istoriia*, no. 3 (1996), 16.

7. Mark von Hagen, *Soldiers in the Proletarian Dictatorship: The Red Army and the Soviet Socialist State, 1917–1930* (Ithaca: Cornell University Press, 1990), 288–294; David M. Glantz, *The Military Strategy of the Soviet Union: A History* (London: Frank Cass, 1992), 57–61.

8. John Barber, "Popular Reactions in Moscow to the German Invasion of June 22, 1941," *Soviet Union*, 18, nos. 1–3 (1991), 6; Heinrich Böll and Lew Kopelew, *Warum haben wir aufeinander geschossen?* (Munich: Deutscher Taschenbuchverlag, 1984), 14.

9. E. S. Seniavskaia, *Psikhologiia voiny v xx veke: istoricheskii opyt Rossii* (Moscow: Rosspen, 1999), 263.

10. Harvard Interview Project on the Soviet Social Structure (hereafter HP), Series A, folder no. 167, ff 22–23, 31; B 182, f 9.

11. *Sovetskaia povsednevnost'*, 109.

12. Seniavskaia, *Psikhologiia voiny*, 264–265; Il'ia Erenburg, *Sobranie sochinenii v deviati tomakh*, vol. 9 (Moscow: Khudozhestvennaia Literatura, 1967), 274.

13. I. V. Stalin, *Works*, supp. vol. 2 [15], ed. Robert H. McNeal (Stanford, Calif.: Hoover Institution, 1967), 7.

14. Anatol Goldberg, *Ilya Ehrenburg: Writing, Politics and the Art of Survival* (London: Weidenfeld and Nicolson, 1984), 197; Konstantin Simonov, *Stikhotvoreniia i poemy* (Moscow: Ogiz, 1945), 5–8. Symptomatically, in some re-editions of this poem, when Soviet editorial policy was once again in a more internationalist mood, the word "German" was replaced by "Fascist." See *Sobranie sochinenii v shesti tomakh*, vol. 1 (Moscow: Khudozhestvennaia Literatura, 1966), 88–90.

15. Ol'ga Berggol'ts, "Iz dnevnikov," *Zvezda*, no. 6 (1990), 171.

16. Katharine Hodgson, *Written with the Bayonet: Soviet Russian Poetry of World War II* (Liverpool: Liverpool University Press, 1996), chap. 2; Robert A. Rothstein, "Homeland, Home Town, and Battlefield: The Popular Song," in Richard Stites, ed., *Culture and Entertainment in Wartime Russia* (Bloomington: Indiana University Press, 1995), 77–94.

17. *Pisateli v otechestvennoi voine, 1941–5gg: pis'ma chitatelei* (Moscow: Goslitmuzei, 1946), 85.

18. Seniavskaia, *Psikhologiia voiny*, 244–245; Simonov, *Stikhotvoreniia i poemy*, 77–79.

19. Lisa Kirschenbaum, "Local Loyalties and Private Life in Soviet World War II Propaganda," *Slavic Review*, 59, no. 4 (Winter 2000), 825–847; quotation on p. 828.

20. Sheila Fitzpatrick, "War and Society in Soviet Context: Soviet Labor before, during, and after World War II," *International Labor and Working-Class History*, no. 35 (Spring 1989), 37–52; John Erickson, "Soviet Women at War," in John Garrard and Carol Garrard, eds., *World War II and the Soviet People* (New York: St Martin's Press, 1993), 50–76.

21. Kirschenbaum, "Local Loyalties," 828; Victoria Bonnell, *Iconography of Power: Soviet Political Posters under Lenin and Stalin* (Berkeley: University of California Press, 1997), 265.

22. Iu. A. Poliakov, "MIFLI 1941 (vospominaniia o M.Ia. Gellere)," *Voprosy istorii,* no. 7 (1999), 110; Viktor Nekrasov, "Tragediia moego pokoleniia," *Literaturnaia gazeta,* September 12, 1990, p. 15.

23. Nina Tumarkin, *The Living and the Dead: The Rise and Fall of the Cult of World War II in Russia* (New York: Basic Books, 1994), 65; Viacheslav Kondrat'ev, "Paradoksy frontovoi nostal'gii," *Literaturnaia gazeta,* May 9, 1990, p. 9.

24. Catherine Merridale, *Night of Stone: Death and Memory in Russia* (London: Granta, 2000), 272; E. S. Seniavskaia, *1941–1945: frontovoe pokolenie* (Moscow: Institut Rossiiskoi Istorii RAN, 1995), 85–86.

25. "*Ia pishu poslednee, byt' mozhet*" *(pis'ma s fronta)* (Omsk: Omskoe Knizhnoe Izdatel'stvo, 1994), 29.

26. Alexander Werth, *The Year of Stalingrad* (London: Hamish Hamilton, 1946), 64.

27. *Velikaia otechestvennaia voina, 1941–1945* (Moscow: Nauka, 1999), book 3 *(Osvobozhdenie),* 349.

28. Ibid., book 1 *(Surovye ispytaniia),* 417; book 3, 353–354.

29. Iu. V. Arutiunian, *Sovetskoe krest'ianstvo v gody Velikoi Otechestvennoi Voiny,* 2nd ed. (Moscow: Nauka, 1970), 84–85, 350–353; John Barber and Mark Harrison, *The Soviet Home Front, 1941–1945: A Social and Economic History of the USSR in World War II* (London: Longman, 1991), 99–104.

30. Elena Zubkova, *Poslevoennoe sovetskoe obshchestvo: politika i povsednevnost', 1945–53* (Moscow: Rosspen, 2000), 62–67.

31. K. B. Toman, "Dni velikikh bedstvii v soznanii sovremennikov," in *Drugaia voina, 1939–1945* (Moscow: Rossiiskii gosudarstvennyi gumanitarnyi universitet, 1996), 302–303.

32. James von Geldern, "Radio Moscow," in Stites, *Culture and Entertainment,* 44–61.

33. Jeffrey Brooks, "*Pravda* Goes to War," in Stites, *Culture and Entertainment,* 9–27; Louise McReynolds, "Dateline Stalingrad: Newspapers at the Front," in ibid., 34.

34. Iu. Vasil'eva, *Russkaia pravoslavnaia tserkov' v politike sovetskogo gosudarstva v 1943–1948gg* (Moscow: Institut Russkoi Istorii RAN, 1999), 110, 44–54; William C. Fletcher, *Nikolai: Portrait of a Dilemma* (New York: Macmillan, 1968), 42–43.

35. Vasil'eva, *Russkaia pravoslavnaia tserkov',* 111–116.

36. T. A. Chumachenko, *Gosudarstvo, pravoslavnaia tserkov', veruiushchie, 1941–1961gg* (Moscow: AIRO-XX, 1999), 23–37.

37. Daniel Peris, "'God Is Now on Our Side': The Religious Revival on Unoccupied Soviet Territory during World War II," *Kritika: Explorations in Russian and Eurasian History,* 1, no. 1 (Winter 2000), 115.

38. *Sovetskaia povsednevnost',* 411–415; Galina M. Yemelianova, *Russia and Islam: A Historical Survey* (Basingstoke: Palgrave, 2002), 120–123.

39. Seniavskaia, *Psikhologiia voiny,* 238–248.

40. Peris, "'God Is Now on Our Side,'" 97–118; quotations on p. 106.

41. Boris Pasternak, *Doktor Zhivago* (Milan: Feltrinelli, 1957), 519; Christopher Barnes, *Boris Pasternak: A Literary Biography,* vol. 2 (1928–1960) (Cambridge: Cambridge University Press, 1998), 181; Boris Pasternak, "Na rannikh poezdakh," in his *Stikhotvoreniia i poemy* (Moscow-Leningrad: Sovetskii Pisatel', 1965), 404–405.

42. Roberta Reeder, *Anna Akhmatova: Poet and Prophet* (London: Allison and Busby, 1995), 258.

43. Ibid., 257–258.

44. Anna Akhmatova, *Stikhotvoreniia i poemy* (Leningrad: Sovetskii Pisatel', 1976), 212.

45. Laurel E. Fay, *Shostakovich: A Life* (Oxford: Oxford University Press, 2000), 131–133.

46. Semen Lipkin, *Stalingrad Vasiliia Grossmana* (Ann Arbor, Mich.: Ardis, 1986), 8; A. Bocharov, *Vasilii Grossman: Zhizn'. Sud'ba. Tvorchestvo* (Moscow: Sovetskii pisatel', 1990), 164–176.

47. Vasilii Grossman, *Zhizn' i sud'ba* (Moscow: Vagrius, 1998), part 1, chaps. 59–61.

48. L. Anninskii, "Mirozdan'e Grossmana," *Druzhba narodov,* no. 10 (1988), 262; John Garrard and Carol Garrard, *The Bones of Berdichev: The Life and Fate of Vasilii Grossman* (New York: Free Press, 1996), 259–262.

49. William O. McCagg, Jr., *Stalin Embattled, 1943–1948* (Detroit: Wayne State University Press, 1978), 104.

50. Milovan Djilas, *Wartime* (New York: Harcourt Brace Jovanovich, 1977), 382.

51. N. K. Petrova, *Antifashistskie komitety v SSSR, 1941–1945gg* (Moscow: Institut Rossiiskoi Istorii RAN, 1999), 123–143, 165–188.

52. Gosudarstvennyi Arkhiv Rossiiskoi Federatsii (hereafter GARF), fond 6646 (Slavianskii komitet SSSR), opis' 1, delo 4 (report on the work of the All-Slav Committee, 1941–44), list'ia 1, 3.

53. Rossiiskii Tsentr Khraneniia i Izucheniia Dokumentov Noveishei Istorii (hereafter RTsKhIDNI), fond 82 (Molotov), op. 2, d. 1011, ll. 1–3; Molotov scribbled a note approving the text for press and radio. The appeal was probably composed by Metropolitan Nikolai of Kiev: see William C. Fletcher, *Nikolai: Portrait of a Dilemma* (New York: Macmillan, 1968), 46.

54. RTsKhIDNI, fond 17 (Central Committee of CPSU), op. 125 (Propaganda and Agitation administration), d. 317, l. 44.

55. A. T. Tvardovskii, *Poemy* (Moscow: Sovetskii Pisatel', 1950), 119.

56. See the Glavlit instruction of January 1943 in Diane P. Koenker and Ronald D. Bachman, eds., *Revelations from the Russian Archives: Documents in English Translation* (Washington, D.C.: Library of Congress, 1997), 172. On the reception of *Vasilii Terkin* see A. L. Grishunin, *Tvorchestvo Tvardovskogo* (Moscow: Izdatel'stvo moskovskogo universiteta, 1999), 40–51.

57. Rogers Brubaker, *Nationalism Reframed: Nationhood and the National Question in the New Europe* (Cambridge: Cambridge University Press, 1996), 20–21.

58. Alexander Werth, *Russia at War* (New York: Carroll and Graff, 1964), 415–416; *Sovetskaia povsednevnost,' 67.*

59. N. Popovich, "Sovetskaia politika po ukrepleniiu russkogo patriotizma i samosoz-

naniia (1935–1945gg)," in *Rossiia v XX veke: istoriki mira sporiat* (Moscow: Nauka, 1994), 468–474.

60. Stalin, *Works,* vol. 2 [15], 203.

61. K. Kromiadi, "Sovetskie voennoplennye v Germanii v 1941-om godu," *Novyi zhurnal,* no. 32 (1953), 194.

62. Pavel Polian, *Zhertvy dvukh diktatur* (Moscow: Rosspen, 2002), 130; Christian Streit, *Keine Kameraden: die Wehrmacht und die sowjetischen Kriegsgefangenen, 1941–1945* (Bonn: Dietz Verlag, 1991), 128; V. N. Zemskov, "K voprosu o repatriatsii sovetskikh grazhdan," *Istoriia SSSR,* no. 4 (1990), 26.

63. Amnon Sella, *The Value of Human Life in Soviet Warfare* (London: Routledge, 1992), 111.

64. Ibid., 100; the decree is published in "Prikaz stavki verkhovnogo glavnogo komandovaniia krasnoi armii," *Voenno-istoricheskii zhurnal,* no. 9 (1988), 26–28.

65. V. B. Konasov and A. V. Tereshchuk, "K istorii sovetskikh i nemetskikh voennoplennykh (1941–1943)," *Novaia i noveishaia istoriia,* no. 4 (1996), 54–72; *Velikaia otechestvennaia voina,* book 3, 357.

66. Catherine Andreyev, *Vlasov and the Russian Liberation Movement* (Cambridge: Cambridge University Press, 1986), 206–209, 46–50; Alex Inkeles and Raymond A. Bauer, *The Soviet Citizen: Daily Life in a Totalitarian Society* (Cambridge, Mass.: Harvard University Press, 1959); M. I. Semiriaga, "Voennoplennye, kollaboratsionisty i general Vlasov," in *Drugaia voina,* 335.

67. V. Shtrik-Shtrikfeldt, *Protiv Stalina i Gitlera: General Vlasov i russkoe osvoboditel'noe dvizhenie* (Frankfurt am Main: Posev, 1975), 190.

68. V. P. Naumov, "Sud'ba voennoplennykh i deportirovannykh grazhdan SSSR. Materialy kommissii o reabilitatsii zhertv politicheskikh repressii." *Novaia i noveishaia istoriia,* no. 2 (1996), 95–96; *Grif sekretnosti sniat: poteri vooruzhennykh sil SSSR v voinakh, boevykh deistviiakh i voennykh konfliktakh* (Moscow: Voennoe Izdatel'stvo, 1993), 385.

69. Zemskov, "K voprosu," 30.

70. Naumov, "Sud'ba voennoplennykh," 92–94, 97–100; the arrival of convicted.re-turnees in the labor camps is described in Aleksandr Solzhenitsyn, *Arkhipelag Gulag,* vol. 1 (Paris: YMCA Press, 1973), 90–97.

71. RBZ, fond R-301 (Sergei Sergeevich Terpilovskii), l. 99; fond R-186 (Evgenii Petrovich Murshel'), l. 157.

72. RBZ, R-186, l. 159.

73. Polian, *Zhertvy,* 532; Naumov, "Sud'ba voennoplennykh," 100.

74. Naumov, "Sud'ba voennoplennykh," 94.

75. Polian, *Zhertvy,* 536–537; Naumov, "Sud'ba voennoplennykh," 101.

76. RBZ, fond R-268 (Alexandra Fedorovna Lychagina), ll. 26–35. Her diary is a handwritten exercise book and gives no account of her ultimate fate. Italics in the original.

77. Naumov, "Sud'ba voennoplennykh," 101–103; *Velikaia otechestvennaia voina, 1941–45,* vol. 4: *Narod i Voina* (Moscow: Nauka, 1999), 133–135; Polian, *Zhertvy,* 592–593.

78. *Velikaia otechestvennaia voina,* vol. 4, 132–135; Bernd Bonwetsch, "Sowjetische Partisanen, 1941–44: Legende und Wirklichkeit des 'allgemeinen Volkskriegs,'" in

Gerhard Schulz, ed., *Partisanen und Volkskrieg: zur Revolutionierung des Krieges im 20ten Jahrhundert* (Göttingen: Vandenhoek und Ruprecht, 1985), 107–115; John A. Armstrong, ed., *Soviet Partisans in World War II* (Madison: University of Wisconsin Press, 1964), 121–135.

79. Seniavskaia, *Psikhologiia voiny,* 226. For a summary of scholarship on the partisans, see Bonwetsch, "Sowjetische Partisanen"; and Leonid D. Grenkevich, *The Soviet Partisan Movement: A Critical Historiographical Analysis* (London: Frank Cass, 1999). On the Ukrainian insurgency, see John A. Armstrong, *Ukrainian Nationalism,* 3rd ed. (Englewood, Colo.: Ukrainian Academic Press, 1990), chaps. 6–7; and Petro R. Sodol, "UPA—the Ukrainian Insurgent Army: An Overview," *Ukrainian Quarterly,* 51 (1995), 139–175.

80. Robert Conquest, *The Nation Killers: Soviet Deportation of Nationalities* (London: Macmillan, 1970); Alexander Nekrich, *The Punished Peoples: The Deportation and Fate of Soviet Minorities at the End of the Second World War* (New York: W. W. Norton and Co, 1978); N. F. Bugai, *Deportatsiia narodov Kryma: dokumenty, fakty, kommentarii* (Moscow: Insan, 2002).

81. Romuald J. Misiunas and Rein Taagepera, *The Baltic States: Years of Dependence, 1940–1990* (London: Hurst, 1993), 42–43, 99, chap. 3; Jan T. Gross, *Revolution from Abroad: The Soviet Conquest of Poland's Western Ukraine and Western Belorussia* (Princeton: Princeton University Press, 1988), 187–199; Charles King, *The Moldovans: Romania, Russia, and the Politics of Culture* (Stanford: Hoover Institution Press, 2000), 93, 96; David R. Marples, *Stalinism in Ukraine in the 1940s* (London: Macmillan, 1992).

82. Conquest, *Nation Killers;* Nekrich, *Punished Peoples.*

83. Alexander Solzhenitsyn, *The Gulag Archipelago,* vol. 3, trans. H. T. Willetts (London: Bodley Head, 1976), 235, 240.

84. The erosion of incipient civil institutions after the war is well treated in Elena Zubkova, *Poslevoennoe sovetskoe obshchestvo: politika i povsednevnost', 1945–1953* (Moscow: Rosspen, 2000); see 35–37.

85. Tumarkin, *The Living and the Dead,* 104.

## 7. The Sweet and Bitter Fruits of Victory

1. Alexander Werth, *Russia at War, 1941–1945* (London: Pan Books, 1965), 867–868.

2. I. V. Stalin, *Sochineniia,* ed. Robert McNeal, vol. 2 (15) (Stanford: Hoover Institution, 1967) xv 203–204.

3. *Sovetskaia zhizn', 1945–1953* (Moscow: Rosspen, 2003), 233–234.

4. Amir Weiner has recently shown how the victory renewed some of the original élan of the Communist project: see Weiner, *Making Sense of War: The Second World War and the Fate of the Bolshevik Revolution* (Princeton: Princeton University Press, 2001).

5. *Sovetskaia zhizn',* 627.

6. HP, A 25, ff 50, 52; A 1101, ff 66–67. It should be noted that the Harvard interview texts represent the interviewer's summary, not the respondent's actual words.

7. M. Ia. Gefter, "Stalin umer vchera . . . ," *Inogo ne dano* (Moscow: Progress, 1988), 305.

8. HP, A 494, ff 59–61; HP, A 33, f 34.

9. HP, B 64, f 54.

10. David Holloway, *Stalin and the Bomb: The Soviet Union and Atomic Energy, 1939–1956* (New Haven: Yale University Press, 1994), 154.

11. Ibid., 184–201.

12. Hugh Seton-Watson, *The East European Revolution* (New York: Praeger, 1951), remains a classic account of this process.

13. Vera Dunham, *In Stalin's Time: Middleclass Values in Soviet Fiction* (Cambridge: Cambridge University Press, 1976).

14. M. Iovchuk, "Leninizm—vysshee dostizhenie russkoi i mirovoi kul'tury," *Kommunist,* no. 1 (1955), 27.

15. F. V. Konstantinov, ed., *Istoricheskii materializm* (Moscow: Politizdat, 1950), 701–702; Stalin, *O velikoi otechestvennoi voine Sovetskogo Soiuza,* 160–161, quoted in Konstantinov, *Istoricheskii materializm,* 704.

16. N. I. Matiushkin, *Chto takoe sovetskii patriotizm?* (Moscow: Goslitizdat, 1955), 21; P. Fedoseev, "Sotsializm i patriotizm," *Kommunist,* no. 9 (1953), 21.

17. Matiushkin, *Chto takoe,* 84–85.

18. Konstantin Simonov, *Glazami cheloveka moego pokoleniia* (Moscow: Kniga, 1990), 111.

19. Fedoseev, "Sotsializm," 23–24.

20. Yuri Slezkine, *Russia and the Small Peoples of the Arctic North* (Ithaca: Cornell University Press, 1994), 304–305.

21. Isaiah Berlin, *The Soviet Mind: Russian Culture under Communism,* ed. Henry Hardy (Washington, D.C.: Brookings Institution Press, 2004), 93.

22. Karen A. Collias, "Making Soviet Citizens: Patriotic and Internationalist Education in the Formation of a Soviet State Identity," in Henry R. Huttenbach, ed., *Soviet Nationality Policies: Ruling Ethnic Groups in the USSR* (London: Mansell, 1990), 73–93.

23. Orest Subtelny, *Ukraine: A History,* 2nd ed. (Toronto: University of Toronto Press, 1994), chap. 23; David R. Marples, *Belarus: A Denationalized Nation* (Amsterdam: Harwood Academic Publishers, 1999), 17–19.

24. Weiner, *Making Sense of War,* 240–244; Timothy Snyder, *The Reconstruction of Nations: Poland, Lithuania, Ukraine, Belarus, 1569–1999* (New Haven: Yale University Press, 2003), 155–200; John A. Armstrong, *Ukrainian Nationalism* (New York: Columbia University Press, 1963), chap. 9.

25. Weiner, *Making Sense of War,* 331–338; see also his "Saving Private Ivan: From What, Whom and How," *Kritika: Explorations in Russian and Eurasian history* 1 (2000), 305–336.

26. On the renewal of the revolutionary spirit, see Weiner, *Making Sense of War.*

27. Juliane Fürst, "Prisoners of the Soviet Self?—Political Youth Opposition in Late Stalinism," *Europe-Asia Studies* 54 (2002), 353–375.

28. As recounted in the memoirs of a participant: Anatolii Zhigulin, *Chernye kamni* (Moscow: Knizhnaia Palata, 1989), 27–29, 35.

29. Werth, *Russia at War,* 554.

30. John Erickson, "Soviet War Losses: Calculations and Controversies," in John Erickson and David Dilks, eds., *Barbarossa: The Axis and the Allies* (Edinburgh: Edinburgh University Press, 1994), 272–274.

31. A report from the Central Committee propaganda organization department: *Sovetskaia zhizn'*, 403–405.

32. Ibid., 406–407.

33. Sonya O. Rose, *Which People's War? National Identity and Citizenship in Britain, 1939–1945* (Oxford: Oxford University Press, 2003), chap. 2, esp. p. 31; *Sovetskaia zhizn'*, 33–35, 90.

34. Elena Zubkova, *Poslevoennoe sovetskoe obshchestvo: politika i povsednevnost', 1945–1953* (Moscow: Rosspen, 2000), 56–58; N. V. Romanovskii, *Liki Stalinizma* (Moscow: n. p., 1995), 13–19. The complaint is from a report by the deputy head of the letters section of *Pravda,* January 1946: *Sovetskaia zhizn'*, 189–191.

35. *Sovetskaia zhizn'*, 80–81.

36. Ibid., 318–319, 322–325; HP B 301, ff 41–43; Nina Tumarkin, *The Living and the Dead: The Rise and Fall of the Cult of World War II in Russia* (New York: Basic Books, 1994), 98; Romanovskii, *Liki Stalinizma*, 24–25.

37. GARF, f. 9541 *(Sovetskii komitet veteranov voiny),* op. 1, d. 40 *(protokol zasedanii sektsii frontovikov,* Dec. 20, 1956), ll. 28–29.

38. Zubkova, *Poslevoennoe,* 42–45.

39. *Sovetskaia zhizn'*, 213–214.

40. Ibid., 228–229, 231.

41. Ol'ga Berggol'ts, "Iz dnevnikov (mai, oktiabr' 1949)," *Znamia,* no. 3 (1991), 162; italics in the original.

42. N. S. Ivanov, "Reskrest'ianivanie derevni (seredina 40-kh-50ye gody)," in N. A. Ivnitskii, ed., *Sud'by rossiiskogo krest'ianstva* (Moscow: RGGU, 1996), 417–418.

43. Zubkova, *Poslevoennoe,* 77; V. F. Zima, *Golod v SSSR 1946–47gg: proiskhozhdenie i posledstviia* (Moscow: Institut Rossiiskoi Istorii RAN, 1996), 11, 168.

44. Ivnitskii, *Sud'by rossiiskogo krest'ianstva,* 425–427.

45. Erickson, "Soviet War Losses," 256–261; Barbara A. Anderson and Brian D. Silver, "Demographic Consequences of World War II on the Non-Russian Nationalities of the USSR," in Susan J. Linz, ed., *The Impact of World War II on the Soviet Union* (Totowa, N.J.: Rowman and Allanheld, 1985), 207–242.

46. *Naselenie Rossii v XX veke: istoricheskie ocherki,* vol. 2, 1940–1959 (Moscow: Rosspen, 2001), 225; Anderson and Silver, "Demographic Consequences"; Liudmila Alexeyeva, *The Thaw Generation: Coming of Age in the Post-Stalin Era* (Boston: Little, Brown, 1990), 11.

47. Tumarkin, *The Living and the Dead,* 104; G. V. Kostyrchenko, *Tainaia politika Stalina: vlast' i antisemitizm* (Moscow: Mezhdunarodnye Otnosheniia, 2001), 291; Robert Service, *Stalin: A Biography* (Basingstoke: Macmillan, 2004), 543–544.

48. Zubkova, *Poslevoennoe,* 37, 35; Emmanuil Kazakevich, *Slushaia vremia: dnevniki, zapisnye knizhki, pis'ma* (Moscow: Sovetskii pisatel', 1990), 28.

49. N. K. Petrova, *Antifashistskie komitety v SSSR, 1941–1945gg* (Moscow: Institut Rossiiskoi Istorii RAN, 1999), 253, 254.

50. RTsKhIDNI, f. 17, op. 125, d. 317, ll. 66–68; GARF, f. 6646, op. 1, d. 172 (2nd plenum of the General Slav Committee in Warsaw, August 15–18, 1947), l. 61.

51. GARF, f. 6646, op. 1, d. 206 *(protokoly zasedanii prezidiuma Slavianskogo Komiteta SSSR za 1949g),* esp. ll. 43–45.

52. Archbishop Antonii of Tula, "Moi vpechatleniia pri vozvrashchenii na rodinu," *Zhurnal Moskovskoi Patriarkhii* no. 9 (1946), 56.

53. Tatiana A. Chumachenko, *Church and State in Soviet Russia: Russian Orthodoxy from World War Two to the Khrushchev Years,* trans. Edward Roslof (Armonk, N.Y.: M. E. Sharpe, 2002), 39–41.

54. William C. Fletcher, *Nikolai: Portrait of a Dilemma* (New York: Macmillan, 1968), 64–77.

55. O. Iu. Vasil'eva, *Russkaia pravoslavnaia tserkov' v politike sovetskogo gosudarstva v 1943–1948gg.* (Moscow: Institut Rossiiskoi Istorii RAN, 1999), 156–170; quotation on pp. 168–169; Chumachenko, *Church and State,* 53–55.

56. Chumachenko, *Church and State,* 63–67, 105–112.

57. M. V. Shkarovskii, "Russkaia pravoslavnaia tserkov' v 1943–1957gg.," *Voprosy istorii,* no. 8 (1995), 47; Chumachenko, *Church and State,* 81–83.

58. William C. Fletcher, "The Soviet Bible Belt: World War II's Effects on Religion," in Susan J. Linz, ed., *The Impact of World War II on the Soviet Union* (Totowa, N.J.: Rowman and Allanheld, 1985), 91–106; *Sovetskaia zhizn',* 640, 643, 652–655.

59. *Sovetskaia zhizn',* 655, 660.

60. Ibid., 645.

61. Chumachenko, *Church and State,* 64–65.

62. Ibid., 52.

63. *Sovetskaia zhizn',* 666–668, 665; Chumachenko, *Church and State,* 96–99, 112–113.

64. Yoram Gorlizki and Oleg Khlevniuk, *Cold Peace: Stalin and the Soviet Ruling Circle, 1945–1953* (Oxford: Oxford University Press, 2004), 87; Werner G. Hahn, *Postwar Soviet Politics: The Fall of Zhdanov and the Defeat of Moderation, 1947–1953* (Ithaca: Cornell University Press, 1982), 122–129; Elena Zubkova, "Kadrovaia politika i chistki v KPSS, 1945–1956," *Svobodnaia mysl',* no. 4 (1999), 102–108; A. Pyzhikov, "Leningradskaia gruppa: put' vo vlast, 1946–1949," *Svobodnaia mysl',* no. 3 (2001), 89–104.

65. Feliks Chuev, *Molotov—poluderzhavnyi vlastelin* (Moscow: Olma Press, 1999), 508–509. Khrushchev in his memoirs recalled that Leningrad had held a large sale of unsold goods without consulting Stalin. See his *Vremia. Liudi. Vlast',* vol. 2 (Moscow: Moskovskie Novosti, 1999), 29. The sale was held on January 10–20, 1949, and was attended by some 2,000 representatives of state and cooperative enterprises: V. A. Kutuzov, "Tak nazyvaemoe 'leningradskoe delo,'" *Voprosy istorii KPSS,* no. 3 (1989), 56n.

66. Dmitrii Volkogonov papers (Davis Center for Russian Studies, Harvard University), Reel 2, Container 3, Folder 14, l. 19. I am grateful to David Brandenberger for drawing this source to my attention.

67. There are indications that Malenkov may have weeded out the files for reasons of his own. See T. B. Toman, "O tak nazyvaemom leningradskom dele," *Izvestiia TsK KPSS,* no. 2 (1989), 133–134.

68. Volkogonov papers, Folder 14, ll. 2–18, 20–30.

69. See the description of Stalin's leadership style in Gorlizki and Khlevniuk, *Cold Peace,* 59, 156.

70. Khrushchev, *Vremia,* vol. 2, 26–27.

71. Ibid., 27–28; *Politburo TsK VKP(b) i Sovet Ministrov SSSR, 1945–1953* (Moscow: Rosspen, 2002), 246–247.

72. Rossiiskii Gosudarstvennyi Arkhiv Sotsial'no-politicheskoi Istorii (hereafter RGASPI), f. 607, o. 1, d. 1–7.

73. David Brandenberger, "Stalin, the Leningrad Affair and the Limits of Postwar Russocentrism," *Russian Review* 63 (2004), 241–255.

74. Werner G. Hahn, *Postwar Soviet Politics: The Fall of Zhdanov and the Defeat of Moderation, 1946–1953* (Ithaca: Cornell University Press, 1982), 123–124, 98–102; Vladimir Dedijer, *Tito Speaks: His Self-Portrait and Struggle with Stalin* (London: Weidenfeld and Nicolson, 1953), 321–322.

75. Vera Tolz, "'Cultural Bosses' as Patrons and Clients: The Functioning of the Soviet Creative Unions in the Postwar Period," *Contemporary European History* 11, no. 1 (Feb. 2002), 87–105.

76. Roberta Reeder, *Anna Akhmatova: Poet and Prophet* (London: Allison and Busby, 1995), 290–307; Christopher Barnes, *Boris Pasternak: A Literary Biography,* vol. 2 (Cambridge: Cambridge University Press, 1998), 233–234.

77. Isaiah Berlin, "Meetings with Russian writers," in Berlin, *The Soviet Mind: Russian Culture under Communism* (Washington, D.C.: Brookings Institution Press, 2004), 78; Anna Akhmatova, *Sochineniia v dvukh tomakh,* vol. 1 (Moscow: Tsitadel', 1996), 230; Reeder, *Akhmatova,* 286–287; György Dalos, *The Guest from the Future: Anna Akhmatova and Isaiah Berlin,* trans. Antony Wood (London: John Murray, 1998), chap. 1. Berlin's own account of the visit is in "Meetings with Russian writers," 70–79.

78. Alexei Kojevnikov, "Rituals of Stalinist Culture at Work: Science and the Games of Intraparty Democracy circa 1948," *Russian Review* 57 (1998), 25–52.

79. Nikolai Krementsov, *Stalinist Science* (Princeton: Princeton University Press, 1997), 96–100, 115–121.

80. Ibid., 131–143.

81. Kostyrchenko, *Tainaia politika,* 298–300.

82. Nikolai Krementsov, *The Cure: A Story of Cancer and Politics from the Cold War* (Chicago: University of Chicago Press, 2002), 117, 125.

83. Ibid., 126–130.

84. David Joravsky, *The Lysenko Affair* (Cambridge, Mass.: Harvard University Press, 1970); Krementsov, *Stalinist Science,* 169–183.

85. Yuri Slezkine, "N. Ia. Marr and the National Origins of Soviet Ethnogenetics," *Slavic Review* 55 (1996), 838.

86. René L'Hermitte, *Marr, Marrisme, Marristes: une page de l'histoire de la linguistique soviétique* (Paris: Institut d'Etudes Slaves, 1987), 11–24.

87. I. V. Stalin, "Marksizm i voprosy iazykoznaniia," reproduced in his *Sochineniia,* vol. 3 (16), 148, 115–116, 119–120; L'Hermitte, *Marr,* 68–73, 79.

88. Stalin did still foresee the possibility of the world proletarian language being constructed out of the mutual enrichment of existing languages—but only after the final defeat of imperialism. See his "Marksizm i voprosy iazykoznaniia," 169.

89. This number included 1.5 million from the pre-1939 Soviet borders, and another 0.5 million from the territories annexed in 1939. See Zvi Gitelman, "Soviet Reactions to the Holocaust, 1945–1991," in Lucjan Dobroszycki and Jeffrey S. Gurock, eds., *The Holocaust in the Soviet Union* (Armonk, N.Y.: M. E. Sharpe, 1993), 3.

90. G. V. Kostyrchenko, *V plenu krasnogo faraona: politicheskie presledovaniia evreev v SSSR v poslednee stalinskoe desiatiletie* (Moscow: Mezhunarodnye otnosheniia, 1994), 15–16.

91. HP, A 417, f 46; A 535, ff 13–14; B 641, ff 1–4.

92. J. Rubenstein and V. P. Naumov, eds., *Stalin's Secret Pogrom: The Postwar Inquisition of the Jewish Anti-Fascist Committee* (New Haven: Yale University Press, 2001), 8–9.

93. Kostyrchenko, *Tainaia politika*, 229–232, 236–242.

94. Kostyrchenko, *V plenu*, 9–13.

95. Petrova, *Antifashistskie komitety*, 260; Kostyrchenko, *Tainaia politika*, 363–365.

96. Benjamin Pinkus, *The Jews of the Soviet Union: The History of a National Minority* (Cambridge: Cambridge University Press, 1988), 161–172.

97. Kostyrchenko, *V plenu*, 124–152; Rubenstein and Naumov, *Stalin's Secret Pogrom*.

98. Kostyrchenko, *V plenu*, chap. 3; Pinkus, *Jews*, 206–208.

99. Pinkus, *Jews*, 187–188; John Garrard and Carol Garrard, *Bones of Berdichev: The Life and Fate of Vasilii Grossman* (New York: Free Press, 1996), 199–214.

100. Kostyrchenko, *Tainaia politika*, 638–645, 650–651, 663–667.

101. Gorlizki and Khlevniuk, *Cold Peace*, 171.

102. I. V. Bystrova and G. E. Riabov, "Voenno-promyshlennyi kompleks SSSR," in Iu. N. Afanas'ev, ed., *Rossiia XX vek: sovetskoe obshchestvo*, vol. 2: *Apogei i krakh stalinizma* (Moscow: RGGU, 1997), 205–206.

## 8. The Relaunch of Utopia

1. Kathleen E. Smith, *Remembering Stalin's Victims: Popular Memory and the End of the USSR* (Ithaca: Cornell University Press, 1996), chap. 2; the most detailed account of the "secret speech" is in William Taubman, *Khrushchev: The Man and His Era* (New York: Free Press, 2003), chap. 11.

2. Barsukov, "Oborotnaia storona ottepeli," *Kentavr*, no. 4 (1993), 133, 136–137.

3. Ibid., 135.

4. A. V. Pyzhikov, *Khrushchevskaia "ottepel'," 1953–1964* (Moscow: Olma-Press, 2002), 192–194.

5. Boris Weil, "Legalität zur Zeit des Tauwetters," in Dietrich Beyrau and Ivo Bock, eds., *Das Tauwetter und die Folgen: Kultur und Politik in Osteuropa nach 1956* (Bremen: Temmen, 1988), 27–28.

6. Ibid., 28–29; Vladimir Bukovsky, *To Build a Castle: My Life as a Dissenter* (London: Andre Deutsch, 1978), 116–126.

7. Weil, "Legalität," 31–36.

8. Christopher Barnes, *Boris Pasternak: A Literary Biography*, vol. 2 (1928–1960) (Cambridge: Cambridge University Press, 1998), 312.

9. Ibid., chaps. 16–17; Dietrich Beyrau, *Intelligenz und Dissens: die russischen Bildungsschichten in der Sowjetunion, 1917 bis 1985* (Göttingen: Vandenhoek and Ruprecht, 1993), 163–170.

10. Raissa Orlowa and Lew Kopelew, *Wir Lebten in Moskau* (Munich: Albrecht Knaus, 1987), 43.

11. Bukovsky, *To Build a Castle*, 117.

12. Ibid., 115.

13. A. V. Pyzhikov, "Sovetskoe poslevoennoe obshchestvo i predposylki khrushchevskikh reform," *Voprosy istorii*, no. 2 (2002), 33–43. Interestingly, Pyzhikov shows that in the early 1950s one of the main opponents of the reforms he later sponsored was none other than Khrushchev himself.

14. Pyzhikov, *Ottepel'*, 115–128.

15. P. H. Juviler, *Revolutionary Law and Order: Politics and Social Change in the USSR* (London: Collier-Macmillan, 1976), 78–79.

16. *Narodnoe khoziaistvo SSSR v 1956g* (Moscow: Gosudarstvennoe Statisticheskoe Izdatel'stvo, 1957), 177; *Narodnoe khoziaistvo SSSR v 1964g* (Moscow: Tsentral'noe Statisticheskoe Upravlenie, 1965), 610; *Narodnoe khoziaistvo SSSR v 1980g* (Moscow: Finansy i Statistika, 1981), 392.

17. Gregory D. Andrusz, *Housing and Urban Development in the USSR* (Basingstoke: Macmillan, 1984), 82–98.

18. Pyzhikov, *Ottepel'*, 125–126, 137; Bernice Q. Madison, *Social Welfare in the Soviet Union* (Stanford: Stanford University Press, 1968).

19. Robert Edelman, *Serious Fun: A History of Spectator Sport in the USSR* (New York: Oxford University Press, 1993), 59–65.

20. Dmitri Sollertinsky and Ludmilla Sollertinsky, *Pages from the Life of Dmitri Shostakovich* (London: Robert Hale, 1980), 93–94.

21. *Sovetskii sport*, October 25, 1975, quoted in Robert Edelman, *Serious Fun: A History of Spectator Sport in the USSR* (Oxford: Oxford University Press, 1993), 177–178.

22. For a full explanation of the propiska hierarchy see G. Hosking, *The First Socialist Society: A History of the Soviet Union from Within*, 3rd ed. (Cambridge, Mass.: Harvard University Press, 1992), 375–376.

23. James Riordan, *Sport in Soviet Society: Development of Sport and Physical Education in Russia and the USSR* (Cambridge: Cambridge University Press, 1977), 173–176, 251.

24. From a Soviet sports handbook of 1973, quoted in ibid., 349.

25. Edelman, *Serious Fun*, 80, 87–91, 119; Riordan, *Sport*, 366.

26. Riordan, *Sport*, 367–374, 378.

27. Dimitry Pospielovsky, *The Russian Church under the Soviet Regime, 1917–1982*, vol. 2 (Crestwood, N.Y.: St Vladimir's Seminary Press, 1982), 357–358.

28. Felix Corley, *Religion in the Soviet Union: An Archival Reader* (Basingstoke: Macmillan, 1996), 221–223.

29. Tatiana A. Chumachenko, *Church and State in Soviet Russia: Russian Orthodoxy from World War Two to the Khrushchev Years*, trans. Edward Roslof (Armonk, N.Y.: M. E. Sharpe, 2002), 153.

30. Pospielovsky, *Russian Church*, vol. 2, 333–335.

31. Arkhiepiskop Vasilii (Krivoshein), "Poslednie vstrechi s Mitropolitom Nikolaem," *Vestnik russkogo khristianskogo dvizheniia*, no. 117 (1976), 209–221.

32. Chumachenko, *Church and State*, 181–186, 159–165.

33. Jane Ellis, *The Russian Orthodox Church: A Contemporary History* (London: Croom Helm, 1986), 53–69; Pospielovsky, *Russian Church*, vol. 2, 335–339.

34. Chumachenko, *Church and State*, 175–177, 187–188.

35. John Anderson, *Religion, State and Politics in the Soviet Union and Successor States* (Cambridge: Cambridge University Press, 1994), 33–34.

36. Pospielovsky, *Russian Church*, vol. 2, 346–349; Ellis, *Russian Orthodox Church*, 32–33; Anderson, *Religion*, 55–59.

37. Arkhiepiskop Vasilii, "Poslednie vstrechi," 213.

38. Anderson, *Religion*, 59–63.

39. Pospielovsky, *Russian Church*, vol. 2, 343–346; Chumachenko, *Church and State*, 168–172.

40. Nathaniel Davis, *A Long Walk to Church: A Contemporary History of Russian Orthodoxy* (Boulder, Colo.: Westview Press, 1995), 204.

41. A copy of a complete report by the deputy head of the Council for Orthodox Church Affairs is in *Vestnik russkogo khristianskogo dvizheniia* 130 (1979), 275–344.

42. Evgenia Ginzburg, *Within the Whirlwind* (London: Collins and Harvill, 1981), 198–199.

43. Nanci Adler, *The Gulag Survivor: Beyond the Soviet System* (New Brunswick: Transaction Publishers, 2002), 22–32, 192.

44. Ibid., 157–161.

45. Lidiia Chukovskaia, *Zapiski ob Anne Akhmatovoi*, vol. 2 (Paris: YMCA Press, 1980), 137.

46. Anne Applebaum, *Gulag: A History* (London: Allen Lane, 2003), 520.

47. Adler, *Gulag Survivor*, 186–187, 190; Applebaum, *Gulag*, 520.

48. Catherine Merridale, *Night of Stone: Death and Memory in Russia* (London: Granta Books, 2000), 342–343.

49. Alice Förster and Birgit Beck, "Post-Traumatic Stress Disorder and World War Two: Can a Psychiatric Concept Help Us Understand Postwar Society?" in Richard Bessell and Dirk Schumann, eds., *Life after Death: Approaches to a Cultural and Social History of Europe during the 1940s and 1950s* (Cambridge: Cambridge University Press, 2003), 15–36.

50. Applebaum, *Gulag*, 525.

51. Adler, *Gulag Survivor*, 110–114.

52. Merridale, *Night of Stone*, 418.

53. Konstantin Tsiolkovsky, *The Will of the Universe* (Moscow: Pamiat', 1992), 7.

54. Ronald B. Humble, *The Soviet Space Programme* (London: Routledge, 1988), 1–4.

55. William Shelton, *Soviet Space Exploration: The First Decade* (London: Arthur Barker, 1969), 52–70, 74–77.

56. Speech of January 22, 1958, quoted in Humble, *Soviet Space Programme*, 5.

57. Shelton, *Soviet Space Exploration*, chap. 7.

58. *Pravda*, April 14, 1961, 1.

59. *Pravda*, April 13, 1961, 4.

60. Shelton, *Soviet Space Exploration*, 119.

61. Aleksandr Fursenko and Timothy Naftali, *"One Hell of a Gamble": The Secret History of the Cuban Missile Crisis* (New York: W. W. Norton, 1997), 52, 55, 180.

62. Ibid., 259–260.

63. Ibid., chaps. 16–17.

64. Adam Ulam, *Expansion and Coexistence: The History of Soviet Foreign Policy, 1917–1967* (New York: Praeger, 1968), 675.

65. Erich Strauss, *Soviet Agriculture in Perspective: A Study of Its Successes and Failures* (London: Allen and Unwin, 1969), 170–175.

66. V. S. Lel'chuk, "1959 god: rasstrel v Temirtau," in Iu. N. Afanas'ev, ed., *Sovetskoe obshchestvo: vozniknovenie, razvitie, istoricheskii final* (Moscow: RGGU, 1997), 296–298.

67. V. A. Kozlov, *Mass Uprisings in the USSR: Protest and Rebellion in the Post-Stalin Years* (Armonk, N.Y.: M. E. Sharpe, 2002), 24–25.

68. Nursultan Nazarbaev, *My Life, My Times and the Future,* trans. and ed. Peter Conradi (Yelverton Manor: Pilkington Press, 1998), 25–26.

69. Kozlov, *Mass Uprisings,* 32–33; Lel'chuk, "1959 god," 276–277, 292–293.

70. Kozlov, *Mass Uprisings,* 34–39.

71. Ibid., chaps. 2, 6; Yoram Gorlizki, "Policing Post-Stalin society: The Militsiia and Public Order under Khrushchev," *Cahiers du Monde Russe* 44 (2003), 465–480.

72. Pyzhikov, *Ottepel',* 128.

73. Kozlov, *Mass Uprisings,* 227–228; Samuel Baron, *Bloody Saturday in the Soviet Union: Novocherkassk 1962* (Stanford: Stanford University Press, 2001), 16–21.

74. Kozlov, *Mass Uprisings,* 228–229, 255–256.

75. Baron, *Bloody Saturday,* 26.

76. Kozlov, *Mass Uprisings,* 231–232; Baron, *Bloody Saturday,* 27, 32–33.

77. Baron, *Bloody Saturday,* 51–57.

78. Kozlov, *Mass Uprisings,* 267–271; Baron, *Bloody Saturday,* 56–61.

79. Baron, *Bloody Saturday,* 70–76, 62–68; Kozlov, *Mass Uprisings,* 267–268.

80. Kozlov, *Mass Uprisings,* 268–274.

81. Ibid., 280–287.

82. Alec Nove, "Agriculture," in Archie Brown and Michael Kaser, eds., *Soviet Policy for the 1980s* (London: Macmillan, 1982), 171.

83. Linda Cook, *The Soviet Social Contract and Why It Failed* (Cambridge, Mass.: Harvard University Press, 1993), 58–67.

84. Kozlov, *Mass Uprisings,* 305.

85. Gregory Gleason, "Leninist Nationality Policy: Its Source and Style," in Henry Huttenbach, ed., *Soviet Nationality Policies: Ruling Ethnic Groups in the USSR* (London: Mansell, 1990), 15.

86. Roman Solchanyk, "Russian Language and Soviet Politics," *Soviet Studies* 34 (1982), 23.

87. S. Enders Wimbush, "The Great Russians and the Soviet State: The Dilemmas of Ethnic Dominance," in Jeremy R. Azrael, ed., *Soviet Nationality Policies and Practices* (New York: Praeger, 1978), 349–360.

88. Kozlov, *Mass Uprisings,* 62–65; on military construction battalions in general, see 50–71.

89. Ibid., 87–89; N. F. Bugai and A. M. Gonov, *Kavkaz: narody v eshelonakh (20–60-e gody)* (Moscow: Insan, 1998), 305–312.

90. Kozlov, *Mass Uprisings,* 97–98.

91. Ibid., 100–109.

92. Ibid., 100–101, 105–106.

93. William J. Tompson, *Khrushchev: A Political Life* (Basingstoke: Macmillan, 1995), 270–276; "Kak snimali N. S. Khrushcheva," *Istoricheskii arkhiv* no. 1 (1993), 7–15.


## 9. The Rediscovery of Russia

1. Mark R. Beissinger, "The Political Elite," in James Cracraft, ed., *The Soviet Union Today: An Interpretive Guide* (Chicago: Bulletin of the Atomic Scientists, 1983), 38–39.

2. Michael Rywkin, "The Russia-Wide Federated Socialist Republic (RSFSR): Privileged or Underprivileged?" in Edward Allworth, ed., *Ethnic Russia: The Dilemma of Dominance* (New York: Pergamon Press, 1980), 182.

3. Mikhail Gorbachev, *Memoirs* (London: Doubleday, 1996), 112, 144; I. Zemtsov, *Partiia ili mafiia? Razvorovannaia respublika* (Paris: Les Editeurs Réunis, 1976).

4. N. Simonov, *Voenno-promyshlennyi kompleks SSSR, 1920ye–1950ye gody* (Moscow: Rosspen, 1996), 329–330; Gorbachev, *Memoirs,* 136, 215–216.

5. Julian Cooper, *The Soviet Defence Industry: Conversion and Reform* (London: Pinter Press for the Royal Institute of International Affairs, 1991), 20–28.

6. *Russkie: etno-sotsiologicheskie ocherki* (Moscow: Nauka, 1992), 98.

7. I. V. Bystrova, *Voenno-promyshlennyi kompleks SSSR v gody kholodnoi voiny (vtoraia polovina 40-kh-nachalo 60-kh godov)* (Moscow: Institut rossiiskoi istorii RAN, 2000), 304–305.

8. Cooper, *Soviet Defence Industry,* 25–28; Viktoriia Glazyrina, "Krasnoiarsk-26: A Closed City of the Defence-Industry Complex," in John Barber and Mark Harrison, eds., *The Soviet Defence Industry Complex from Stalin to Khrushchev* (Basingstoke: Macmillan, 2000), 195–202; Andrei Sakharov describes Arzamas-16 in his *Memoirs* (London: Hutchinson, 1990), chap. 7.

9. Bystrova, *Voenno-promyshlennyi kompleks,* 309–310.

10. Ludmila Selezneva, *Growing Up Russian: Letters from Ludmilla* (Moscow: n.p., 2002), 46–47.

11. Robert J. Kaiser, *The Geography of Nationalism in Russia and the USSR* (Princeton: Princeton University Press, 1994), 203.

12. A. S. Seniavskii, *Rossiiskii gorod v 1960–80ye gody* (Moscow: Institut Rossiiskoi Istorii RAN, 1995), 235, 106–131.

13. Ibid., 131–147.

14. V. P. Perevedentsev, *Molodezh' i sotsial'no-demograficheskie problemy SSSR* (Moscow: Nauka, 1990), 133–135.

15. D. J. Peterson, *Troubled Lands: The Legacy of Soviet Environmental Destruction* (Boulder, Colo.: Westview Press, 1993), 29, 36–37, 41, 142.

16. Ibid., 58–66, 102–105.

17. Perevedentsev, *Naselenie SSSR* (Moscow: Nauka, 1972), 3, 9.

18. A. G. Kharchev and S. I. Golod, *Professional'naia rabota zhenshchin i sem'ia* (Leningrad: Nauka, 1971), 42.

19. V. Perevedentsev, "Sem'ia: vchera, segodnia, zavtra: zametki sotsiologa," *Nash*

*sovremennik,* no. 6 (1975), 118–131; V. Perevedentsev, "Naselenie: prognoz i real'nost," *Nash sovremennik,* no. 11 (1975), 131–132.

20. Perevedentsev, "Sem'ia," 128.

21. Seniavskii, *Rossiiskii gorod,* 166–181; Perevedentsev, *Naselenie SSSR,* 9.

22. Hedrick Smith, *The Russians* (New York: Quadrangle, 1976), 341.

23. Blair A. Ruble, "From *khrushcheby* to *korobki,*" in William Craft Brumfield and Blair A. Ruble, eds., *Russian Housing in the Modern Age: Design and Social History* (Cambridge: Cambridge University Press, 1993), 249–251.

24. Alan Sillitoe, *Road to Volgograd* (London: Macmillan, 1969), 14.

25. Hilary Pilkington, *Russia's Youth and Its Culture: A Nation's Constructors and Constructed* (London: Routledge, 1994), 64–71.

26. V. N. Shkurin, *Neformal'nye molodezhnye ob"edineniia* (Moscow: Ministerstvo Kul'tury, 1990), 56.

27. Ibid., 66–67, 98–100; I. Iu. Sundiev, "Neformal'nye molodezhnye ob"edneniia: opyt ekzpozitsii," *Sotsiologicheskie issledovaniia,* no. 5 (1987), 59–60; also his "Samodeiatel'nye ob"edineniia molodezhi," *Sotsiologicheskie issledovaniia,* no. 2 (1989), 56–62; on outbreaks of gang warfare among soccer fans in the early 1980s, see John Bushnell, *Moscow Graffiti: Language and Subculture* (London: Unwin Hyman, 1990), 31–39.

28. E. B. Nikitaeva, "Ischezaiushchaia derevnia (1960-seredina 80-kh godov)," in N. A. Ivnitskii, ed., *Sud'by rossiiskogo krest'ianstva* (Moscow: RGGU, 1996), 455–459. One of the most haunting Russian novels of the 1970s, Valentin Rasputin's work *Proshchane s Materoi* concerns the resettlement of elderly people from an ancient island village, now being flooded for a hydroelectric scheme, to a bare and exposed multistory settlement on the mainland (see p. 330).

29. Nikitaeva, "Ischezaiushchaia derevnia," 439; L. N. Denisova, *Ischezaiushchaia derevnia Rossii: nechernozem'e v 1960–80-ye gody* (Moscow: Institut Rossiiskoi Istorii RAN, 1996), 58–63, 49.

30. Denisova, *Ischezaiushchaia derevnia Rossii,* 39.

31. Ibid., 45, 146. The letter is quoted from the archive, so presumably it was not published in the newspaper at the time.

32. Ibid., 174.

33. Ibid., 164–169.

34. Ibid., 133, 141.

35. Ibid., 134–136, 141.

36. Ibid., 141.

37. Ibid., 206.

38. Marie-Rose Rialand, *L'Alcool et les Russes* (Paris: Institut des Etudes Slaves, 1989), 29–35.

39. Denisova, *Ischezaiushchaia derevnia Rossii,* 205–209.

40. Selezneva, *Letters from Liudmila,* 18–19.

41. RBZ, R-385 (Beliaev, Viktor Petrovich), ll. 9–10.

42. *Russkie,* 33; V. Kabuzan, *Russkie v mire* (St. Petersburg: Blits, 1996), 244–253.

43. *Russkie,* 105–108, 129.

44. V. A. Alpatov, *150 Iazykov i Politika, 1917–1997gg* (Moscow: Institut Vostokovedeniia, 1997), 97–99.

45. *Russkie,* 192–193, 210–213; Kaiser, *The Geography of Nationalism,* 318–319; R. Karklins, *Ethnic Relations in the USSR: The Perspective from Below* (Boston, Mass.: Allen and Unwin, 1986), 36–41.

46. *Russkie,* 197–200.

47. Karklins, *Ethnic Relations,* 215.

48. Kabuzan, *Russkie v mire,* 240–241, 263–265; Kaiser, *The Geography of Nationalism,* 166–170, 181, chap. 6; L. L. Rybakovskii and N. V. Tarasova, "Migratsionnye protsessy v SSSR: novye iavleniia," *Sotsiologicheskie issledovaniia,* no. 7 (1990), 32–42; I. Erofeeva, "Slavianskoe naselenie Vostochnogo Kazakhstana v xviii–xx vekakh: migratsionnoe dvizhenie, stadii sotsiokul'turnoi evoliutsii, problemy reemigratsii," in *Etnicheskii natsionalizm i gosudarstvennoe stroitel'stvo* (Moscow: IV RAN—Natalis, 2001), 358–360; V. I. Kozlov, "Russkie v novom zarubezh'e," in *Russkie v sovremennom mire* (Moscow: Institut Etnologii i Antropologii RAN, 1998), 21–23.

49. M. Guboglo, *Sovremennye etno-iazykovye protsessy v SSSR* (Moscow: Nauka, 1984), 64–72.

50. Roman Solchanyk, "Russian Language and Soviet Politics," *Soviet Studies* 34 (1982), 23–42.

51. Ibid., 23; see above, p. 299.

52. Alpatov, *150 Iazykov,* 99–100.

53. Steven L. Guthier, "The Belorussians: National Identification and Assimilation, 1897–1970," *Soviet Studies* 29 (1977), 273–275, 280–281.

54. Solchanyk, "Russian Language," 25–26.

55. Ronald G. Suny, *The Making of the Georgian Nation,* 2nd ed. (Bloomington: Indiana University Press, 1994), 309.

56. Toivo U. Raun, *Estonia and the Estonians,* 2nd ed. (Stanford: Hoover Institution Press, 1991), 195–197. The text of one of the letters is in *Radio Liberty Research Report,* no. 477 (December 15, 1980).

57. Alpatov, *150 Iazykov,* 103; *Russkie,* 289–292, 300–302.

58. Alpatov, *150 Iazykov,* 108–111.

59. Solchanyk, "Russian Language," 37–38; Ivan Dziuba, *Internationalism or Russification? A Study in the Soviet Nationalities Problem,* 2nd ed. (London: Weidenfeld and Nicolson, 1970), 99, 137.

60. Christel Lane, *The Rites of Rulers: Ritual in Industrial Society—The Soviet Case* (Cambridge: Cambridge University Press, 1981), 210–220.

61. Ibid., 79; *Russkie,* 335–354.

62. Lane, *Rites of Rulers,* 91–96.

63. T. A. Listova, "Narodnaia religioznaia kontseptsiia zarozhdeniia i nachala zhizni," in V. A. Aleksandrov, I. V. Vlasova, and N. S. Polishchuk, eds., *Russkie* (Moscow: Nauka, 1997), 700–701.

64. *Russkie,* 318–321; Natalia Sadomskaya, "New Soviet Rituals and National Inte-

gration in the USSR," in Henry Huttenbach, ed., *Soviet Nationality Policies: Ruling Ethnic Groups in the USSR* (London: Mansell, 1990), 94–120.

65. Catherine Merridale, *Night of Stone: Death and Memory in Russia* (London: Granta Books, 2000), 169–173, 356–359; I. A. Kremleva, "Pokhoronnye-pominal'nye obychai i obriady," in Aleksandrov, *Russkie,* 530–532.

66. *The Village of Viriatino,* trans. and ed. Sula Benet (New York: Anchor Books, 1970), 275–276.

67. *Russkie,* 357–359; Lane, *Rites of Rulers,* 82–86.

68. Raissa Orlowa and Lew Kopelew, *Wir Lebten in Moskau* (Munich: Albrecht Knaus Verlag, 1987), 62–63.

69. Lane, *Rites of Rulers,* chap. 13; quotation on p. 251.

70. Nina Tumarkin, *The Living and the Dead: The Rise and Fall of the Cult of World War II in Russia* (New York: Basic Books, 1994), 33–39.

71. Michael Ignatieff, "Soviet War Memorials," *History Workshop,* no. 17 (Spring 1984), 157–163; quotation on p. 162.

72. A variant of *nam ostochertelo,* "we got fed up with."

73. Evgenii Evtushenko, *Bratskii GES: stikhi i poemy* (Moscow: Sovetskii Pisatel', 1967), 238.

74. Valentin Rasputin, "Proshchanie s Materoi," *Nash sovremennik,* no. 10 (1976), 68.

75. Oleg Kharkhordin, *The Collective and the Individual in Russia: A Study of Practices* (Berkeley: University of California Press, 1999), 323–324: modified translation of Zinovev, *Reality of Communism,* 114.

76. This aspect of Soviet society is well analyzed in Alena Ledeneva, *Russia's Economy of Favours: Blat, Networking and Informal Exchange* (Cambridge: Cambridge University Press, 1998).

77. Zinovev's ideas are most conveniently set out in his book *The Reality of Communism,* trans. Charles Janson (London: Gollancz, 1984). For a brief exposition of his ideas, see Geoffrey Hosking, "Mediocrity for the Millions," *Times Literary Supplement,* May 23, 1980, 571–572; Philip Hanson, "Alexander Zinoviev: Totalitarianism from Below," *Survey* 26, no. 1 (Spring 1982), 29–48.

78. Alexander Pyzhikov, *Khrushchevskaia Ottepel'* (Moscow: OLMA Press, 2002), 248–249.

79. Ibid., 247, 253.

80. Quoted in Efim Etkind, *Protsess Iosifa Brodskogo* (London: Overseas Publications Interchange, 1988), 16, 22.

81. Ibid., 61.

82. Kharkhordin, *Collective,* 303–311.

83. Ibid., 312–313; William E. Odom, *The Collapse of the Soviet Military* (New Haven: Yale University Press, 1998), 286–292; "'Dedovshchina' na vesakh zakona," *Kommunist vooruzhennykh sil,* no, 24 (1989), 50–58; "'Dedovshchina': realii i prognozy," *Kommunist vooruzhennykh sil,* no. 22 (1989), 44–52.

84. In 1989 the party's military journal conducted a questionnaire among 1,153 military personnel, from which much of my evidence is taken. See *Kommunist vooruzhennykh sil,* no. 18 (1989), 61–66; no. 22 (1989), 44–52; no. 24 (1989), 50–58.

85. Odom, *Collapse*, 250–251.

86. Ibid., 196–199, 267–268.


## 10. The Return of Politics

1. Joseph Brodsky, *Less Than One: Selected Essays* (New York: Farrar Straus Giroux, 1986), 28–29.

2. Oleg Kharkhordin, *The Collective and the Individual in Russia: A Study of Practices* (Berkeley: University of California Press, 1999), 313–322.

3. Alla Latynina, "Pora gasit' kostry," *Novyi mir* 6 (2003), 170.

4. Quoted in Petr Vail' and Aleksandr Genis, *60-ye: mir sovetskogo cheloveka* (Moscow: Novoe Literaturnoe Obozrenie, 1996), 104.

5. Philip Boobbyer, "Truth-Telling, Conscience and Dissent in Late Soviet Russia: Evidence from Oral Histories," *European History Quarterly* 30 (2000), 557–558.

6. At a public lecture in London in June 1988, Archbishop Kirill of Smolensk (now Metropolitan, and in change of the external affairs of the Russian Orthodox Church) admitted that the church had not been able to fulfill its proper function of providing spiritual enlightenment in Soviet society, and that that function had been taken over by literature.

7. A. Tvardovskii, "Po sluchaiu iubileia," *Novyi mir* 1 (1965), 13–14.

8. Ibid., 13; On *pravda zhizni* see T. A. Snigireva, *A. T. Tvardovskii: poet i ego epokha* (Ekaterinburg: Izdatel'stvo ural'skogo universiteta, 1997) 231–237.

9. In this respect he probably reflected the assumptions of many Russian readers, which is why the journal was so popular. See the remarks by Peter Reddaway and Dmitri Glinski, *The Tragedy of Russia's Reforms: Market Bolshevism against Democracy* (Washington, D.C.: U.S. Institute of Peace Press, 2001), 102.

10. A. Tvardovskii, "Neskol'ko slov k chitateliam *Novogo mira*," *Novyi mir* 12 (1961), 252; Snigireva, *Tvardovskii*, 223–224, 231–237.

11. Edith Rogovin Frankel, *Novyi mir: A Case Study in the Politics of Literature, 1952–58* (Cambridge: Cambridge University Press, 1981), 125; the atmosphere is captured in the diary of one of the editors, A. Kondratovich, *Novomirskii dnevnik, 1967–1970* (Moscow: Sovetskii Pisatel', 1991).

12. Recounted in detail in Kondratovich, *Novomirskii dnevnik.*

13. Tvardovskii, "Po sluchaiu iubileia," 5, 7.

14. Snigireva, *Tvardovskii*, 277–311.

15. On this role, see Steven Marks, *How Russia Shaped the Modern World: From Art to Anti-Semitism* (Princeton, N.J.: Princeton University Press, 2003).

16. Leopold Labedz, ed., *Solzhenitsyn: A Documentary Record* (London: Allen Lane, 1970), 15–16.

17. Snigireva, *Tvardovskii*, 162–163.

18. In conversation with me in December 1988, Vladimir Lakshin suggested that Tvardovskii himself approved their decision once *Novyi mir* was no longer his journal; he said Tvardovskii was impressed with the *narodnyi* character of *Nash sovremennik* and thought it promised well for the future.

19. This process is examined in Dina Zisserman-Brodsky, *Constructing Ethnopolitics in the Soviet Union: Samizdat, Deprivation and the Rise of Ethnic Nationalism* (London: Palgrave, 2003).

20. Stanislav Kuniaev, "Poeziia. Sud'ba. Rossiia." *Nash sovremennik* 1 (1999), 142.

21. Kuniaev, "Poeziia," *Nash sovremennik*, 2 (1999), 118.

22. Albert Todd and Max Hayward, eds., *Twentieth Century Russian Poetry* (London: Fourth Estate, 1993), 805–807.

23. M. R. Zezina, *Sovetskaia khudozhestvennaia intelligentsiia i vlast', 1950–60-ye gody* (Moscow: Dialog-MGU, 1999), 151.

24. Nikolai Mitrokhin, *Russkaia partiia: dvizhenie russkikh natsionalistov v SSSR, 1953–1985* (Moscow: Novoe Literaturnoe Obozrenie, 2003), 147.

25. Zezina, *Sovetskaia,* 147–152.

26. Mitrokhin, *Russkaia partiia,* 146–150; Zezina, *Sovetskaia,* 226–228.

27. Yitzhak M. Brudny, *Reinventing Russia: Russian Nationalism and the Soviet State* (Cambridge, Mass.: Harvard University Press, 1998), 77.

28. This example is taken from one of the earliest works of the genre: Nikolai Zhdanov, "Poezdka na rodinu," *Literaturnaia Moskva,* vol. 2 (Moscow: Khudozhestvennaia Literature, 1956), 407.

29. Geoffrey Hosking, *Beyond Socialist Realism: Soviet Fiction since Ivan Denisovich* (London: Elek Books, 1980), 59–62.

30. Anthony D. Smith, *National Identity* (London: Penguin, 1991), 91.

31. Philip T. Grier, *Marxist Ethical Theory in the Soviet Union* (Dordrecht: D. Reidel, 1978), 108; the text of the Moral Code is in Richard T. De George, *Soviet Ethics and Morality* (Ann Arbor: University of Michigan Press, 1969), 83.

32. See the suggestive study by Steven Shapin, *A Social History of Truth: Civility and Science in Seventeenth-Century England* (Chicago: University of Chicago Press, 1994).

33. Andrei Sakharov, *Memoirs,* trans. Richard Lourie (London: Hutchinson, 1990), 96–98.

34. Ibid., 225.

35. Ibid., 229.

36. Harrison E. Salisbury, ed., *Sakharov Speaks* (London: Collins and Harvill, 1974), 143–144.

37. Andrei Sakharov, *V bor'be za mir* (Frankfurt am Main: Posev, 1973), 9–65.

38. Mark Hopkins, *Russia's Underground Press: The Chronicle of Current Events* (New York: Praeger, 1983).

39. De George, *Soviet Ethics,* 83.

40. Derek Offord, *"Lichnost':* Notions of Individual Identity," in Catriona Kelly and David Shepherd, eds., *Constructing Russian Culture in the Age of Revolution: 1881–1940* (Oxford: Oxford University Press, 1998), 13–25.

41. Evgenii Vagin, "Interv'iu Vestniku RKhD," *Vestnik RKhD* 122 (1977), 252–262.

42. Aleksandr Solzhenitsyn, *Sobranie sochinenii v 9-i tomakh,* vol. 7 (Moscow: Terra—knizhnyi klub, 2001), 95–99.

43. Douglas R. Weiner, *A Little Corner of Freedom: Russian Nature Protection from Stalin to Gorbachev* (Berkeley: University of California Press, 1999).

44. Mitrokhin, *Russkaia partiia,* 303.

45. Ibid., 300–308; Brudnyi, *Reinventing Russia,* 67–68.

46. A. Korobov et al., "Kak dal'she stroit' Moskvu?" *Moskva* 3 (1962), 147–160, quotation on p. 150; Timothy Colton, *Moscow: Governing the Socialist Metropolis* (Cambridge, Mass.: Belknap Press of Harvard University Press, 1995), 419–421.

47. Mitrokhin, *Russkaia partiia,* 308–315.

48. Brudny, *Reinventing Russia,* 69–70; John B. Dunlop, *The Faces of Contemporary Russian Nationalism* (Princeton: Princeton University Press, 1983), 66.

49. Dunlop, *Faces,* 74–76.

50. Mitrokhin, *Russkaia partiia,* 318–325; Sergei Semanov, "Russkii klub," *Moskva* 3 (1997), 177–182.

51. Douglas R. Weiner, *A Little Corner of Freedom: Russian Nature Protection from Stalin to Gorbachev* (Berkeley: University of California Press, 1999), 312–339.

52. Ibid., 319–333.

53. Ibid., 334–339.

54. Geoffrey Hosking, *The Awakening of the Soviet Union* (Cambridge, Mass.: Harvard University Press, 1990), 55–57; Weiner, *A Little Corner,* 355–373.

55. T. H. Rigby, "The Soviet Regional Leadership: The Brezhnev Generation," *Slavic Review* 37 (1978), 1–24.

56. Brudny, *Reinventing Russia,* 15–19, 102–110.

57. Ibid., 61–62.

58. Mitrokhin, *Russkaia partiia,* 276–283.

59. V. Chalmaev, "Filosofiia patriotizma," *Molodaia gvardiia* 10 (1967), 285.

60. D. Balashov, "Svet iz glubiny," *Molodaia gvardiia* 9 (1966), 293; Il'ia Glazunov, "Doroga k tebe," *Molodaia gvardiia* 6 (1966), 262.

61. V. Soloukhin, "Pis'ma iz russkogo muzeia," *Molodaia gvardiia* 9 (1966), 243.

62. Chalmaev, "Filosofiia," 288.

63. Ibid., 274; V. Chalmaev, "Neizbezhnost'," *Molodaia gvardiia* 9 (1968), 272.

64. M. Lobanov, "Zhiznennost' slova," *Molodaia gvardiia* 9 (1967), 259.

65. See above, p. 280.

66. A. G. Dement'ev, "O traditsiiakh i narodnosti," *Novyi mir* 4 (1969), 215–235, quotation on p. 235.

67. Brudny, *Reinventing Russia,* 88–93; Vol'fram Eggeling, *Politika i kul'tura pri Khrushcheve i Brezhneve, 1953–1970gg* (Moscow: AIRO-XX, 1999), chap. 9.

68. Peter J. S. Duncan, *Russian Messianism: Third Rome, Revolution, Communism and After* (London: Routledge, 2000), 89–96.

69. Aleksandr Solzhenitsyn, "Pis'mo vozhdiam Sovetskogo Soiuza," *Sobranie sochinenii,* vol. 7 (Moscow: Terra, 2001), 60–94.

70. Ibid., quotation on p. 75.

71. Karen Brutents, *Tridtsat' let na staroi ploshchadi* (Moscow: Mezhdunarodnye Otnosheniia, 1998), 187–192. Brutents was a consultant with special responsibility for Africa.

72. G. A. Arbatov, *Zatianuvsheesia vyzdorovlenie: svidetel'stvo sovremennika, 1953–1985* (Moscow: Mezhdunarodnye Otnosheniia, 1991), 67–75, 381–399.

73. When he became general secretary, Gorbachev gleaned many of his ideas from the International Department; see his *Memoirs* (London: Doubleday, 1996), 166.

74. On Eurasianism, see Nicholas V. Riasanovsky, "The Emergence of Eurasianism," *California Slavic Studies,* 4 (1967), 39–72; for Gumilev's biography, see S .B Lavrov, *Lev Gumilev: sud'ba i idei* (Moscow: Svarog i K, 2000). For my account of Eurasianism and Gumilev I am much indebted to my former research student Alexander Titov.

75. L. N. Gumilev, "Biografiia nauchnoi teorii, ili avtonekrolog," *Znamia* 4 (1988), 205.

76. A. Kuz'min, "Sviashchennye kamni pamiati," *Molodaia gvardiia,* 1 (1982), 252–266, actually accused Gumilev of being a Russophobe.

77. Gumilev's main ideas are expounded in his *Etnogez i biosfera zemli* (Leningrad: Izdatel'stvo leningradskogo universiteta, 1989), and *Drevniaia Rus' i velikaia step'* (Moscow: Mysl', 1989). See Ryszard Paradowski, "The Eurasian Idea and Leo Gumilev's Scientific Ideology," *Canadian Slavonic Papers* 41 (1999), 19–32, and Marlène Laruelle, "Lev Nikolaevic Gumilev (1912–1992): biologisme et eurasisme dans la pensée russe," *Revue des Etudes Slaves* 72 (2000), 163–189.

78. V. Kozlov, "O biologo-geograficheskoi kontseptsii etnicheskoi istorii," *Voprosy istorii* 12 (1974), 83, 85.

79. Vadim Kozhinov, "I nazovet menia vsiak sushchii v nei iazyk," reprinted in his *O russkom natsional'nom soznanii* (Moscow: Algoritm, 2002), 133–180; quotations on pp. 134, 136, 178–179.

80. Ibid., 174–176.

81. Igor' Shafarevich, "Sotsializm kak iavlenie mirovoi istorii," in his *Sochineniia v trekh tomakh* (Moscow: Feniks, 1994), vol. 1.

82. I. R. Shafarevich, "Russkii vopros," ibid., vol. 2, 110–120.

83. Ibid., 111, 123, 132, 160.


## 11. An Unanticipated Creation

1. Robert Strayer, "Decolonization, Democratization, and Communist Reform: The Soviet Collapse in Comparative Perspective," *Journal of World History* 12, no. 2 (Fall 2001), 380.

2. *Pravda,* January 16, 1989, 1.

3. Geoffrey Hosking, *The Awakening of the Soviet Union* (Cambridge, Mass.: Harvard University Press, 1990), 64–67; Michael Urban, with Vyacheslav Igrunov and Sergei Mitrokhin, *The Rebirth of Politics in Russia* (Cambridge: Cambridge University Press, 1997), 95–99.

4. Peter Reddaway and Dmitri Glinski, *The Tragedy of Russia's Reforms: Market Bolshevism against Democracy* (Washington, D.C.: United States Institute of Peace Press, 2001), 122–123; Urban, *Rebirth,* 101–106.

5. Hosking, *Awakening,* 67.

6. Geoffrey A. Hosking, "The Beginnings of Independent Political Activity," in Geoffrey A. Hosking, Jonathan Aves, and Peter J. S. Duncan, *The Road to Post-Communism: Independent Political Movements in the Soviet Union, 1985–1991* (London: Pinter Publishers, 1992), 18.

7. A. V. Gromov and O. S. Kuzin, *Neformaly: kto est' kto?* (Moscow: Mysl', 1990), 107.

8. Alexander Lukin, *The Political Culture of the Russian "Democrats"* (Oxford: Oxford University Press, 2000), 77–79.

9. Hosking, *Awakening,* 71–72.

10. John Dunlop, *The Rise of Russia and the Fall of the Soviet Empire* (Princeton, N.J.: Princeton University Press, 1993), 79–81.

11. Mark R. Beissinger, *Nationalist Mobilization and the Collapse of the Soviet Union* (Cambridge: Cambridge University Press, 2002), 394.

12. *Pervyi s'ezd narodnykh deputatov SSSR: stenograficheskii otchet,* vol. 2 (Moscow: Izdanie Verkhovnogo Soveta, 1989), 458–459.

13. Dunlop, *Rise of Russia,* 81–85.

14. Ibid., 92–93, 102–106; Urban, *Rebirth,* 182–193.

15. Aleksandr Prokhanov, "Tragediia tsentralizma," *Literaturnaia Rossiia,* no. 1 (January 5, 1990), 4.

16. Dunlop, *Rise of Russia,* 125, 127.

17. Peter J. S. Duncan, "The Rebirth of Politics in Russia," in Hosking et al., *Road to Post-Communism,* 84.

18. Hosking, *Awakening,* 92.

19. Dunlop, *Rise of Russia,* 136.

20. Jonathan Aves, "The Russian Labour Movement, 1989–91: The Mirage of a Russian Solidarność," in Hosking et al., *Road to Post-Communism,* 140–142.

21. Valerii Solovei, "Russkie natsionalisty i vlast' v epokhu Gorbacheva," in P. Goble and G. Bordiugov, eds., *Mezhnatsional'nye otnosheniia v Rossii i SNG* (Moscow: AIRO-XX, 1994), 61–62.

22. *Literaturnaia Rossiia,* no. 38 (September 22, 1989), 5; *Literaturnaia Rossiia,* no. 52 (December 29, 1989), 2.

23. Dunlop, *Rise of Russia,* 142–143, 19.

24. John Morrison, *Boris Yeltsin: From Bolshevik to Democrat* (London: Penguin Books, 1991), 142.

25. Beissinger, *Nationalist Mobilization,* 411–412.

26. Morrison, *Yeltsin,* 142–144; Beissinger, *Nationalist Mobilization,* 411; Valerie Bunce, *Subversive Institutions: The Design and the Destruction of Socialism and the State* (Cambridge: Cambridge University Press, 1999), 108–109.

27. Beissinger, *Nationalist Mobilization,* 411–412.

28. Reddaway and Glinski, *Tragedy of Russia's Reforms,* 170–178.

29. Ibid., 334–335.

30. Beissinger, *Nationalist Mobilization,* 419–420.

31. *Current Digest of the Soviet Press* 43, no. 33 (1991), 1–2.

32. Aleksandr Lebed', *Za derzhavu obidno* (Moscow: Moskovskii Rabochii, 1995), 390.

33. Dunlop, *Rise of Russia,* 212–218.

34. Urban, *Rebirth,* 257.

35. Dunlop, *Rise of Russia,* 271–276; Reddaway and Glinski, *Tragedy of Russia's Reforms,* 274–275.

36. Urban, *Rebirth,* chap. 1.

37. Liliia Shevtsova, "Puti konsolidatsii vlasti," in *God posle avgusta: gorech' i vybor. Sbornik statei i interv'iu* (Moscow: Izdatel'stvo "Literatura i Politika," 1992), 124.

38. Urban, *Rebirth,* 200.

39. Lukin, *Political Culture,* 293.

40. John Lloyd, *Rebirth of a Nation: An Anatomy of Russia* (London: Michael Joseph, 1998), 218.

41. Lukin, *Political Culture,* 289; Reddaway and Glinski, *Tragedy of Russia's Reforms,* 236–241; Viktor Iaroshenko, "Popytka Gaidara," *Novyi mir* 3 (1993), 115.

42. Lloyd, *Rebirth of a Nation,* 277–279; Thane Gustafsson, *Capitalism Russian-Style* (Cambridge: Cambridge University Press, 1999), chap. 5; Olga Kryshtanovskaya and Stephen White, "From Soviet *nomenklatura* to Russian Elite," *Europe-Asia Studies* 48 (1996), 711–733; Reddaway and Glinski, *Tragedy of Russia's Reforms,* 233–236.

43. Janine Wedel, *Collision and Collusion: The Strange Case of Western Aid to Eastern Europe* (Basingstoke: Macmillan, 1998), chap. 4.

44. Alena V. Ledeneva, *Russia's Economy of Favours: Blat, Networking and Informal Exchange* (Cambridge: Cambridge University Press, 1998), chap. 6; Lukin, *Political Culture,* chap. 5.

45. Robert Service, *Russia: Experiment with a People* (London: Macmillan, 2002), 309.

46. G. F. Morozova, "Sovremennye migratsionnye iavleniia: bezhentsy i emigranty," *Sotsiologicheskie issledovaniia* 3 (1992), 34–40; K. T. Toshchenko, "Russkie bezhentsy: tragediia ili izderzhki imperskogo soznaniia?" *Sotsiologicheskie issledovaniia* 3 (1992), 59–64.

47. Galina Litvinova, "I snova o bezhentsakh: unizhenie prodolzhaetsia," *Literaturnaia Rossiia,* no. 25 (June 22, 1990), 16.

48. "Kuda bezhat'?" *Literaturnaia Rossiia,* no. 5 (February 2, 1990), 3.

49. Neil Melvin, *Russians beyond Russia: The Politics of National Identity* (London: RIIA, 1995), 17.

50. The actual figures may well have been higher. Reddaway and Glinski, *Tragedy of Russia's Reforms,* chap. 7, esp. 426–429.

51. Melvin, *Russians,* 18.

52. Gerhard Simon, "Are the Russians a Nation?" in Matti Kotiranta, ed., *Religious Transition in Russia* (Helsinki: Kikimora Publications, 2000), 12–13.

53. Robert Service, "Zhirinovskii: Ideas in Search of an Audience," in Geoffrey Hosking and Robert Service, eds., *Russian Nationalism, Past and Present* (Basingstoke: Macmillan, 1998), 179–197.

54. Gennadii Ziuganov, *Za gorizontom,* 2nd ed. (Orel: Veshnie Vody, 1995), 74; Gennadii Ziuganov, *Derzhava* (Moscow: Inforpechat', 1994), 43.

55. Gennady Ziuganov, *My Russia: The Political Autobiography of Gennady Zyuganov,* ed. Vadim Medish (Armonk: M. E. Sharpe, 1997), 12–13, 15.

56. Joan Barth Urban and Valerii D. Solovei, *Russia's Communists at the Crossroads* (Boulder, Colo.: Westview Press, 1997), 103.

57. Ziuganov, *My Russia,* 10–11.

58. Luke March, *The Communist Party in Post-Soviet Russia* (Manchester: Manchester University Press, 2002), chap. 4, esp. 106.

59. Ziuganov, *Za gorizontom,* 47–49.

60. Mitropolit Ioann, "Bitva za Rossiiu," *Russkii uzel: stat'i, besedy, obrashcheniia* (Saint Petersburg: Tsarskoe Delo, 2000), 63–74; see Wendy Slater, "A Modern-Day Saint? Metropolitan Ioann and the Post-Soviet Russian Orthodox Church," *Religion, State and Society* 28 (2000), 313–325.

61. S. B. Filatov, *Religiia i obshchestvo: ocherki religioznoi zhizni sovremennoi Rossii* (Moscow: Letnii Sad, 2002), 470–484.

62. Ralph Della Cava, "Reviving Orthodoxy in Russia: An Overview of the Factions in the Russian Orthodox Church in the Spring of 1996," *Cahiers du Monde Russe* 38 (1997), 387–414.

63. Iu. A. Levada et al., eds., *Sovetskii prostoi chelovek: opyt sotsial'nogo portreta na rubezhe 90-kh* (Moscow: n.p., 1993), 13–26.

64. Service, *Russia,* 197–202; Richard Sakwa, *Putin: Russia's Choice* (London: Routledge, 2004), 164–166; G. V. Vilinbakhov, *Gerb i flag Rossii: x–xx vekov* (Moscow: Iuridicheskaia Literatura, 1997), 495, 500–512.

65. Service, *Russia,* 198–199, 211–212.

66. Oleg Platonov, *Ubiistvo tsarskoi sem'i* (Moscow: Sovetskaia Rossiia, 1991), 3; Wendy Slater, "Relics, Remains and Revisionism: Narratives of Nicholas II in Contemporary Russia," unpublished paper.

67. For a full examination of them, see Vera Tolz, "Conflicting 'Homeland Myths' and Nation-State Building in Postcommunist Russia," *Slavic Review* 57 (1998), 267–294.

68. Dmitri V. Trenin and Aleksei Malashenko, with Anatol Lieven, *Russia's Restless Frontier: The Chechnya Factor in Post-Soviet Russia* (Washington, D.C.: Carnegie Endowment for International Peace, 2004), 2–3.

## Conclusion

1. Karl Deutsch, *Nationalism and Social Communication,* 2nd ed. (New York: MIT Press, 1966); Ernest Gellner, *Nations and Nationalism* (Oxford: Basil Blackwell, 1983); John Breuilly, *Nationalism and the State,* 2nd ed. (Manchester: Manchester University Press, 1993).

2. This process is explained at length in Geoffrey Hosking, *Russia: People and Empire, 1552–1917* (Cambridge, Mass.: Harvard University Press, 1997), 75–94.

3. John Breuilly, "The State and Nationalism," in Montserrat Guibernau and John Hutchinson, eds., *Understanding Nationalism* (Cambridge: Polity, 2001), 32.

4. Breuilly, *Nationalism and the State,* 373–374.

5. Benedict Anderson, *Imagined Communities: Reflections on the Origin and Spread of Nationalism* (London: Verso, 1991).

6. Vera Tolz, *Inventing the Nation: Russia* (London: Longman, 2001), esp. 94–99, 181–188.

7. Valerii Solovei, "Russkie protiv imperii," *Svobodnaia mysl',* no. 12 (2002), 82.

8. Richard Sakwa, *Putin: Russia's Choice* (London: Routledge, 2004), 168.

# INDEX